I0729472

My nickname **PaperBlue** is a combination of my favorite things, the **color blue** and **paper**. It is not blue paper, though.
I particularly like blue, so I used to paint a lot of blue paintings back in the day.
That is **why I picked** the word **blue**. And **why paper**?
As an artist, **you can create anything on paper**.

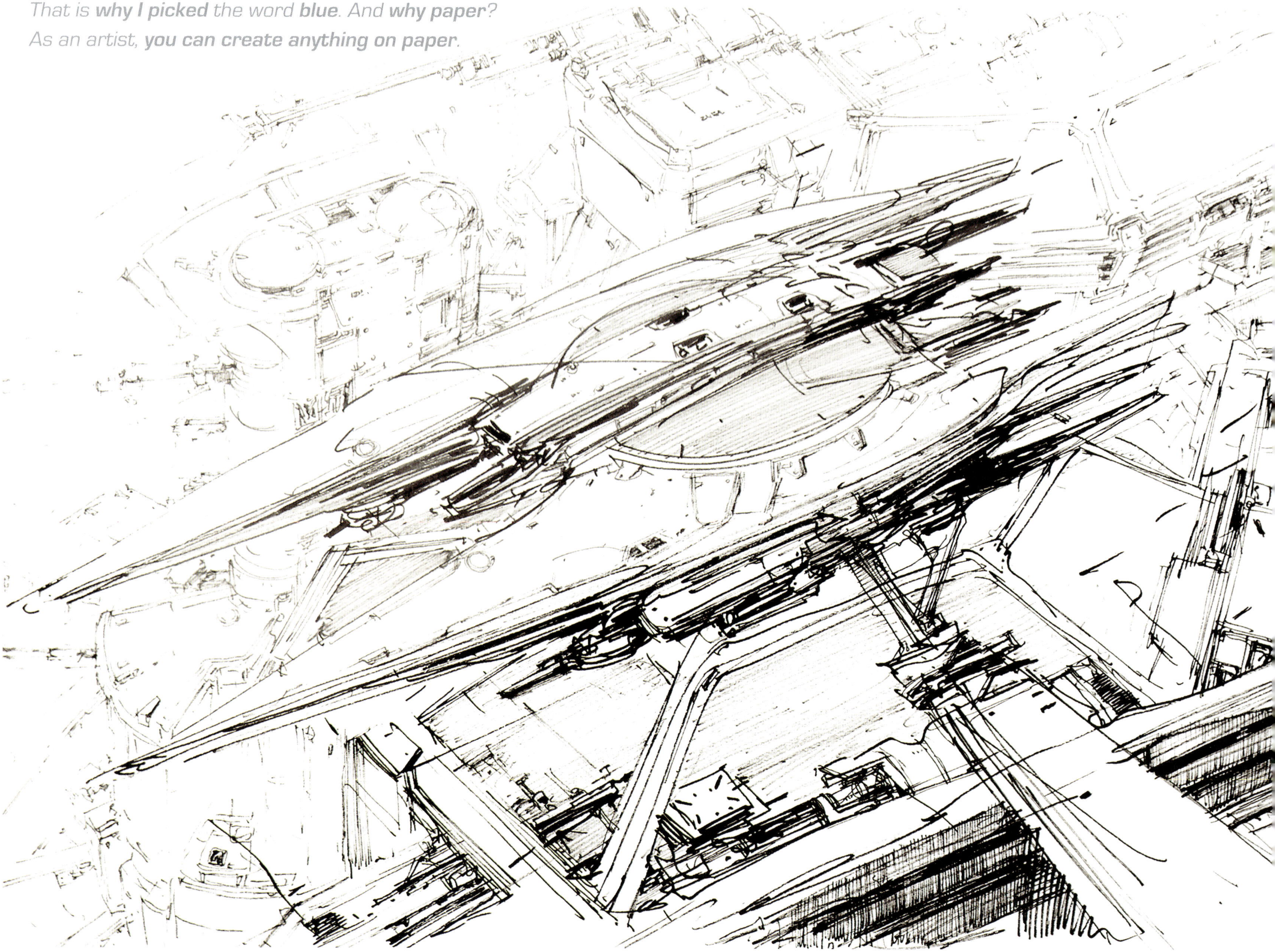

I would say paper is the starting base of all my creativity.

The Art of PAPER BLUE

an instructional companion
for the digital artist

Jae-Cheol Park

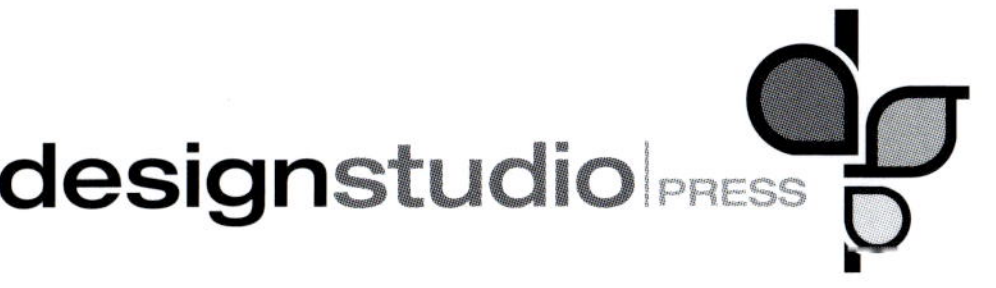

Editor | Peter C. Lee
Designer | Christopher J. De La Rosa
Art Direction | Scott Robertson
Copy Editors | Teena Apeles, Jessica Hoffmann

Publisher | Design Studio Press
Website | www.designstudiopress.com
E-mail | info@designstudiopress.com

Printed in China • First Edition • November 2014

10   9   8   7   6   5   4   3   2
Library of Congress Control Number: 2014941261
ISBN: 978-162465014-7

TABLE OF CONTENTS

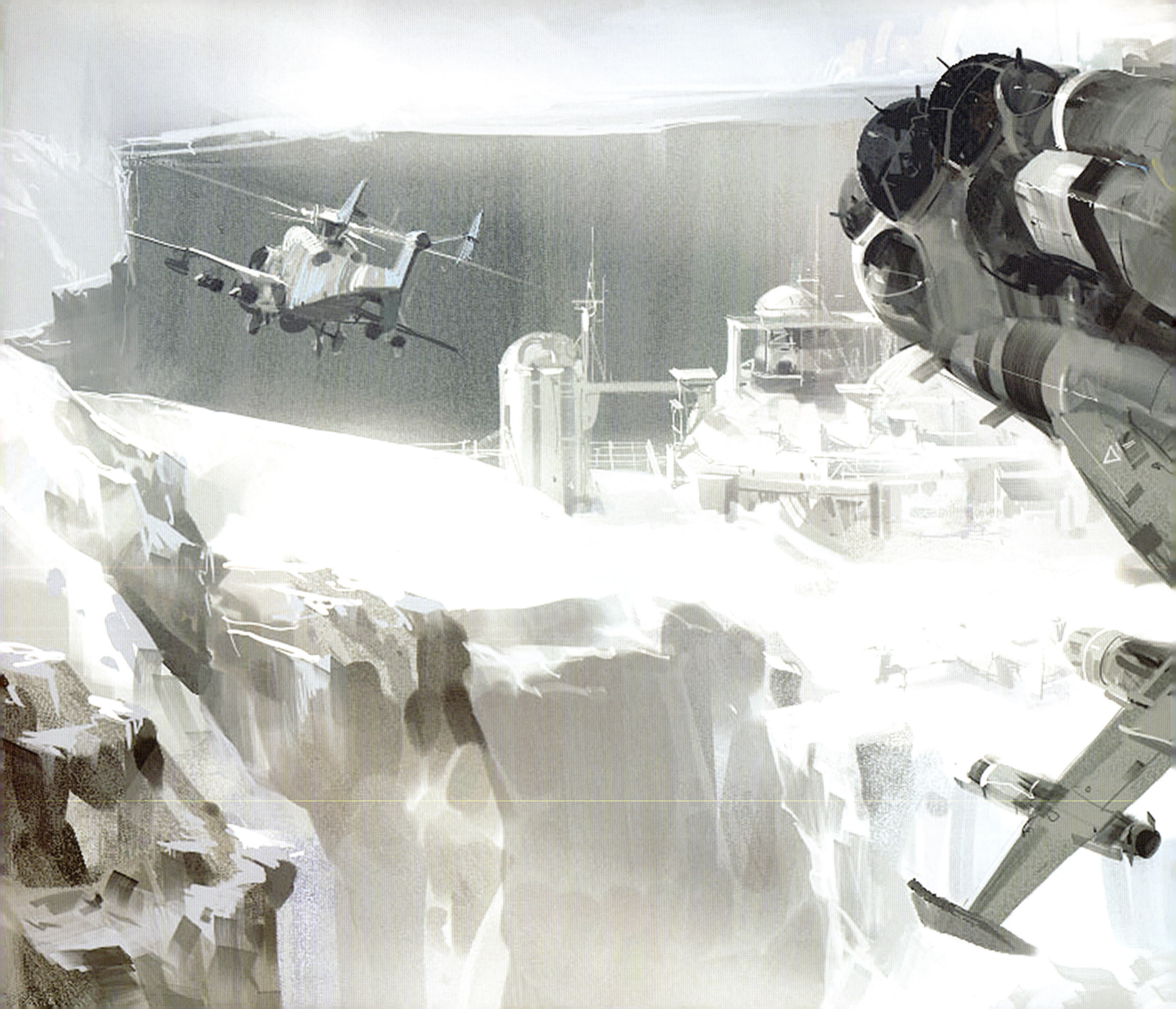

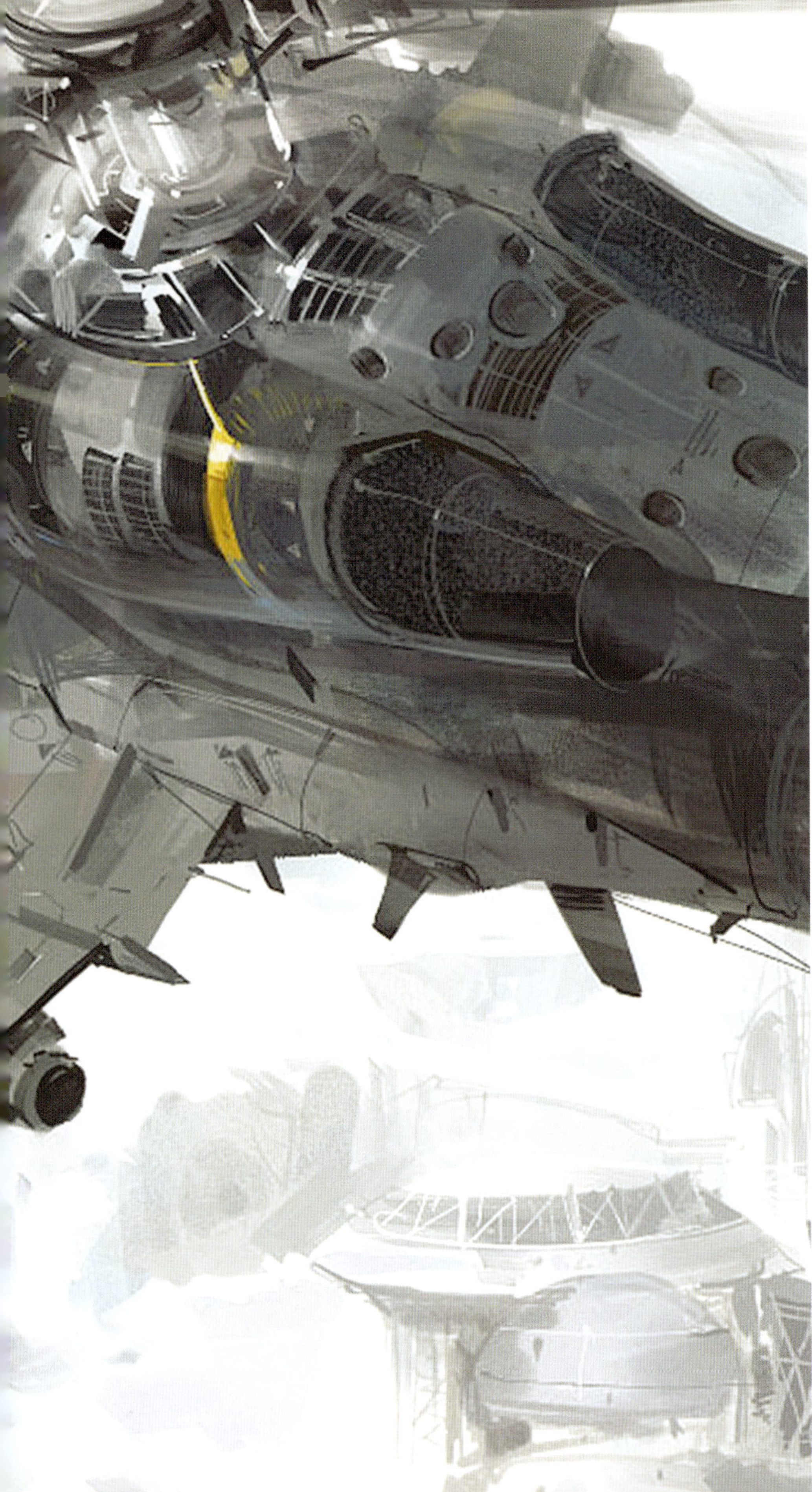

FOREWORD

The Art of PaperBlue is a book I'm very happy to publish. I have been a fan of Jae-Cheol's illustrative style and aesthetic range for years now, and the fact that this book includes a diverse collection of tutorials on his process makes it that much more special. To top it off, having his methods translated into English now brings his knowledge and experience to us in the West.

I hope you enjoy learning about his process as much as I have, and realize that hard work and practice can help any artist improve their skills, especially when great artists share their techniques as generously as Jae-Cheol has done here. Educational books are much more difficult to put together and write than portfolio-style books. We should all feel very grateful that this incredible artist was willing to put in the extra effort to share his techniques with the world.

Thank you, Jae-Cheol.

Scott Robertson
President, Design Studio Press

Los Angeles, California
May 30, 2014

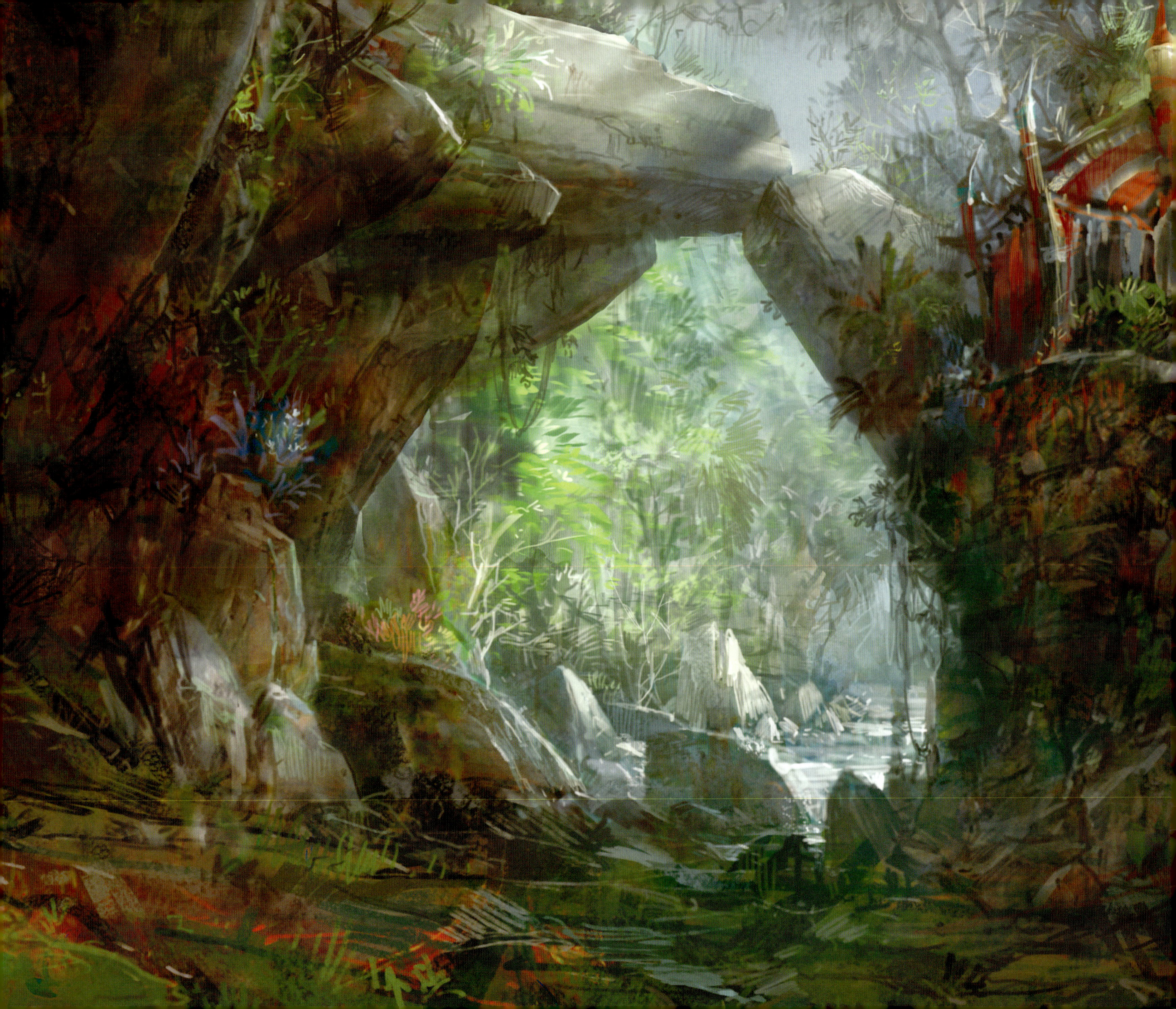

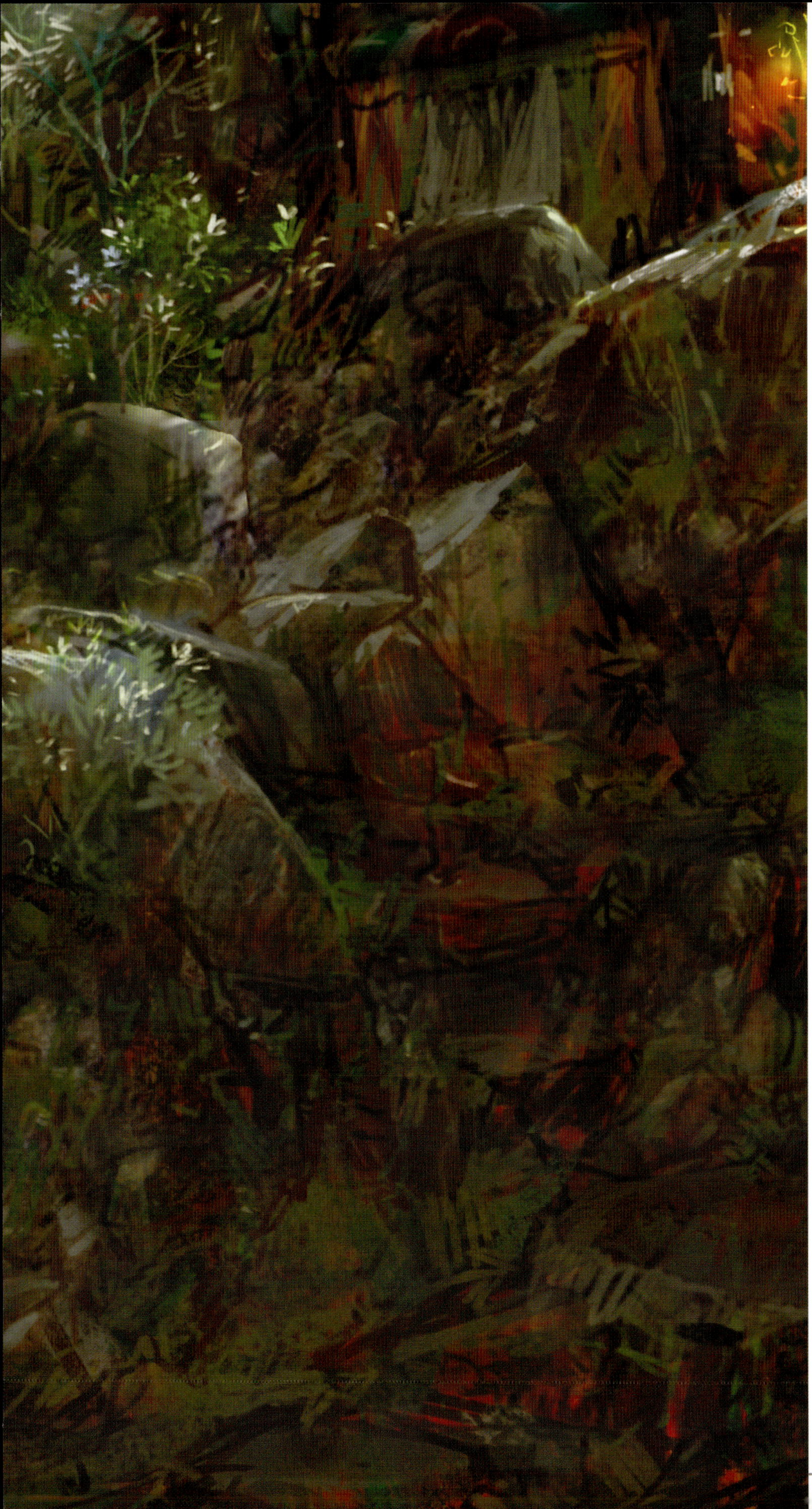

INTRODUCTION

As a concept artist for more than a decade, I have been lucky enough to create environment concept paintings for many movies and games, including *Lineage, Sun, The Day, Ion,* and *Blade and Soul.* When I was a student trying to learn conceptual painting, there was little information available, and no school taught the subject. So there was only one path: become a self-taught artist. I learned digital painting by studying Hayao Miyazaki's animation backgrounds.

Aware of the difficulties in learning this craft, I wrote *The Art of PaperBlue* to help anyone who wants to improve his or her artistic skills. In this book, you will find 10 step-by-step tutorials with detailed explanations, links to six video demos, numerous quick sketches, and more than a hundred of my paintings—from sci-fi environment paintings and vehicle designs to natural landscapes and much more. I cover creating and using custom brushes, smudge tools, color theories, compositions, and many other techniques helpful in creating imaginative artwork.

I hope that by sharing my knowledge of creating environment concept paintings for the entertainment world, you can hone your skills.

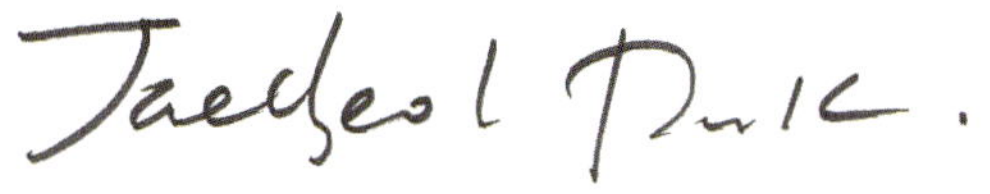

Jae-Cheol Park
Seoul, Korea
Winter 2013

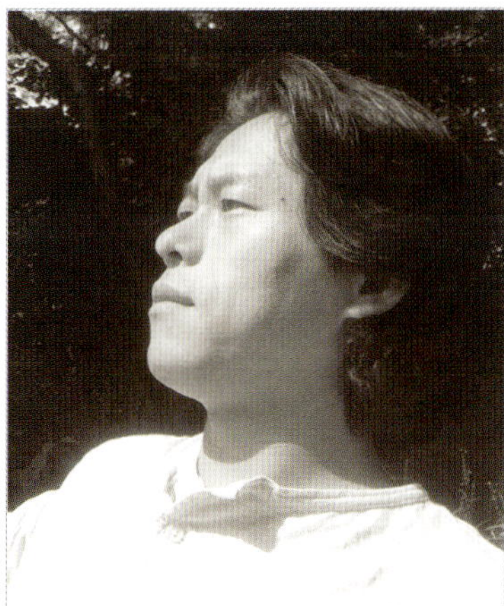

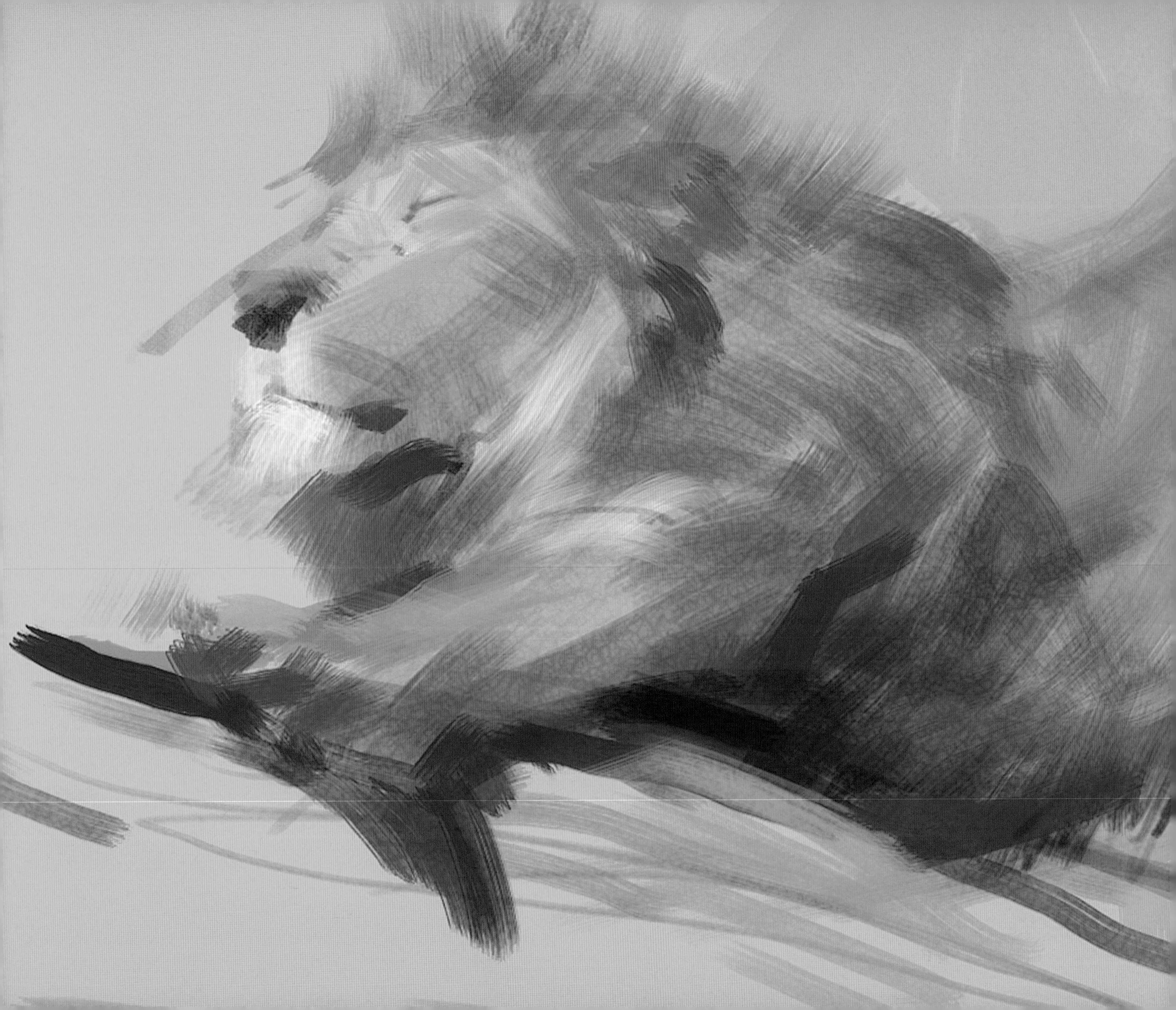

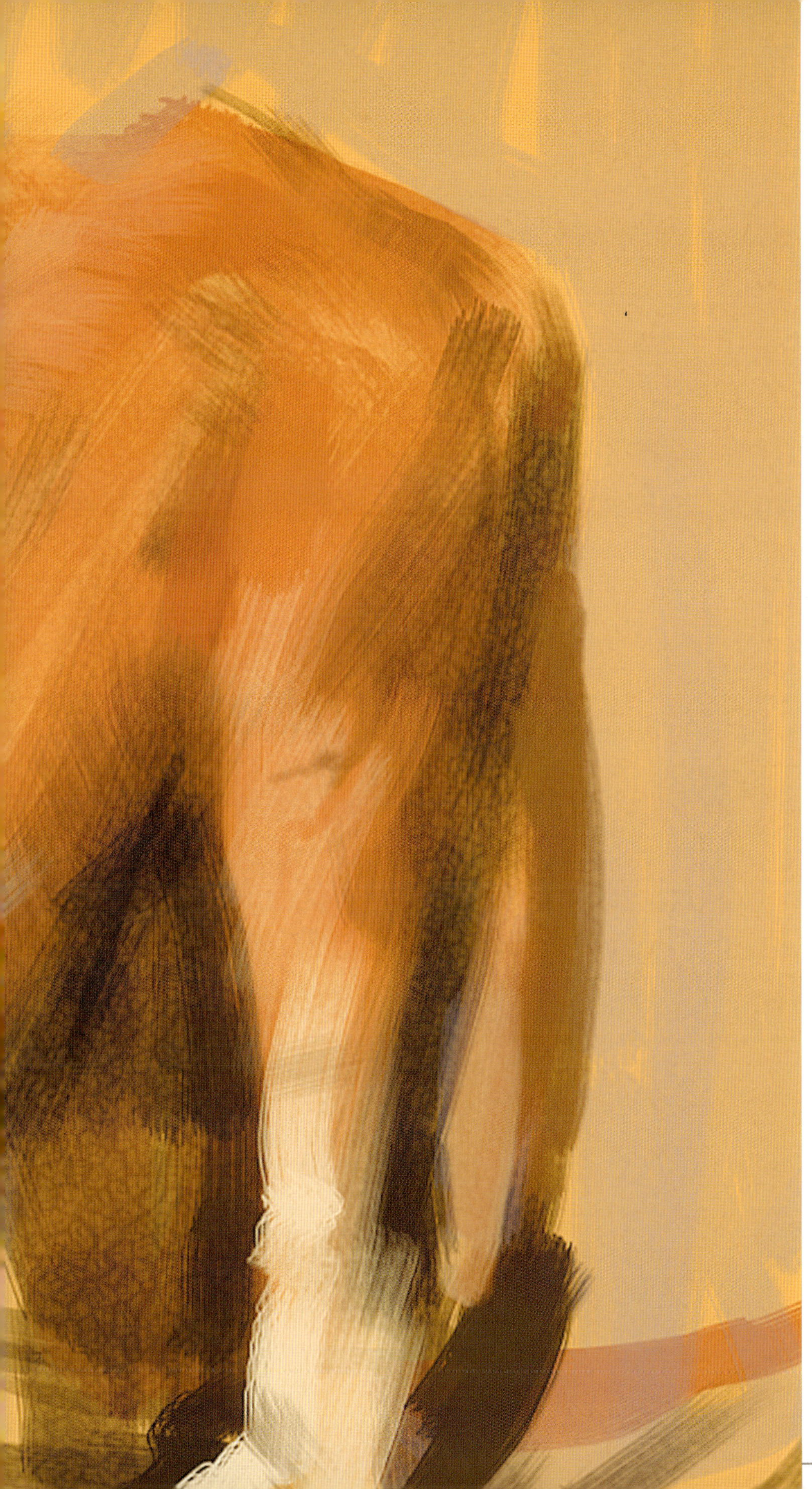

chapter **01**

BRUSH TUTORIALS

In this chapter, I will explain how to make and use a custom brush. Creating a brush should be a thoughtful process; a random brush pattern will not create meaningful painting strokes. After explaining the basic philosophy of brush making, I will show some paintings I created by using textured brushes.

Brushes

Cross-hatching transparent brushstrokes makes interesting patterns and gives a translucent feel to the strokes (a).

In this test sample, I used a very low-opacity brush (10%) and stacked up the strokes to build up the opacity. When I paint blue (10% opacity) on top of a yellow background, the result is a gray color that has a slightly bluish tone.

Fig. 1.1

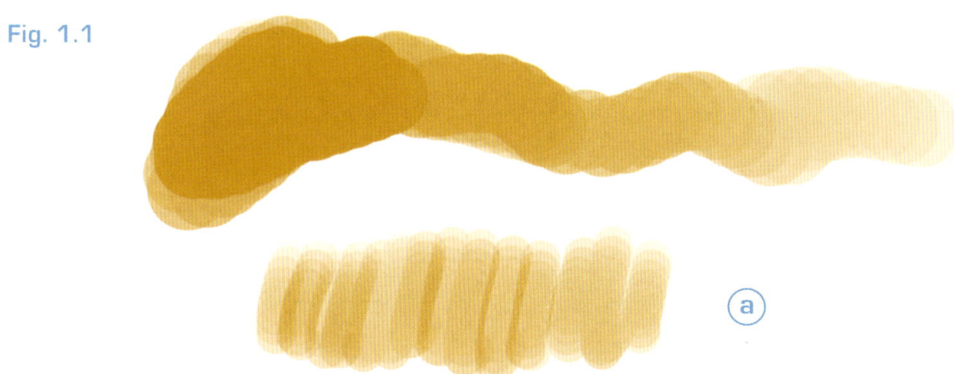

Fig. 1.2

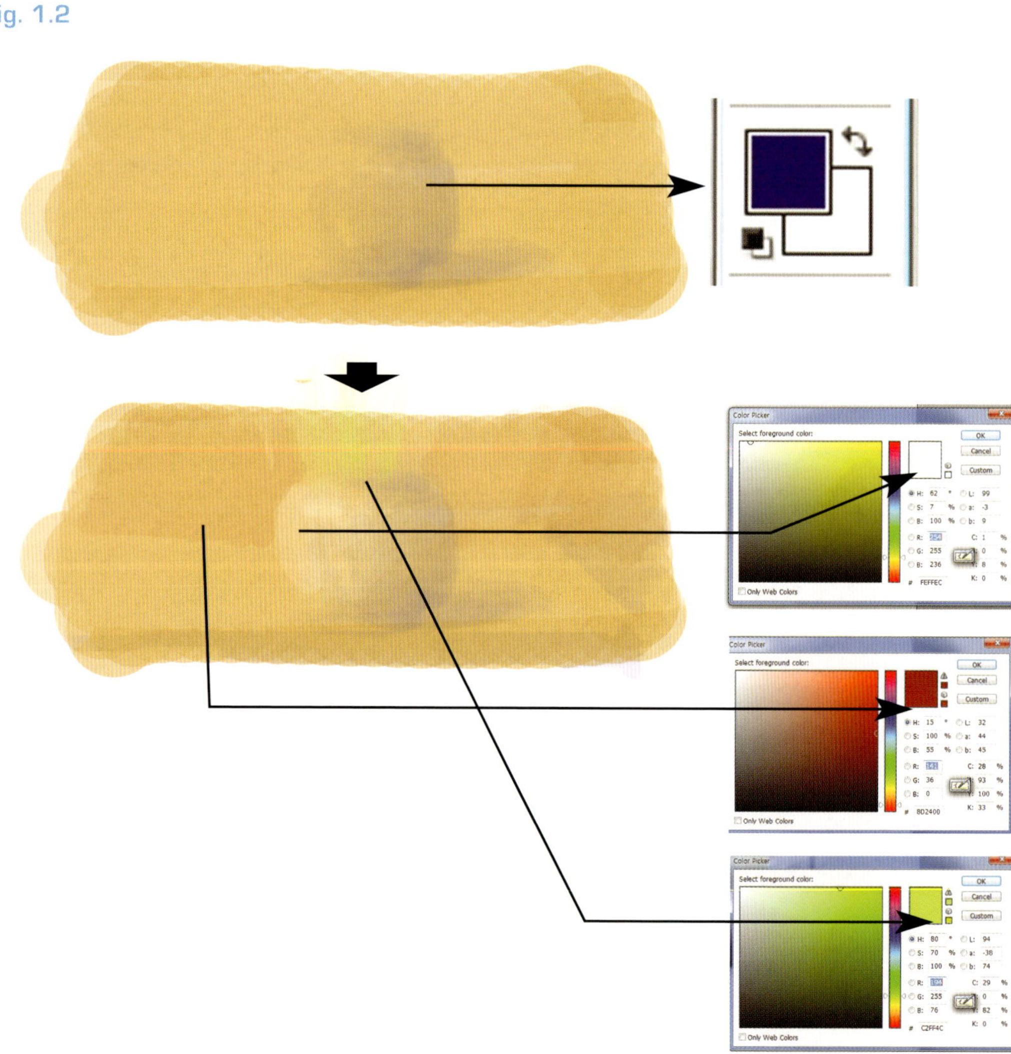

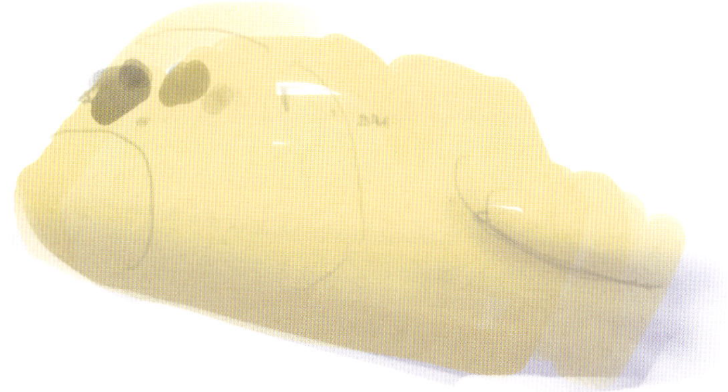
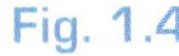

Fig. 1.3

This is an example of how I would apply that low-opacity brush in my painting process. First, by using a normal brush with a higher opacity, I draw the big shape. Then I use a dark blue color to paint the shadow, using a 30% opacity airbrush. This gives a very transparent feel to the paint stroke, and allows me to save the sketch as well.

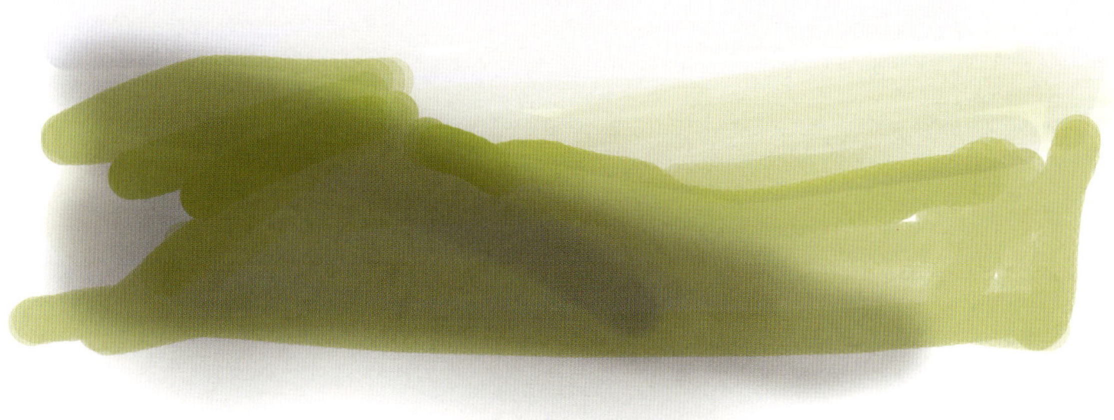
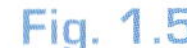

Fig. 1.4

The same rule applies when painting nature. First, draw the mountain range with a normal brushstroke. Then, using a 50% black airbrush, add a shadow layer.

Fig. 1.5

Here is a small exercise that shows everything I have explained here. First, draw a big shape with a basic brush. Next, paint the shadow of the cloud with an airbrush. Then, apply cross-hatching to the strokes to create a lost-edge effect. Opaque strokes result in a sharper edge.

Fig. 1.6

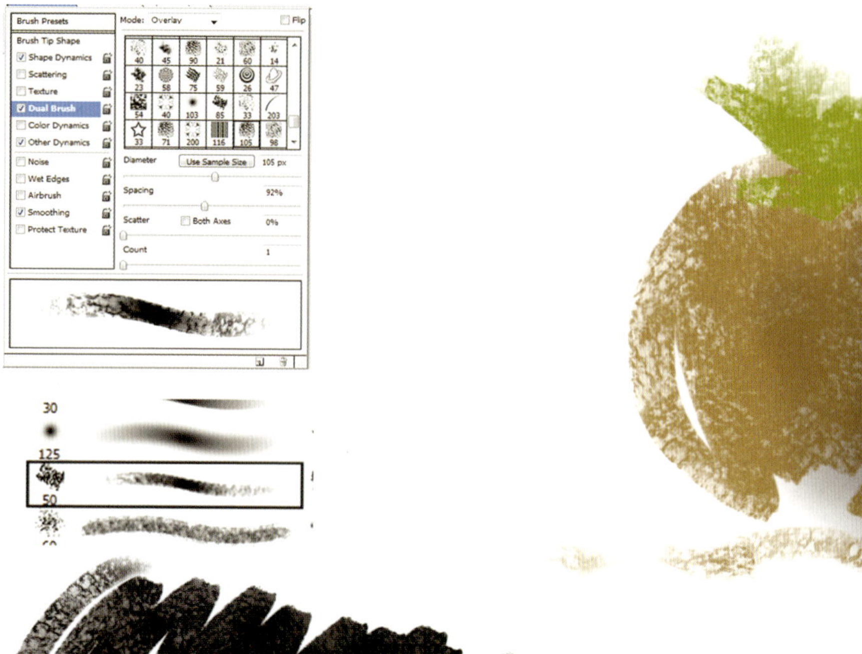

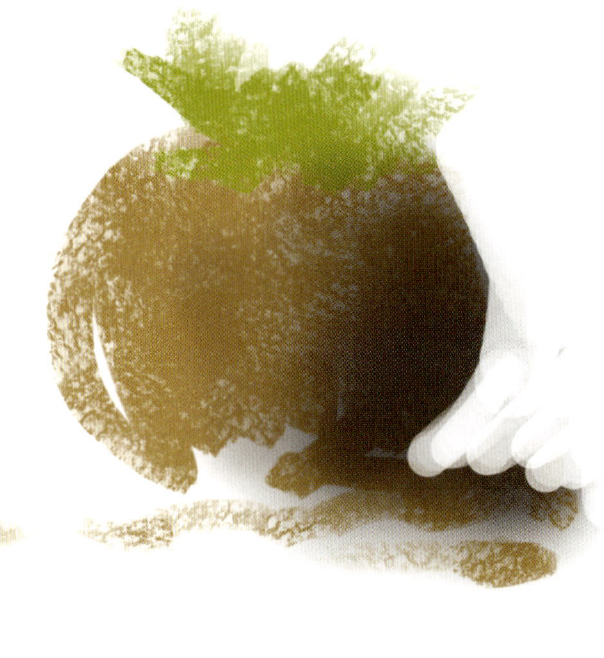

Now I will explain how to use the texture settings in the brush control menu. Following the steps in the previous test sample, first draw a big shape, this time using a textured brush. Then apply a shadow with a low-opacity airbrush. This creates a fun texture for the painting. The airbrush finishes the painting with a soft-edge control.

Here is another exercise. First, draw the shape with a rough texture brush.

Fig. 1.7

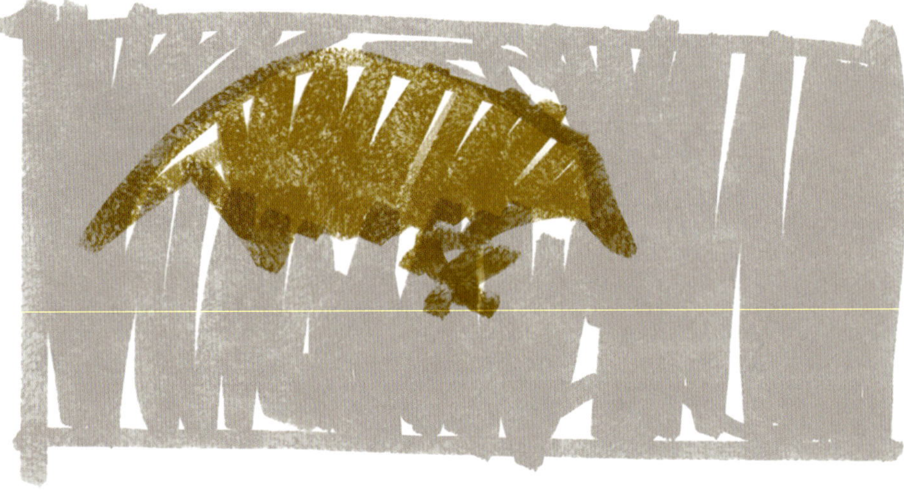

Chapter 01 - Brush Tutorials

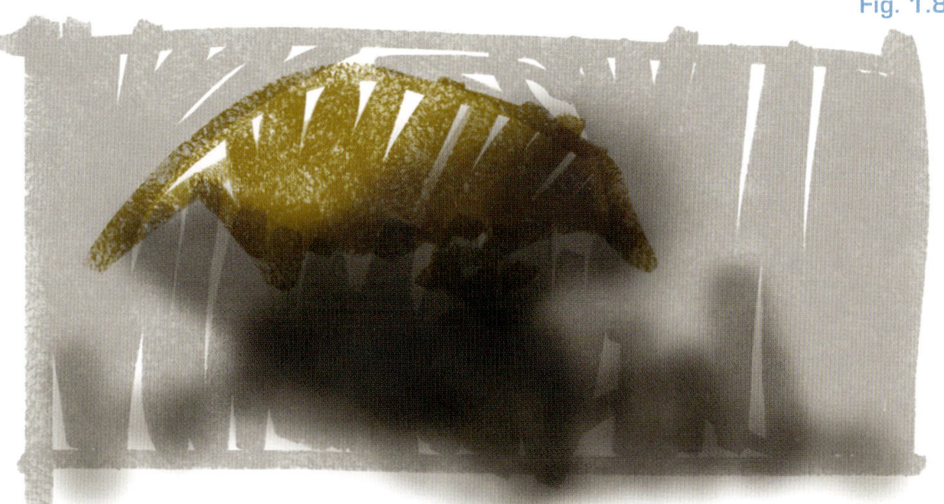

Fig. 1.8

Second, use a 50% opacity airbrush to draw the silhouette in the shadow.

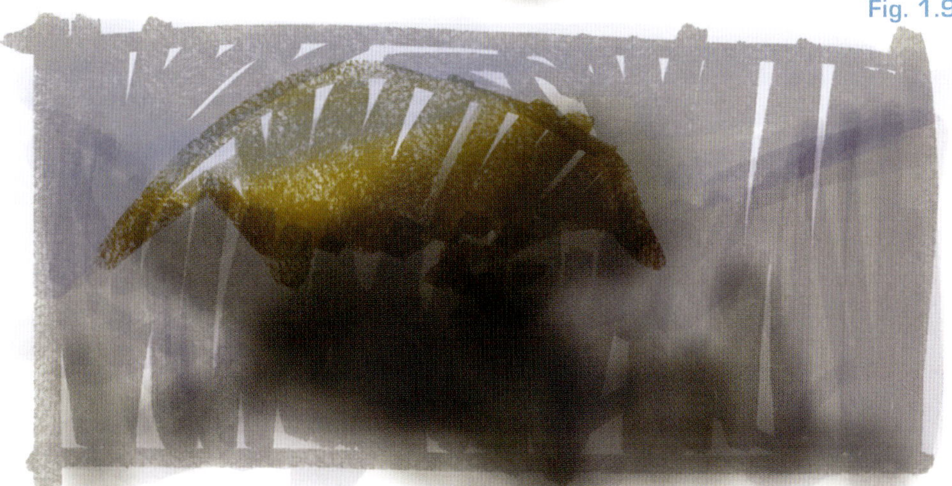

Fig. 1.9

Then, use a basic brush to draw the background. Its simplicity works well for the background shape in the distance.

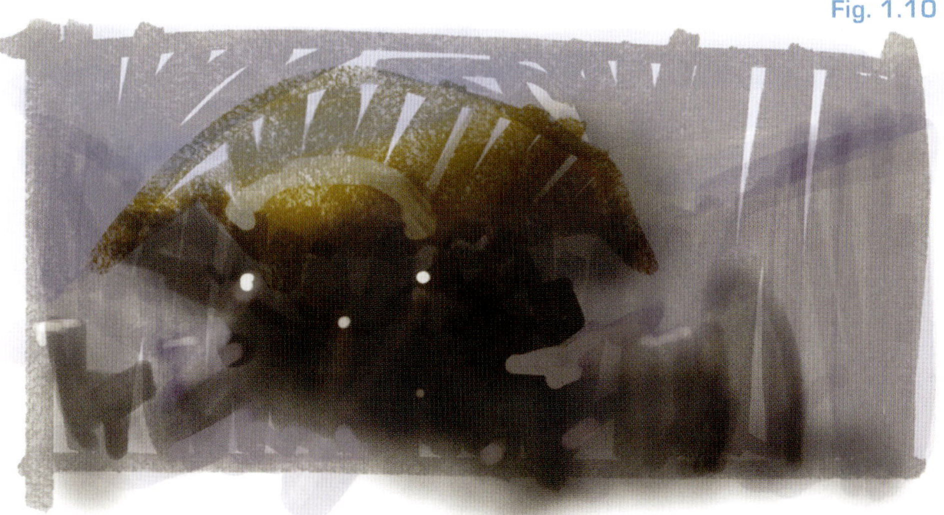

Fig. 1.10

The shape created with an airbrush doesn't have a clear form or clean edge, so I took a hard-edge brush with full opacity to carve in the silhouette shape more clearly. After, indicate a light source with white color.

Here is another example of using custom brushes. I used a low-opacity (10%) blue color in the background to produce a subtle color shift. An important thing to note here is that even though I tinted the background, I did not cover up every part evenly. I intentionally left gaps between brushstrokes to create a more natural feel. When I use blue on top of yellow, it creates a nice grayish tone, which creates a nice color balance in the painting. I also added a bit more red to the lion's fur to give it more color accents.

These are samples of the brushes I used in this example. Here, I used big brushstrokes in the shadow areas to create more size contrast between brushstrokes. Where a clean end was needed, I used an opaque brush to create a more solid, hard edge.

Fig. 1.11

Fig. 1.12

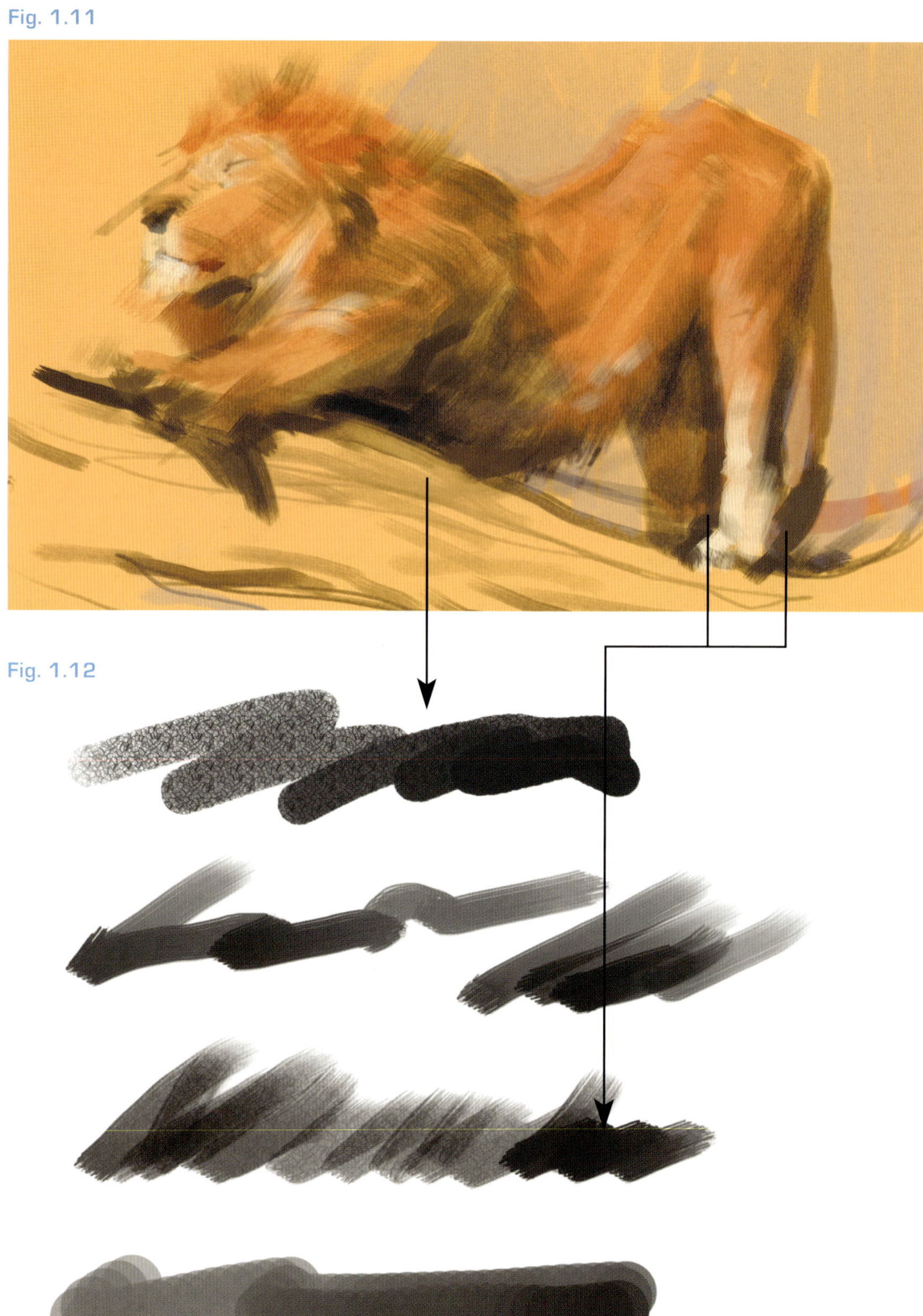

Fig. 1.13

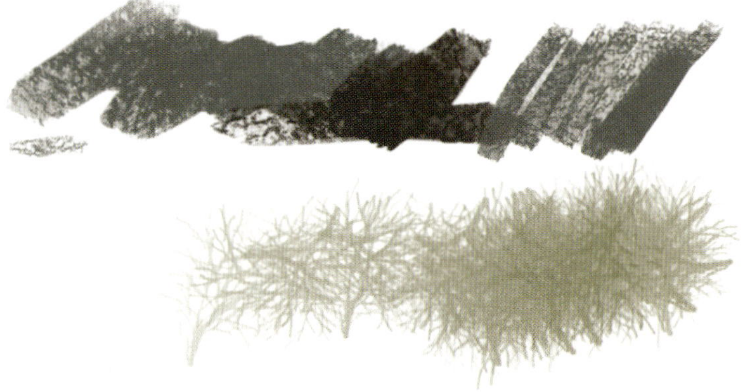

The following sketches are examples of how I would use a texture brush in my painting. These are the two main texture brushes I am using for this painting other than the default brush.

Fig. 1.14

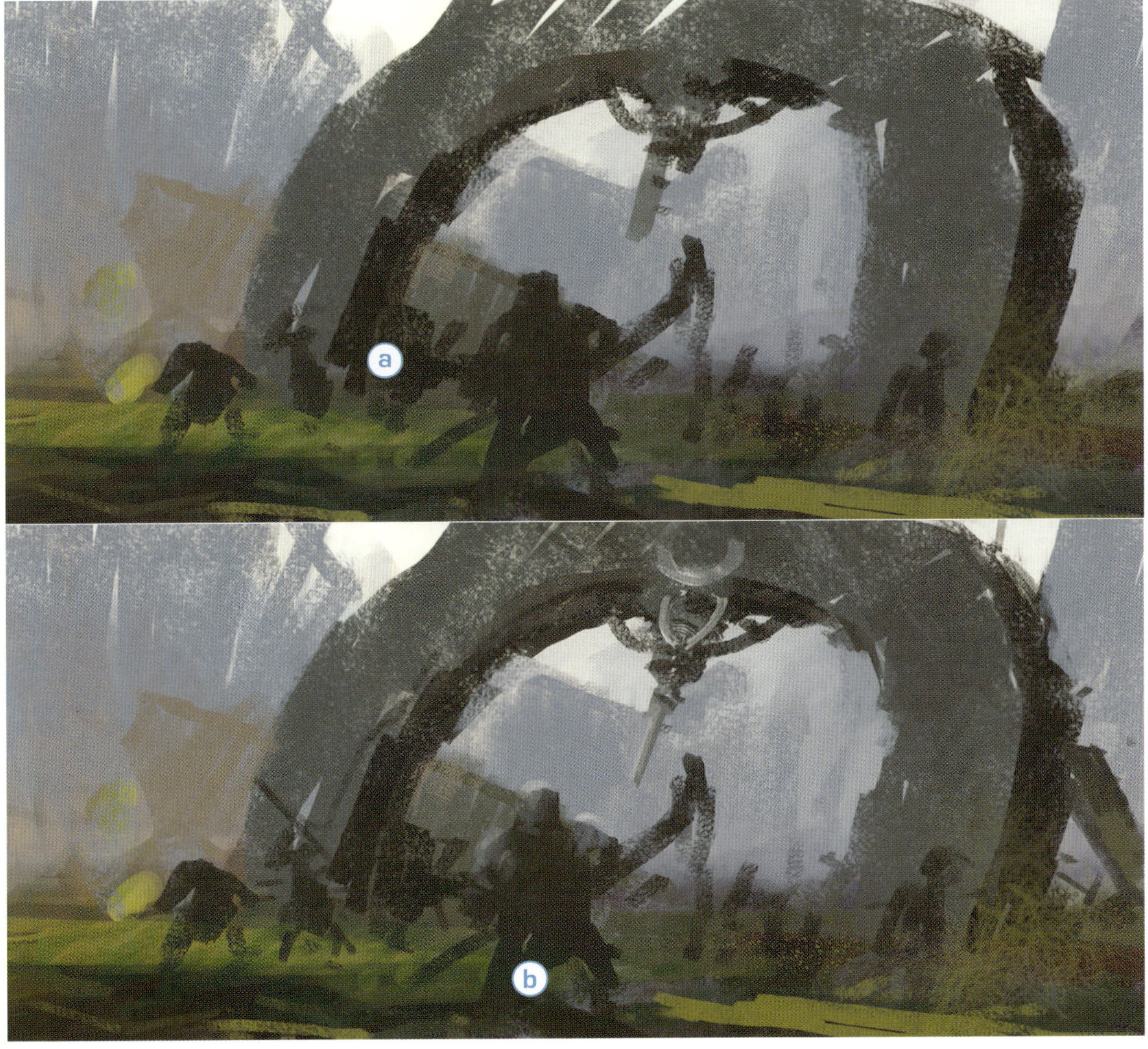

I start with the main subject of the painting. Then I get the big shapes down, and clarify the design of the objects. The main subject can be either the arch (a) or the soldier in the foreground (b).

The next step is to add a clear light source. Since most of the painting is a cool color, I painted a red cape on the soldier.

I have used a low-opacity (10–30%) texture brush to suggest the look of grass on the field. Also, darker value was added to the soldier to tighten up the value structure. I would leave the background as loose as it is. I can also tighten up the focal point to make this painting look more finished if I want to.

Fig. 1.15

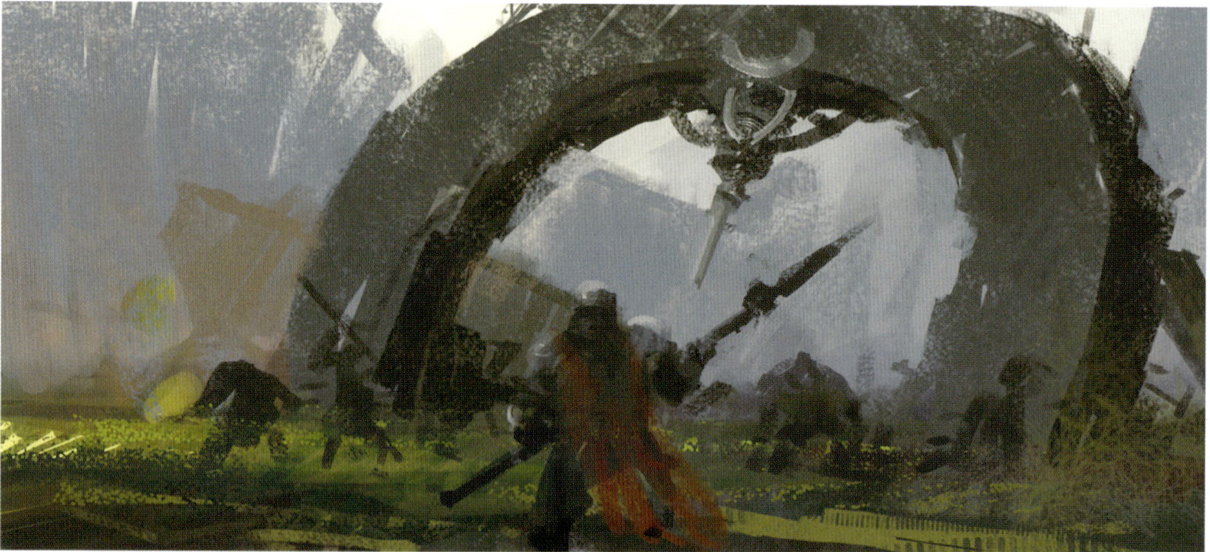

Fig. 1.16

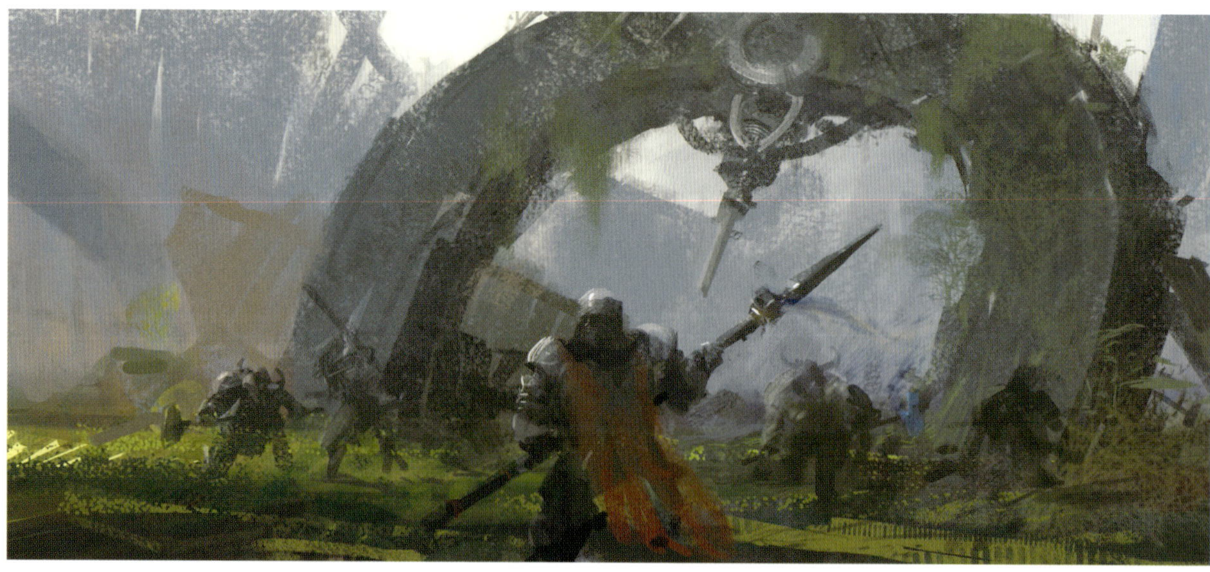

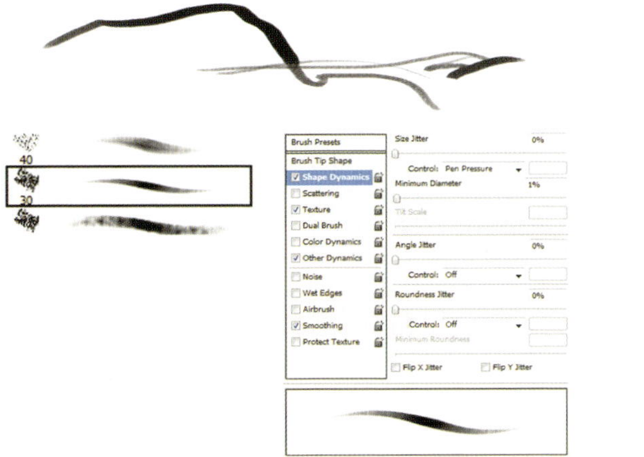

Fig. 1.17

Fig. 1.18

This time I played with the Shape Dynamics in the Brush Preset window. I set the size jitter at Pen Pressure. This setting results in more natural-looking traditional brush marks.

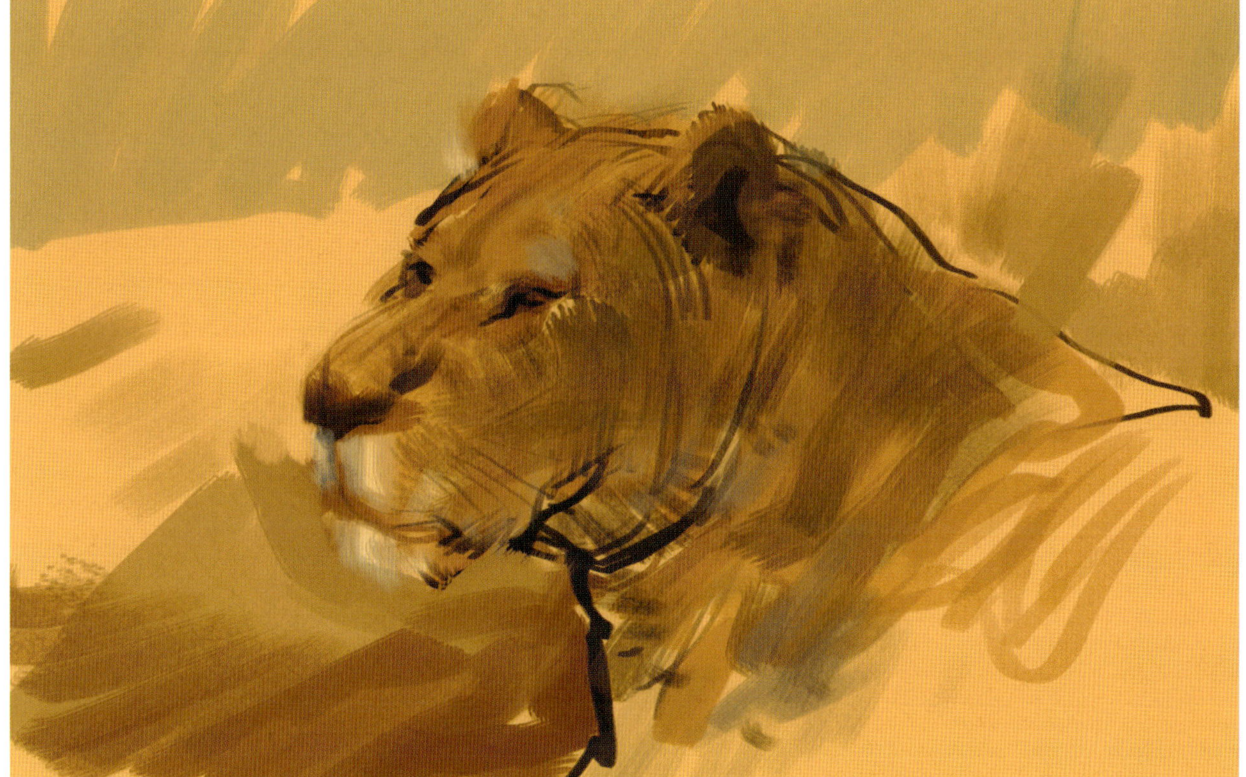

Fig. 1.19

I used a gray color around the mouth and in the background. It works great as a mid-tone neutral color in this painting. It widens the color spectrum. The gray color used around the mouth of the lion looks bluish, but it is still in the orange family. I changed the saturation of the color, which made it look much cooler than it really is against the orange background.

These are two different brushes I used to paint the lion fur. The one on the left (Fig. 1.19a) has a drier brush texture, and creates very rough marks, which is very useful for expressing individual hair marks. On the other hand, the one on the right (Fig. 1.19b) has more of a wet brush feel, which is smoother and softer. I used this one to block in the big shape before I used the dry brush for the hair.

This is the last exercise of the brush tutorial. For this particular painting, I started with an acrylic painting as a base. I took a photo of my acrylic painting and brought it into Photoshop. I used a very rough texture brush in order to get a rough tree-bark look.

Then, I start to add more lighting information to the painting. Here, I have added a little bit of gray to make my color palette more abundant in its range.

Fig. 1.20

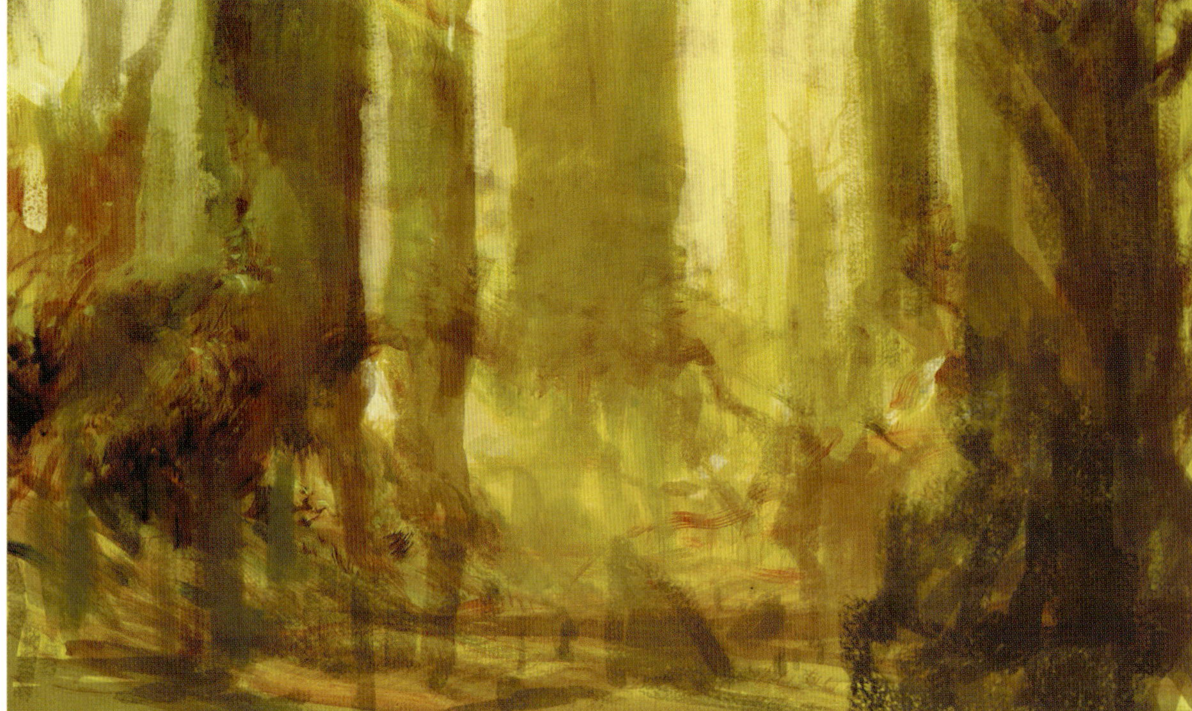

Fig. 1.21

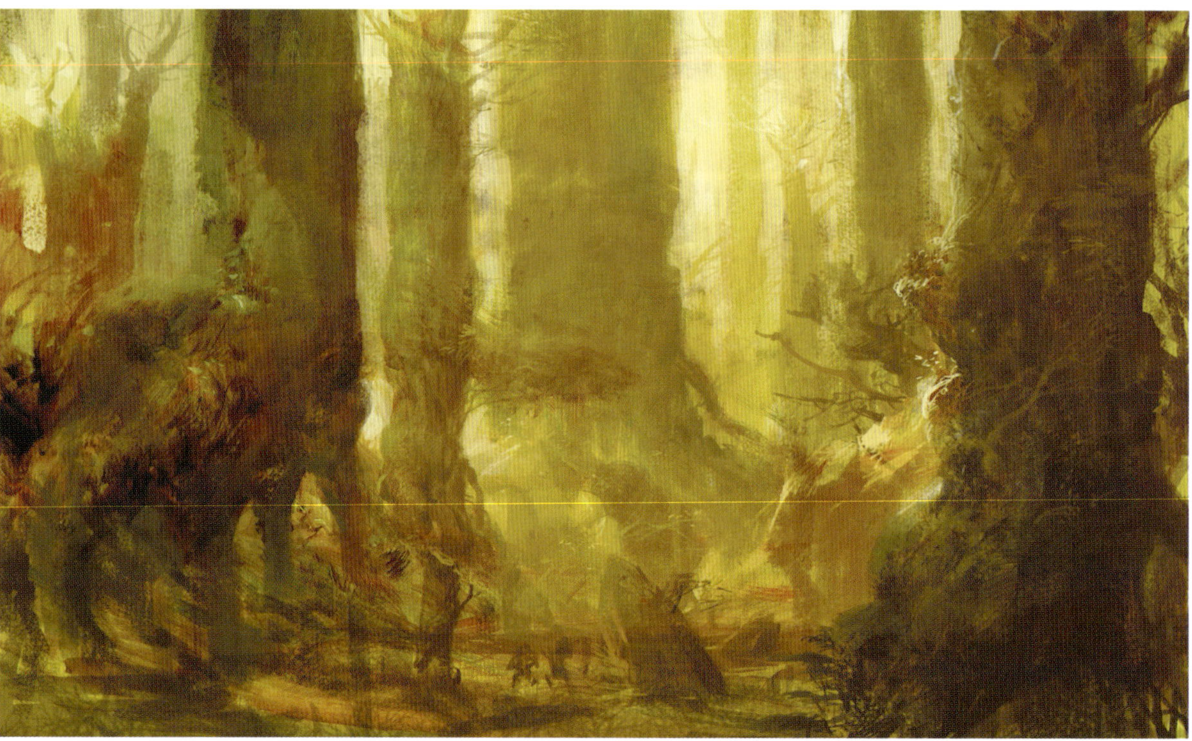

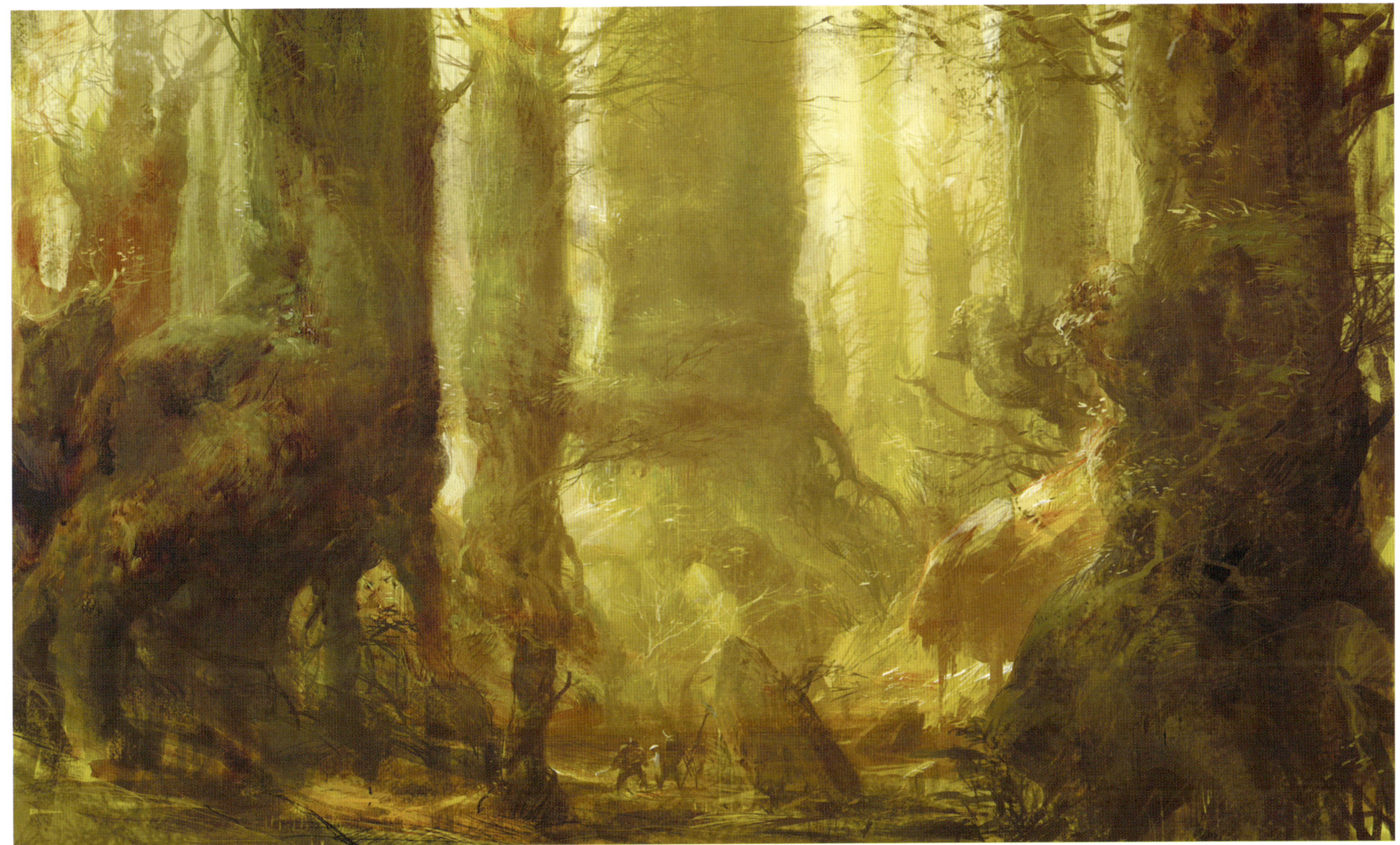

There are several different ways to paint the details and bring up the finish level. The first one is by using the Lasso tool. The result is a very clean and sharp look. Another way is by using lines. This is a more organic way to add more natural-looking brush marks. Also, by mixing these different painting techniques, it is possible to get a wide variety of different brush marks in a painting.

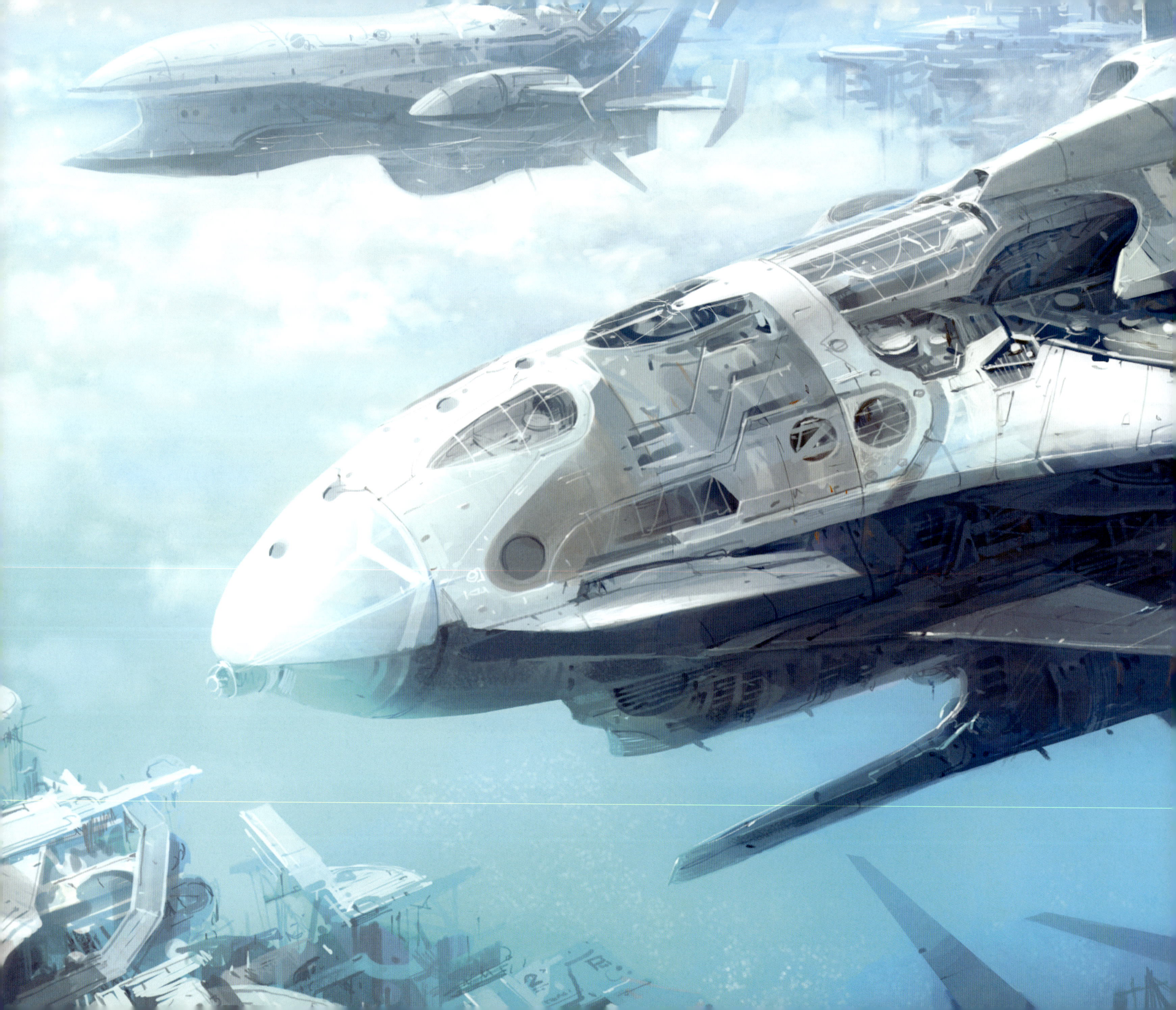

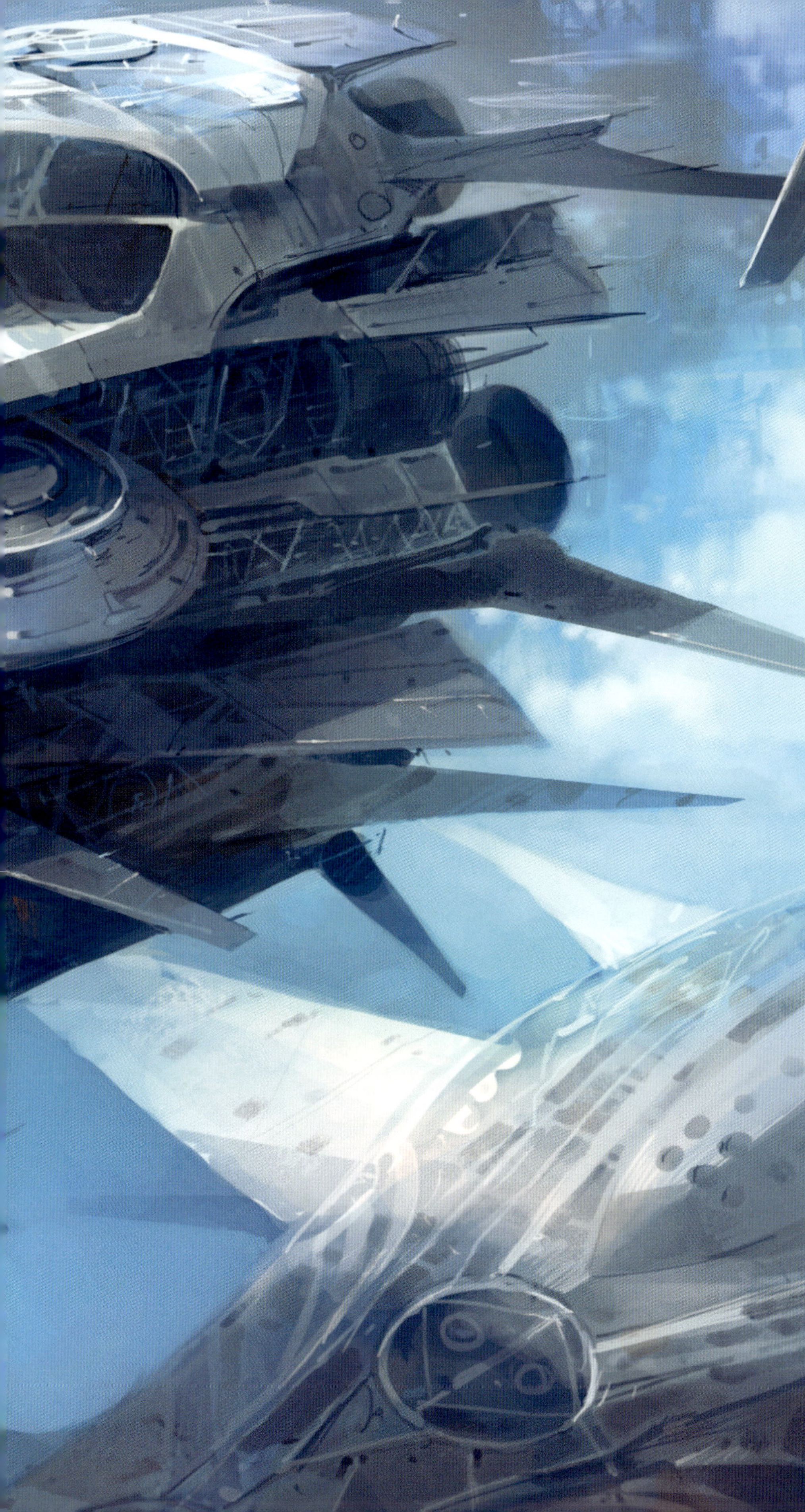

VEHICLE TUTORIALS 02

In this chapter, I will demonstrate how to create a series of vehicle designs, including hard-surface mechanical subjects like spaceships, helicopters, tanks, and flying ships. You will learn about the forms and shapes of vehicle design and how to create interesting-looking vehicles. And rather than just feature vehicles in isolation, I put them in environments to create more interesting storytelling settings, because it is important to harmonize a vehicle with the background.

Space Fighter

Fig. 2.1

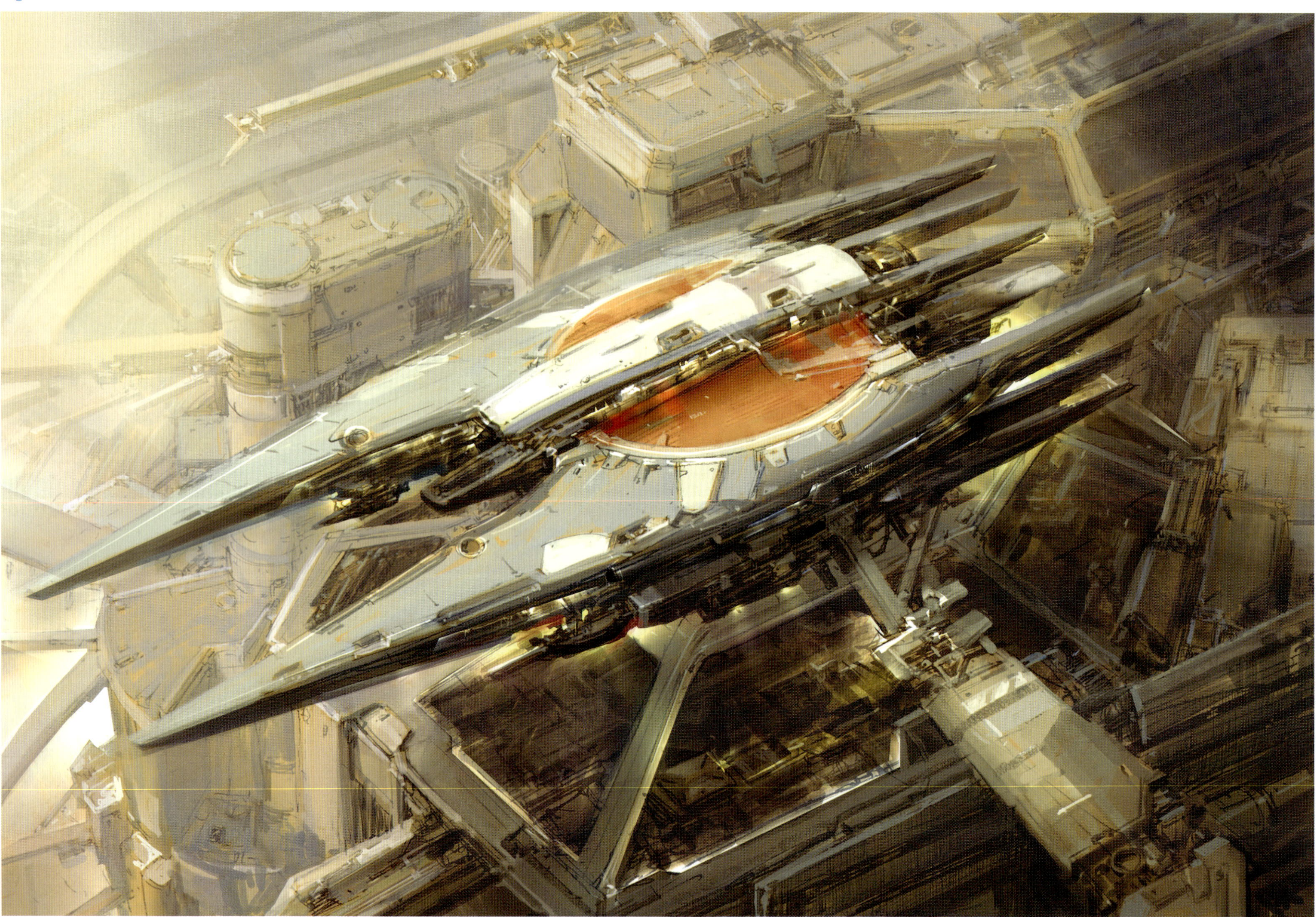

Fig. 2.2

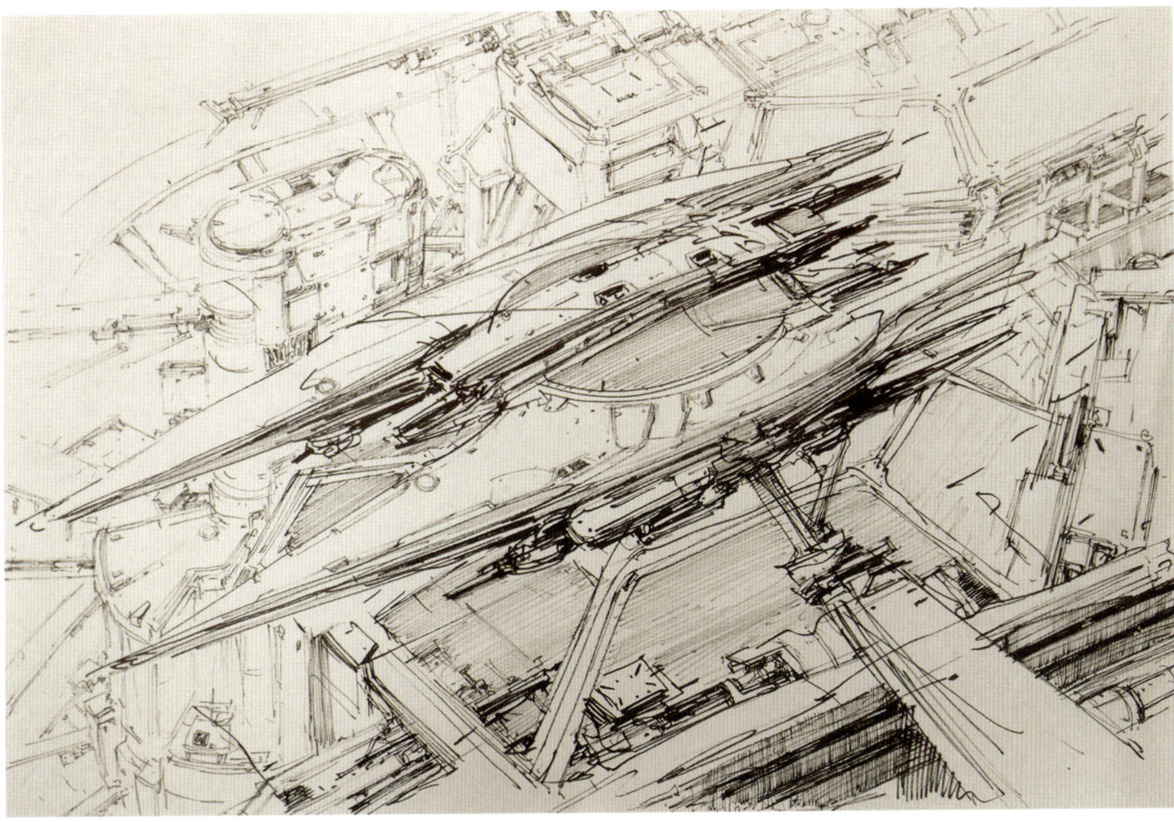

I start my sketch with a Stylo pen on A4-sized paper. In the background, you can see there is a difference in line weight. It gets lighter in the background because I used a dried-out Stylo pen for those marks. The subject for this scene is a space fighter docked in a hangar, located in a corner of a city. The ship has a big, generally curved shape with small-scale straight lines. This is a typical small-scale fighter-ship design that I enjoy drawing from time to time. This time, I started with an isometric top-down view.

Fig. 2.3

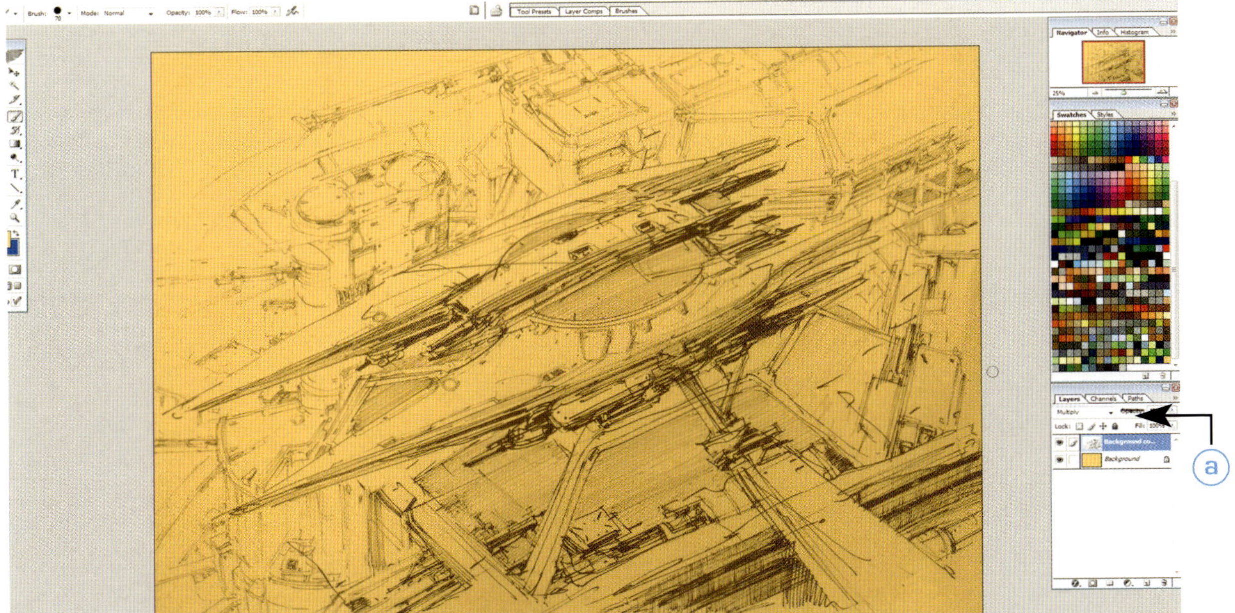

Once I am happy with the line work, I scan it and bring it into Photoshop. Then I create a Multiply layer and fill it with golden brown. This golden brown base tone creates a very warm feeling for the painting. If I want to see quicker results, I start with the main color that I am going to use for the hangar (in this case, that would have been gray and orange). However, since I wanted to explore more color variation in this painting, I started with this golden brown as a base tone.

Fig. 2.4

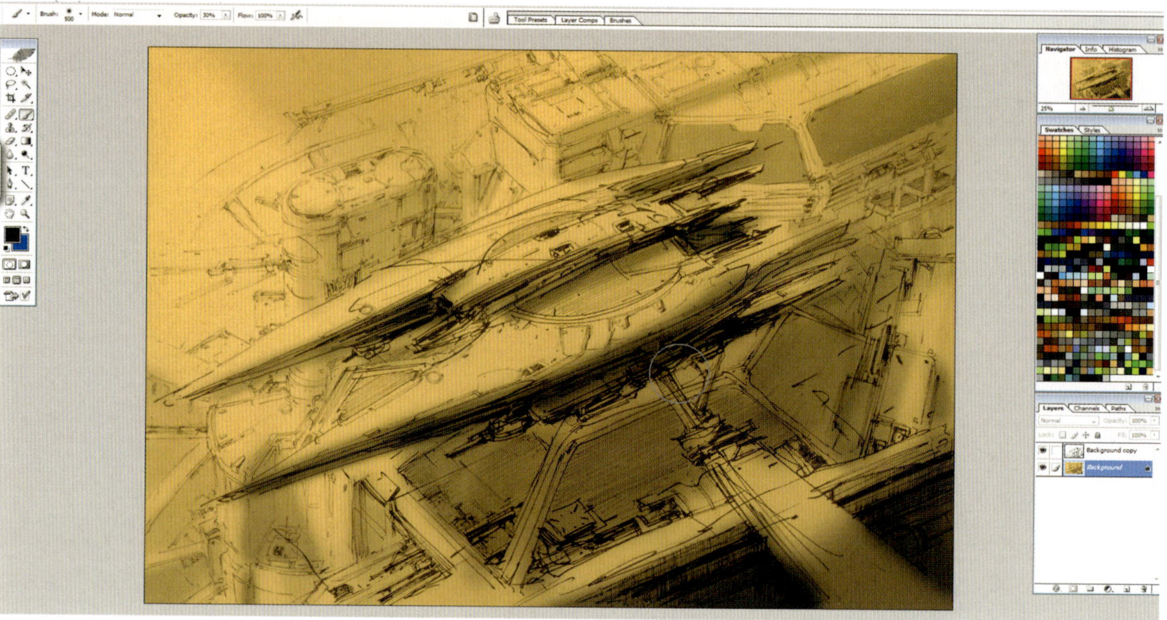

On the same Multiply layer, I begin to block in a big shadow with a soft airbrush.

Then, I paint the main colors for the battleship. Here I chose gray, white, and orange. Since these are the main theme colors for the painting, I had to be accurate with these color choices. Choosing the right kind of gray was especially important. I picked the bright gray containing a little bit of greenish tone, which has a warm and heavy feel. If I start a painting with a lighter color—perhaps the lightest color of the painting—it helps me to establish a brighter feeling for its mood. Yet, at the same time, I have to work with a darker value as well as a lighter tone in order to understand the full value range of the painting.

Sometimes I use the Burn tool to darken the whole portion. A good thing about this tool is that you can darken the value while keeping the original texture. Once I put down the base color, I use the Burn tool to create a darker shadow color, and to repaint on top of that color. This is just one of the many ways I could start my painting.

Fig. 2.5

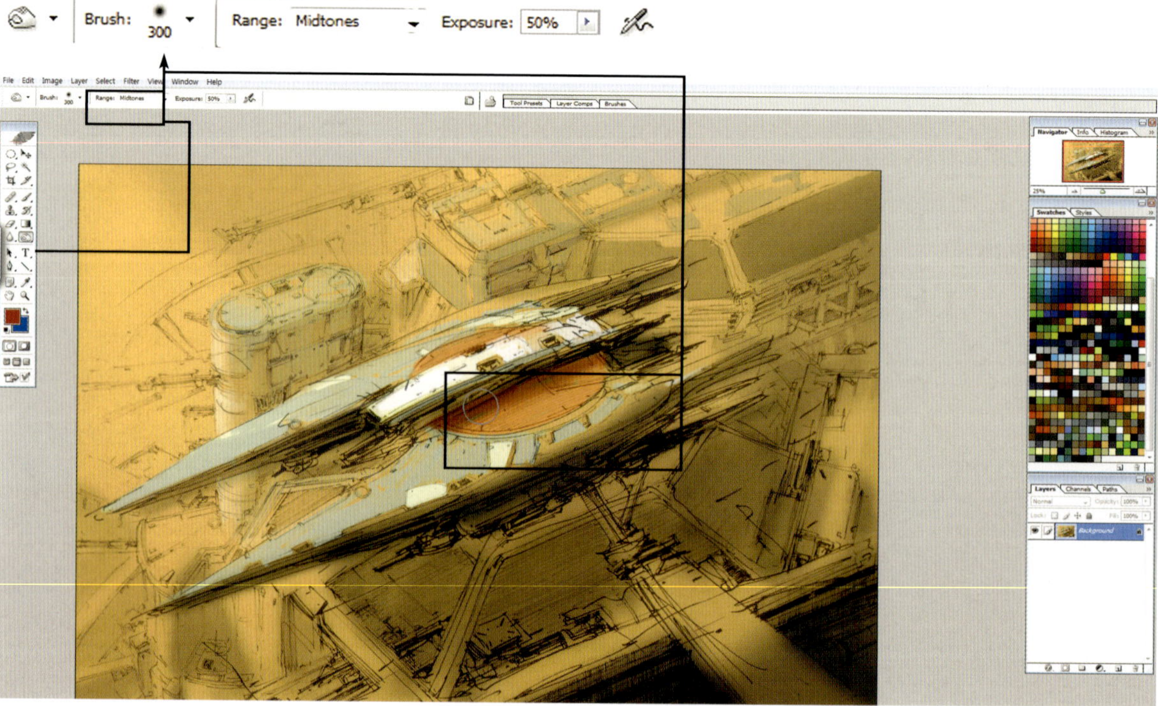

Chapter 02 - Vehicle Tutorials

Fig. 2.6

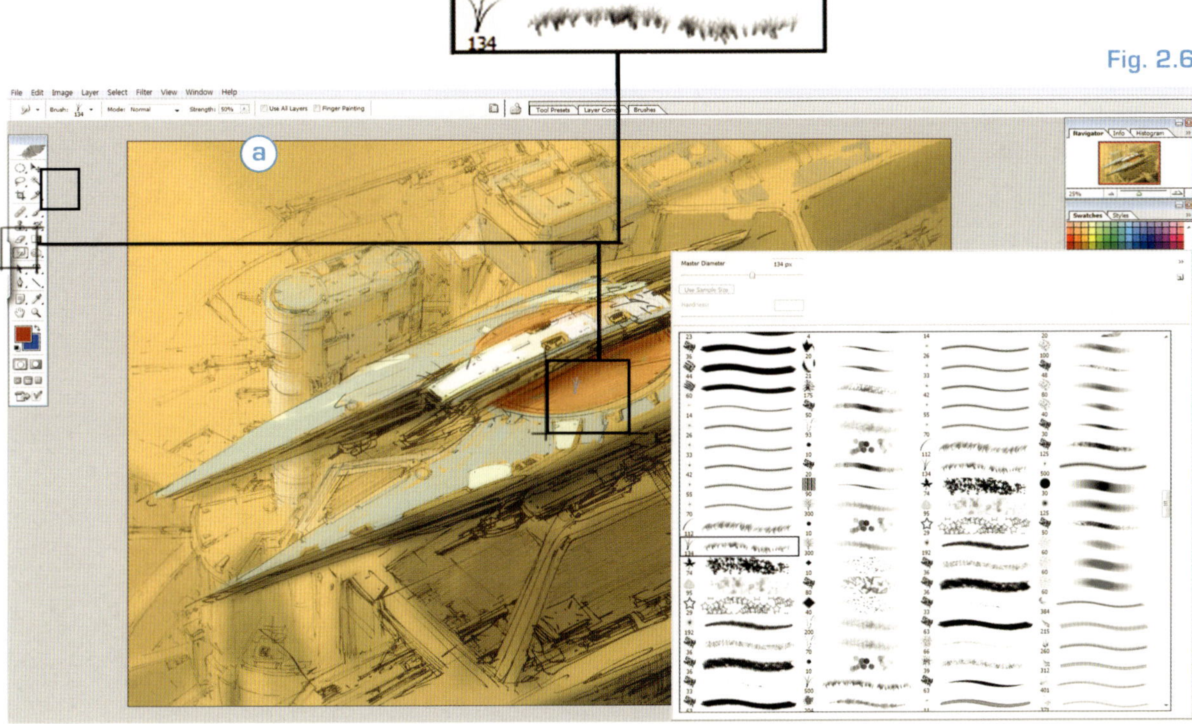

Fig. 2.7

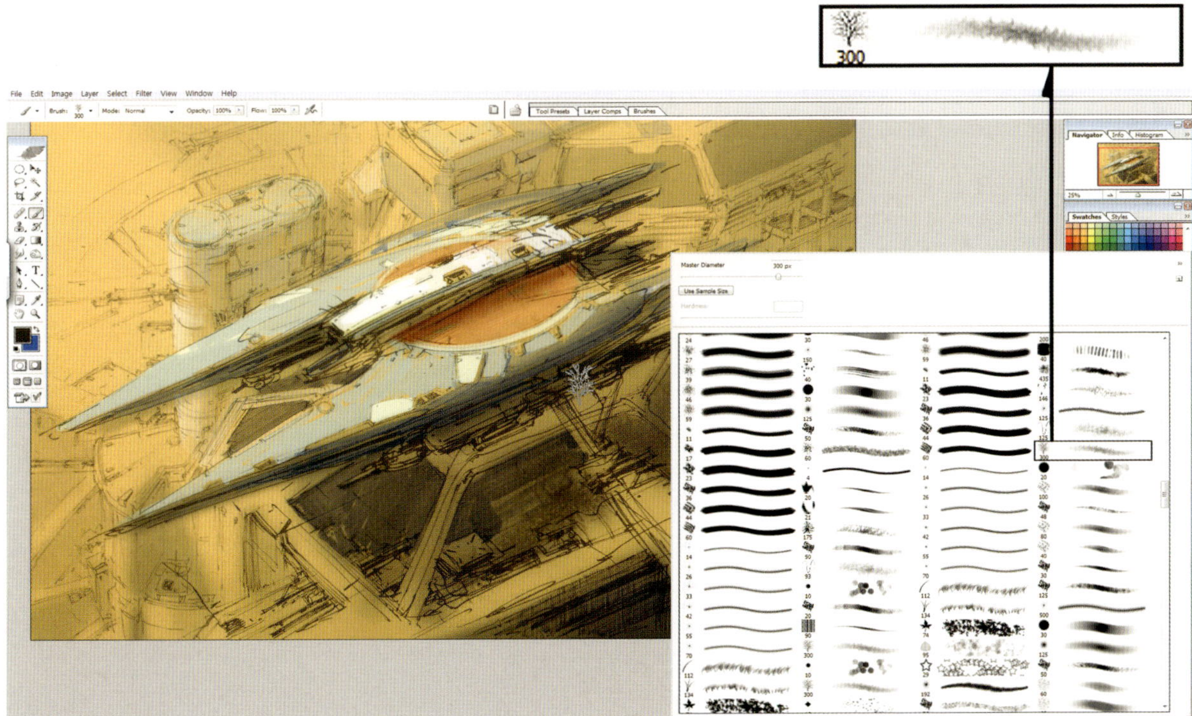

Smudge tool: This is one of the tools that I use most often when I am painting. It is a good tool to use to soften the brushstroke. I usually use it with 50% pressure, but sometimes I push it up to full opacity. When I use this tool, I enjoy the texture it creates while it mixes base colors.

Next, I use some texture brushes. I do not use these much when I paint mechanical subjects. However, in a case in which a softer edge or lost edge is needed— like the shadow area in the example painting—texture brushes create a subtle color mix.

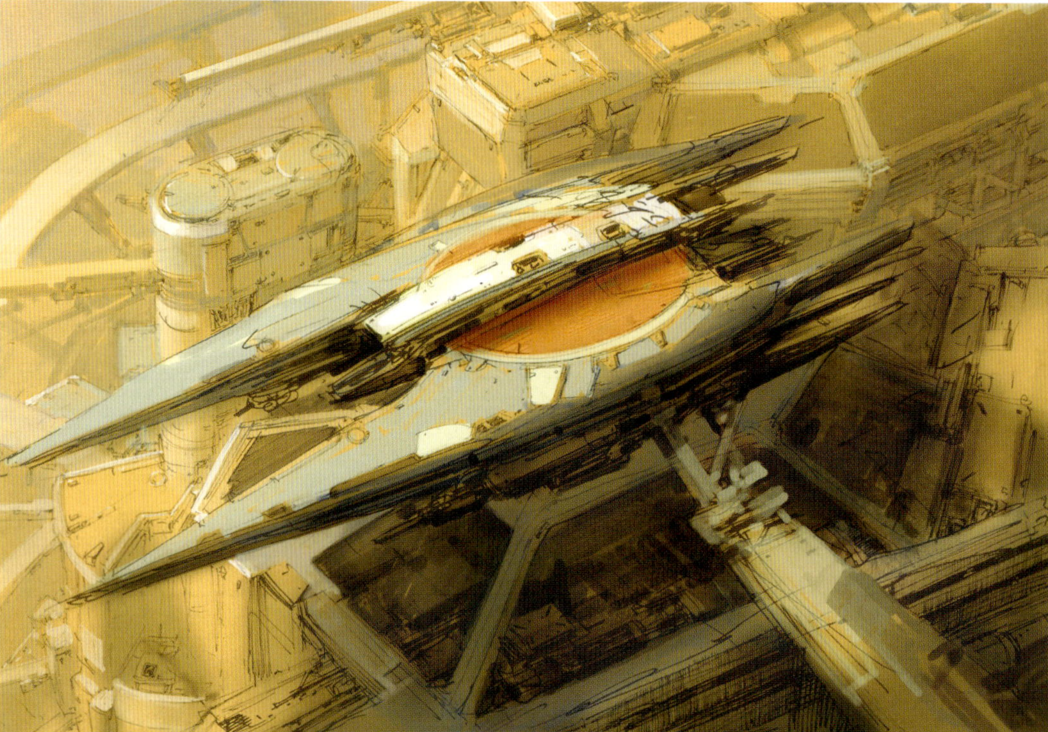

Then I add more local colors to the painting. Even though I set my brush opacity at 30% to paint most of the painting, I also used some full-opacity brushstrokes to give more clear definition to the form. It creates a greater contrast between soft brushstrokes and hard brushstrokes.

Rather than adding any new color at this point, I tend to use the Eyedropper tool to pick colors that already exist on the palette and emphasize the harmony of the existing color in the painting.

I tried to use as many different hues of gray as possible (a). If only one hue of gray were used, the painting would appear too simple and boring. In order to make the dark area more colorful, I added a bit more blue. On the white surface, I added a bit more Persian blue to give more color variation (b). I used the Lasso tool to make a clean selection on the front side of the ship, since that is the most important part of the ship design (c).

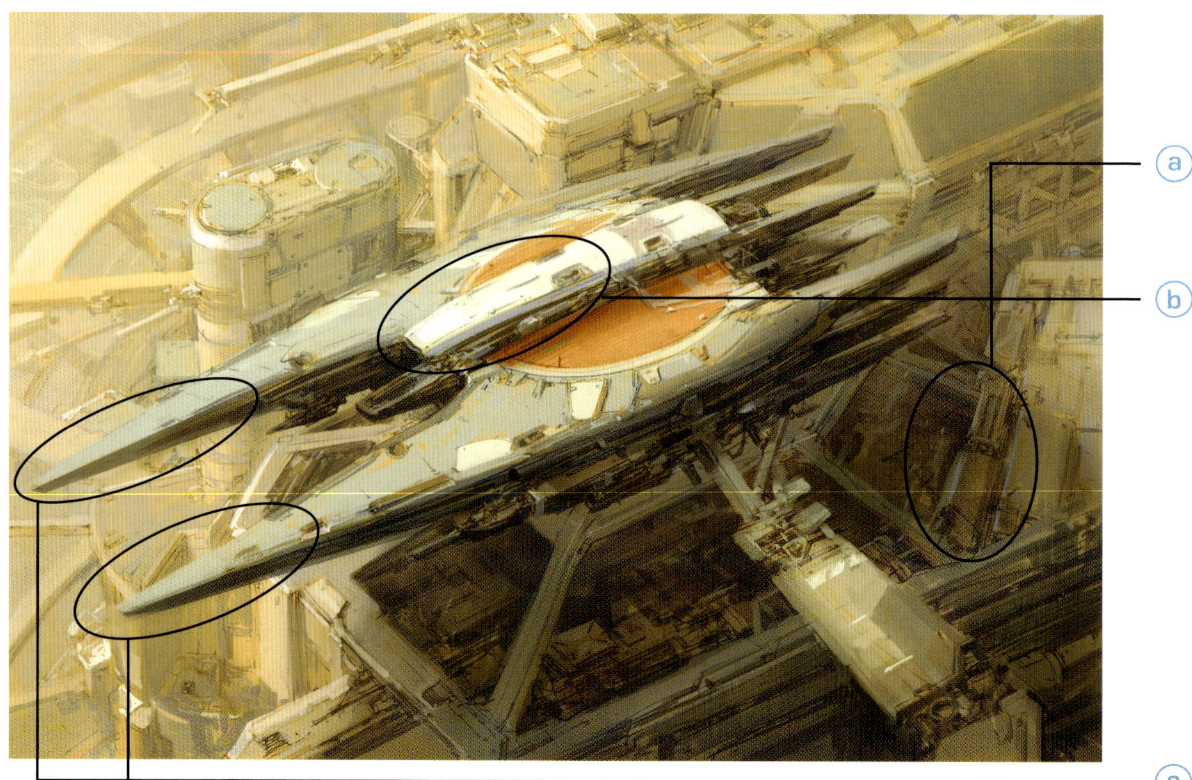

Fig. 2.10

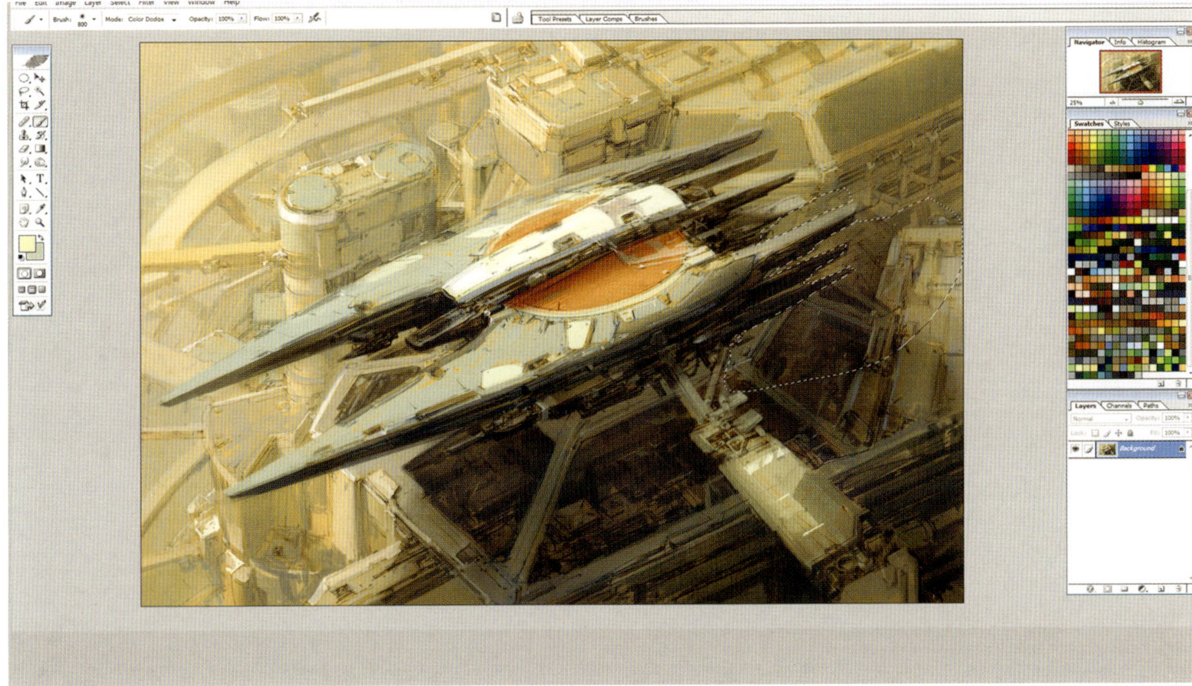

Using the Lasso tool, I make a selection behind the ship.

Fig. 2.11

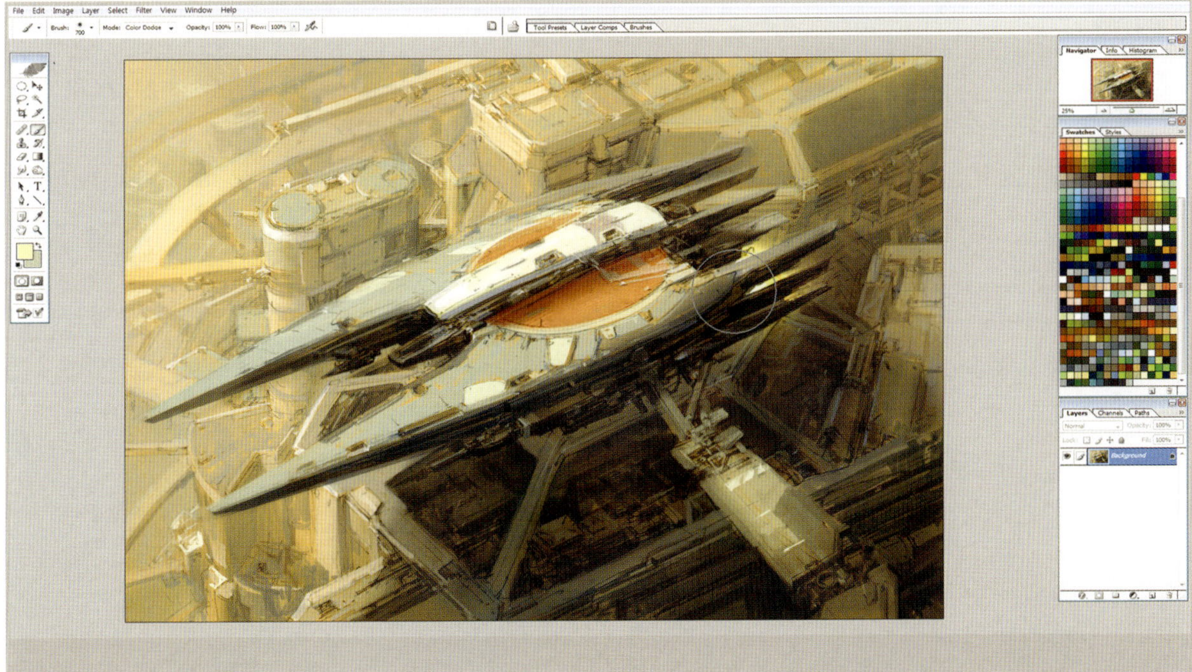

After hiding the selection, I set the Brush mode to Color Dodge, and then paint in an engine glow behind the ship.

I repeat the process on other areas that need engine-glow effects.

I then change the Brush mode to Normal, and break the evenness of the glow effects by painting a few brushstrokes at low opacity (a).

Fig. 2.12

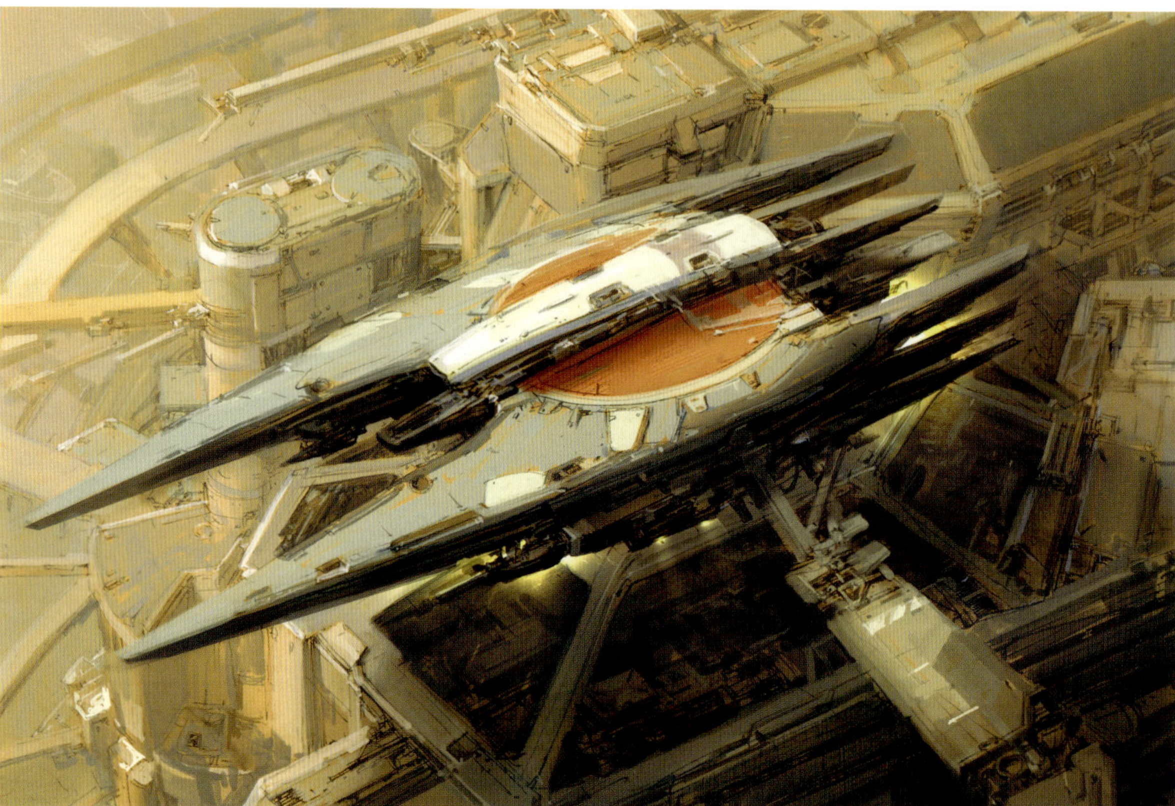

Fig. 2.13

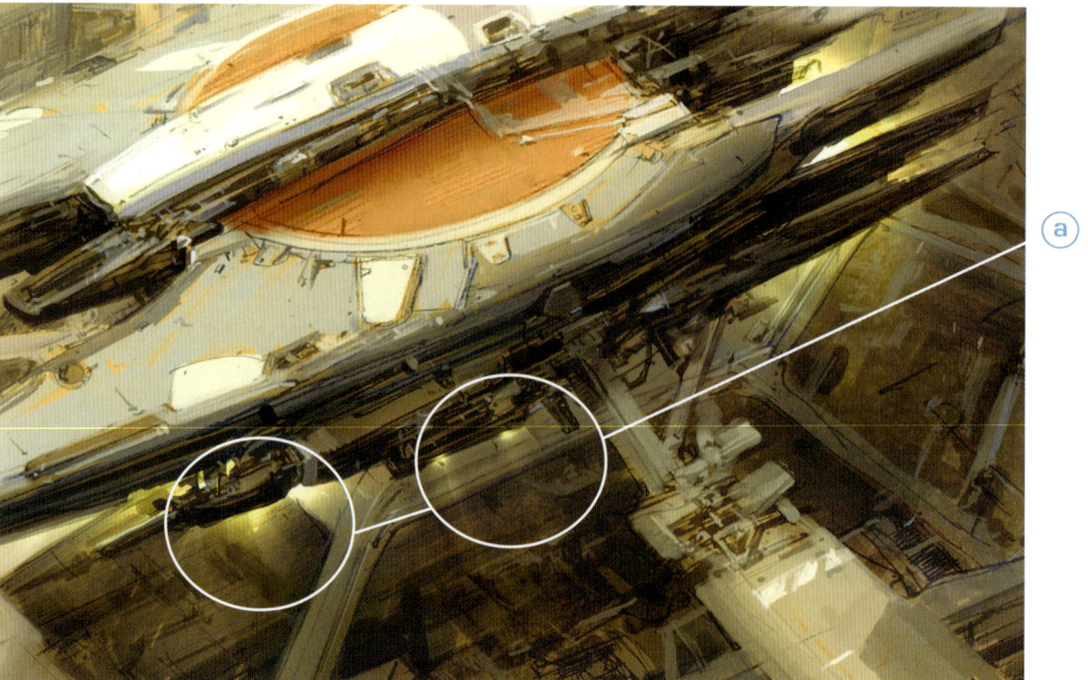

Fig. 2.14

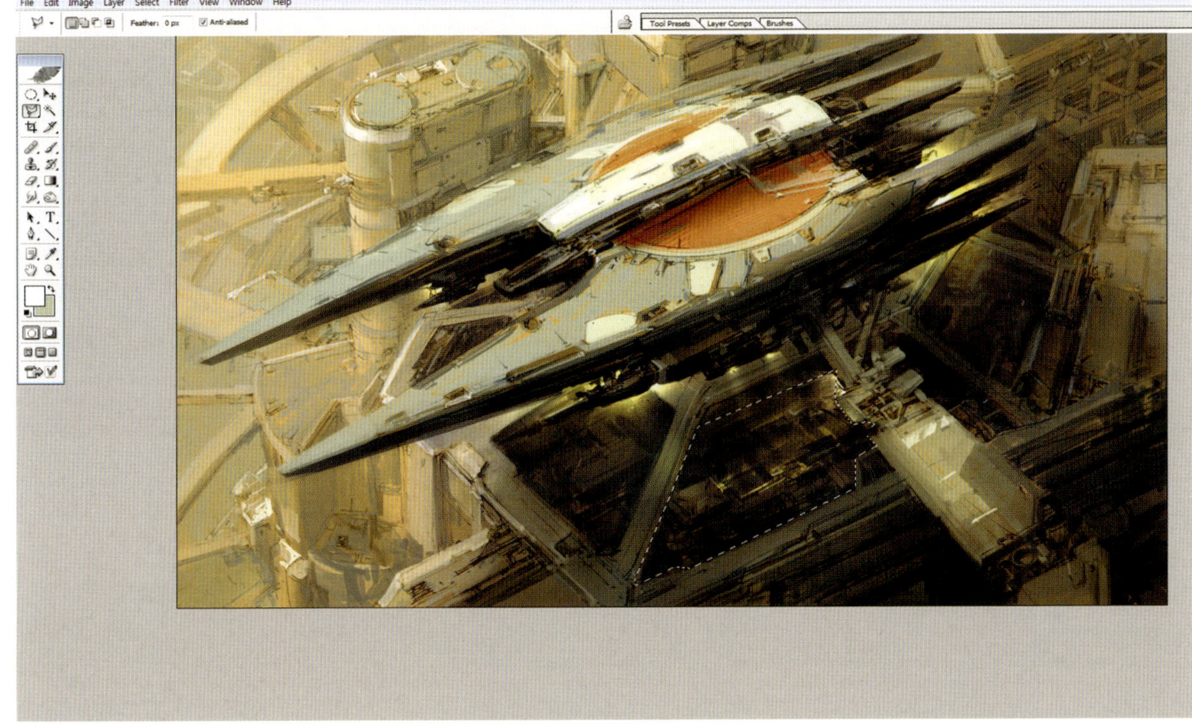

Next step, I select the main frame.

Fig. 2.15

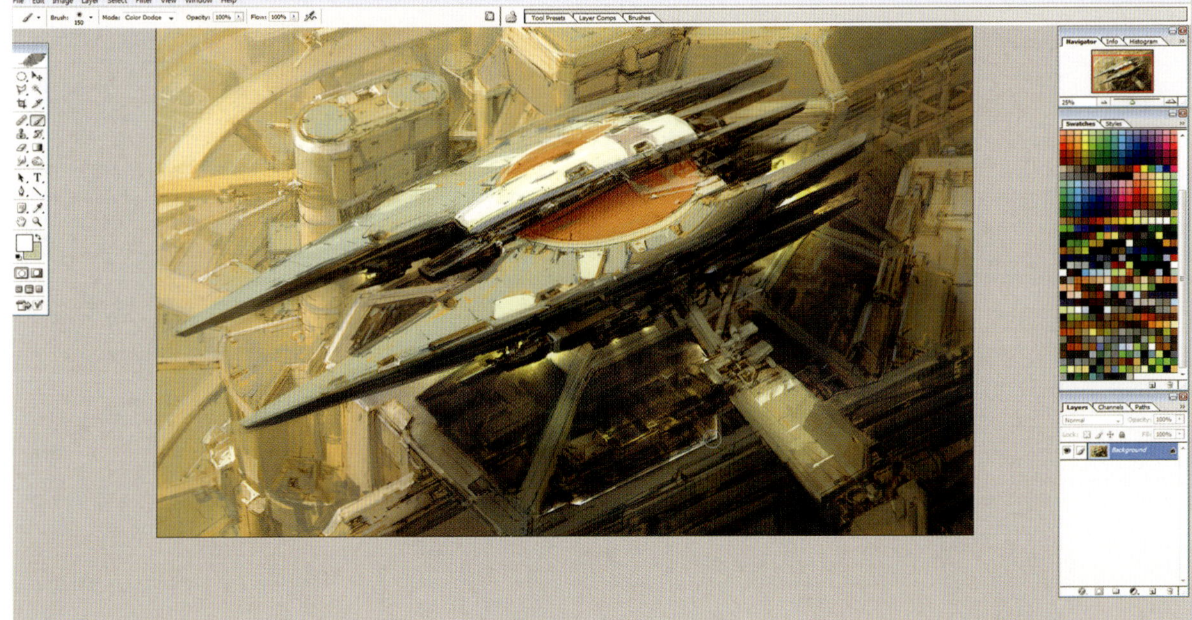

After hiding the selection, I use an Airbrush (Color Dodge mode) to paint the thickness of the frame. Note that I picked a normal round brush to paint straight edges. When using the Lasso tool to paint straight edges like this, don't try to paint corner to corner. It is better to suggest the form by painting the beginning and the end, and letting other areas breathe.

I repeat the process of lassoing and airbrushing with Color Dodge mode until I have enough details (a). I add more details using smaller touches. One advantage of using the Color Dodge brush is that I can save the drawing lines and underpainting brushstrokes. A more natural look is achieved when one can see the layers of the brushstrokes instead of painting over everything.

By using a 10 to 30% low-opacity brush, I tinted a bit more navy blue, which makes the whole painting feel more colorful. Be careful not to add too much of it, or it will make everything appear too saturated and too colorful. That would change my whole plan for this painting. As you can see, I preserved the pencil marks as much as possible, since I wanted to use them as another cool texture to the painting.

Fig. 2.16

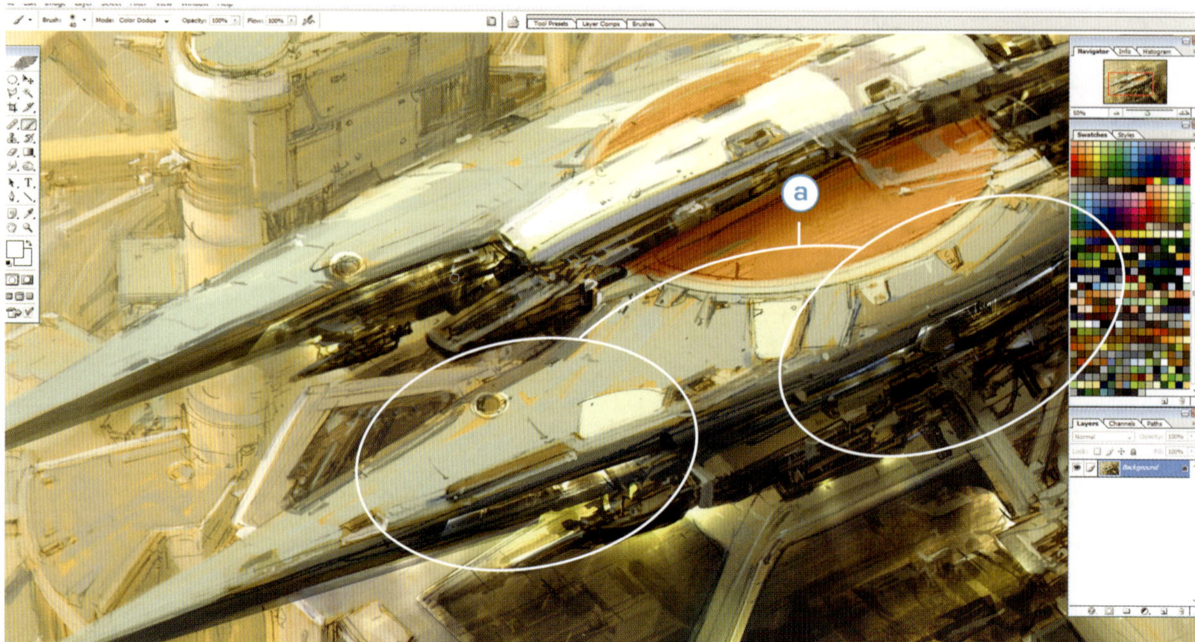

Fig. 2.17

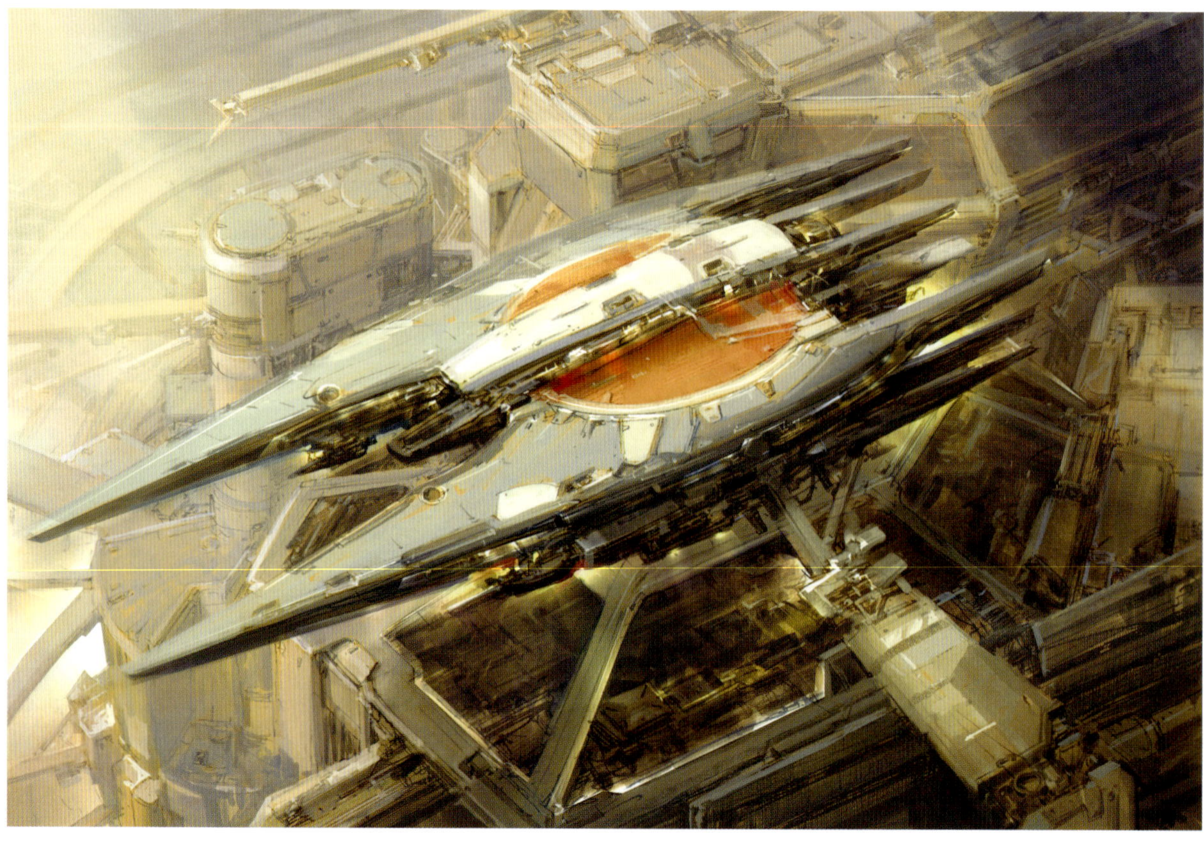

Ship in the Hangar

Fig. 2.18

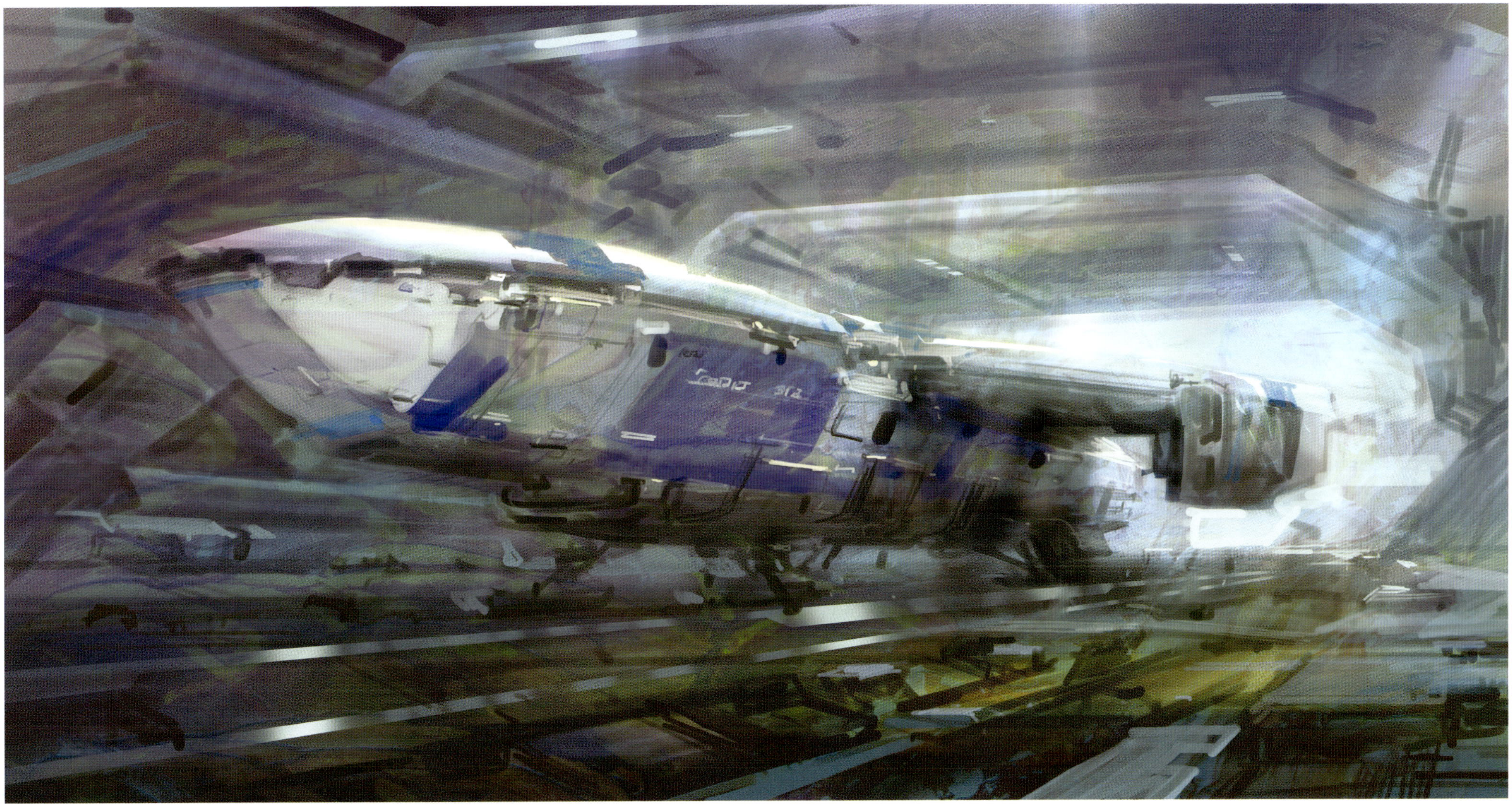

Ready to see how I created this painting from start to finish? This is the first of six video demonstrations in the book that captures my every line and brushstroke to complete a painting.

Docking Station

Fig. 2.19

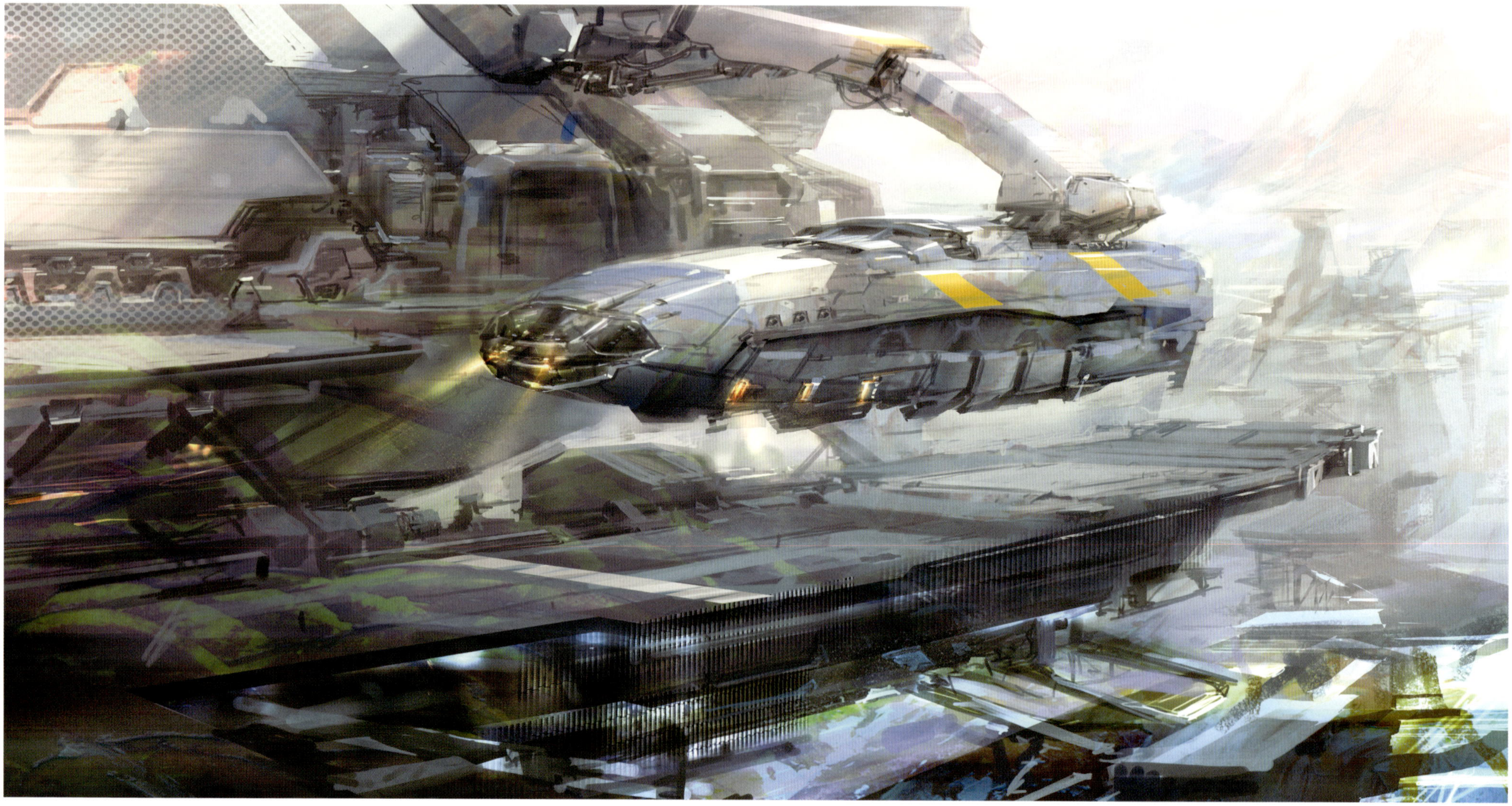

Being able to **CREATE** what I have in my mind is the most rewarding feeling I can have **AS AN ARTIST.**

Fighter Ship

Fig. 2.20

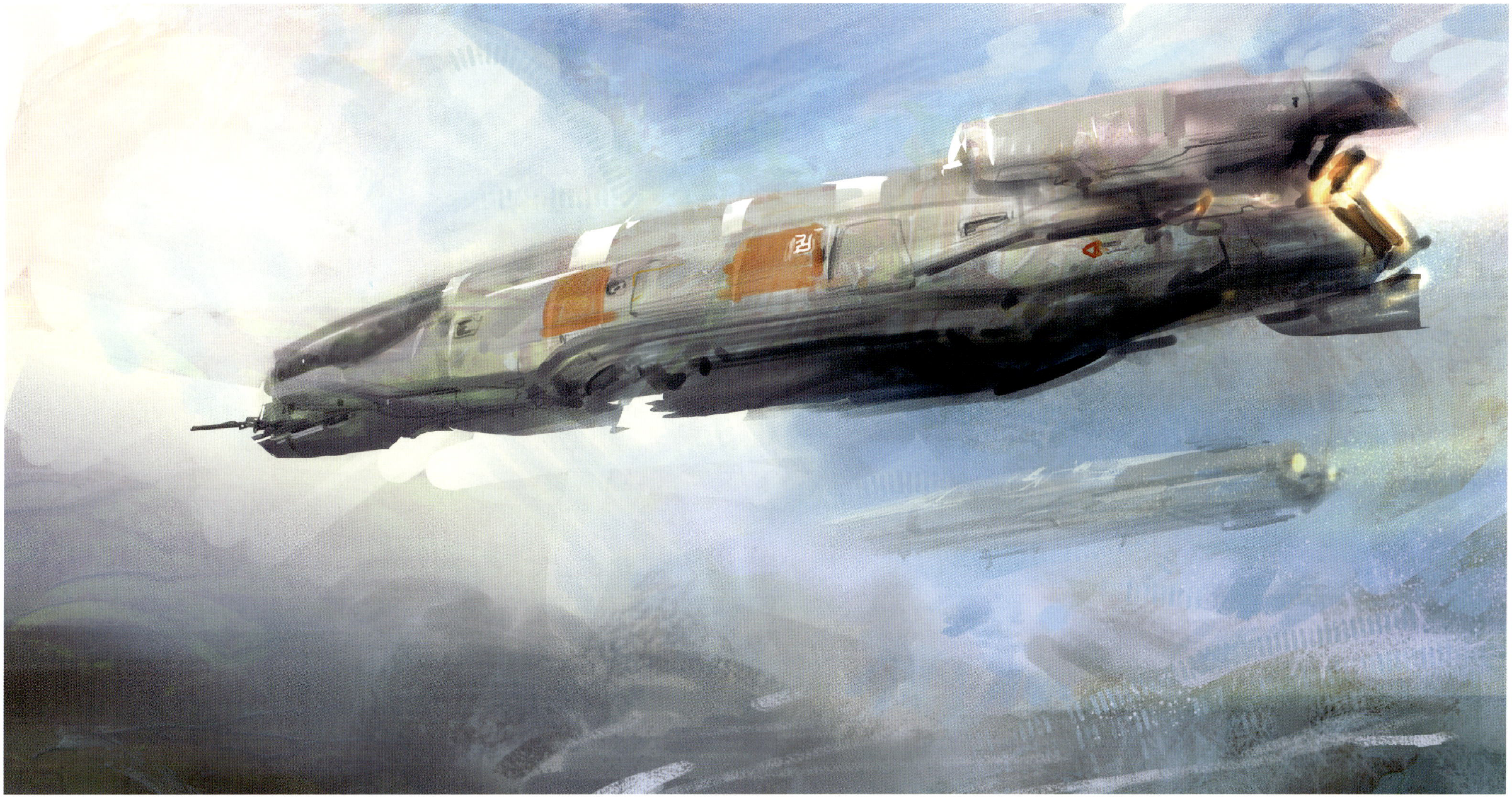

Flying Helicopter

Fig. 2.21

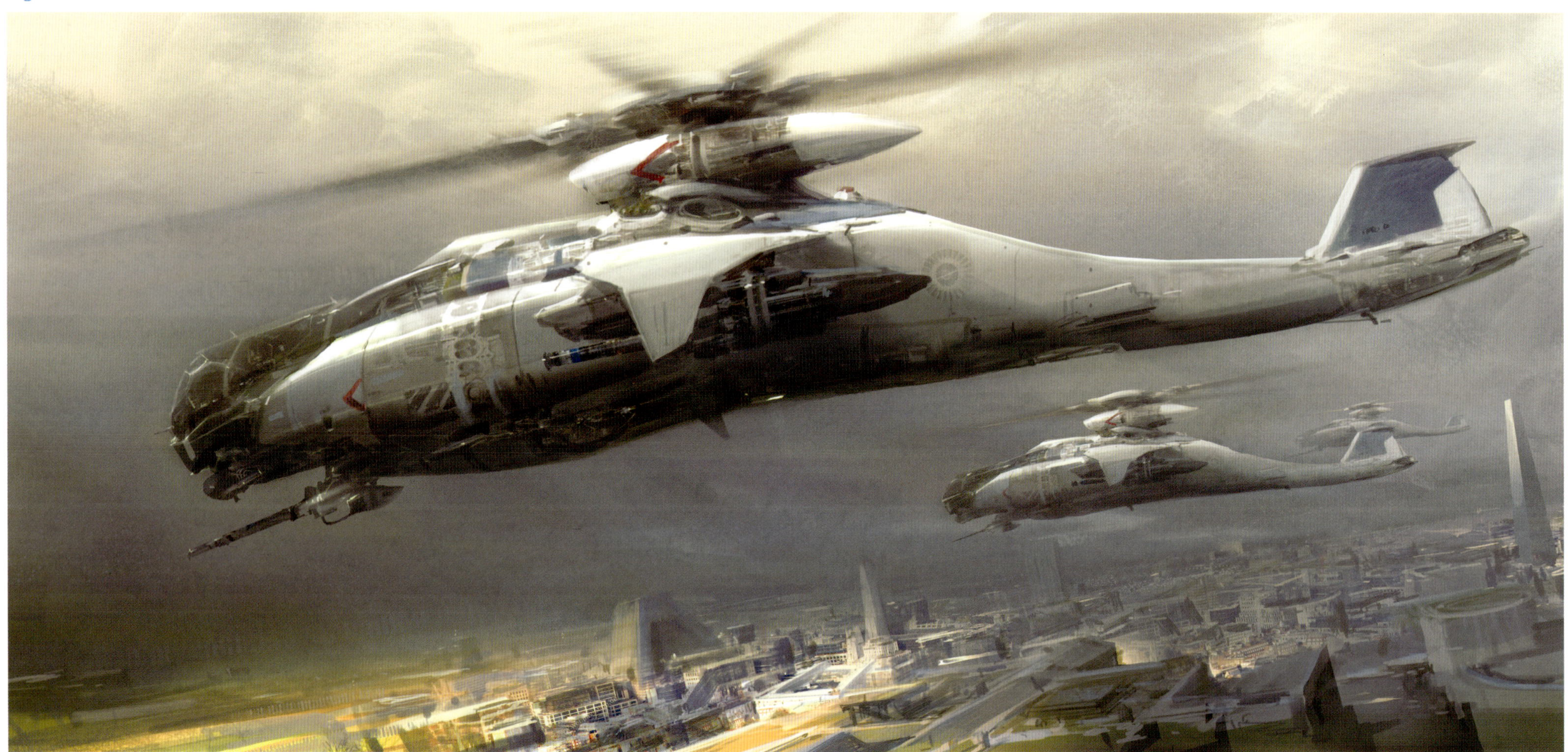

In this tutorial, I am going to demonstrate how to create a flying vehicle with a simple cityscape in the background.

Fig. 2.22

I made a back plate to use as a starting background. This particular back plate has a lot of medium-value color, which is a very useful color as a starting point.

Fig. 2.23

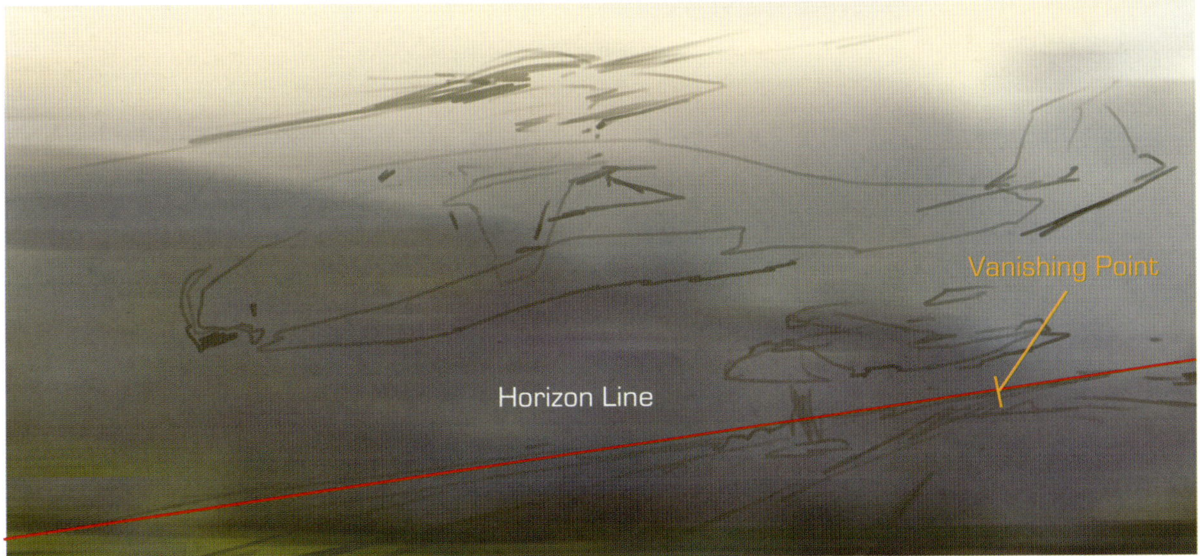

First, I block in the rough shape of the main subject, a helicopter. Note that the propeller is tilted slightly forward to make it look as if it is moving at a fast speed. I used a more curved shape instead of a straight line in order to make it appear more aerodynamic. When starting my sketch, I tend not to draw a perspective grid at first. Once I draw a precise perspective grid, I tend to stick to that grid, and my drawing becomes very stiff. After blocking in the big shape, I then draw the perspective grid based on my sketch. In this way, I can draw a more dynamic composition without it getting too stiff because of the perspective grid.

Fig. 2.24

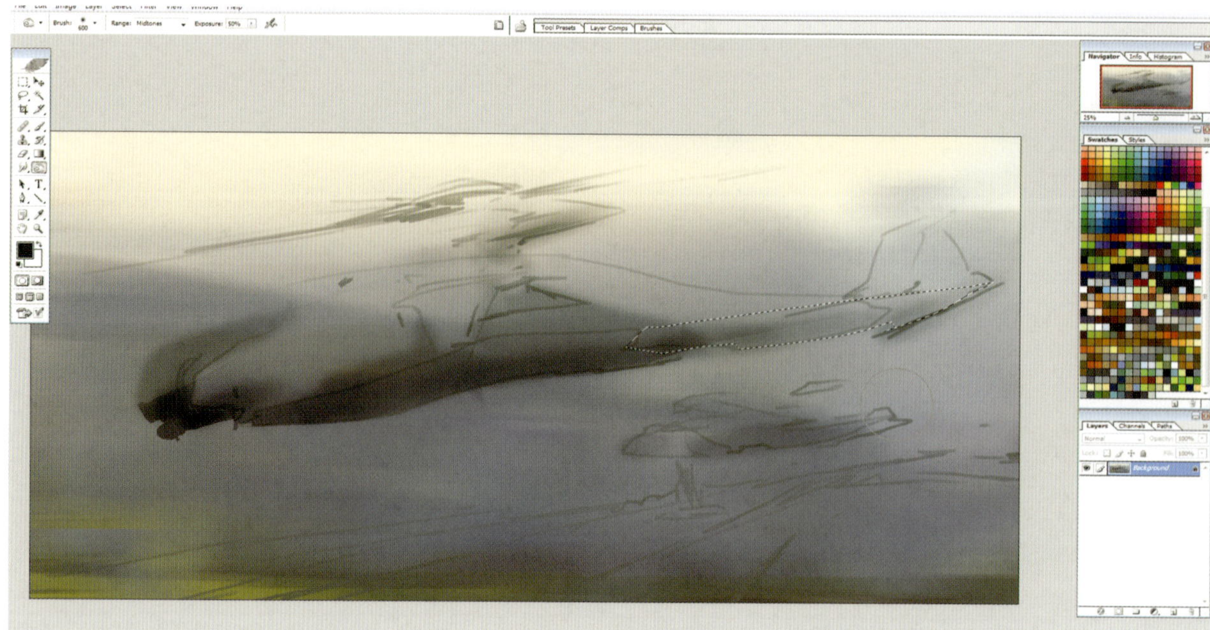

In this figure, I roughly blocked in a shadow shape by using the Lasso tool.

After selecting an area, I use the Burn tool (set to Midtones) to darken the selected area. I use both Airbrush mode and the Burn tool. One advantage of using the Burn tool is that the picture can be darkened without losing the background texture.

Fig. 2.25

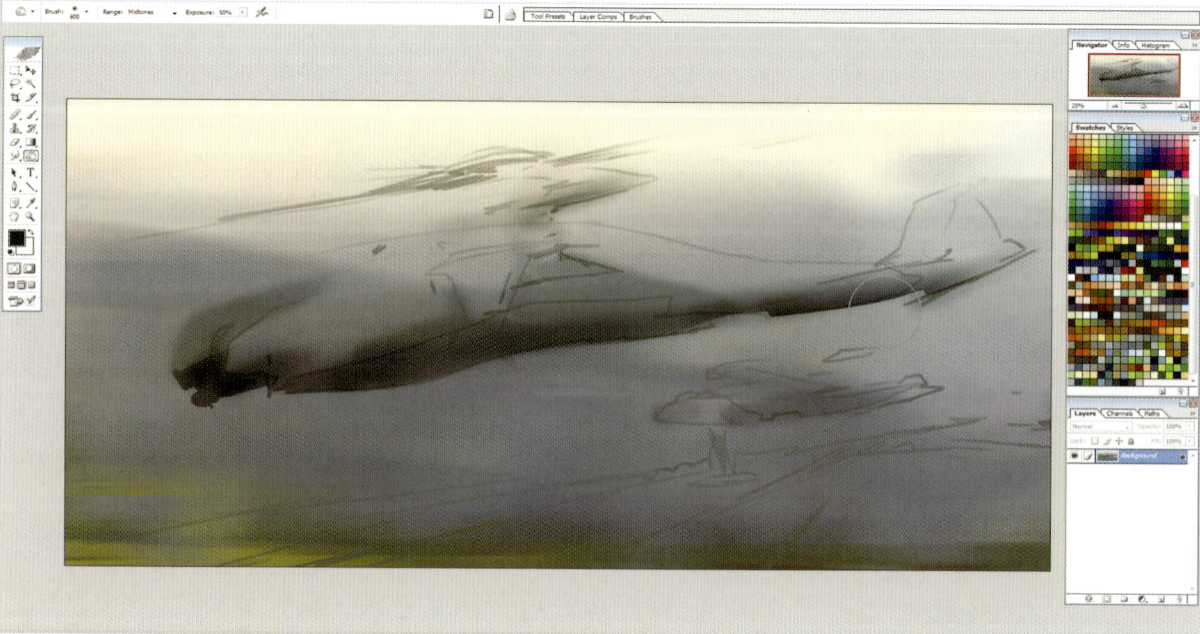

Fig. 2.26

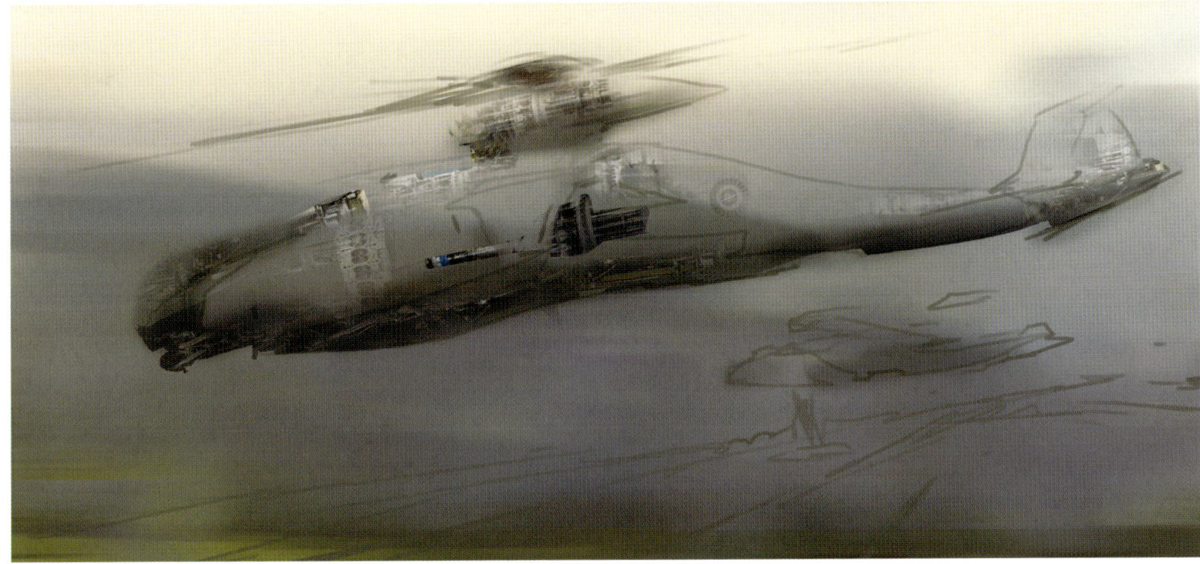

In this figure, I used a photo source. After applying the photo source, I erased a portion of it to let it blend into the base picture.

Fig. 2.27

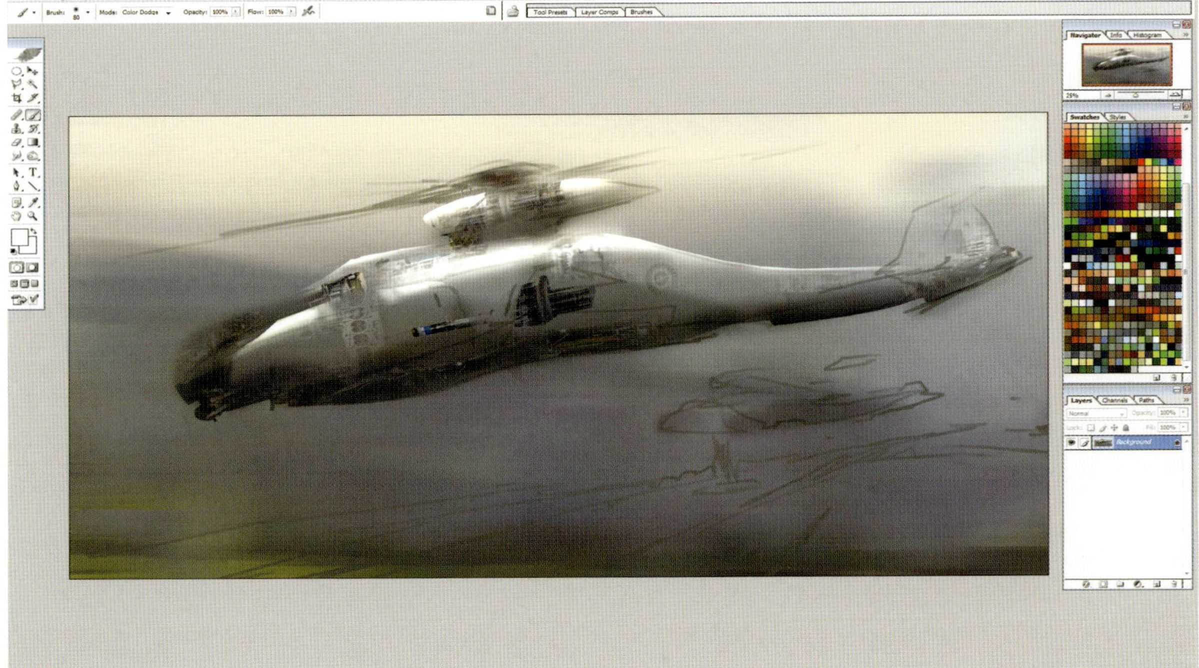

Just as I used the Lasso tool to paint the shadow side in Fig. 2.21, I have used it to paint the light side in this step. This time I used an airbrush (Color Dodge mode).

After blocking in the largest light and shadow shapes, I continue to draw more big shapes to refine the subject. I also add a bit more photo source as a texture. Its shape is getting clearer bit by bit.

I use the Smudge tool quite often. Using it almost feels like I am using my finger to smudge an oil painting (a). If I set the pressure to 100%, it picks up the colors from the base layer and mixes them together. However, for this figure, I set my brush pressure at 50% because I wanted to use it as a blending brush rather than as a mixing brush. I enjoy using this tool a lot, so I set up a shortcut key in Photoshop. Using it is very efficient when I want to add a more traditional look to my painting.

Fig. 2.28

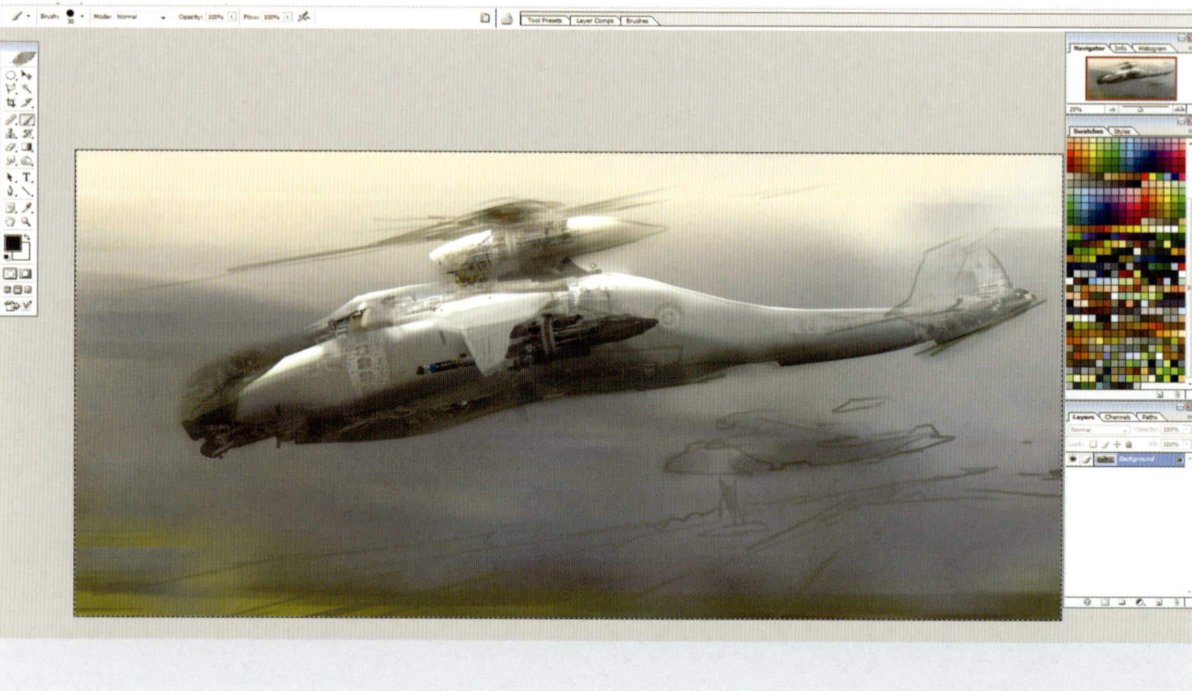

Fig. 2.29

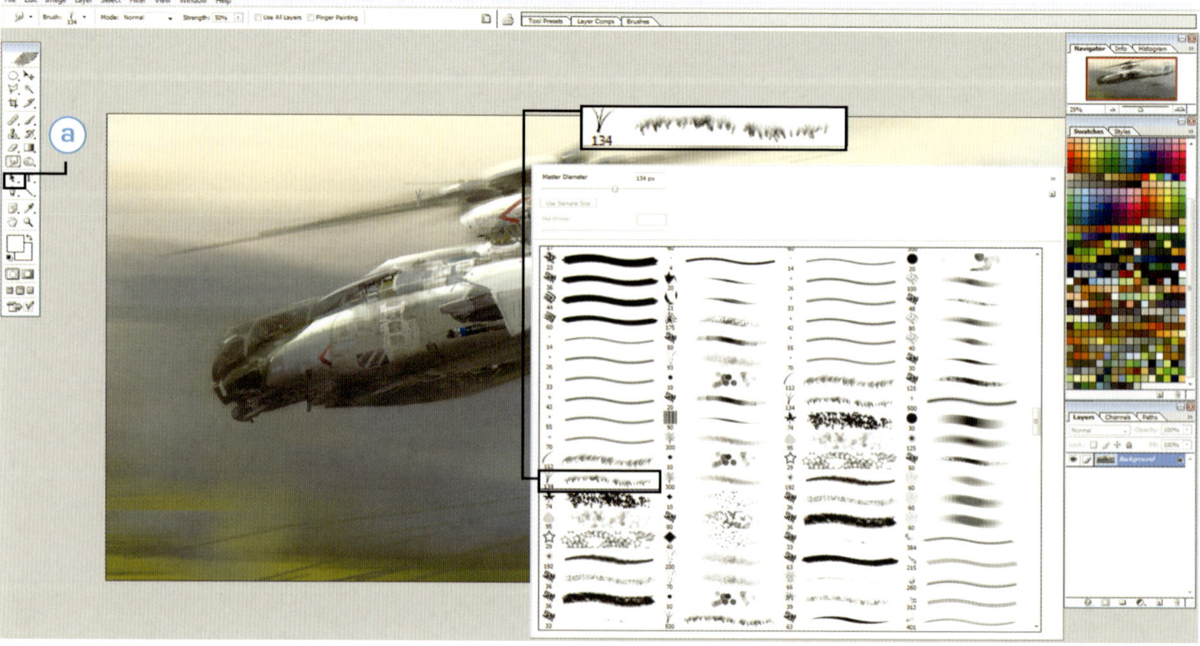

Fig. 2.30

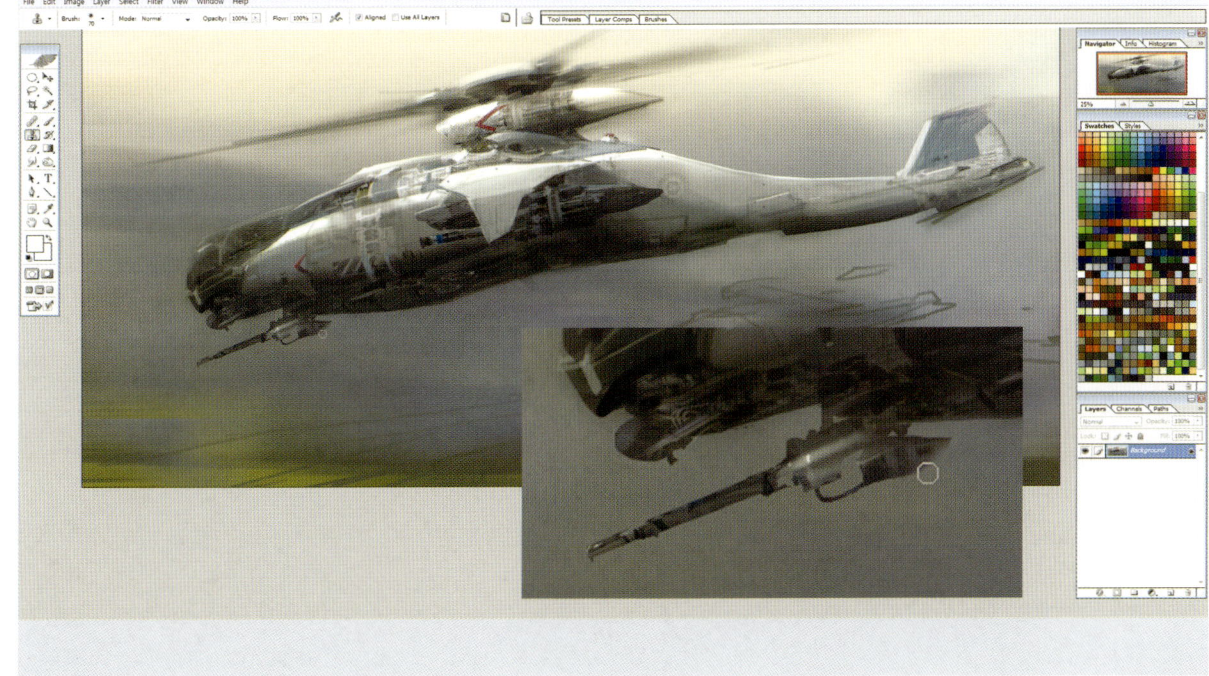

I add more details to the painting as I make more progress. In this figure, I show how to paint the gun part. Draw the silhouette of the gun with the Lasso tool first. Then use the Stamp tool to clone the other part of the helicopter. As the Stamp tool picks up the details from the other part of the helicopter, it adds a very interesting texture and fine details to the gun.

Fig. 2.31

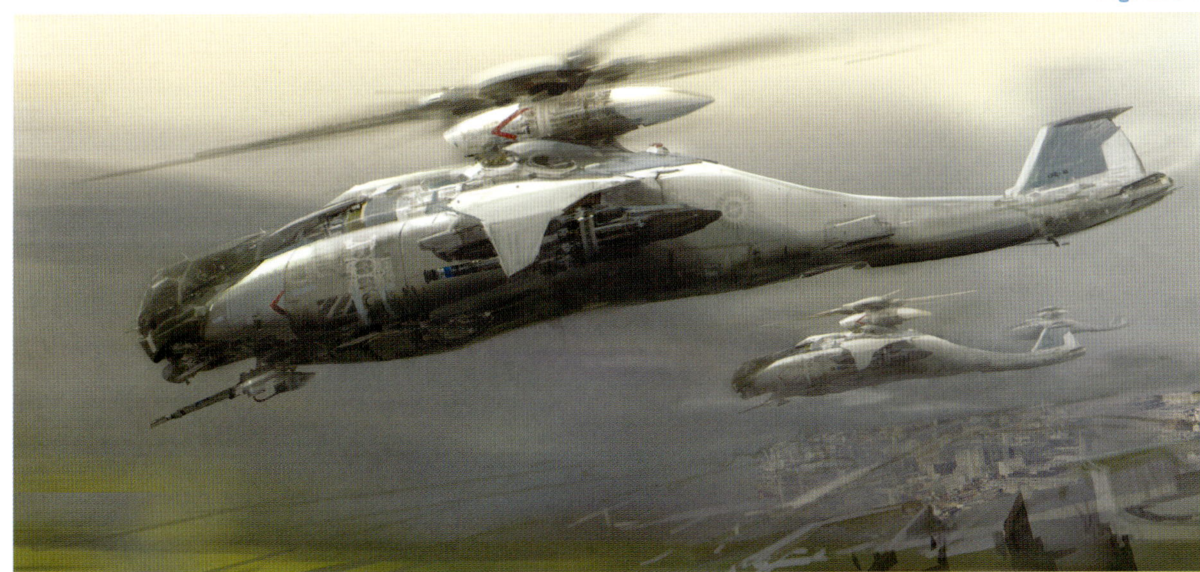

The next step is to paint the background. Here, I picked a cityscape photo and matched it with my perspective grid. I erased the sections that were not needed and kept only the portions that were to be used in the painting. I have used this city background as a simple backdrop just to add more flavor, so I am not worried about making it look perfect with my perspective.

To give the painting volumetric light, I select a section with the Lasso tool. Then I set my brush at Color Dodge mode and paint the atmosphere. This technique creates more depth in the painting. After adding atmosphere, I repaint the outline of the foreground buildings to make them look clean and sharp.

In this figure, I am double-checking the perspective to be sure that I have followed the initial direction that I had planned at the beginning of the work.

Fig. 2.32

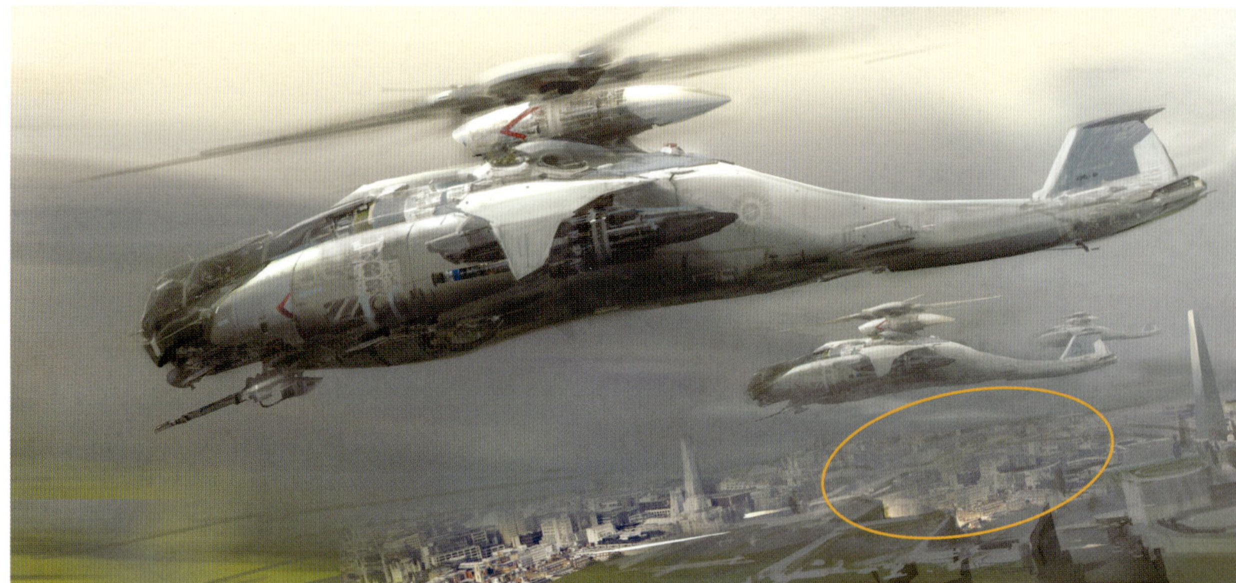

Fig. 2.33

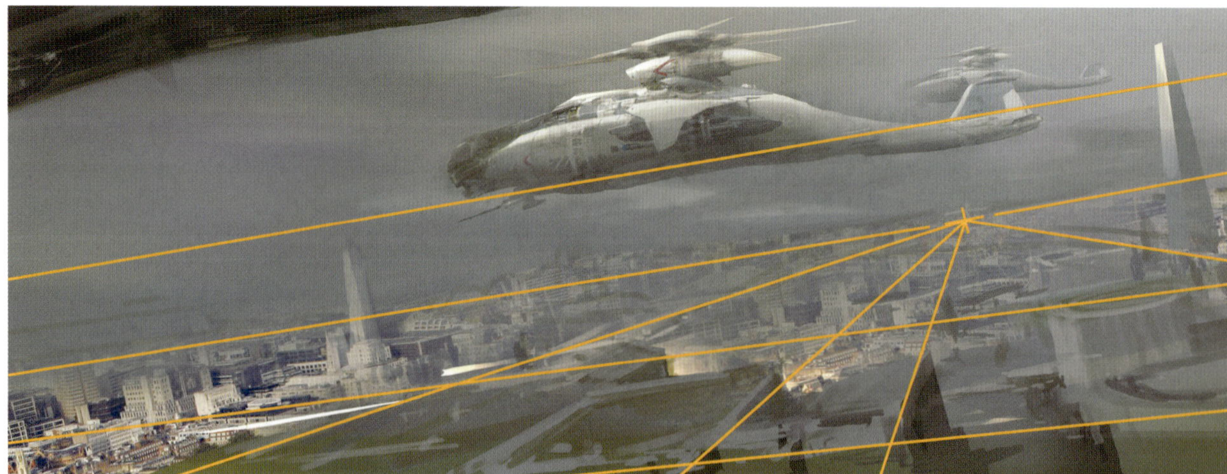

Fig. 2.34

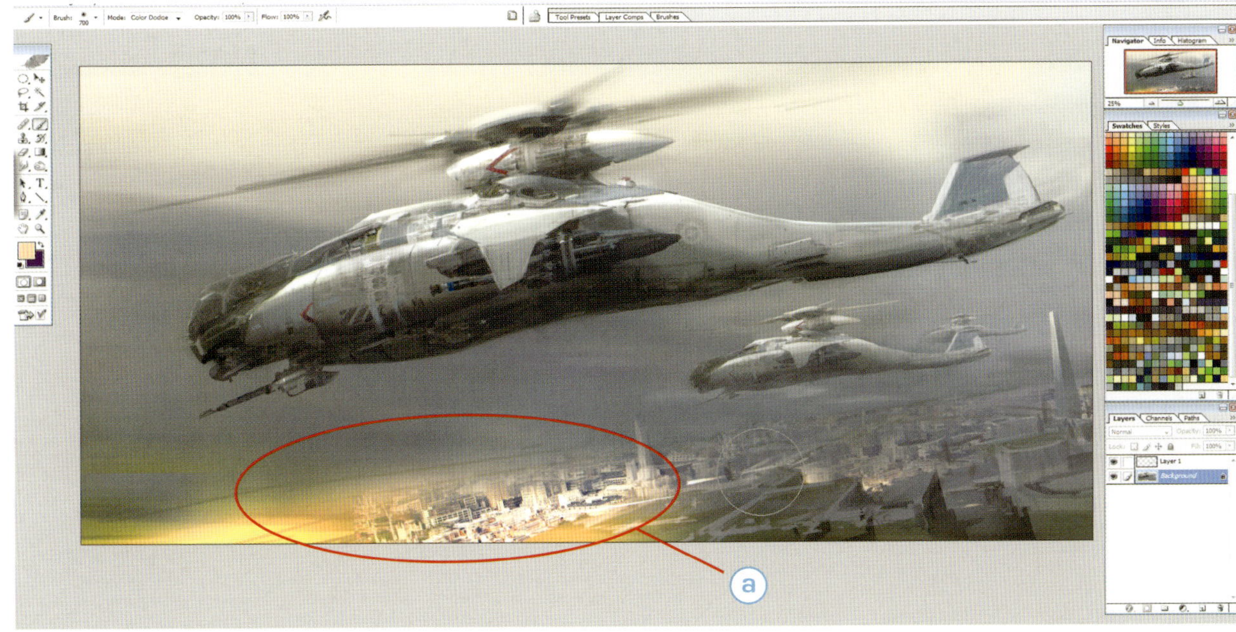

The whole painting looked too desaturated, so I decided to add stronger color pop. I added a golden light in the left corner. I could have added golden color to the sky and clouds, but I wanted the helicopter to be the main focal point of the painting. I did not want a saturated sky to fight with the main subject. Notice that when one paints an orange/golden color on top of neutral gray with the Color Dodge brush, the result is a beautiful late-afternoon lighting.

Fig. 2.35

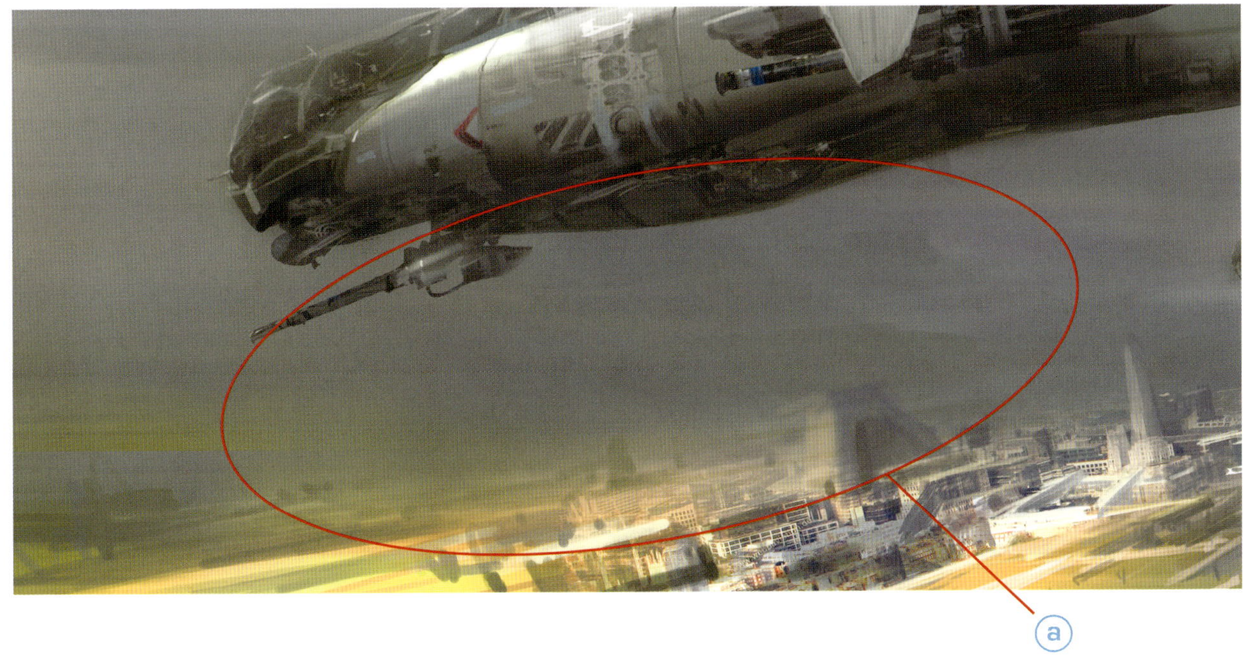

Here, I add additional building shapes with big brushstrokes. The shapes don't need to be too precise since they will remain in the background. I also wanted to add scattered light effects in the sky. To achieve this effect (a), I set the brush at 10% opacity and overlap the brush marks. But if I overlap them too much, the sky looks very opaque, which is not a proper way to paint it. So be careful not to overdo the overlapping of brush marks.

Fig. 2.36

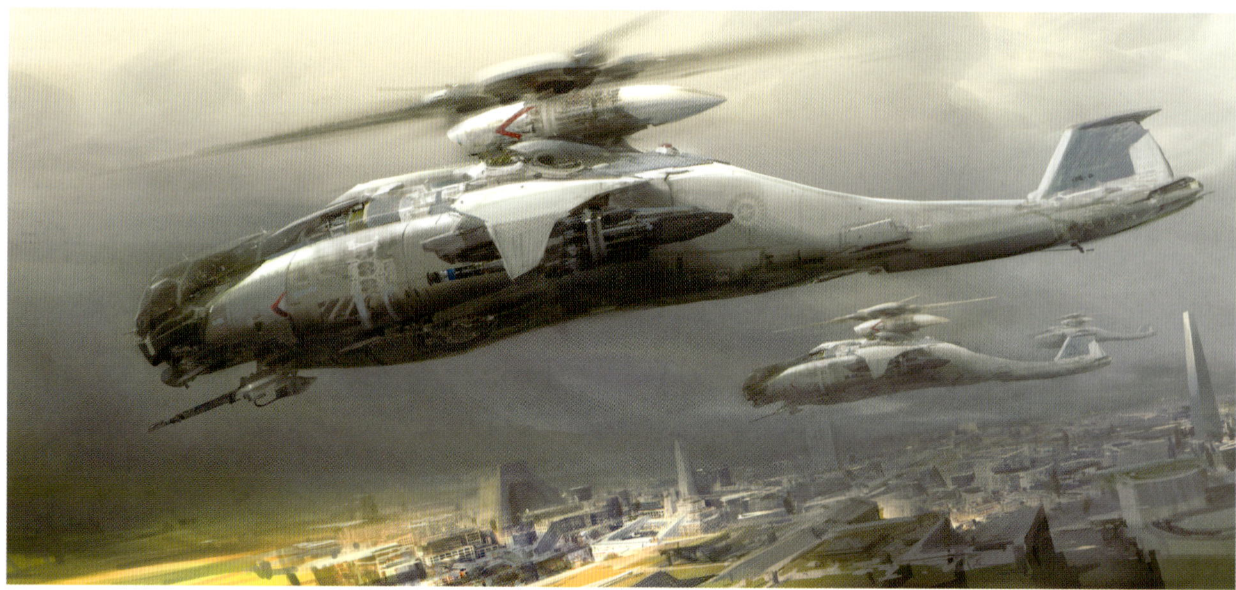

It is time to paint clouds into the painting. Block in the big shapes of the clouds by using a normal brush (100% opacity). When painting clouds, it is always better to keep it simple. Use simple brushstrokes and make them very light. I darken the left corner with a heavy cloud to give more tension to the painting. Compositionally, it helps to stop the eye flow from leaving the page too easily.

I add a slight blue tint to give more color to the painting.

Fig. 2.37

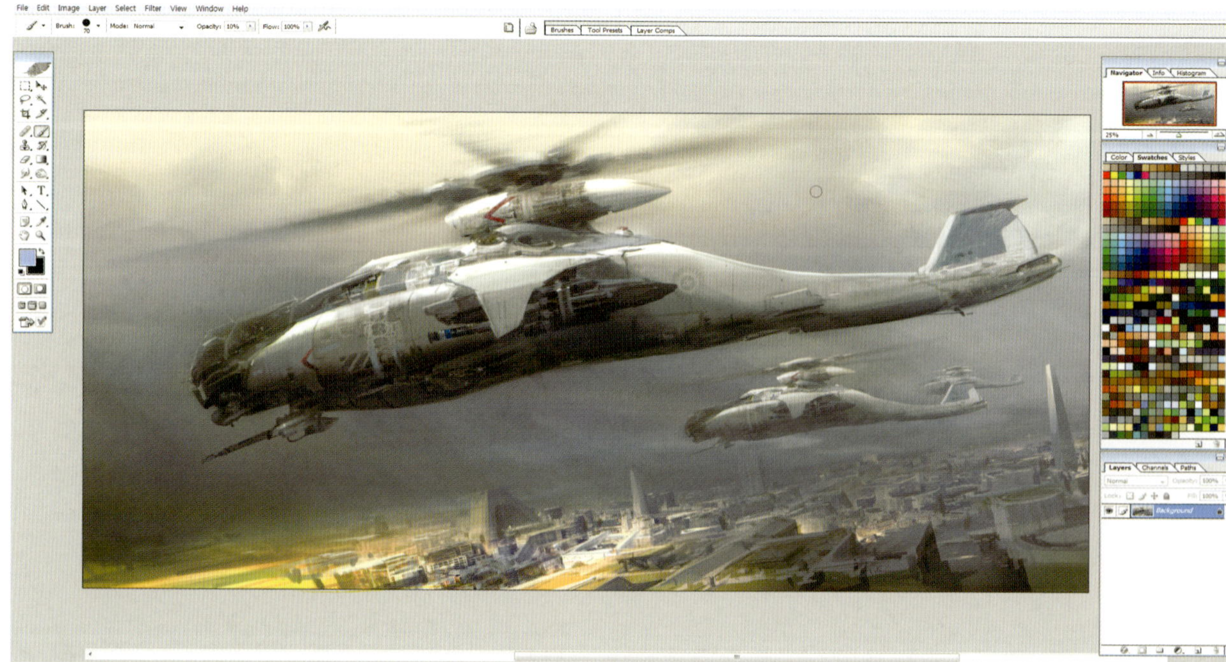

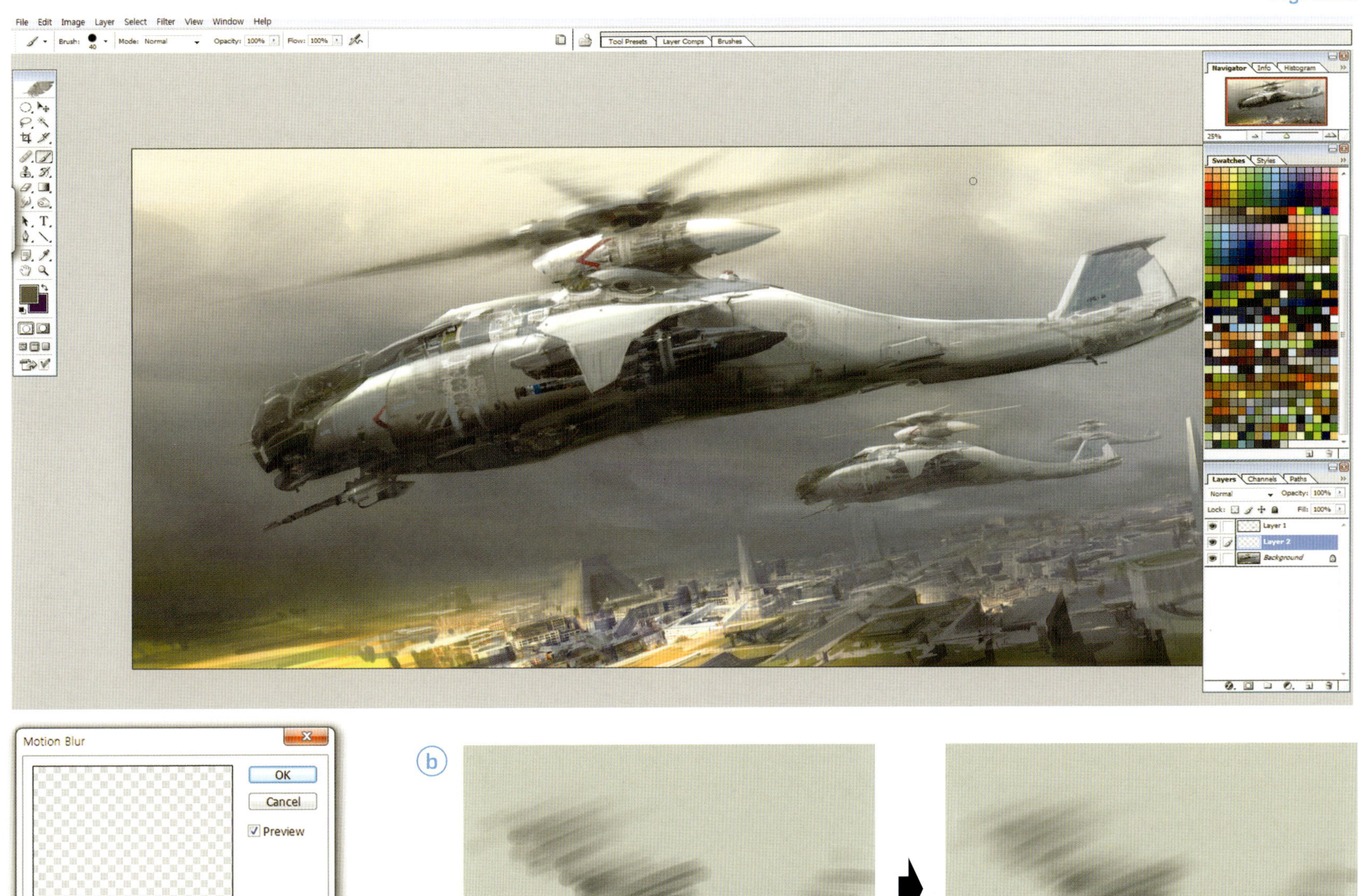

Now it's time to draw a propeller on the flying helicopter. First, paint a moving propeller, and add a Motion Blur filter to it. Depending on how the angle and the distance (a) are modified, the outcome can be dramatically different, as shown in the example (b). It can be modified depending on how much blur effect is desired.

Fig. 2.39

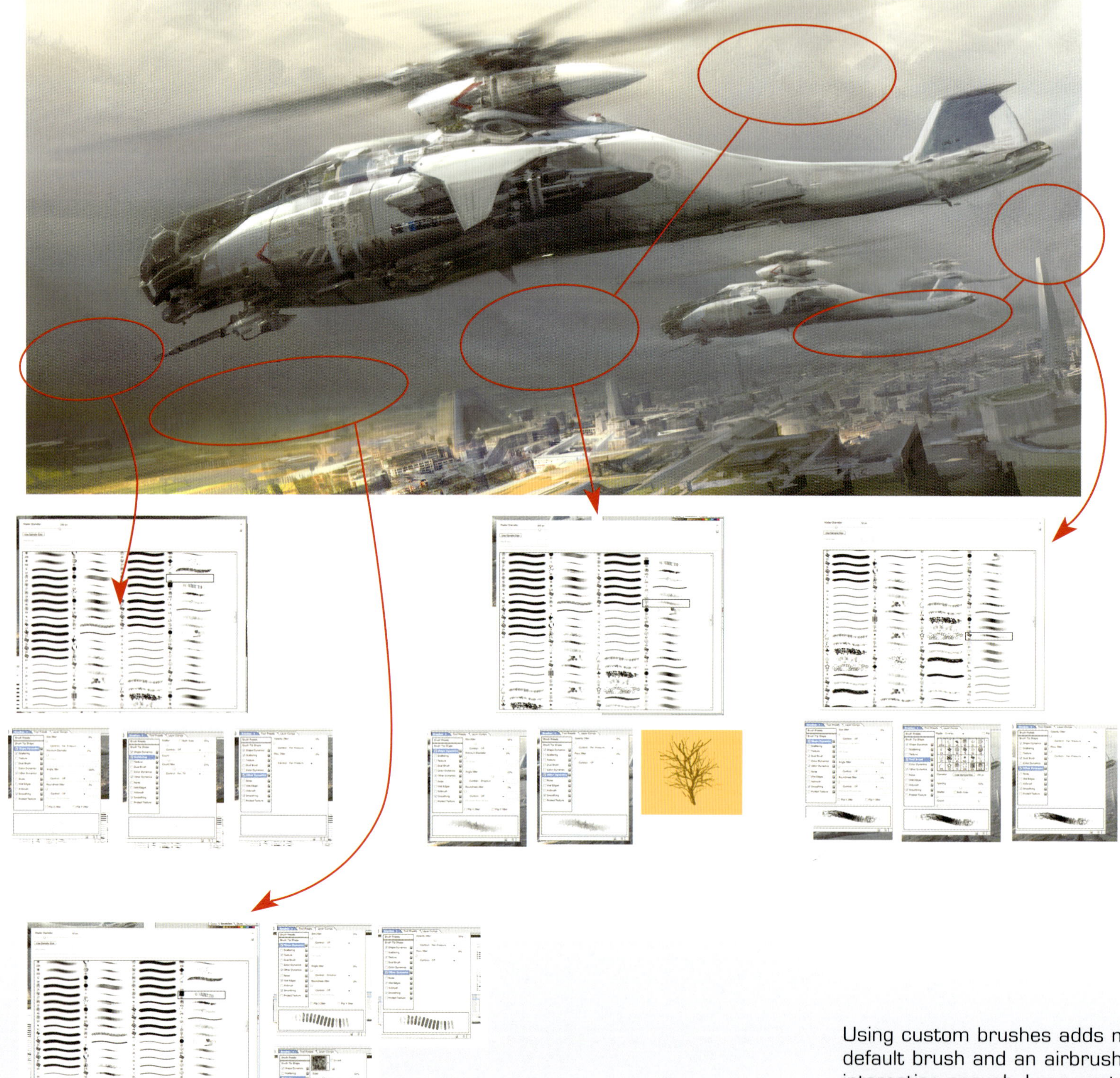

Using custom brushes adds more interesting brush marks. When I work with a default brush and an airbrush, my painting often looks a bit flat and not visually interesting enough. I use custom brushes to add more interesting texture to the painting. Nevertheless, one should be careful not to overdo it. This figure shows the copyright-free brushes I collected from the Internet. There are countless numbers of good brushes, but these are the brushes I use most often when doing my work.

Landed Helicopter

Fig. 2.40

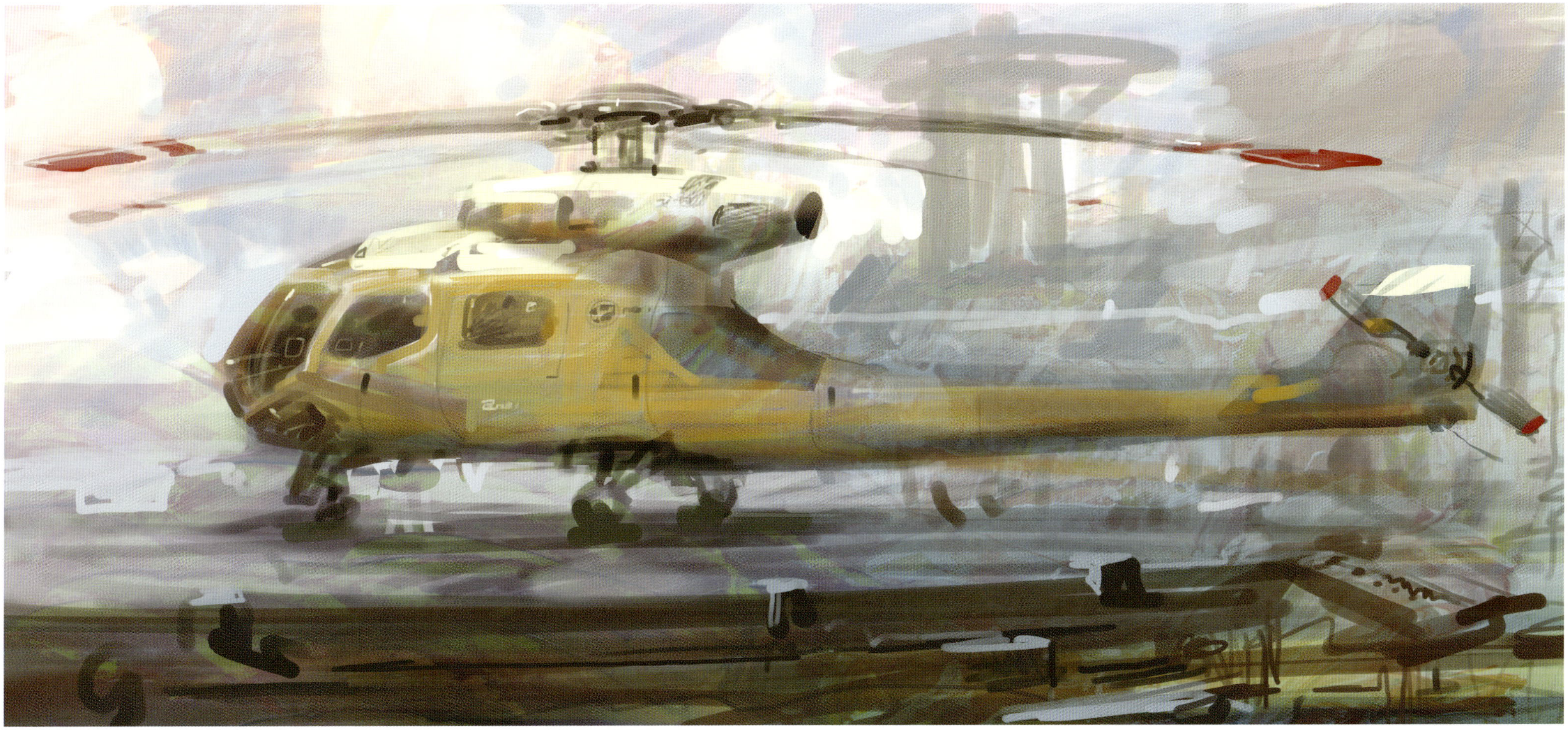

Now that you've learned how to depict a helicopter in flight, watch this video demo by scanning the QR code, or visiting pg. 4 for the URL, to see how I created this painting of a helicopter that just landed.

Abandoned Tank

Fig. 2.41

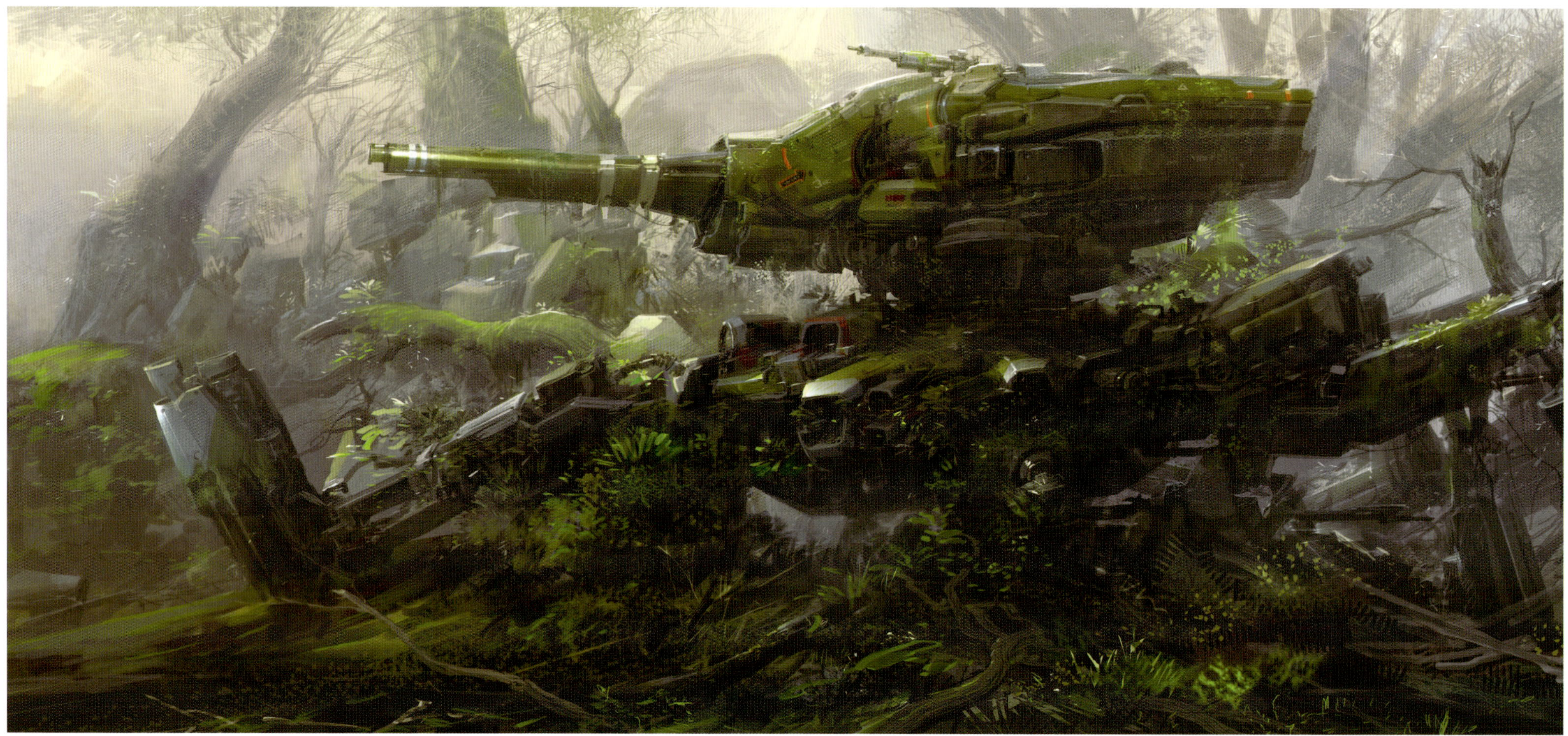

This tutorial will cover how to paint a mechanical subject: a destroyed, abandoned tank. Perhaps this tank was on a mission in a forest, but the army got ambushed by its enemy. As time goes by, the tank has been overgrown by a forest, and has become a part of the forest. In contrast with other tutorial paintings, I started this painting directly in Photoshop instead of creating a pencil sketch first.

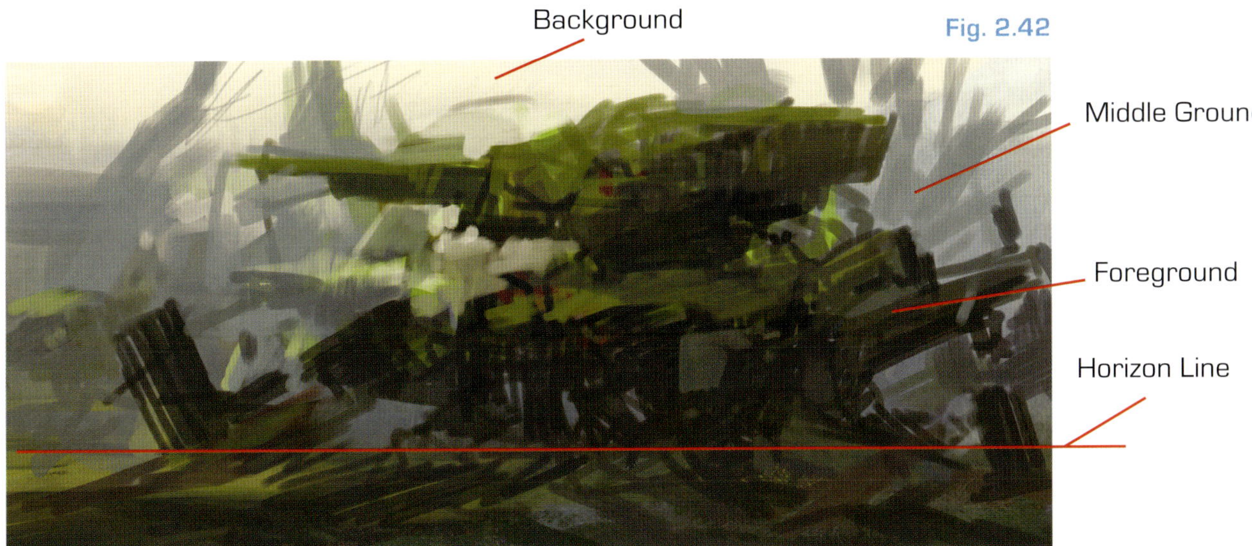

I block in a general shape of the subject by using a rough texture brush. I will make the tank a green color since it needs a camouflage color in the forest. Therefore, green will be a main color of this painting, especially in the foreground and middle ground. I will leave the background a bit more desaturated and lighter, so that it can sit subtly in the back and support the main subject.

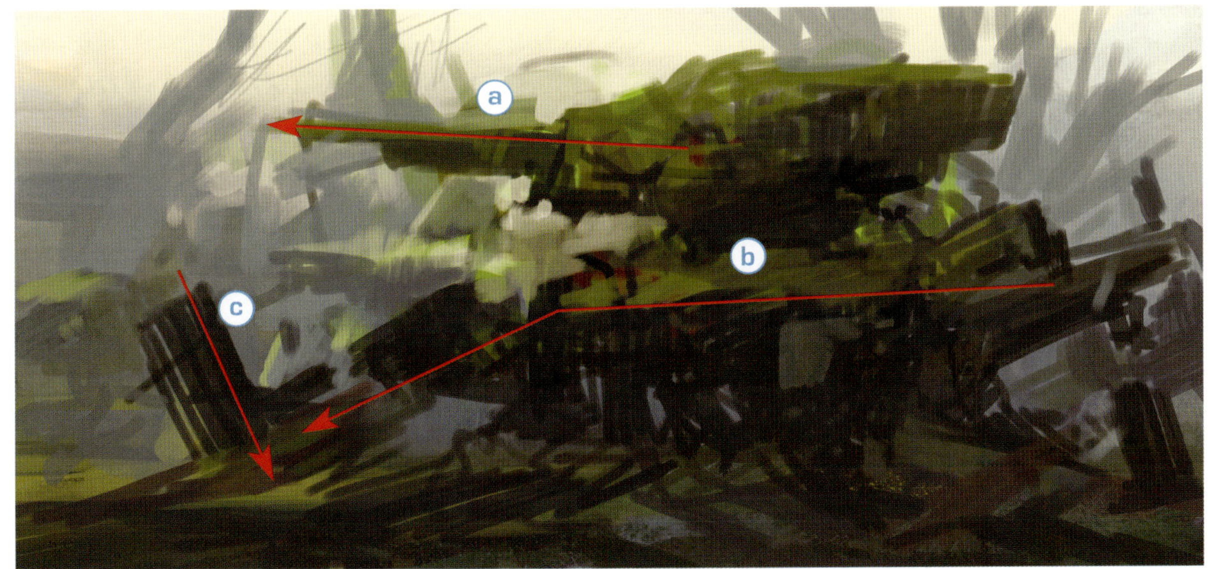

I make the main cannon facing slightly upward (a), instead of making the angle flat. On the other hand, the body is facing down, to counterbalance the main cannon (b). Setting up different angles for different objects will create a more interesting visual flow to the main subject. To stop the viewer's eyes from leaving the page, I placed a stake on the ground (c). All of the design decisions that I have described in this figure so far were made to enhance the visual movement in this painting.

Fig. 2.44

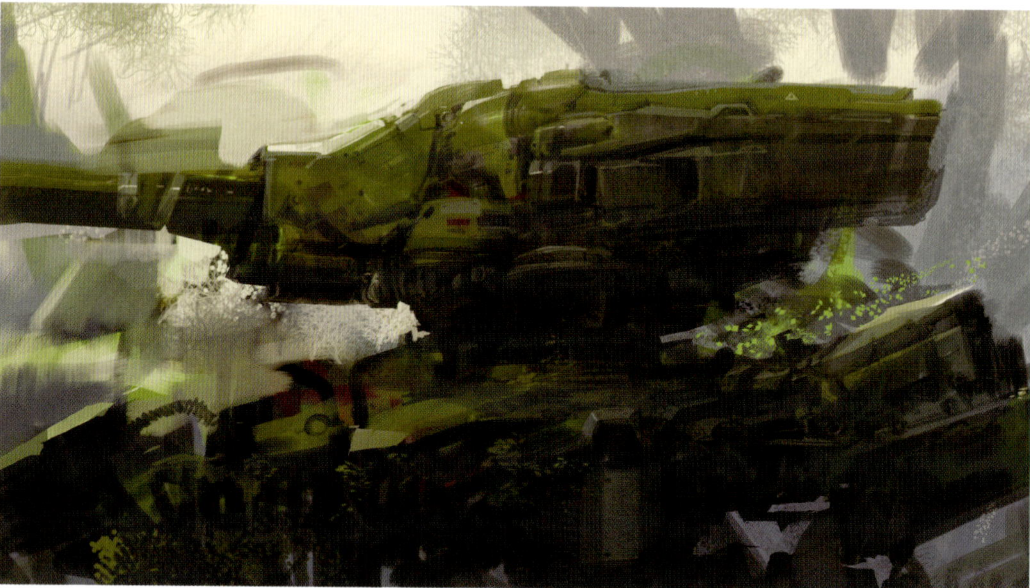

This next step involves using a brush, as shown in the example (brush setting window). I start to render the main subject. Placing strong highlights in a selected area is not a bad idea, since it creates an interesting visual contrast.

I use many different types of texture brushes in this painting. It is a good idea to try out types of brushes other than what I have shown in the example (a). The most important exercise here is to try as many different brushes as possible and find ones that work for the painting as well as one's painting style (b).

Fig. 2.45

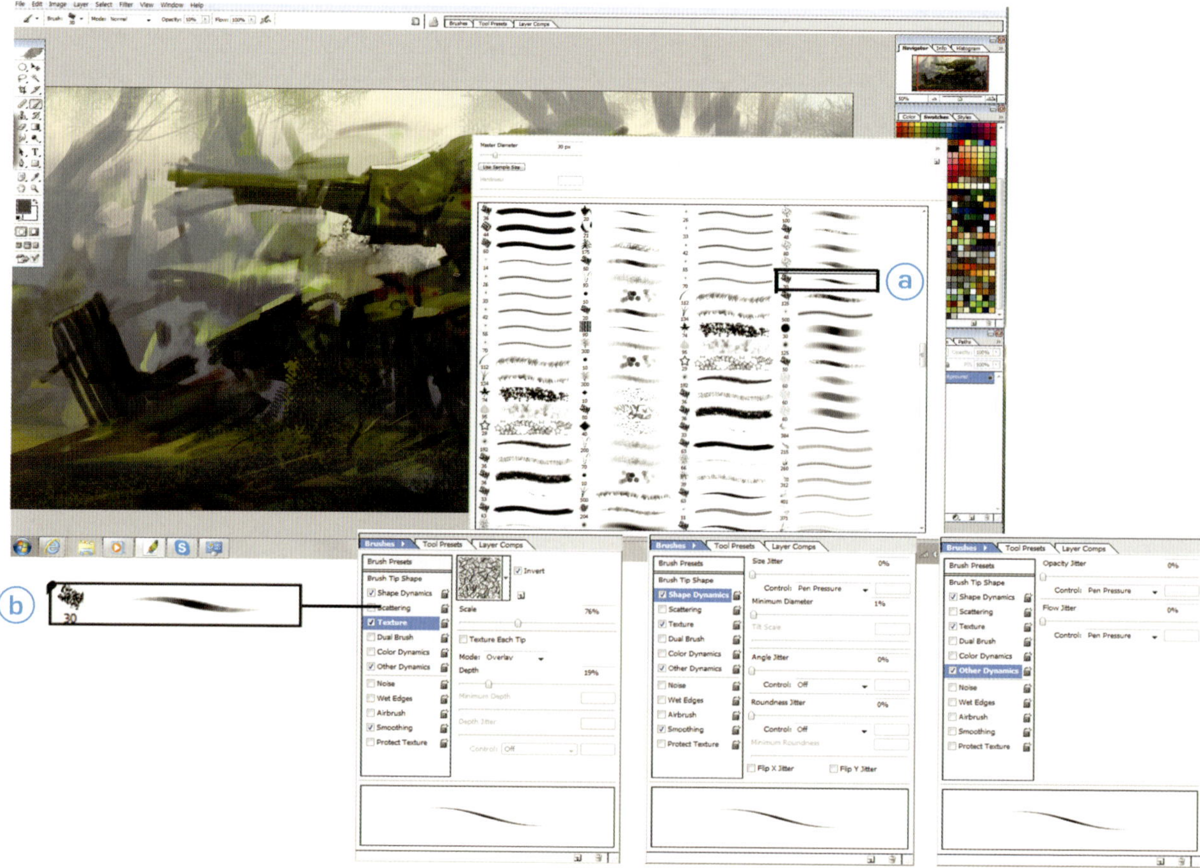

Fig. 2.46

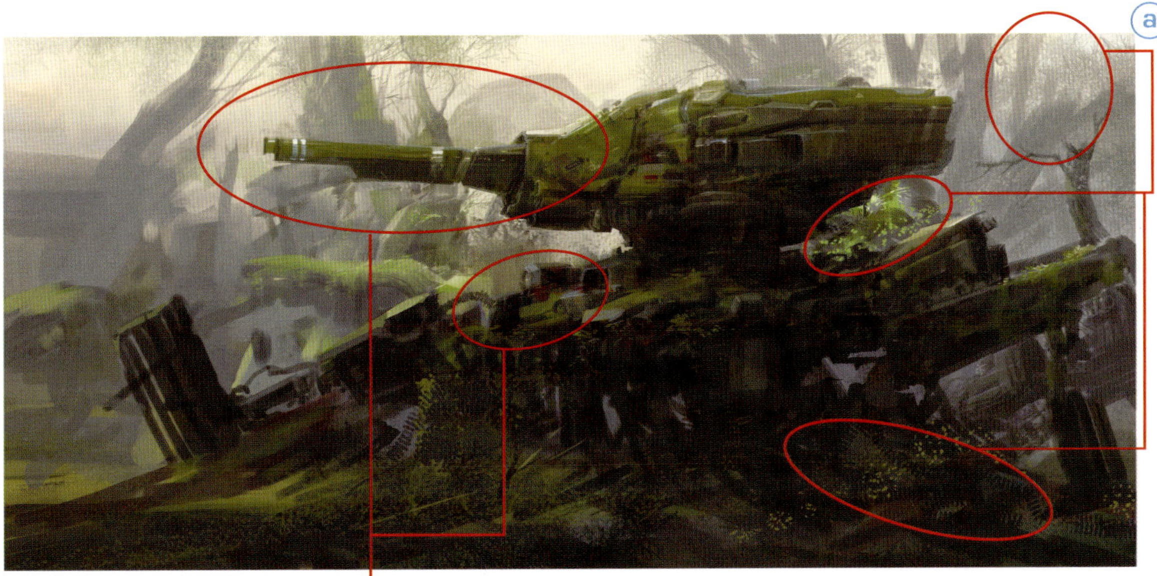

As I develop more details on the tank, it is a good time to introduce secondary details and colors on its surface. Since the main color is green, I add white and gray to break the pattern on the green surface (a). Adding small decals and warning signs creates more believable surface detail (b).

Fig. 2.47

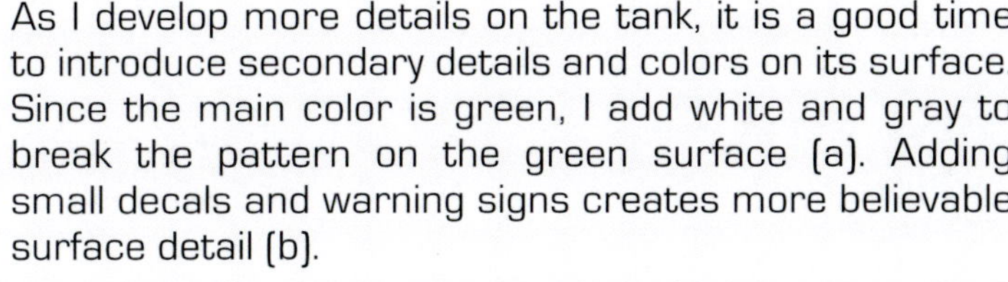

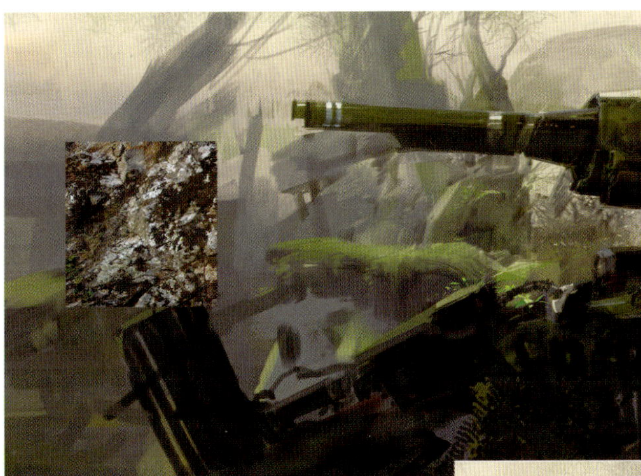

Next, I am going to develop the background more. When using a photo source to paint over, I oftentimes set a photo source as either an overlay layer or a normal layer.

Fig. 2.48

In this step, I erase the parts that I do not need for the painting and keep the detail information that I do need. It is important to pay attention to the detail information of the photo source. As this figure shows, there are many scattered dots on the surface of a rock, which is a very common pattern on natural rock. I can either use a photo source to capture that, or I can use my texture brush to create that effect.

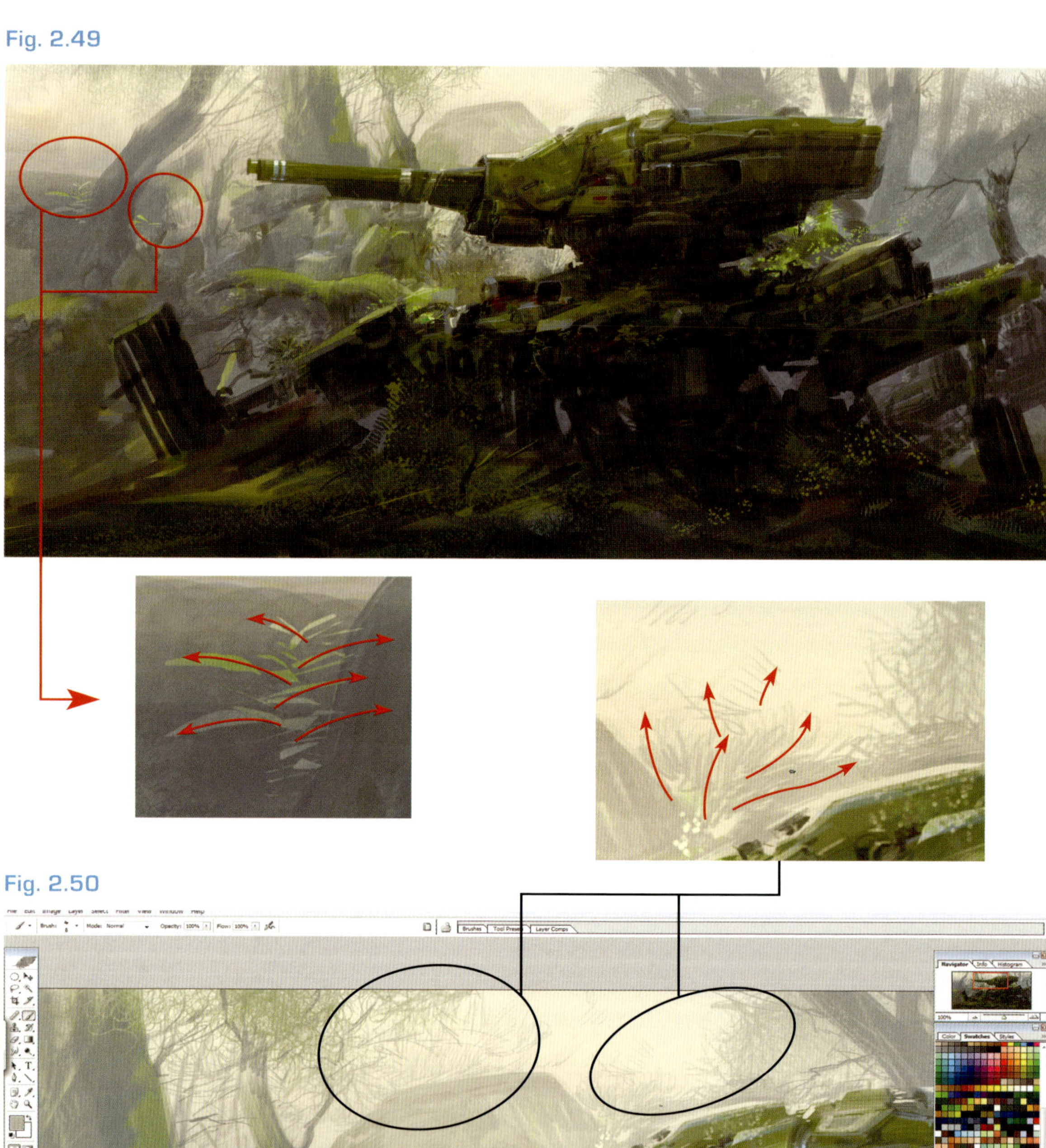

Fig. 2.49

The Lasso tool is perfect for painting leaves. Select the leaf shape with the lasso and paint the leaves with a low-opacity brush. It is important to observe plants in their natural state whenever possible. It is amazing how many different plants grow in nature. Observe them carefully, and memorize their shapes, so that this information can be used whenever it is needed.

I paint a few more trees by hand drawing, without using any fancy texture brush. Painting gets too computerized after using a texture brush for a while. To break that digitized look and to add a more natural look back into a painting, paint over more trees with freehand brushstrokes. Remember to keep the flow and direction of the tree branch.

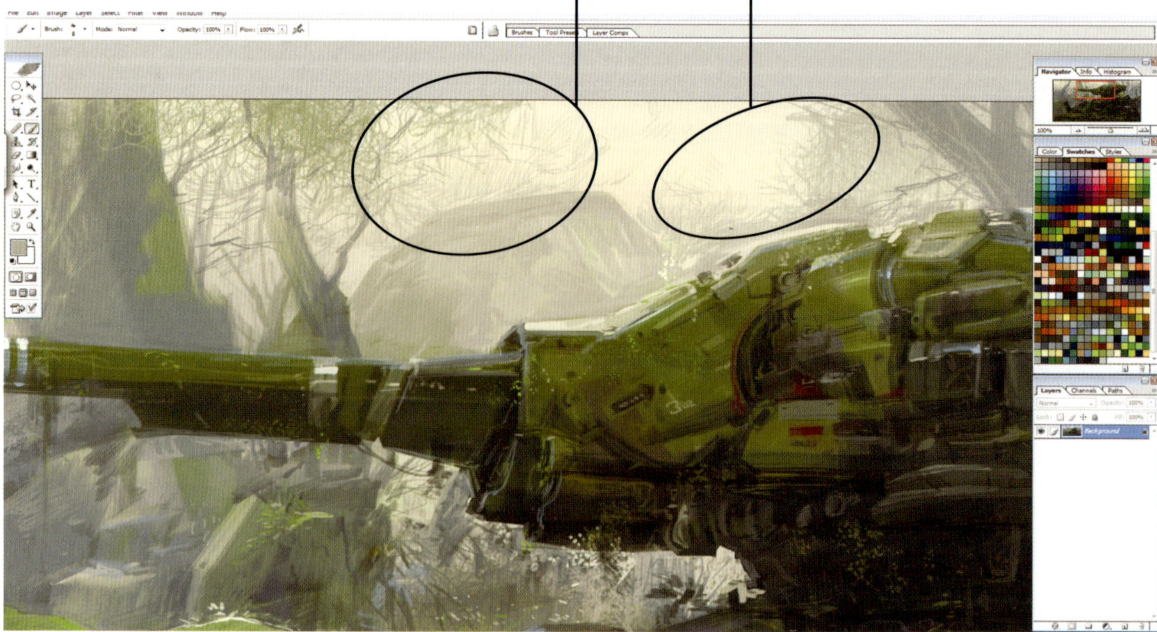

Fig. 2.50

Fig. 2.51

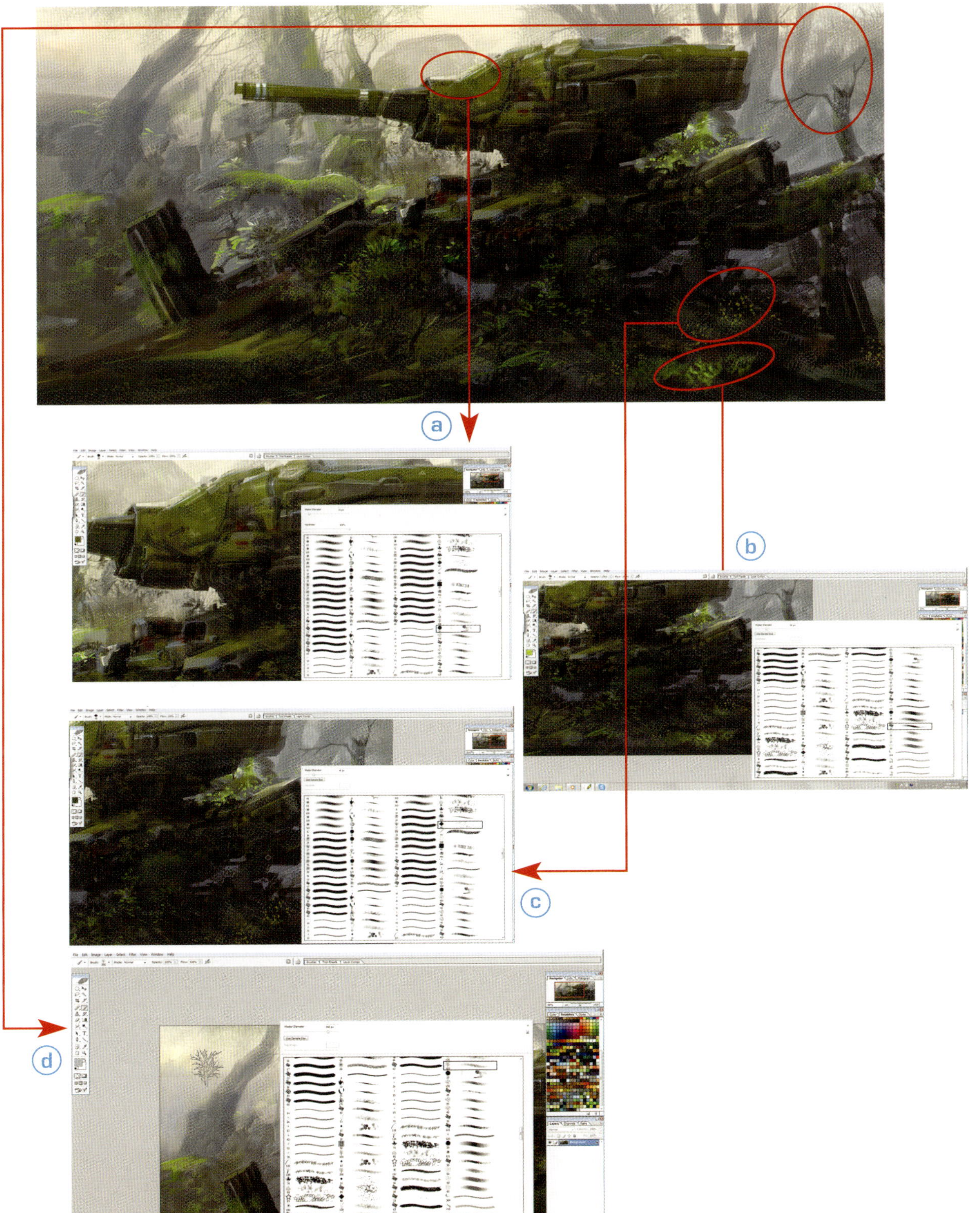

In this figure, I am going to share some brush setting information for some of the texture brushes I have used in this painting.

First, this is a good brush (a) to render small leaves. However, try not to overuse this brush; it gets too busy too quickly because of its high-frequency brush marks. Second, there is a default chalk brush (b). Scale this brush up and use it as a rough texture brush with its grains. The next brush (c) is similar to the brush used for small leaves (a).

One reason I used multiple brushes for a similar outcome is that if I use the same brush too much it creates boring brush marks. Vary the brush shapes and textures as much as possible. The more variety that can be seen in a painting, the more dynamic the painting. The last brush (d) is a tree-shaped brush. This brush is not a default brush in Photoshop, but anyone can easily make one. This brush is particularly good when painting leaves in the far distance. It mimics the spreading effect in a watercolor painting.

I use all these different types of brushes in Photoshop because otherwise it is very difficult to obtain the result I want. When painting with traditional paintbrushes, it is possible to get many different effects with one brush. But because of the technical limitations of using a digital painting program, the only way to get the effects I wanted was to use multiple brushes.

The next stage involves adding a warmer sky color in the background to make the color palette richer (a). It also adds a more sophisticated lighting effect to the painting. Note that I also painted roots and tree branches on the ground with strong directional shapes to draw the visual focus back to the main subject. However, I also wanted to counterbalance the repeated patterns by adding a few branches that go in the opposite direction. This results in a more natural look as opposed to making every branch flow in one direction.

Here, I use an orange color to create the small decals as a secondary color pop. This orange color creates a more interesting visual balance. I also paint a small gun turret as a fine detail of the tank. It adds more variation to the silhouette design and to the shape design. Most of the shapes were too big in this painting. Adding a smaller shape like the gun turret creates more visual balance. Again, I paint more grass with the Lasso tool to add more fine detail to the scene.

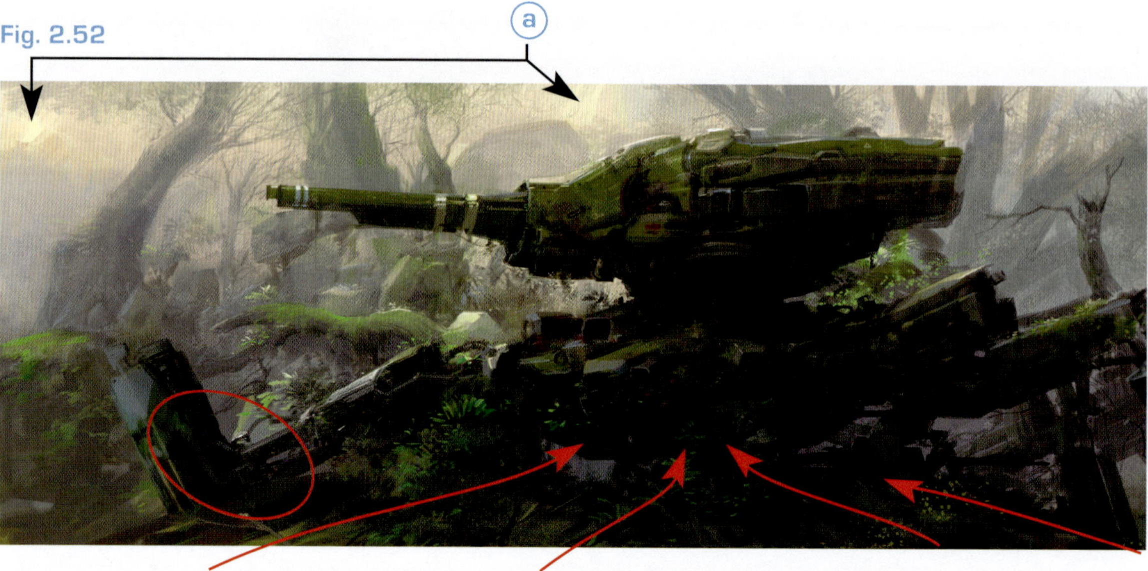

Fig. 2.52

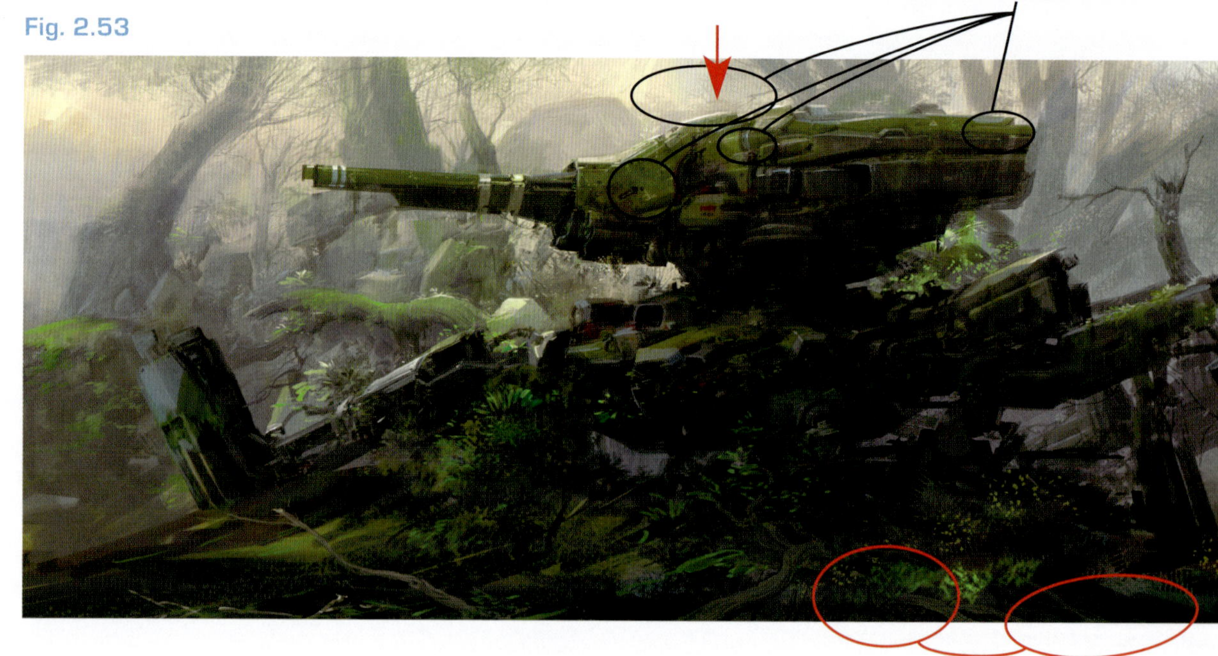

Fig. 2.53

Fig. 2.54

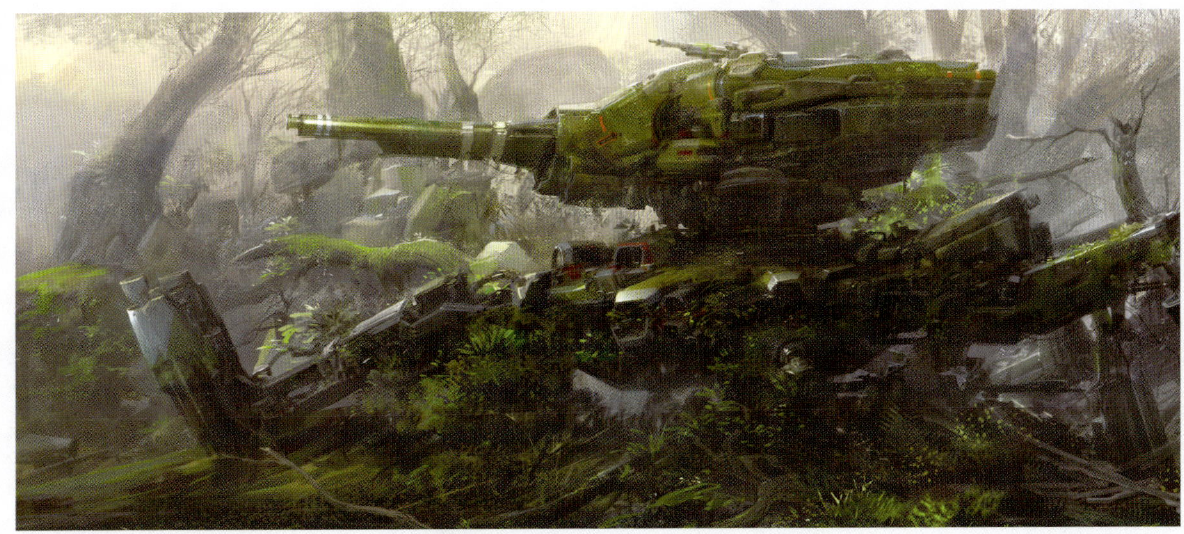

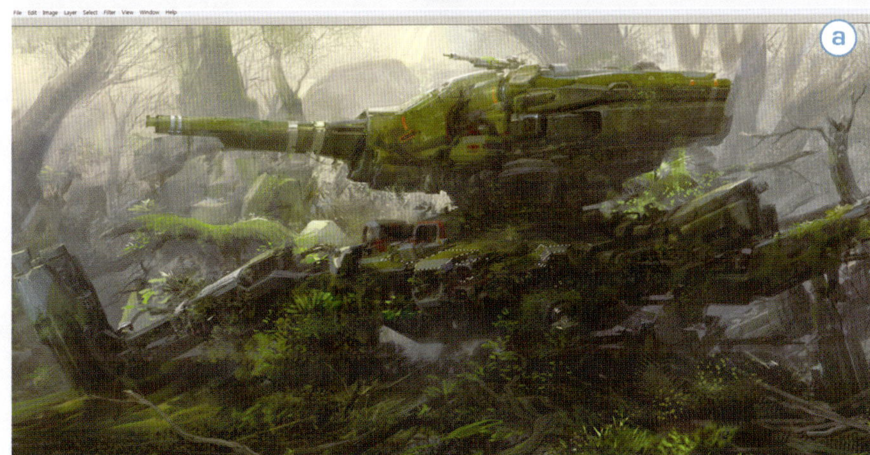

The last step is to add more detailed lighting information to the painting to clarify the atmosphere. I paint more atmospheric effects with an airbrush at 10 to 30% opacity. I choose a bluish color to paint the air. After doing so, I make a selection with the Lasso tool (a), which is particularly good when I want to make a very sharp edge selection. Adding sharp edges creates visual tension, so I use this technique during the last stage of the painting process.

Then, by using a Color Dodge brush, I paint more lighting effects to the selected area (b). I also make very small selections (almost like dots) in the upper right-hand corner (c) to paint more of the noise details. These small selections may seem, at quick glance, not to do anything to the painting, but all of these little details make a big difference overall.

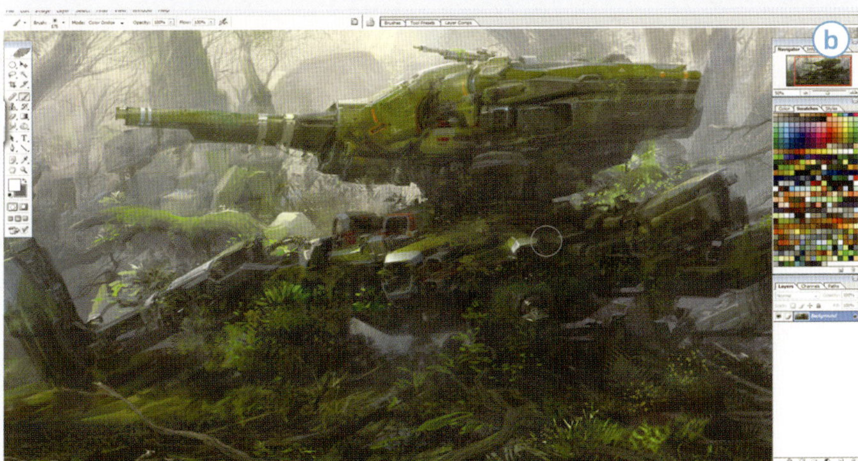

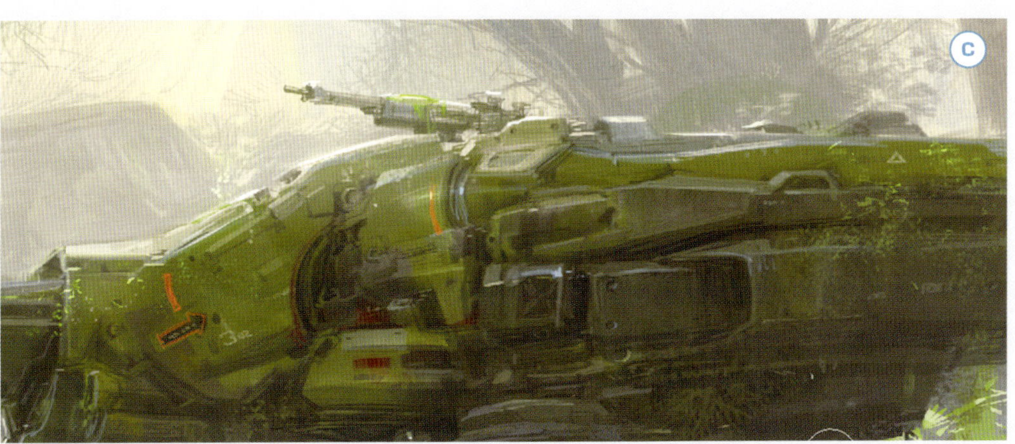

Space Shuttle

Fig. 2.55

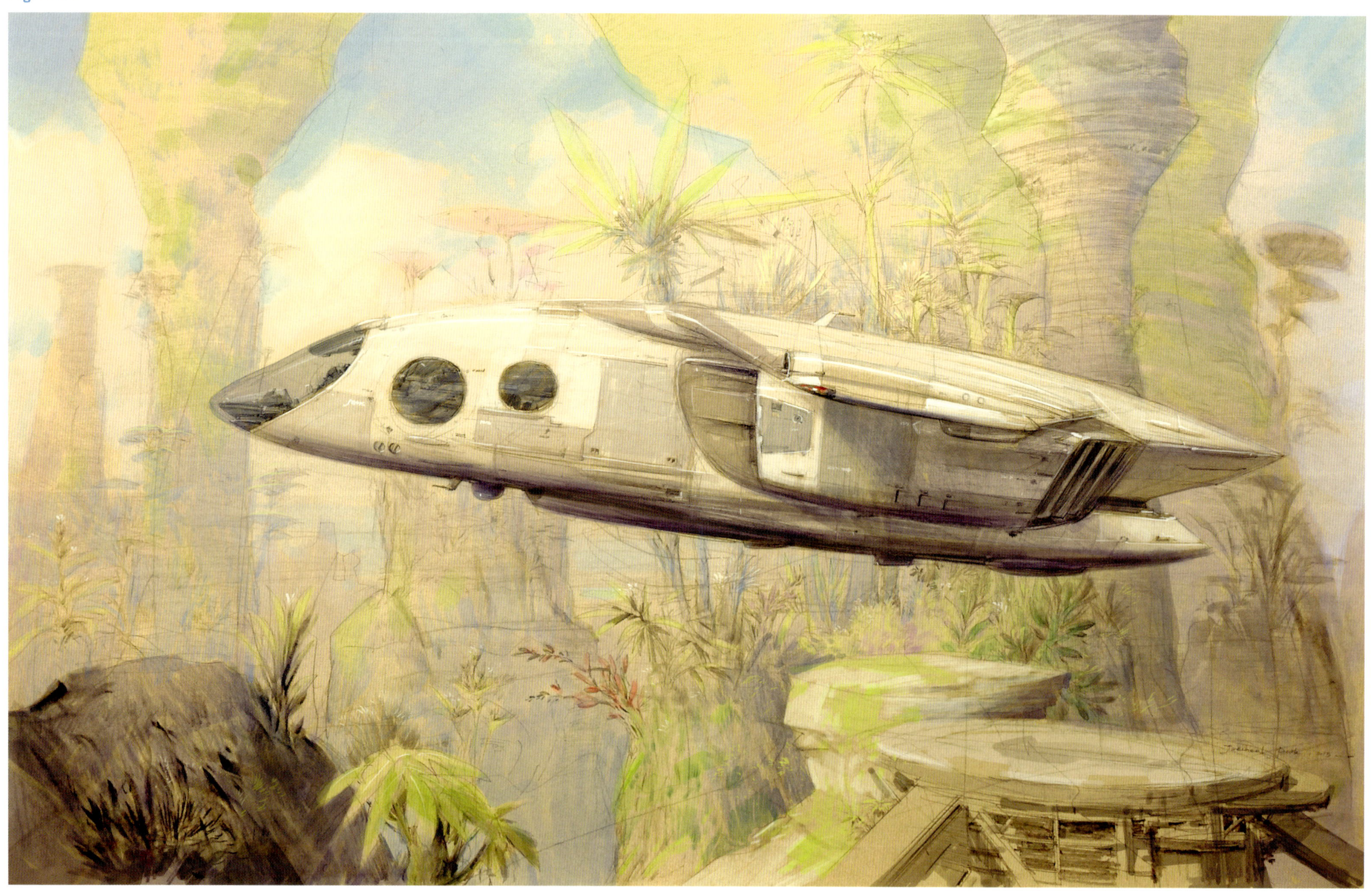

Fig. 2.56

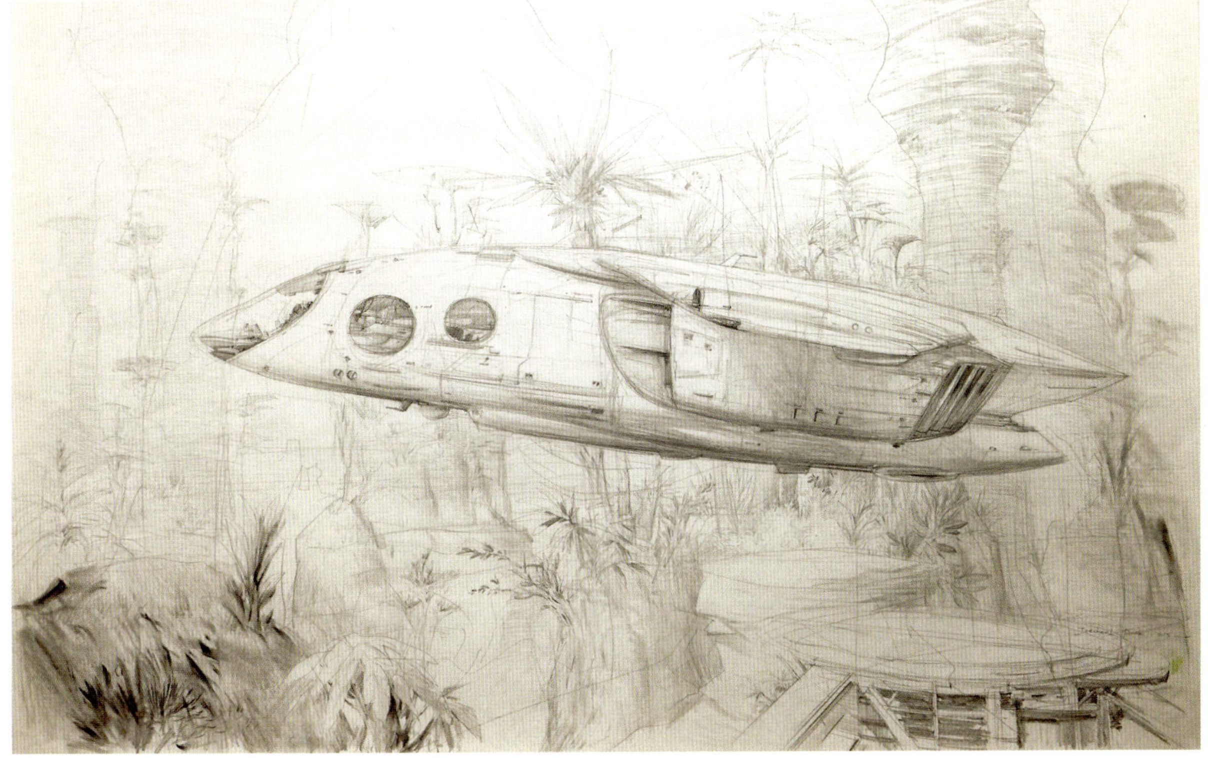

In this example, I am using a pencil sketch as a starting base. This time, I want to make this painting almost like a watercolor painting, which has more transparency than other paintings. I approach the aircraft using a design that I could find in real life, and add a slightly more futuristic feel to it (this is how I design most of my aircraft). I reference my memory for the plants. I quite often go out in nature or to the mountains and observe plants. It is amazing how many different plants grow in one place. There are many plants much smaller than a fingernail. I am always surprised to see new plants every time I go out in the wilderness. Also, covering the rocks with moss gives the painting a more lush vibe.

Next, I tone the canvas with warm brown. I will try to have this background color bleed out as if I were painting a watercolor painting on toned paper.

Fig. 2.57

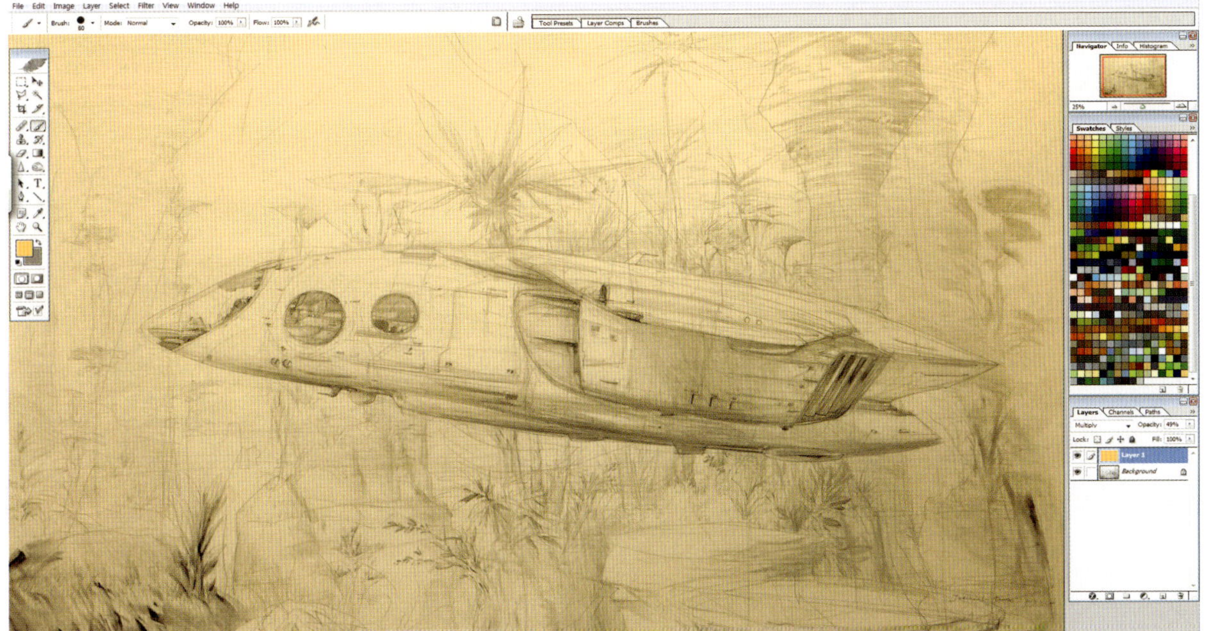

This time, I have use the most basic brush on this painting.

The next step is glazing, which is done with a low-opacity brush (30%). The most important part of doing this glazing technique is choosing the right color. Using a low-opacity brush means having a lot more color mix with base layers, so be very careful and accurate about the original color choice.

At this stage, use big brushstrokes. Since this is a very early stage of the painting, try not to use too many smaller brushstrokes. Since I am using a very low-opacity brush, I should be able to see my base drawing at all times, and it should feel more like a watercolor painting with dried water marks (a).

Fig. 2.58

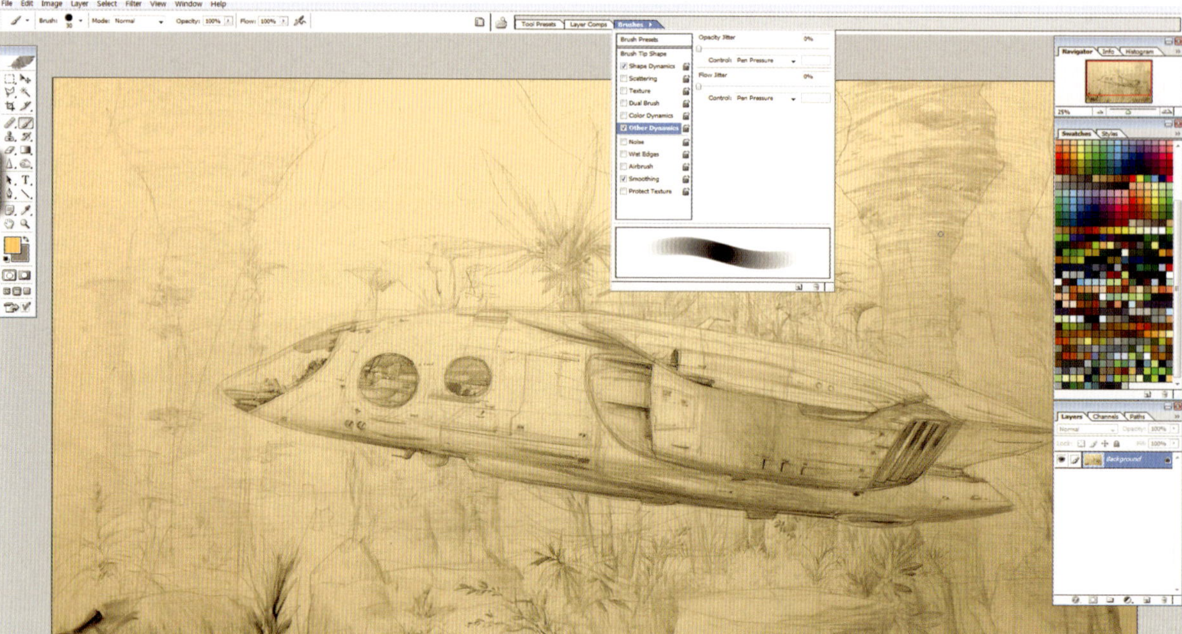

Fig. 2.59

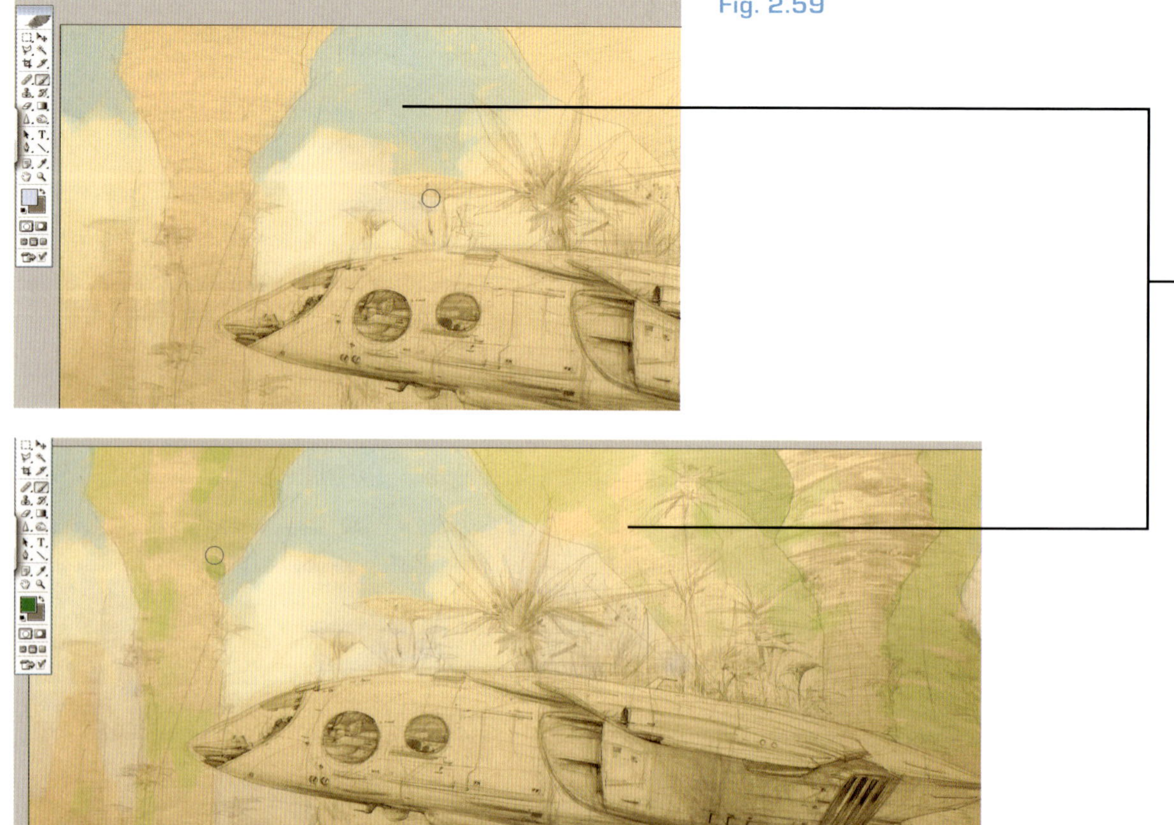

(a)

Fig. 2.60

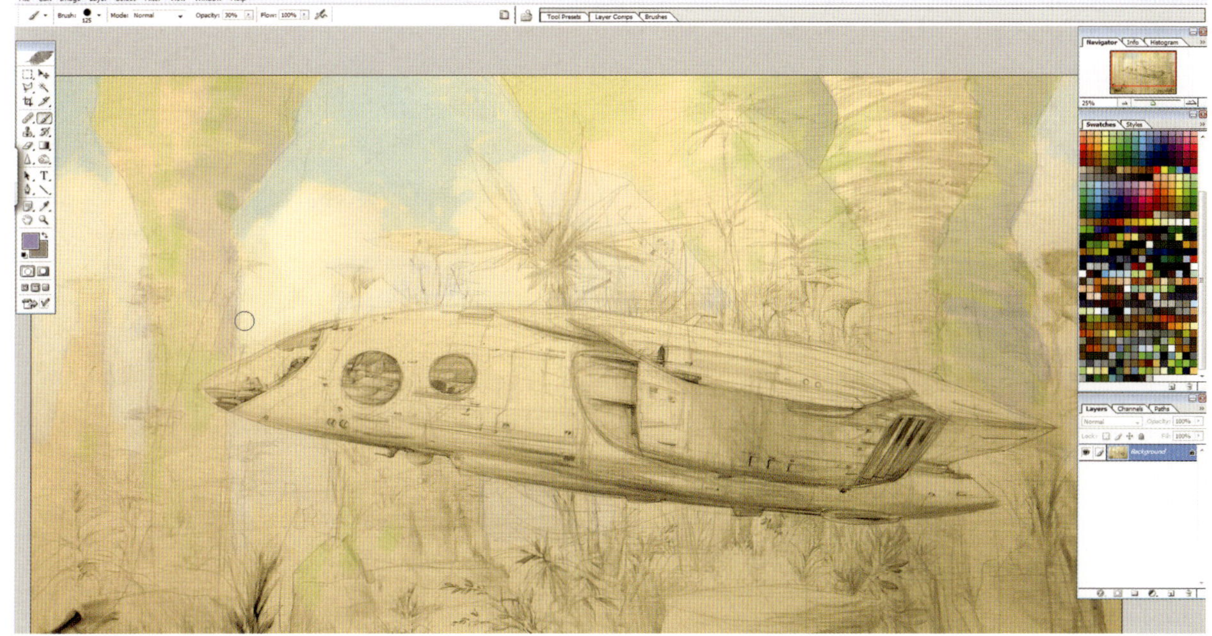

Fig. 2.61

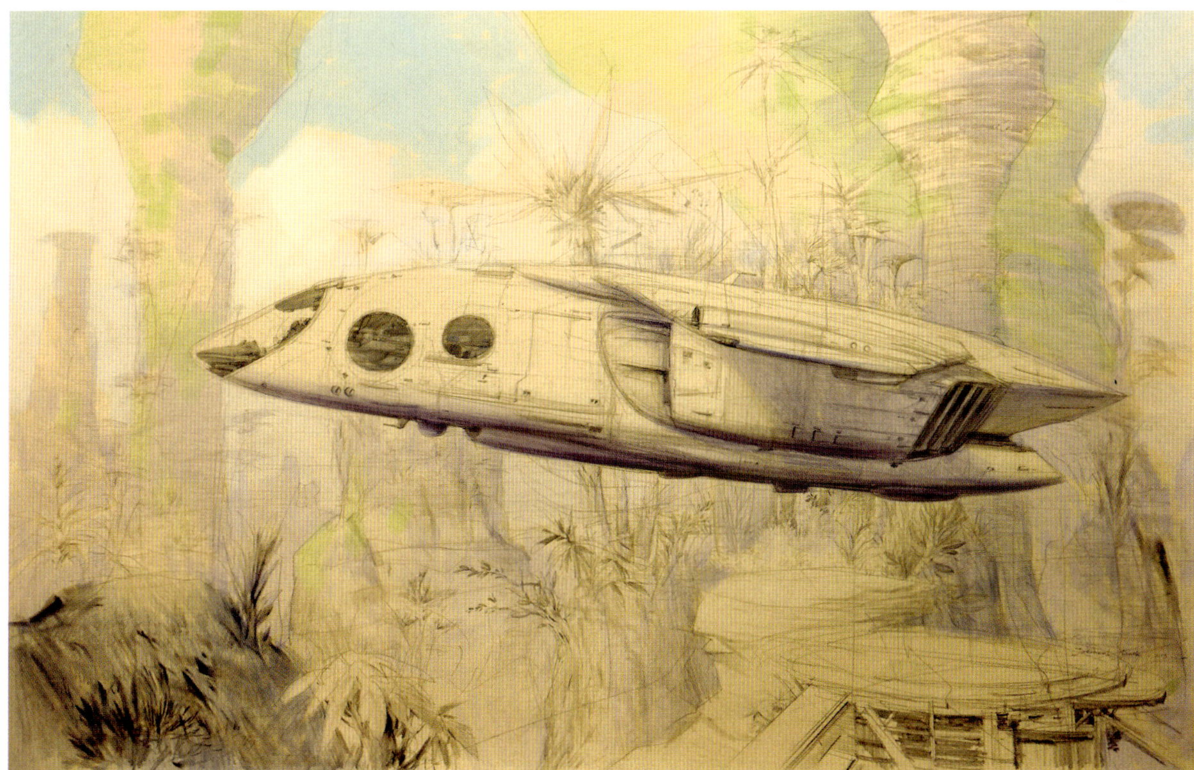

Here, I use purple to create the rock shadows. The purple shouldn't be too dark; otherwise, it defeats the goal of making the painting look like a watercolor. When the light purple I used here gets mixed with a darker base tone, it creates a very warm, tranquil feeling.

Once I have some basic color painted in, I then use the Brightness/Contrast tool to pump up the contrast a bit to give it a clearer look.

To make this painting more colorful, I add a few color pops such as pink, blue, and red (a). Now, I need to decide the color for the aircraft. I have been asking myself which color was the best since starting this painting. I considered white, blue, and red. I even thought of using black so I could make a military version of the aircraft. Several colors fit the bill. After a long, thoughtful decision-making process, I decide to go with white, which is the most basic color scheme that best fits the mood of the painting as a whole.

I finish the painting with some opaque brushstrokes to give it more sharpness and clarity. Even though this painting is not as intense as other paintings, I like the looseness of it, and how each subtle stroke turned out to almost look like a watercolor glazing (a). This final result allows maximum usage of the initial sketch as a big part of the finished product.

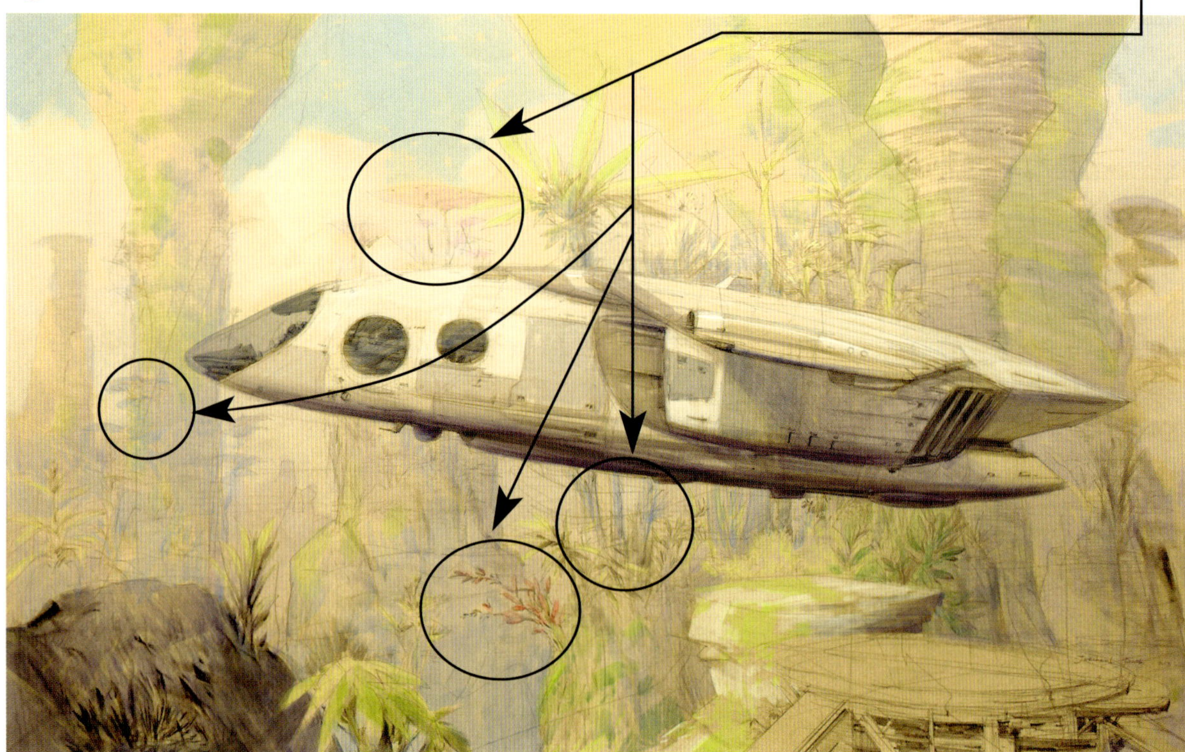
Fig. 2.62

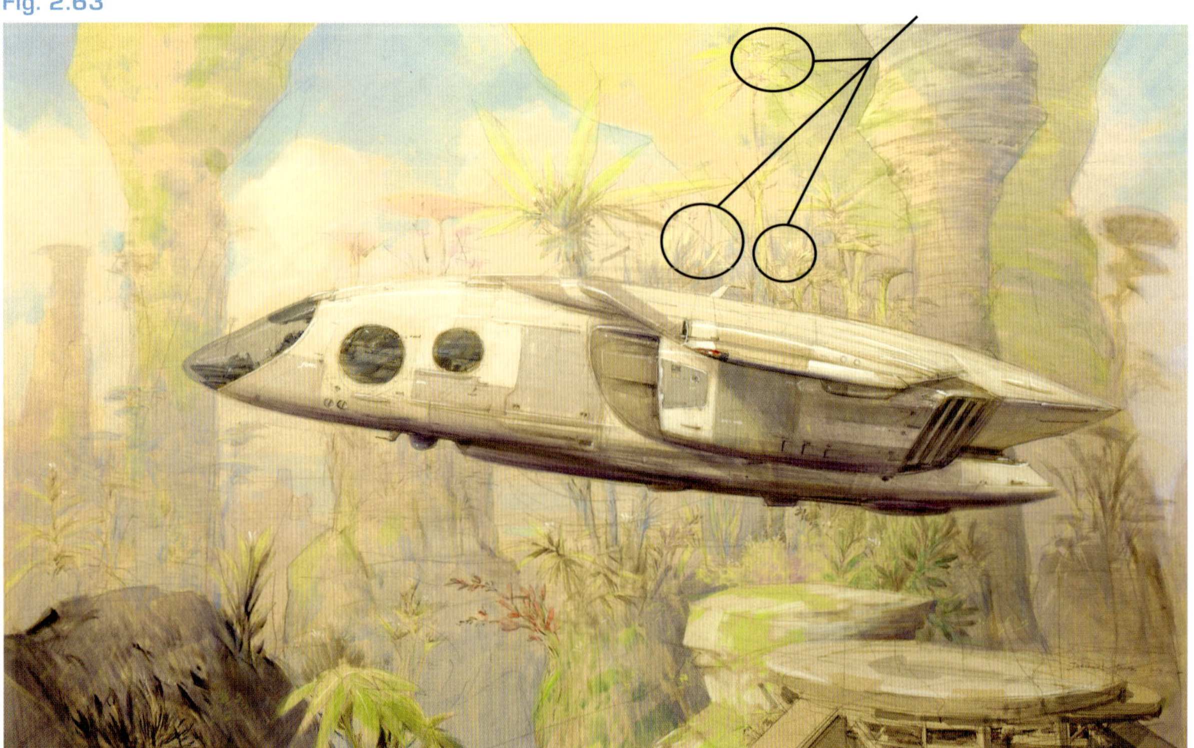
Fig. 2.63

Shuttle in the Station

Fig. 2.64

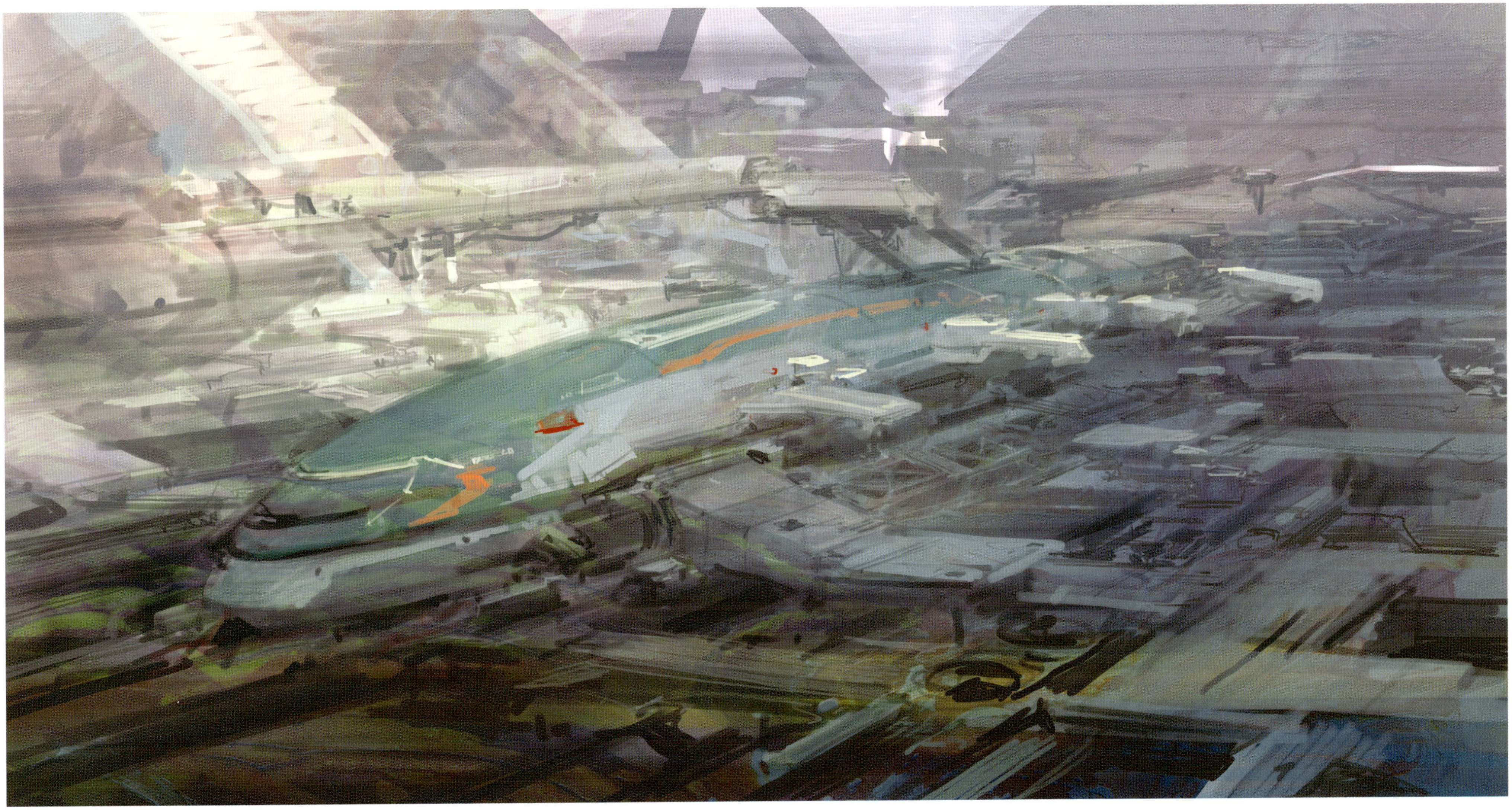

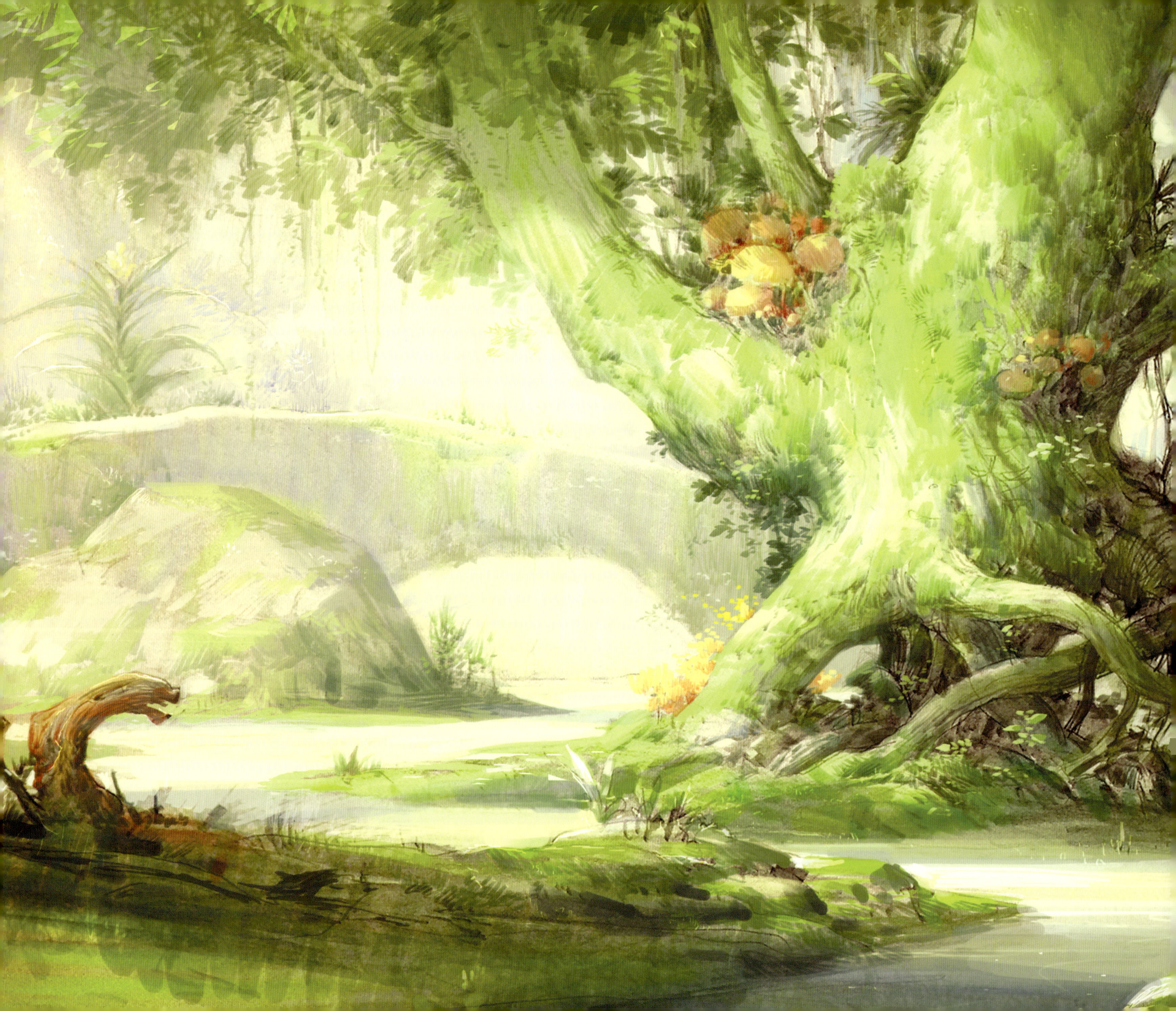

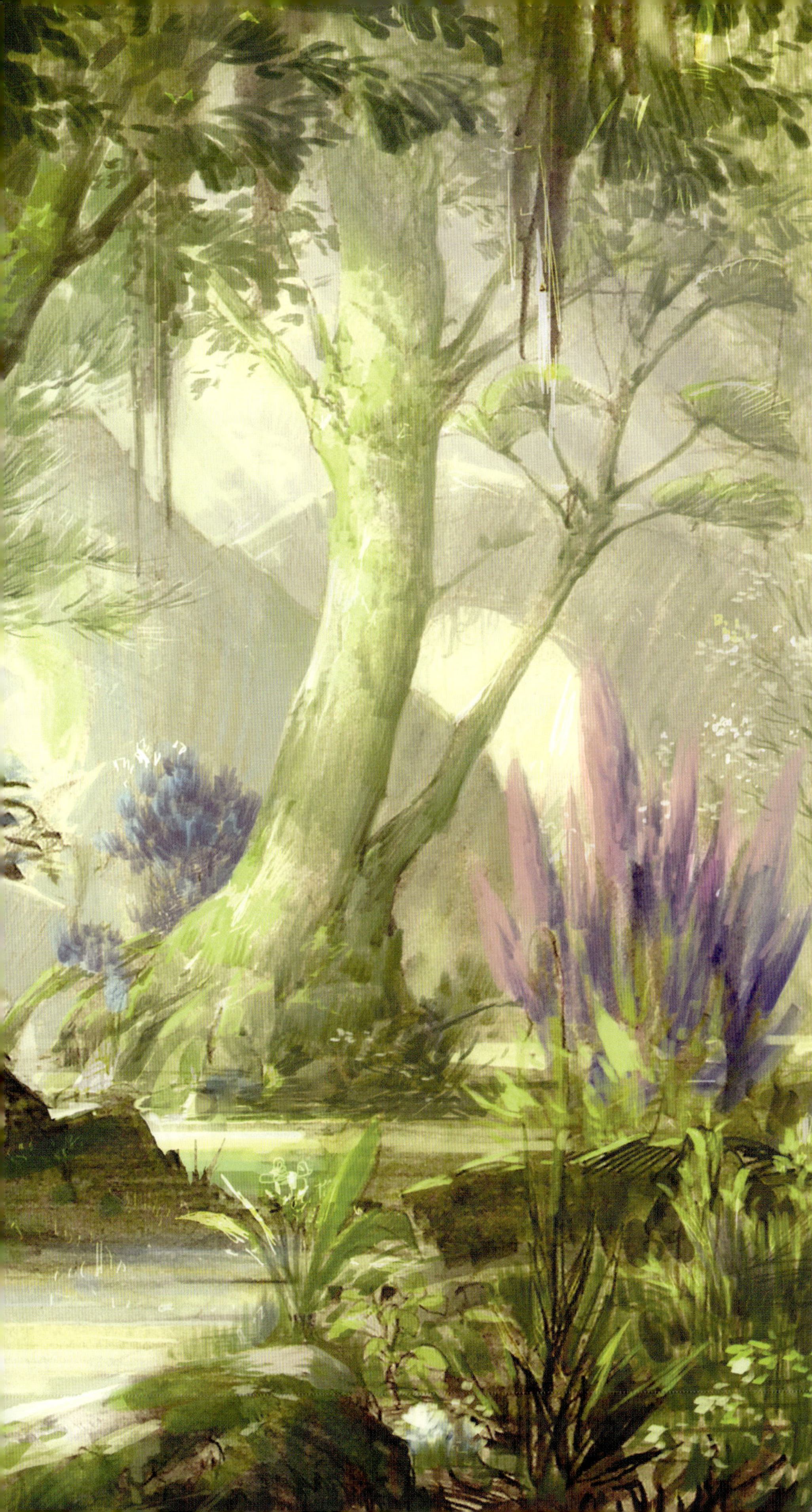

chapter 03
LANDSCAPE TUTORIALS

In this chapter, I will demonstrate how to create environments, cityscapes, nature scenes, and various fantasy settings by covering the basics of perspective and color theory, how to use custom brushes to paint nature, and how to create atmospheric effects, such as depth. Plus, you will learn how to use the visual flow of a painting to get the viewer's attention.

Mech City

In this tutorial, I will cover how to draw a complex
perspective drawing.

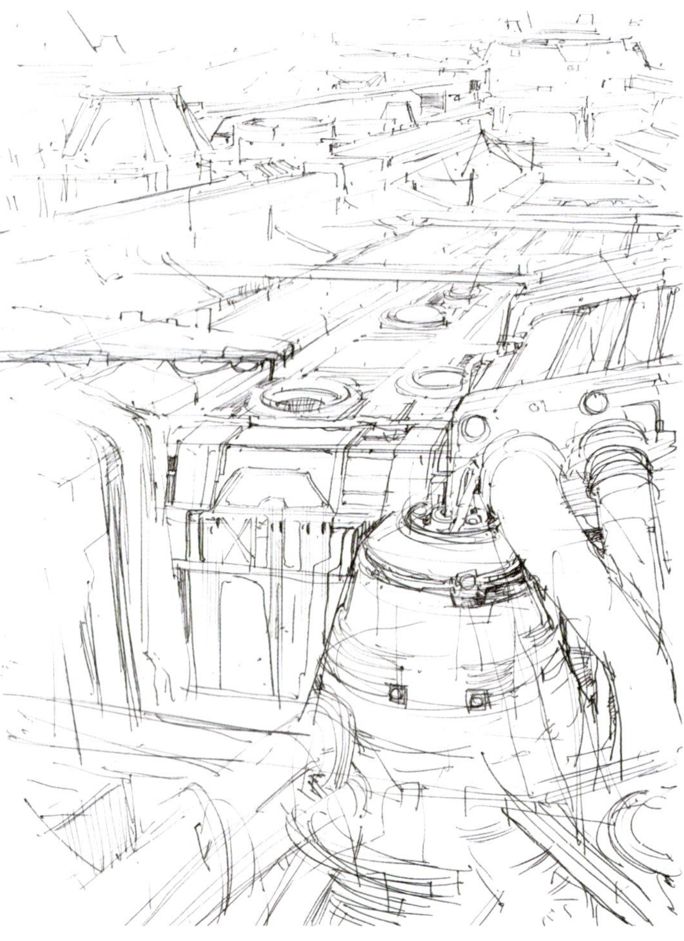

Fig. 3.1

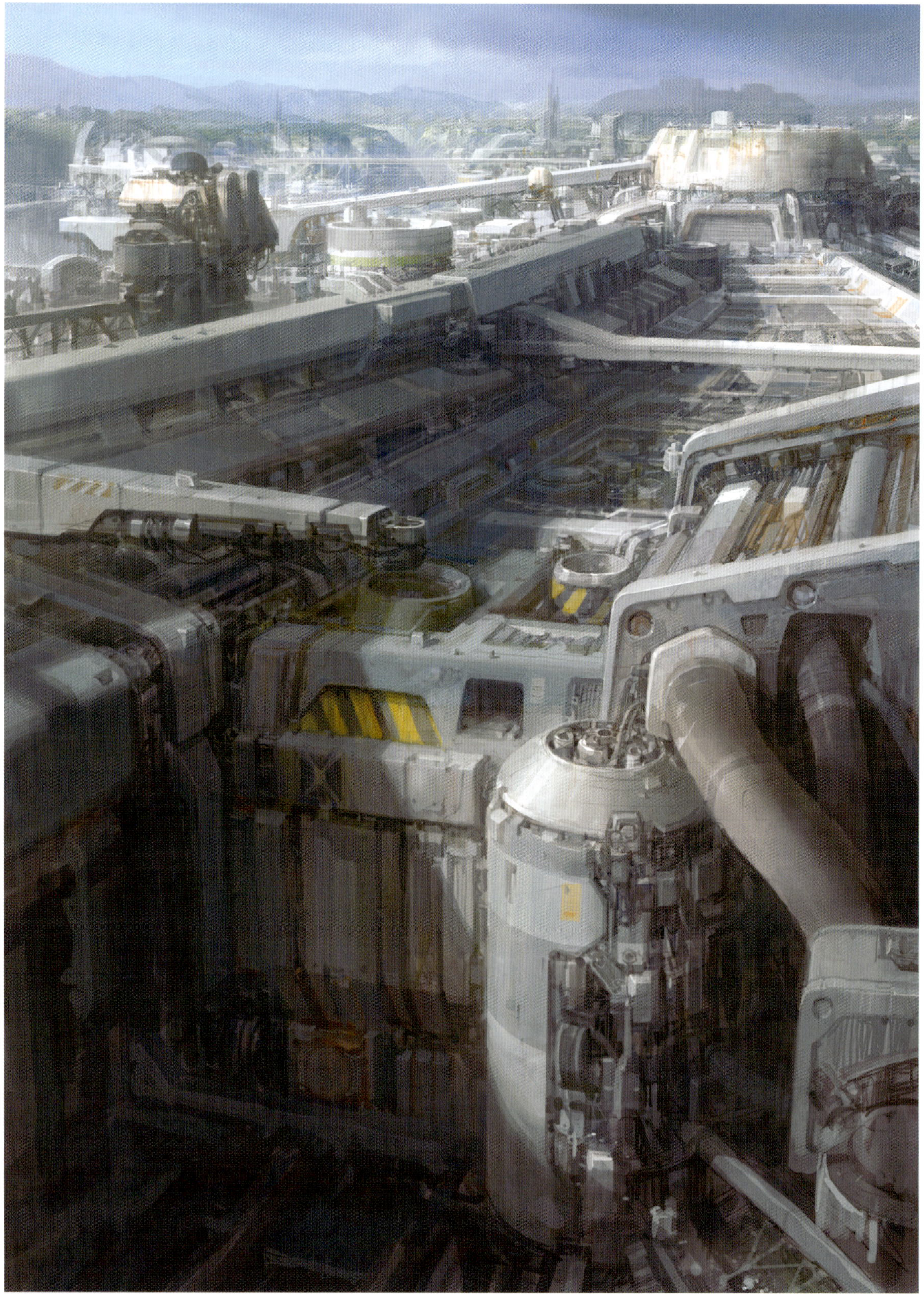

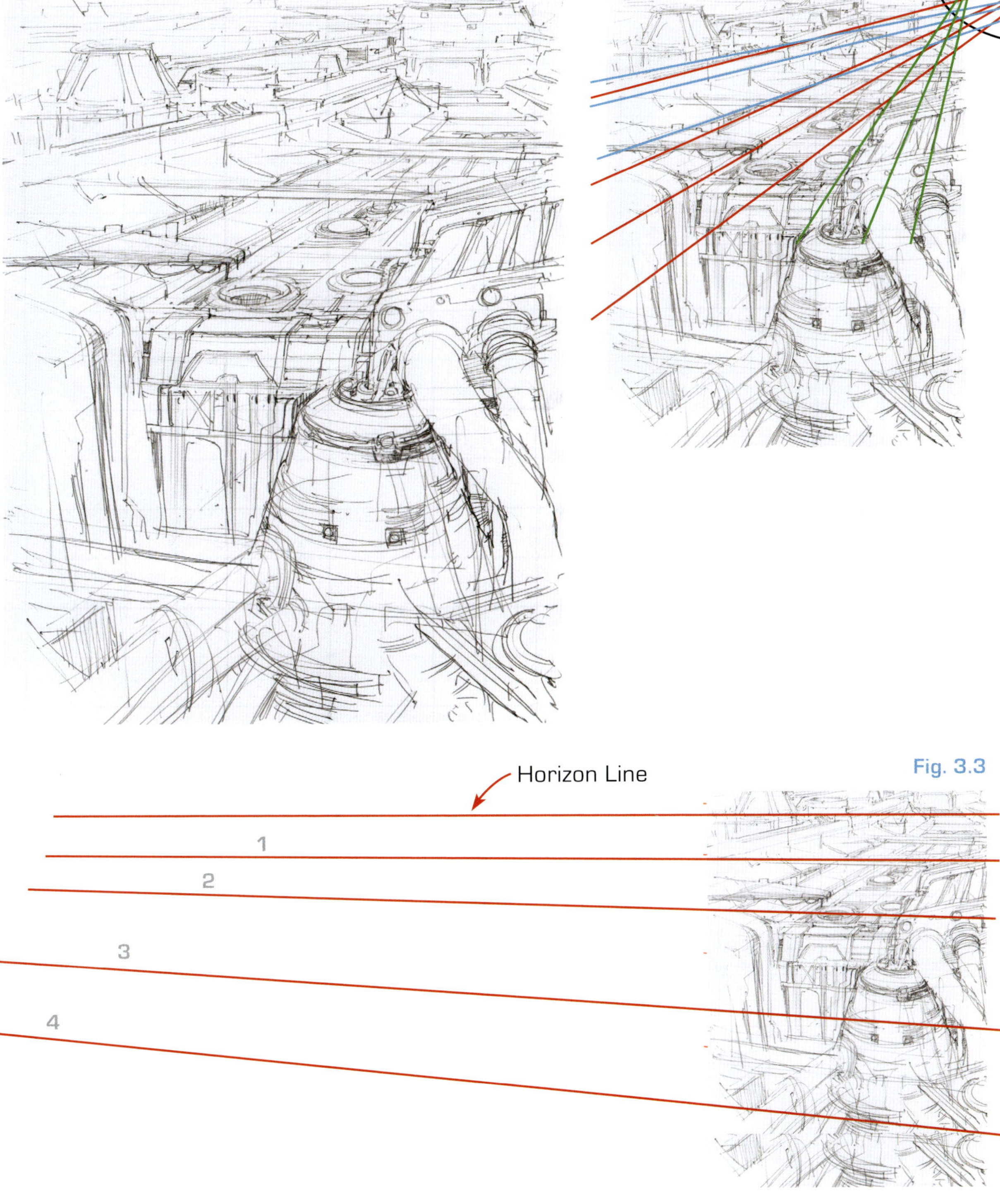

Fig. 3.3

This painting has an advanced two-point perspective grid. One set of vanishing points (1) is going toward the foreground on the right side of the image, and two other sets of vanishing points (2, 3) are going more toward the foreground on the left side. This is because any object that is rotated relative to any other object sitting parallel to a ground plane has its own set of vanishing points. I only marked three vanishing points in this example, but there are many other vanishing points in this painting. Remember, all the vanishing points will converge to the same horizon line if the surfaces of an object are parallel to the ground.

Since this is a two-point perspective painting, there are also sets of vanishing points (Fig. 3.3) that go toward the left vanishing points of the objects in the scene. Obviously these vanishing points converge to the same horizon line as those in Fig. 3.2; they're just going 90° in perspective to those lines. Since the left vanishing point is far away from the edge of the image, it is wise to first set a converging perspective line (4) that is farthest away from the horizon line as a starting point. Then fill the gap between the horizon line and the converging line with more perspective lines converging to the left vanishing point.

To draw an ellipse in perspective: Its minor axis—a line dividing the ellipse in half symmetrically across its shortest dimension—will stay perpendicular to the ground plane if the surface defined by the ellipse is parallel to the ground plane (Fig. 3.4). The degree of the ellipse—how wide or narrow it is along the minor axis—will become narrower as it gets closer to the horizon line as you are seeing less and less of that surface of the ellipse. As I did in Fig. 3.2 with my perspective lines, draw an ellipse near the bottom of the image as a starting point and then draw more ellipses in perspective. The ellipses' minor axes will be parallel to any vertical lines in the scene and follow the same perspective grid. If the vertical lines in the scene are converging to a third vanishing point below the image, be sure to make your minor axis lines converge to this vanishing point as well. It is a good exercise to draw several ellipses with minor axes for practice (a).

In this figure, I block in the large shapes with simple color and value (a). I place my line drawing on a separate Multiply layer for now so that I can see my sketch as I paint in the big shapes (b–c). Then I collapse the drawing layer with the painting layer because it is easier to control the whole painting that way. Nevertheless, I am paying attention not to paint over the whole drawing. Probably some of the lines will get painted over completely (d), but I want to save as many drawing lines as possible because it looks much more natural that way. In some places I even used a photograph to add more texture to the painting.

Fig. 3.4

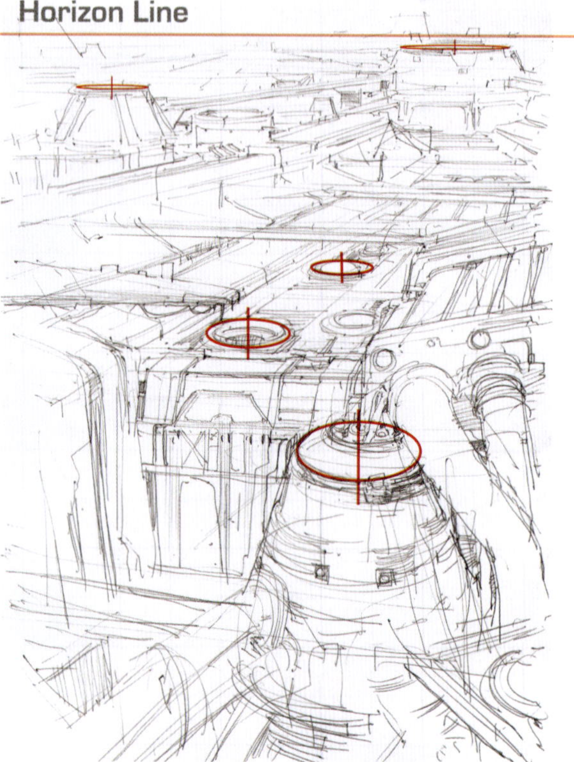

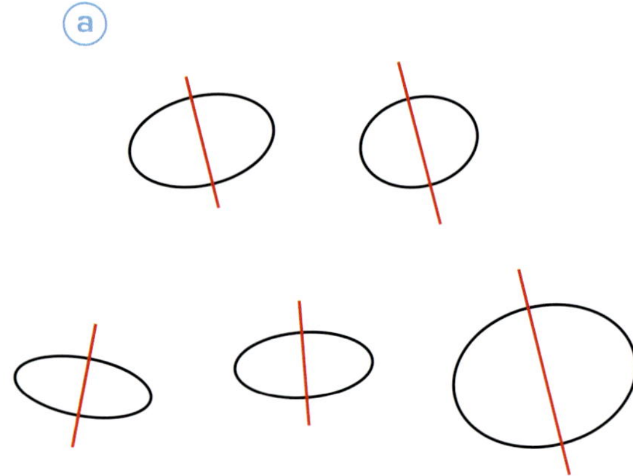

Fig. 3.5

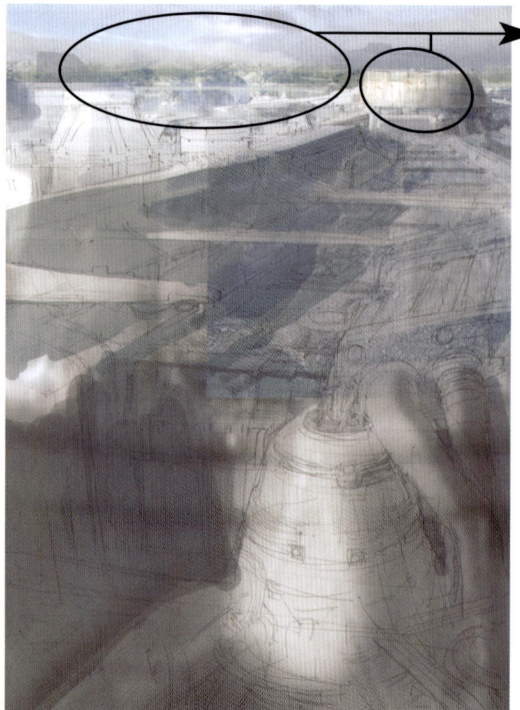

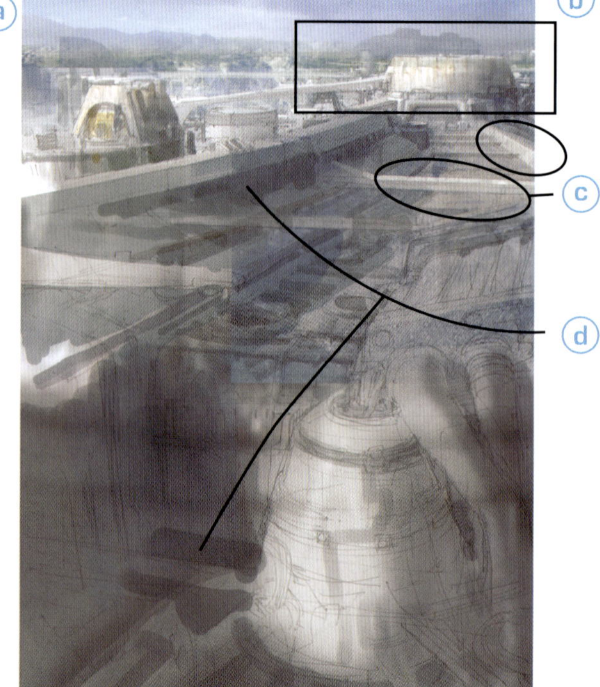

Fig. 3.6

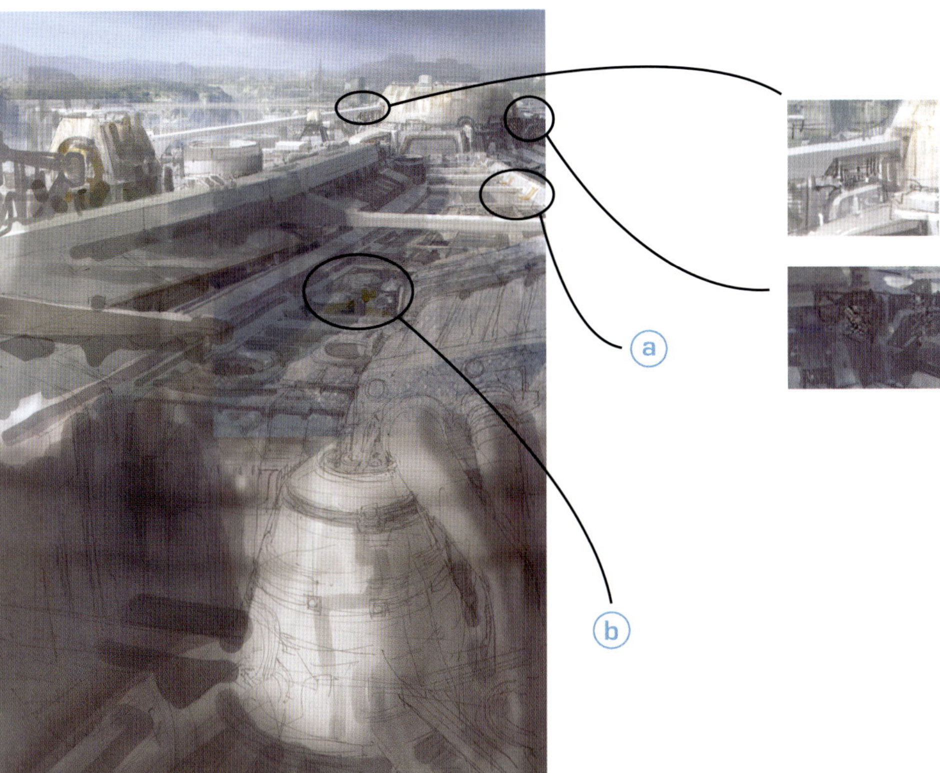

With digital painting, I try not to zoom in too much. I would like to see the whole painting as I make progress. Otherwise, I get lost in smaller details too easily. There are many ways to draw the detail in the painting. One way, as seen here, is to roughly indicate the look of it with lines and big marks (a). Furthermore, I am designing the painting not only with shapes, but also with colors. Adding a rusty orange color to a bluish painting like this tends to work really well. It seems like I have too much blue in the dark area. So I decided to add a bit more greenish colors in the dark (b).

As I make large shapes by using big brushstrokes, I also counterbalance them with small and sharp details (a). Adding greenish gray to the metal surfaces gives a very heavy feel to the material. It works well when I draw a mechanical subject (b).

Fig. 3.7

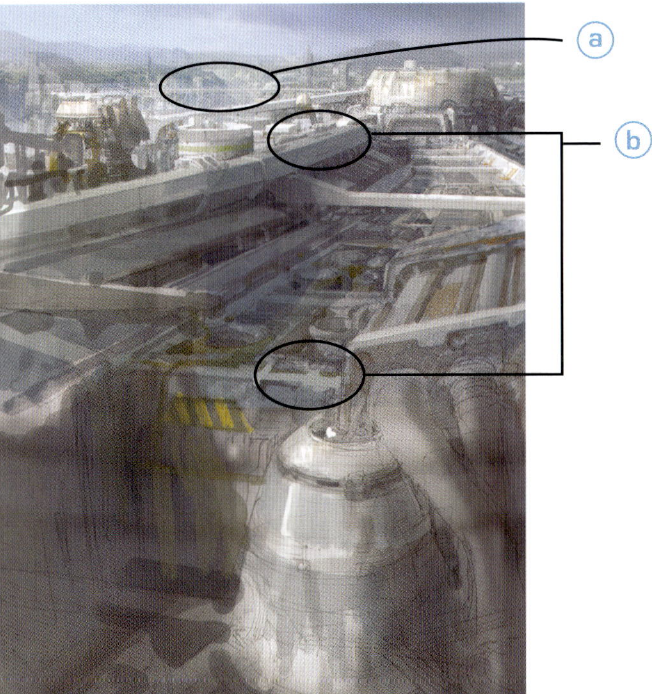

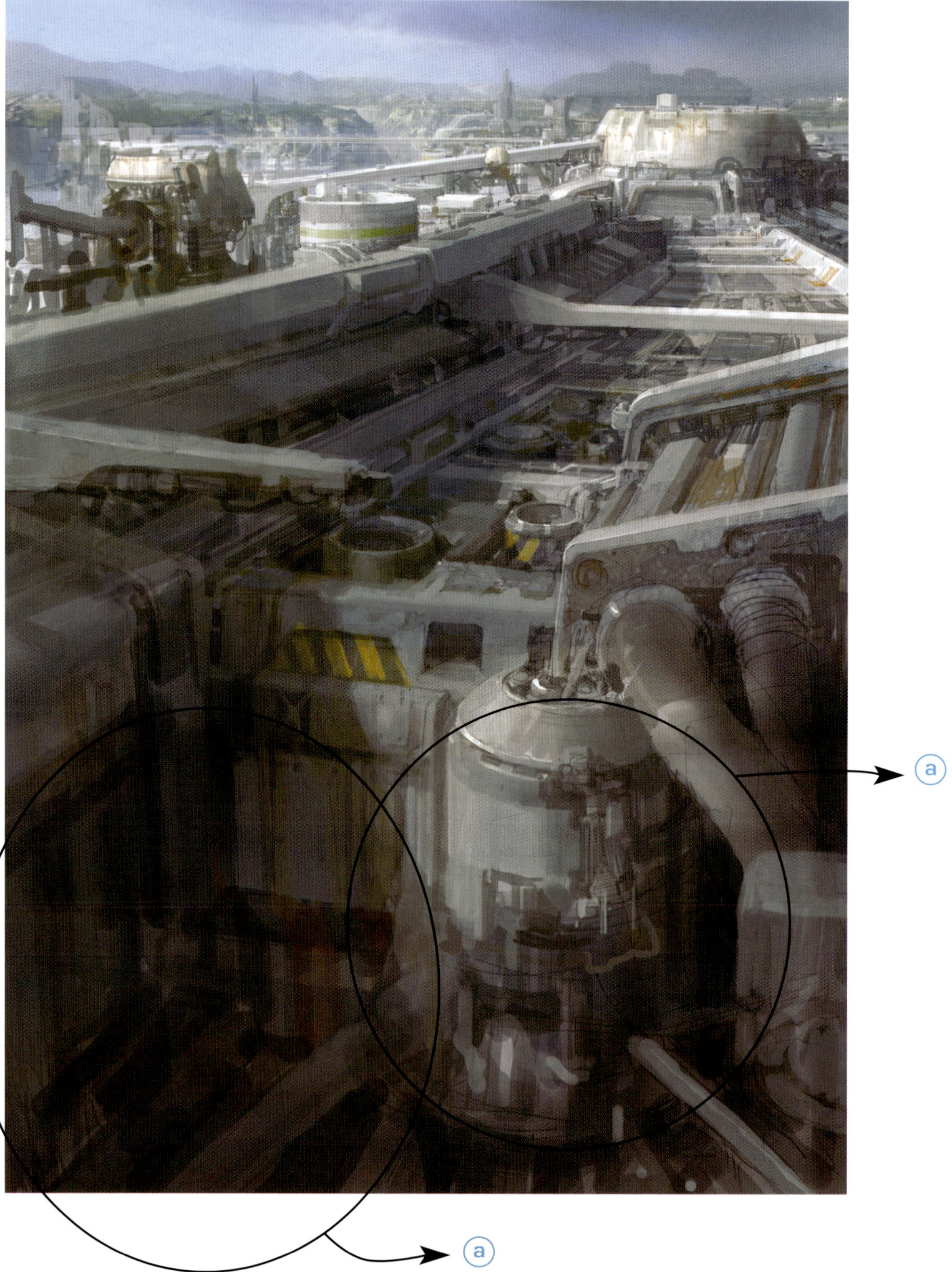

Fig. 3.8

I change the design of the main cylinder a little bit since I did not like how it flares out at the bottom. This is one big advantage of working loosely. I can change and update the design on the fly as I want to. I start to paint in the detail on the top side and left the bottom portion as a sketch for now. I will get back to it later as I make more progress.

Whenever I feel stuck with one part of the painting, feeling that I can never make it right, I just leave it as it is for a time and move on to another part of the painting. I come back to it later with fresh eyes. One way that I make myself feel refreshed while working on a painting is to work with a few different painting techniques. I believe it is a good habit to switch your painting techniques from time to time and not stick to one corner of the painting for too long. Keep moving around the page and see the whole picture as you make progress.

I decide to finish this painting with this bottom section being loosely painted, without too much detail (a). This creates a more painterly feel compared to other parts of the painting. But even in this loose area, I need to add sharp edges in some places to make the painting looks more finished. By mixing these tight details with loose brushstrokes, it is possible to achieve the desired feeling of control and/or naturalness (b).

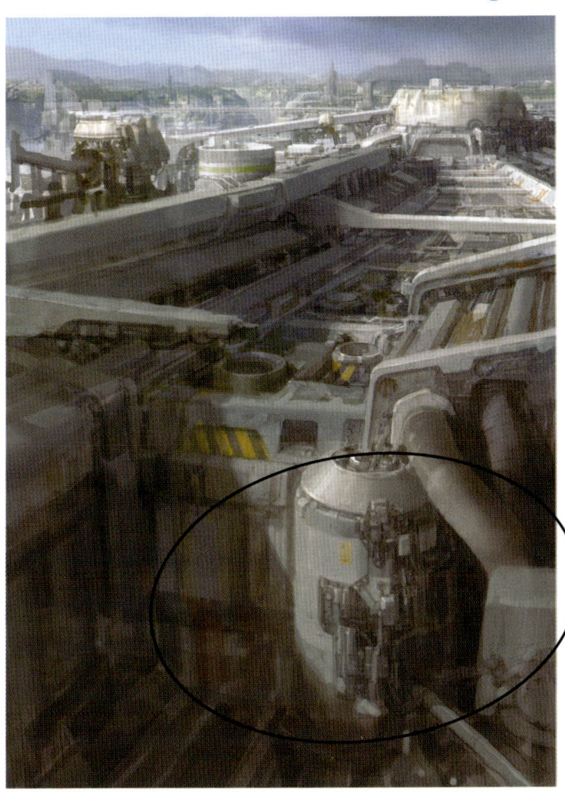

Fig. 3.9

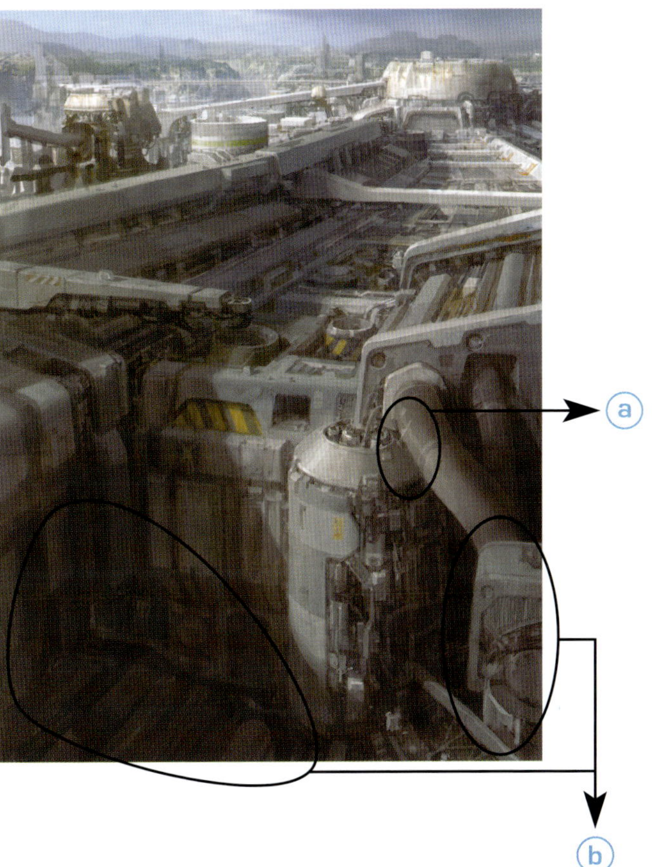

Fig. 3.10

Here, I start to bring up the detail level of the painting. Even in this process, I do not want to detail everything evenly. I am still trying to keep the good balance of loose and tight contrast in my expression.

Sometimes, a brushstroke makes for a happy accident. For example, in this portion of the painting, the gaps between brushstrokes make a very interesting texture. It almost looks like a dent mark on a metal pipe or a water mark on a watercolor painting (a). I like that happy-accident mark, so I try to mimic more of those brushstrokes on the other part of the painting (b).

Fig. 3.11

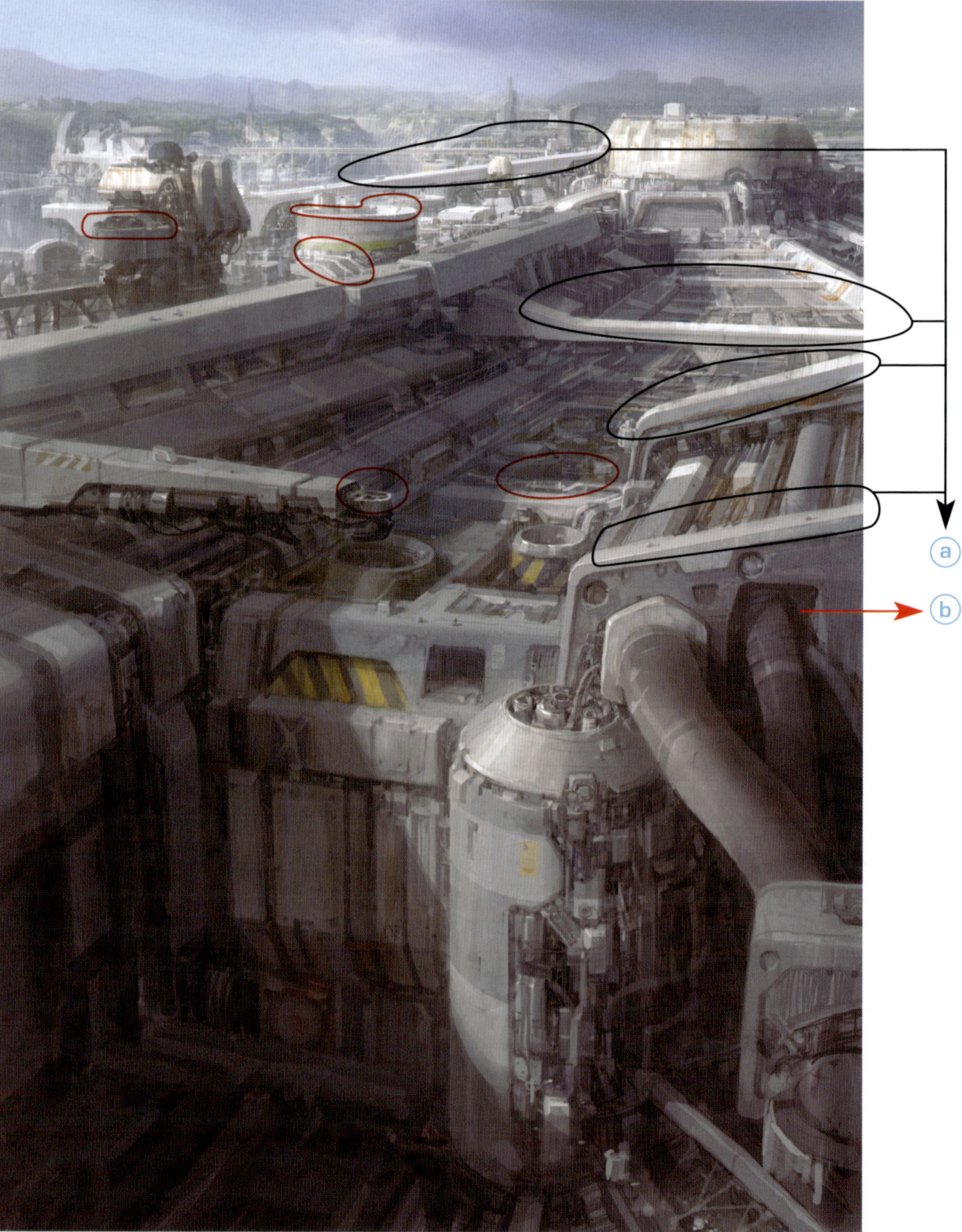

To finish off the painting, I use the Lasso tool to create the clean, sharp edges. After selecting an area, do not fill it with flat color. Try to use more varied brushstrokes to create a more interesting effect (a). These strokes should vary in thickness and value to create more interesting highlights. The red circles in the example indicate the areas where I am using a very sharp, bright color to create the highlight (b).

Fantasy Cityscape

Fig. 3.12

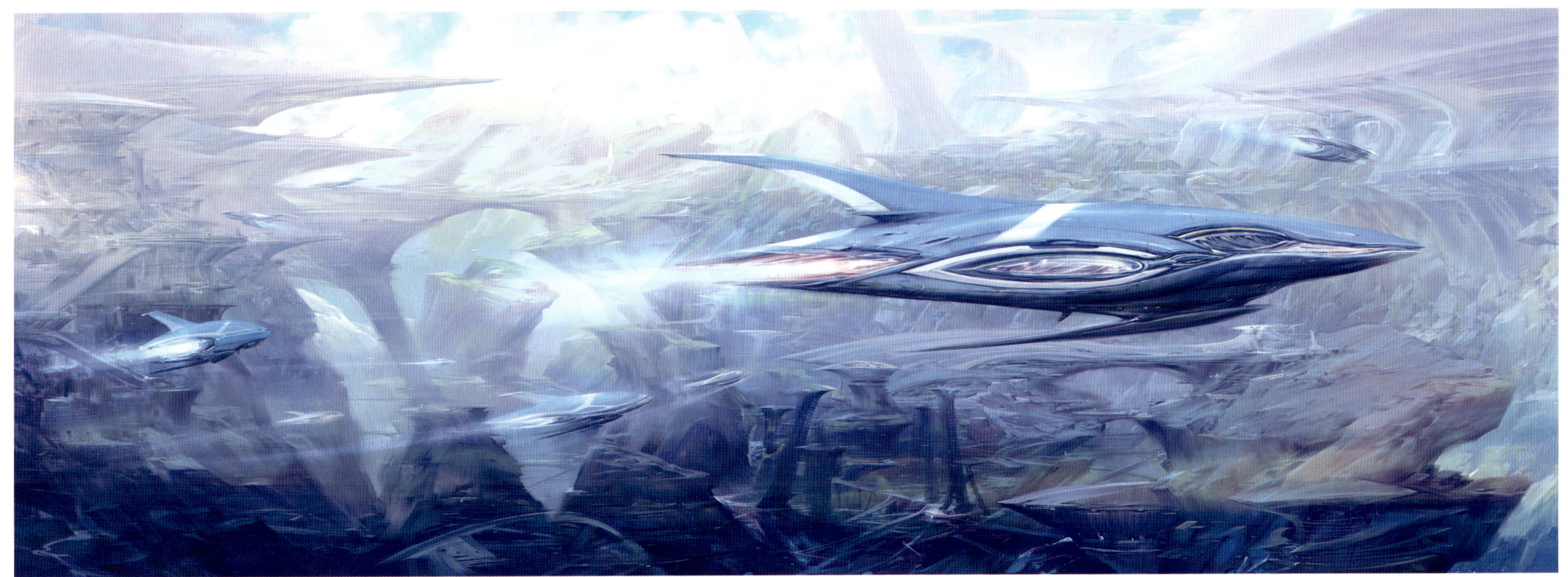

This tutorial will cover how to paint a futuristic cityscape from imagination. This particular series is different from the others because I am going to use Corel Painter instead of Photoshop. Since I previously explained my Photoshop painting technique in great detail, here I will focus more on the painting principles than the techniques.

Fig. 3.13

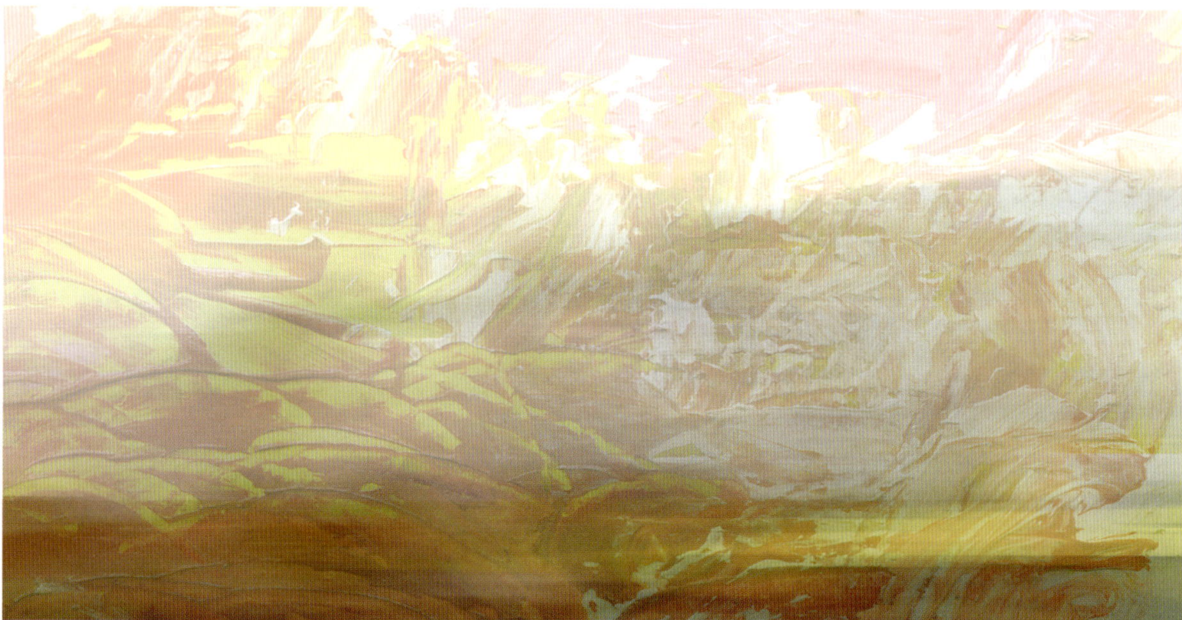

I start to paint a random background texture by using acrylic paint on paper. I use a palette knife to create the texture I want for my base layer. The base layer can be any color. The color choice depends on the main color scheme of the painting. Here, I used a yellowish pink. Once I am happy with the result, I take a snapshot of it and bring that photo into Painter.

Fig. 3.14

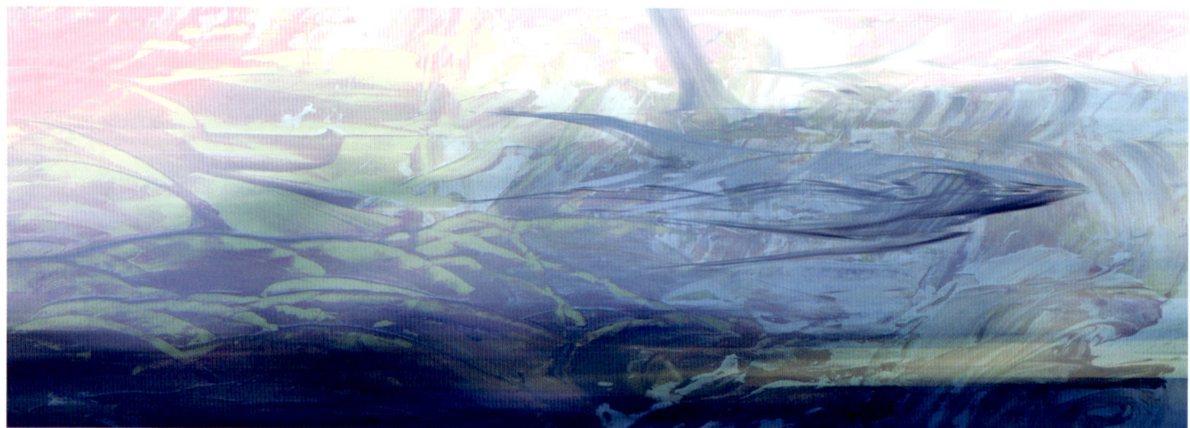

After I have brought the snapshot into Painter, I tint the whole bottom of the page with dark blue.

Fig. 3.15

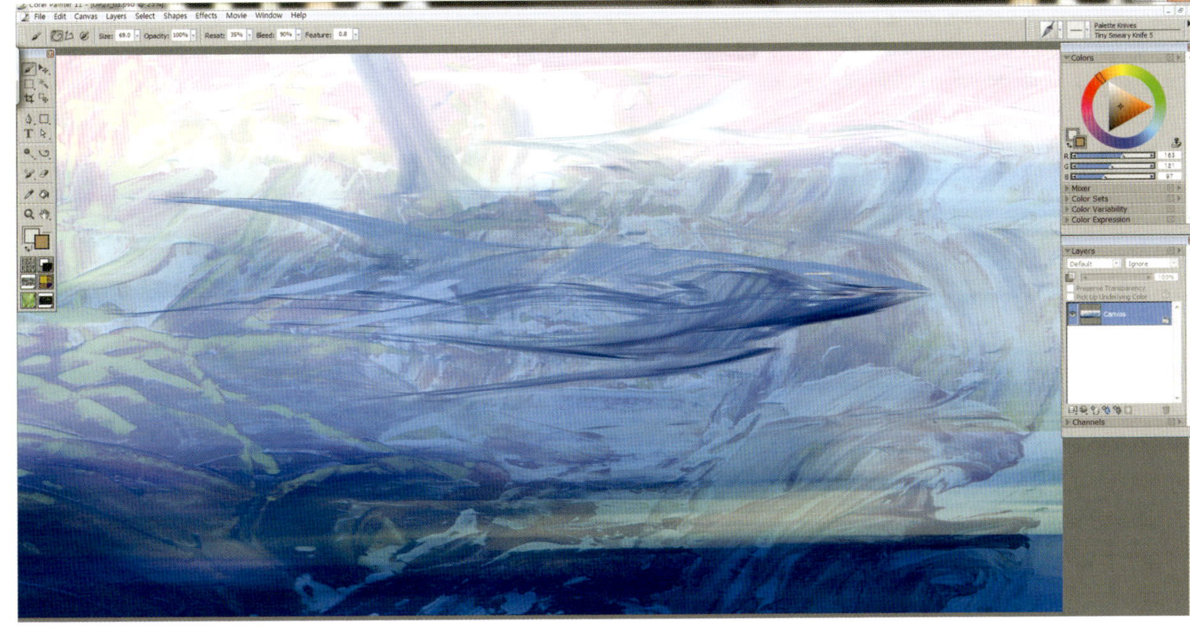

Now, I am going to use Painter's Palette Knife tool. With one exception, I normally use this tool without changing any presets from default. The only setting that I change is the Resat (or Resaturation, in some versions of Painter). Once the Resat number gets closer to 100, the Palette Knife does not pick up the base color. For lower numbers, the Palette Knife picks up more of the base color and mixes it with the foreground color, so choose the Resat number carefully to get the desired effect.

Fig. 3.16

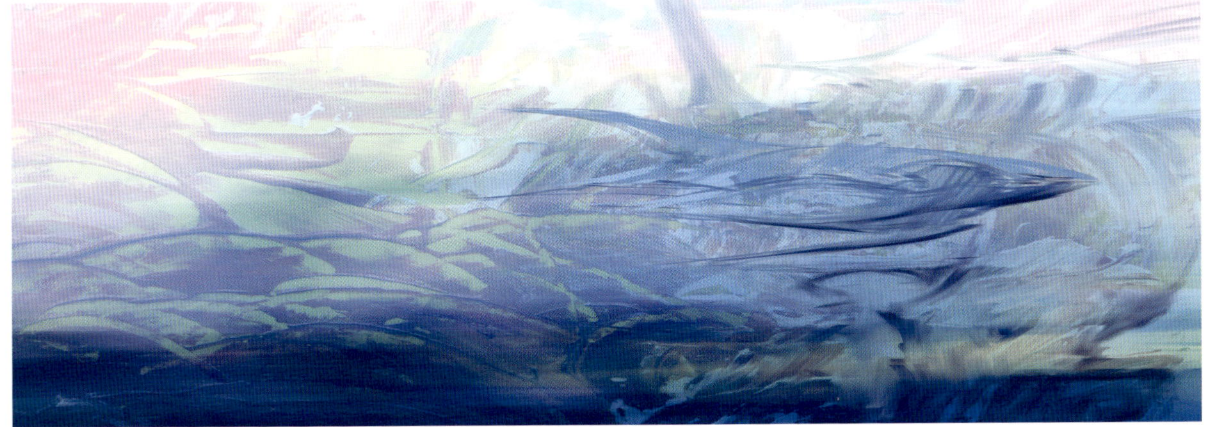

Here I start to paint the sky. Even though it is still an early stage, in order to set up the color scheme of the whole picture, I have to add a sky color in the background now. However, do not cover up the base layer completely. Take advantage of the beautiful background color. If I set the Resat at 30-50, the Palette Knife tool will pick up the color from the base layer and beautifully mix it with a foreground color.

Fig. 3.17

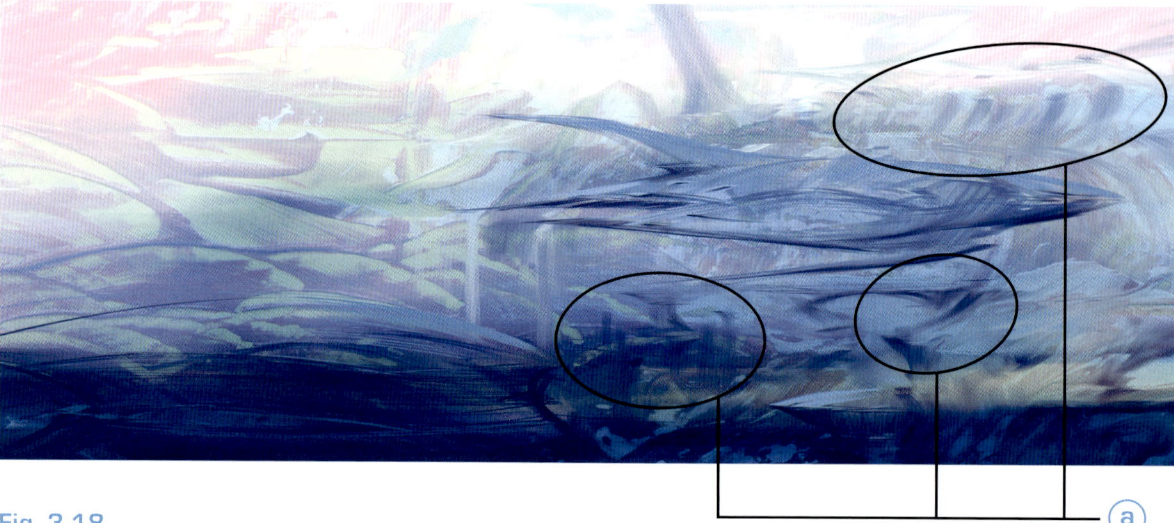

Just as if I am using a real palette knife, I use Painter's Palette Knife to drag and smudge the paint on the canvas (a). When doing so, I block out the big shapes first, then make smaller shapes.

Fig. 3.18

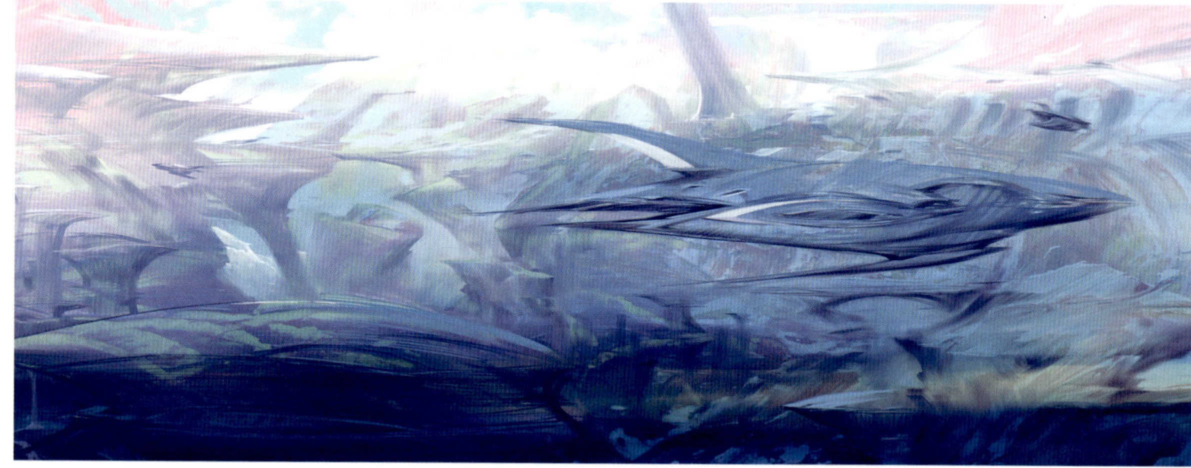

I continue to develop more design for the background city and the spaceship. I give a whale shape to this spaceship, which will be the main subject of the painting.

Fig. 3.19

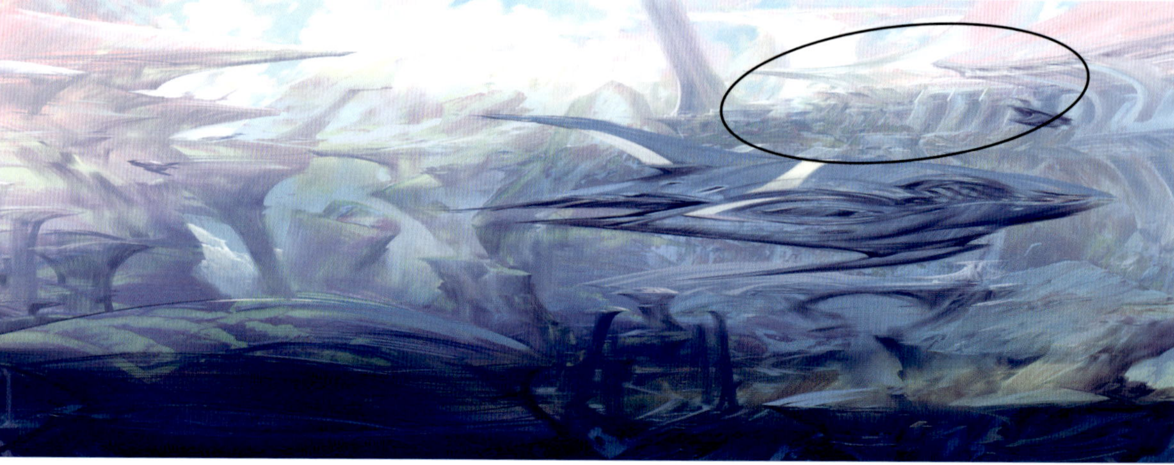

Regardless of which program I use to paint, the philosophy remains basically the same. As I have explained in other tutorials, select the section that gets the most light and make it sharp and clear. That will draw the viewer's attention and will make the painting look more defined.

Fig. 3.20

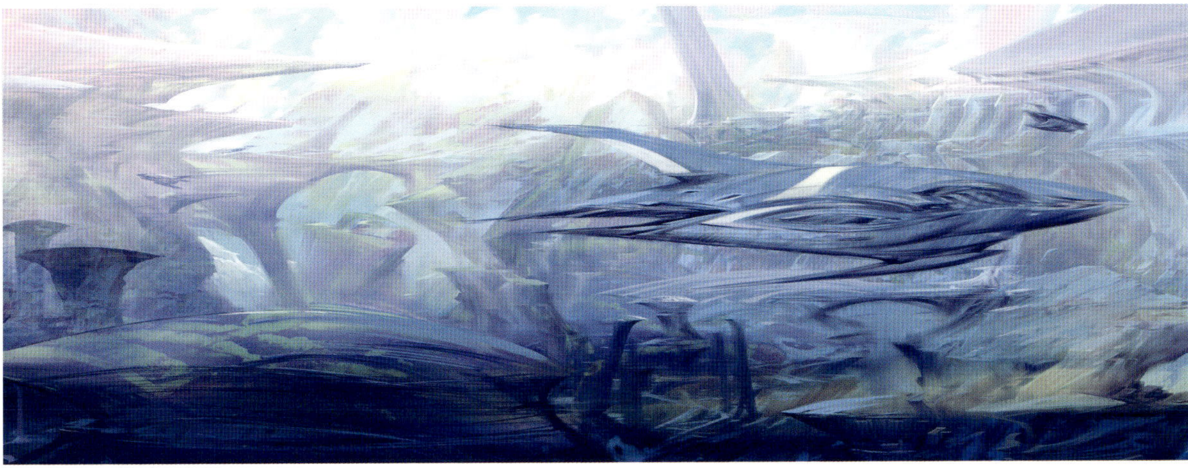

I keep developing the details.

Fig. 3.21

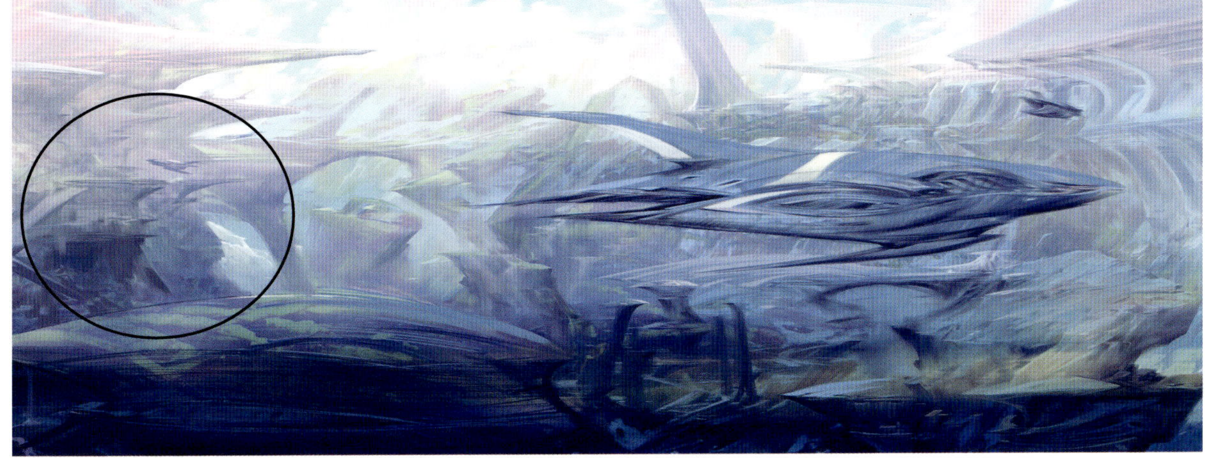

In this step, I change the design of the city buildings a bit so it matches the visual language of other parts of the painting.

Fig. 3.22

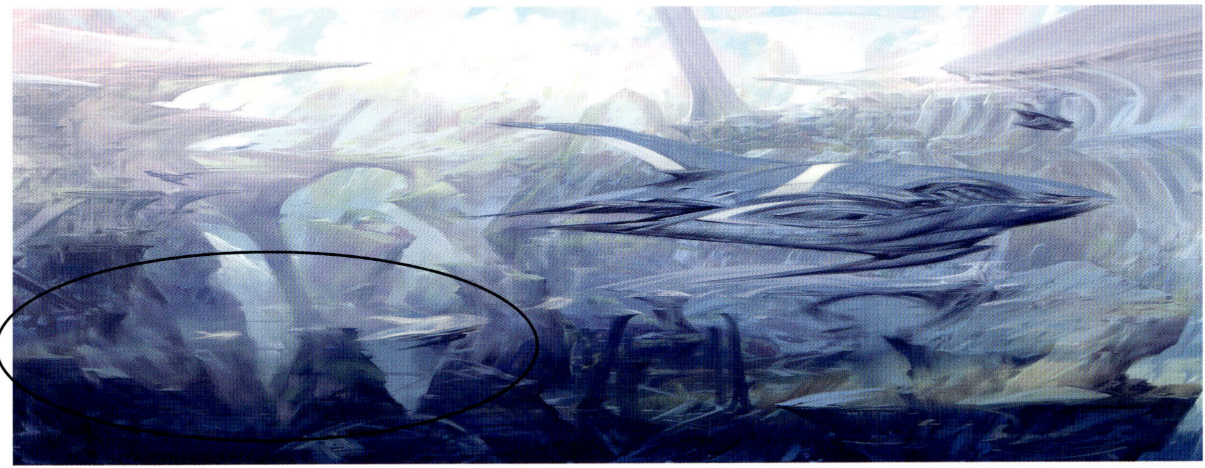

Just as I did in the previous step, I change the design of the foreground building structure to open up the eye flow, so that it does not stop the visual flow. As I have shown elsewhere and in these figures, do not get too bound to the original design. If necessary, modify the design anytime. I also add a few more aircraft to add more interesting storytelling elements to the picture.

Here, I paint engine-glow effects behind the aircraft. This will give the ships a sense of direction. I make sure to create many variations among them. In fact, I make one of them fly faster than the others, have some going downward, or make some of the ships fly in opposite directions.

The next step is to add more definition and details to the middle ground. Because there were not enough middle-ground elements in the painting, I add stronger contrast to them.

To make those small lighting effects on the building structure in the foreground, I used a Color Dodge brush in Photoshop.

Fig. 3.23

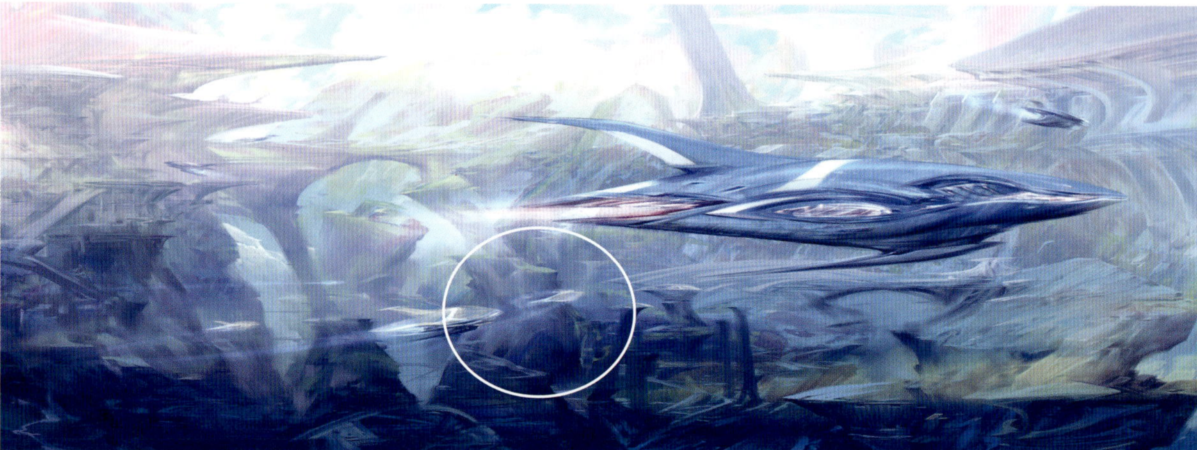

Fig. 3.24

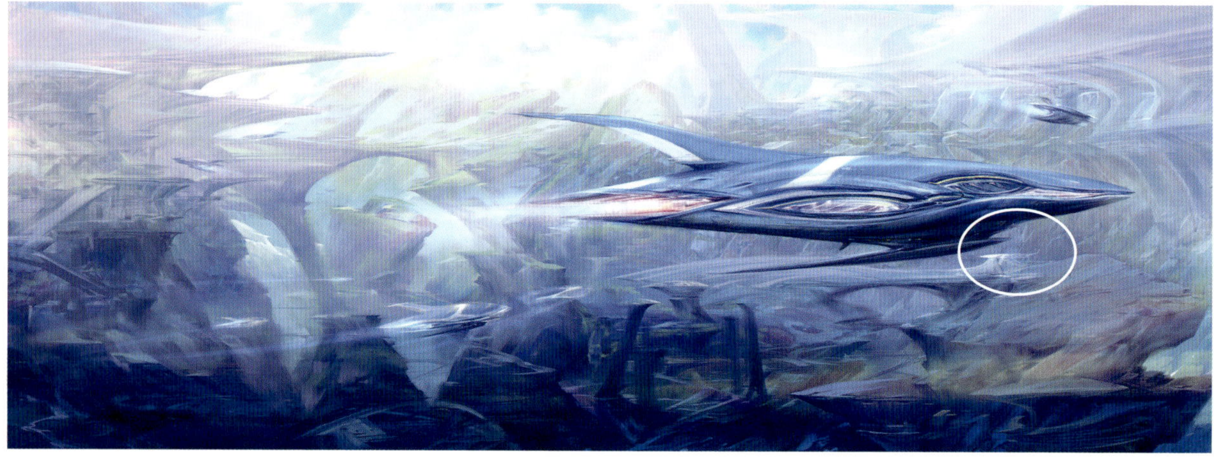

Fig. 3.25

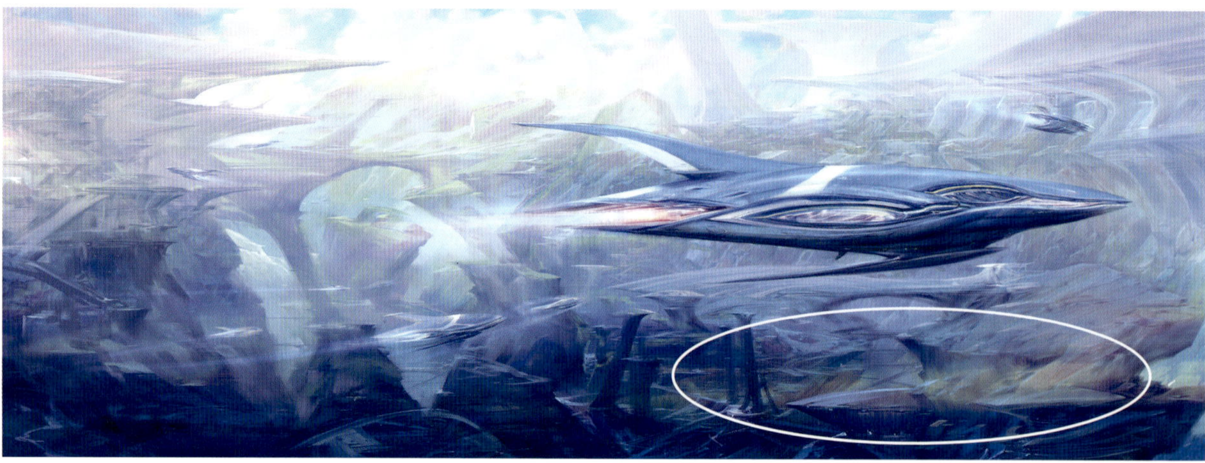

Fig. 3.26

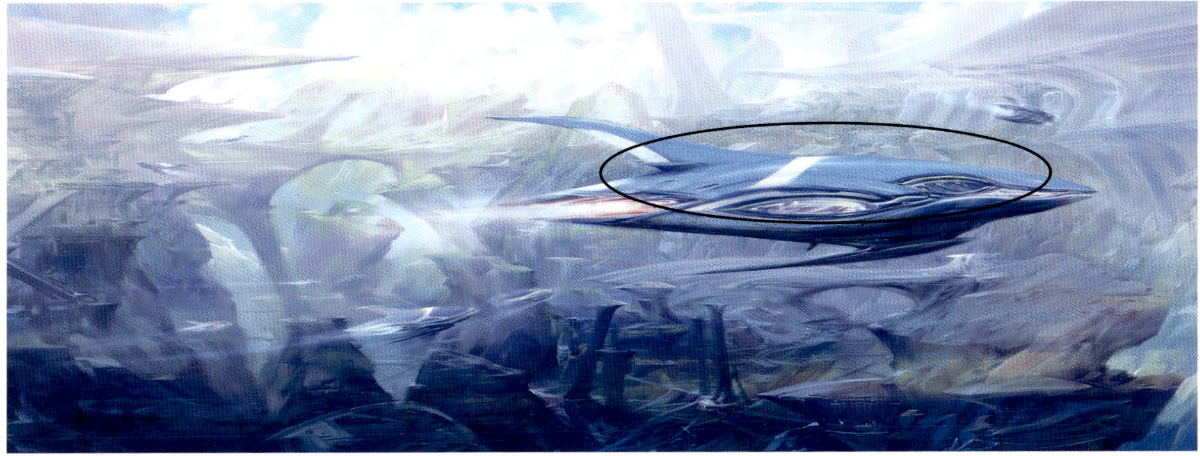

Then, I paint more details on the main spaceship. Since the main subject was a little underdeveloped compared to the background, I added sharper details to its body.

Fig. 3.27

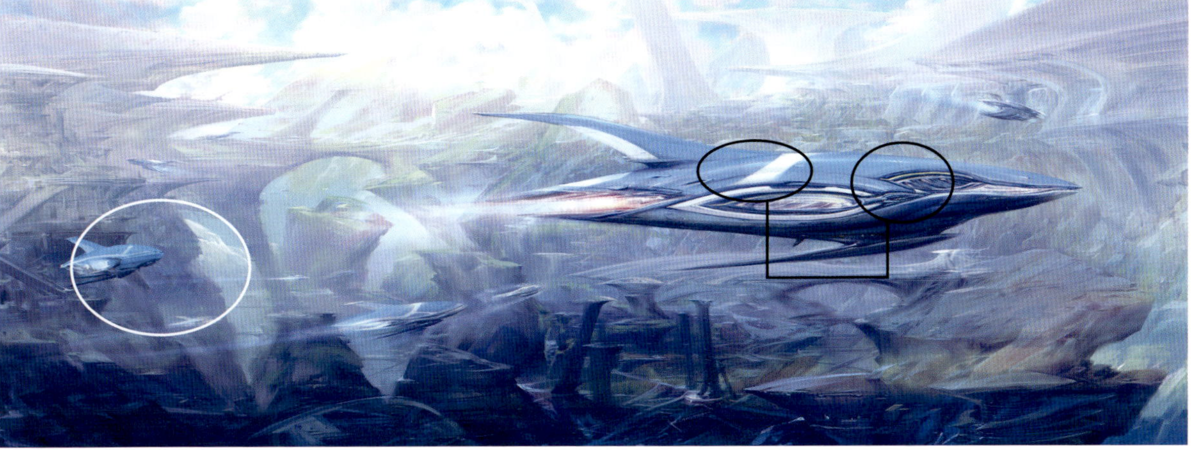

Next, I add a few more sharp design lines on the main aircraft and one more ship that is entering the painting from the outside of the page to create that fake illusion of three-dimensionality.

Fig. 3.28

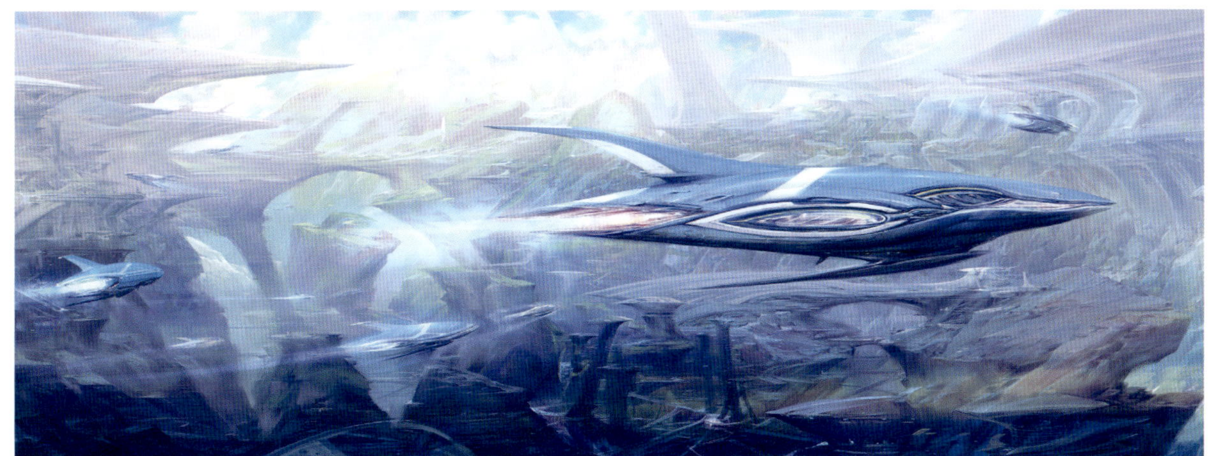

Finally, I finished the painting by showing more detail.

Forest

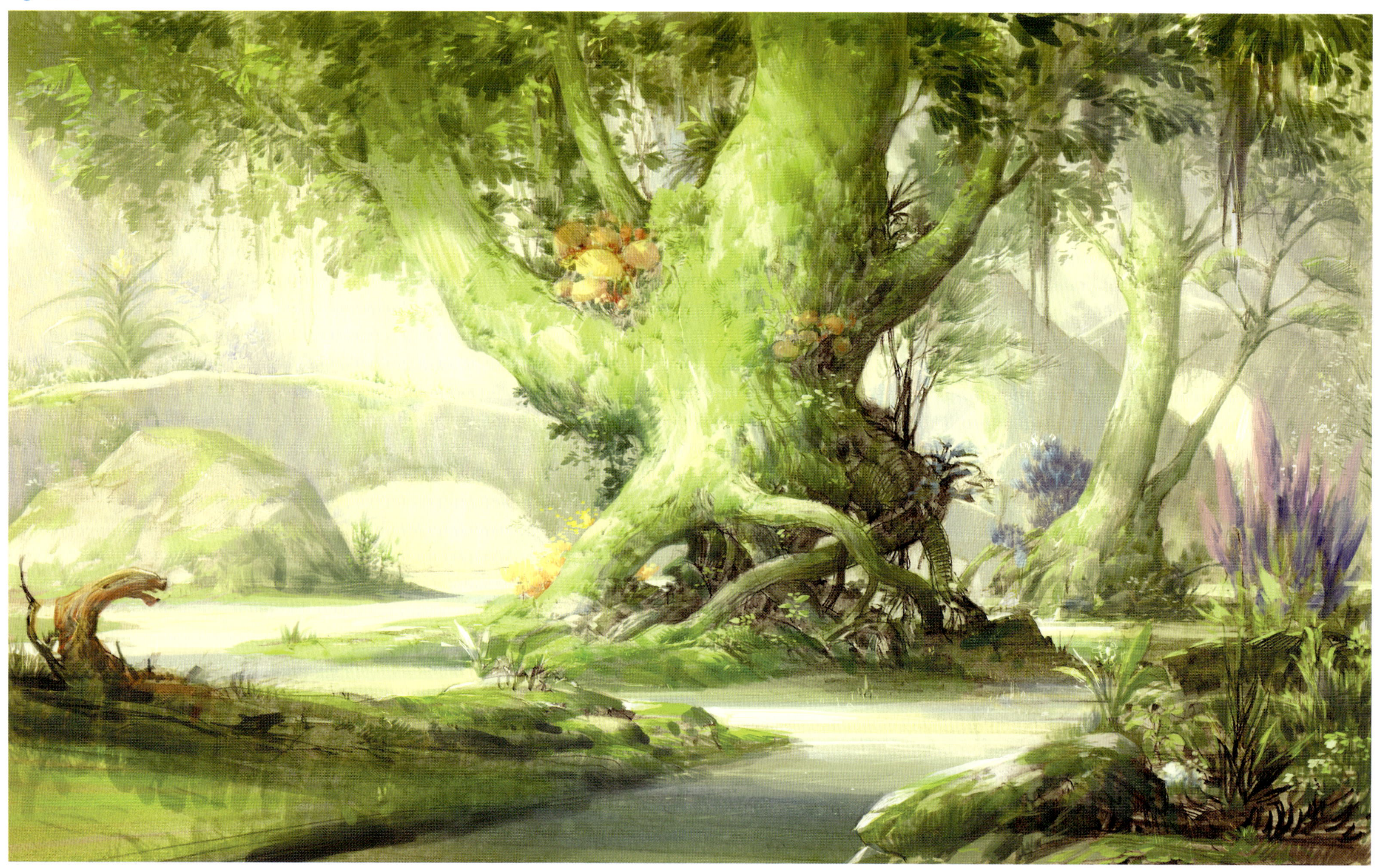

In this installment, I am going to revisit nature, and show you how to draw a painting with an organic environment. I did not use any perspective grid this time other than a horizon line. Drawing nature is quite different from drawing a cityscape. Using a perspective grid is very efficient when drawing a cityscape, but when drawing an organic environment, use visual balance rather than a mathematical grid.

Fig. 3.30

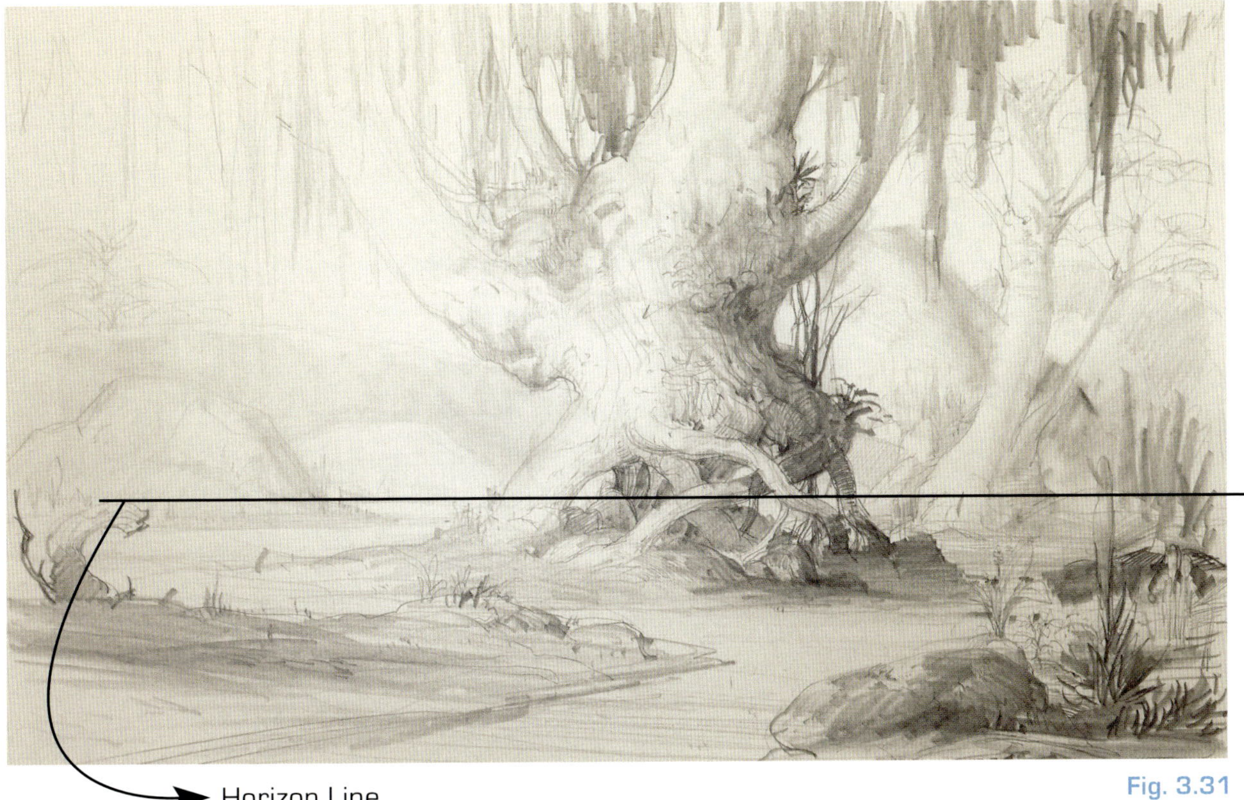

Horizon Line

Fig. 3.31

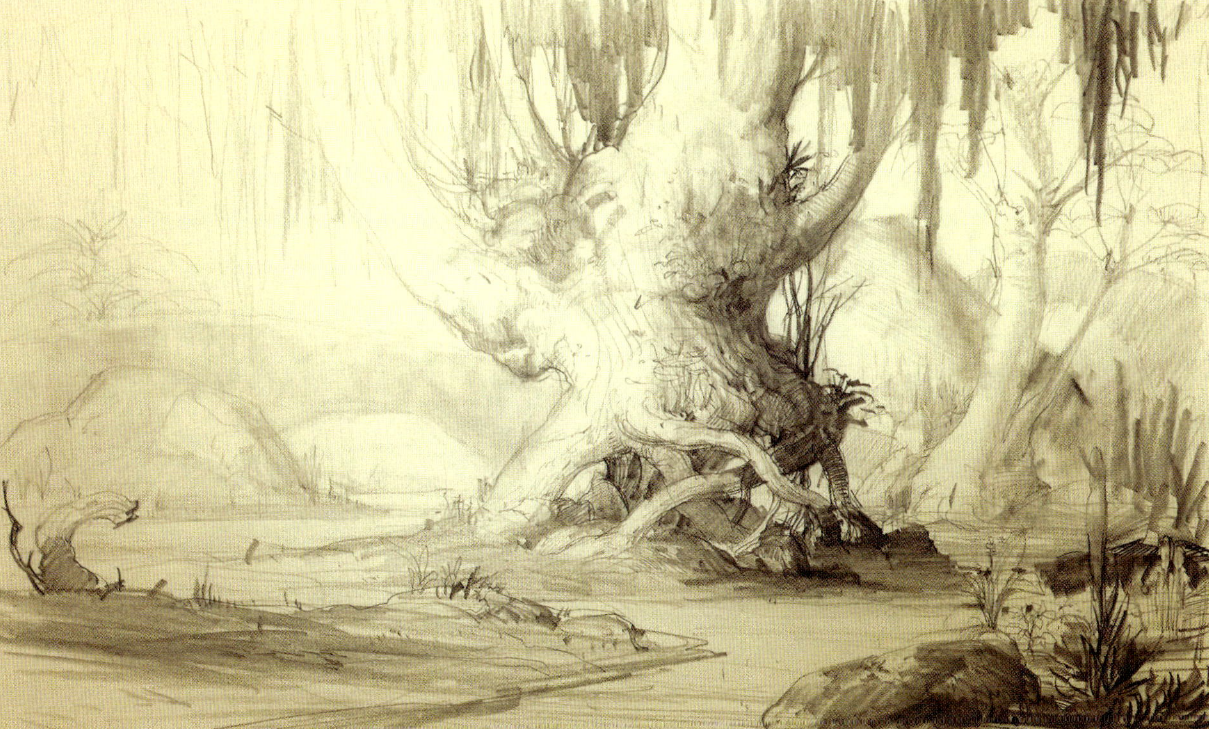

First, I used a 4B pencil to draw this initial sketch on paper. Since I want a big tree to be the main focal point of this painting, I place this tree in the center of the page. I also place a couple of smaller trees on the right side of the page to support the main subject. Adding a stream is the perfect element for creating an S curve flow in a painting. This S curve will help the painting have more visual rhythm. As usual, I reference my memory for plants. Painting a natural scene is such a fun experience, and always gives me a very tranquil feeling.

After doing the main sketch and adding the brown base, the next step is glazing, which is done with a low-opacity brush at 30%. I use only two different shades of green to block in a base color. With these two different green colors and a brown base tone, I am able to create the proper amount of base colors for the painting.

The next step is applying the texture brush.

a. First, I lay in a base color with a tree brush before I paint the tree leaves.

b. When I need to draw a tree in the far distance, I also use this brush to create a generic base tone; then I draw a few tree leaves with the default brush on top of that base tone.

c. This texture brush is also useful in creating soft edges between light and shadow areas.

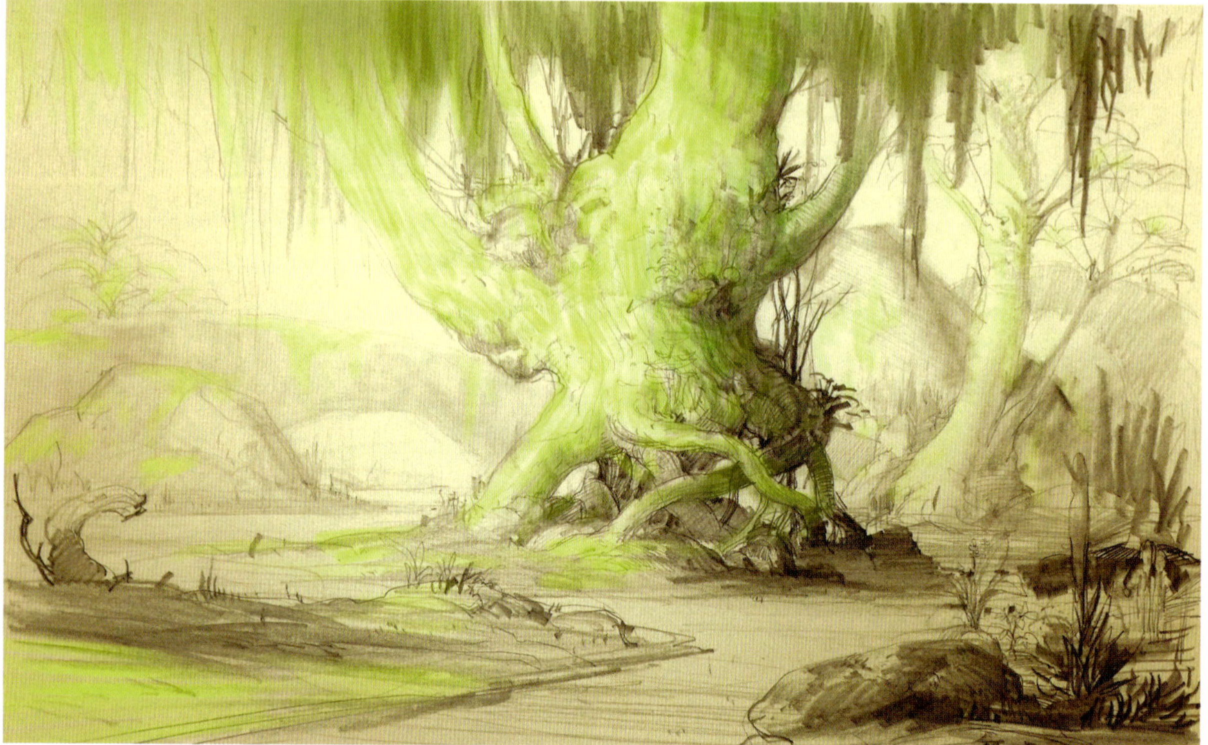

Fig. 3.32

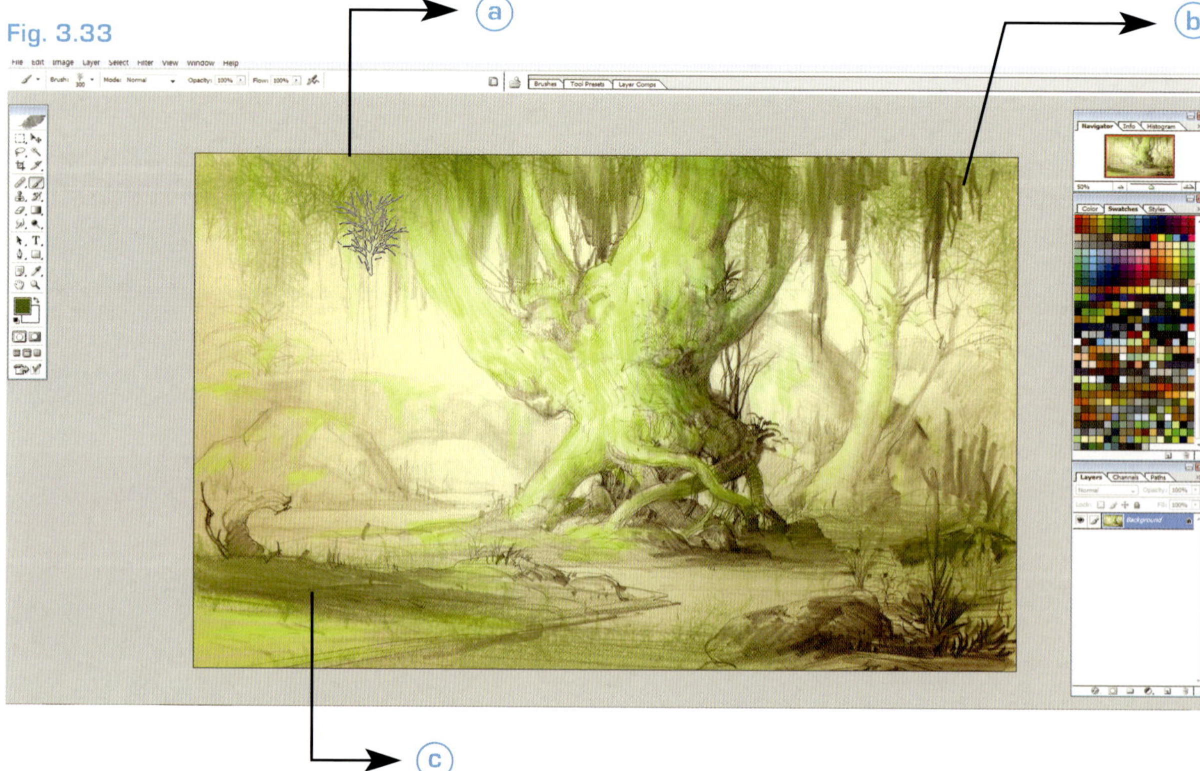

Fig. 3.33

Fig. 3.34

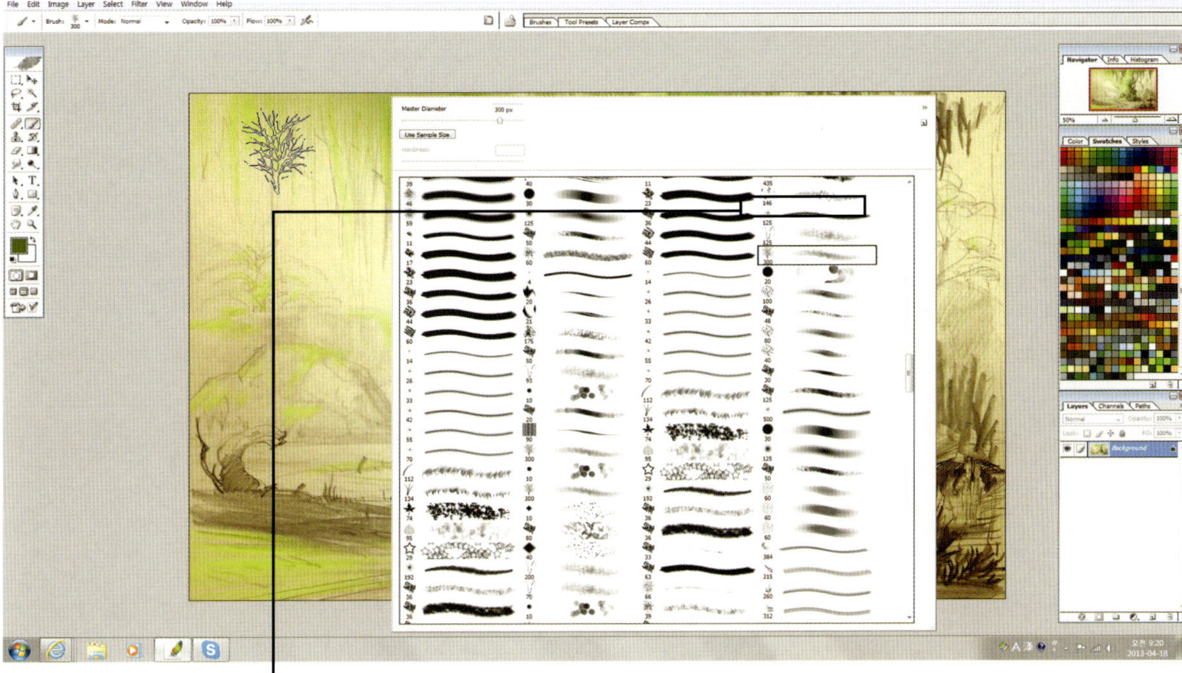

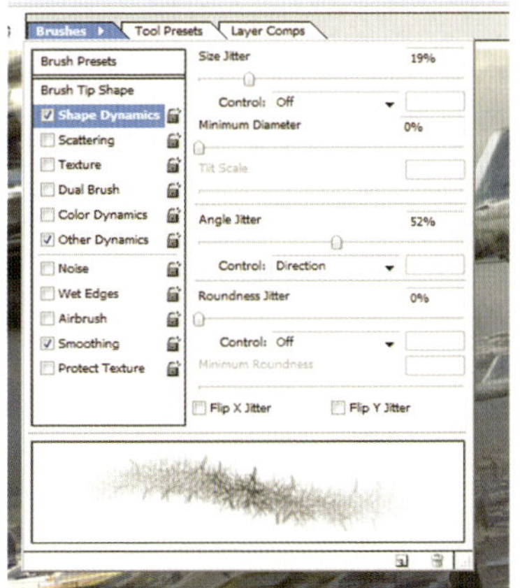

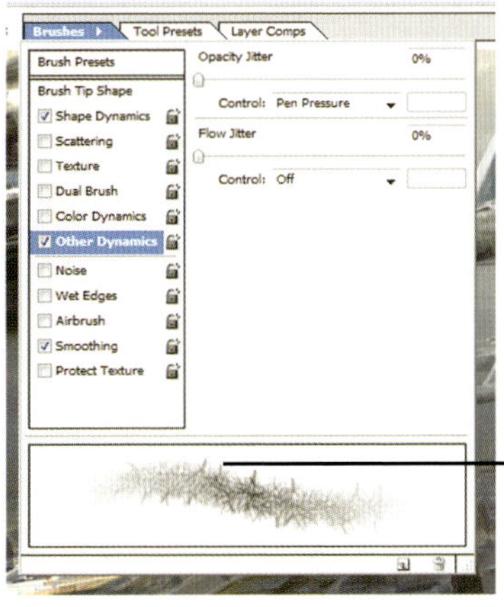

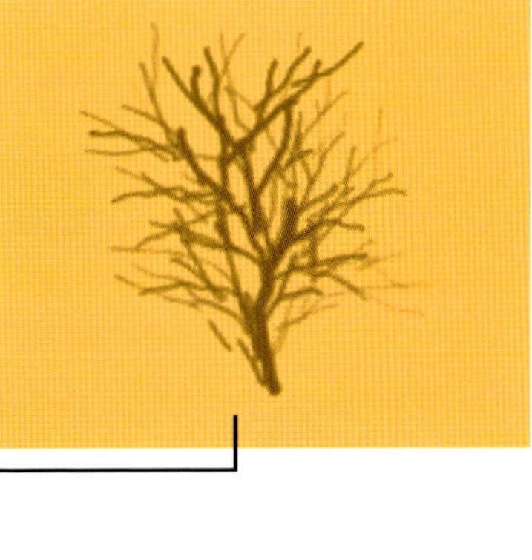

Fig. 3.35

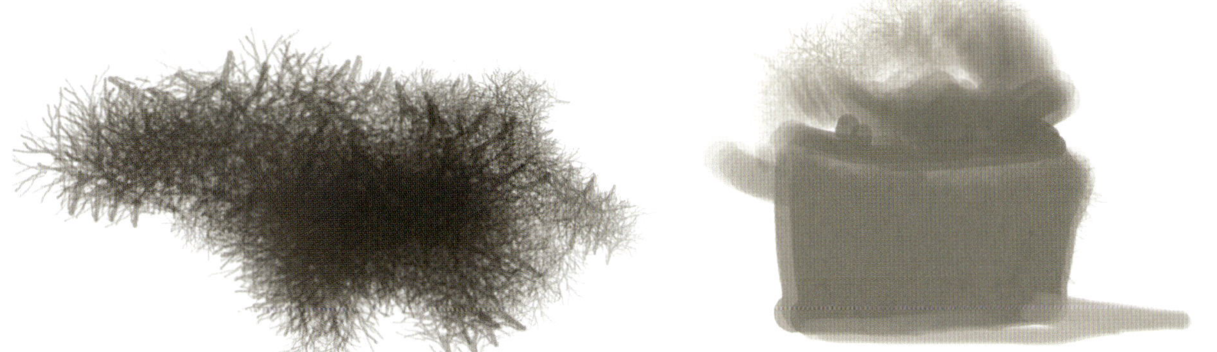

Before I move on to the next step, I will demonstrate how to make one of my favorite brushes, a tree brush. First, draw a simple tree shape as a base. Second, play with brush settings such as Size Jitter, Angle Jitter, and Opacity Jitter, as shown in the figure. Then test the brush with different brush sizes. Paint a big brushstroke, a medium brushstroke, and a small brushstroke. See if this new brush is holding its quality on many different scales.

Here, I made a really simple sample to show how I would use this brush in a painting environment. I have used the most basic brush to block in the large shape, and used this tree texture brush to indicate some bush effects. The painting would probably have looked a bit flat by using the default brushstrokes alone. However, when I added more texture with a texture brush, it created a lot more visual interest.

Chapter 03 - Landscape Tutorials

Now is a good time to add more color to the painting. Since it is still an early stage of the process, I still want to use big strokes with bold colors instead of creating refined detail.

a.   First, I add warm colors on the main tree to bump up the saturation.

b.   Second, because adding a yellow color was not enough to create a colorful palette, I also add a few more colorful bushes using blue and purple. When I go out into the wilderness, I can easily spot dozens of different-colored plants. I want to mimic what Mother Nature does in my painting.

c.   Next, I add stronger lighting information on a rock in the foreground.

d.   Then I paint sharper edge strokes with higher contrast. Up to this point, I have used a lot of loose-edge brushmarks. However, as I make more progress on the painting, I have to use both loose-edge and hard-edge brushstrokes to keep the visual balance. For example, a painting would look too blended if I use only loose-edge strokes. On the other hand, everything would look too sharp if I only use the hard-edge strokes. I keep repeating this process of using both types of brushstrokes until this painting is finished.

e.   Note that I have used a hot brown color for the tree stump. It doesn't have to be a realistic color. This hot brown will help the painting to become more colorful.

f.   At this stage, I try to keep the background objects as simple and clear as possible. Do not add too many details in the background area yet. Just use a simple brush.

g.   Make sharp definition on the surfaces that receive a lot of light, since it helps to indicate a clear form.

I try to **MIMIC** what
MOTHER NATURE does.

Fig. 3.36

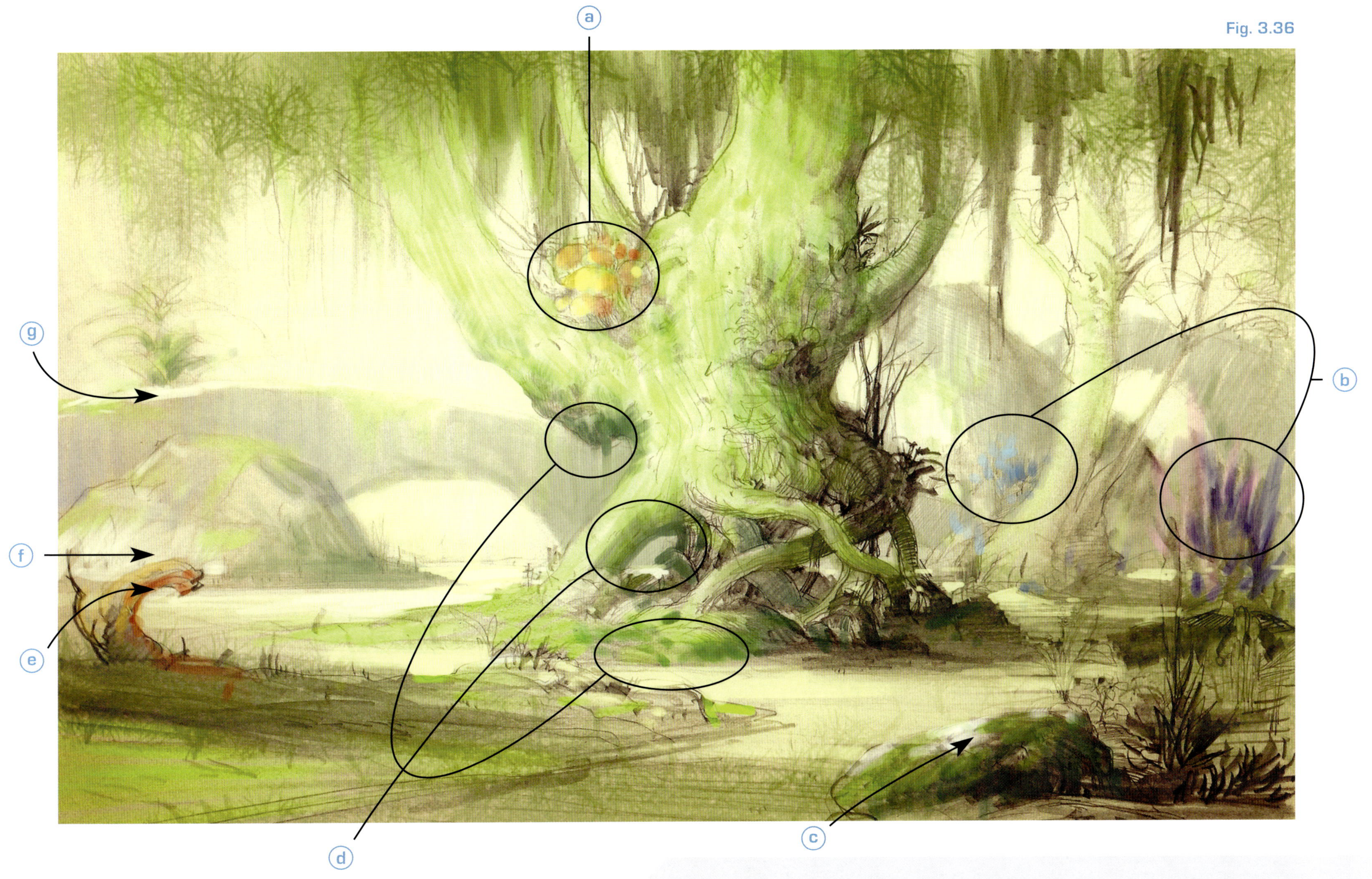

During the rendering of this painting, I make another brush for the tree leaves. This brush has a sharp end point. I add a slight texture to the brush as well. This brush can be very useful when painting tree foliage, branches, or wooden panels.

In this scene, I paint more details with the pointy end brush mentioned in the previous step. This branch also gives a calligraphy-brush feeling, which is a useful tool when painting the foliage. As I have shown in this figure, stacking up the brushstrokes results in awesome textured shapes from a far distance.

Fig. 3.37

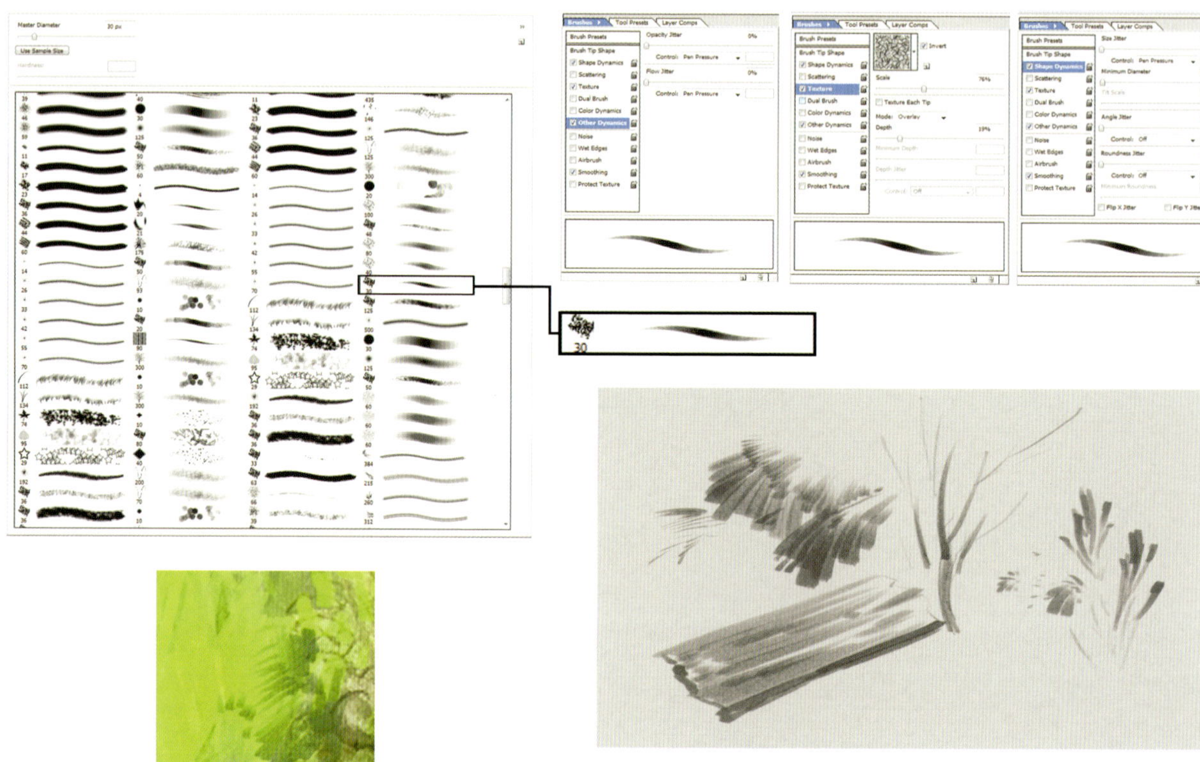

Fig. 3.38

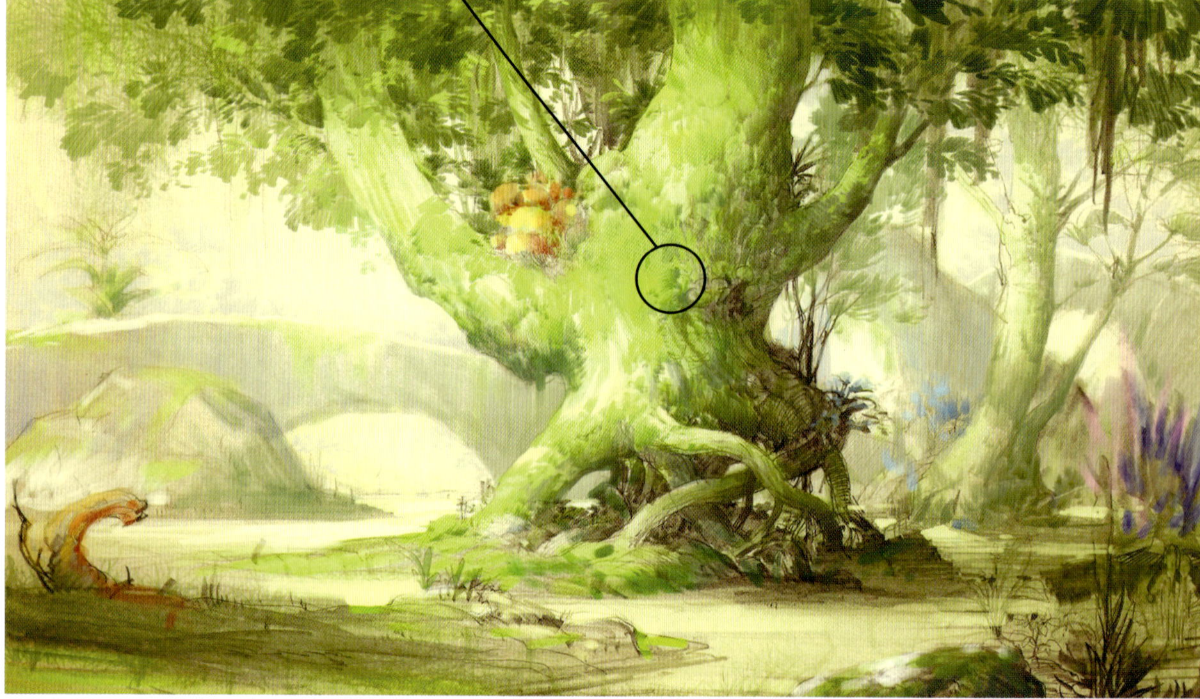

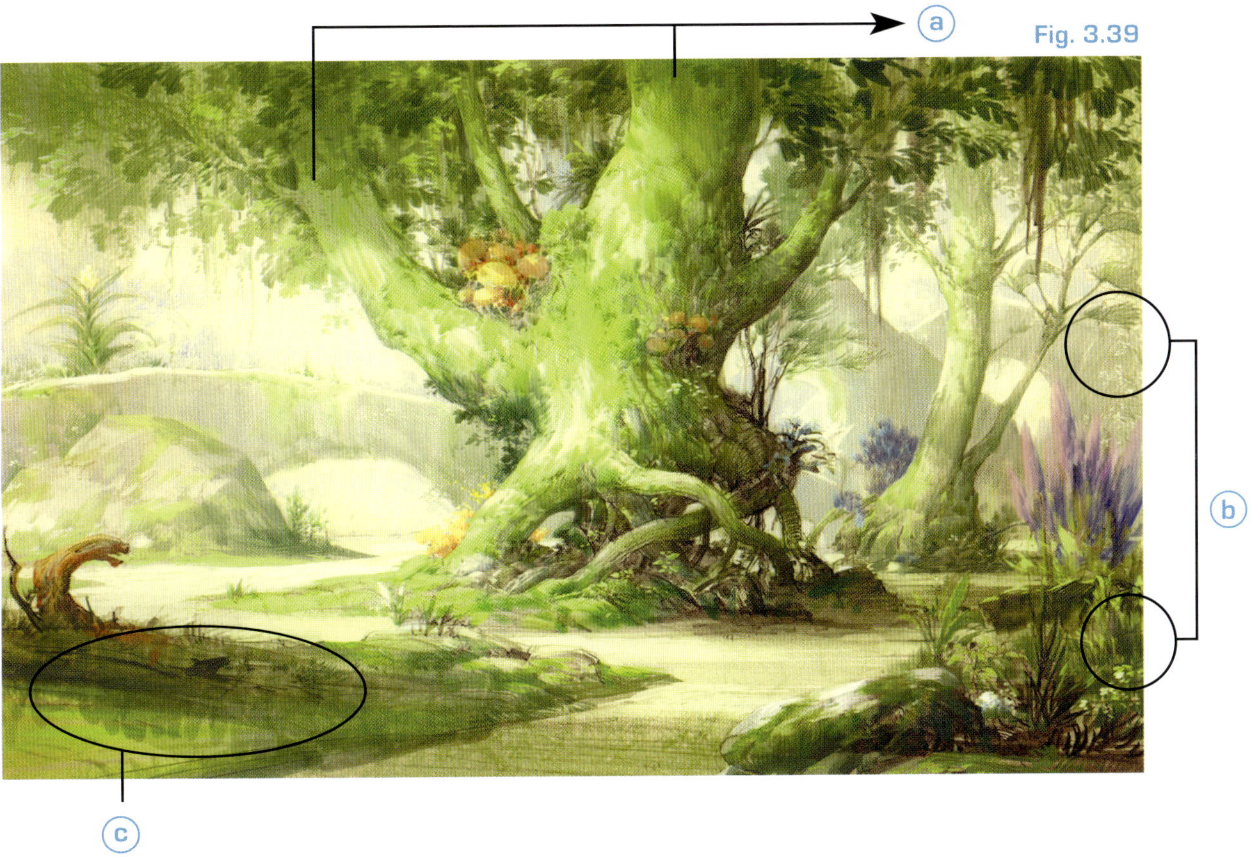

Fig. 3.39

a. The next step is to tie the whole painting together with more atmosphere information. I have built up enough details so far. To create such effects, I use an airbrush and a simple default brush with very low opacity (10-30%). An airbrush can create a soft atmosphere, and a simple brush works well when I want to create a few brushstrokes. Here, I darken the top portion of the main tree.

b. I also paint small, scattered dots in some areas. These patterns are easily found in nature. This kind of smaller shape counterbalances the big shapes like the main tree. These scattered dot patterns not only add more believability, but they also raise the quality of the finished painting.

c. I also paint big brush marks at 30% opacity in the left corner to add variety to the texture of the painting. Rough brushstrokes like these increase the fun visual element.

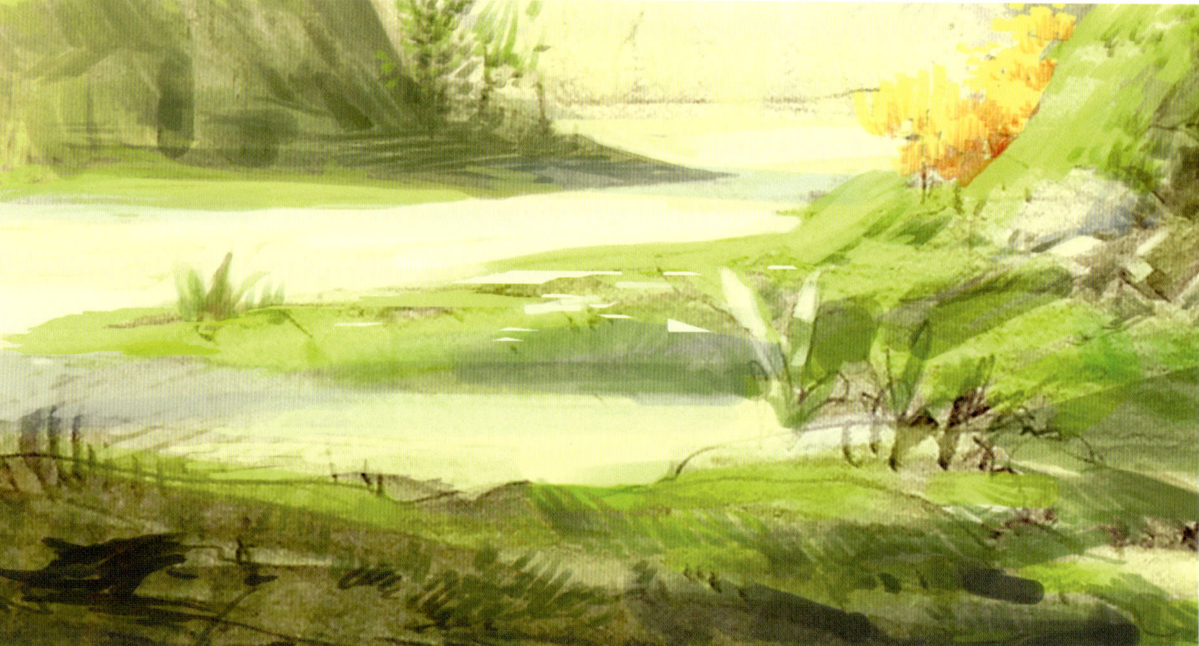

Fig. 3.40

Next, using the Lasso tool, I make several small, sharp selections to paint the small rocks on the ground. I did not try to make them look realistic; rather, I want to create a more impressionistic effect.

Just as I painted the small rocks in the previous step, here I make more selections on the tree leaves and paint lighting effects on the foliage.

a. In this last step, I paint scattered light sources, which shine through the forest, with a basic brush with low opacity (10%). I also add a slight blue in the air to enhance the color harmony of the painting.

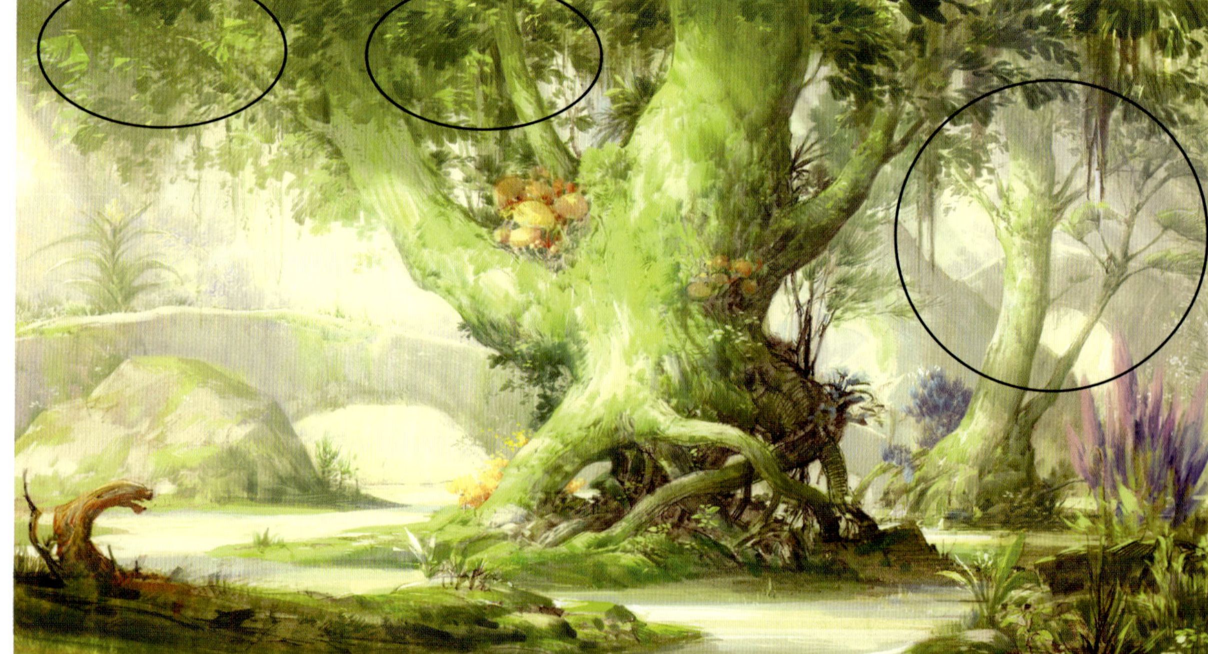

Fig. 3.41

Fig. 3.42 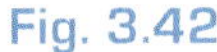

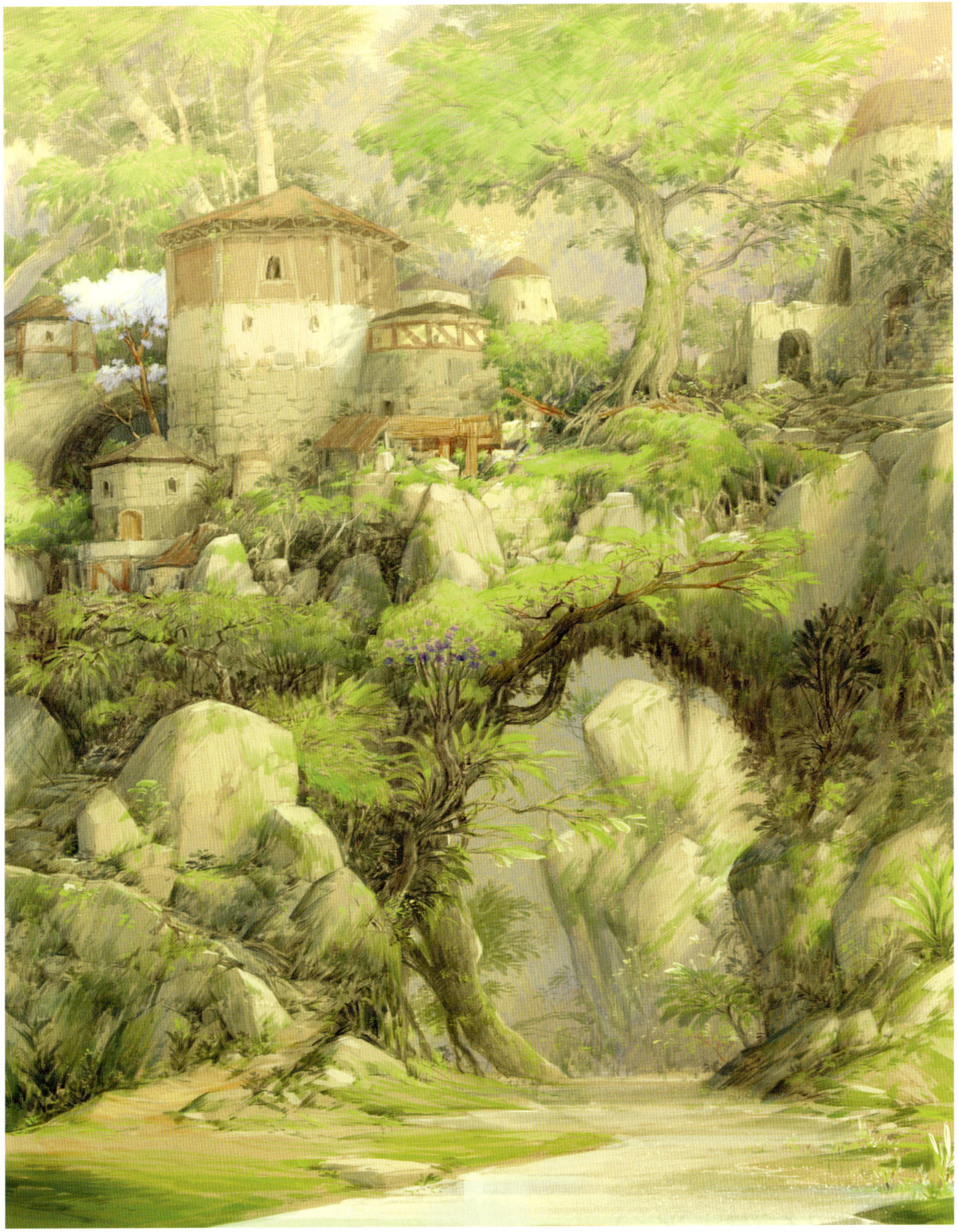

Forest Town

In this tutorial, I am going to paint a peaceful town located deep inside a forest. We can see a lot of trees and moss growing on top of rocks, and a stream flows through the town.

I frequently paint streams because of childhood memories. When I was a child, I often played with friends in a stream, catching little fish all day long. I also sketch in narrow pebble steps on the left bottom corner of the painting so that little boys have a pathway home when their playtime in the water is over. This is the place where I want to relive memories. Rather than creating a realistic painting, I want to paint a more impressionistic picture with vibrant colors for this tutorial.

Fig. 3.43

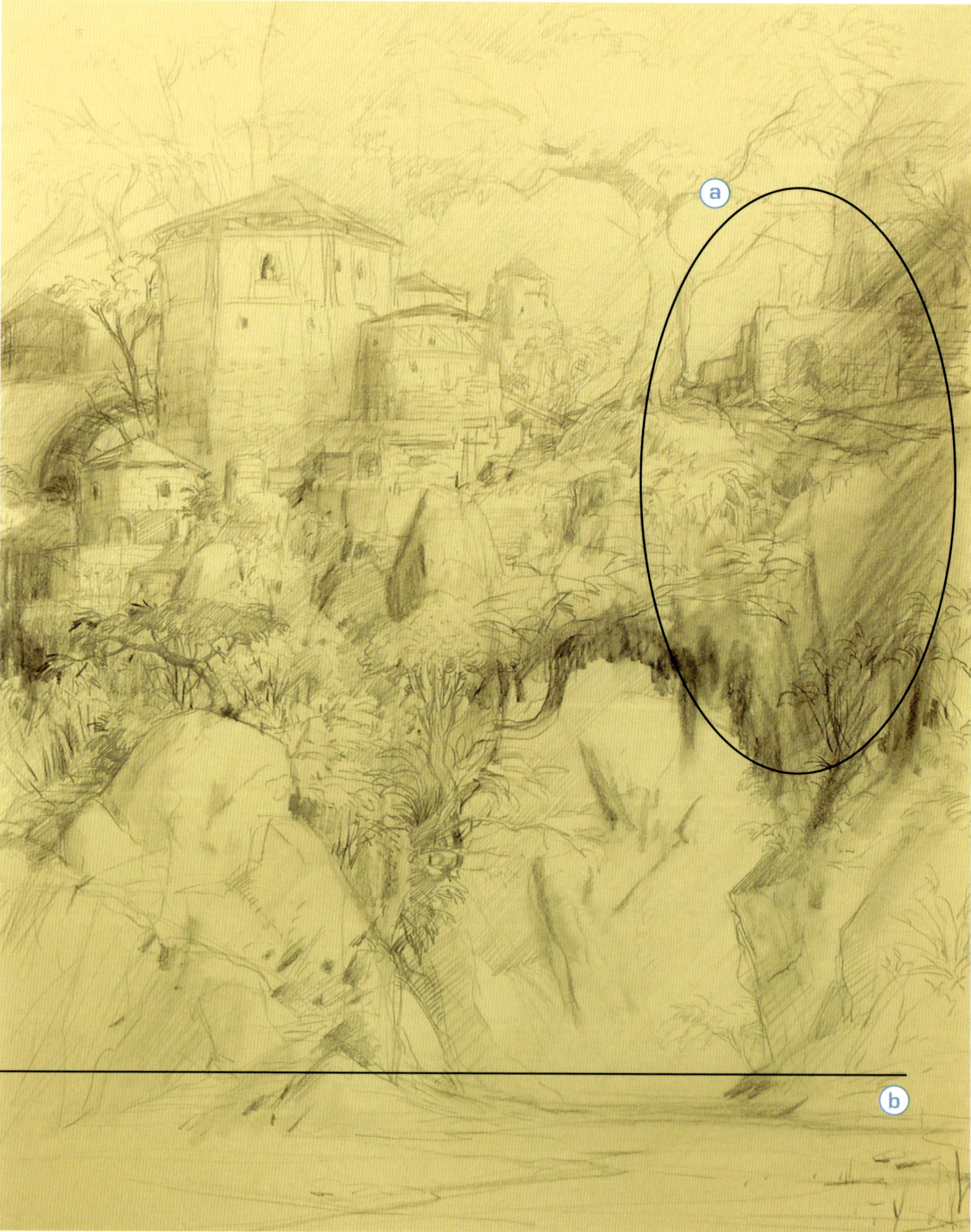

a. I start the painting by sketching with pencil on paper, and add theatrical lighting to the painting by placing a big shadow on the right side (a). After the initial sketch is done, I scan the pencil sketch and import it to Photoshop.

b. I then add a brown base tone to the sketch. Also, I indicate a simple horizon perspective line on the sketch for future reference.

Fig. 3.44

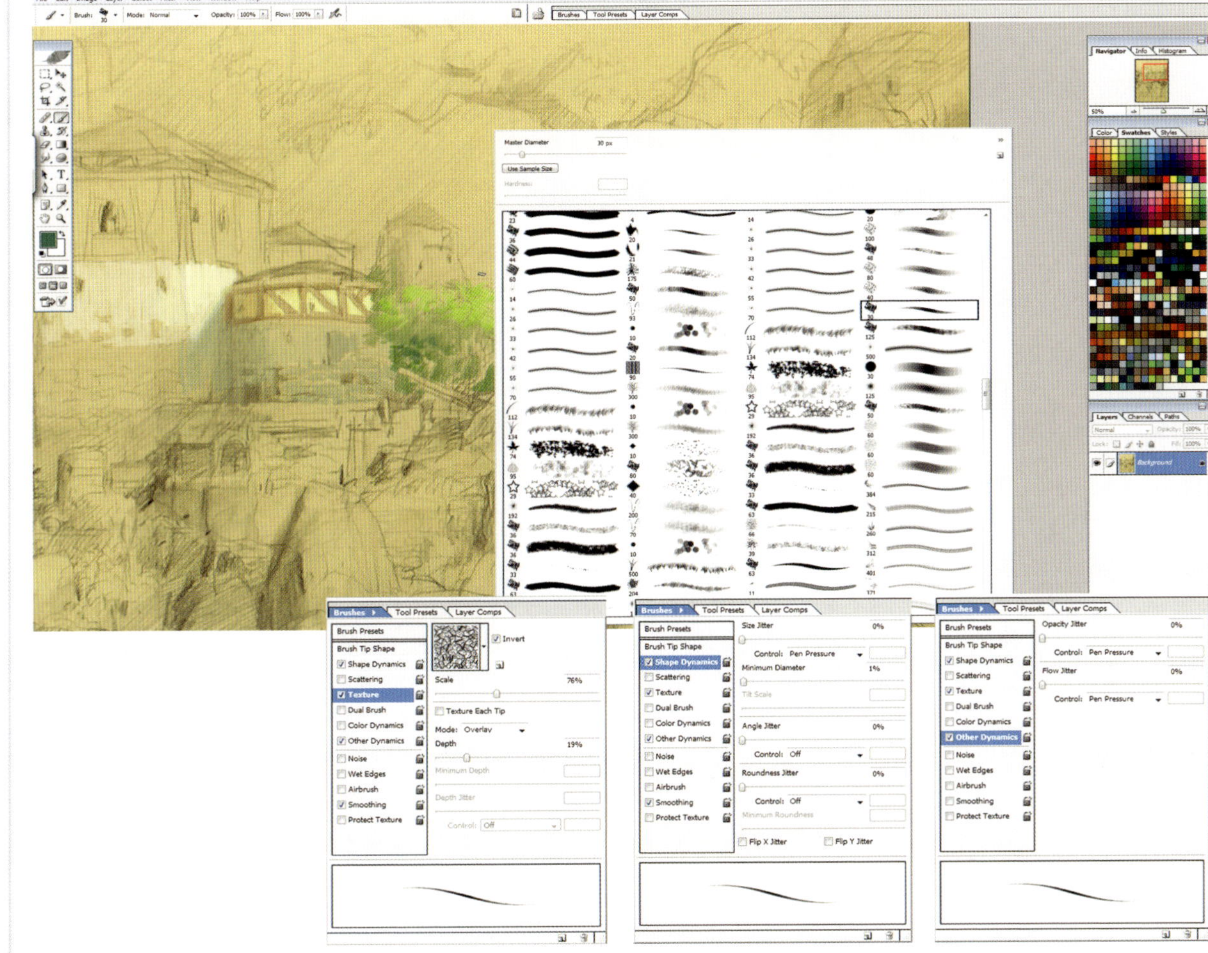

Fig. 3.45

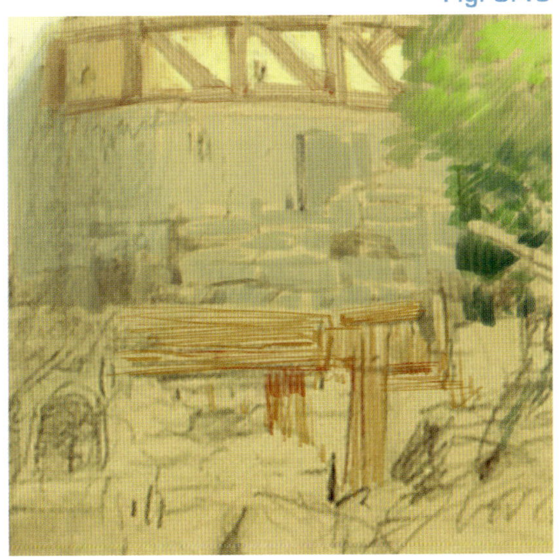

In this painting, I am mainly going to use a brush that has a sharp end point with some rough texture. This brush is good to use when drawing a nature scene. I try to preserve the base tone as much as possible, and add a light touch of colors on top of it. Keeping the taste of the pencil mark is the key to this work. I want to maintain an antique look in this painting because this matches my childhood memory.

When painting wooden panels, I make sure that the brushstrokes follow the direction of the panel. It will make the painting more believable.

The next step is blocking in the dark shadow. I picked a dark green for this. This is one of the colors that I enjoy using quite often because it reminds me of emerging spring and the lush green of early summer; it always makes me feel renewed. In addition, I mixed this dark green with many different shades of green, to give more variety to the color scheme.

Then I start to paint more foliage, making more progress by covering a broader area using the same colors and technique.

Fig. 3.46

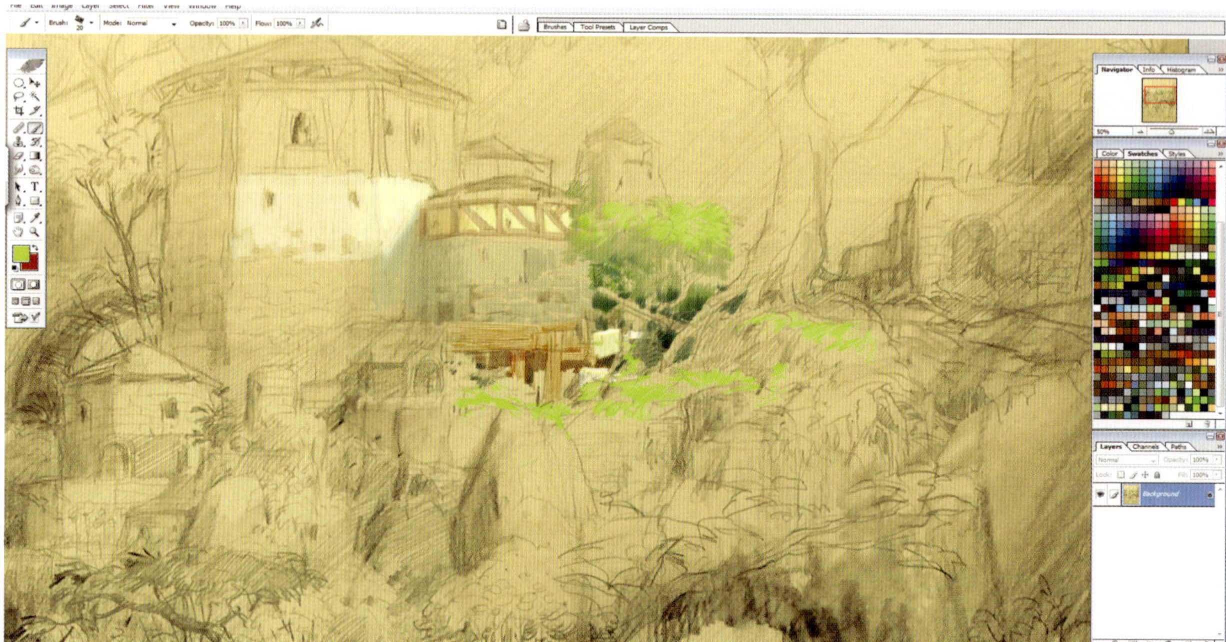

Fig. 3.47

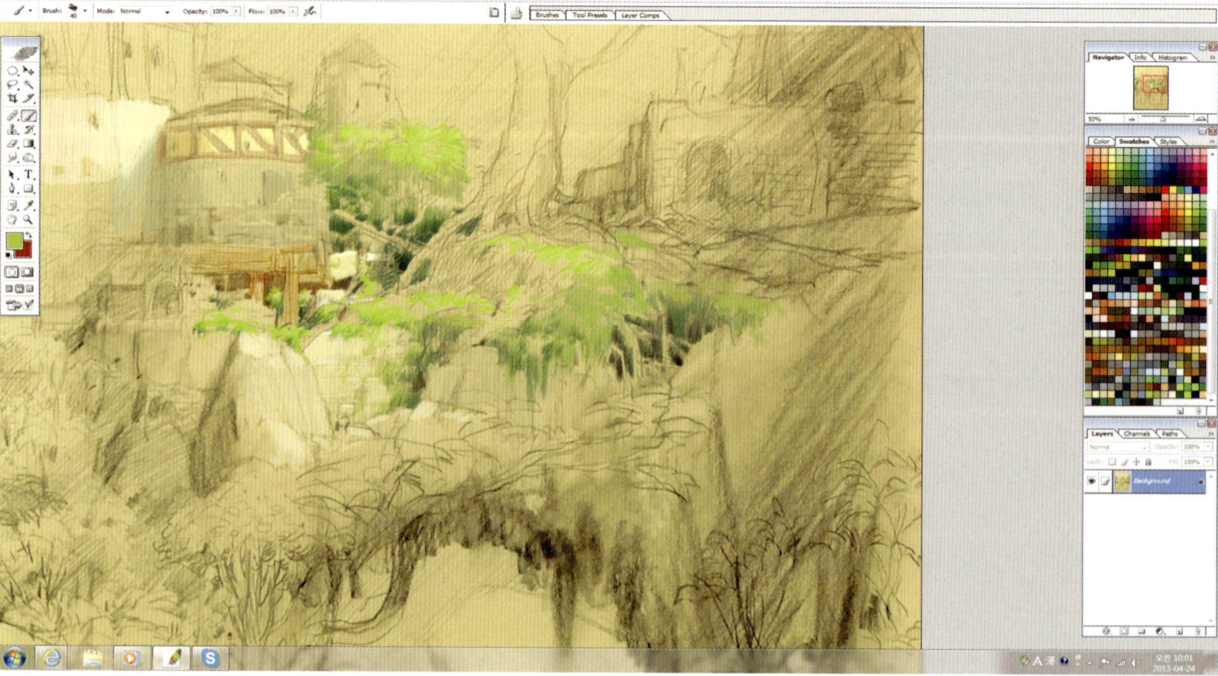

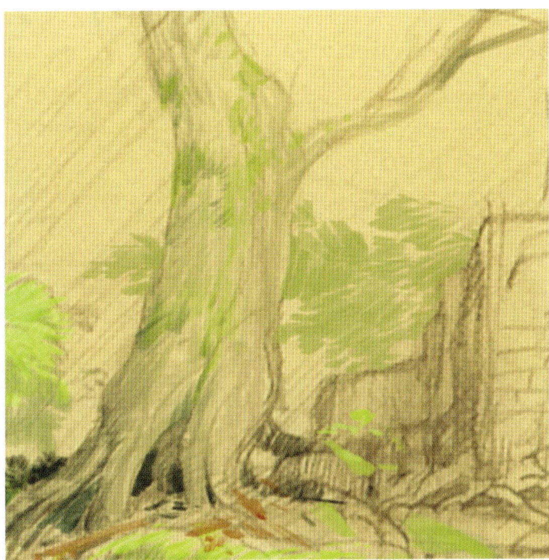

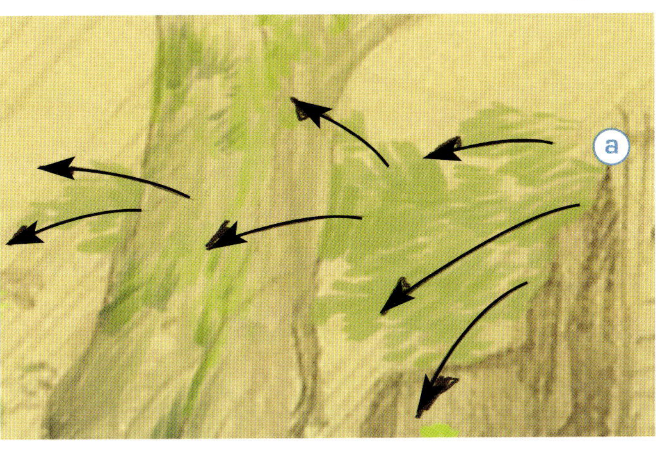

Fig. 3.48

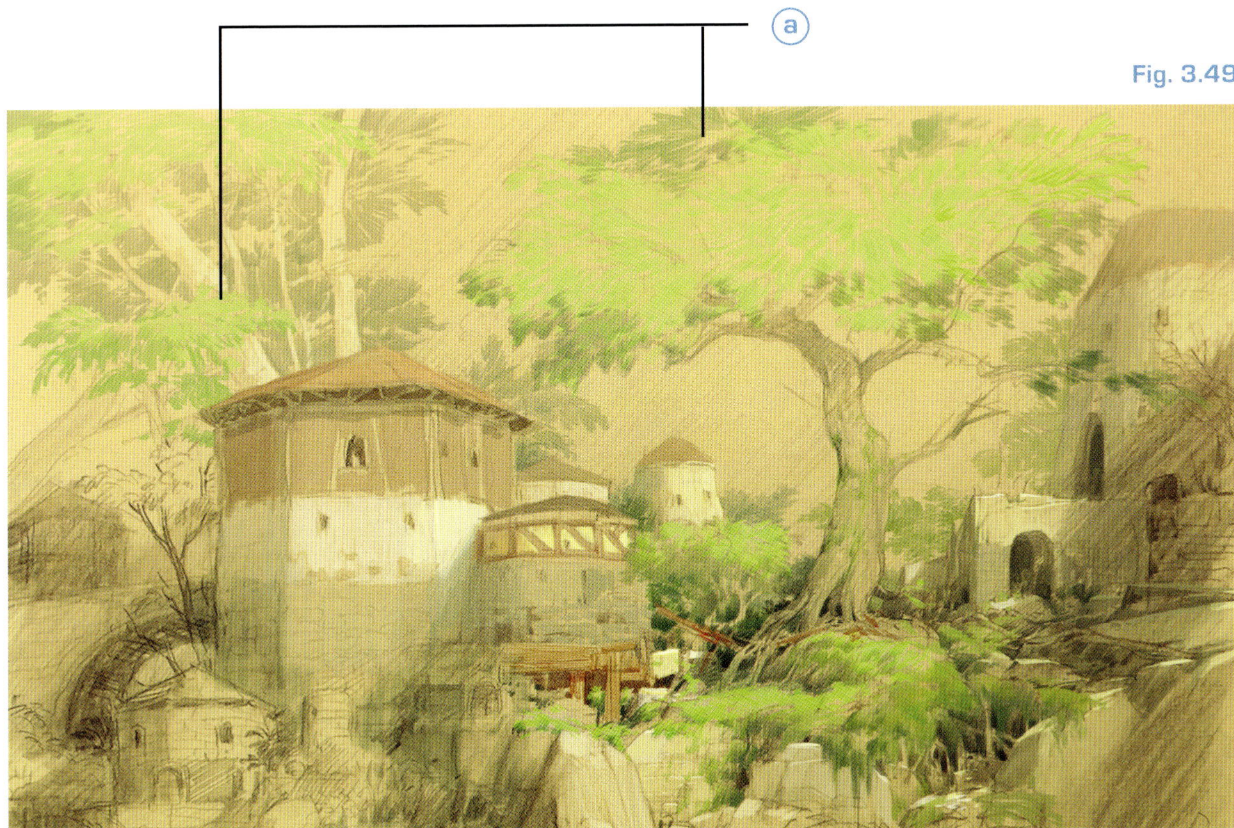

Fig. 3.49

A key point to remember when painting a tree is to not paint the entire surface with a brushstroke. Leave gaps between brushstrokes. Let the background color bleed through these brushstrokes as if this were a watercolor painting. Also, when making brushstrokes for leaves, it is important to give the strokes a directional flow (a). That is what nature does.

It does not matter whether one paints a small tree or a big one. Keep the rhythm of the flow, as well as the balance. Don't add too much strong color too quickly. Rather, build up the layers of leaves one by one (a).

After laying the basic greens down on the page, the next step is to add more color pops, which will counterbalance the green. I add a white tree to make the painting feel more tranquil. I also use a slight dark blue for the shadow color on this tree. Then I add a purple bush to widen the color spectrum of this painting. I usually paint a painting from dark to light, but sometimes adding the dark on top of the light surface creates an interesting result. This town is starting to get prettier and more colorful. This gives me, as well as the viewer, a happier feeling.

Figure 3.51 shows some samples of different tree shapes that I painted for this piece. When I walk in the wilderness, I always observe the trees. Each tree has a variety of distinctive shapes. No tree looks like another; each one is unique. However, when I observe a tree carefully, I often find repeated patterns inside of chaotic shapes. There is flow and rhythm within each tree.

Fig. 3.50

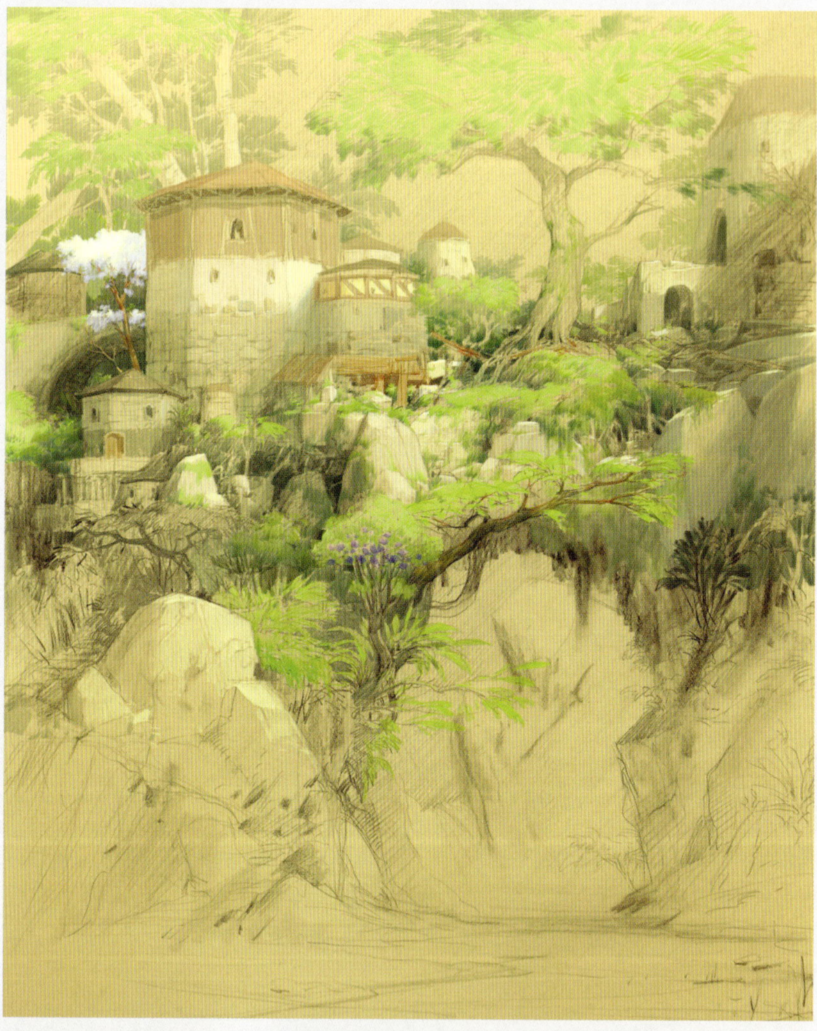

Fig. 3.51

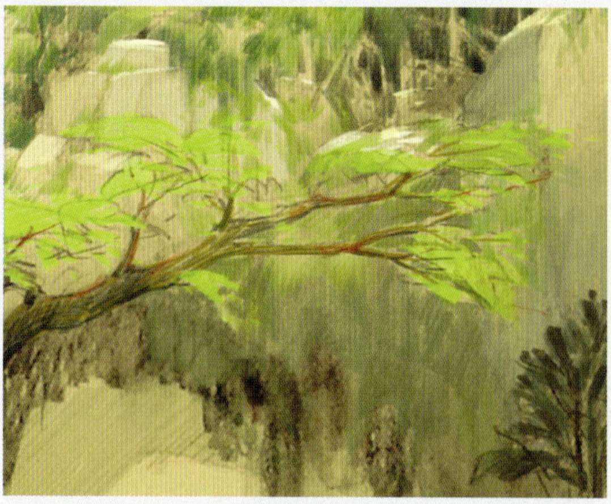
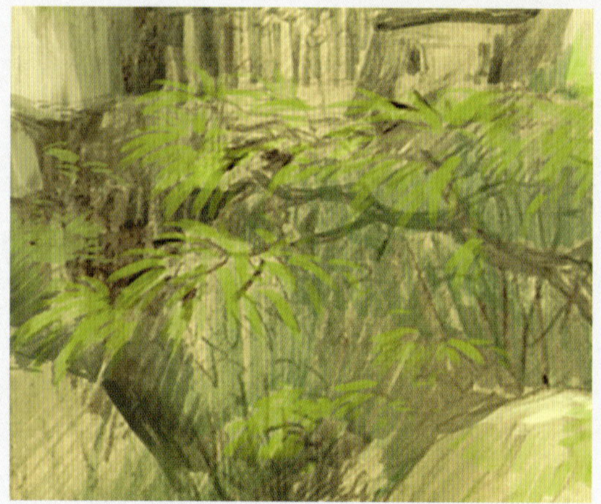
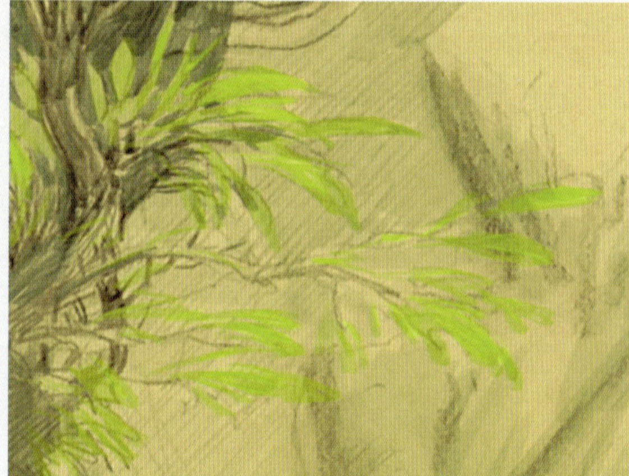

Fig. 3.52

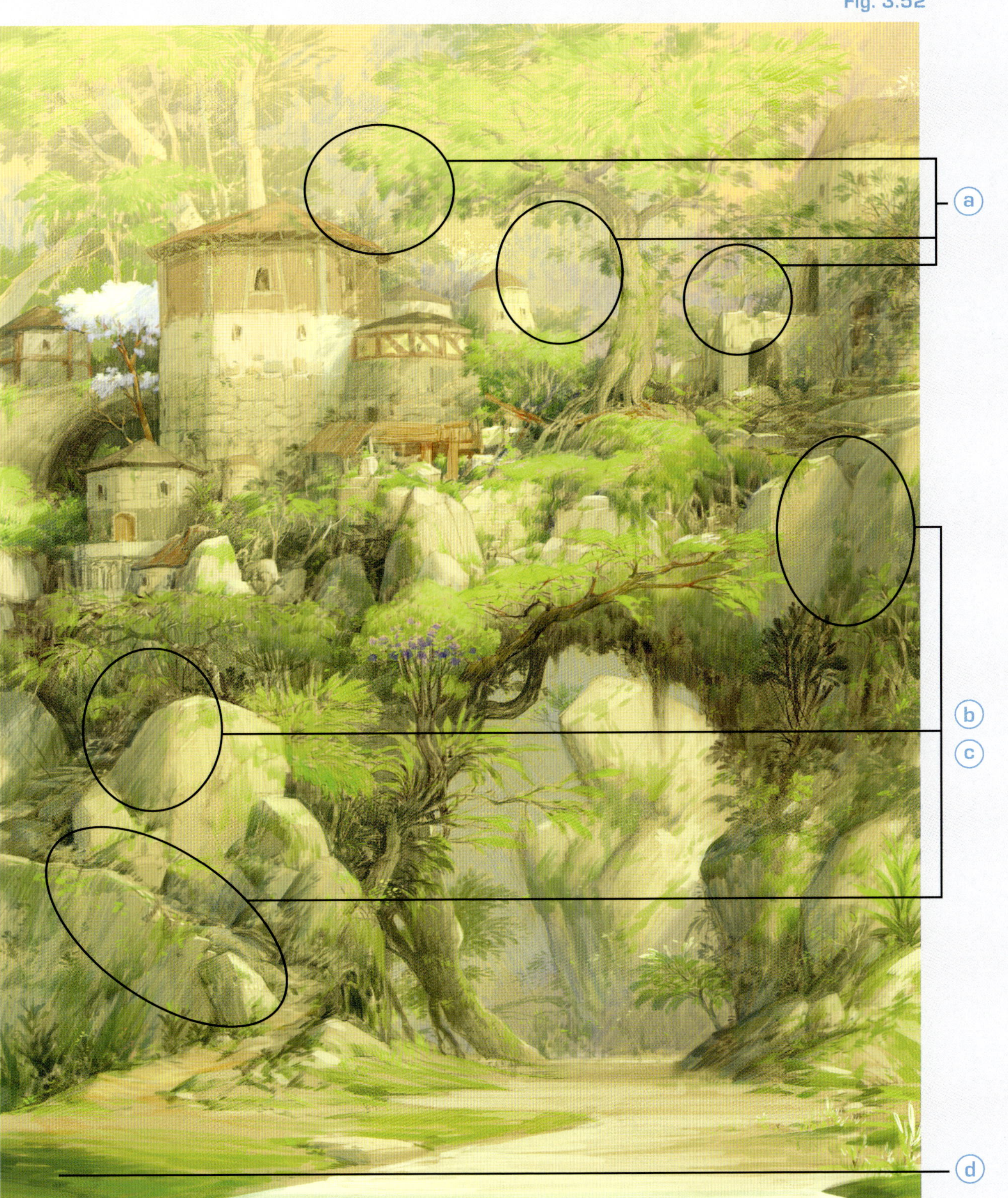

a. I add a light purple to the background to push it back. In this process, I use a very low-opacity brush because I did not want to draw people's attention to the background. By using a 10% opacity brush, I add cooler color to the background to knock it back without making the painting too desaturated.

b. As the painting progresses toward completion, I keep checking the color balance of the whole painting. Rather than adding any new color at this point, I emphasize the harmony of the existing color in the painting.

c. If some areas get too desaturated, or do not have enough color variation, I use a simple brush at 30% opacity and glaze over the blue tint.

d. Since the bottom corners did not have strong value contrast compared to other parts of the painting, I add shadow in those corners to frame the picture with darker value.

Fig. 3.53

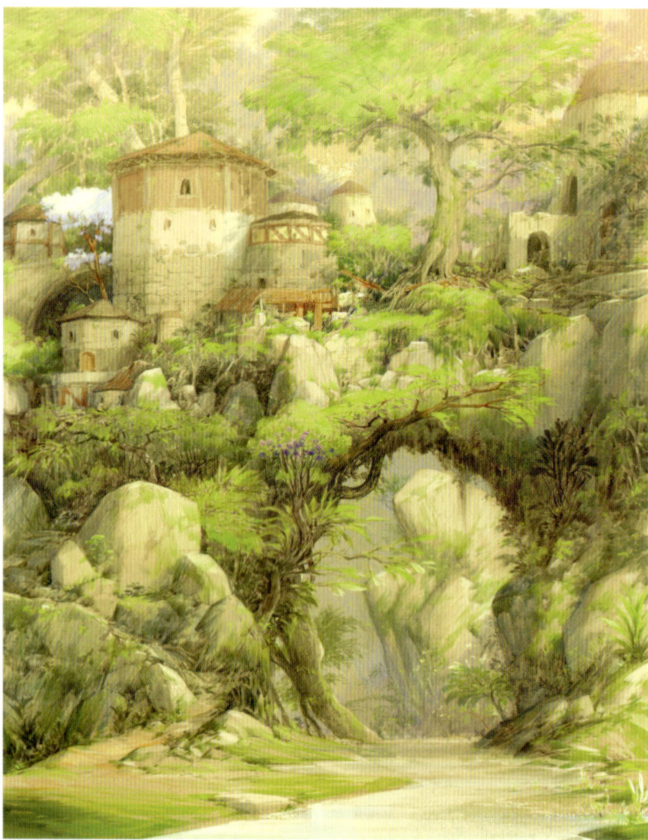

Fig. 3.54

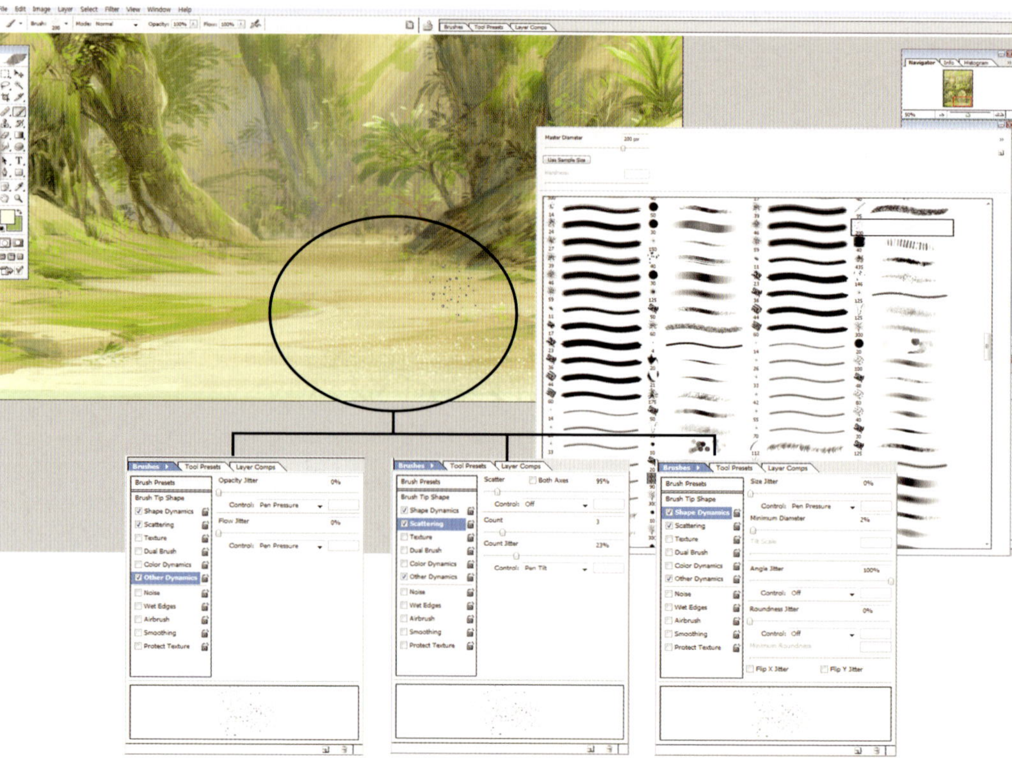

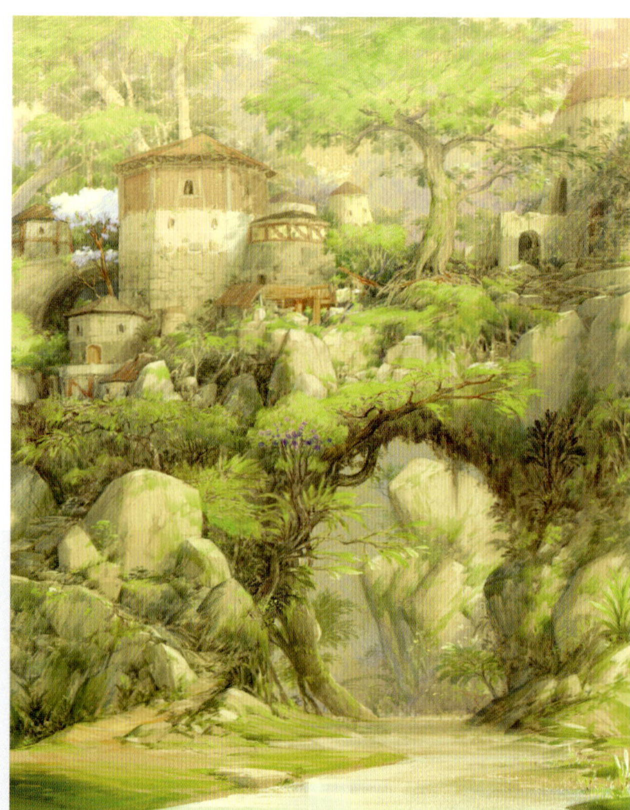

As a last step, I darken the treetops on the upper portion of the painting. The most important thing for this last step is to keep the balance of the painting. Balance includes, but is not limited to, light balance, color balance, and detail balance. I keep tweaking all of the elements until the painting gets the right balance.

One last tip: The scattered-dot brush can be used to express scattering light effects on the stream.

Lava Fortress

Fig. 3.55

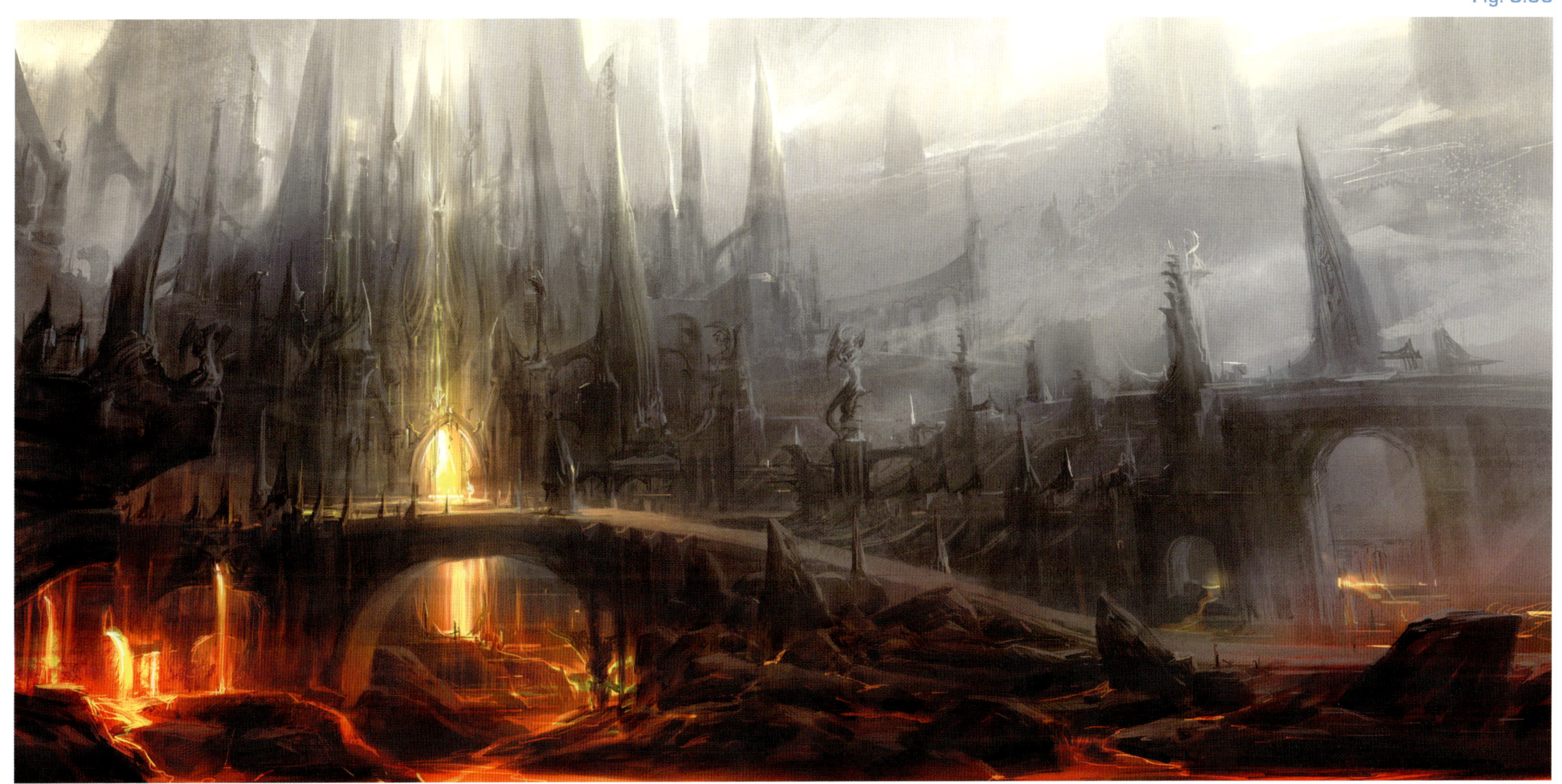

In this tutorial, I create a fantasy fortress. Hot lava is flowing around the castle, making it an invincible fortress. The overall design of this fortress is very sharp and spiky. I will save the most intense saturation for the lava and let other parts be a little desaturated.

I start with one of my favorite base-color templates that I use often. Before I draw any perspective grid on the page, I tend to enjoy drawing the initial sketch, and then I retrofit the perspective grid to match the drawing. After drawing a rough sketch, I add a horizon line to the painting, as I have done here.

To develop the painting more, I put down several textured brushstrokes (a) to create points of interest, and to give it a more interesting color blending.

Fig. 3.56

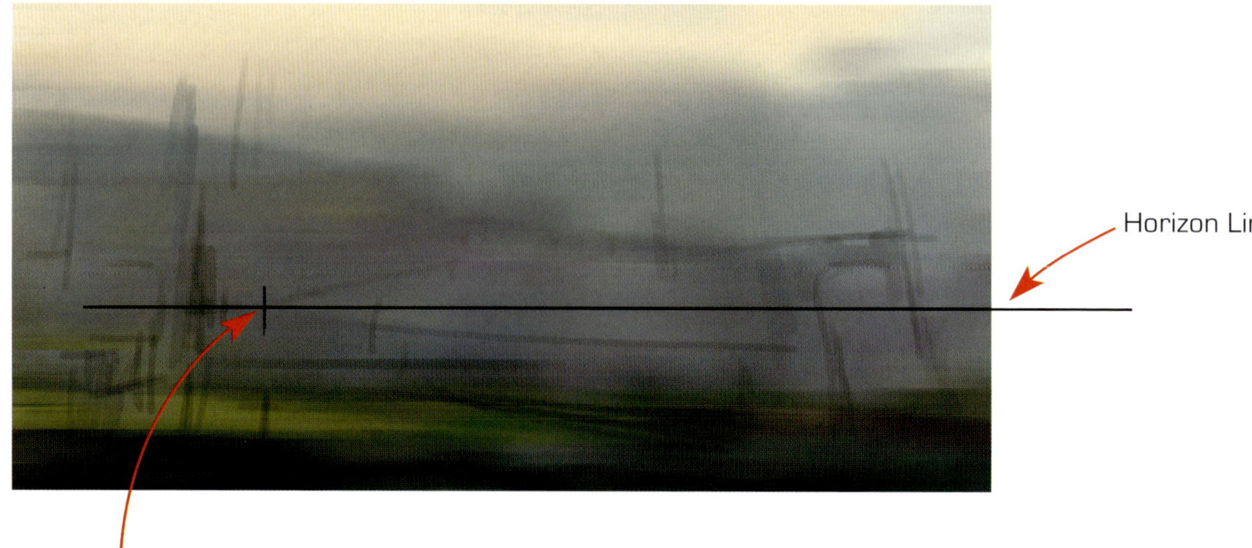

Fig. 3.57

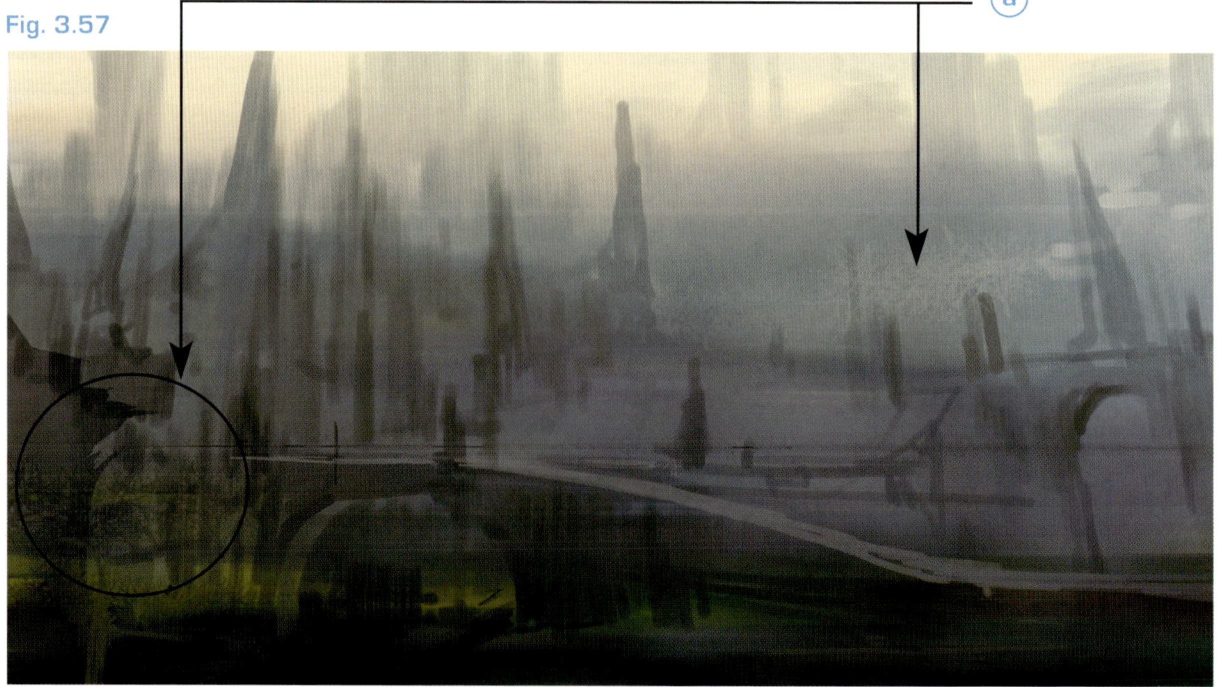

Fig. 3.58

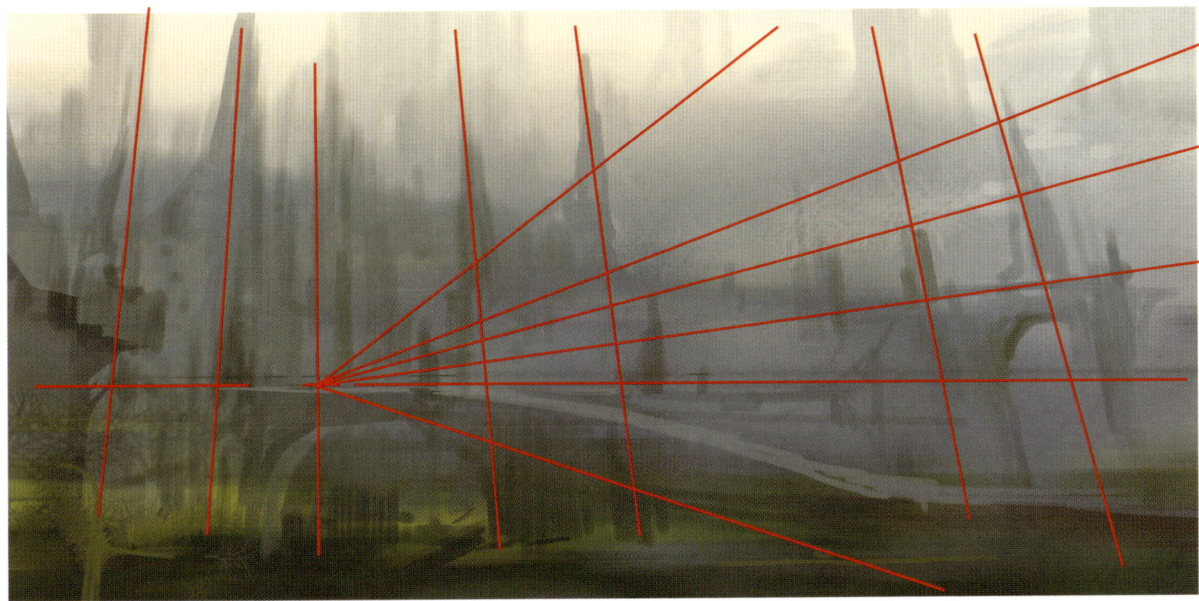

Note that I have used three-point perspective in this painting. Since the vertical perspective lines are very important for three-point perspective, I draw many guidelines on a separate layer so that I can refer back to them later.

Next, I make a new layer, and set it as a color mode. I use this layer in preparation for painting the lava using a Color Dodge brush. If the base tone is too hot, the Color Dodge brush bleaches out the color too quickly. Therefore, I paint the base layer with yellowish brown.

Fig. 3.59

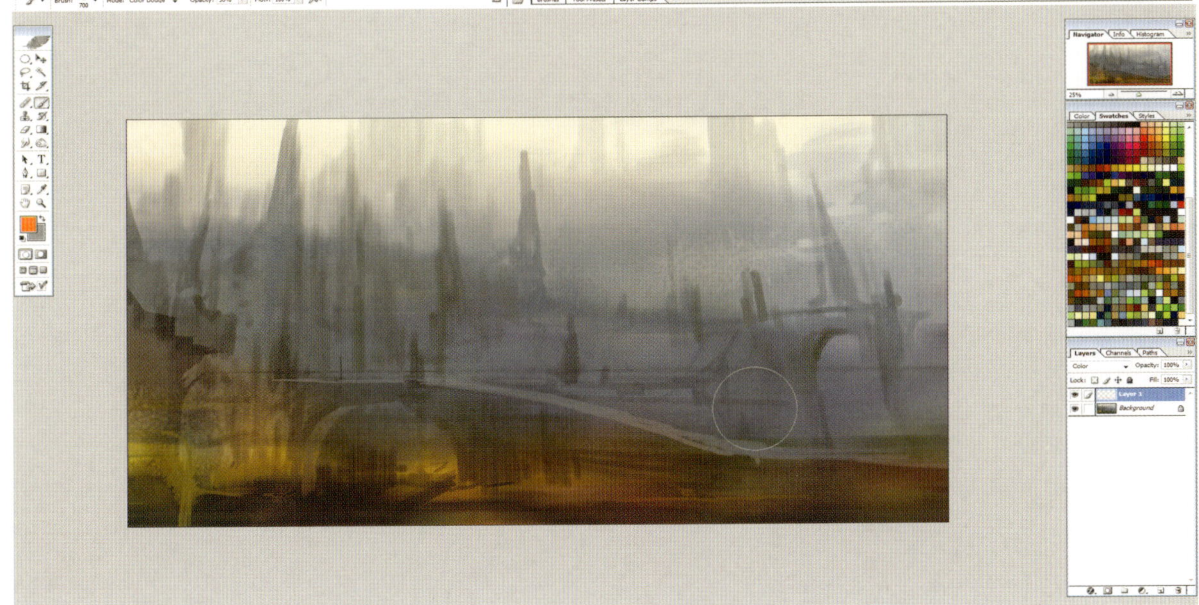

Fig. 3.60

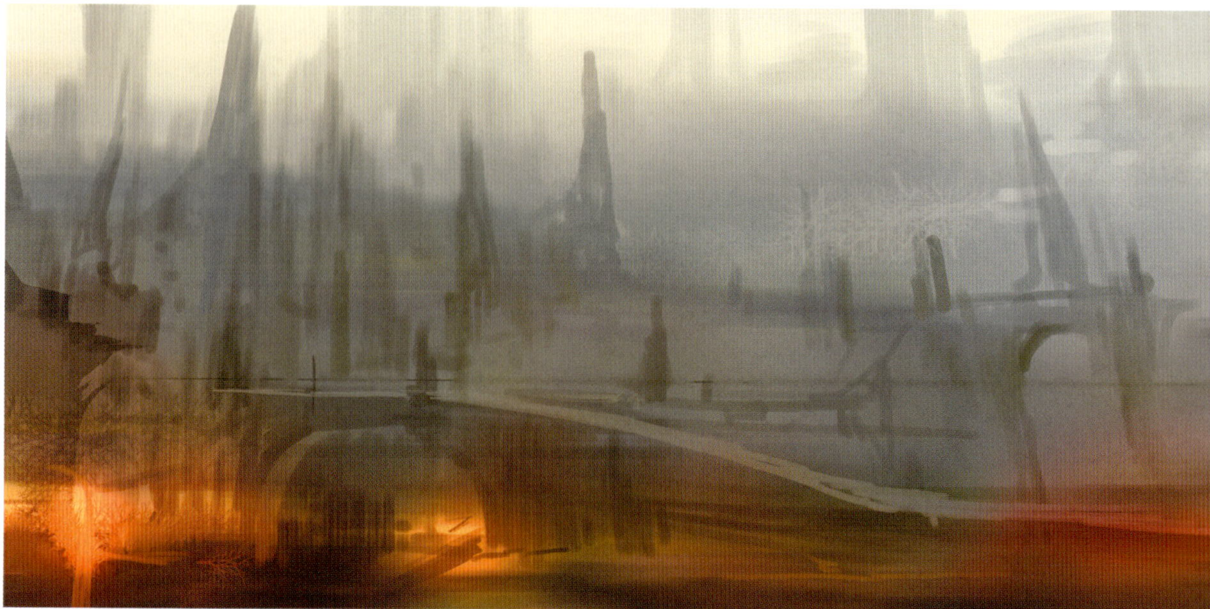

With the preparation stage completed, the lava is ready to be painted. I use the color dodge brush to paint the lava, and then pick an orange-yellow color and set the brush mode to the Color Dodge. Then I slowly paint in the hot lava color on the page. The neutral gray color I used in the background makes this hot orange look more saturated and strong.

Once I establish the overall color and temperature of the lava, I add a few big lavafalls. I choose a simple round brush and set it to Color Dodge mode. Next, I draw the lavafalls and lava splashes, using a light yellow color (a).

Fig. 3.61

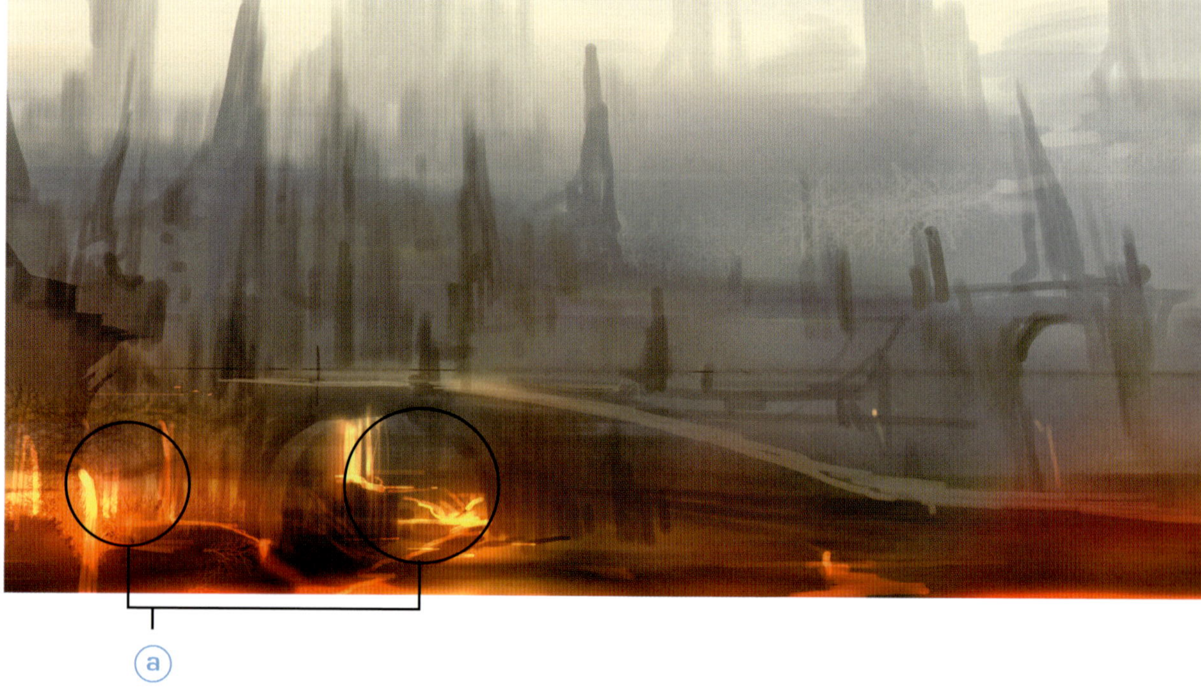

Fig. 3.62

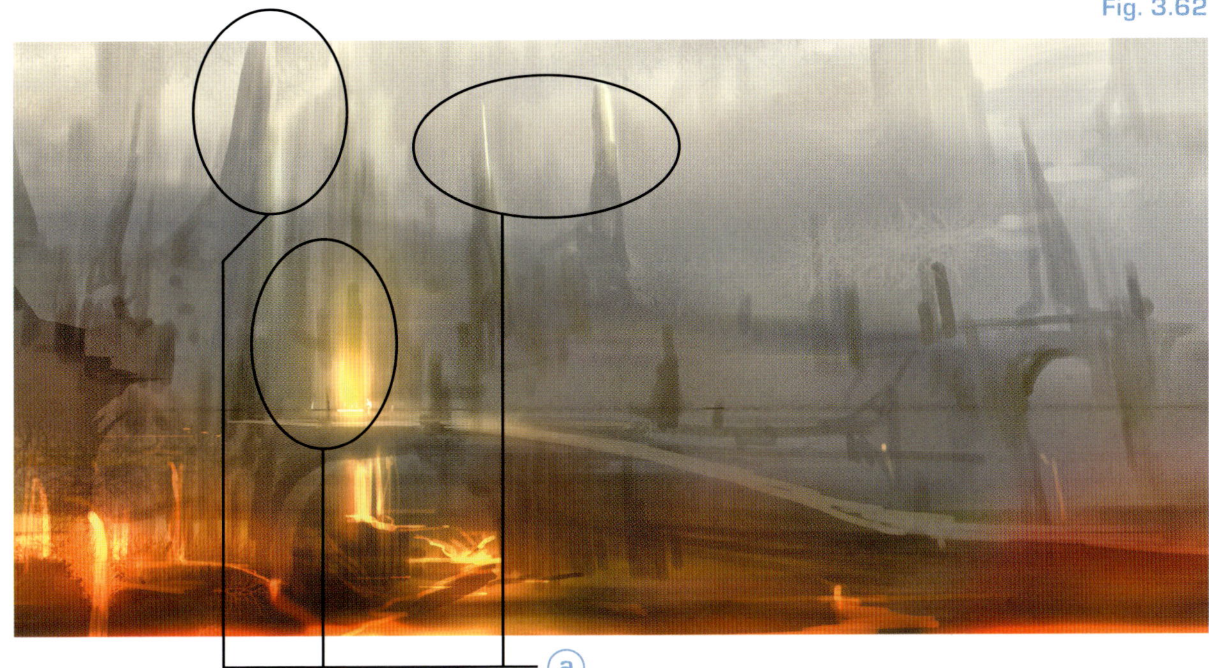

Fig. 3.63

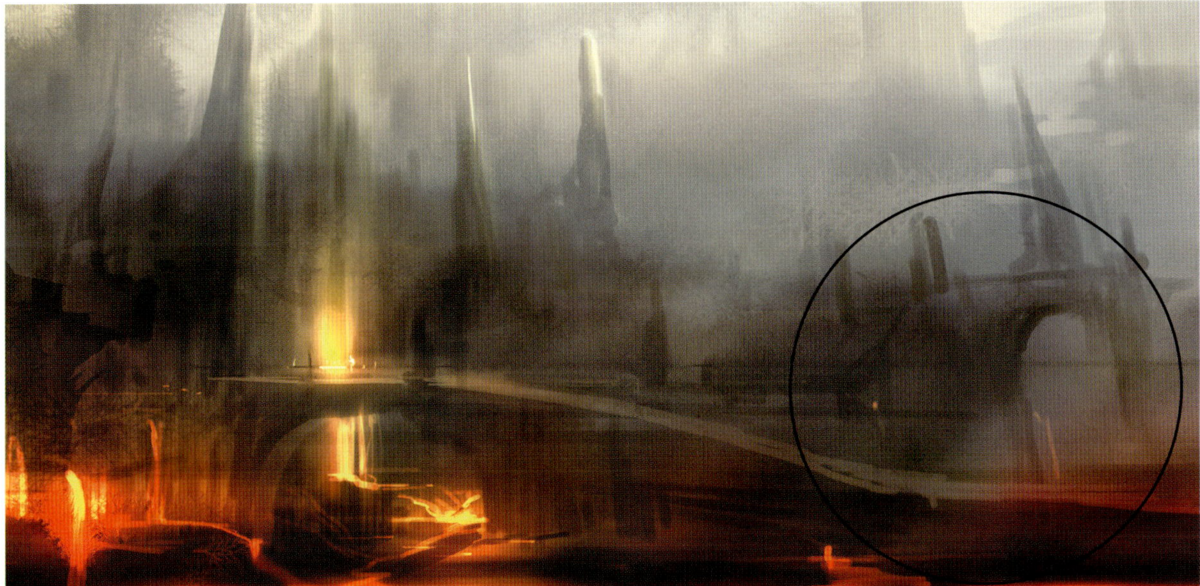

I add some textured strokes to the sky to indicate clouds and fog. I also paint lighting effects around the focal area (the main entrance). Then I paint sunlight hitting the tops of the towers (a). In my imagination, this castle exists in a very foggy area, so most of the castle is under shadow. That is why only some sections of the castle get sunlit.

Since good progress has been made in adding lights to the painting, it is time to add more darks. First I choose the section I want to make darker, then I darken it by using the Burn tool. Subsequently, I paint more textured strokes on the spot where I have used the Burn tool to add more texture grits. After all that is done, I paint the beams of light that shine through the bridge by using the same technique. It creates more dramatic lighting.

Next step is to bring up the detail level of the main subject. I start by drawing big silhouettes and designing the architectural elements. This initial shape-designing step is the most crucial footprint of the design process.

Once the silhouette design is done, I paint in more details. Here I use a toned-down light color because it is sitting under the shadow area.

Fig. 3.64

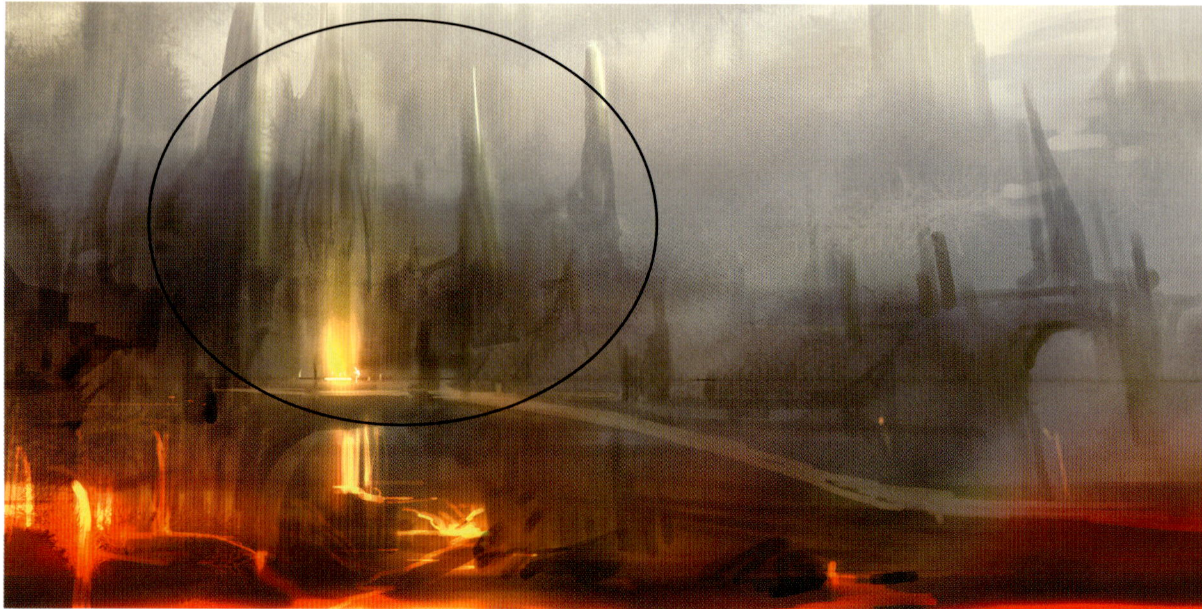

Fig. 3.65

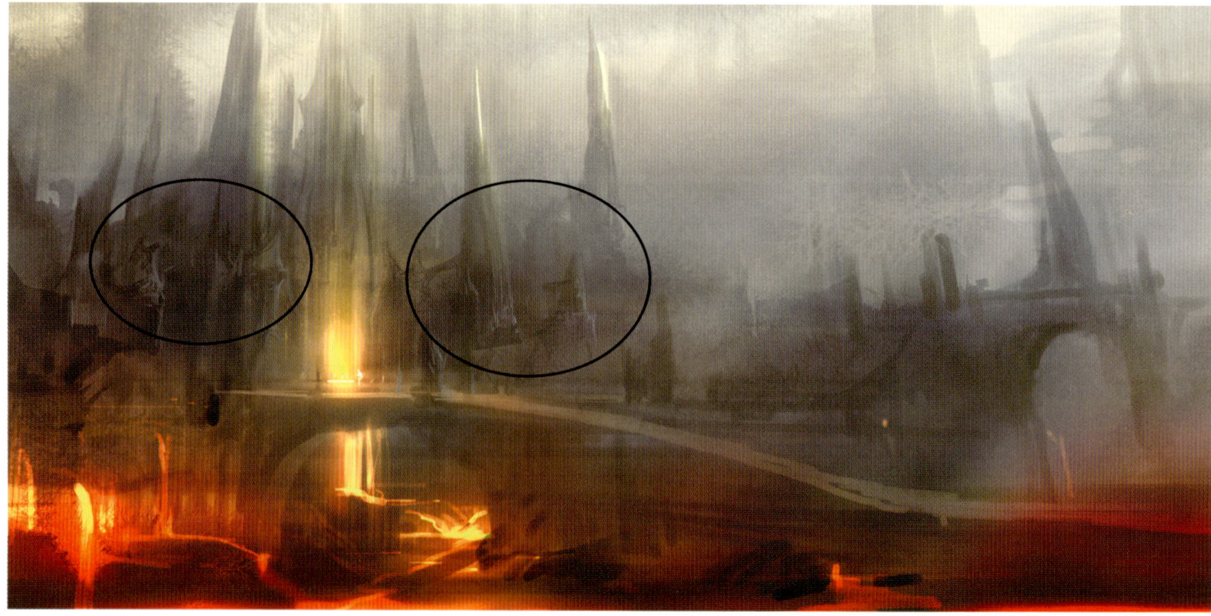

Fig. 3.66

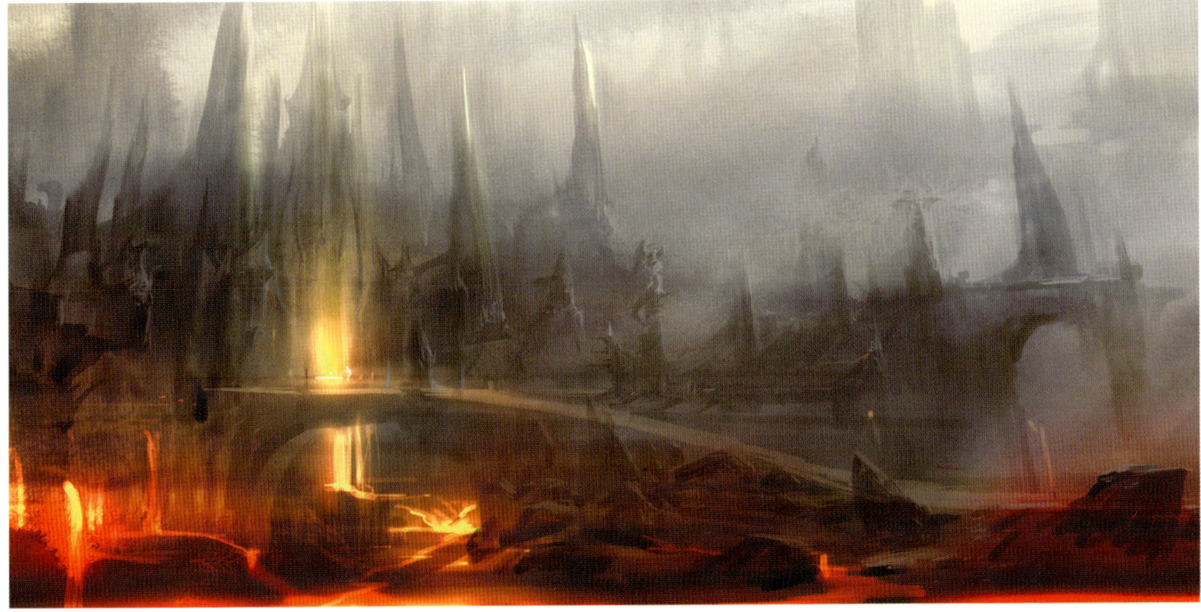

I continue what was done in the previous step to the right side of the building. Instead of drawing every single detail, I try to leave some sections with a suggestion of an expression without any details.

Since I have added a good amount of detail, it is now time to reintroduce bigger shapes to add heavier weight to the painting. On the left and right side of the bridge (a), I start to add more details with a darker value.

Fig. 3.67

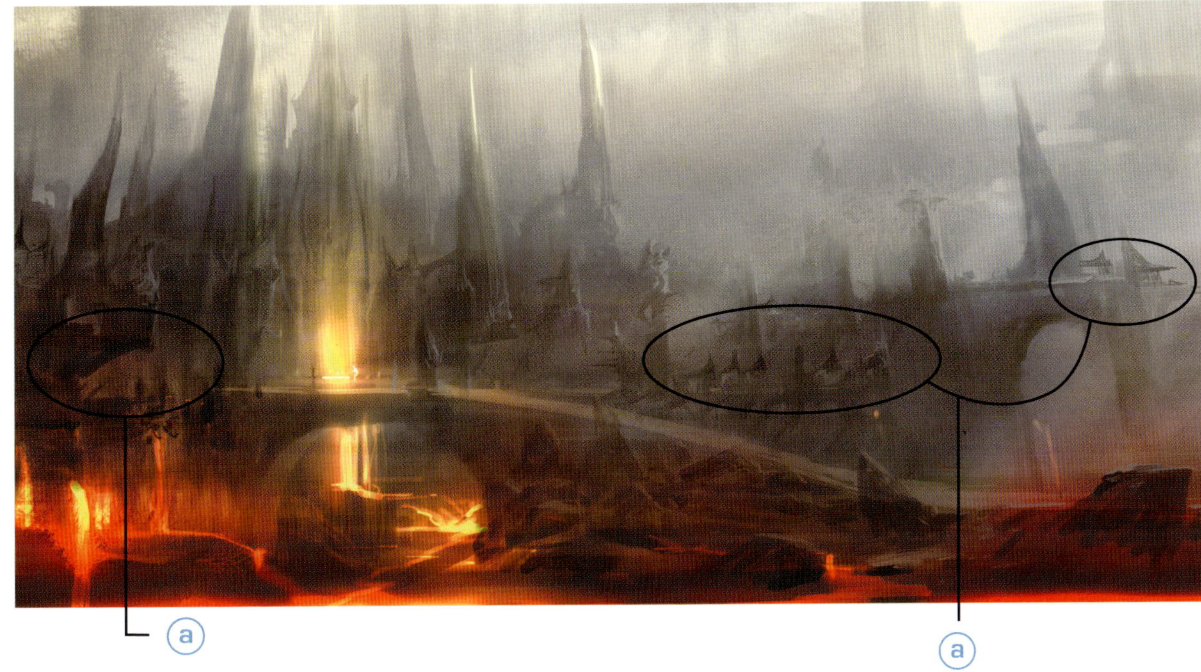

Now it is time to jump back to the main subject. I never complete a painting by finishing each section separately. Rather, I develop the painting as a whole by jumping from section to section, all the while keeping an eye toward maintaining the balance of the picture.

To make the main focal point more intriguing, I add a few more towers and arches. I scale up some of the towers as well. Introducing more repetitive shapes in the far distance gives a greater sense of scale and perspective. Along with all of these enhancements, adding a big, round wall in the background creates an illusion of having even bigger buildings in the far distance.

Fig. 3.68

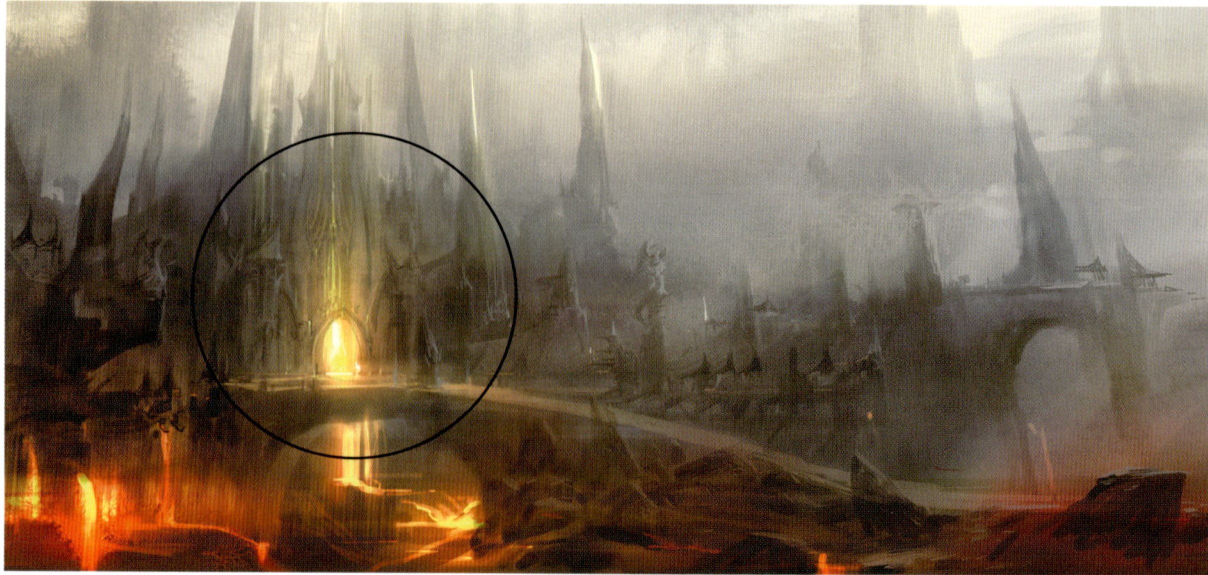

Fig. 3.69

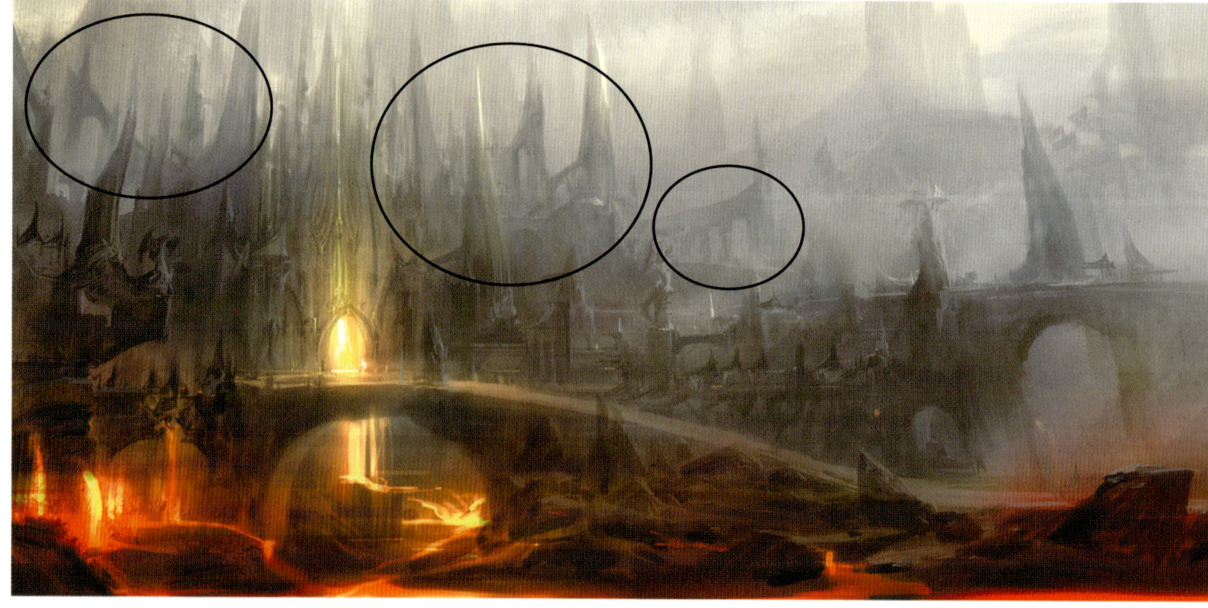

Fig. 3.70

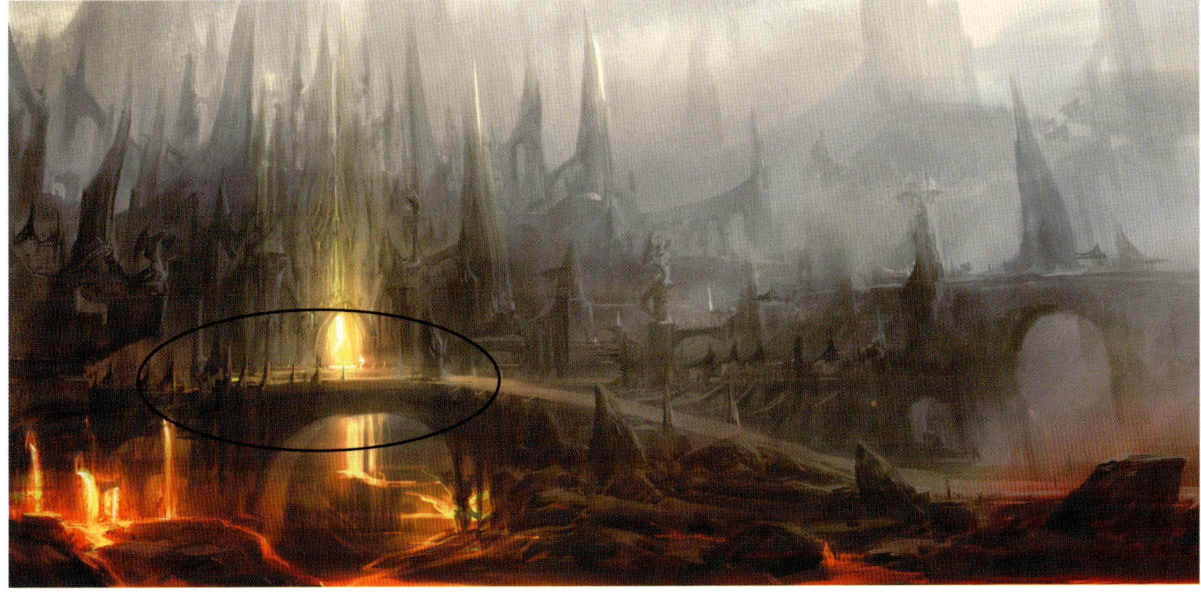

Following the above enhancements, I now turn to painting more details on the bridge. I keep reinforcing the shape language by consistently using similar shapes. Even on the bridge, I keep using a spike theme to reinforce the shape unification.

Fig. 3.71

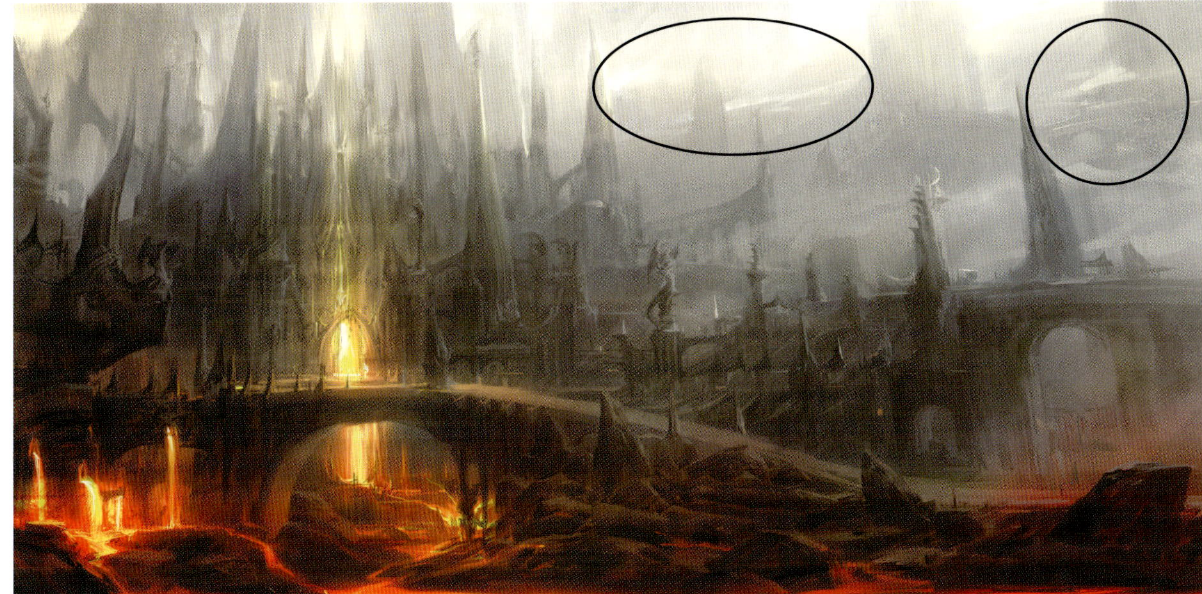

Next I paint more atmospheric effects to create more atmospheric depth and a magical mood. Adding a zigzag-shaped fog in the background helps to create a more dynamic visual flow. To draw the fog like this, first draw a shape with light color. Then pick a slightly darker color (at 30% opacity) and blend it. It is possible to get a very naturalistic result this way. I also use a dot brush to indicate some particles in the air.

Fig. 3.72
This figure shows how the air flows in this painting indicated by the red arrows (a). For the lava in the foreground, take a very small brush (Color Dodge mode) and paint it with a bright orange color, almost as if making an etching (b).

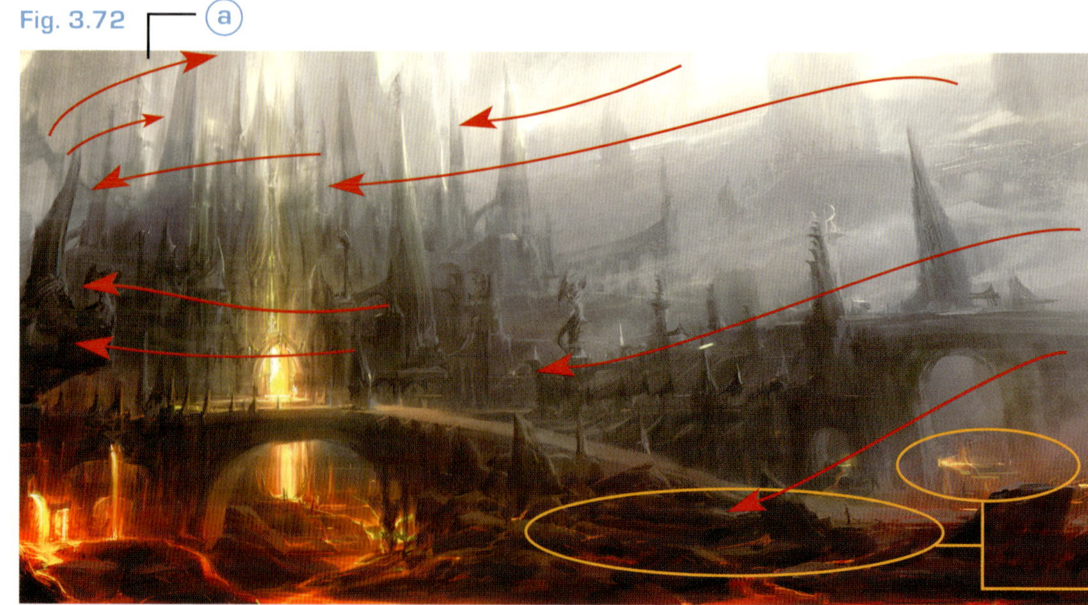

Fig. 3.73

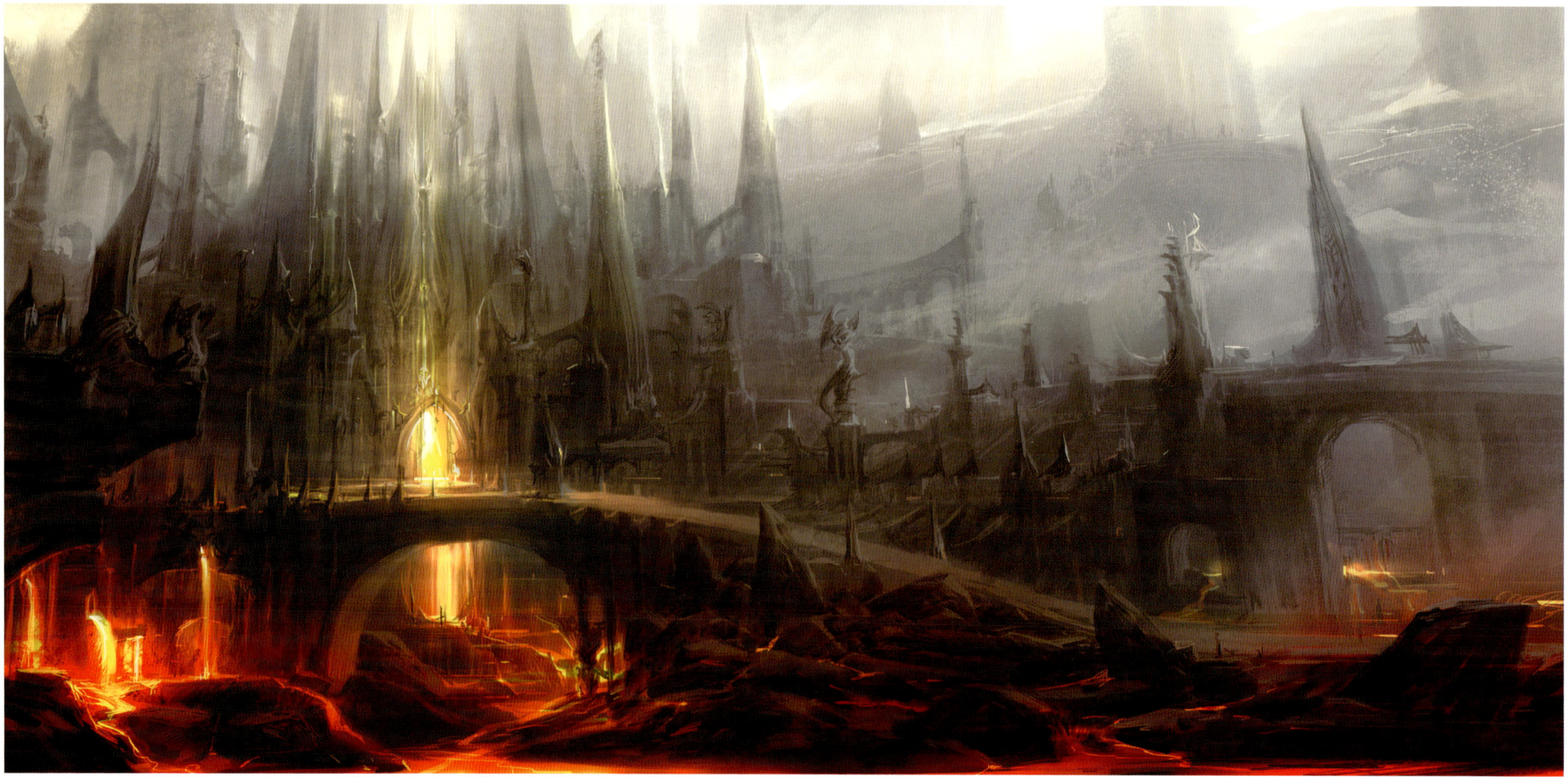

Frozen Castle

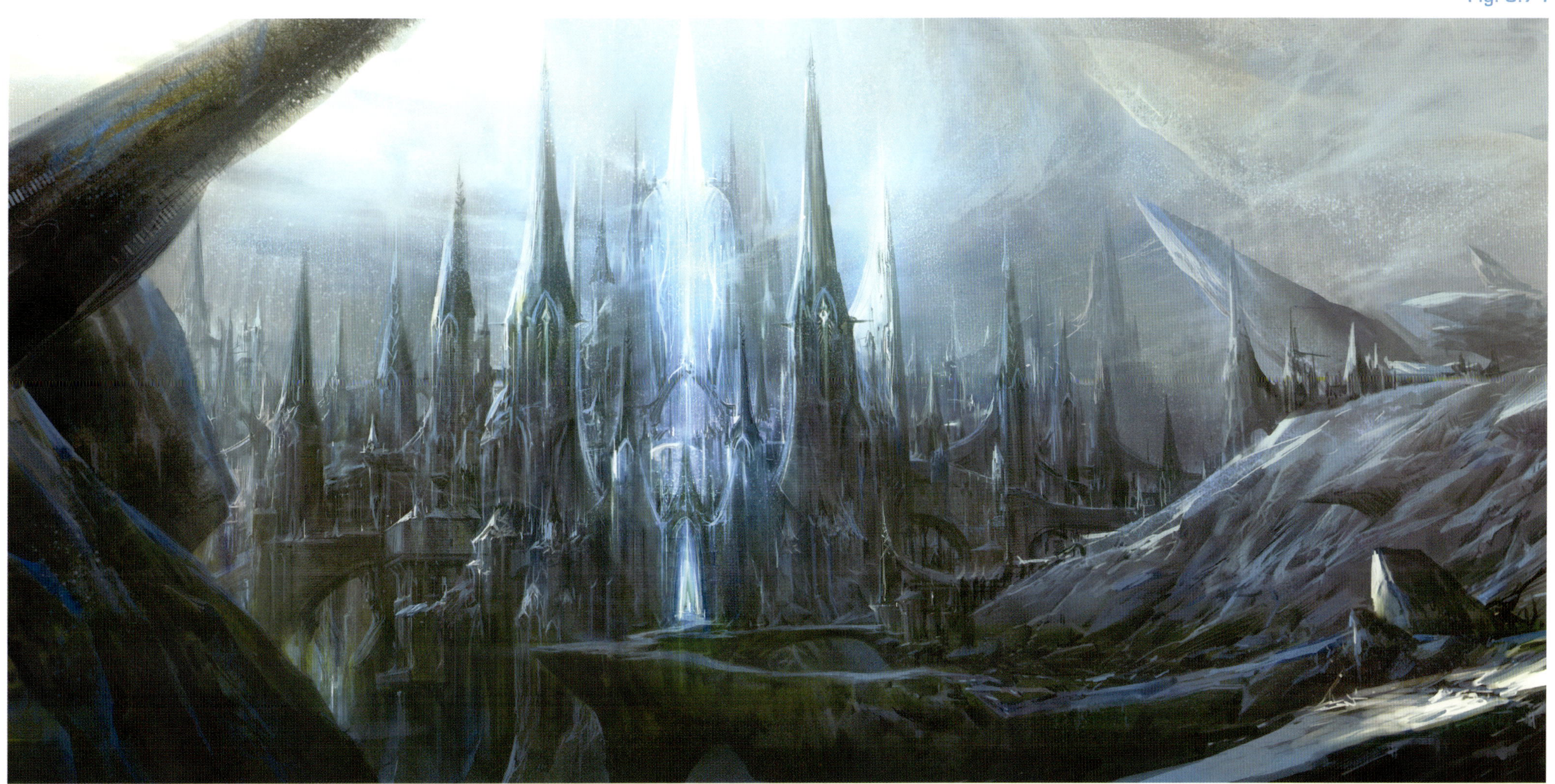

Fig. 3.74

In this tutorial, I am going to demonstrate how to paint a castle in a fantasy world. Instead of starting with a pencil sketch, I started my drawing on top of a rough, base-color background.

I sketch a rough silhouette of the castle with a very simple vanishing point in the middle. I also indicate a horizon line on a separate drawing layer.

I add a giant rock diagonally on the right side of the page. Since the base composition is a very simple one-point perspective, I want to create more visual interest by adding an element that has directional movement in form and design.

Fig. 3.75

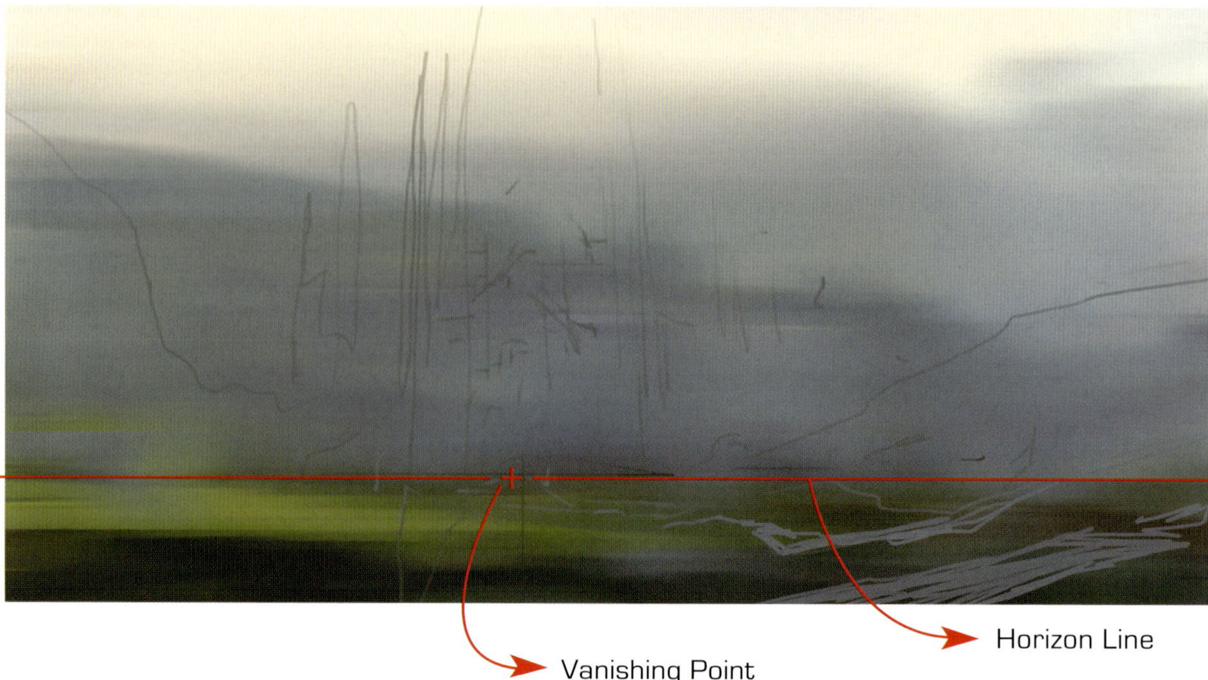

Fig. 3.76

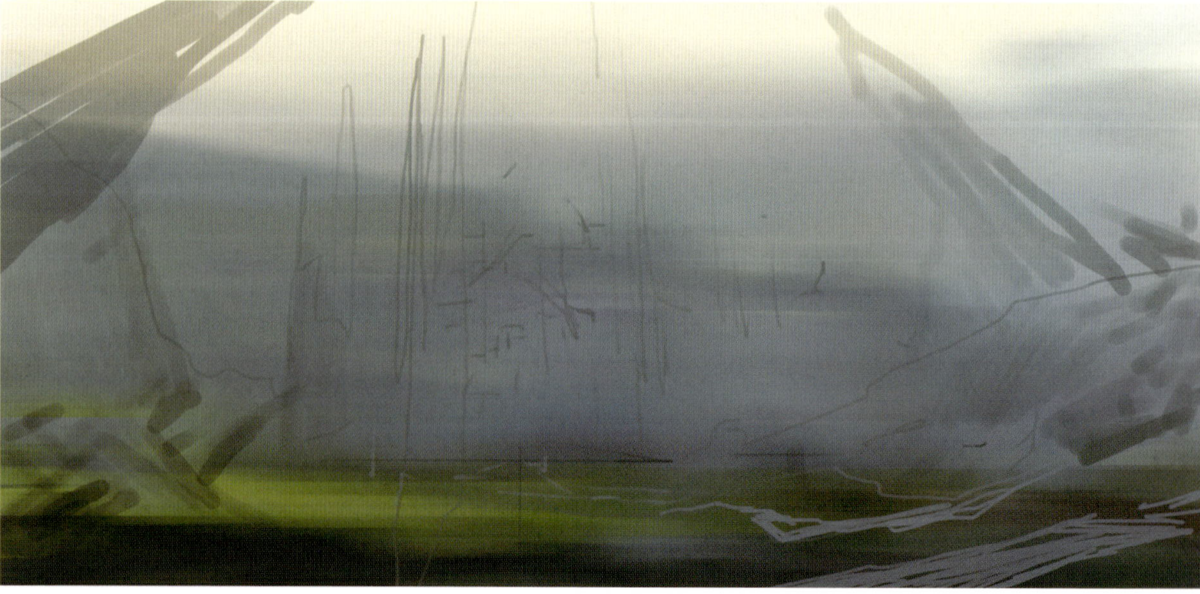

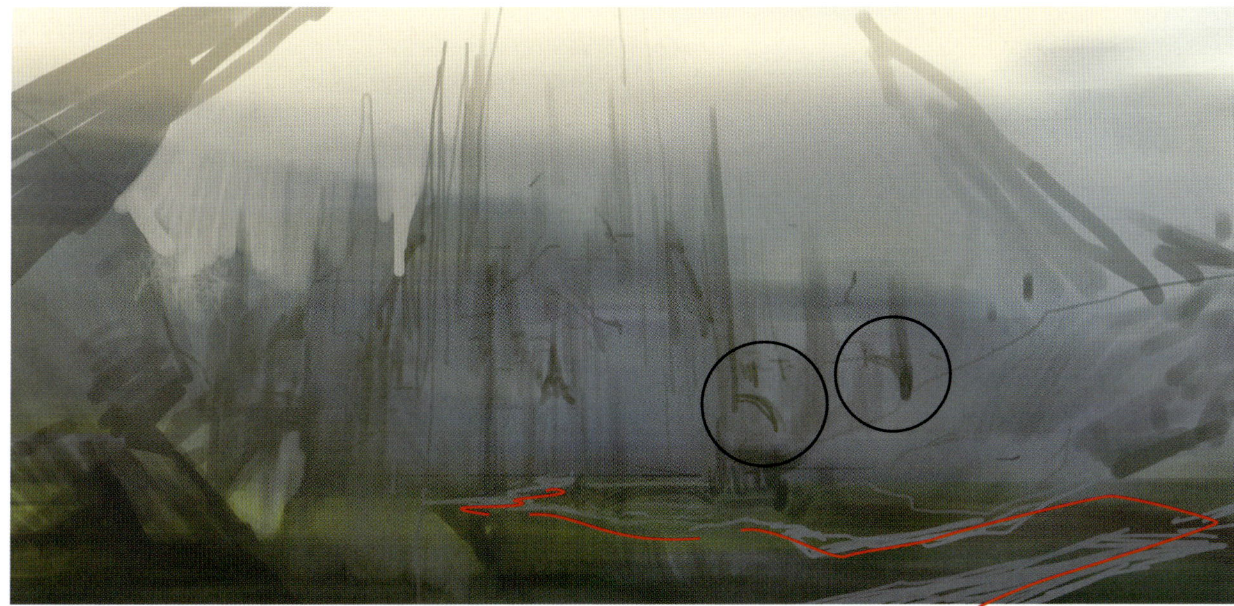

Fig. 3.77

In this third drawing, I paint more compelling visual elements into the picture. I add a couple of tower shapes, more arch shapes, and a bridge. Basically, I am trying to add more interesting storytelling objects. I also paint a zigzag-shaped road to introduce an S-curve flow to the picture. These additions all add more depth and visual flow to the painting.

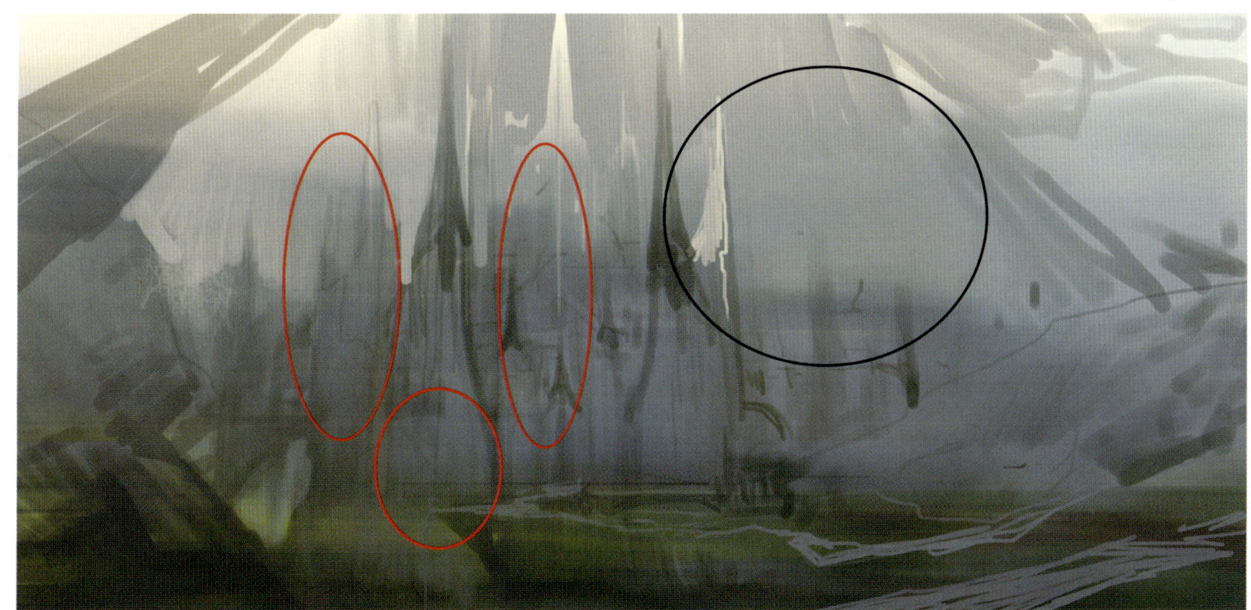

Fig. 3.78

Next, I develop the design of the main spire of the tower. Since this spire is the main focal point, I want to create an interesting design for it prior to adding any other components. I also start painting the background. This figure also shows that a mountain shape has been blocked in with rough brushstrokes. It is better to make big strokes like this in the early stages of the painting, since it adds a more painterly feel. I will keep it rough like this for now.

The next step is to apply more lighting information to the picture. Here, I show that the direct light hits only the top portion of the tower roof. I let other parts of the castle stay in the shadows. Adding more value contrast increases the visual tension. Also, adding more of the small buildings around the big castle increases the scale contrast, thus creating more visual tension.

After developing the contrast and tension, I use an airbrush (in Color Dodge mode with a blue color) to give an overall color tint to the bright side of the picture. Then for the dark area, I use a dark green tone to give the picture a heavier look. Because of this dark green, the light blue looks even lighter in the scene.

Fig. 3.79

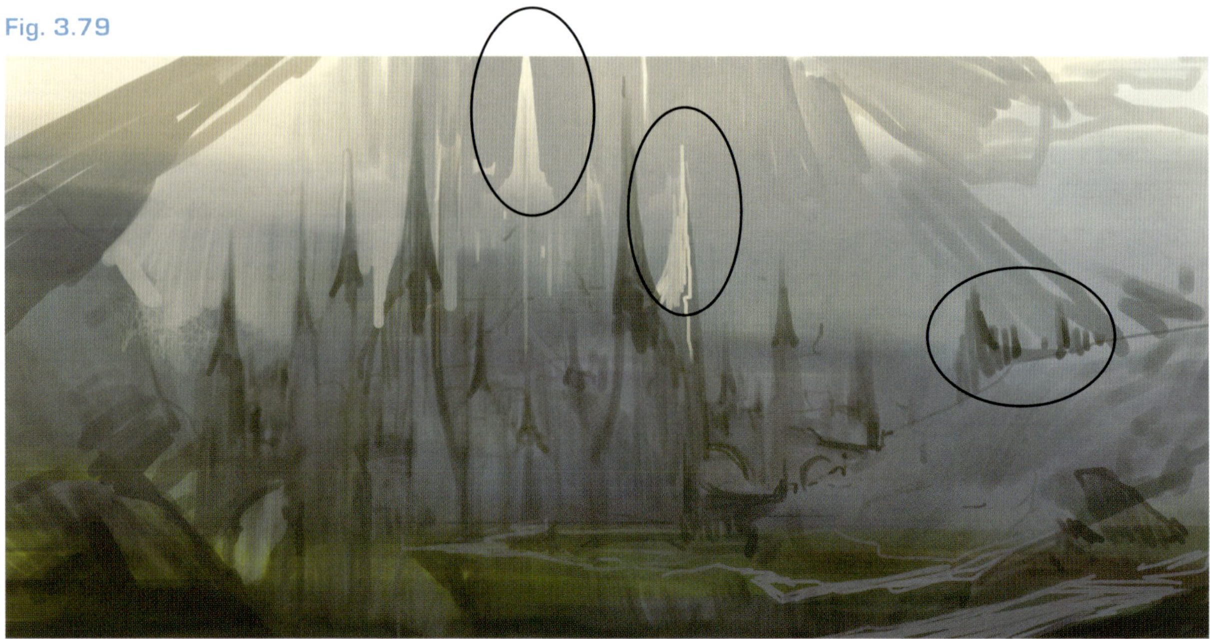

Fig. 3.80

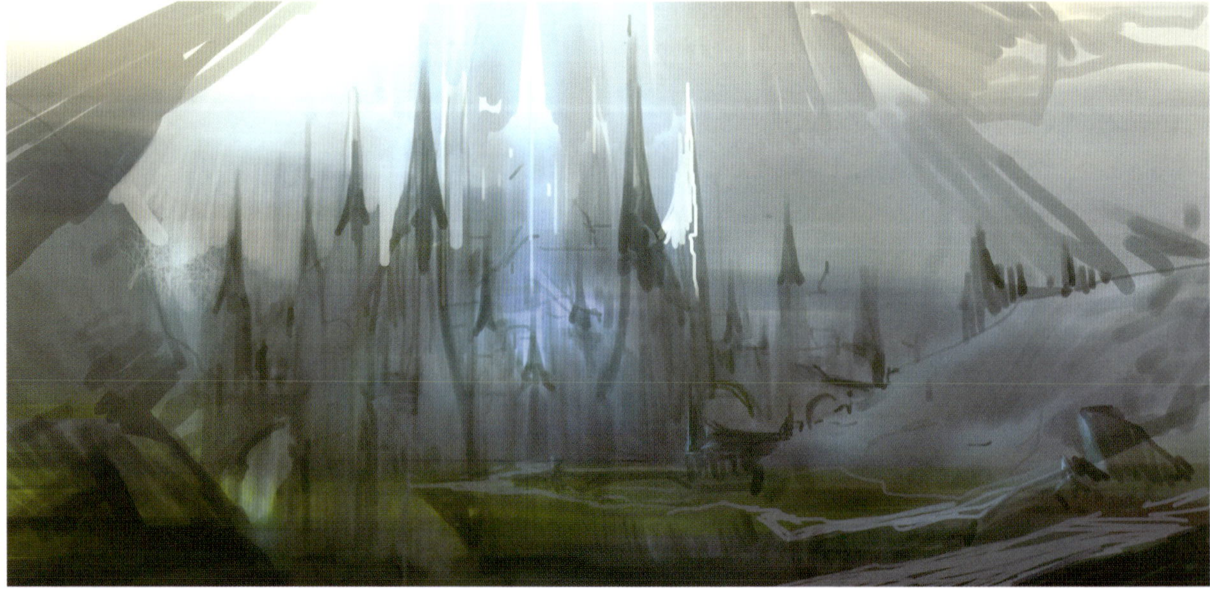

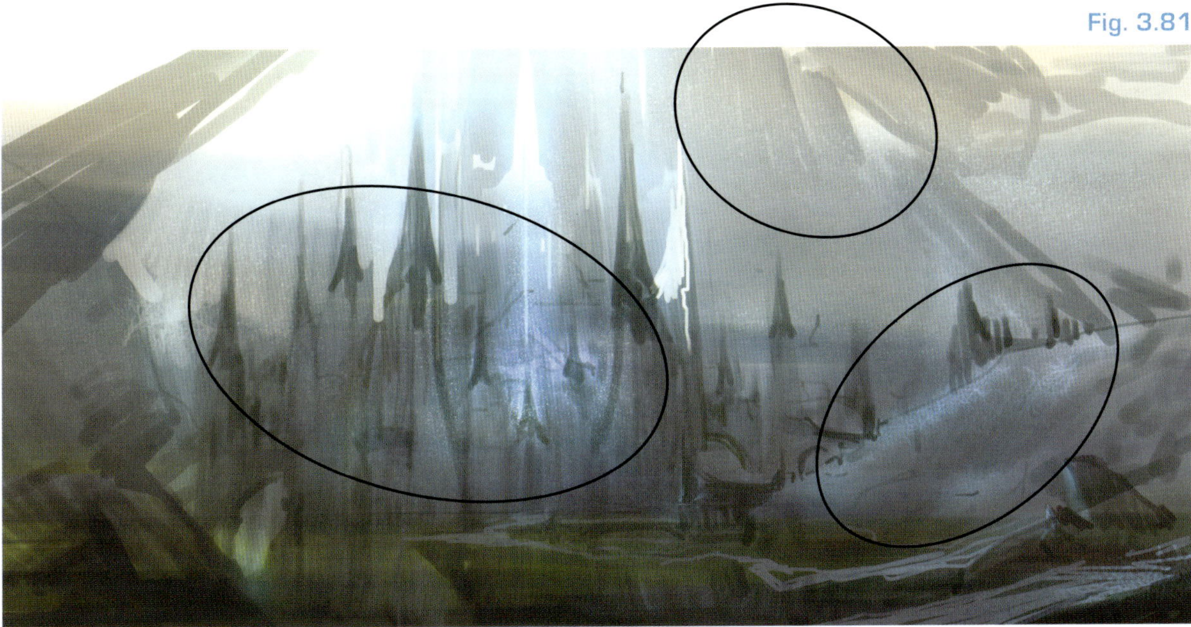

Fig. 3.81

To add a more intriguing base texture, I use a texture brush (set in Color Dodge mode) and paint some random textures. These base textures will help subsequent painting strokes look more compelling.

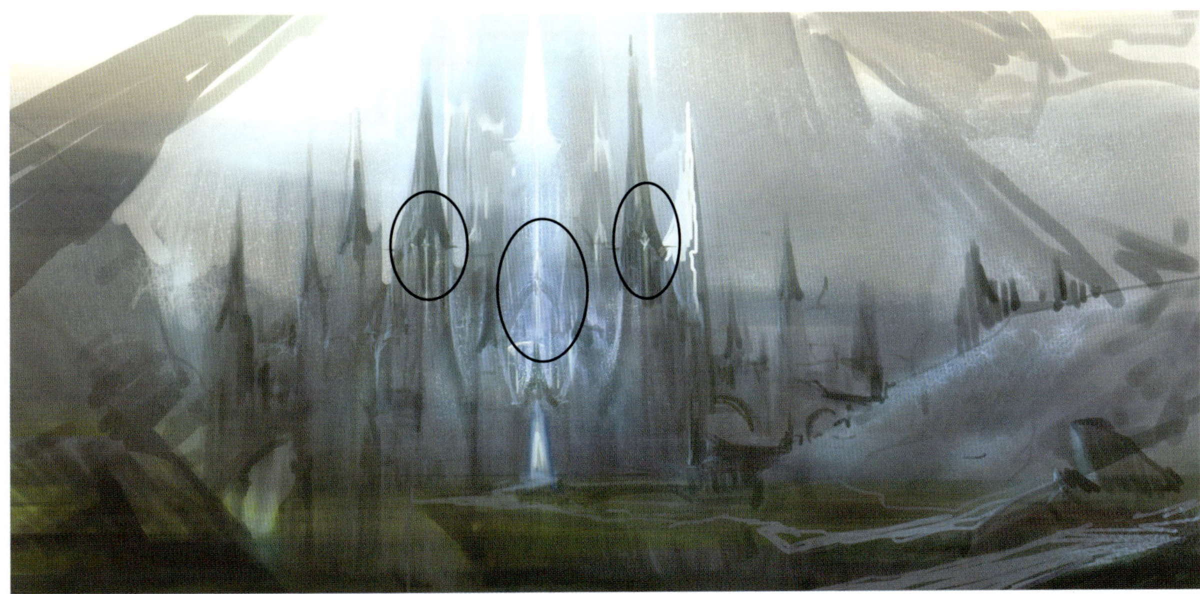

Fig. 3.82

Now it is time to add a more refined design to the picture. Up to this point, I have worked on creating the overall mood and setting the tone of the painting. There has been little focus on the smaller details. It is a good time to start painting more details. First, draw some large shapes. Then make an interesting silhouette with a simple stroke. I will get to the finer details later.

Once the large shapes and silhouette are drawn, I start to render the details on the bright side with a turquoise blue color. When painting a detail, zoom out enough so that the whole picture is visible. If you are zoomed in too far, you can only see a small section of the painting and you will lose perspective of the overall detail balance. Also, watch out for repetitive renderings. Try to create as many variations as possible within the boundary of the cohesiveness of the design.

Here, I create a very fun texture in the foreground by using a texture brush. I paint multiple strokes with a texture brush, thus giving it a splattered effect like in a watercolor painting. Furthermore, it also looks like a rock texture.

Fig. 3.83

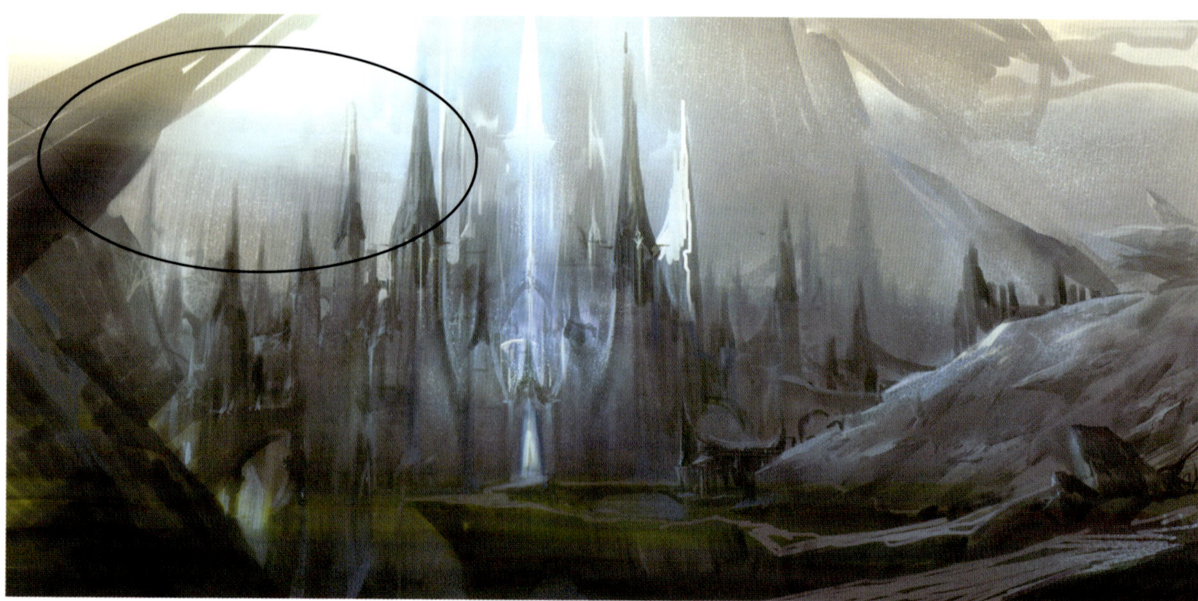

Fig. 3.84

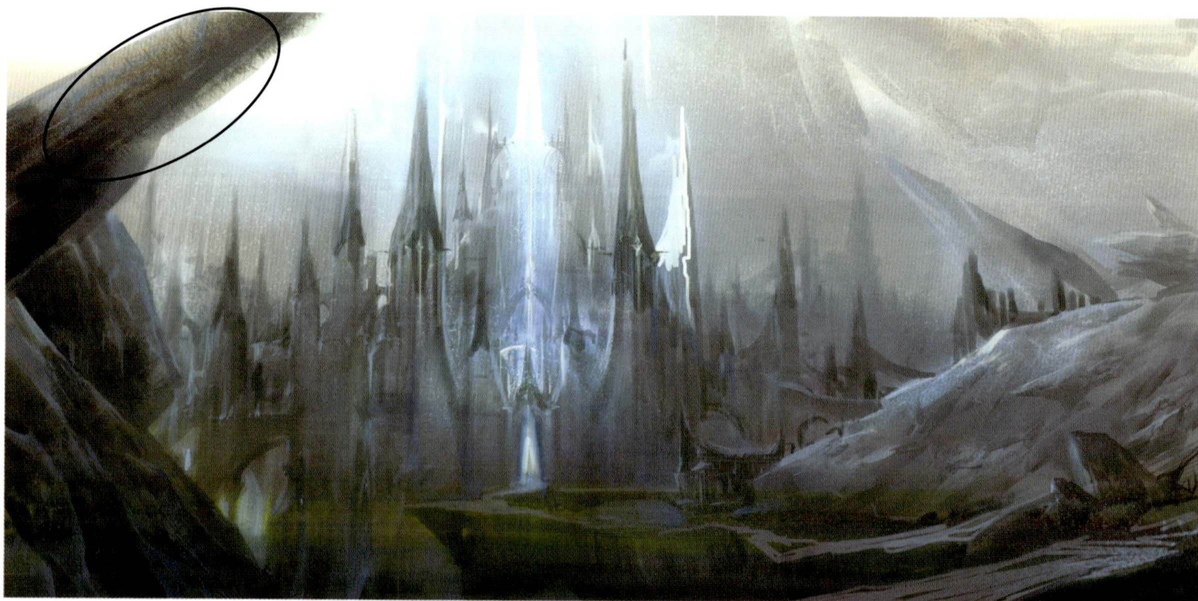

Fig. 3.85

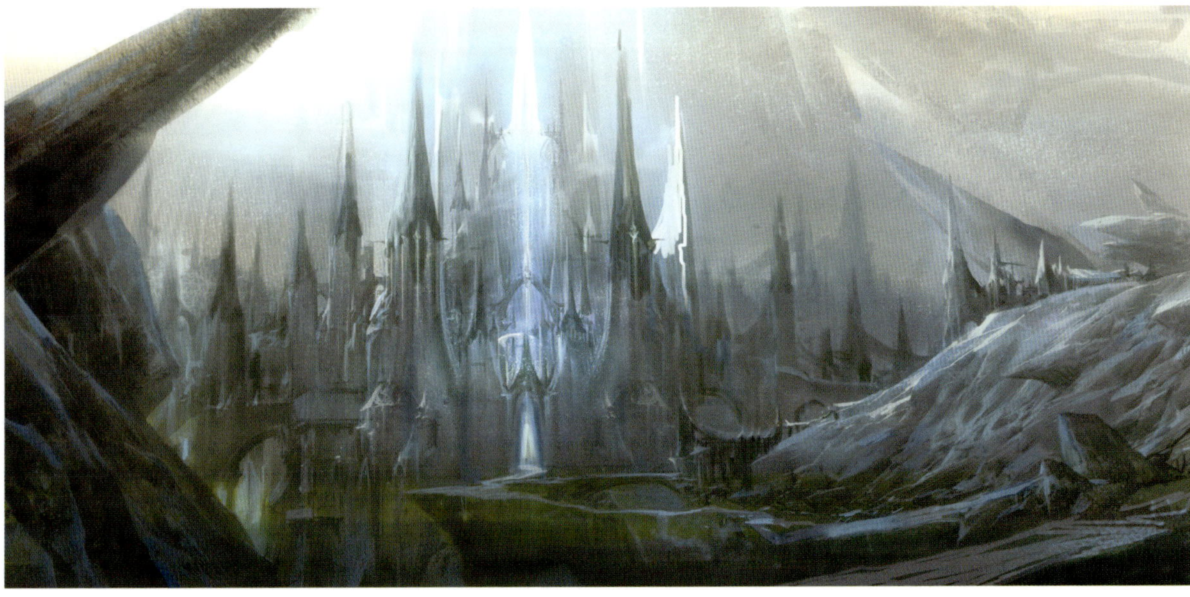

At this point of the painting's progression, I keep adding more details.

Fig. 3.86

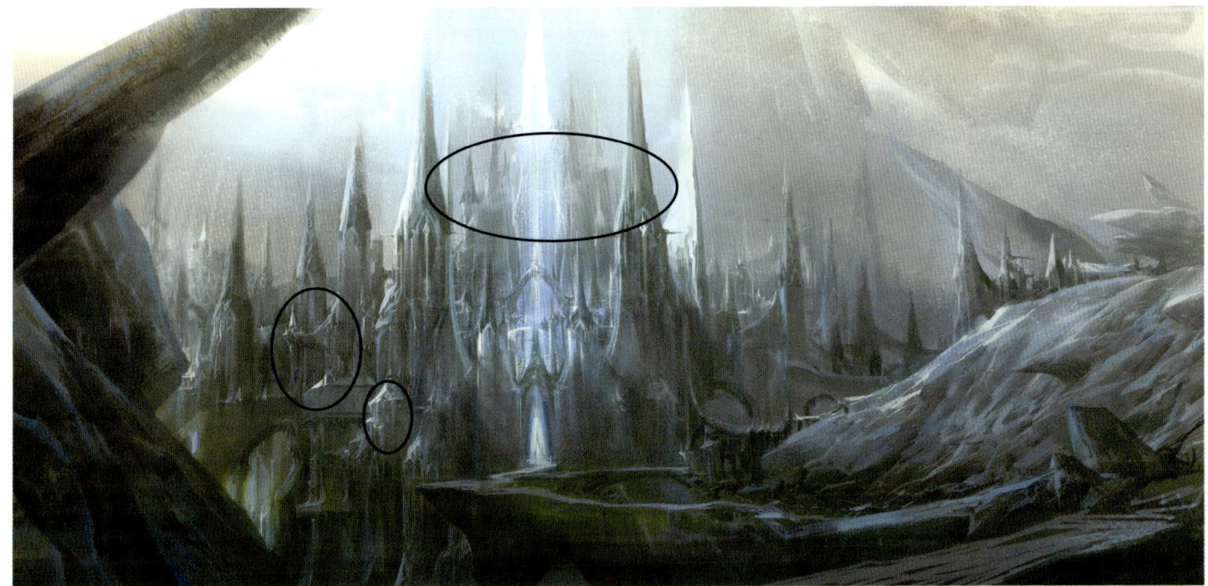

Here, I paint the magical effects, which almost look like light is swiveling around the main tower and blown away by the wind. In addition, I add a bit more atmospheric fog to create more depth in the painting. I also paint a very sharp and bright color to indicate a strong light source hitting the rooftops. I make sure not overdo it; otherwise, it is going to break the flow of the main light source.

Now it is time to define more details in the sky. I pay extra attention when painting the sky and fog because I want to create more slight movement in them—almost as if the cloud is hugging the main tower, but not too aggressively. It has to be subtle enough to create a more magical feeling. The way I painted this cloud's motion is very subtle, yet the scale of its movement is big.

Adding a small pool of light in the foreground helps to maximize the depth of the painting, and creates a more sophisticated light setting.

Fig. 3.87

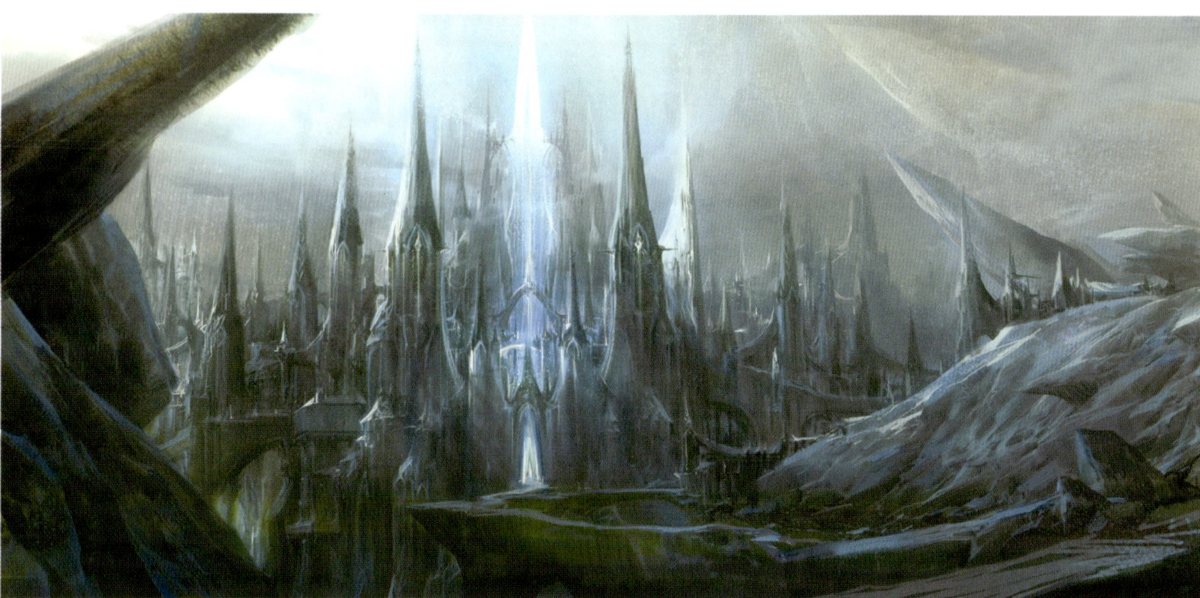

Fig. 3.88

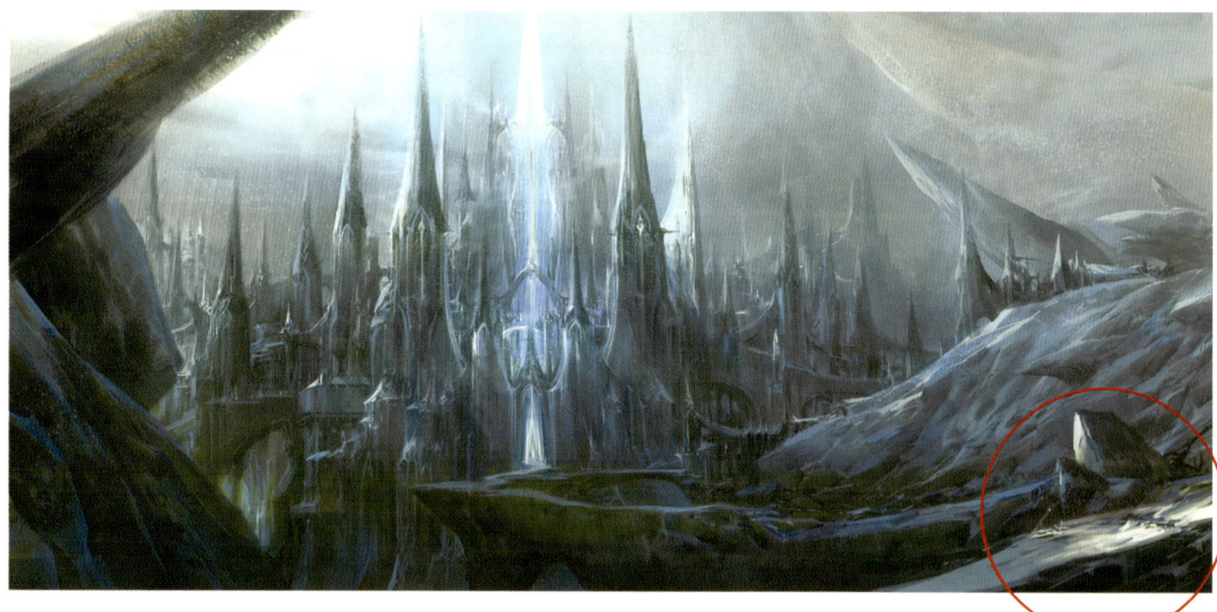

Fig. 3.89

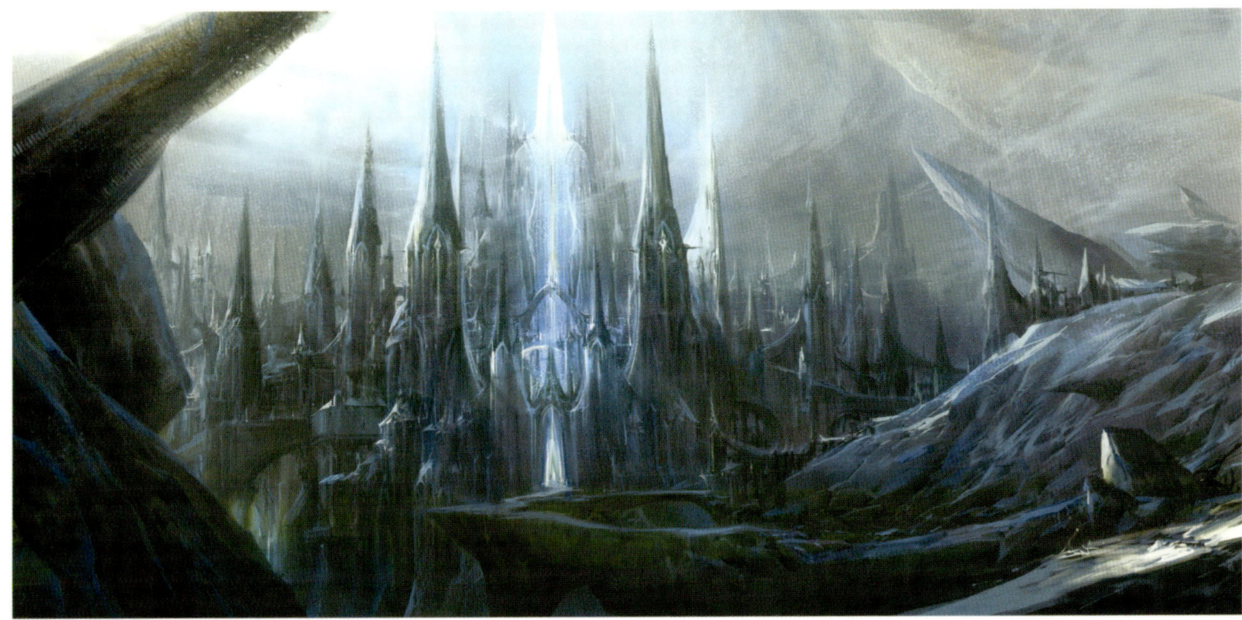

Before moving on to the last stage, I paint in more atmospheric effects. I push the background even further back on the right side, so that I can emphasize the main tower as the focal point. Additionally, I render the cloud shape more clearly to make it very obvious that a magical force is swiveling around the castle.

Lastly, I bump up the saturation of the castle area to create more saturation contrast in the painting.

Fig. 3.90

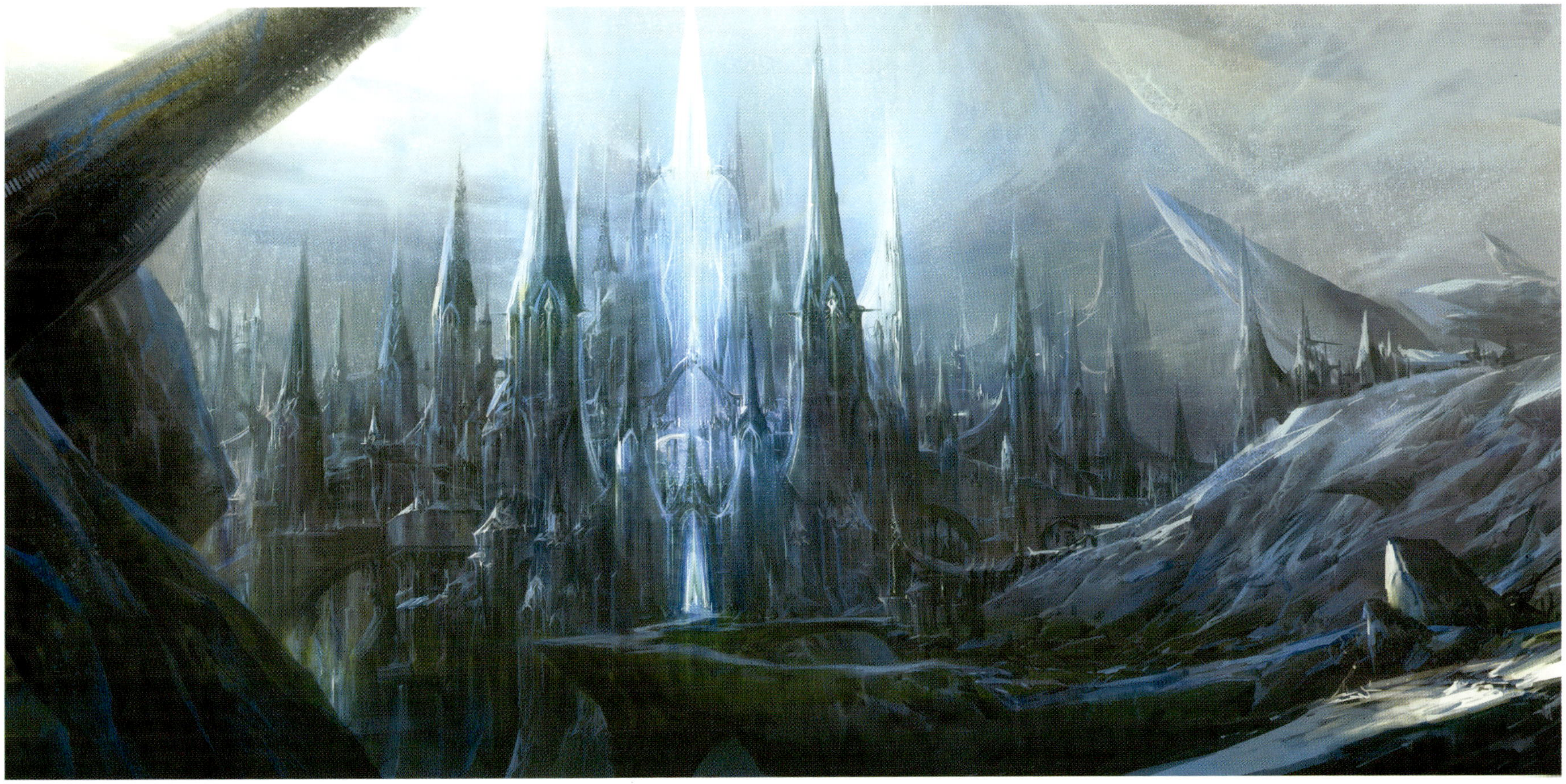

Fantasy Landscape

Fig. 3.91

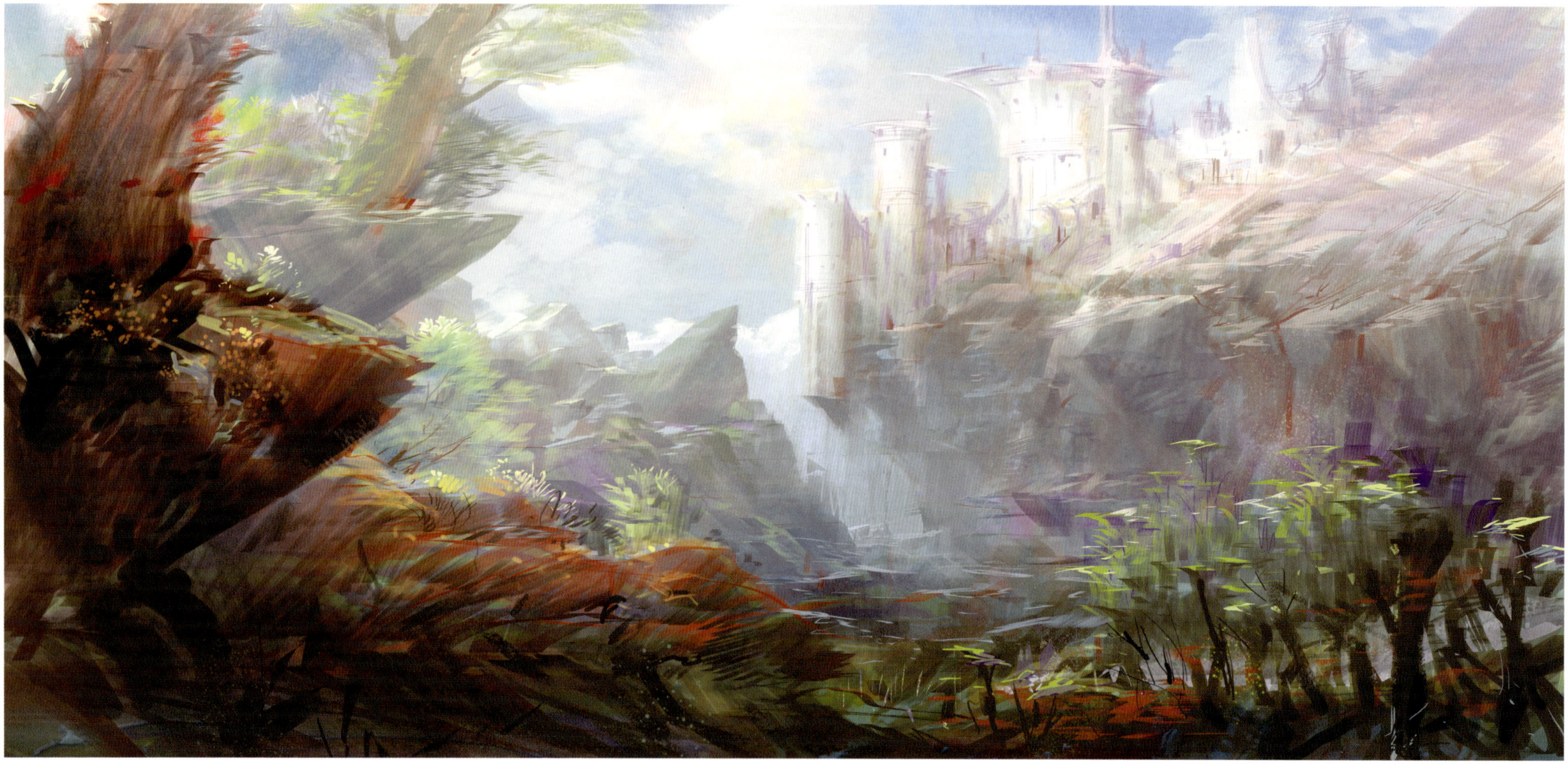

I get my inspiration from nature and beautiful paintings. After seeing a masterpiece, it makes me think of a lot of different things and I get mixed emotions about the artwork. That becomes my motivation and inspiration. I also have a similar feeling when I go out in nature and walk in a forest.

DK online. Copyright RPG Factory

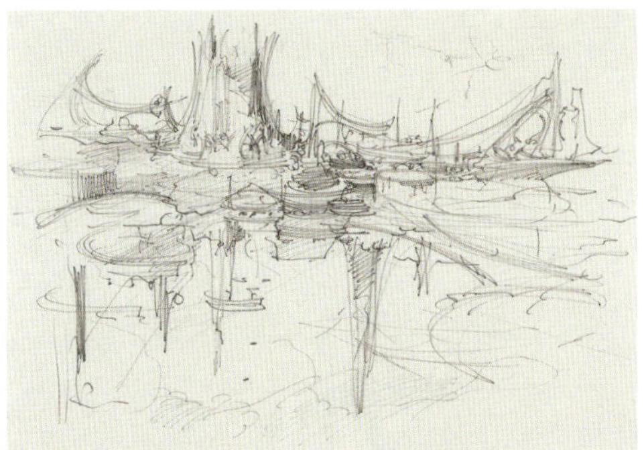 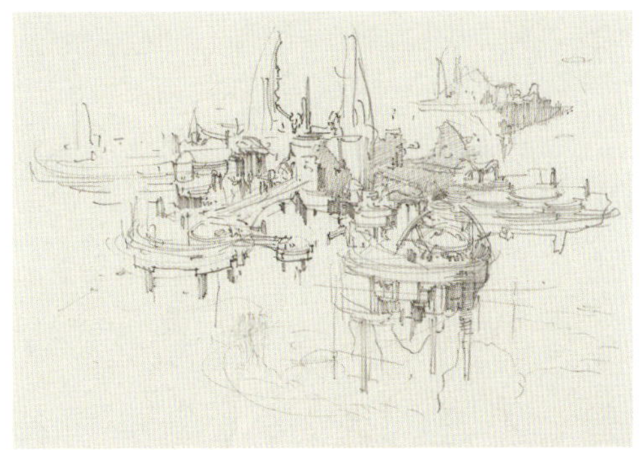 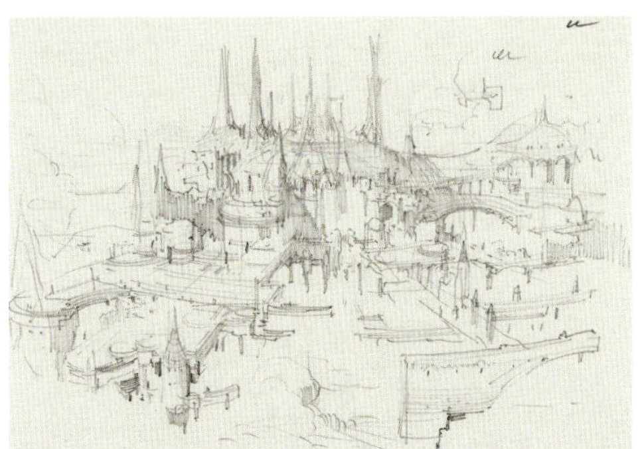 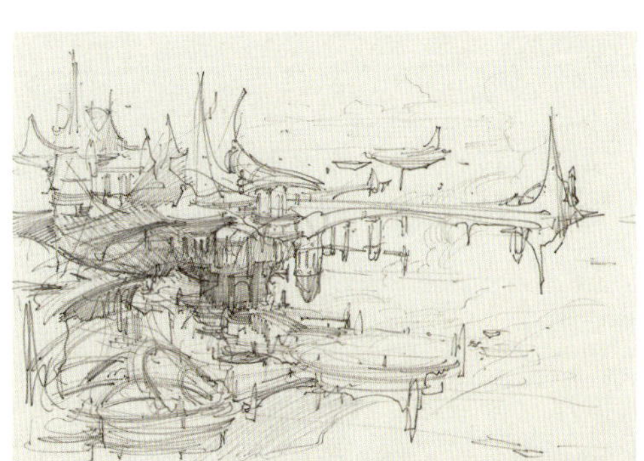

Chapter 03 - Landscape Tutorials

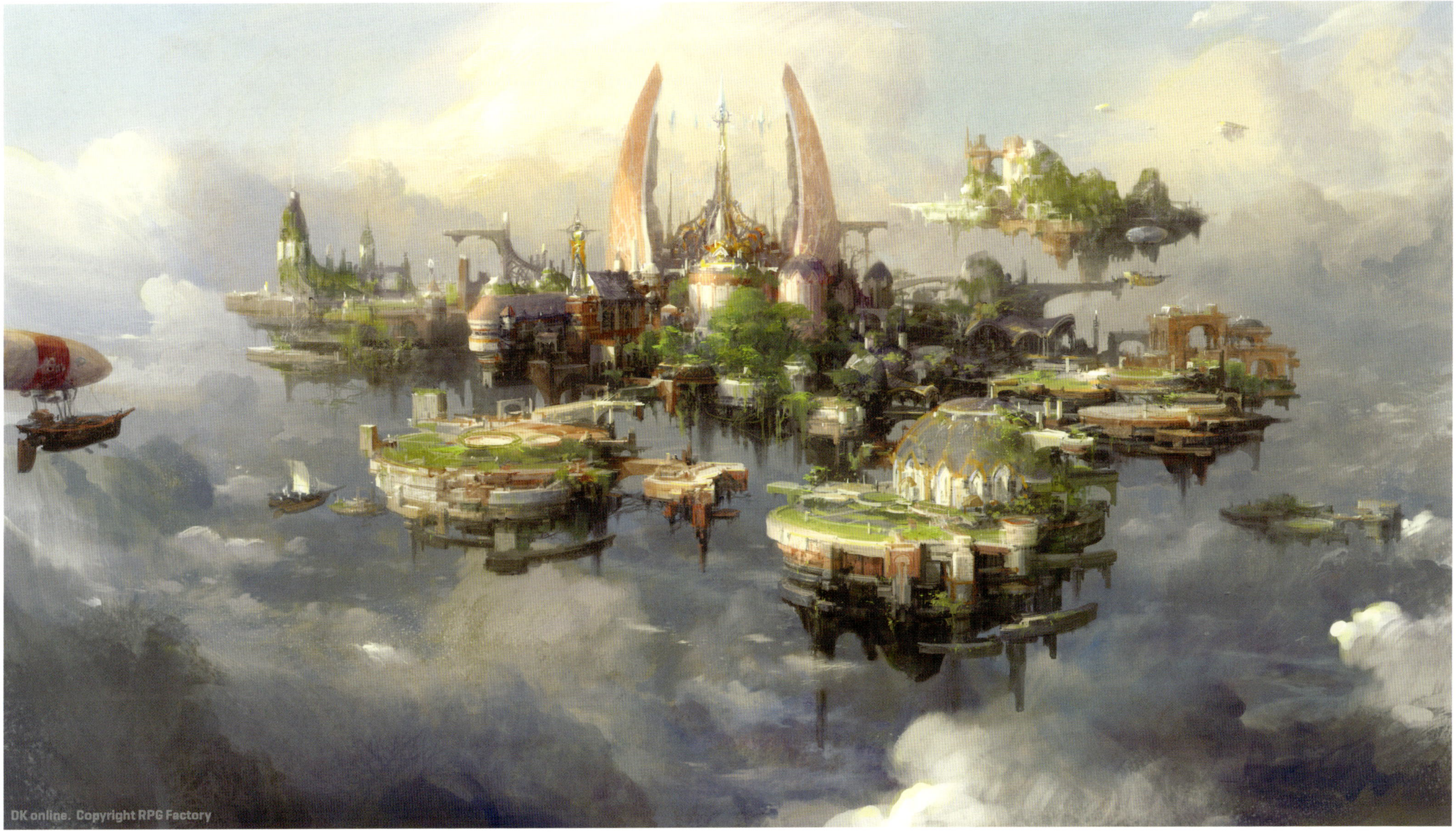

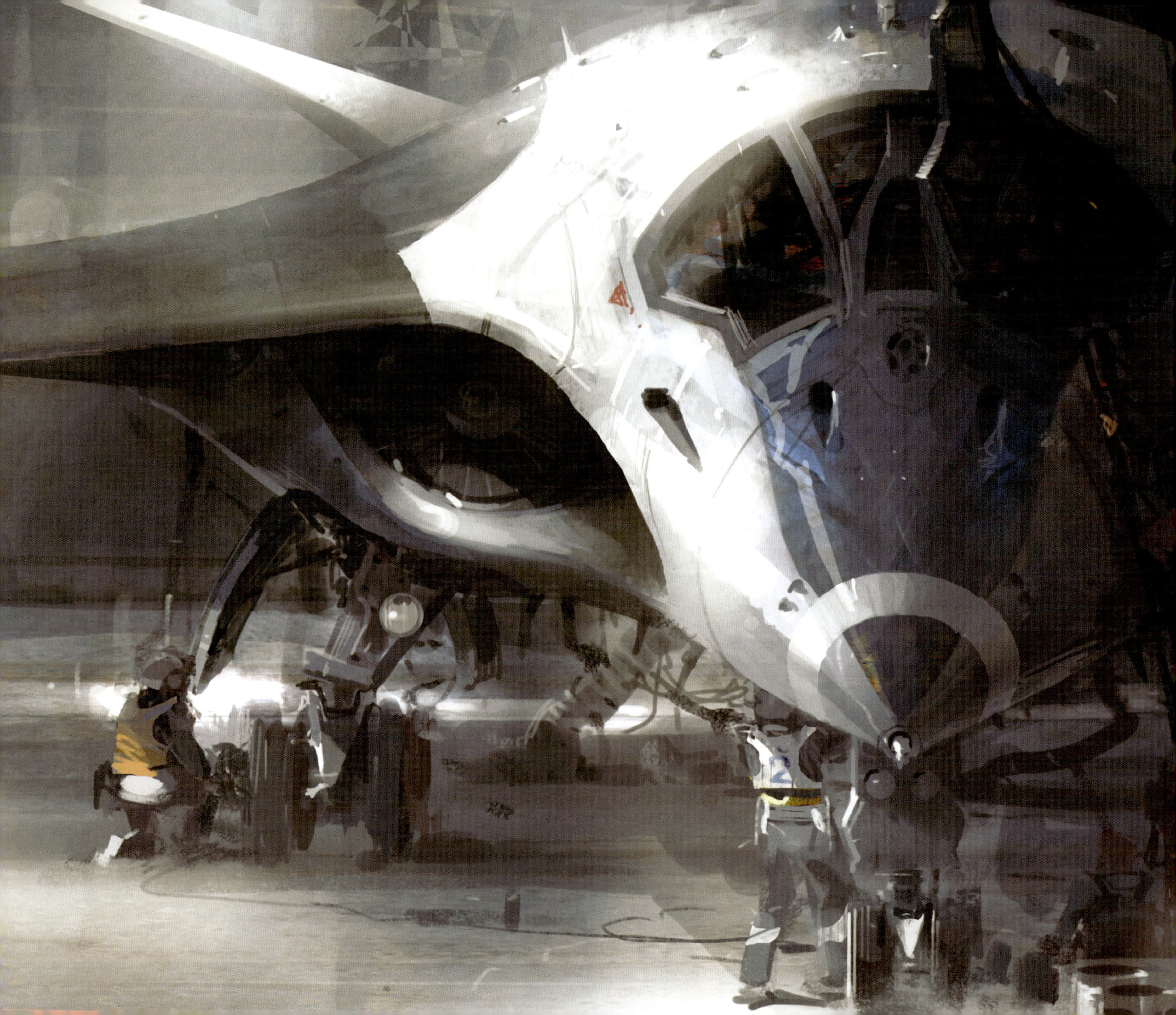

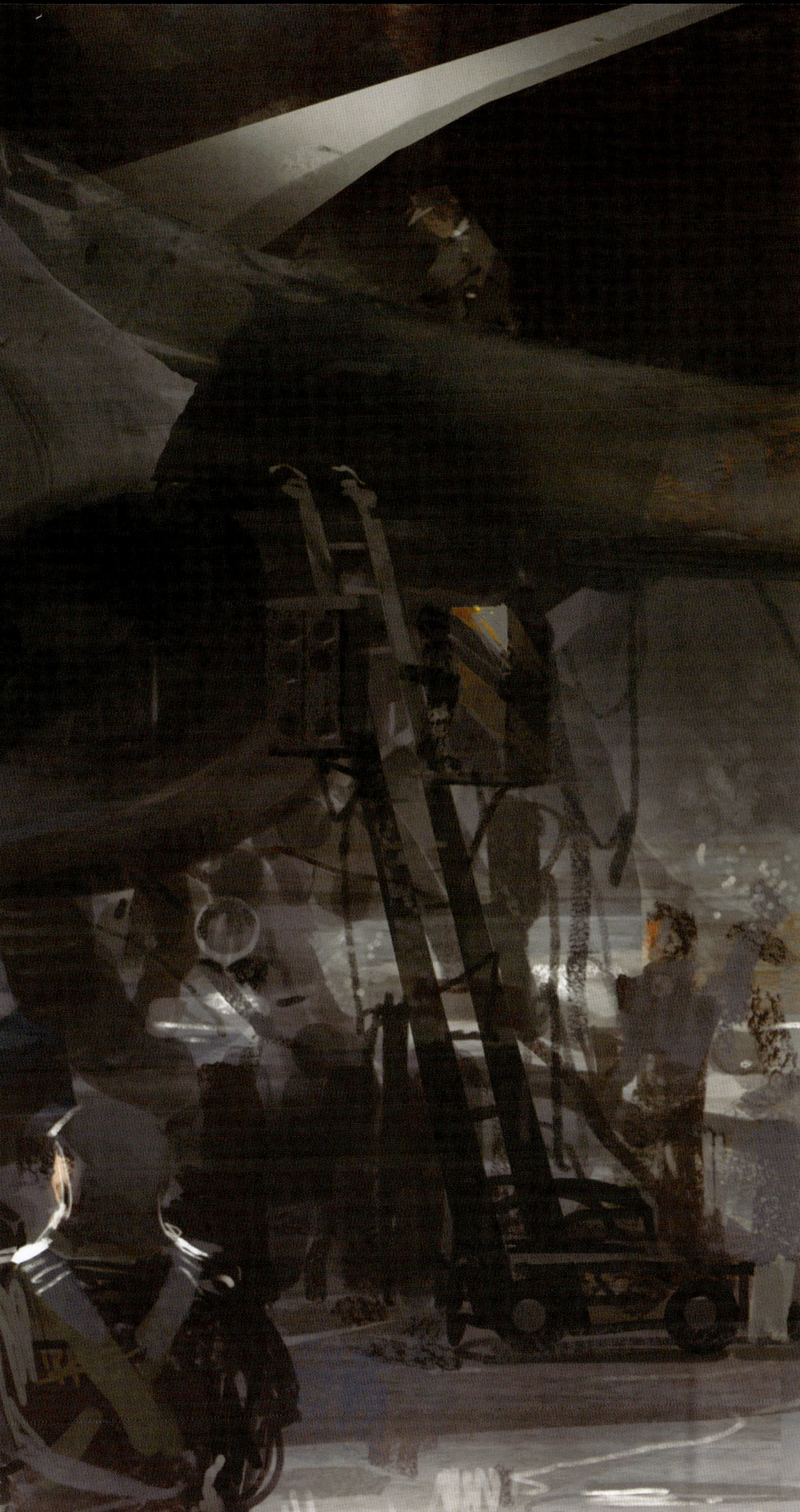

MINI TUTORIALS 04

In this chapter, I will share many mini tutorials with less detailed descriptions. Since I explained painting principles in great detail in previous tutorials, here I want to share more progress shots with minimal explanation. I will show a finished painting in four to six progress steps, revealing how I started the painting and how I advanced to the final stage. This should make perfect sense by now since we have already covered the whole process in the preceding tutorials. Seeing the process from start to finish should distinguish what makes a finished painting versus a painting in progress.

Fig. 4.1

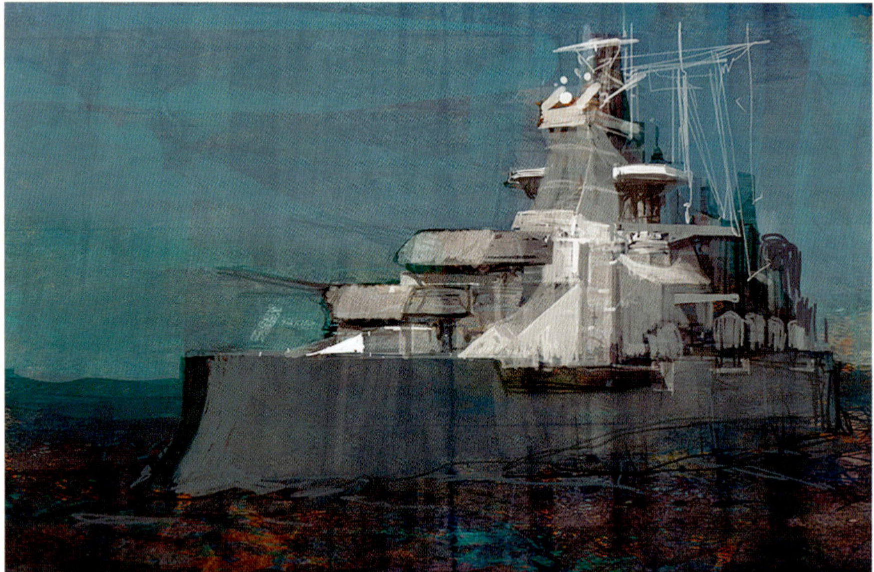

Fig. 4.2

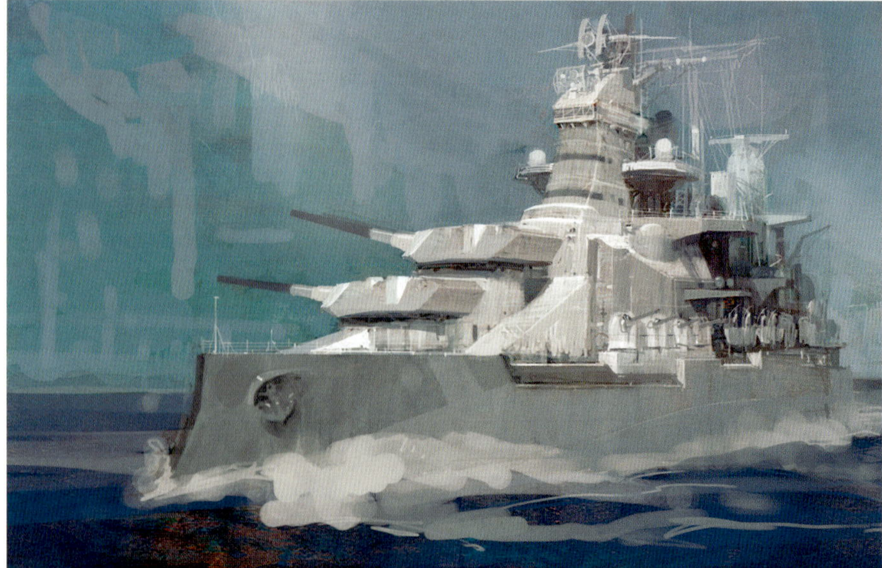

Fig. 4.3

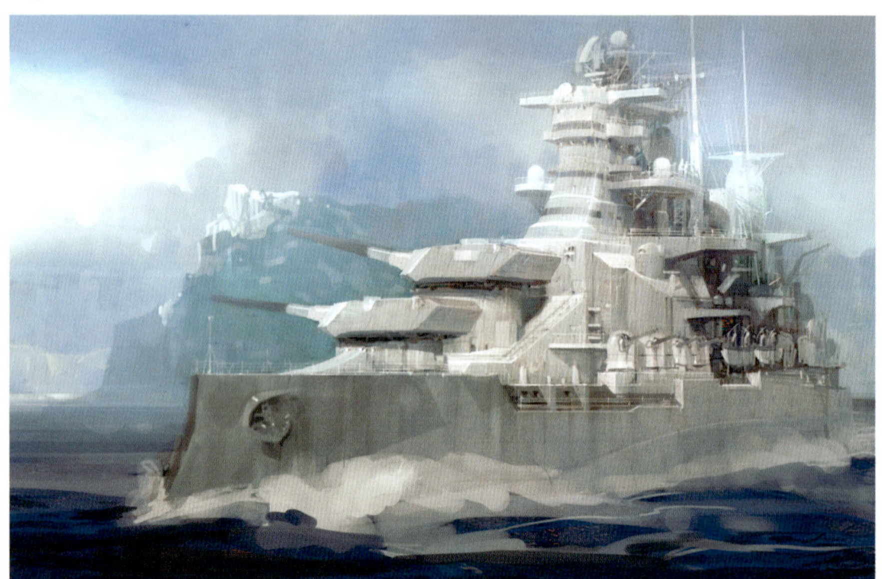

Fig. 4.4

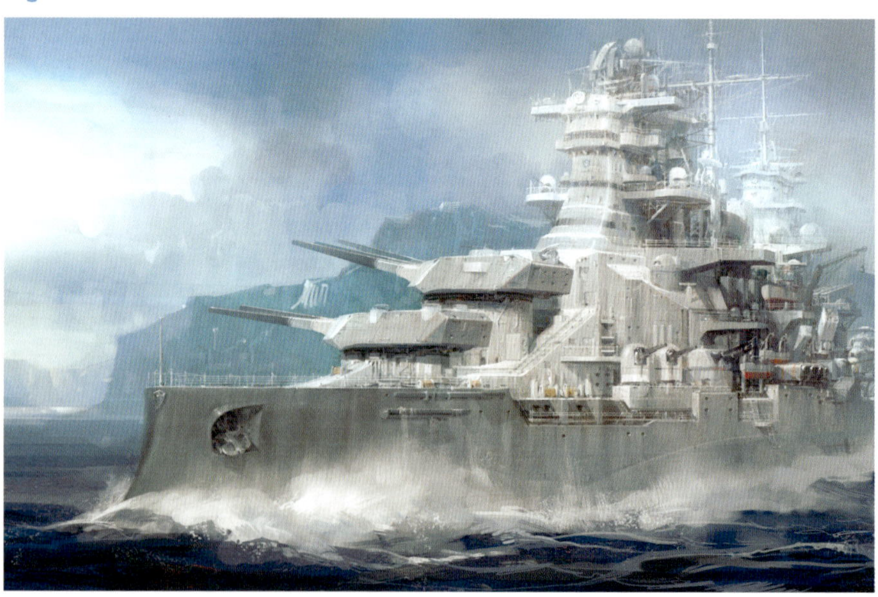

First, I start to paint a background texture by using acrylic paint on paper (Fig. 4.1). I use thick paint marks to create the texture I want for my base layer. The base-layer painting can be any color, but I used a bluish tone to match the subject I want to paint.

Second, after bringing the snapshot into Photoshop, I start to paint in the big shapes of the ship and ocean (Fig. 4.2).

Then, I start to paint the sky and background (Fig. 4.3). However, I do not cover up the base layer completely; I take advantage of the background texture.

Next, I bring up the details without breaking the big shape (Fig. 4.4).

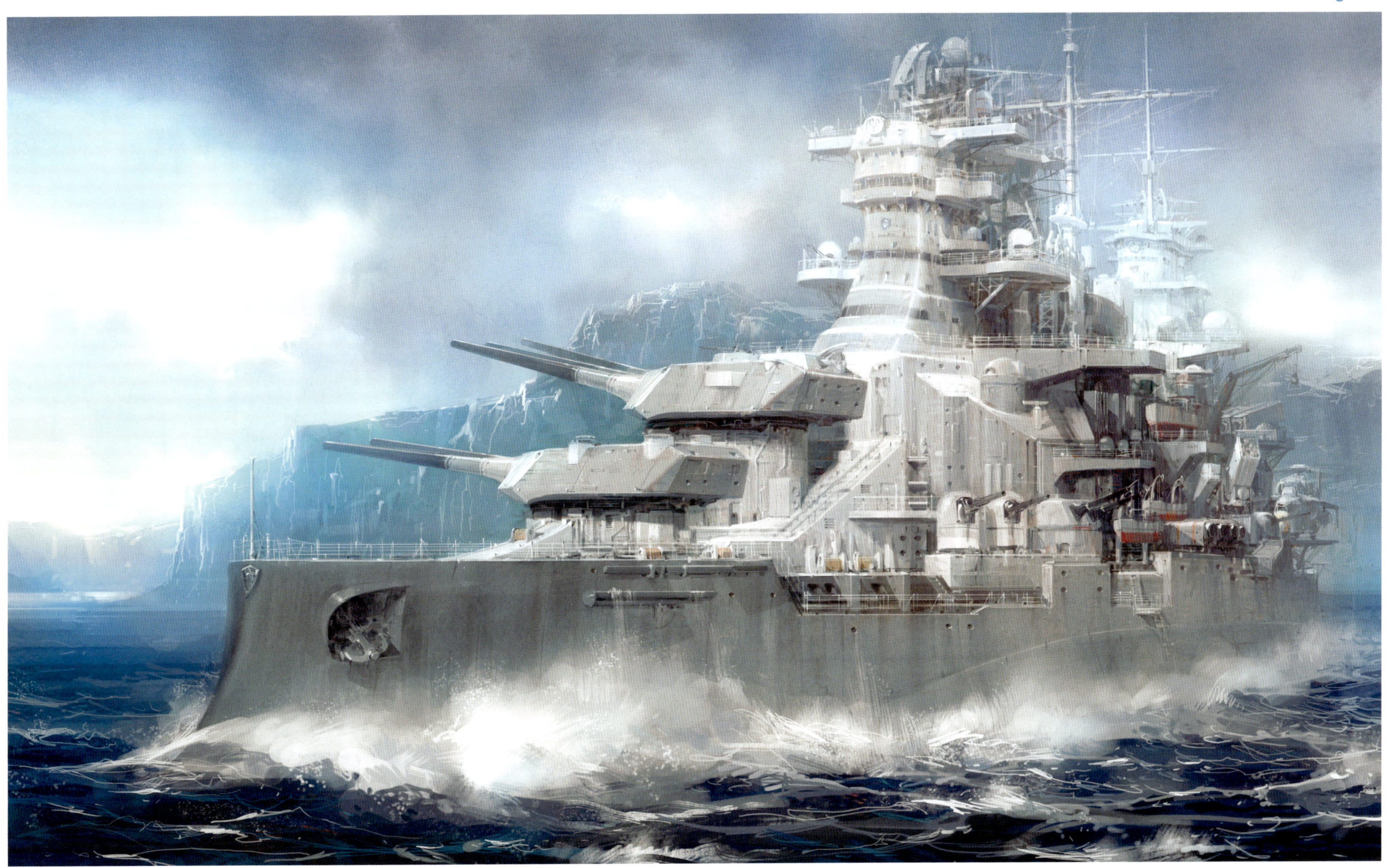

I then select the section that gets the most light and make it sharp and clear to draw the viewer's attention. And I make the paint look more defined and keep developing the details as I go. As I explained many times in previous tutorials, do not get too bound to the original design. Modify the design anytime it is necessary.

The last step in this process is painting more details on the main ship. Since the main subject was a little underdeveloped compared to the background, I add sharper details to its body.

Fig. 4.6

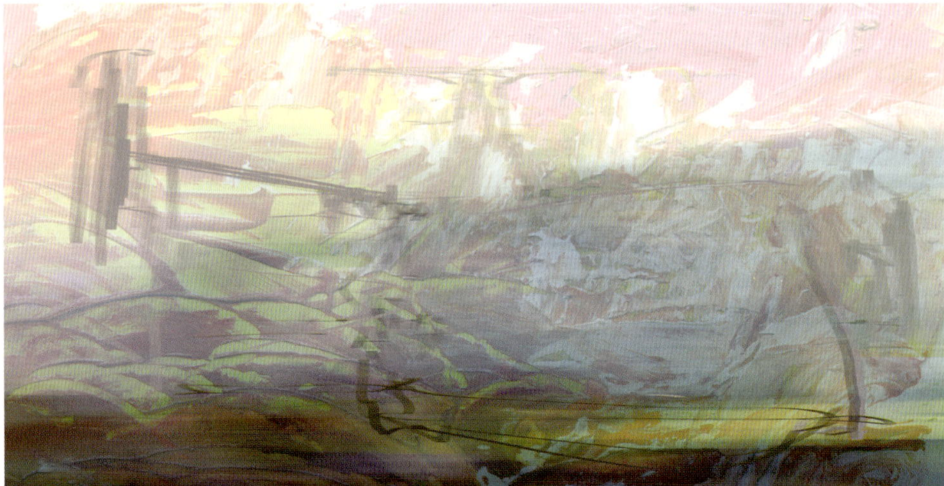

Fig. 4.7

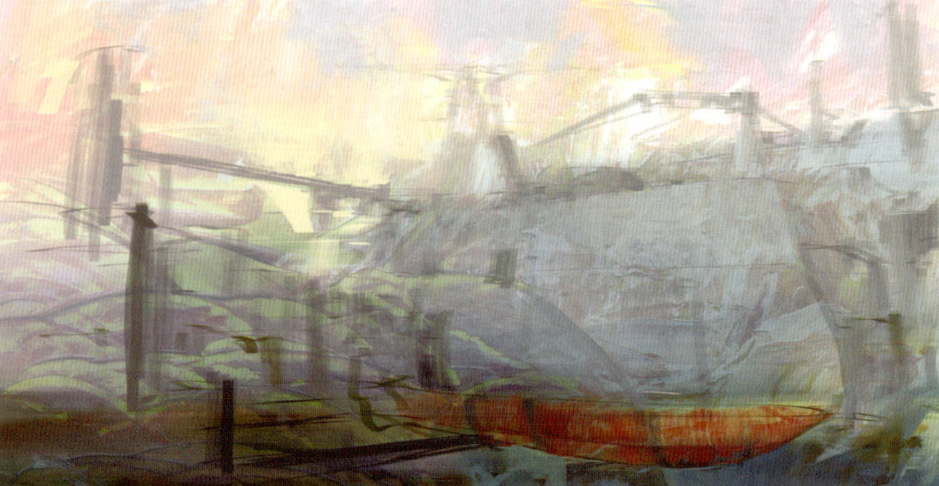

Fig. 4.8

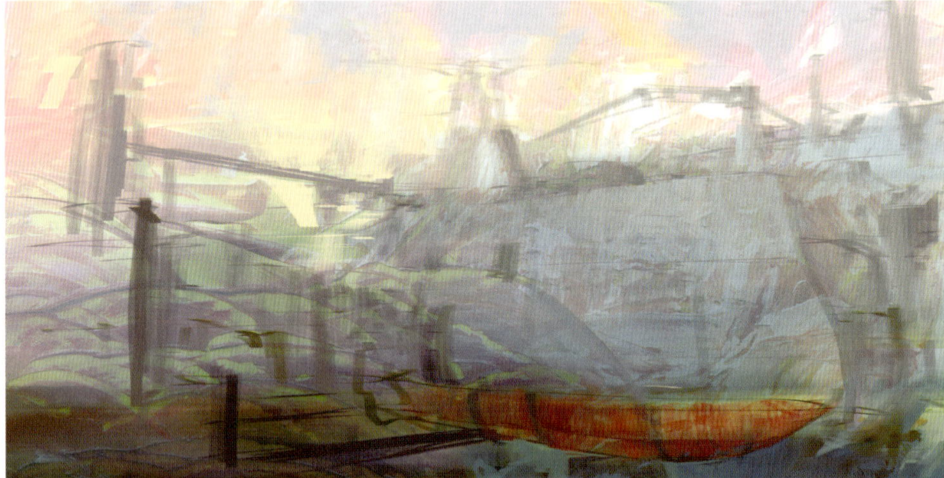

Fig. 4.9

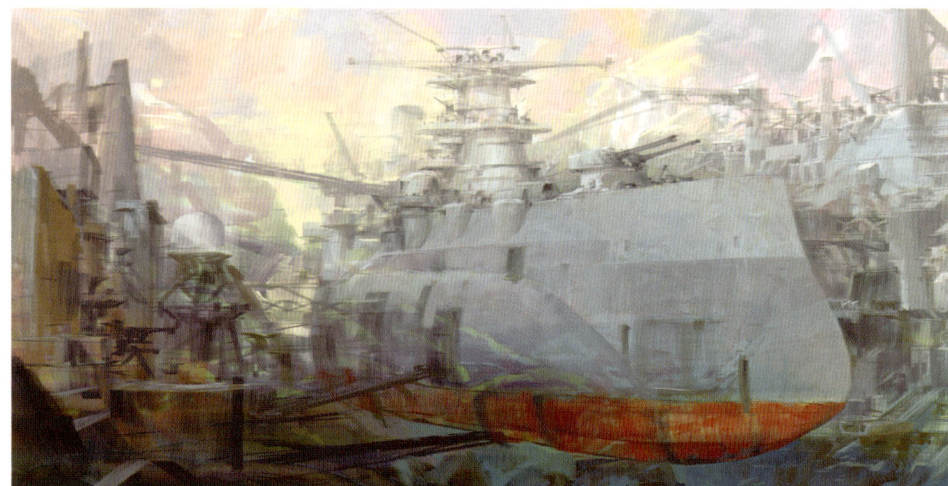

Fig. 4.10

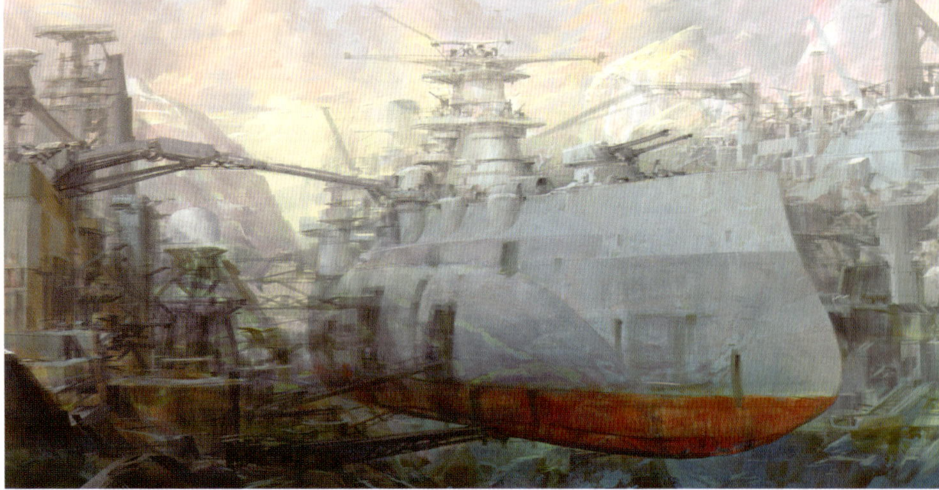

Fig. 4.11

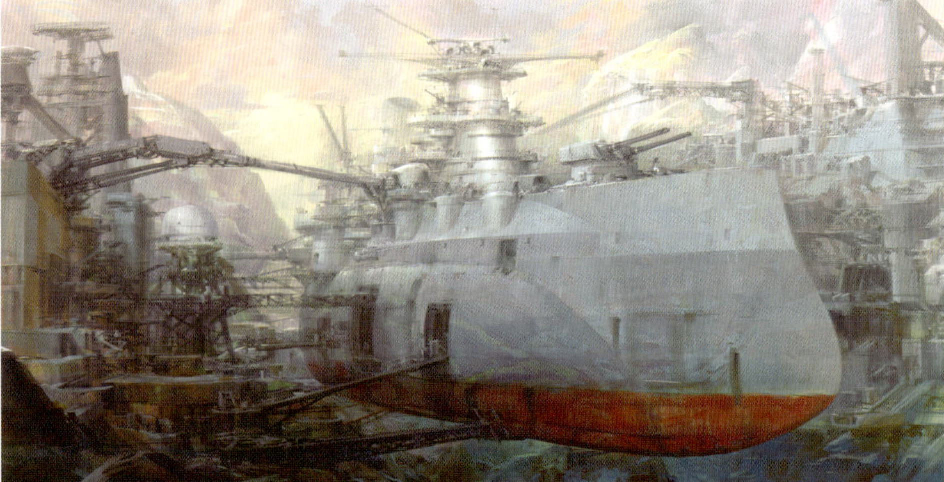

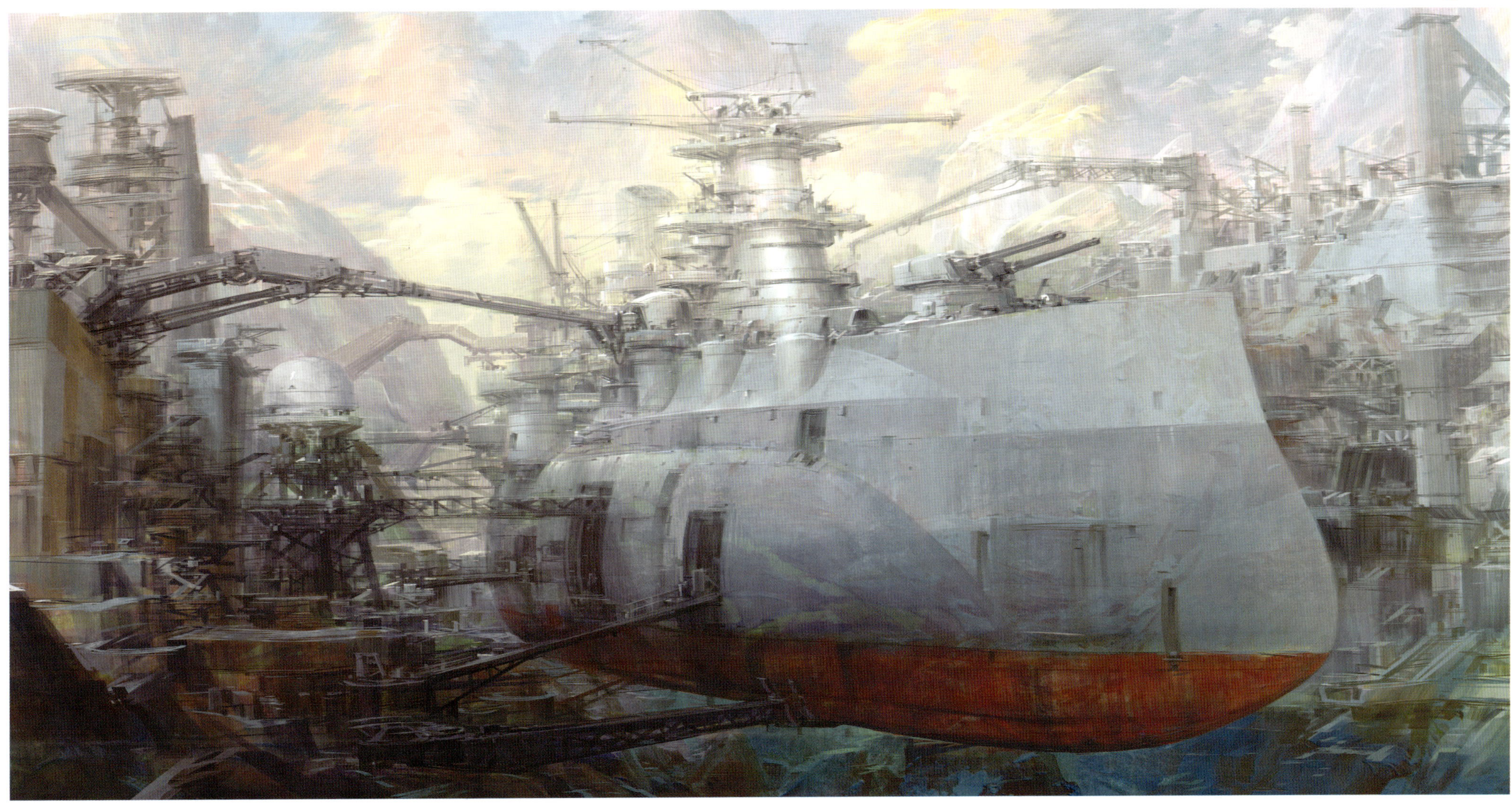

Again, I start to paint a random background texture by using acrylic paint on paper. I use a palette knife to create the texture I want for my base layer. The base-layer painting can be any color. The color choice depends on the main color scheme of the painting. Here, I used a yellowish pink. Once I am happy with the result, I take a snapshot of it and bring that photo into Photoshop and start to paint as usual. As I make progress on the painting, I try to use the base color as much as possible. Covering up the base color kills the color variation of a painting too quickly. Note that this is just one of the many ways I could start my painting. There are various ways to start a painting; I am sharing some options to create more interesting paintings.

Fig. 4.13

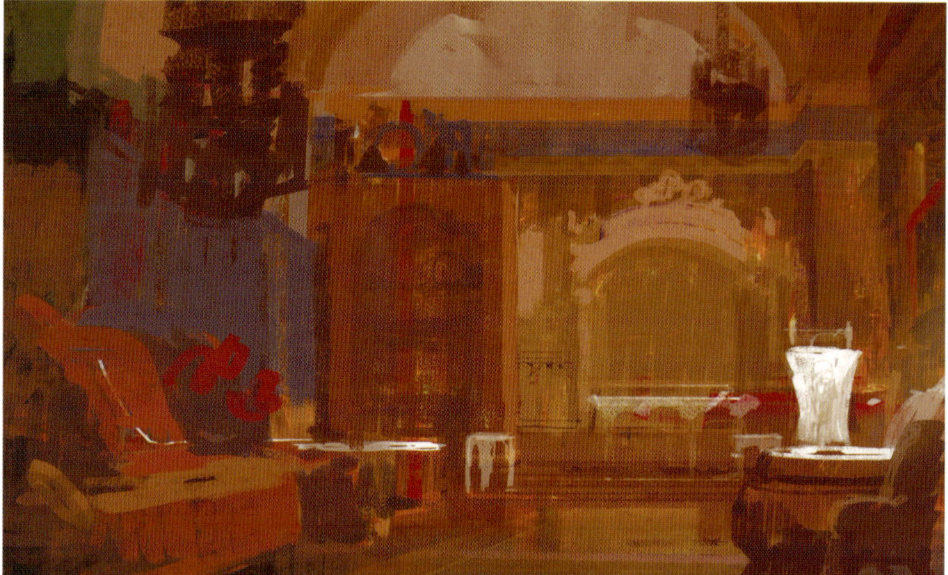

Fig. 4.14

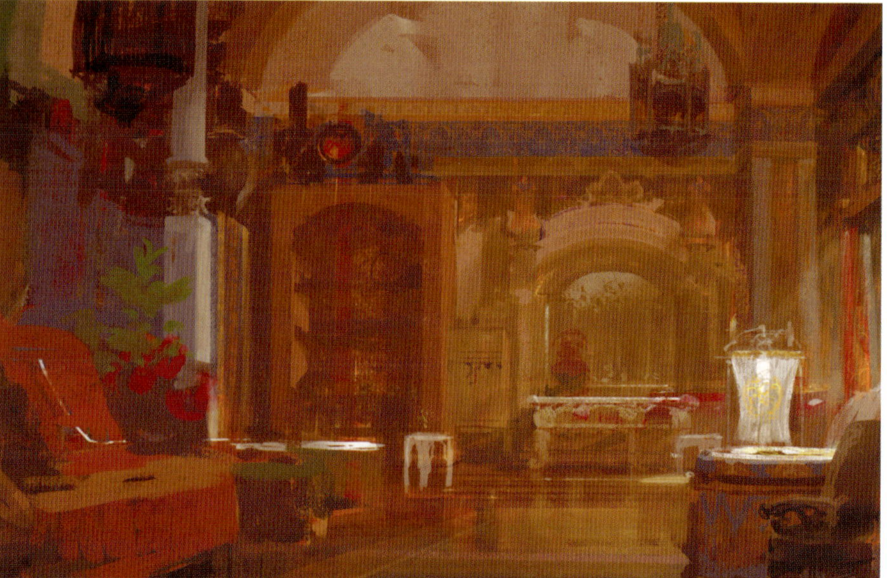

Fig. 4.15

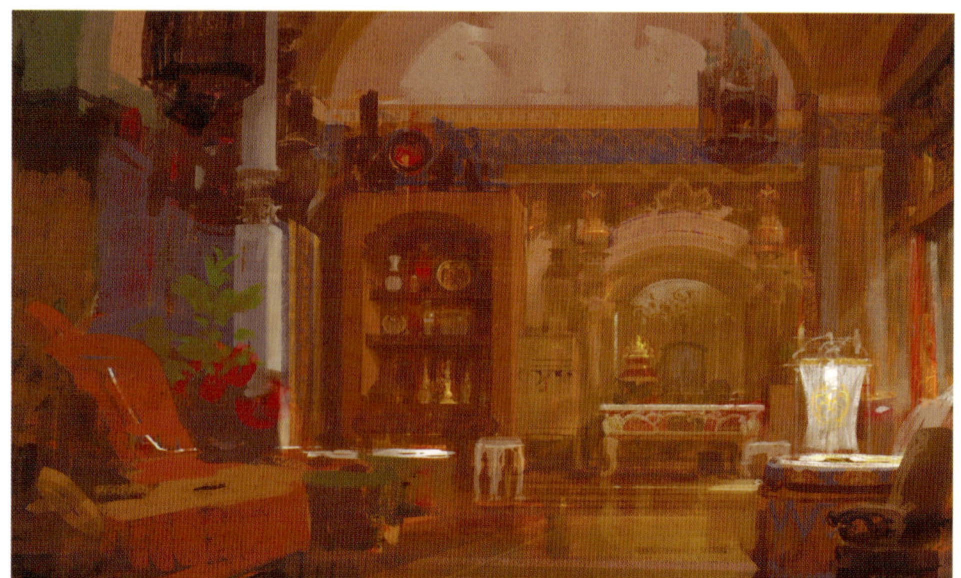

Fig. 4.16

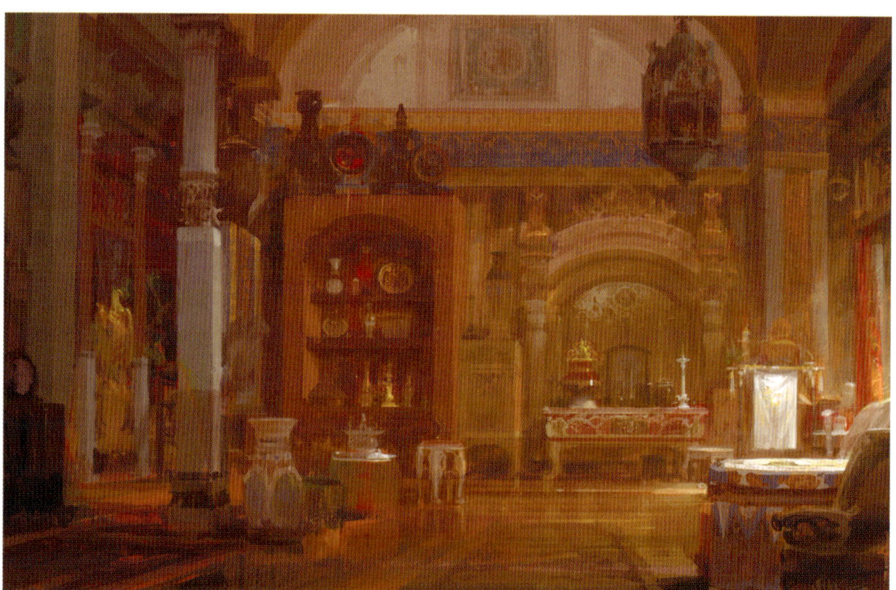

In this example, I paint the main color of the room a reddish brown. I start with local color, without worrying about the color of light at first (Fig. 4.13–14). As I make more progress, I add more lighting information and more colors (Fig. 4.15). Yet at the same time, I have to work with a darker value as well as a lighter tone in order to understand the full value range of the painting. Sometimes I use the Burn tool to darken the whole portion. A good thing about this tool is that you can darken the value while keeping the original texture. Once I put down the base color, I use the Burn tool to create a darker shadow color, and to repaint on top of that color. I also use some full-opacity brushstrokes to give clearer definition to the form and to create a greater contrast between soft and hard brushstrokes (Fig. 4.16).

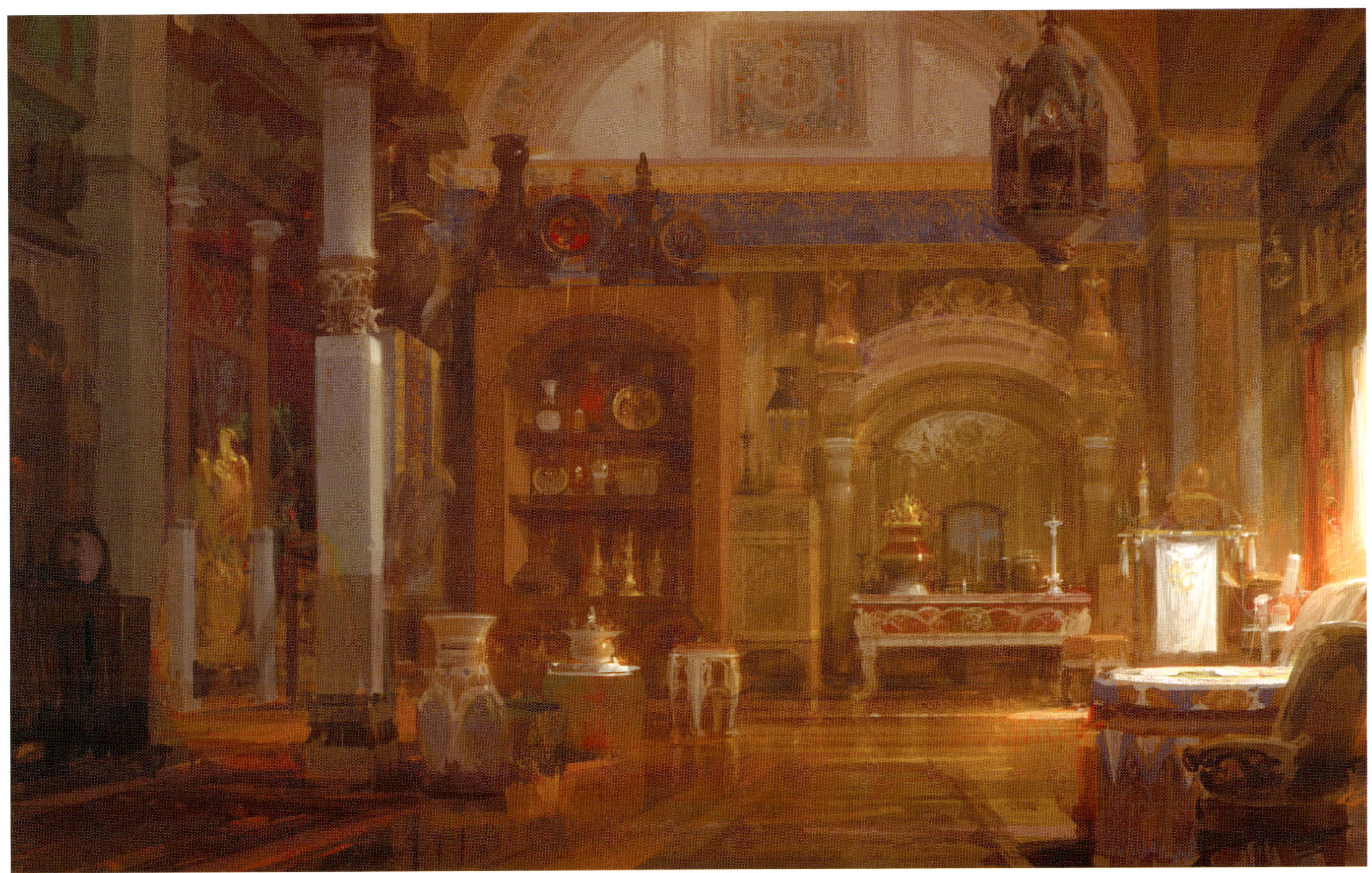

By the end of the process I tend to use the Eyedropper tool to pick colors that already exist on the palette and emphasize the harmony of the existing color in the painting. I use the Lasso tool to make a clean selection on a certain part of the painting, where I add crisp, clean lines to make the painting look tighter. But one thing to remember when using the Lasso tool to paint straight edges: don't try to paint corner to corner, it is better to suggest the form by painting the beginning and the end, and letting other areas breathe.

In this tutorial, similar to the one on the previous pages, I am going to demonstrate how to create a room interior with natural lighting in the background. First, I block in starting background colors. These background colors have a lot of medium-value color, which is very useful as a starting point.

One advantage of using the Color Dodge brush is that I can save the drawing lines and underpainting brushstrokes. A more natural look is achieved when one can see the layers of the brushstrokes; this necessitates not painting over everything. Be careful not to add too much color, or it will make everything appear too saturated and too colorful.

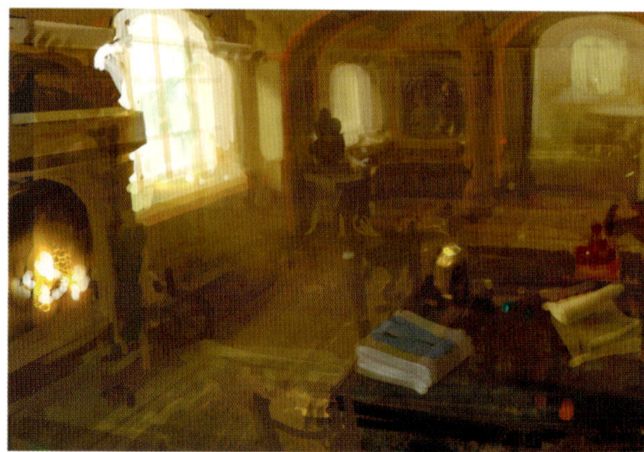

Fig. 4.18

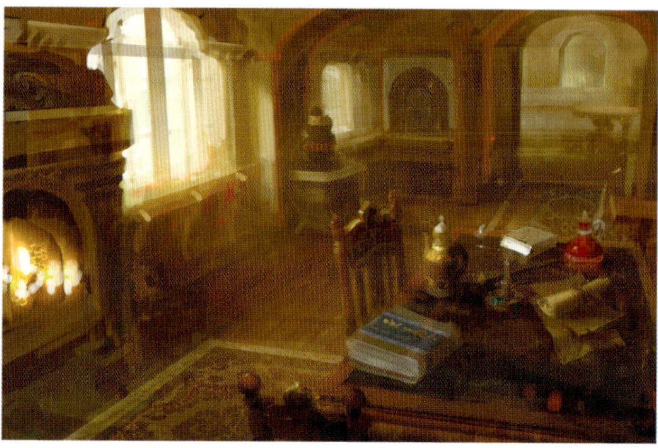

Fig. 4.19

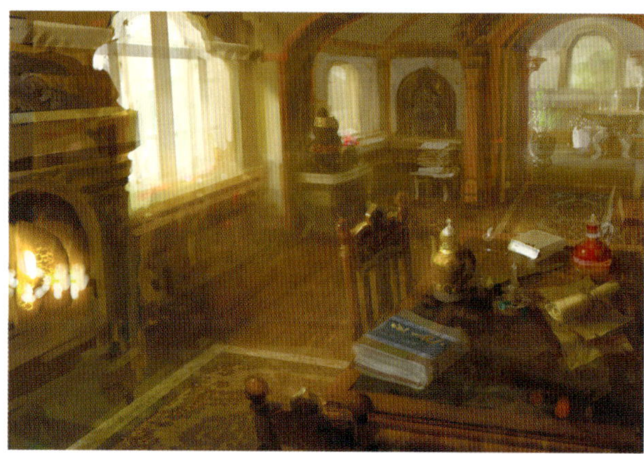

Fig. 4.20

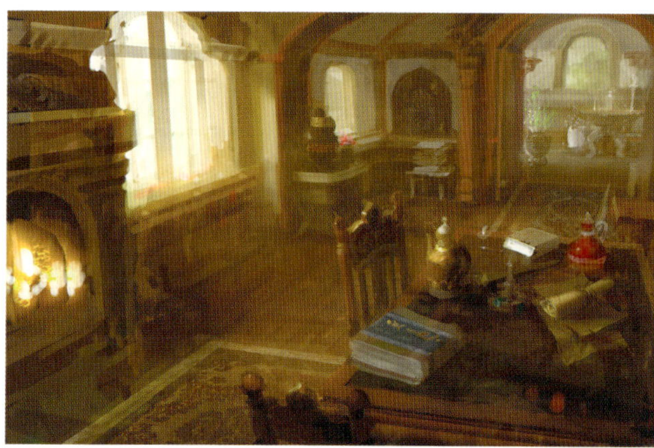

Fig. 4.21

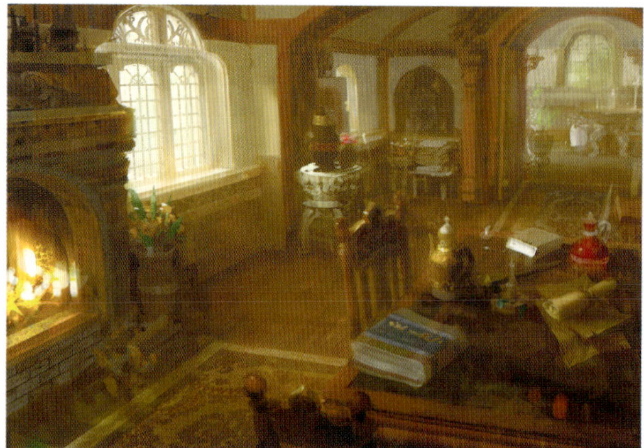

Fig. 4.22

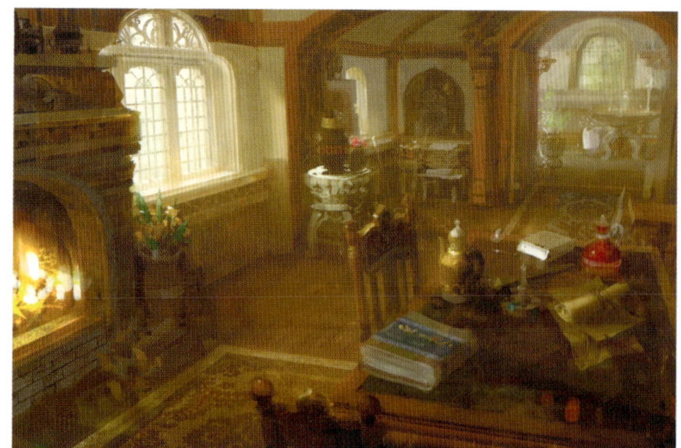

Fig. 4.23

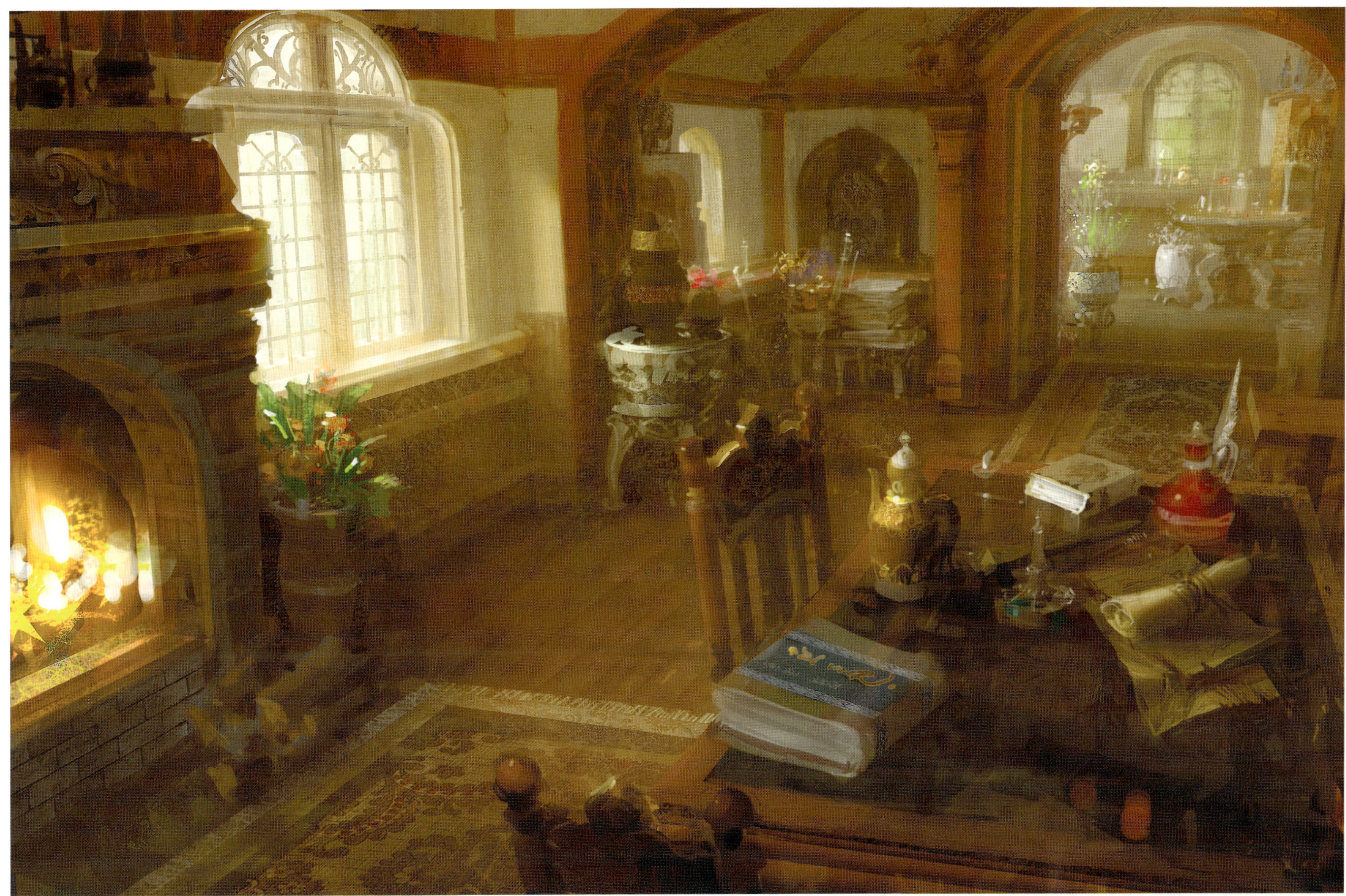

To give the painting volumetric light, I selected a section with the Lasso tool. Then I set my brush at Color Dodge mode and painted the atmosphere. This technique creates more depth in the painting. After adding atmosphere, I repainted certain sections to make them look clean and sharp. I double-checked the perspective to be sure that I had followed the initial direction that I had planned at the beginning of the work.

Fig. 4.25

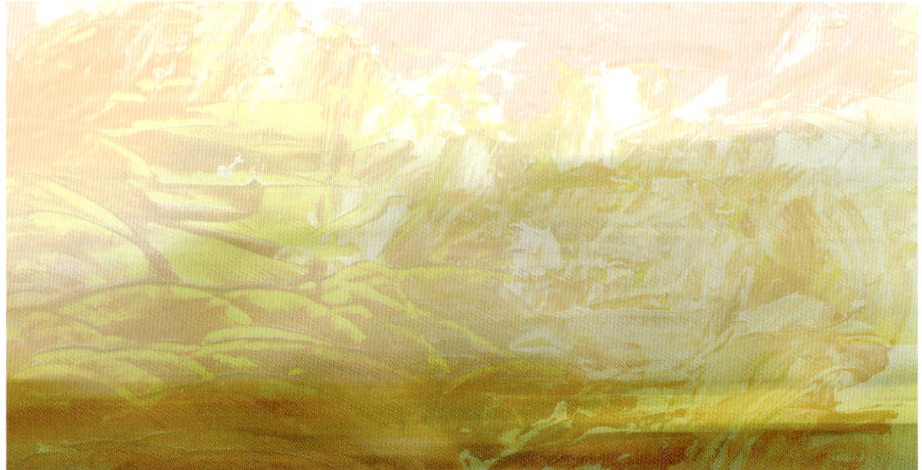

Fig. 4.26

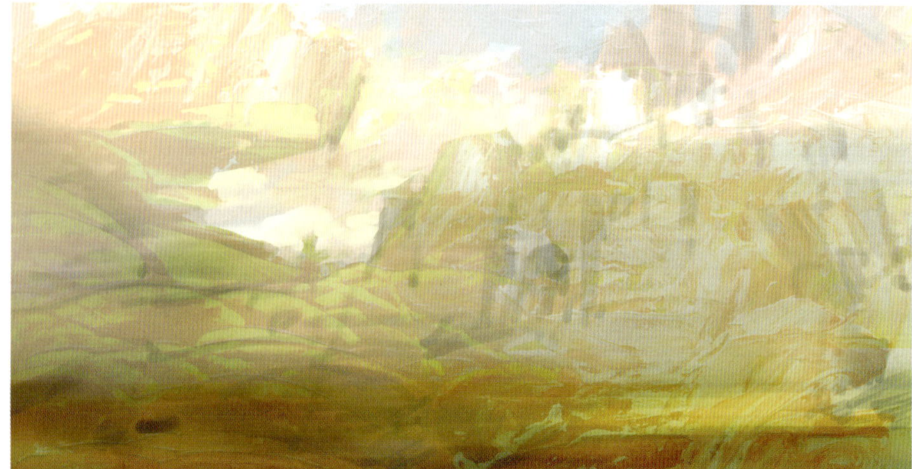

Fig. 4.27

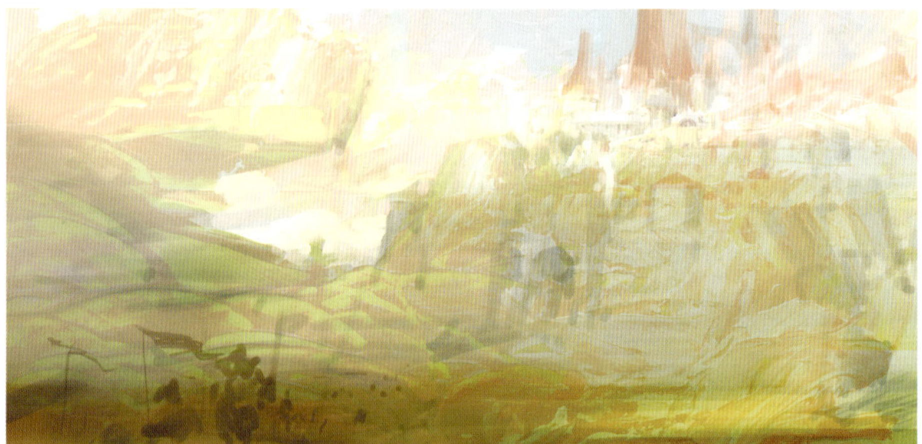

Fig. 4.28

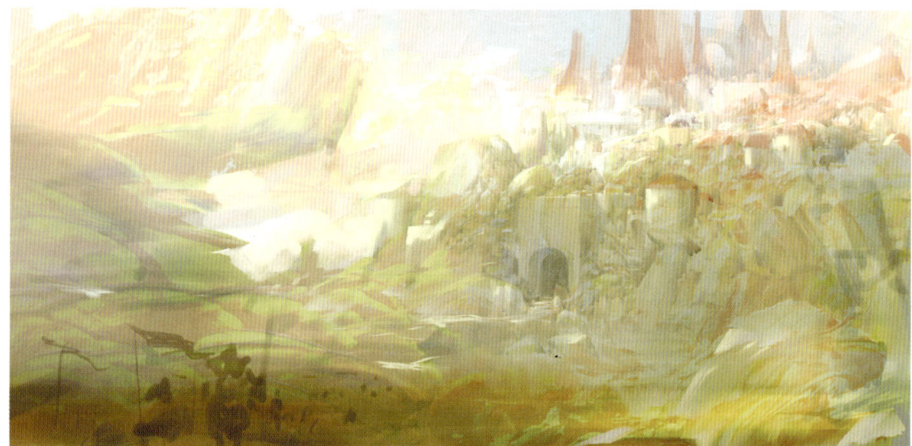

Fig. 4.29

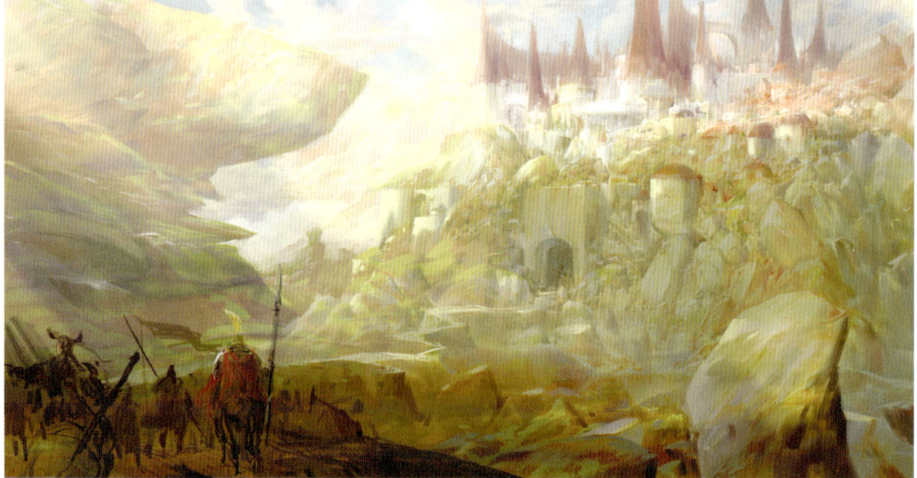

Fig. 4.30

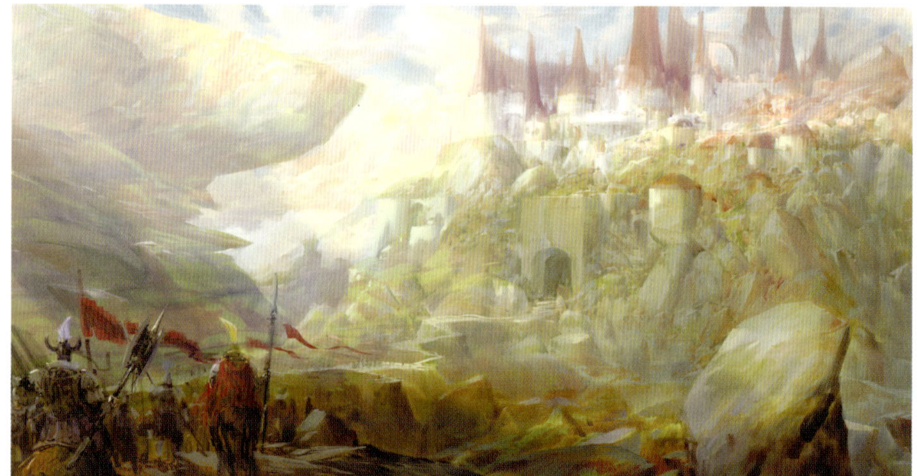

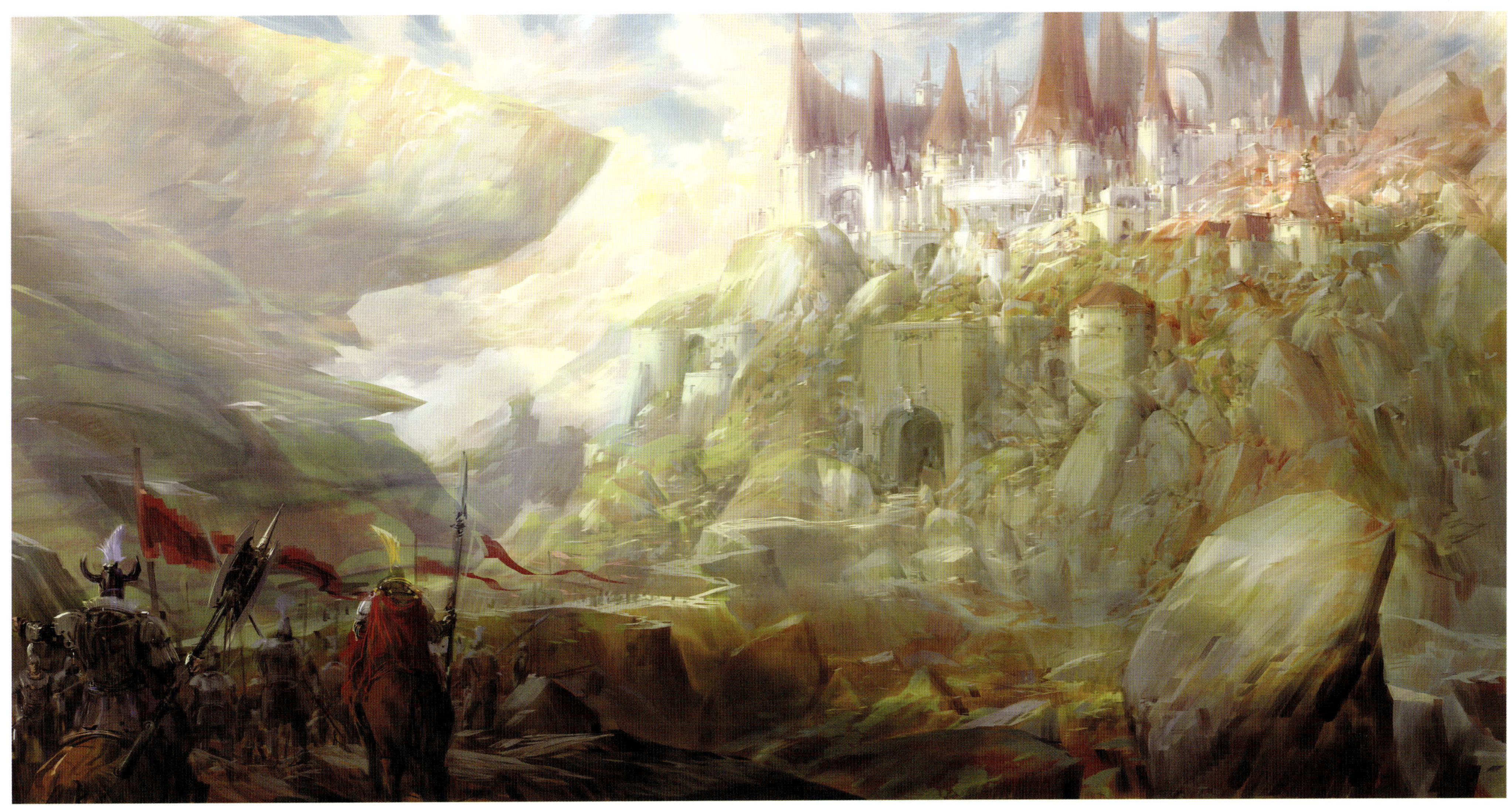

In Fig. 4.25, I started with the same acrylic base texture that I used for the Fantasy Cityscapes tutorial (Fig 3.13). Then I started to block in the big shape, and slowly added the local color of the main subject: the castle (Fig. 4.26). I added more details as I went on, including darkening the foreground to give more contrast (Fig. 4.27-28). This helps to create a more atmospheric effect. As part of this process, I painted figures in the foreground as a storytelling element (Fig. 4.29-30). I keep developing a picture until I feel like it has a nice balance overall (Fig. 4.31).

Fig. 4.32

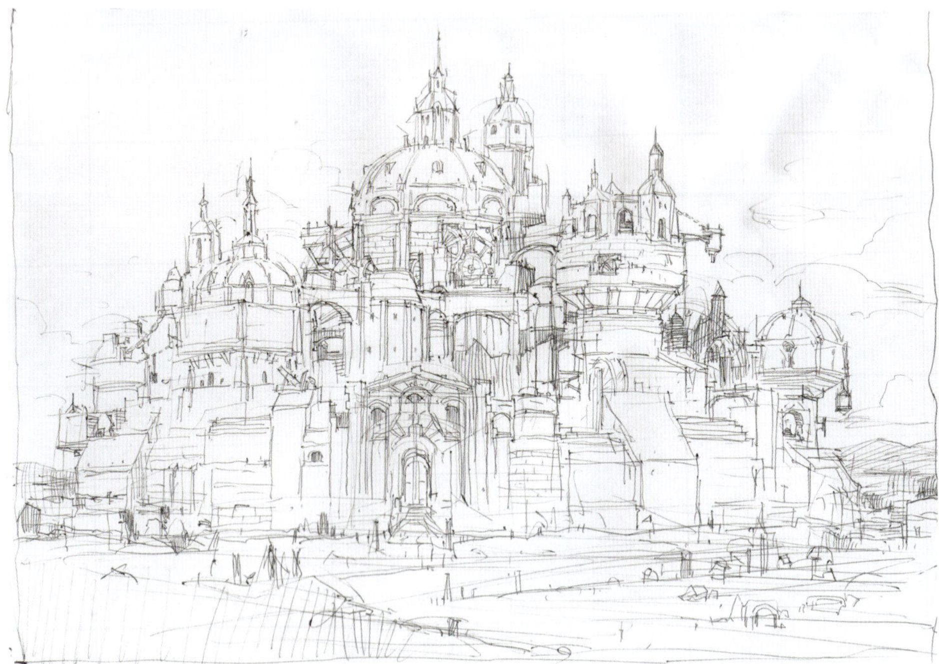

Fig. 4.33

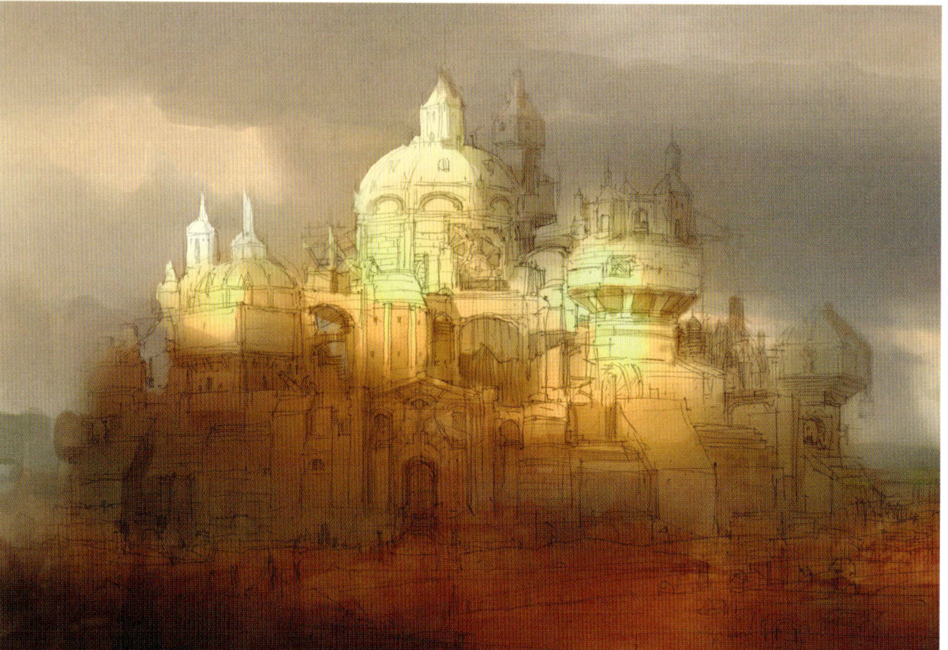

Fig. 4.34

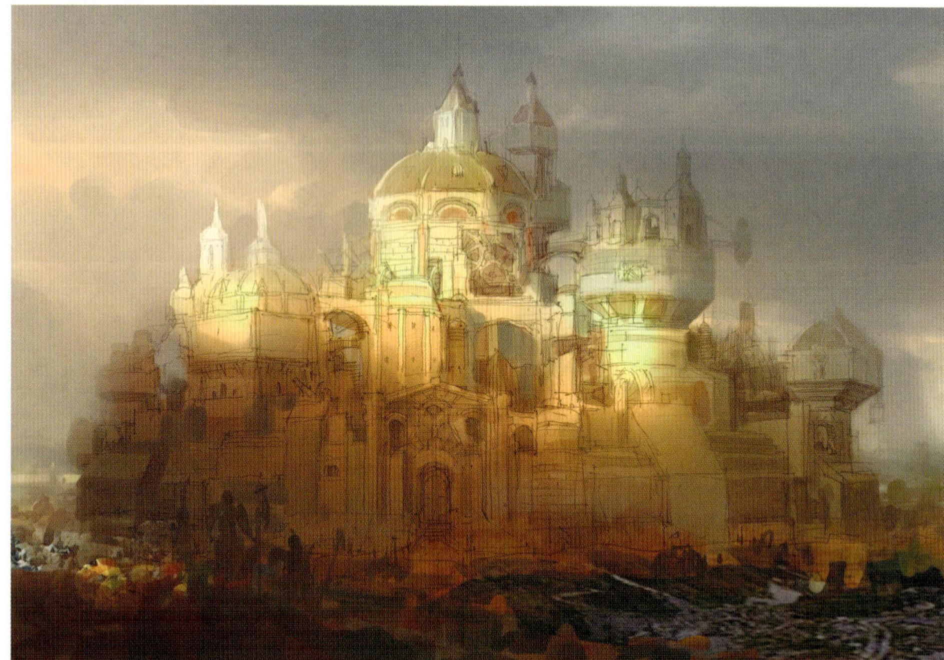

Fig. 4.35

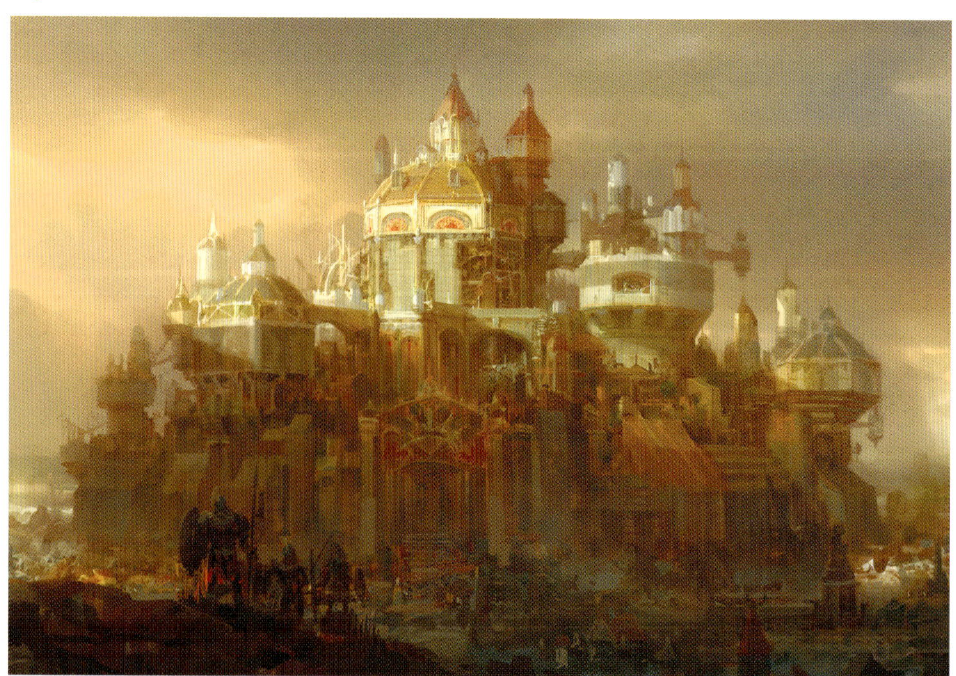

In this painting, I started with a pen sketch I did on A4 paper (Fig. 4.32). Once I am happy with a sketch, I scan it and set it up as a Multiply layer in Photoshop. I blocked in background color with a lot of medium-value color, which is very useful as a starting point. As in prior pieces, I generally block in the big shape first and then add more details (Fig. 4.33–34). It's important to try to keep a balance of shapes unbroken as you add details (Fig. 4.35). Once again, I have preserved the pencil marks as much as possible, since I always want to use them as another cool texture in the painting.

Fig. 4.36

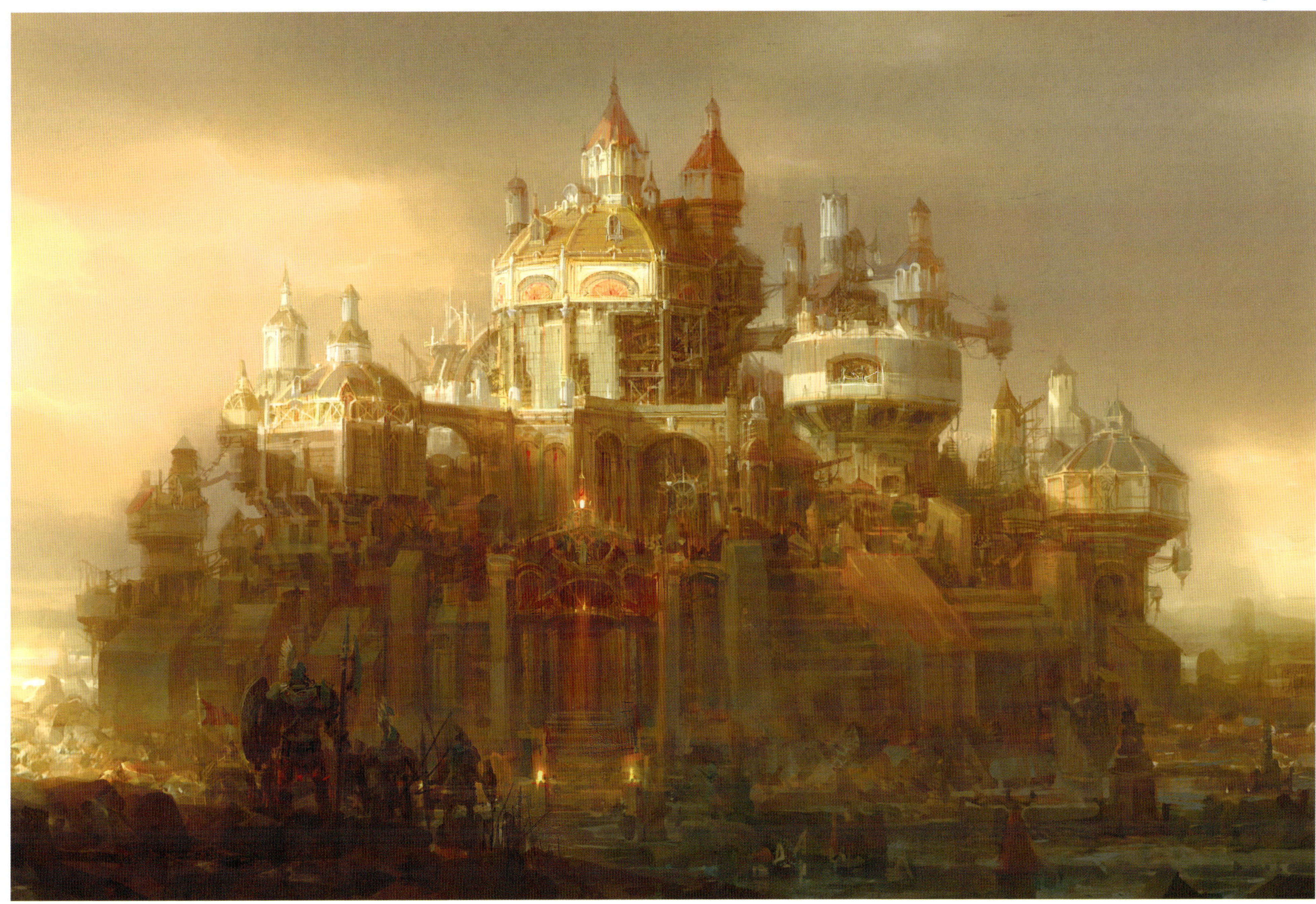

Different light and shadow shapes create different feels. It was getting a little too dark in the shadow area, so I added a bit more torch light to counterbalance it (Fig. 4.36). This also gives a good scale indicator to the painting.

Fig. 4.37

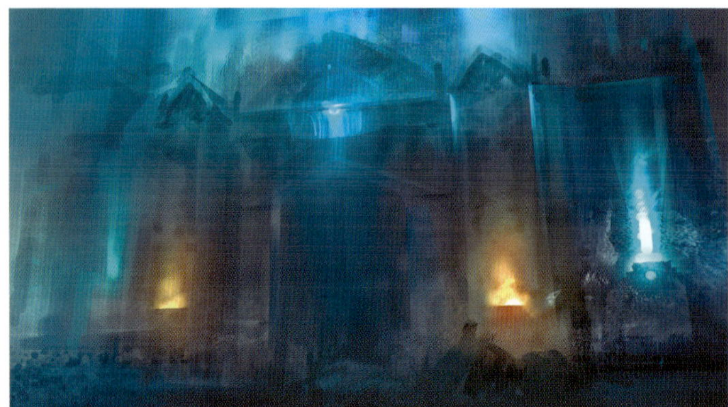

Fig. 4.38

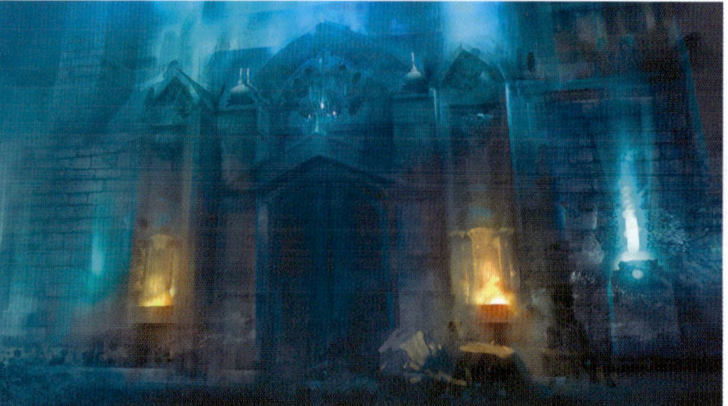

Fig. 4.39

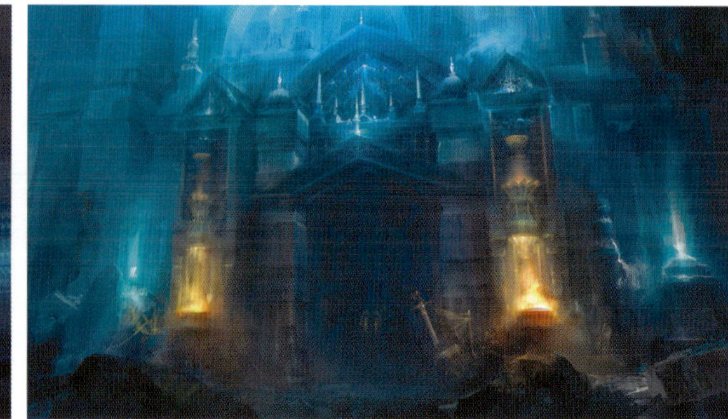

Fig. 4.40

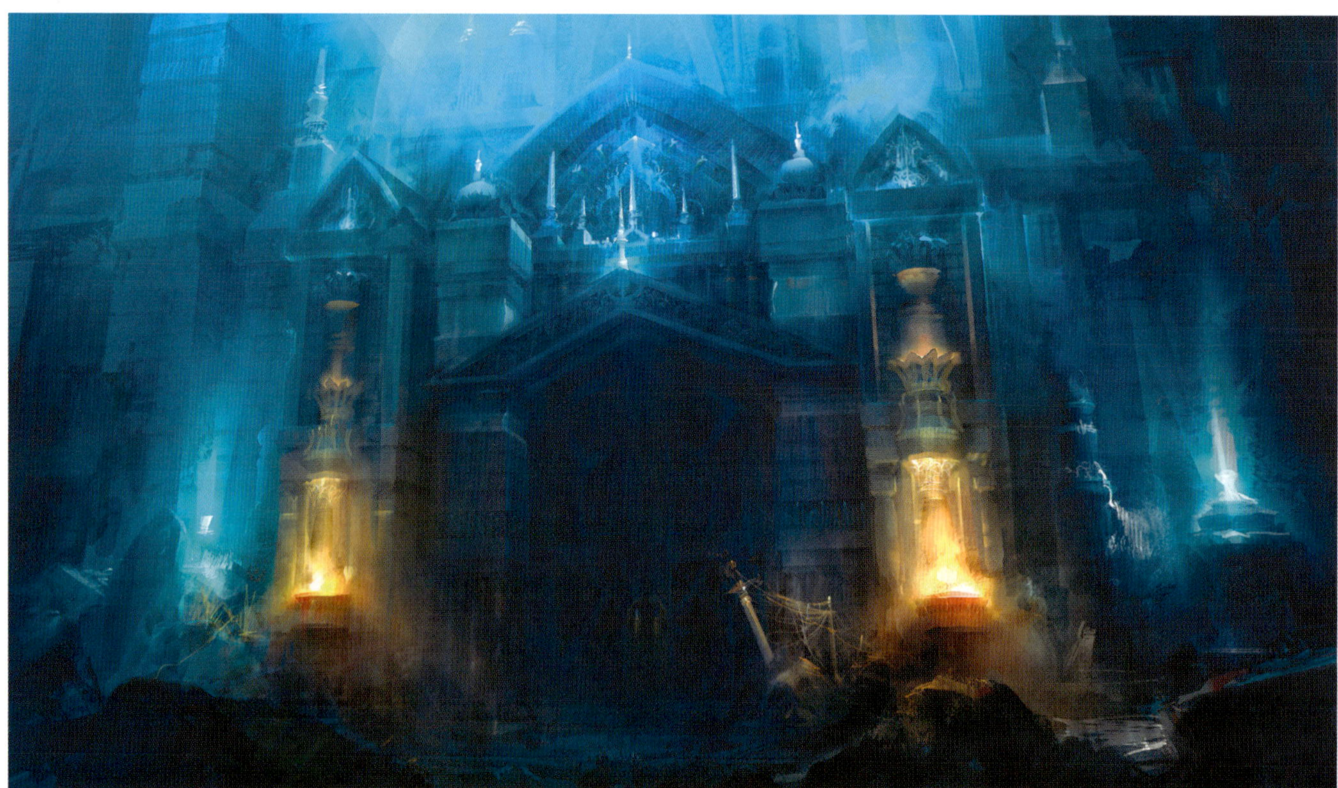

For this dungeon, I started with a rough color block and then focused on setting overall mood and tone of the painting instead of painting the detail too early. Once I was happy with the mood, I started to develop more detail on the painting, adding more details only on important focal points, leaving other parts of the painting a bit loose. This created more interesting visual contrast and helped to bring audience's attention back to the focal point.

Fig. 4.41

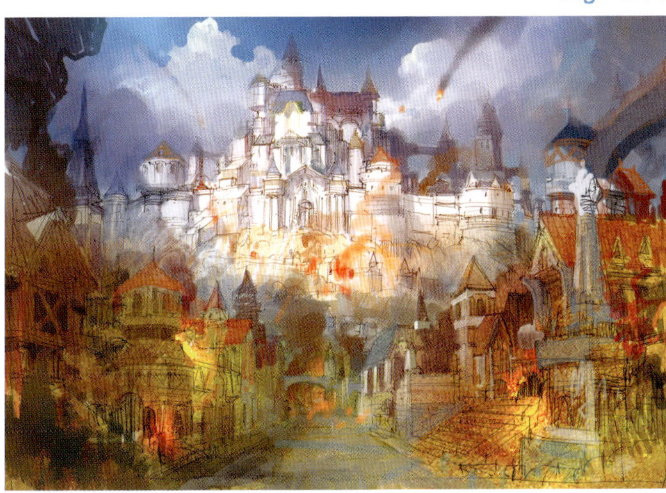

Fig. 4.42

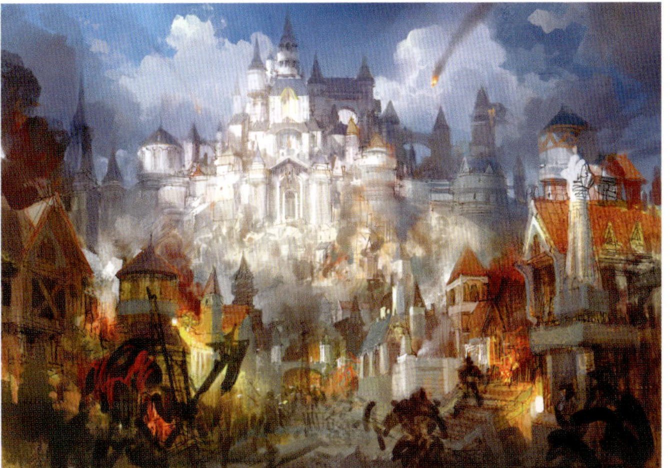

Fig. 4.43

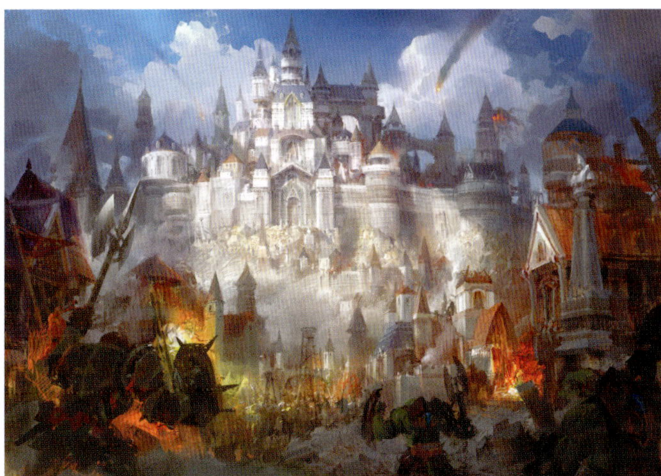

Fig. 4.44

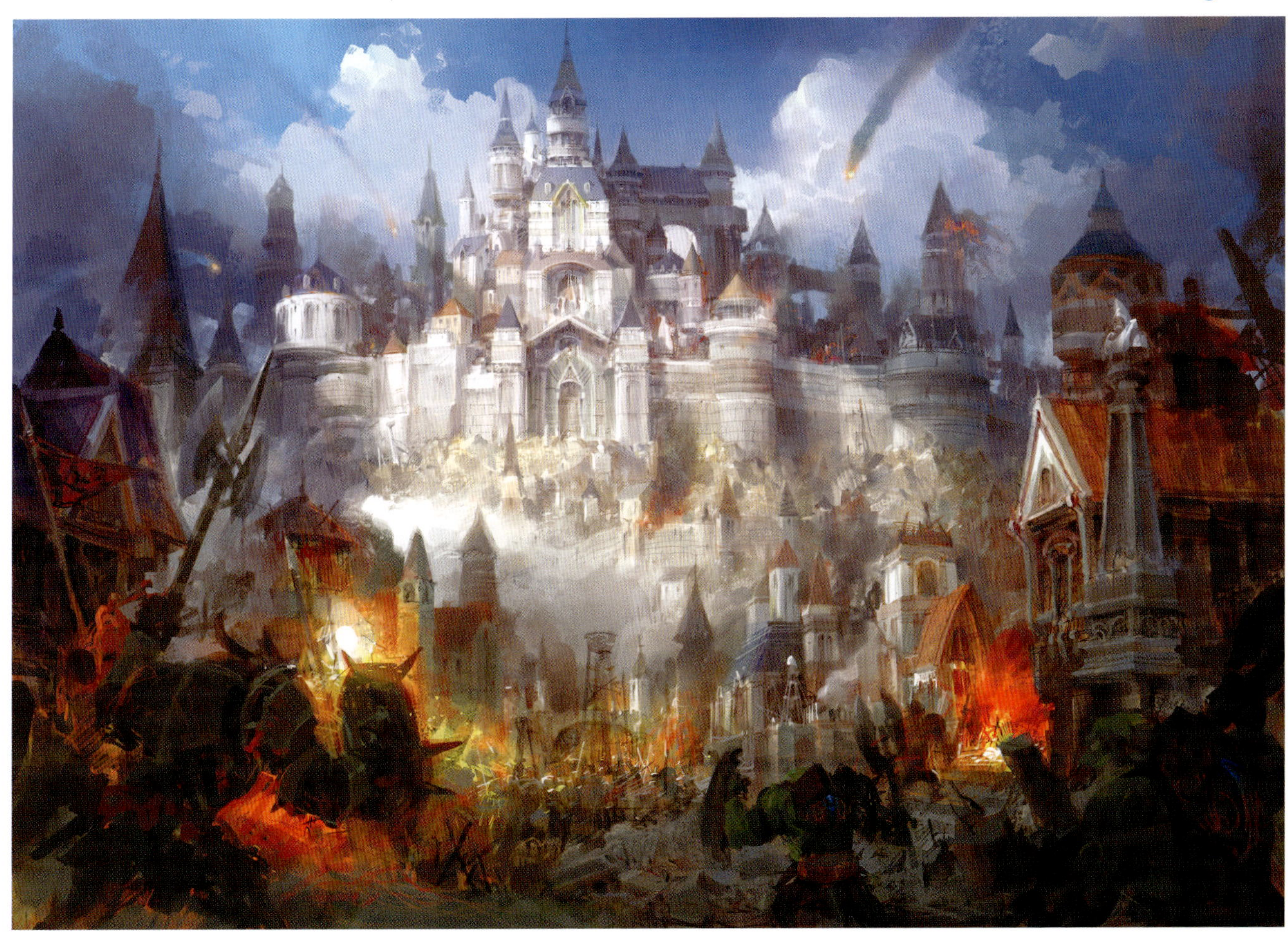

I started this painting with a pen sketch on paper. Then I scanned that image into Photoshop. I also used an acrylic base texture that I painted. Then I painted building shapes with big brushstrokes. The shapes didn't need to be too precise because they will remain the background. But if I overlap them too much, the brushstrokes get very opaque, which is not a proper way to paint. As mentioned previously, be careful not to overdo the overlapping of brushstrokes. I shifted the color scheme a bit to unify the whole painting.

Fig. 4.45

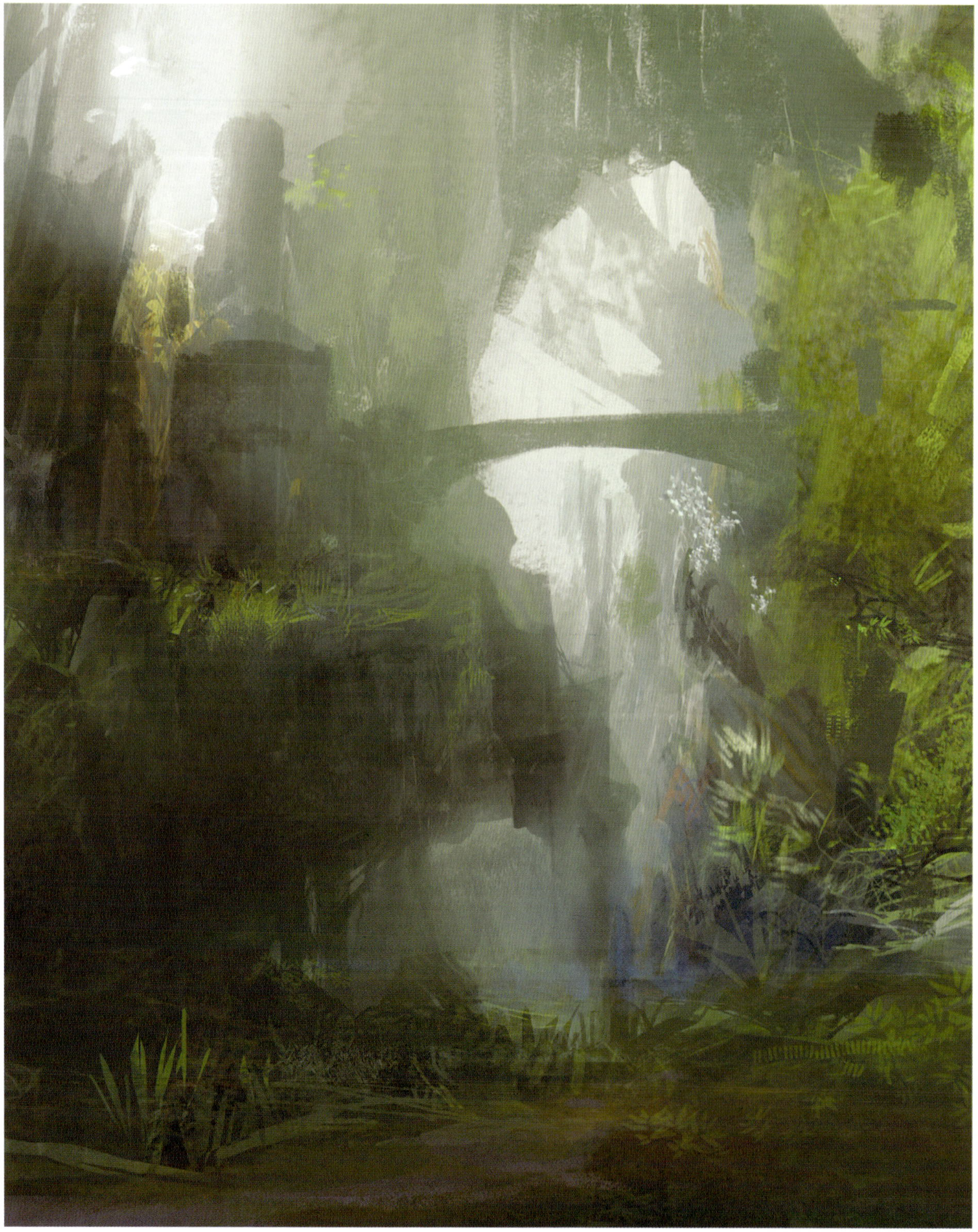

Fig. 4.46

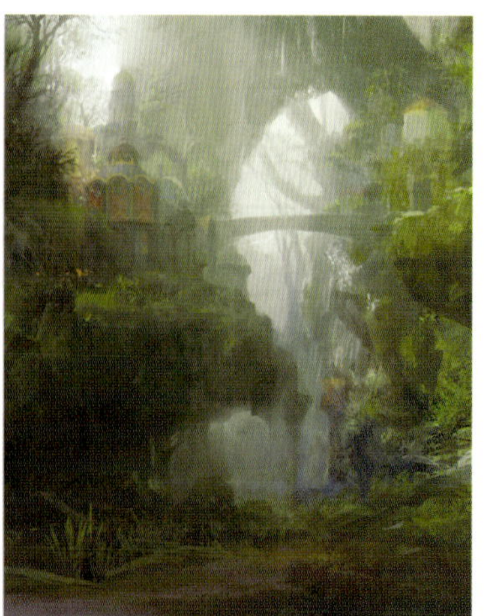

Fig. 4.47

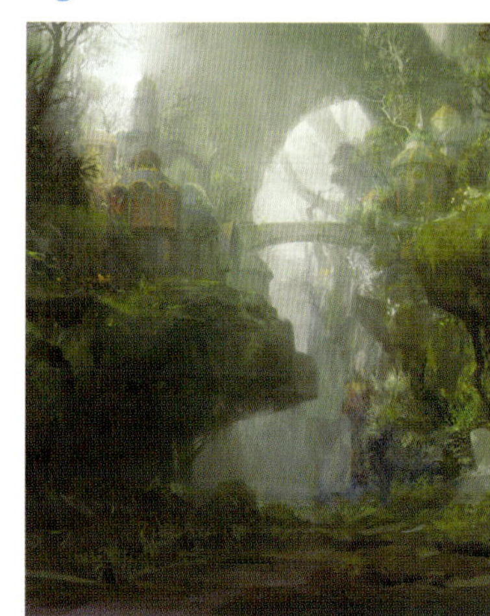

Fig. 4.48

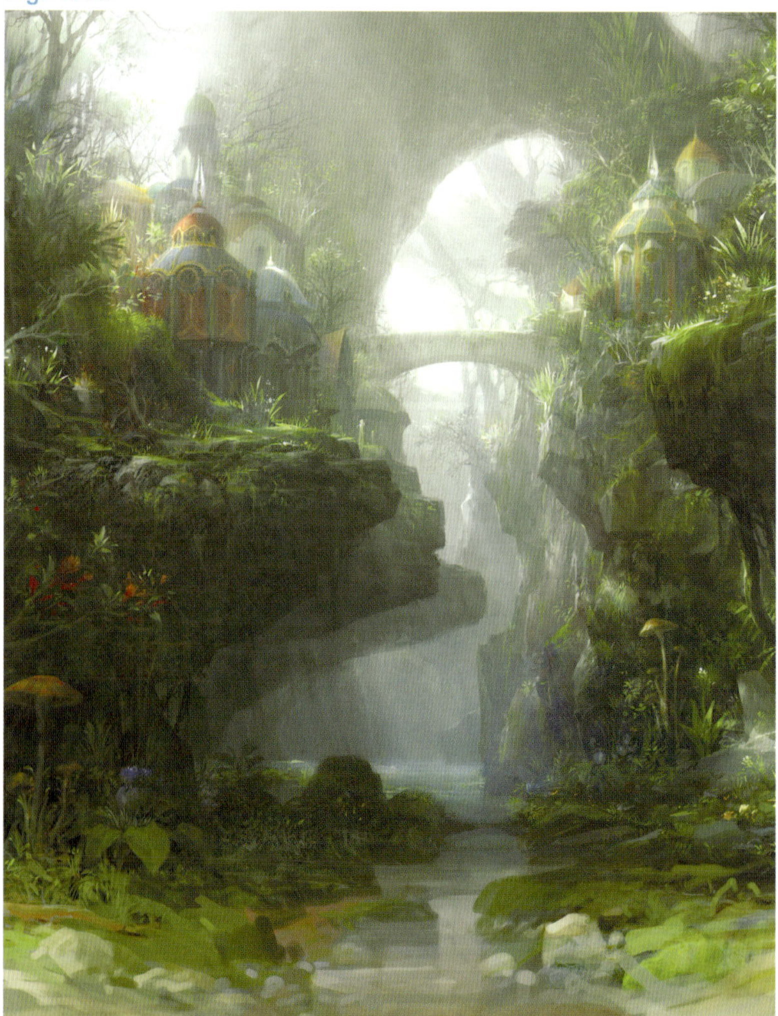

Fig. 4.49

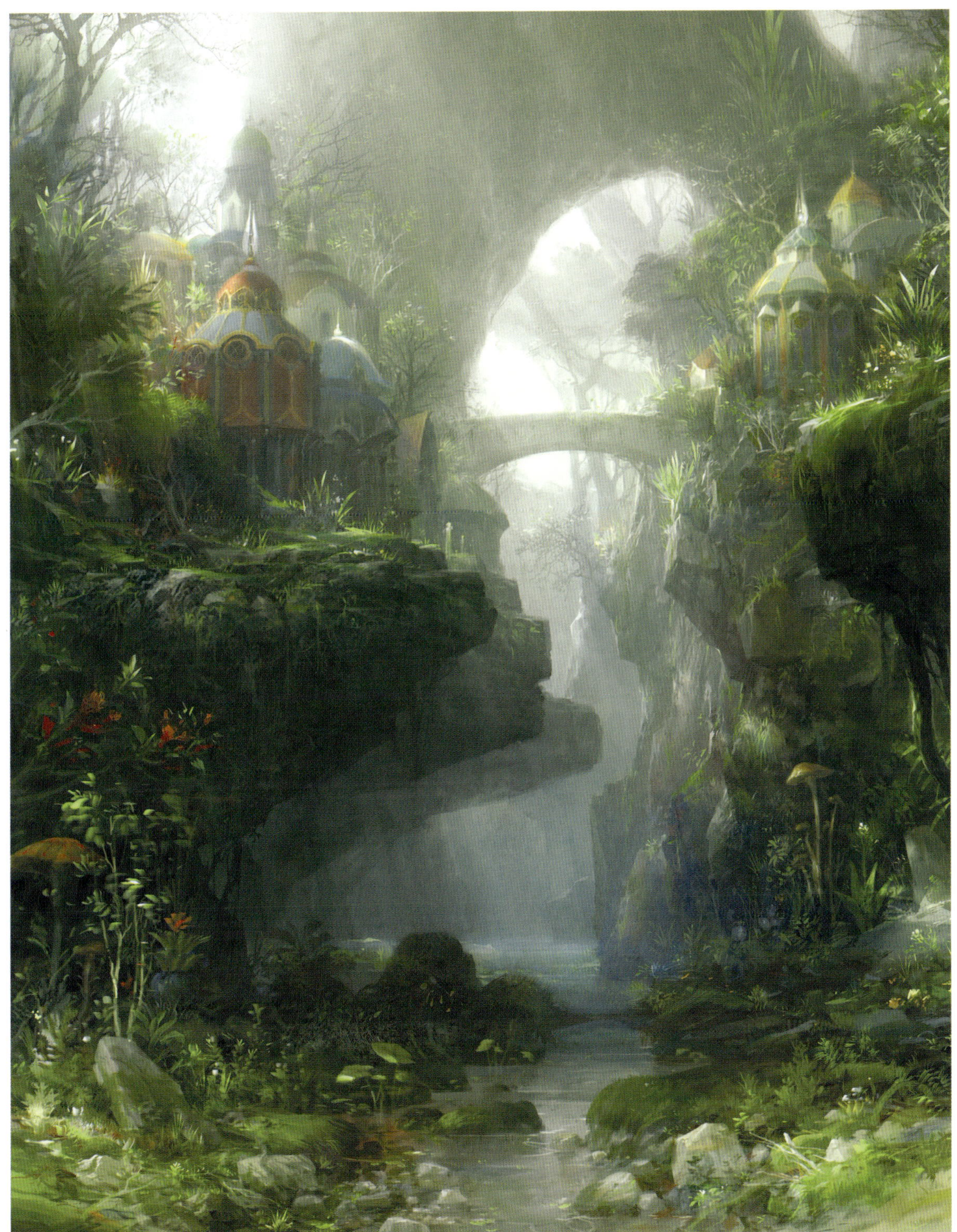

In this example, I painted a magical castle located deep inside a forest, where you can see a lot of trees and moss growing on top of rocks. A stream also flows below the castle. I wanted to paint an impressionistic picture with vibrant colors.

First, I added a greenish base tone to the sketch (Fig. 4.45). The next step was blocking in the dark shadow. I picked a dark green that I enjoy using quite often. I mixed this dark green with many different shades of green to give more variety to the color scheme. It does not matter whether one paints a small tree or a big one. Keep the rhythm of the flow, as well as the balance. Don't add too much strong color too quickly. Rather, build up the layers of leaves one by one (Fig. 4.46–47).

As the painting progresses toward completion, keep checking the color balance of the whole painting. Rather than adding any new color at this point, emphasize the harmony of the existing color in the painting. If some areas get too desaturated, or do not have enough color variation, the best thing to always do is use a simple brush at 30% opacity and glaze over the blue tint (Fig. 4.48). As always, he most important thing for this last step is to keep the balance of the painting. Again, balance includes, but is not limited to, light balance, color balance, and detail balance. Continue tweaking all of the elements until the painting gets the right balance (Fig. 4.49).

Fig. 4.50

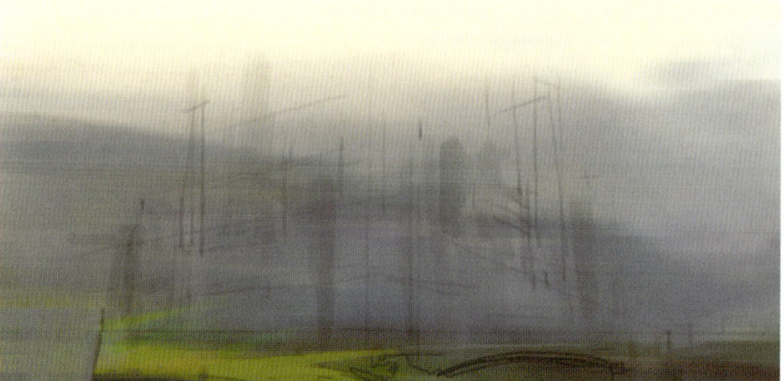

Fig. 4.51

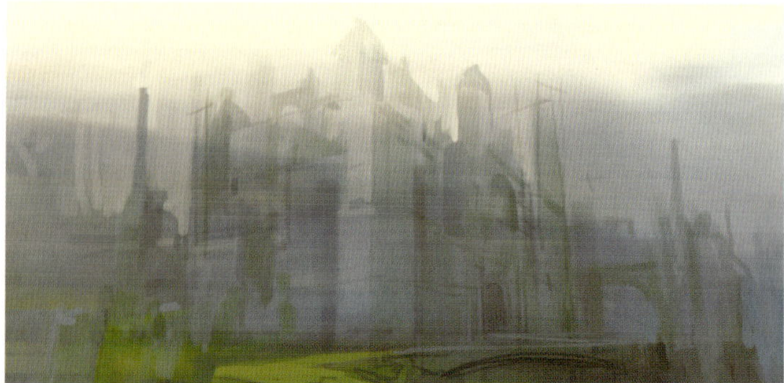

Fig. 4.52

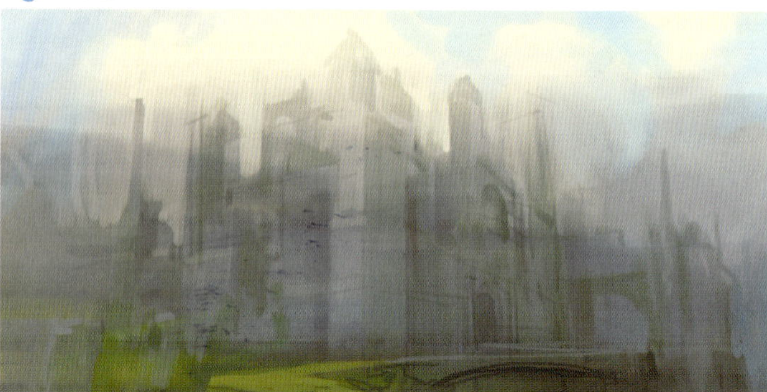

Fig. 4.53

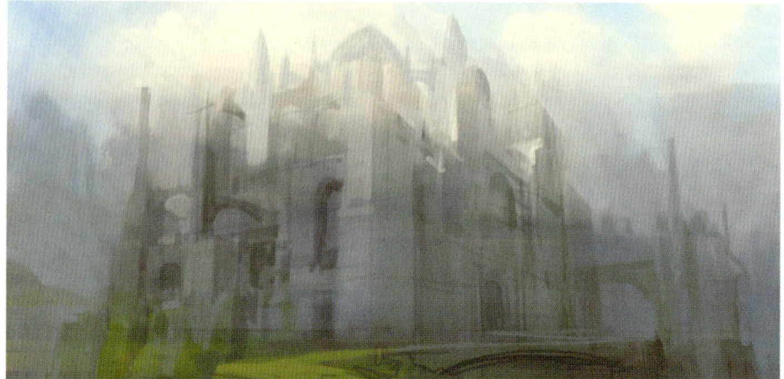

Fig. 4.54

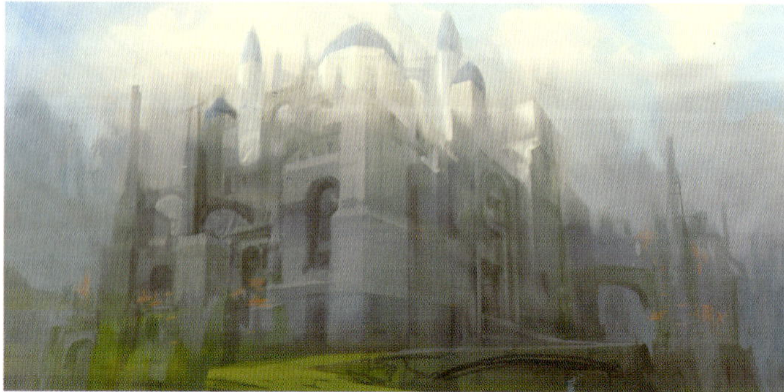

Fig. 4.55

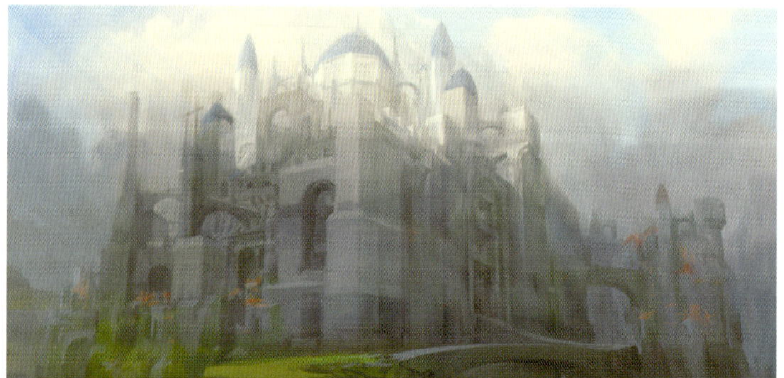

Fig. 4.56

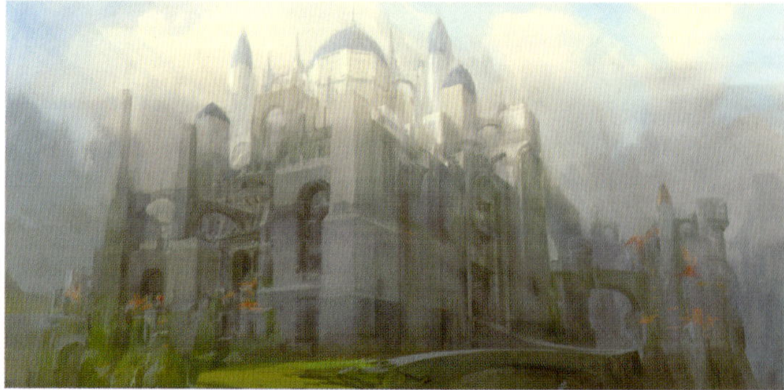

Fig. 4.57

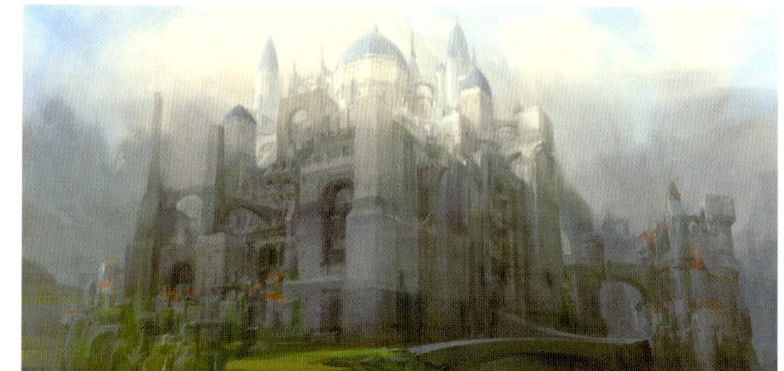

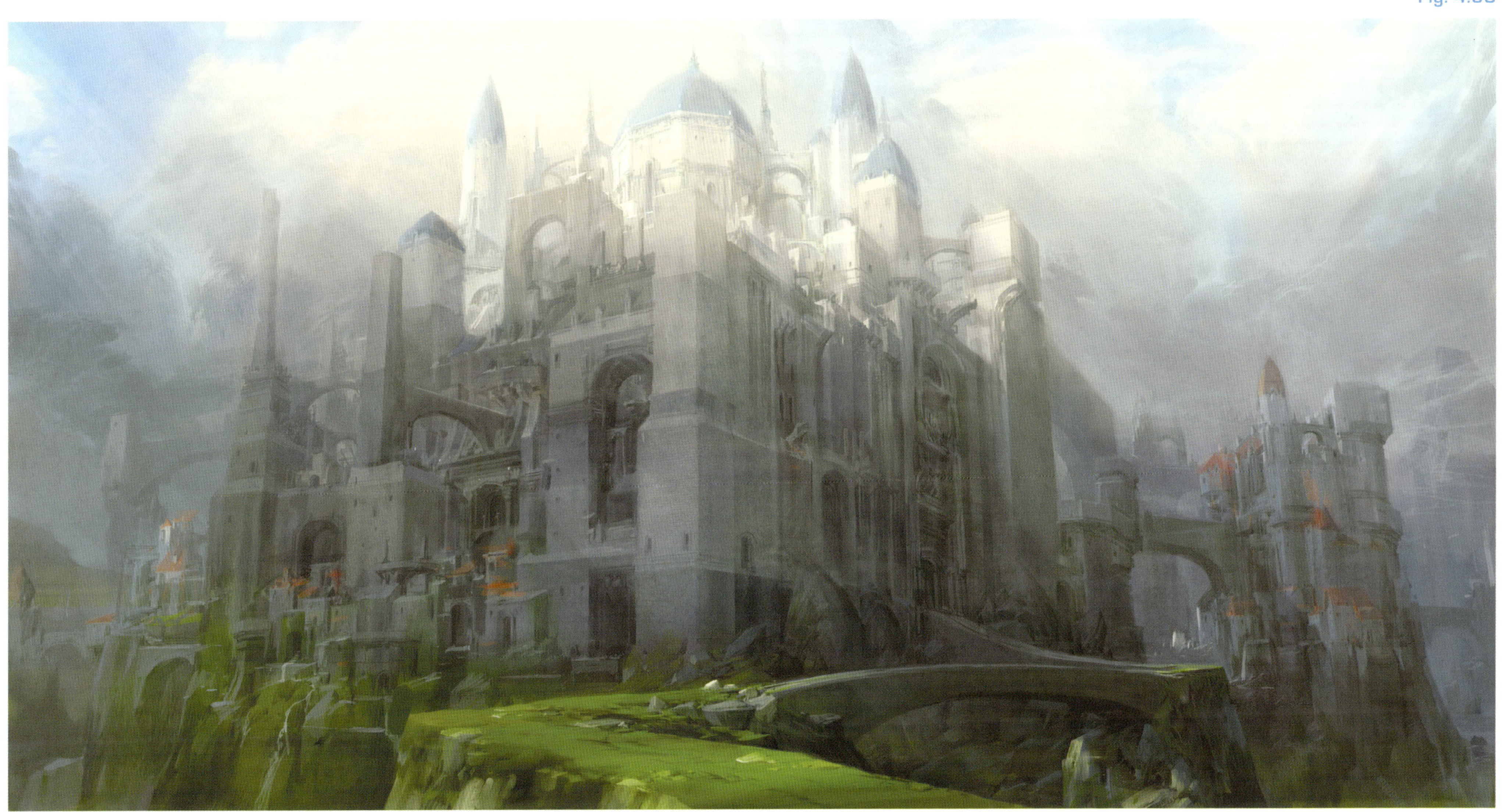

For this painting, I made a back plate to use as a starting background (Fig. 4.50). Instead of starting with a pencil sketch, I started my drawing on top of a rough base-color background.

Before I draw any perspective grid on the page, I tend to enjoy drawing the initial sketch, and then I retrofit the perspective grid to match the drawing. I blocked in with rough brushstrokes. It is better to make big strokes like this in the early stage, since it adds a more painterly feel (Fig. 4.52–53). The next step is to apply more lighting information (Fig. 4.54). Here, I have shown that the direct light hits only the top portion of the tower roof. I let other parts of the castle stay in the shadows. Adding more value contrast increases the visual tension (Fig. 4.55–57). I finished by adding more details (Fig. 4.58).

Fig. 4.59

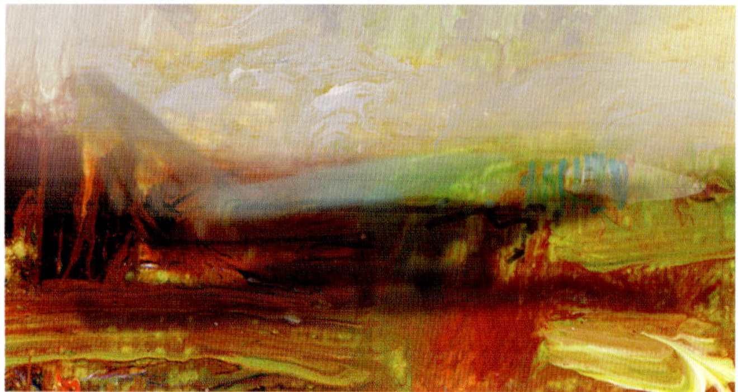

Fig. 4.60

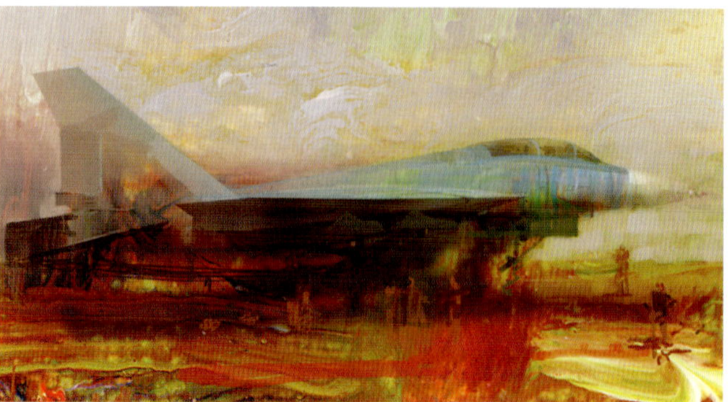

Fig. 4.61

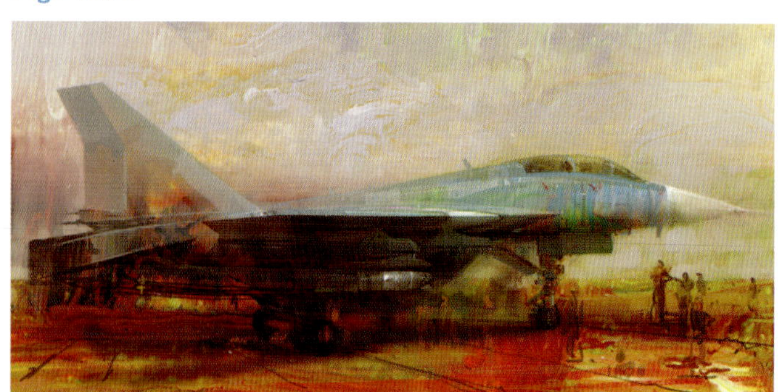

Fig. 4.62

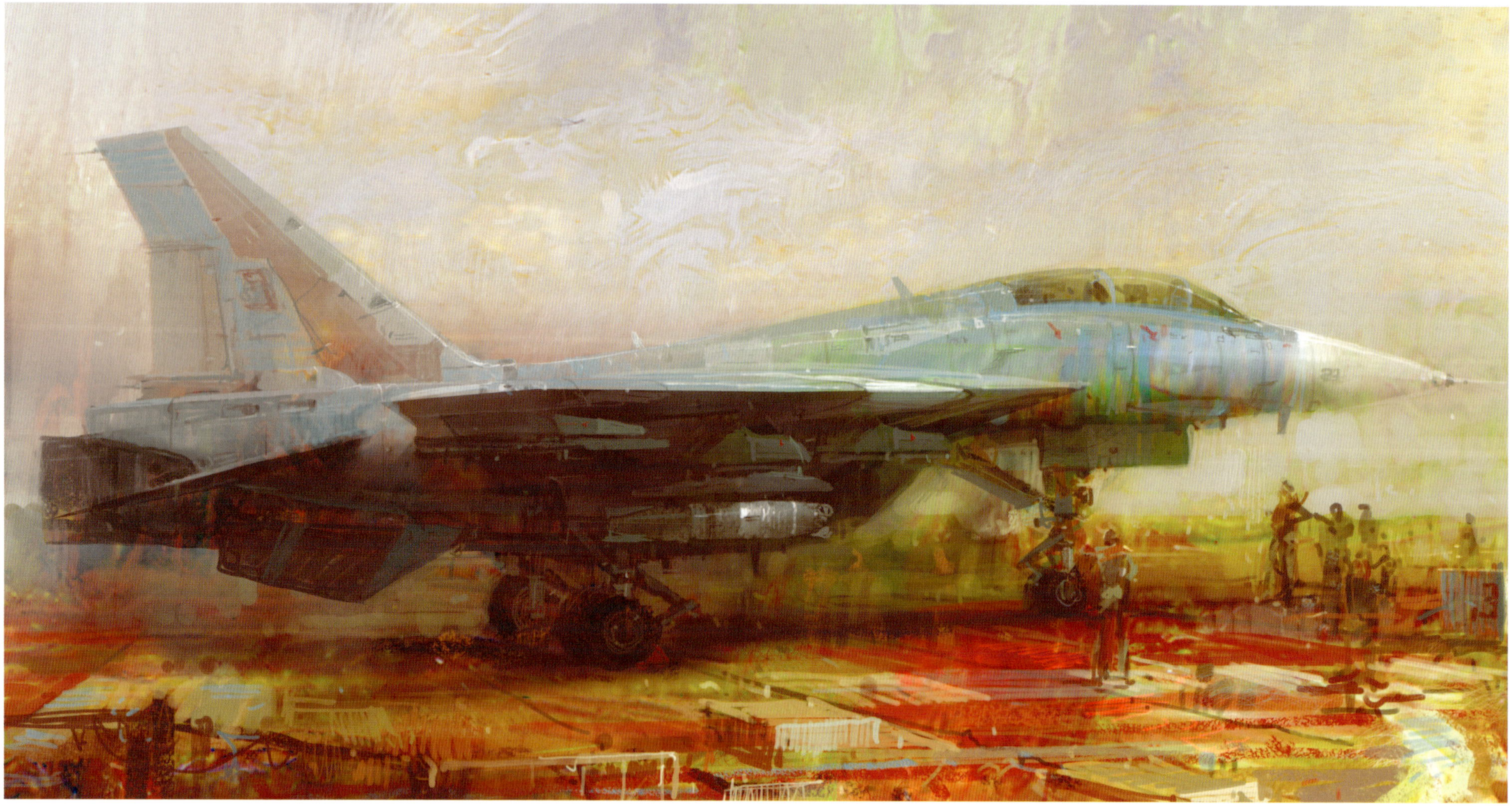

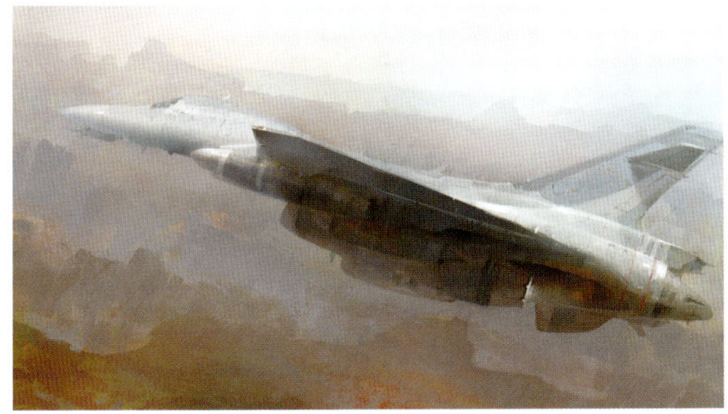

Fig. 4.63

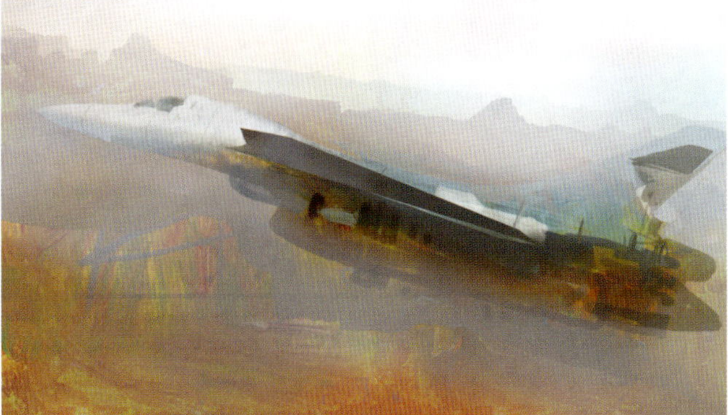

Fig. 4.64

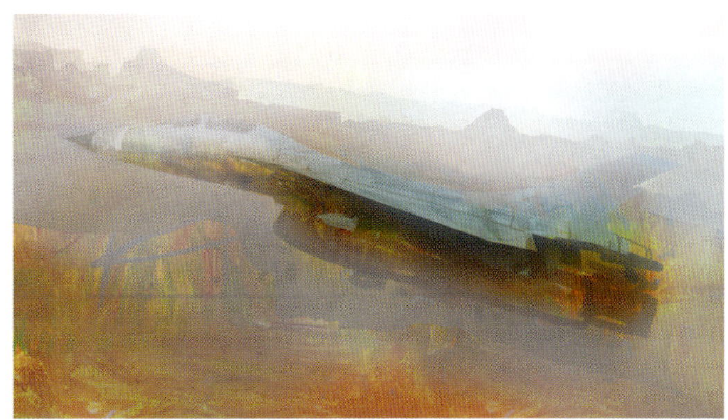

Fig. 4.65

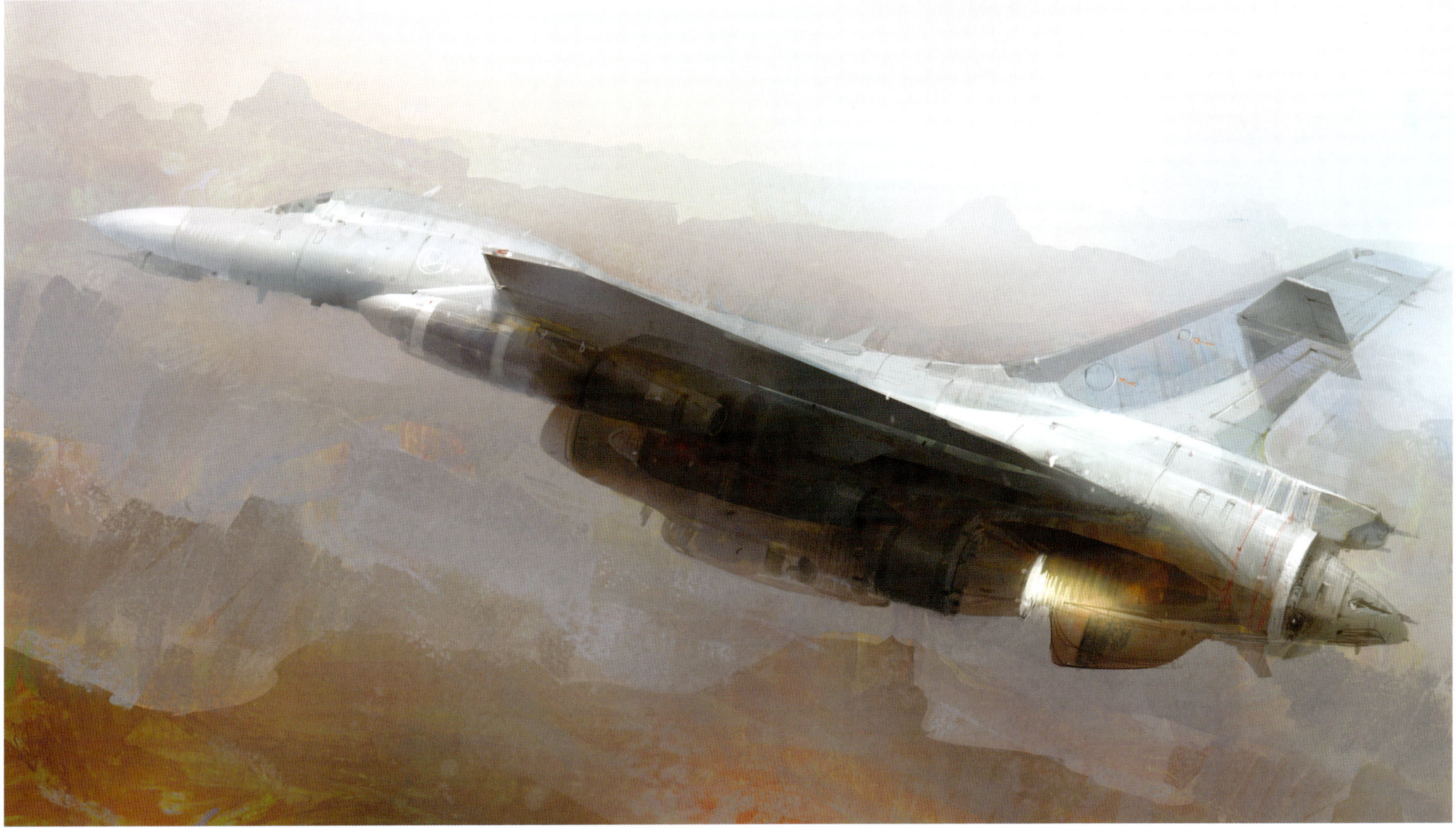

Fig. 4.66

Fig. 4.67

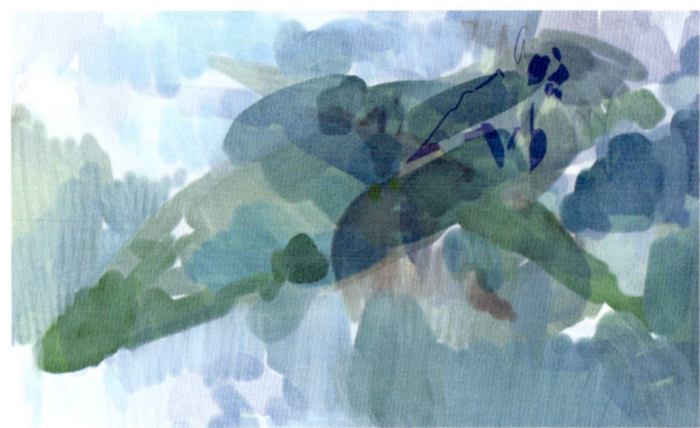

Fig. 4.68

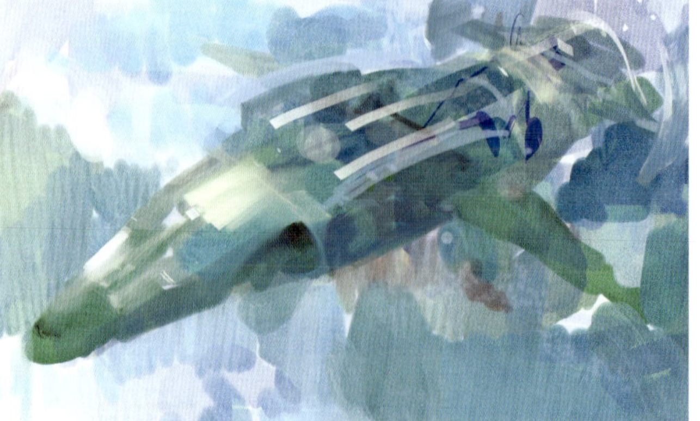

Fig. 4.69

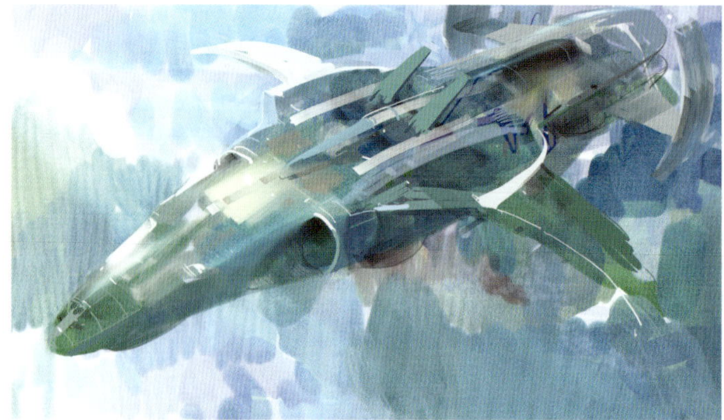

Fig. 4.72

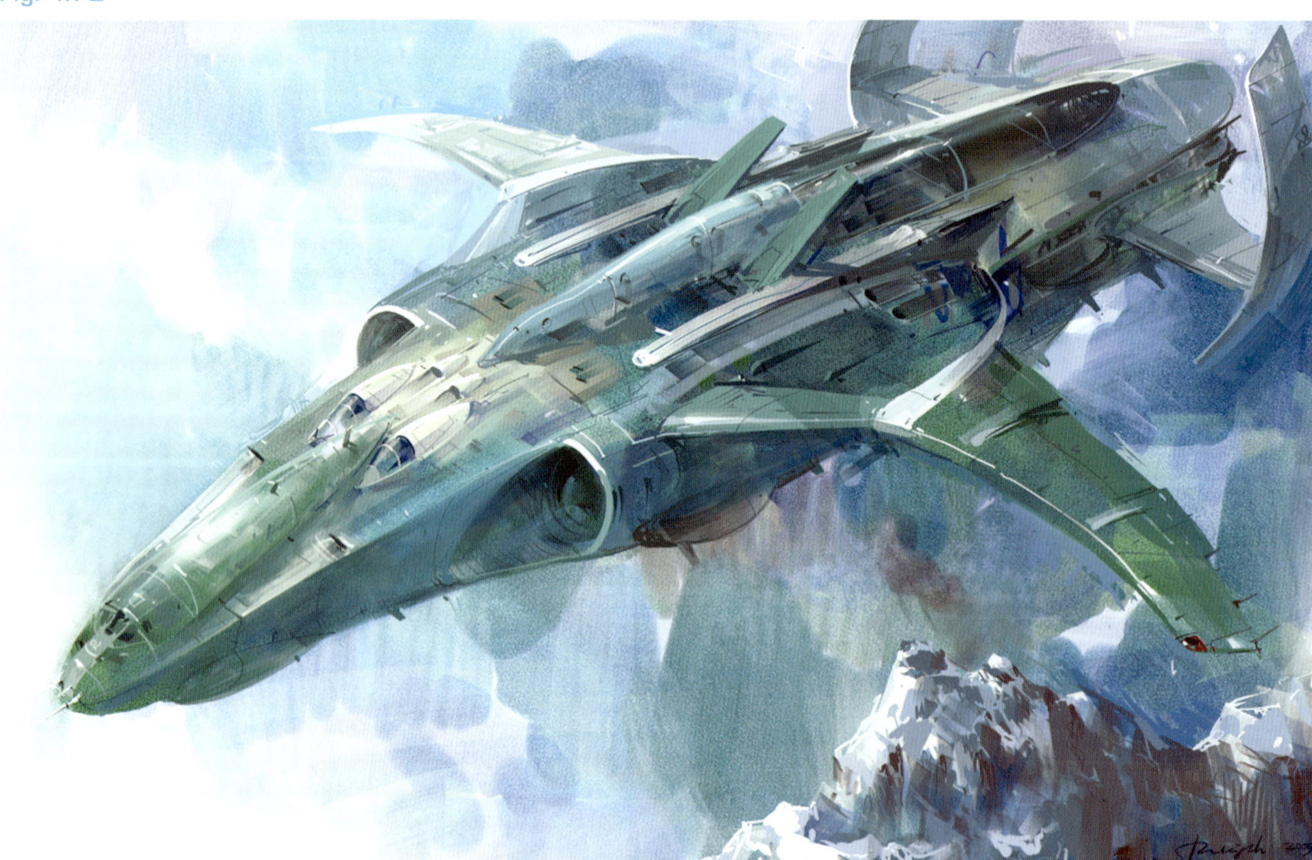

Fig. 4.70

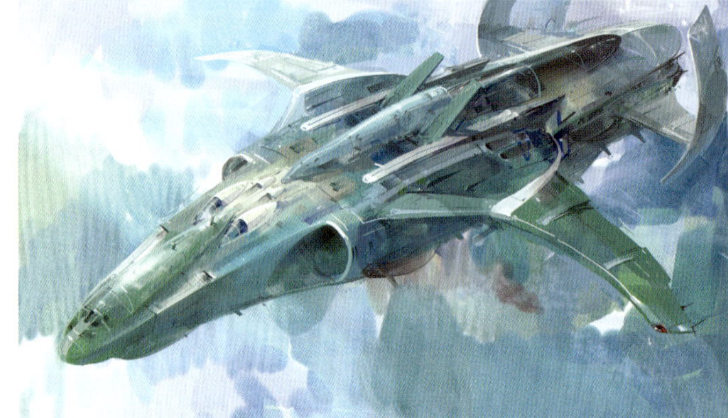

Fig. 4.71

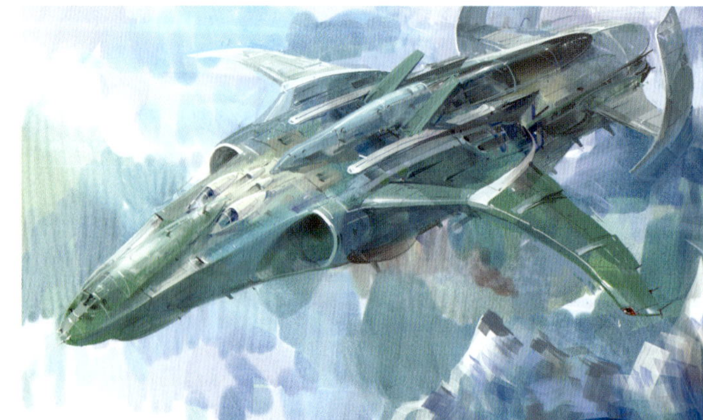

I started this picture with a watercolor base. By using watercolor and watercolor paper, I can quickly block in the basic shape and color. Once I am happy with the result, I scan it into Photoshop and start to paint digitally from that point on. First, I focus on the main subject, and then I move on to the background. To finish, I move back to the main subject.

Fig. 4.73

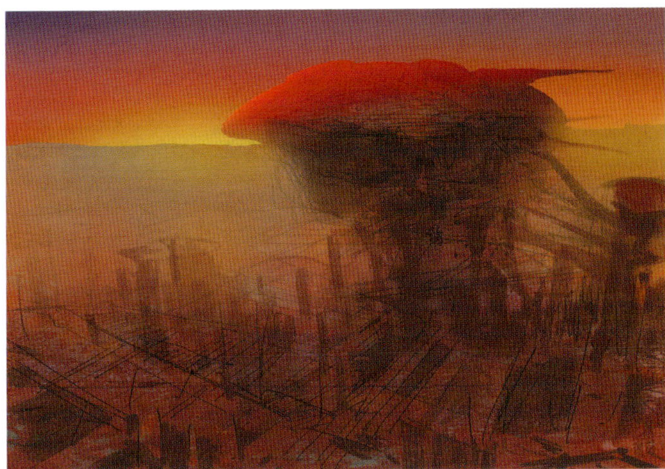

Fig. 4.74

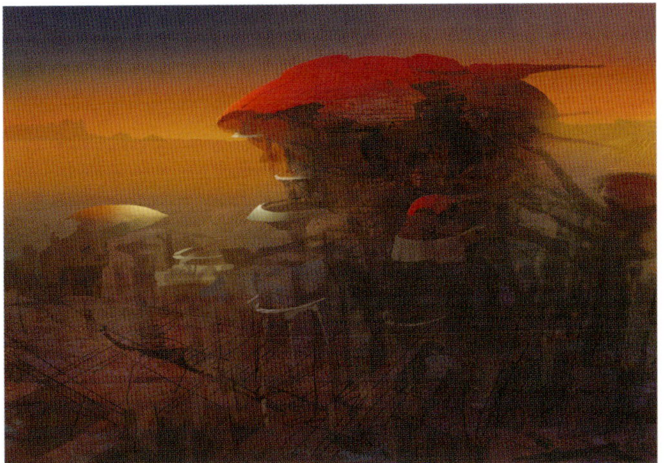

Fig. 4.75

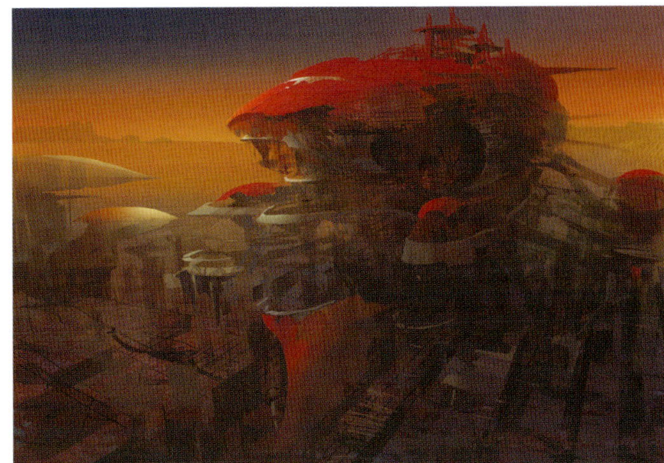

Fig. 4.76

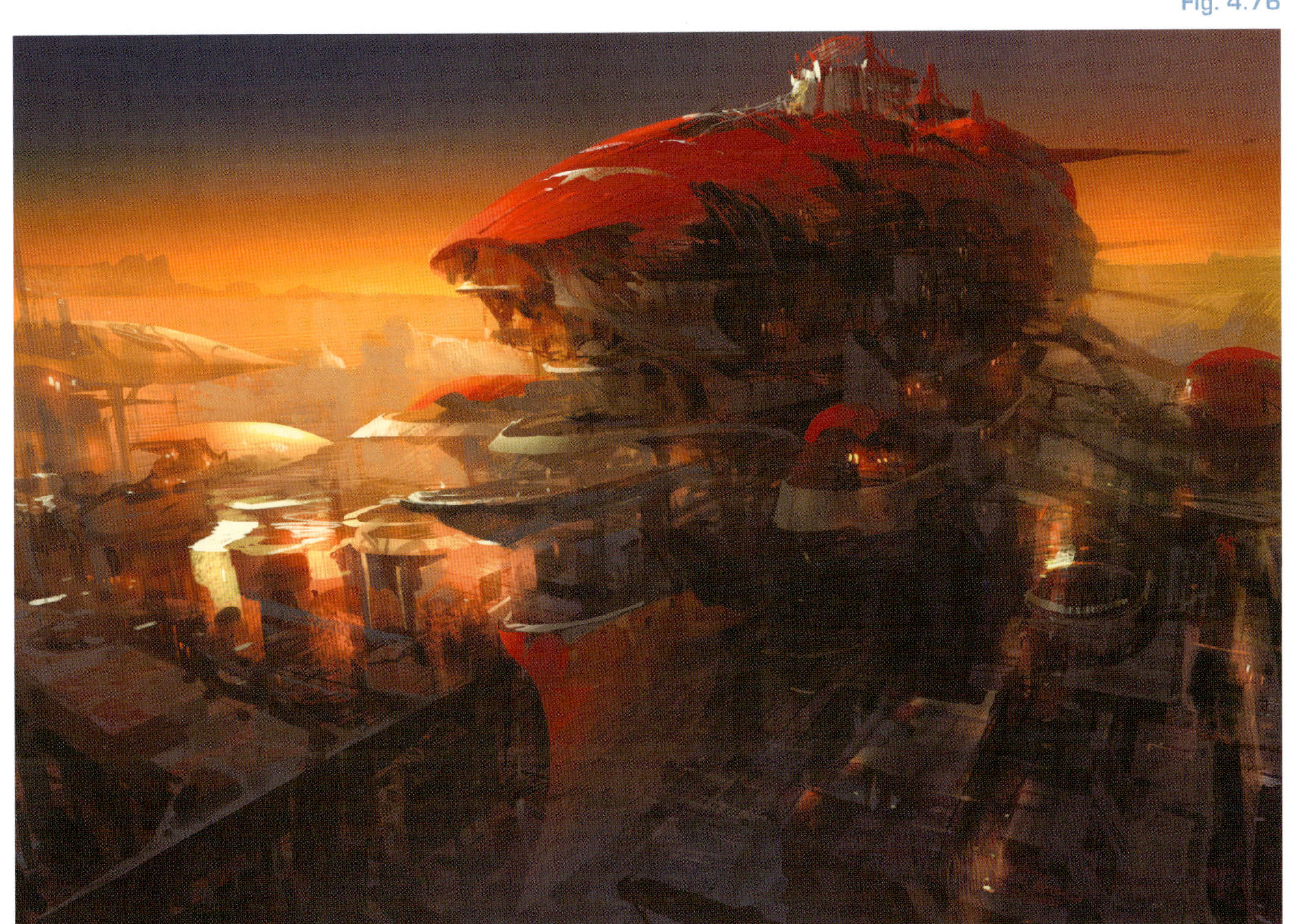

To create this piece, I blocked in the rough shape of the main subject, a spaceship (Fig. 4.73). I used a more curved shape instead of a straight line in order to make it appear more aerodynamic.

After blocking in the big shape, I draw the perspective grid based on my sketch. In this way, I can draw a more dynamic composition than if I had drawn the perspective grid first.. Then I roughly blocked in a shadow shape using the Lasso tool (Fig. 4.74). After blocking in the largest light and shadow shapes, I continued to draw more big shapes to refine the subject (Fig. 4.75). I added more details to the painting as I went along (Fig. 4.76).

Fig. 4.77

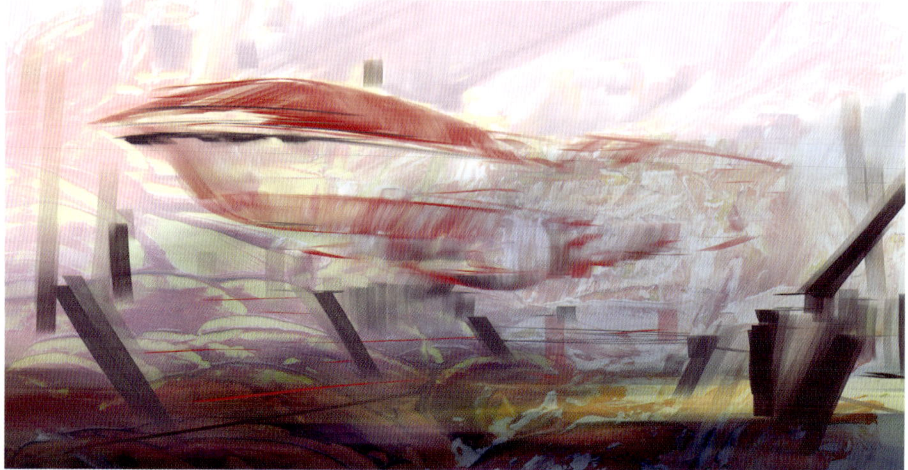

Fig. 4.78

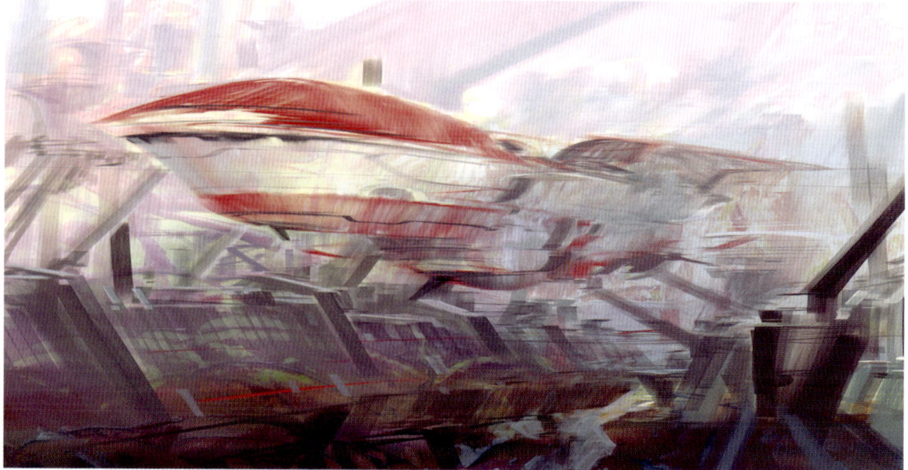

Fig. 4.79

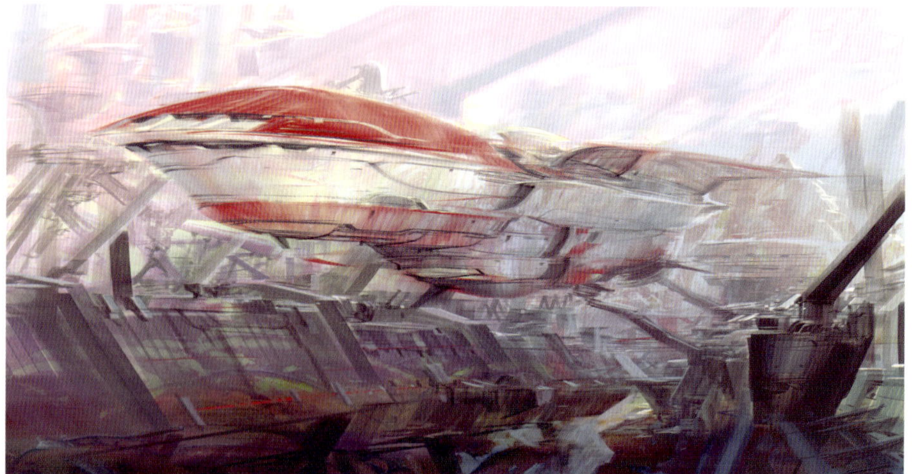

Fig. 4.80

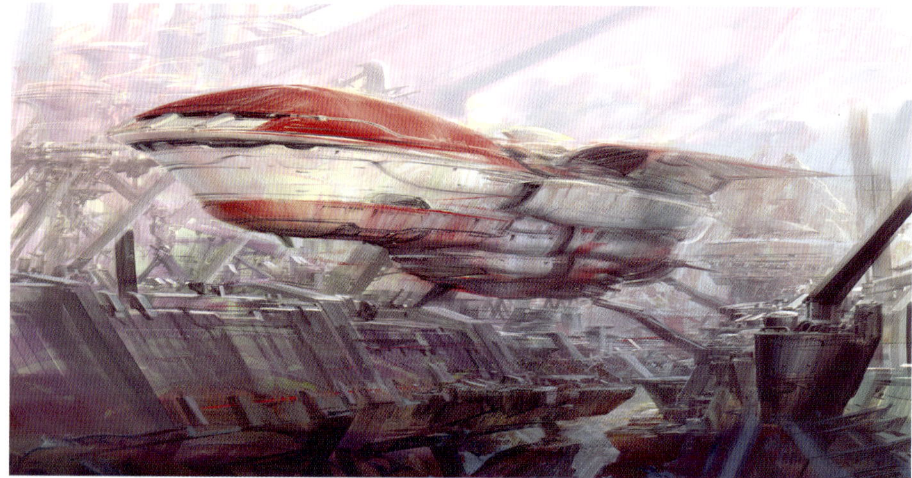

Fig. 4.81

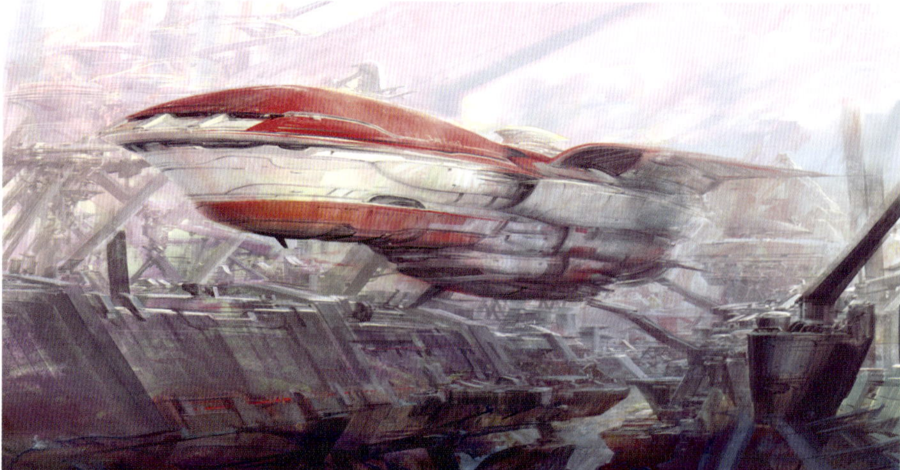

Fig. 4.82

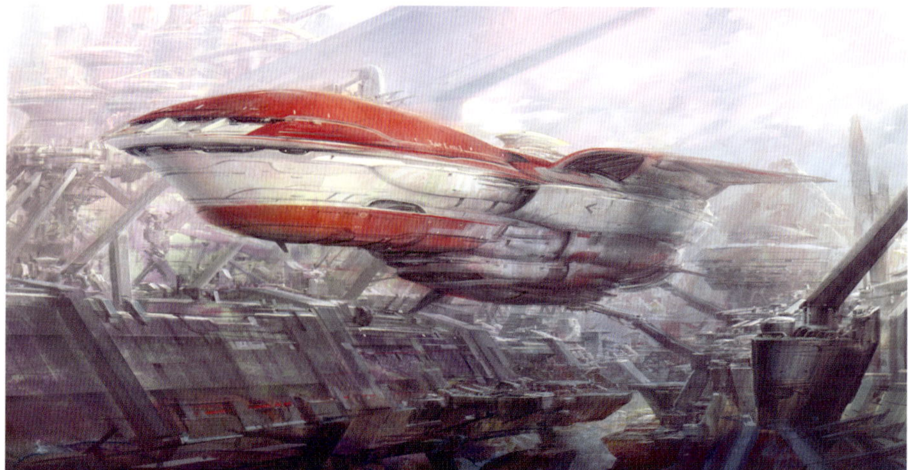

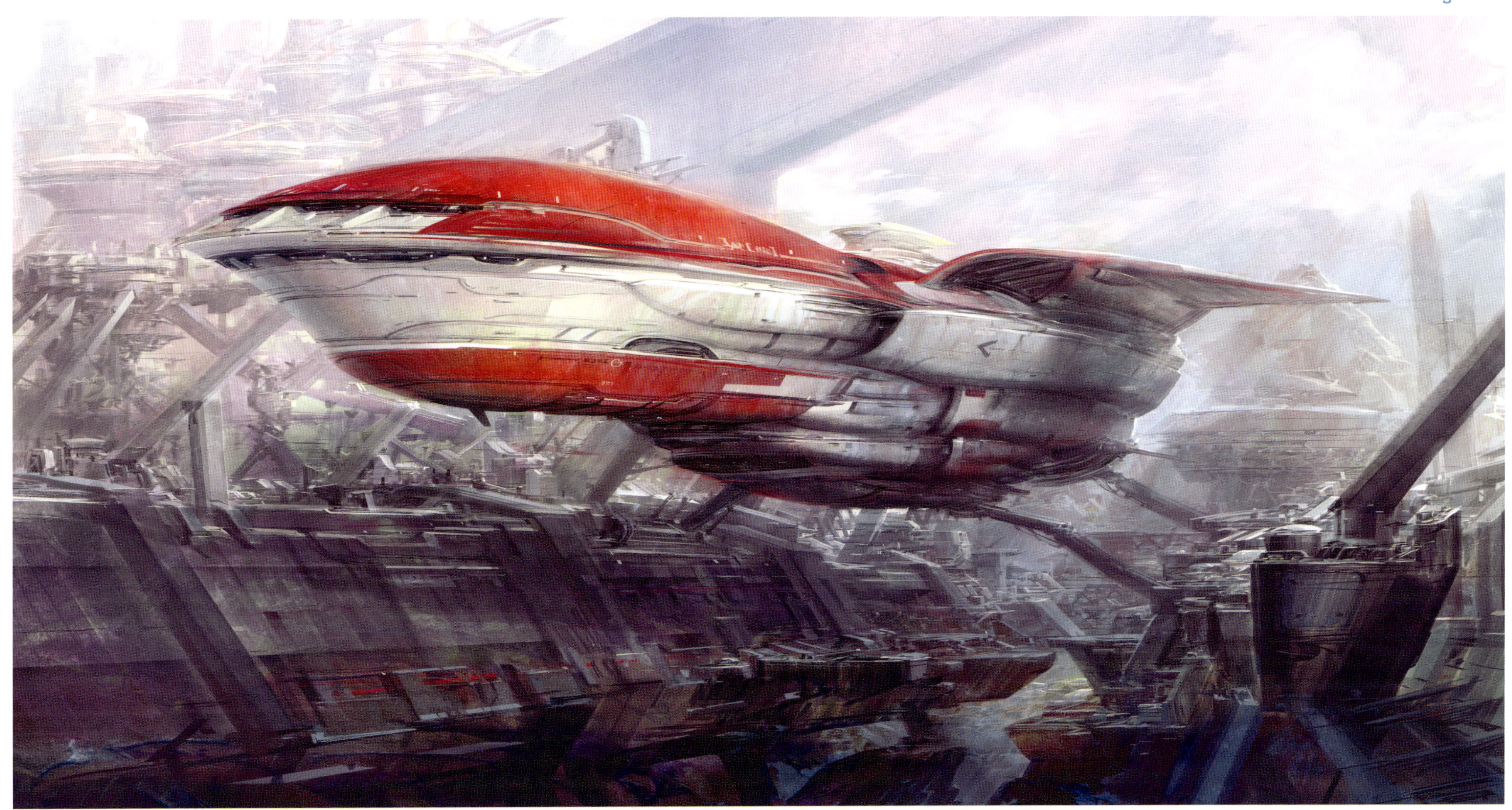

I use big brushstrokes to block in the big shape. In the early stage of a painting, I try not to use too many smaller brushstrokes. Once I have some basic color painted in, I use darker colors to pump up the contrast a bit to give the painting a clearer look. A big shadow gives the painting the proper sense of scale. I finished the painting with some opaque brushstrokes to give it more sharpness and clarity.

Fig. 4.84

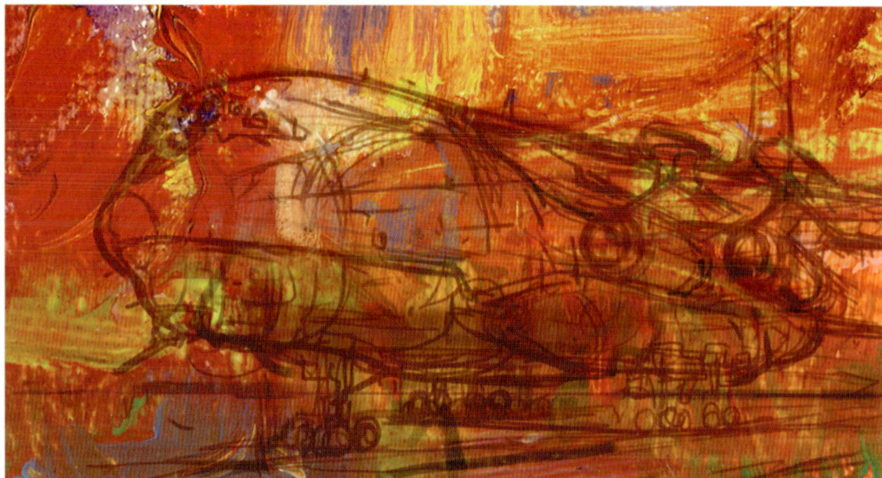

Fig. 4.85

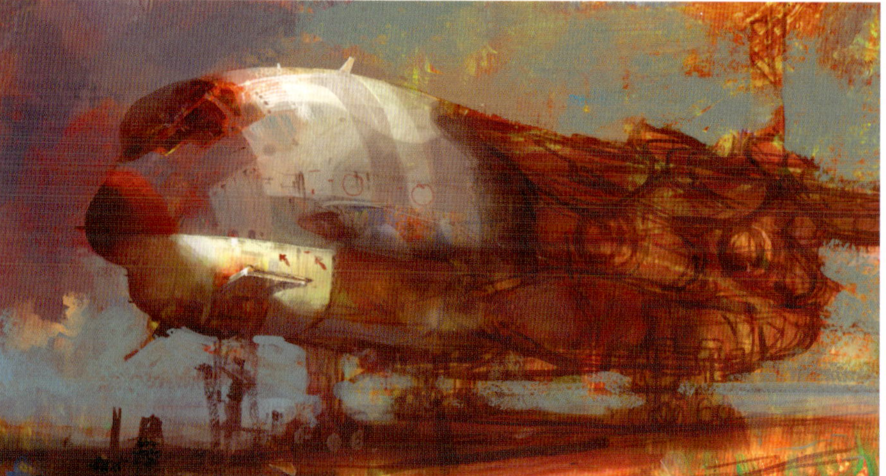

Fig. 4.86

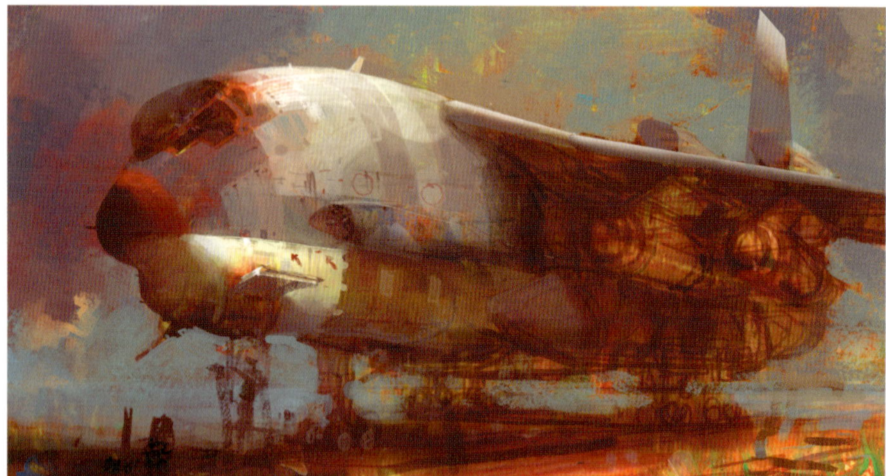

Fig. 4.87

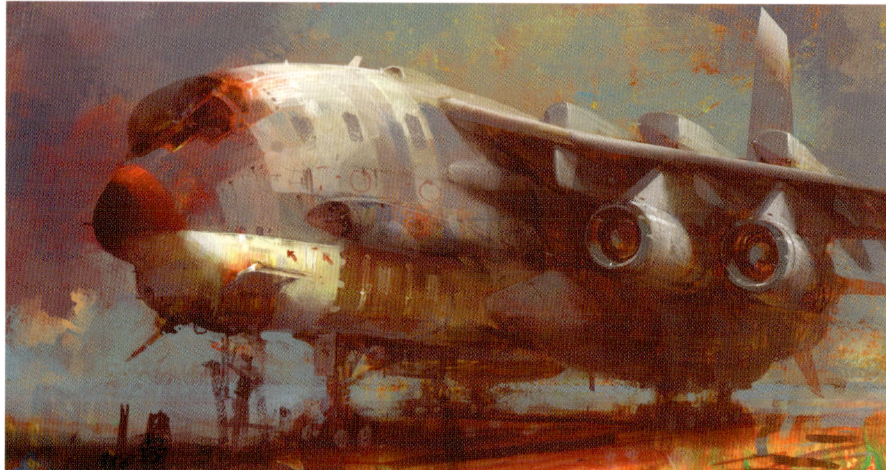

Fig. 4.88

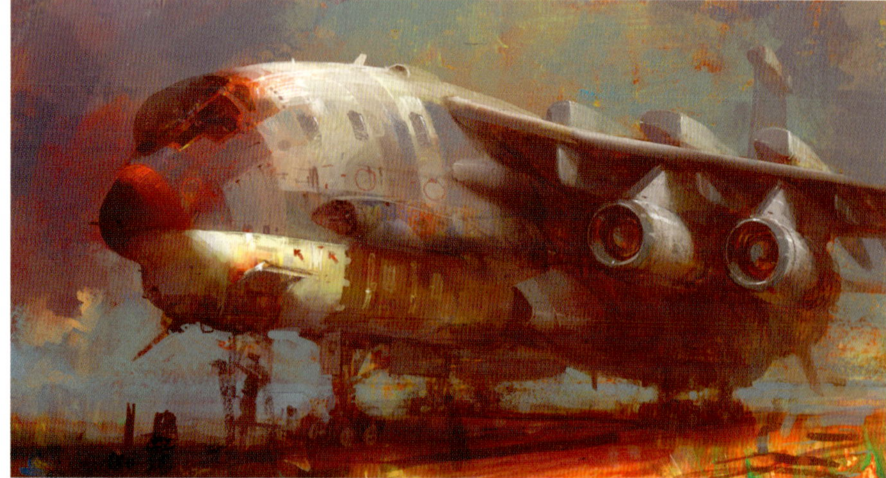

Fig. 4.89

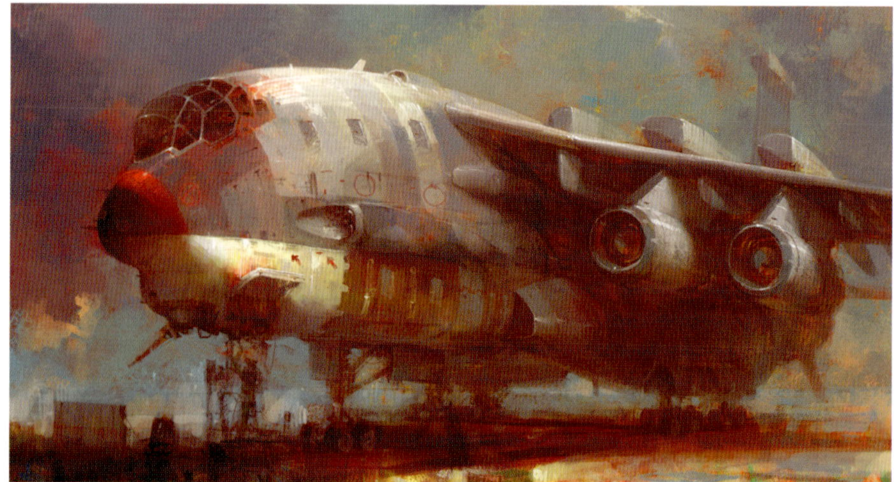

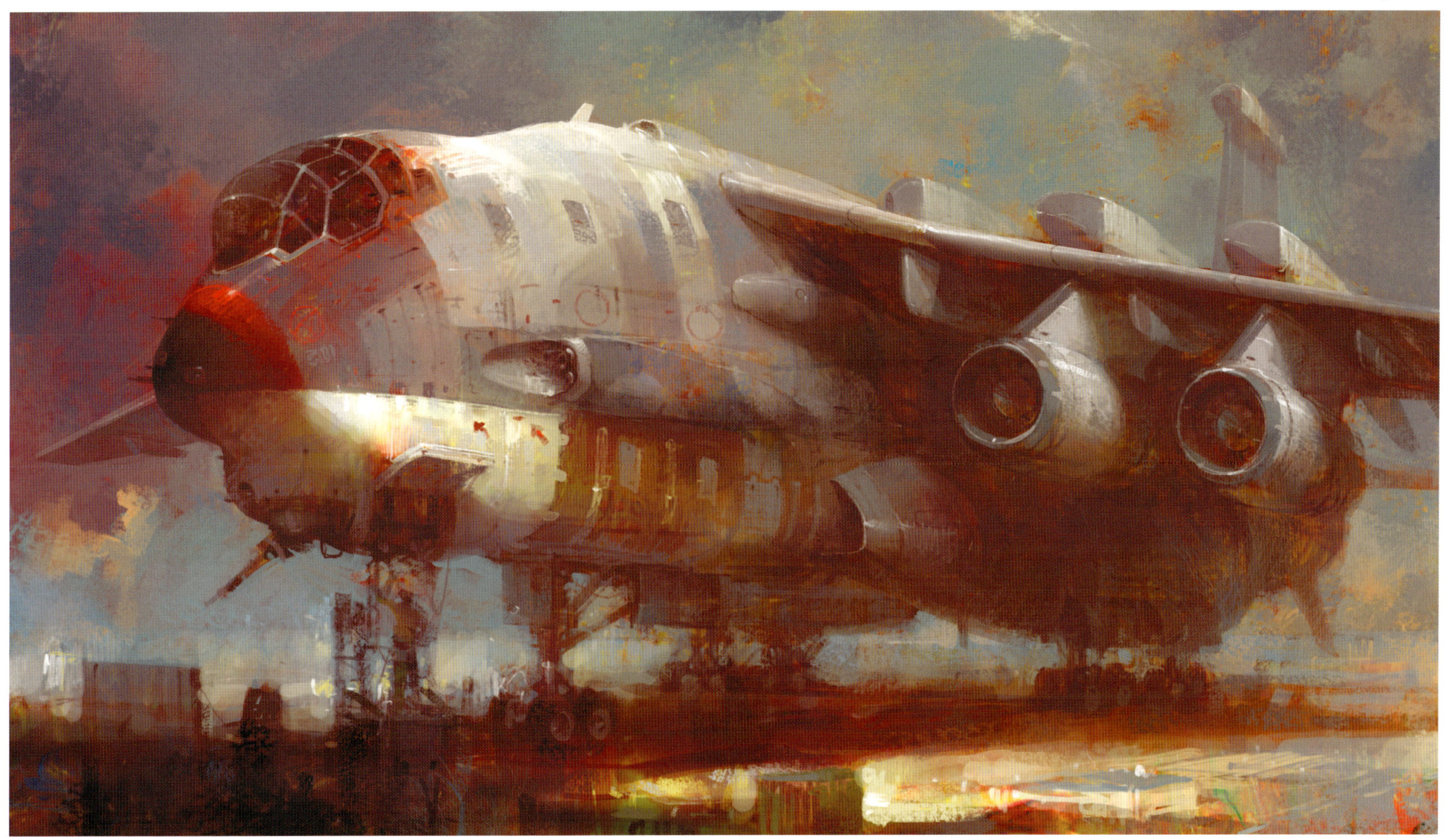

I started this painting with oil paint on a canvas. I mixed a few very intense colors on the canvas and scanned it into Photoshop. Then I started to sketch digitally. I used gray as a main color for the main subject, but used the vibrant background color as much as possible. It gives a very warm underpaint feel. I started with big shapes and, as I made progress, I elaborated the details on the bomber. I finished it with a very sketchy look, yet it looks finished because I successfully controlled the contrast of loose and tight sections.

Fig. 4.91

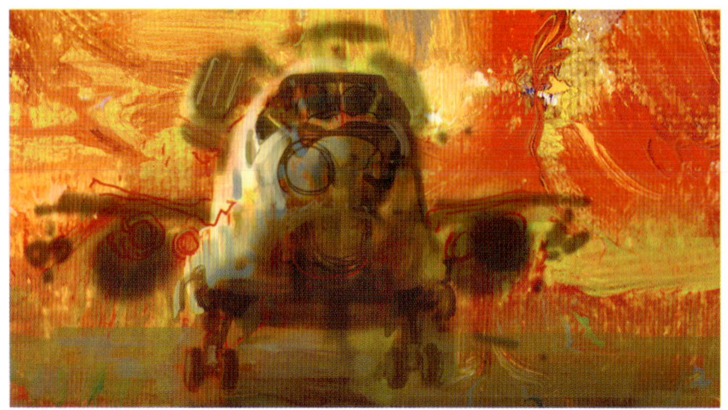

Fig. 4.92

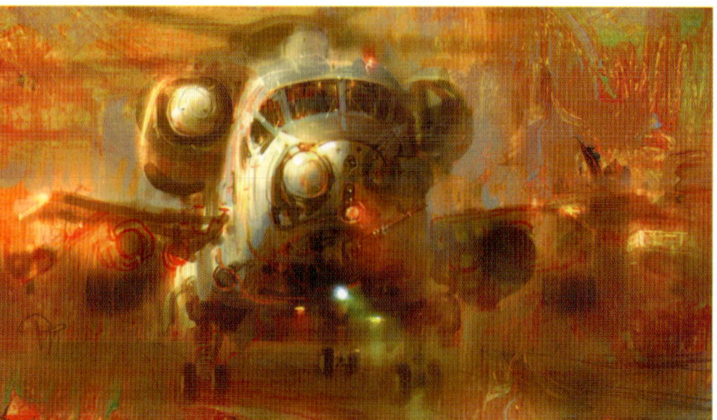

Fig. 4.93

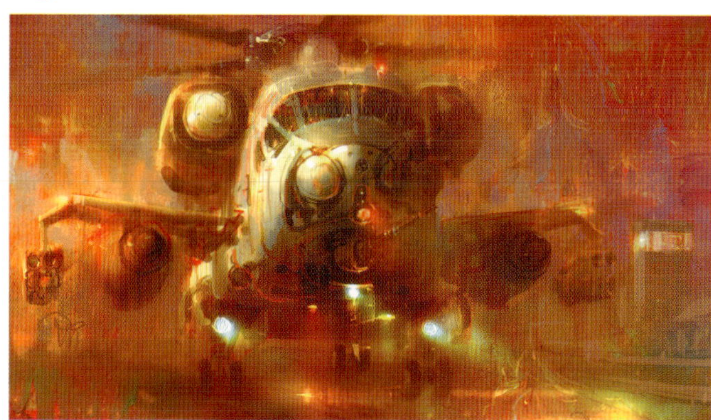

Fig. 4.94

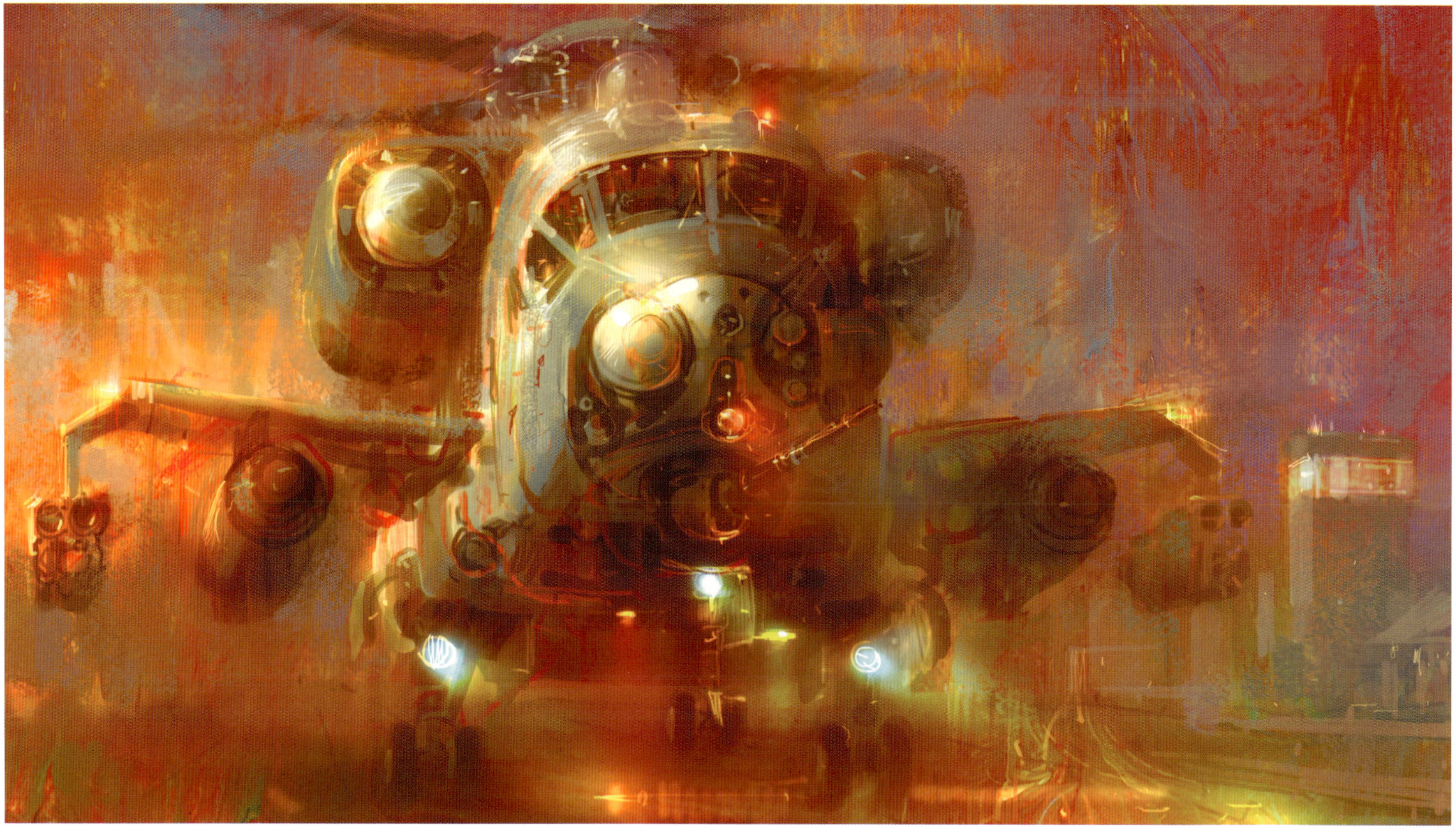

Fig. 4.95

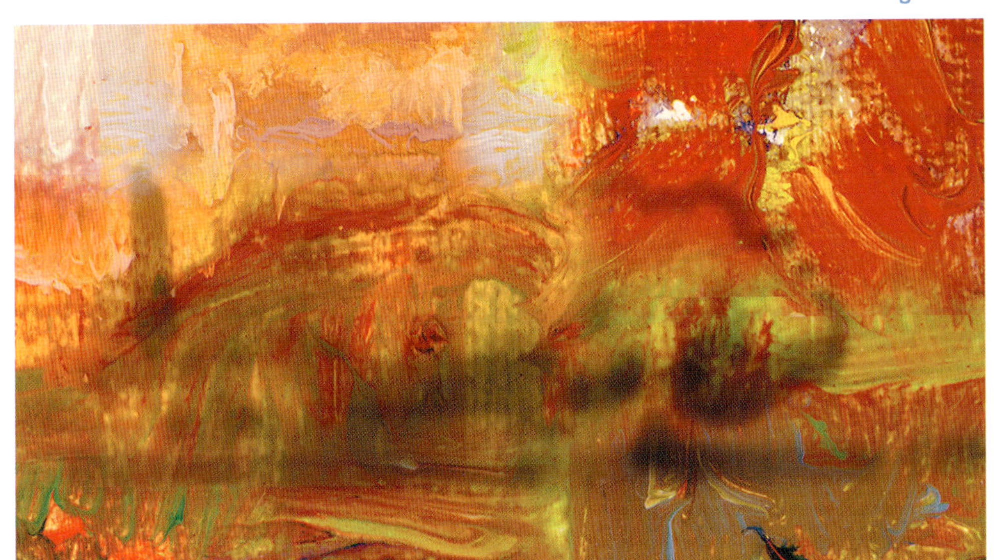

Fig. 4.97

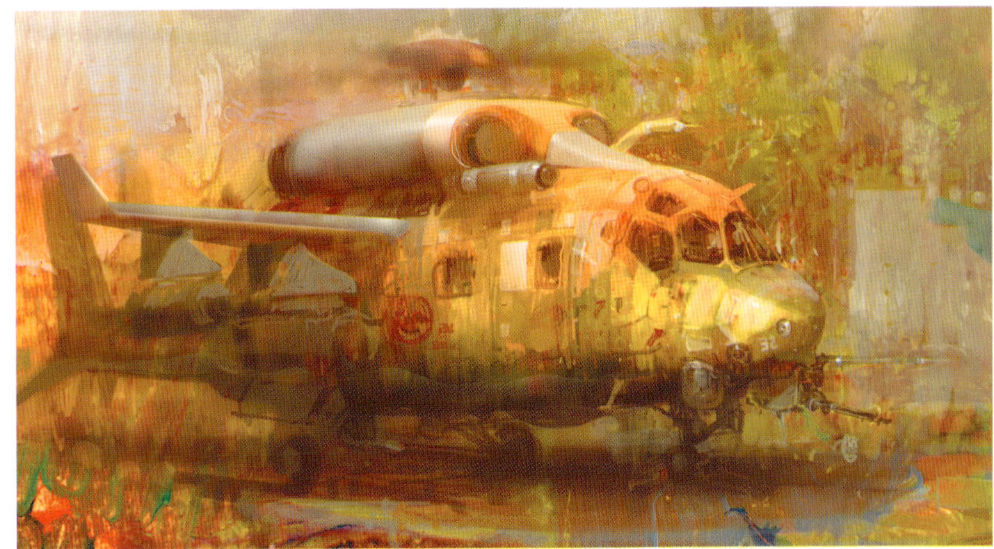

Fig. 4.96

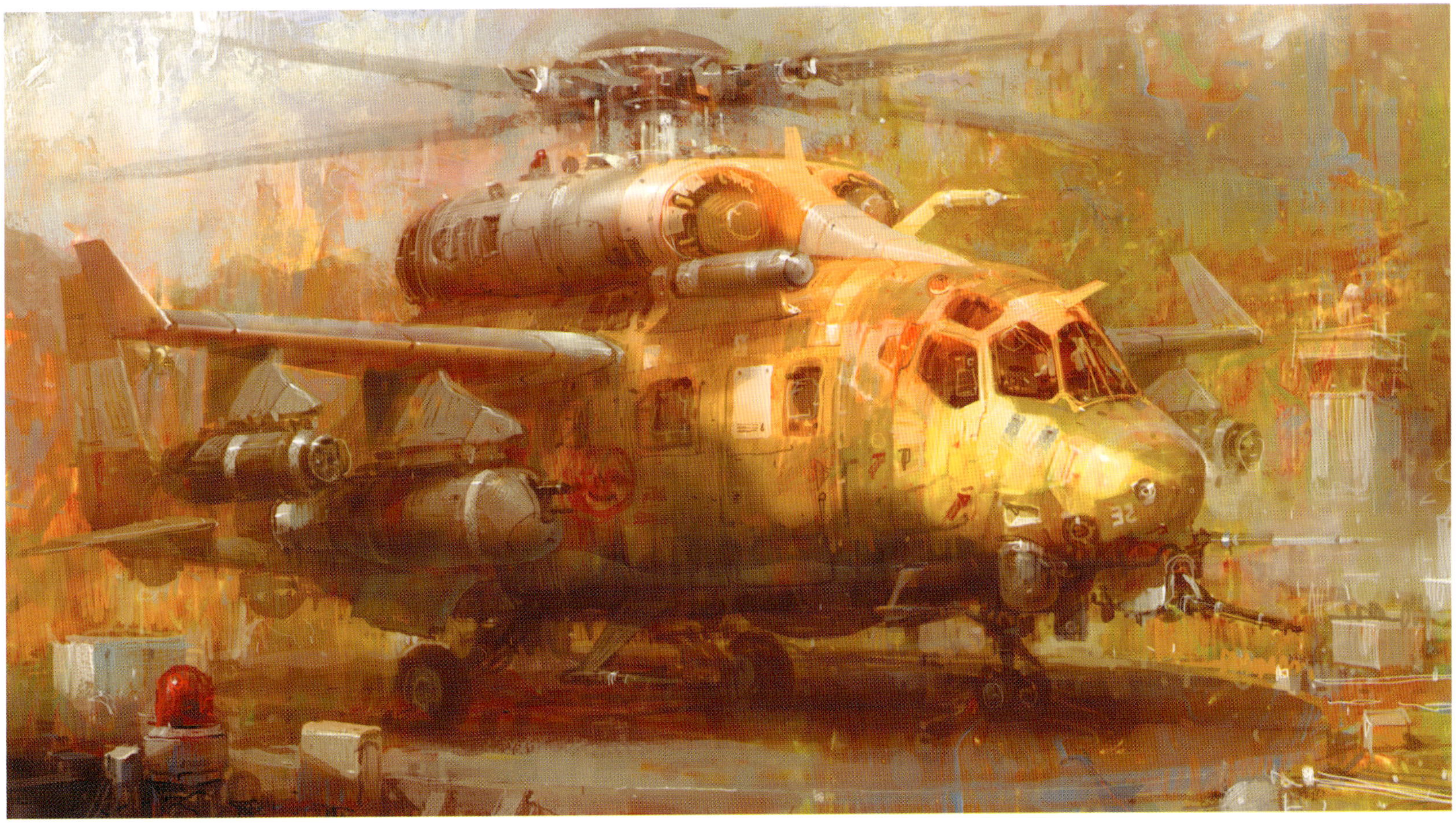

Fig. 4.98

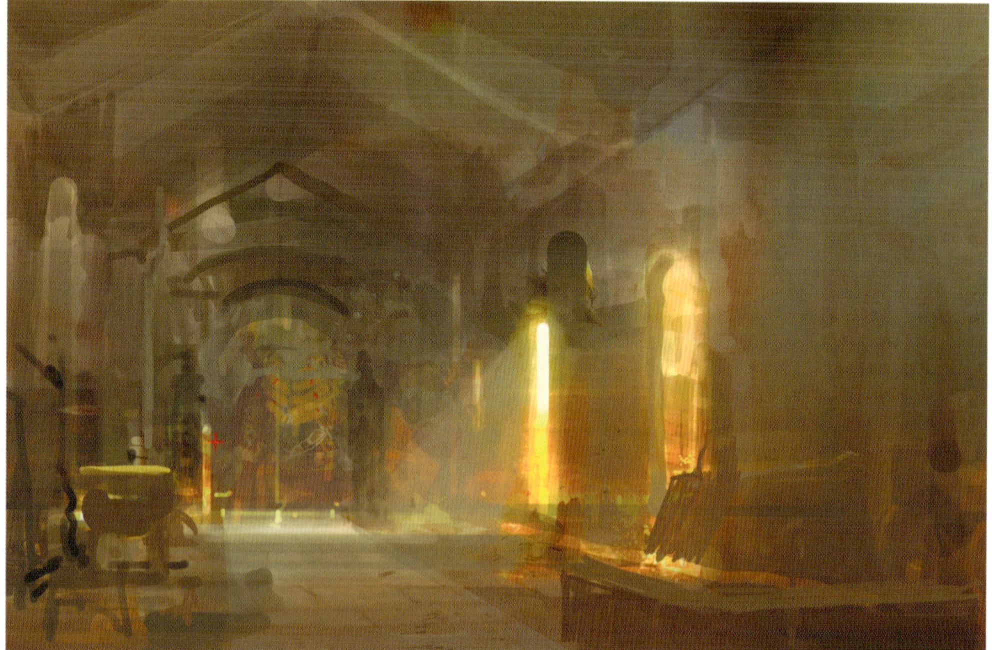

Fig. 4.99

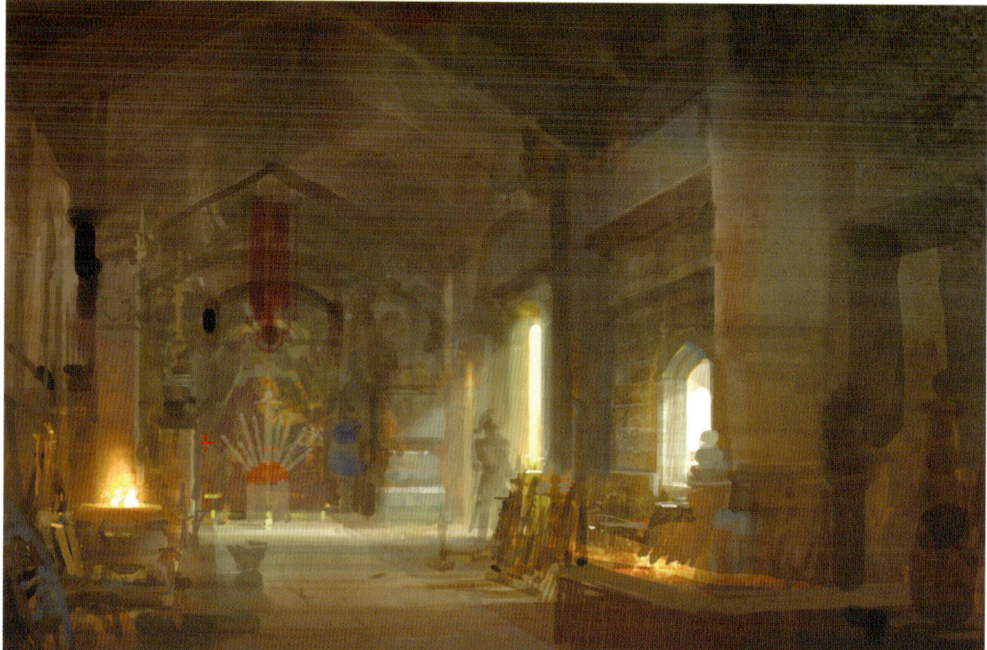

Fig. 4.100

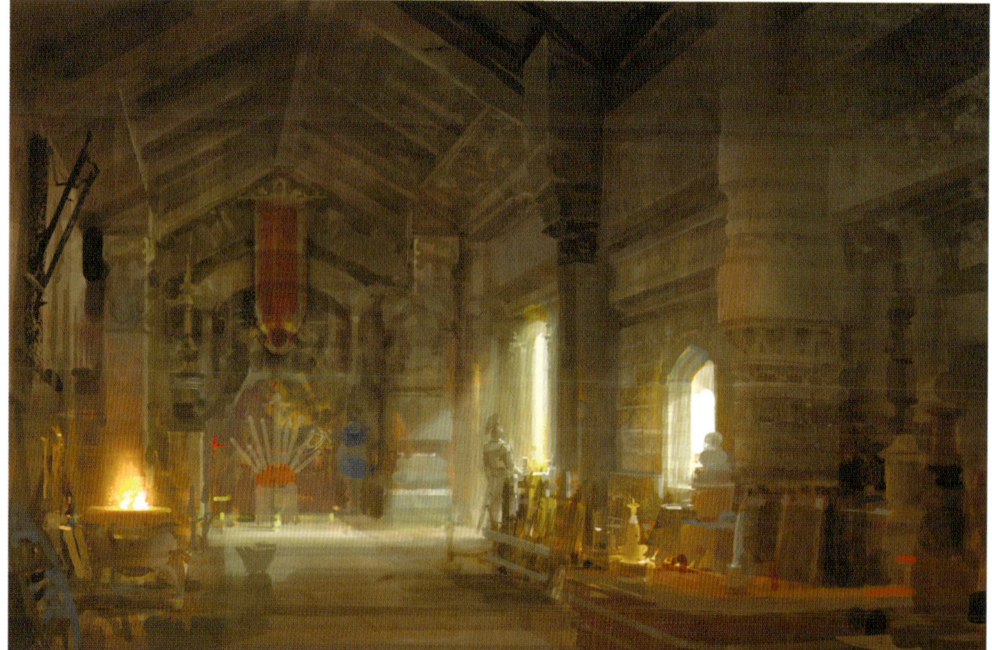

Fig. 4.101

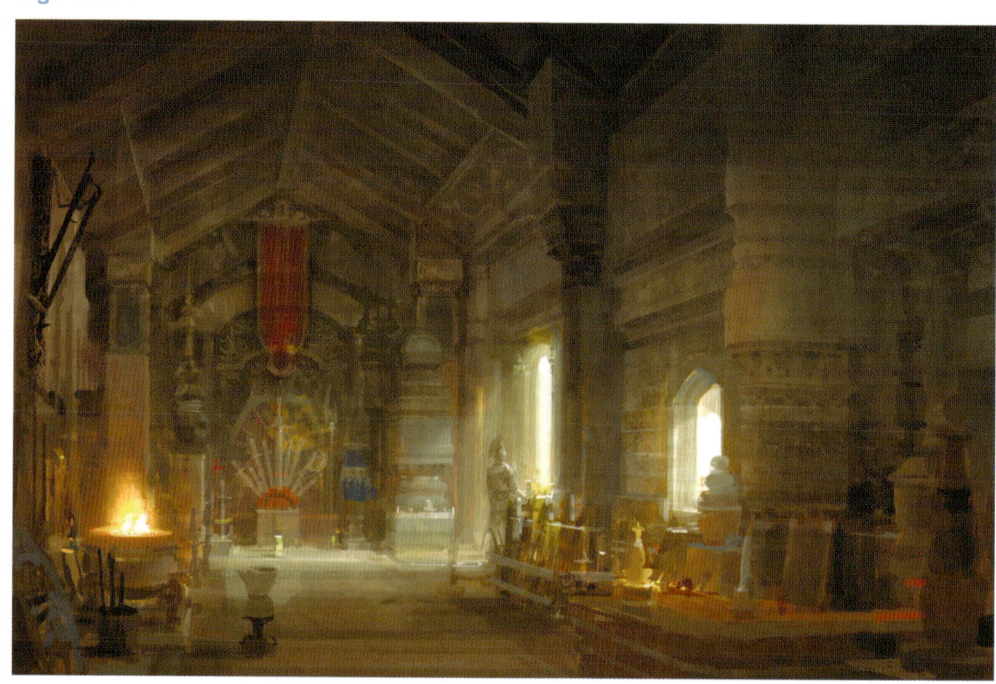

For this room, I started the painting with big shapes, and then I blocked in the local color of the objects. Next, I indicated general lighting information from the window. Do not pay too much attention to the individual objects in the room; pay more attention to the big feeling of the scene. By using value grouping, you can paint more objects into a scene without making it too busy.

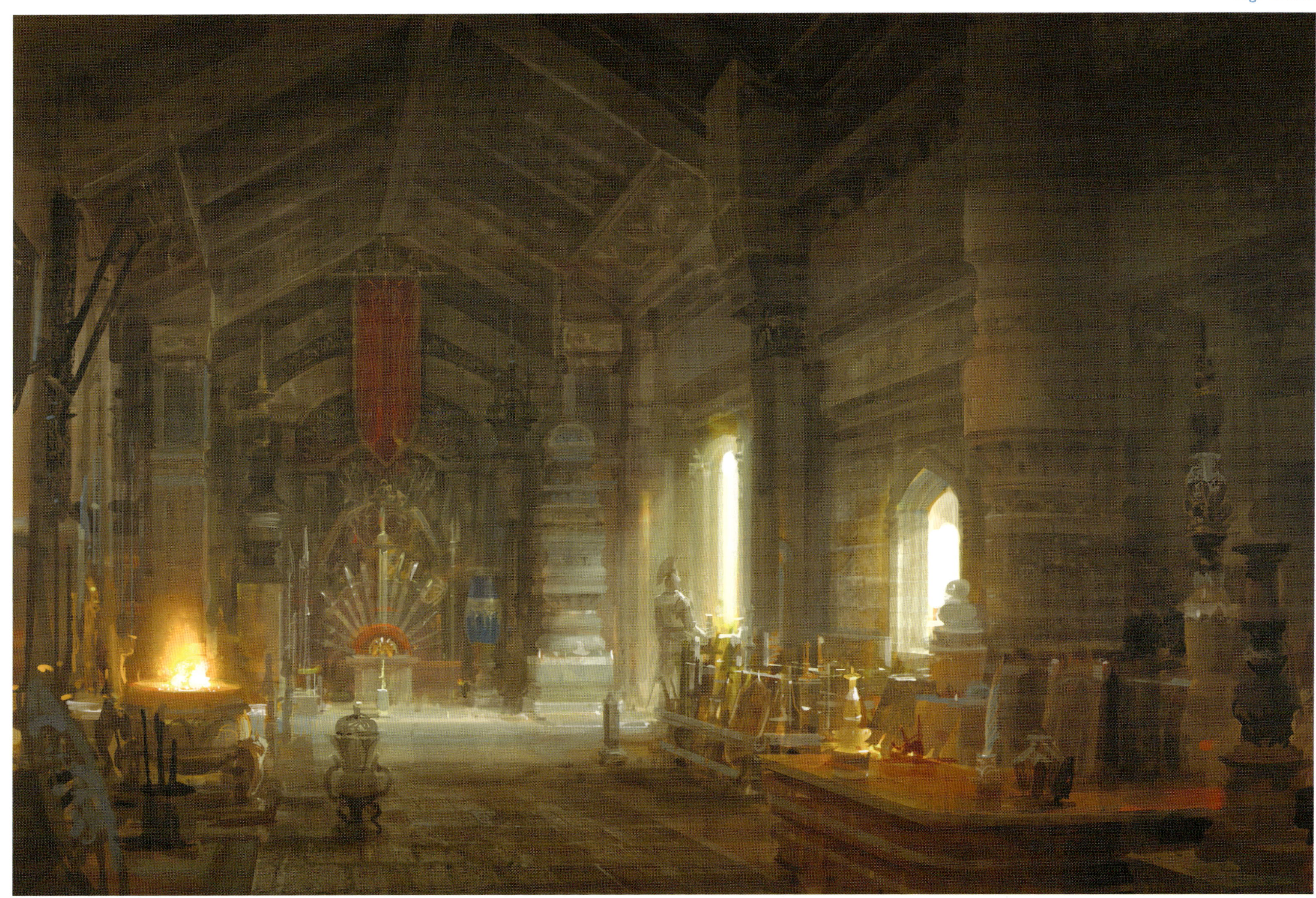

A bounce light gives a cool illusion to the atmosphere in the room. To finish off the painting, I used the Lasso tool to create the clean, sharp edges. I also varied brushstrokes to create a more interesting effect. In some areas, I used a very sharp, bright color to create the highlight. That brought up the contrast of the painting and made the painting look more finished and interesting.

Fig. 4.103

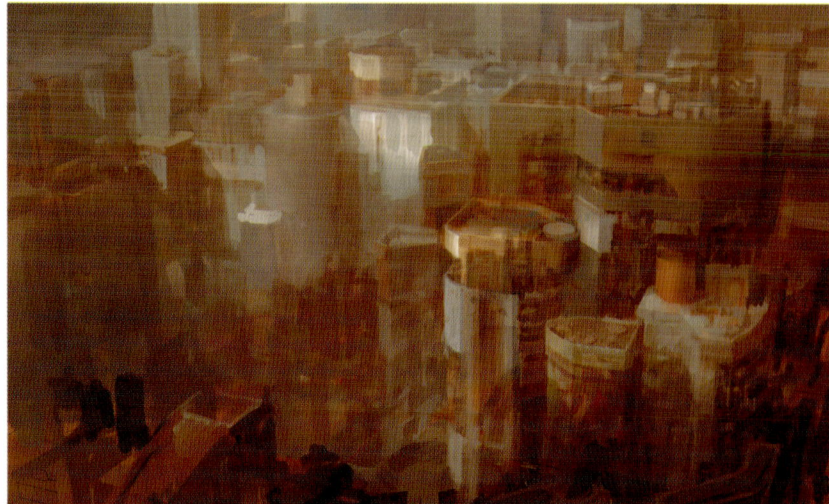

Fig. 4.104

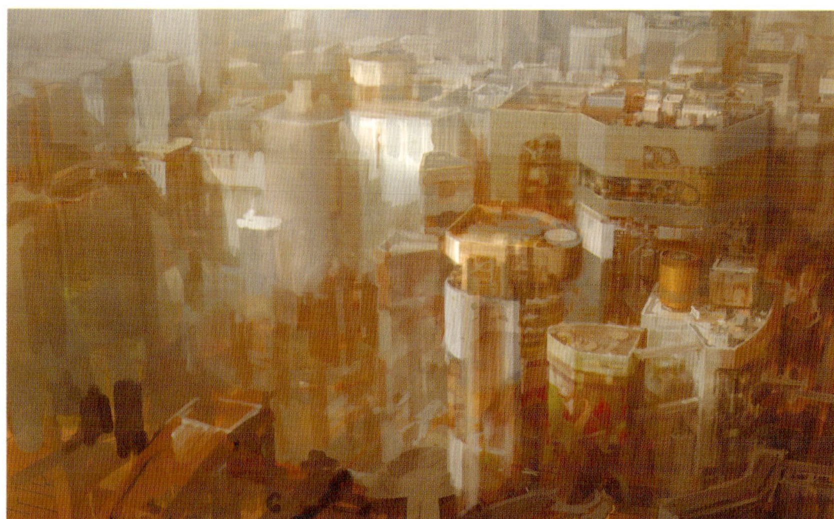

Fig. 4.105

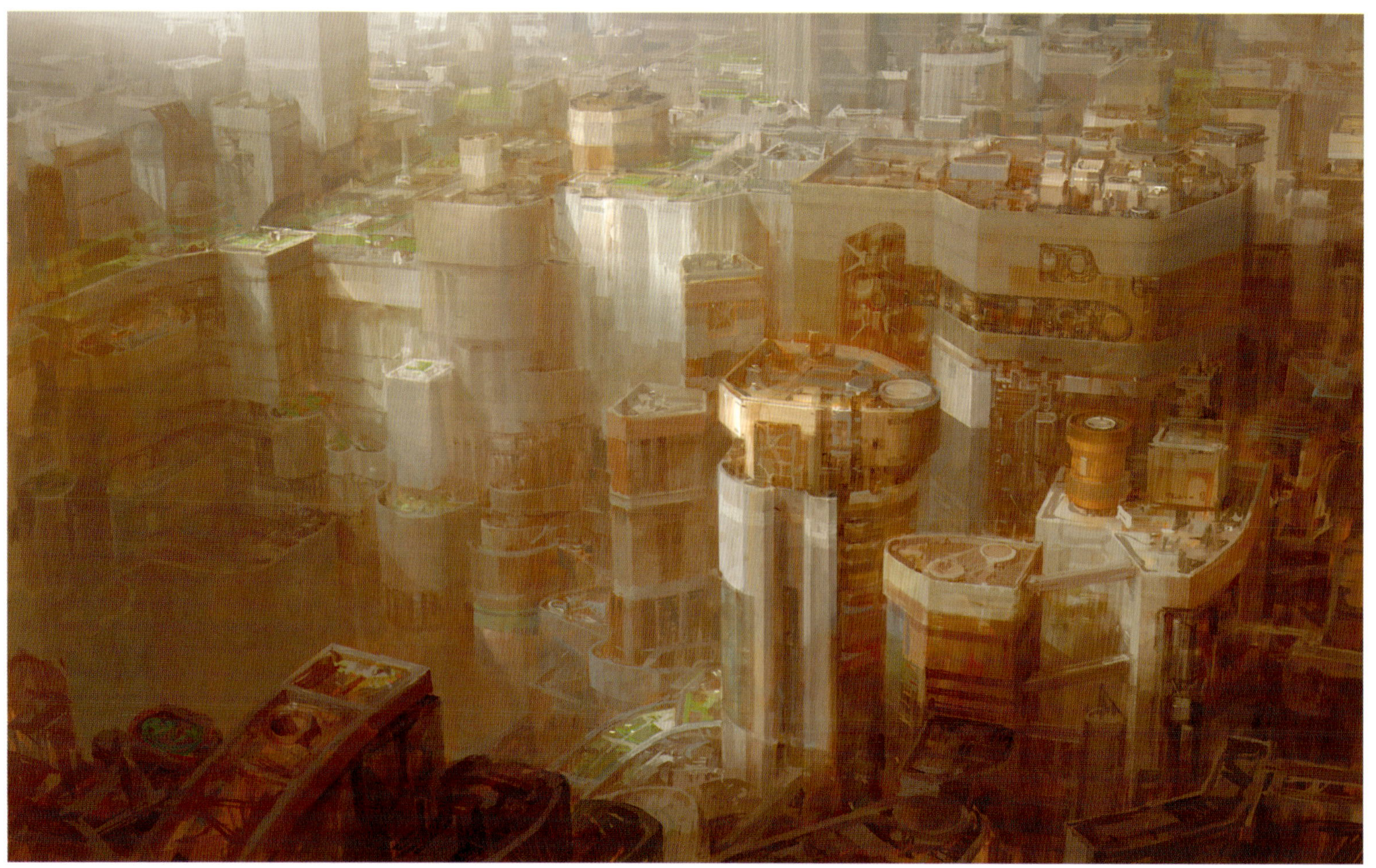

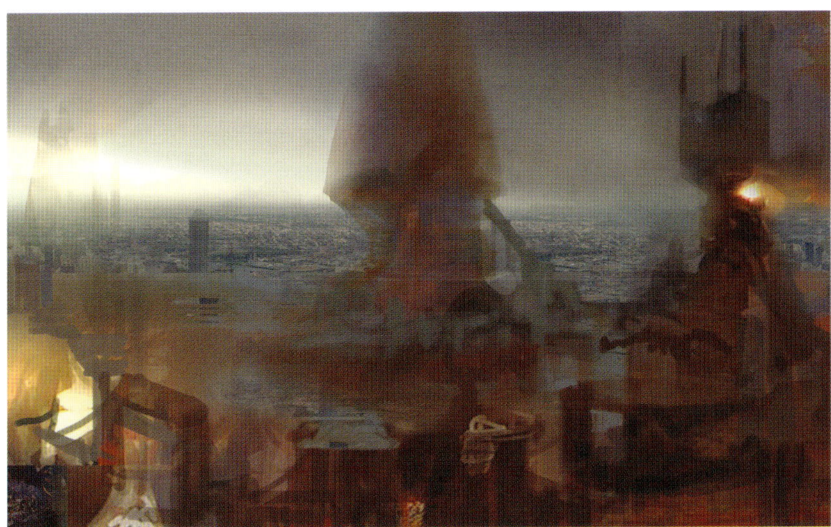

Fig. 4.106

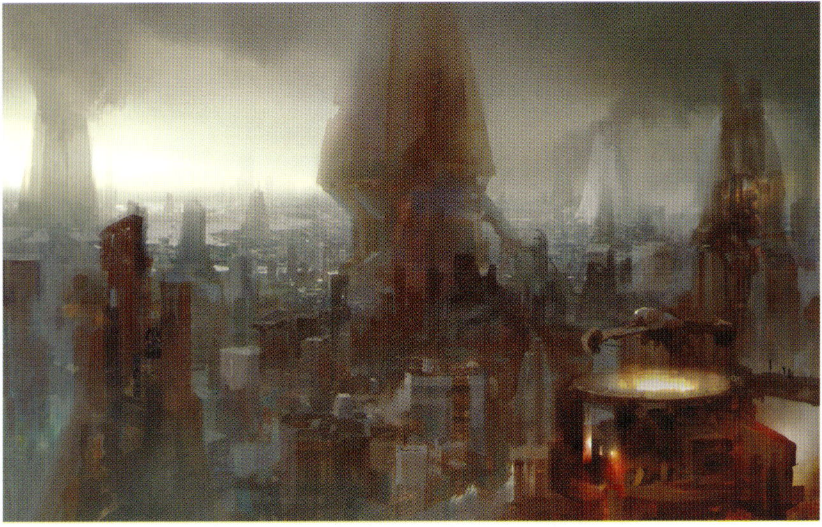

Fig. 4.107

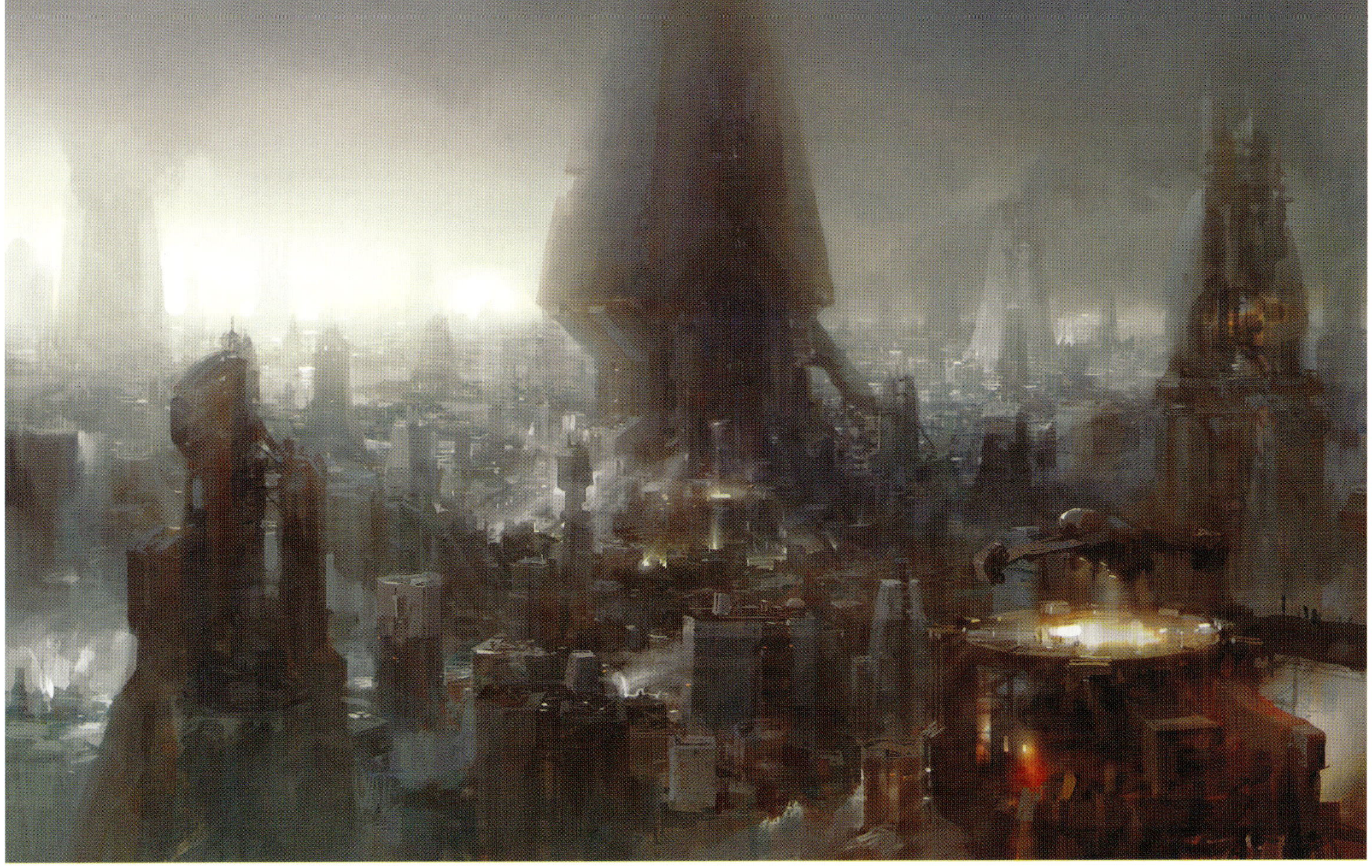

Fig. 4.108

Fig. 4.109

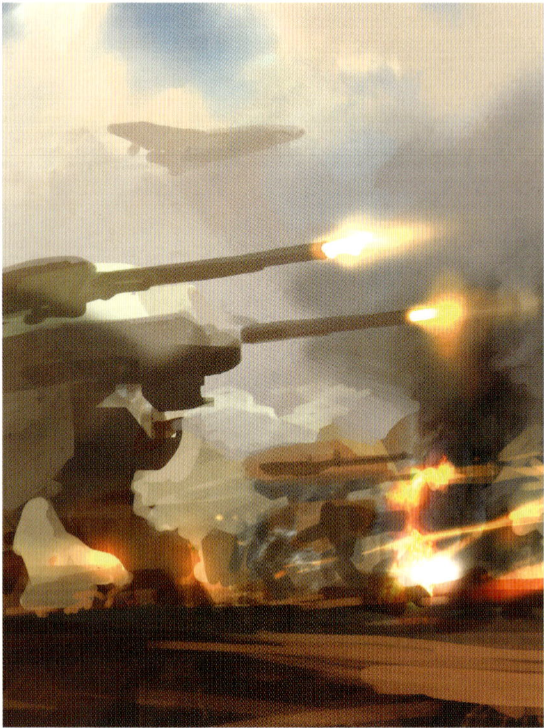

Fig. 4.110

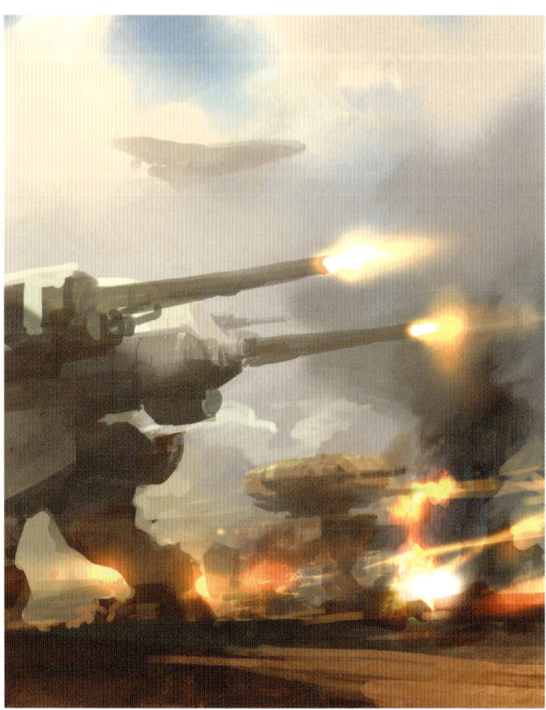

Fig. 4.111

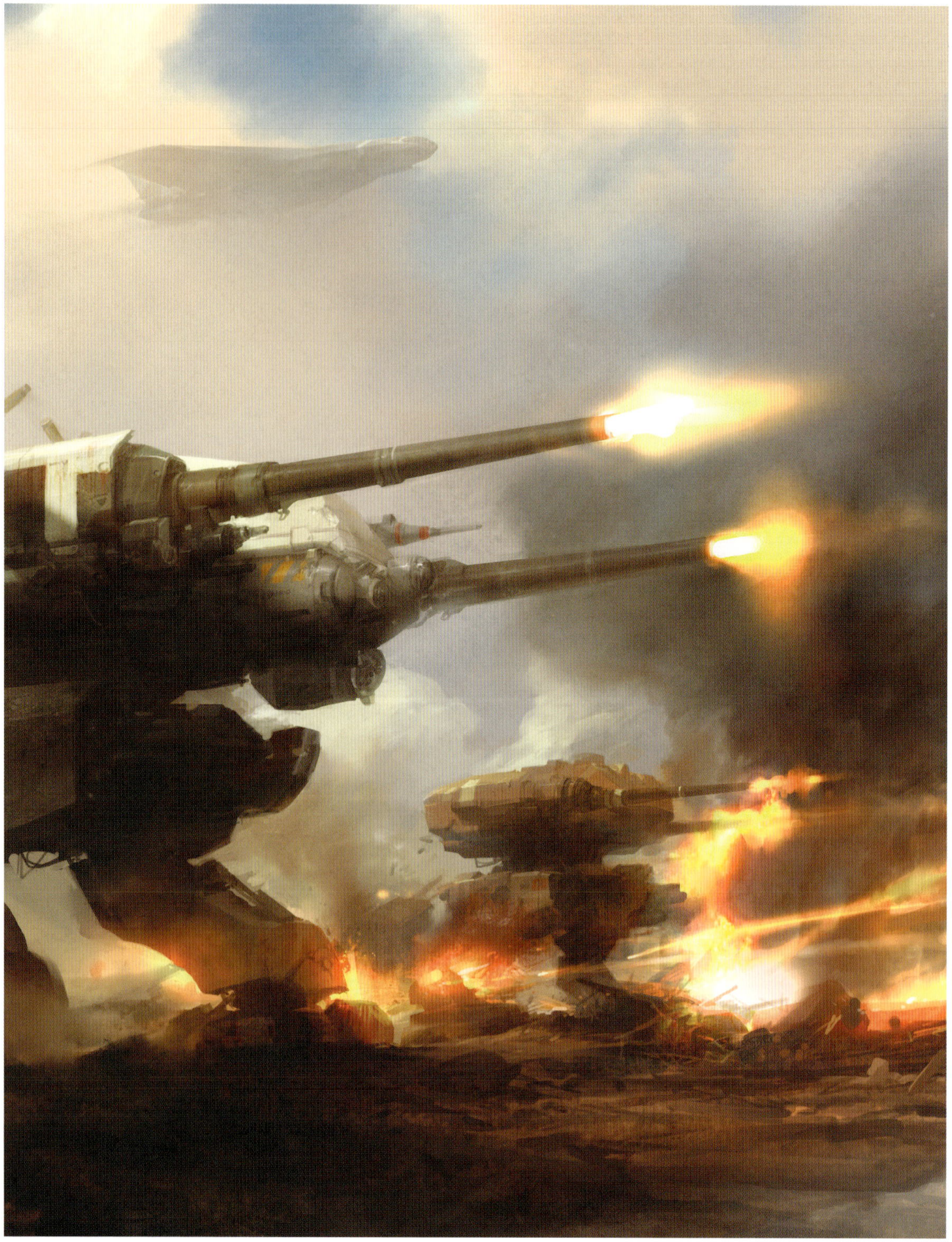

Fig. 4.112

Fig. 4.113

Fig. 4.114

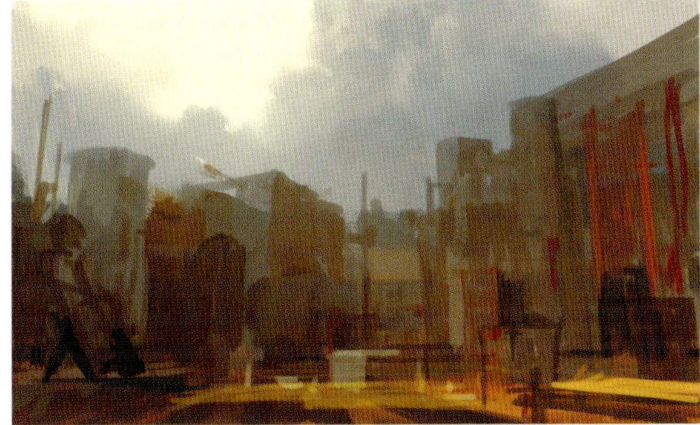

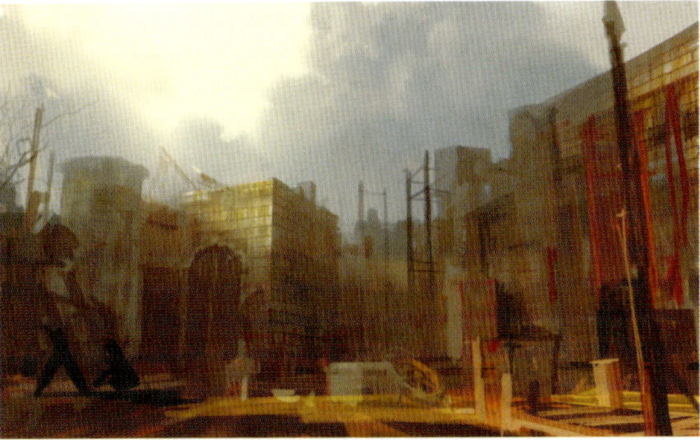

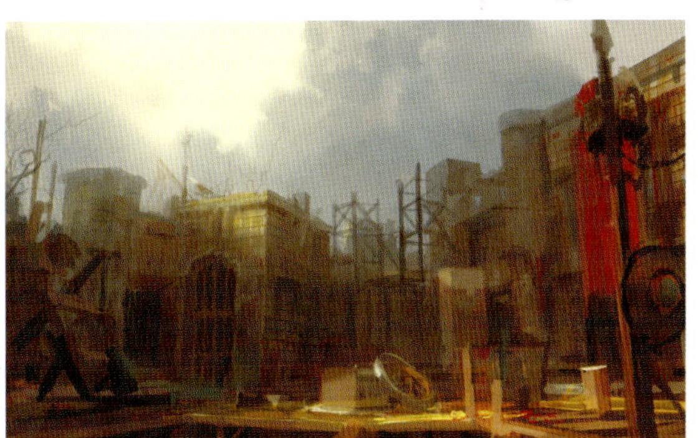

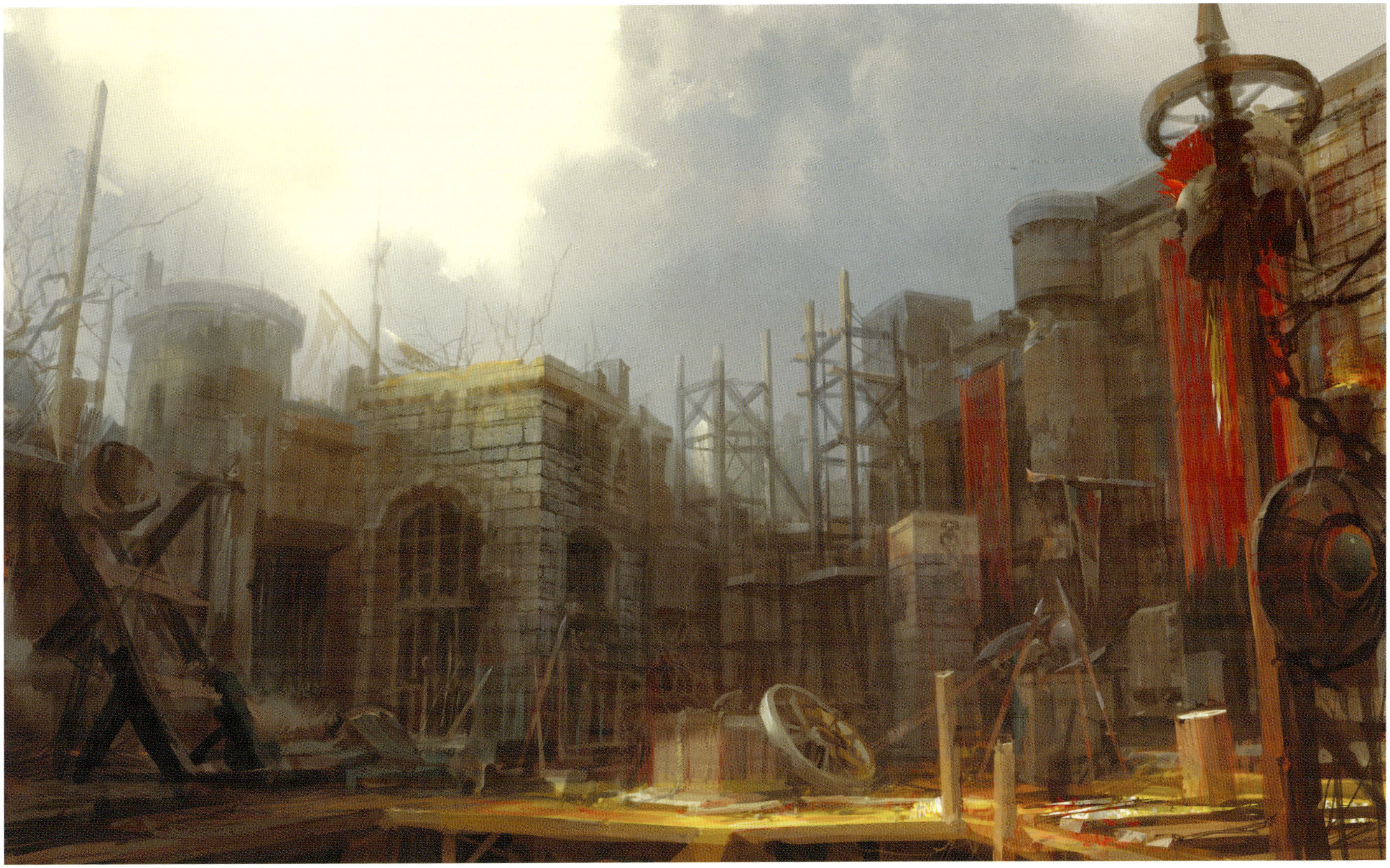

Fig. 4.115

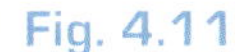

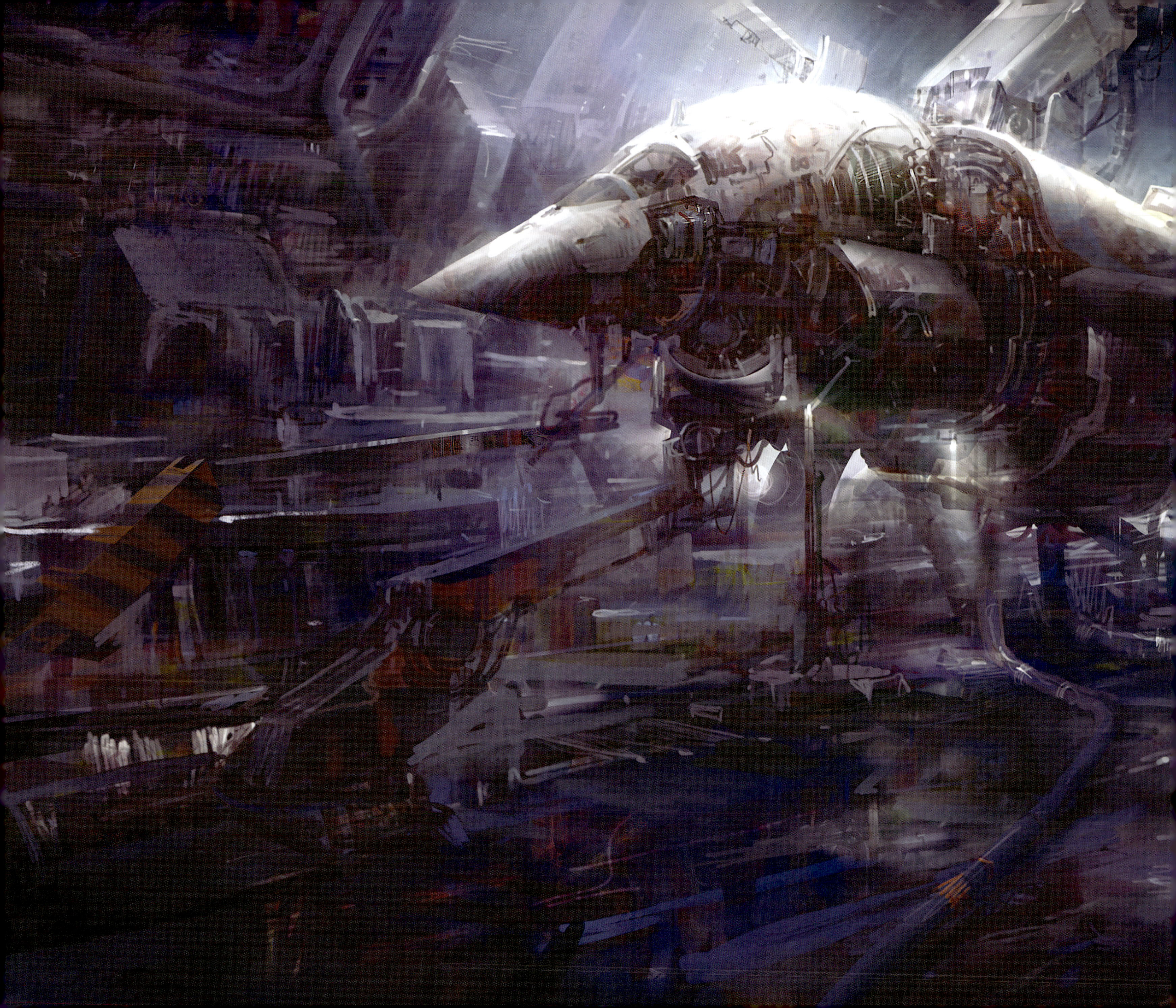

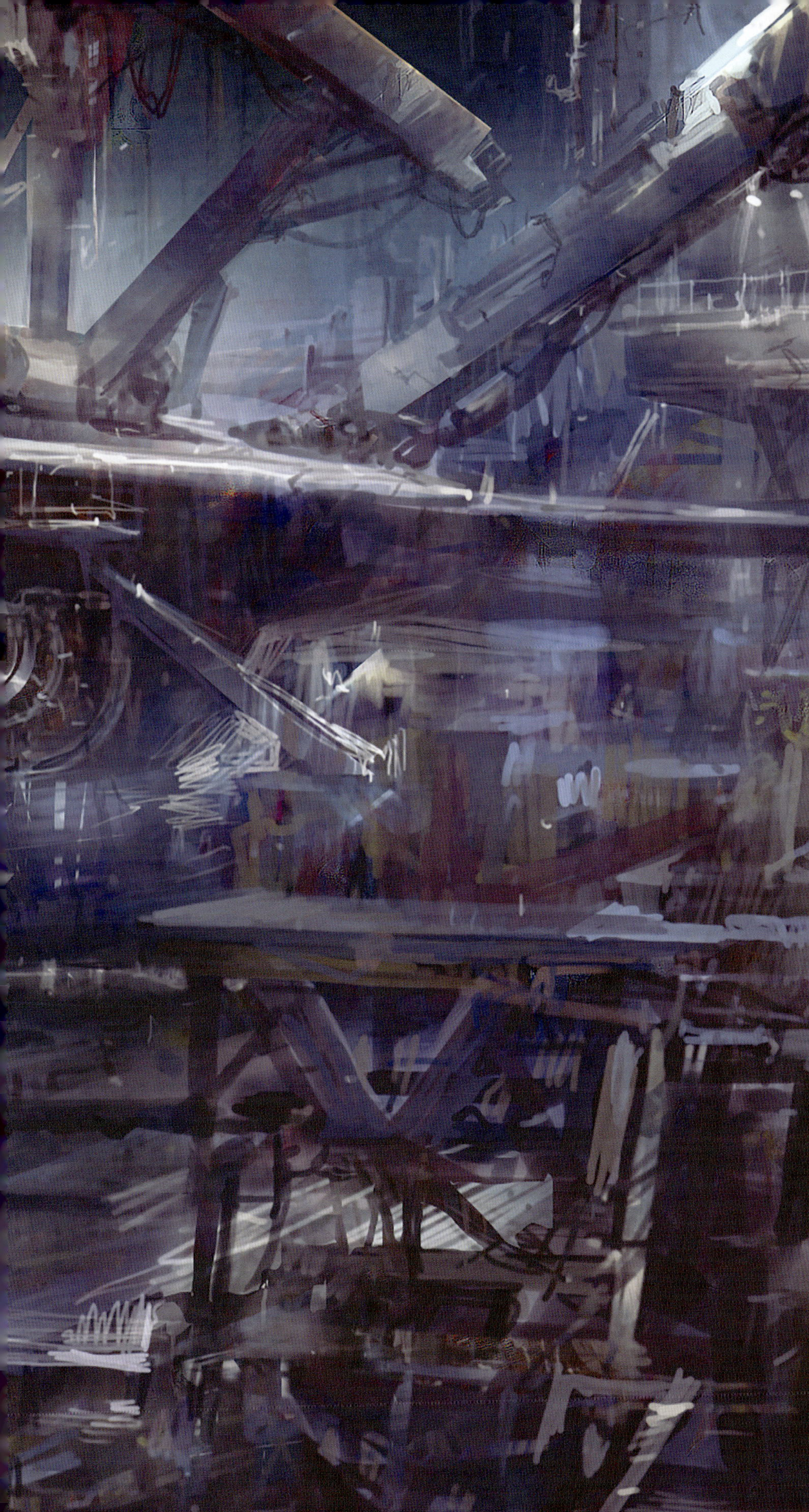

In this last section, I will share finished paintings that are a mix of my personal and professional work. Most of them were done in a digital medium, but as I showed in many tutorials, there are many pieces that started as traditional paintings and finished digitally. I mostly used Photoshop to create these paintings, but a few of them were done in Painter. In addition to these finished works, I included some rough sketches. With this collection, I have tried to show a variety of different subjects and painting techniques.

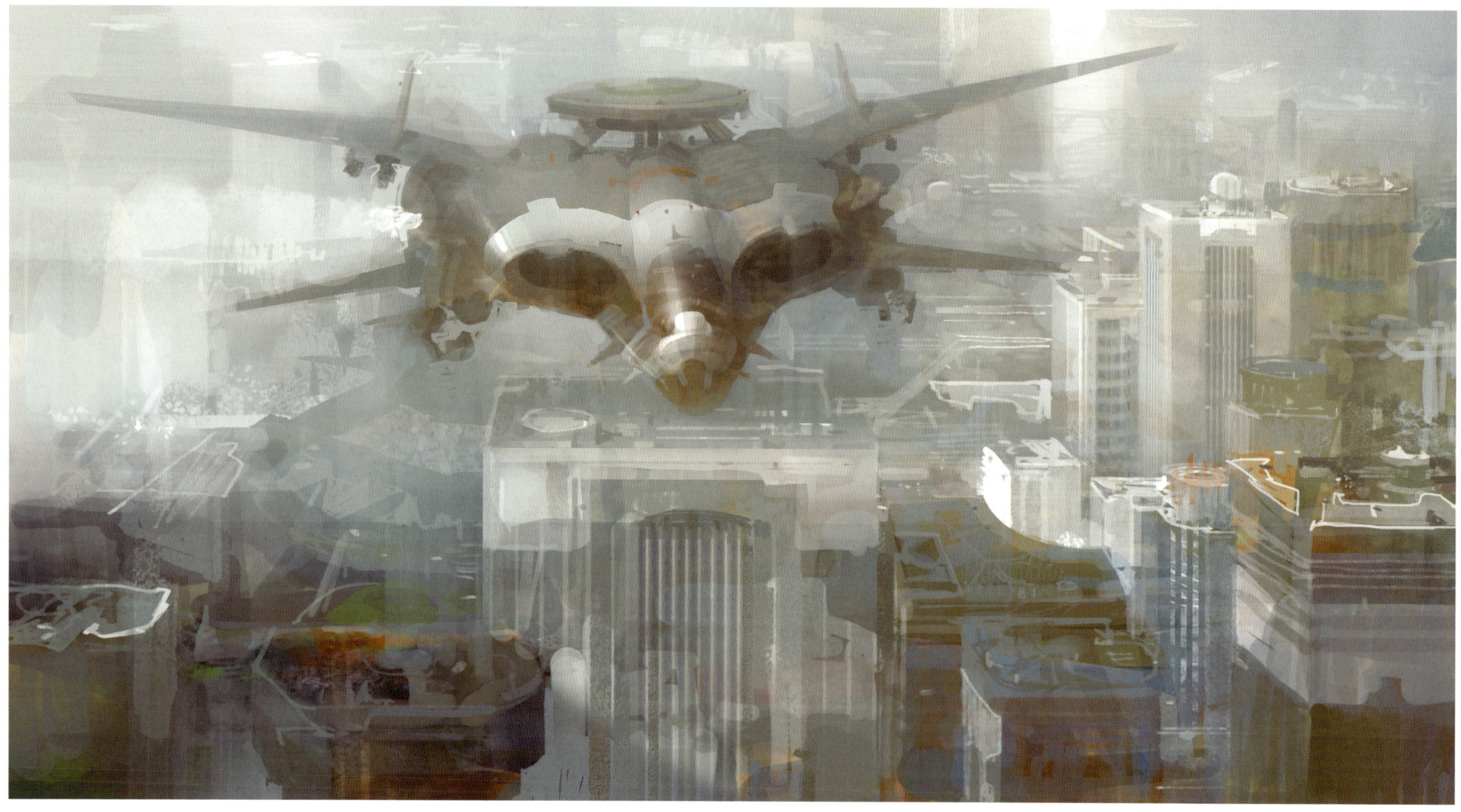

I NEVER complete a painting by **FINISHING** each section separately. **RATHER,** I develop the painting as a whole by **JUMPING** from section to section . . .

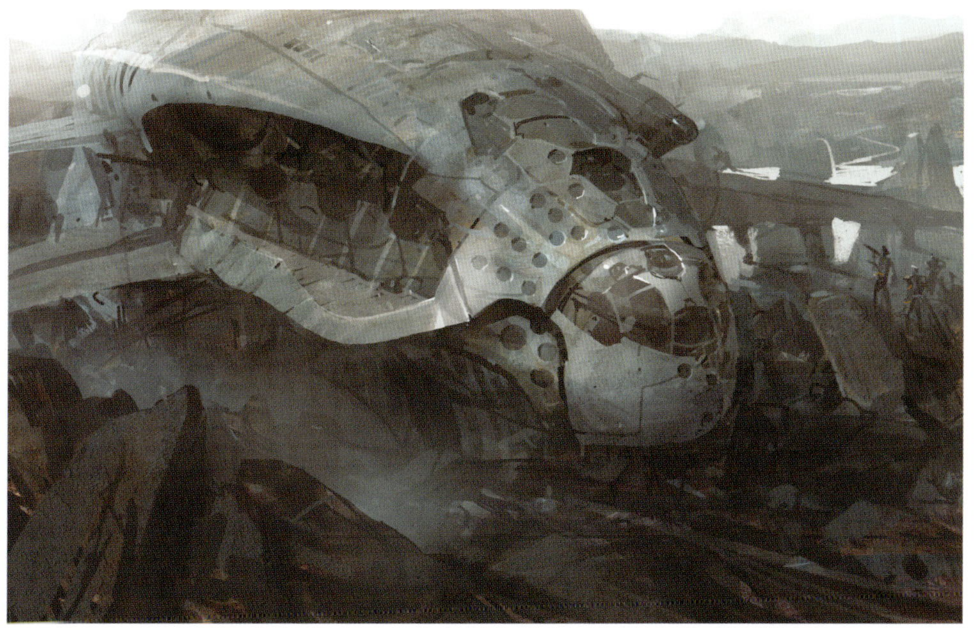

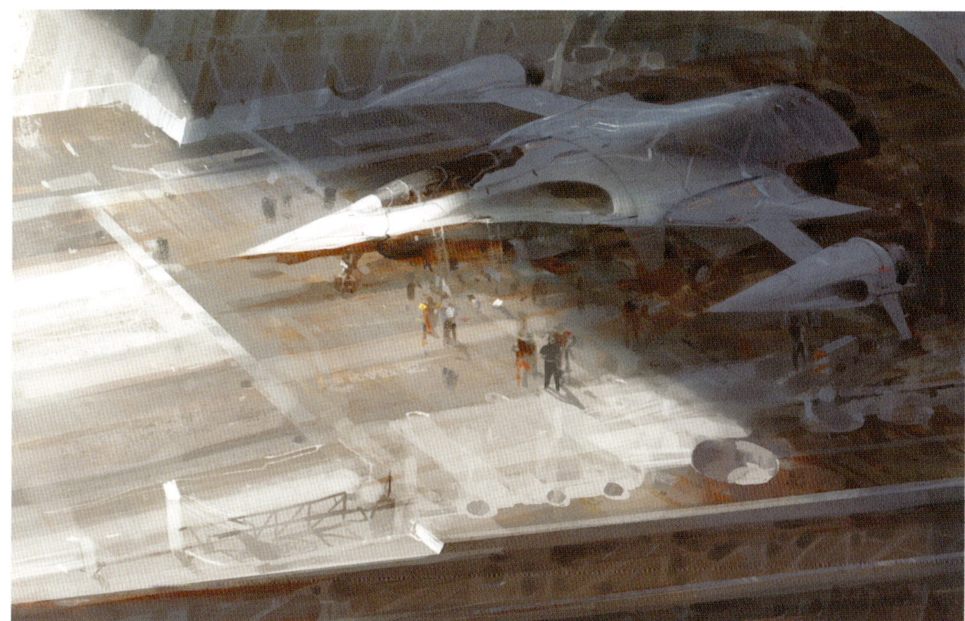

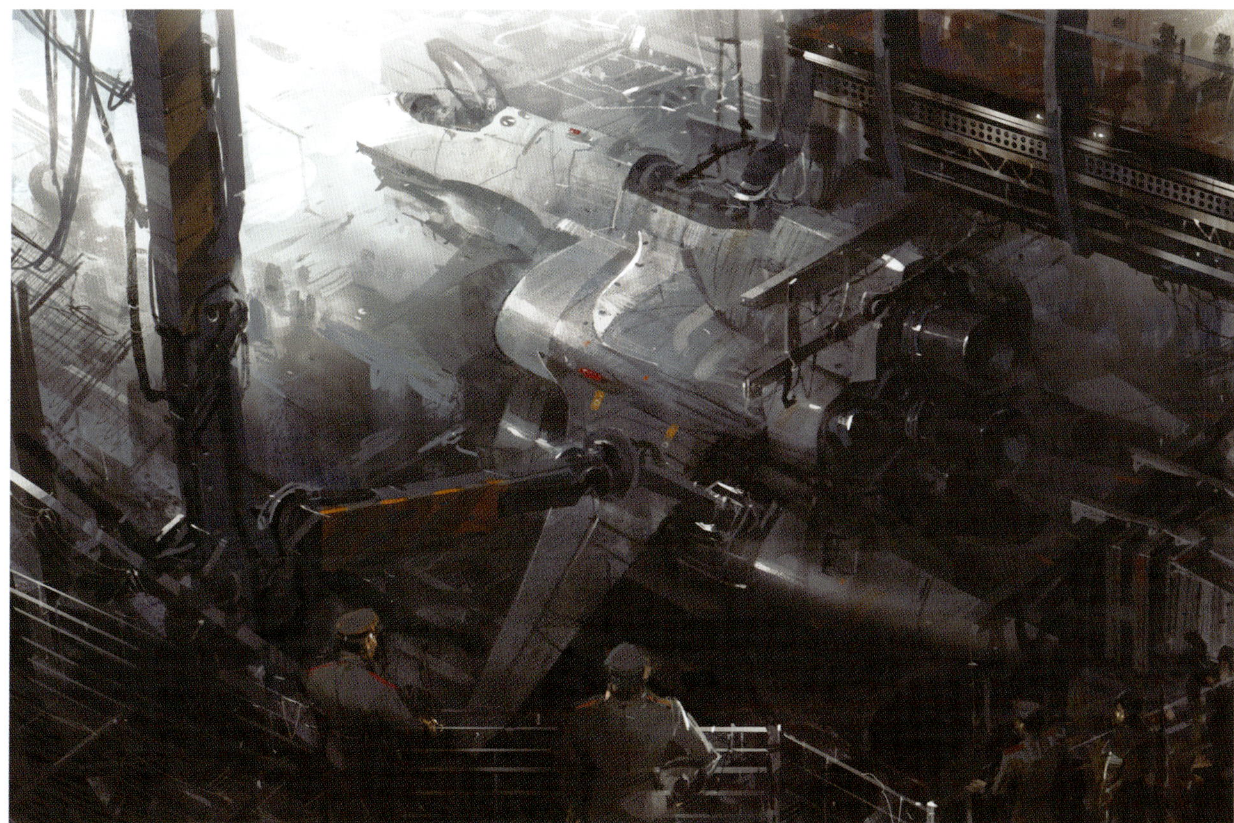

. . . all the while keeping an eye toward maintaining the **BALANCE** of the picture.

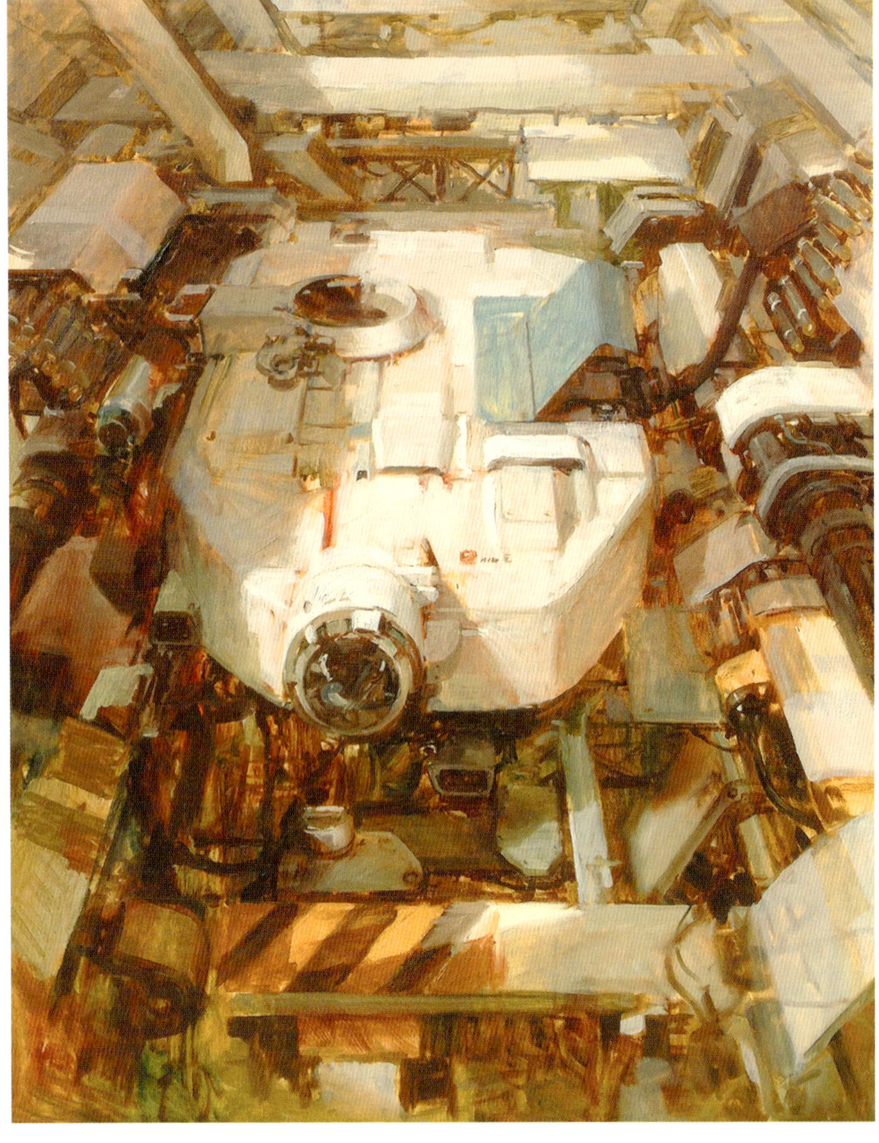

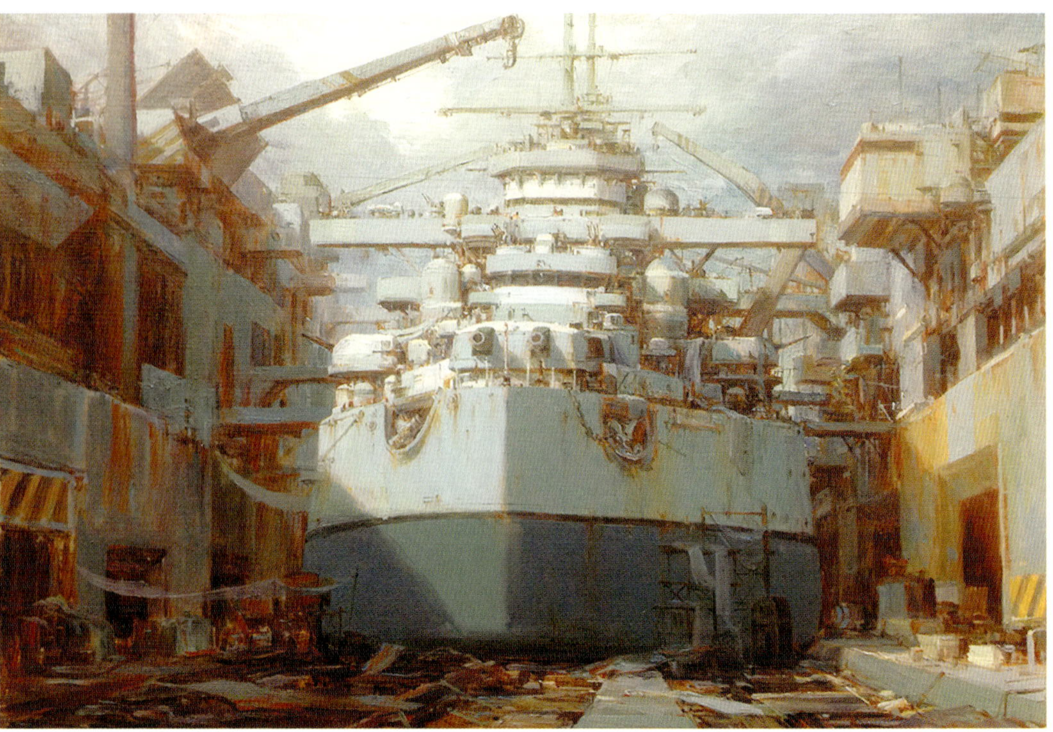

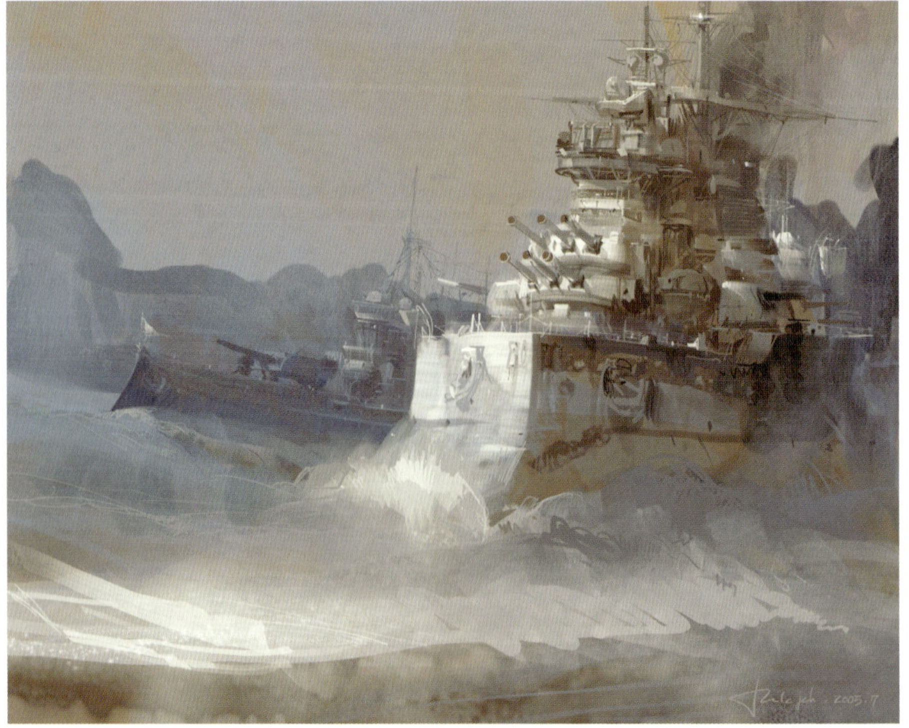

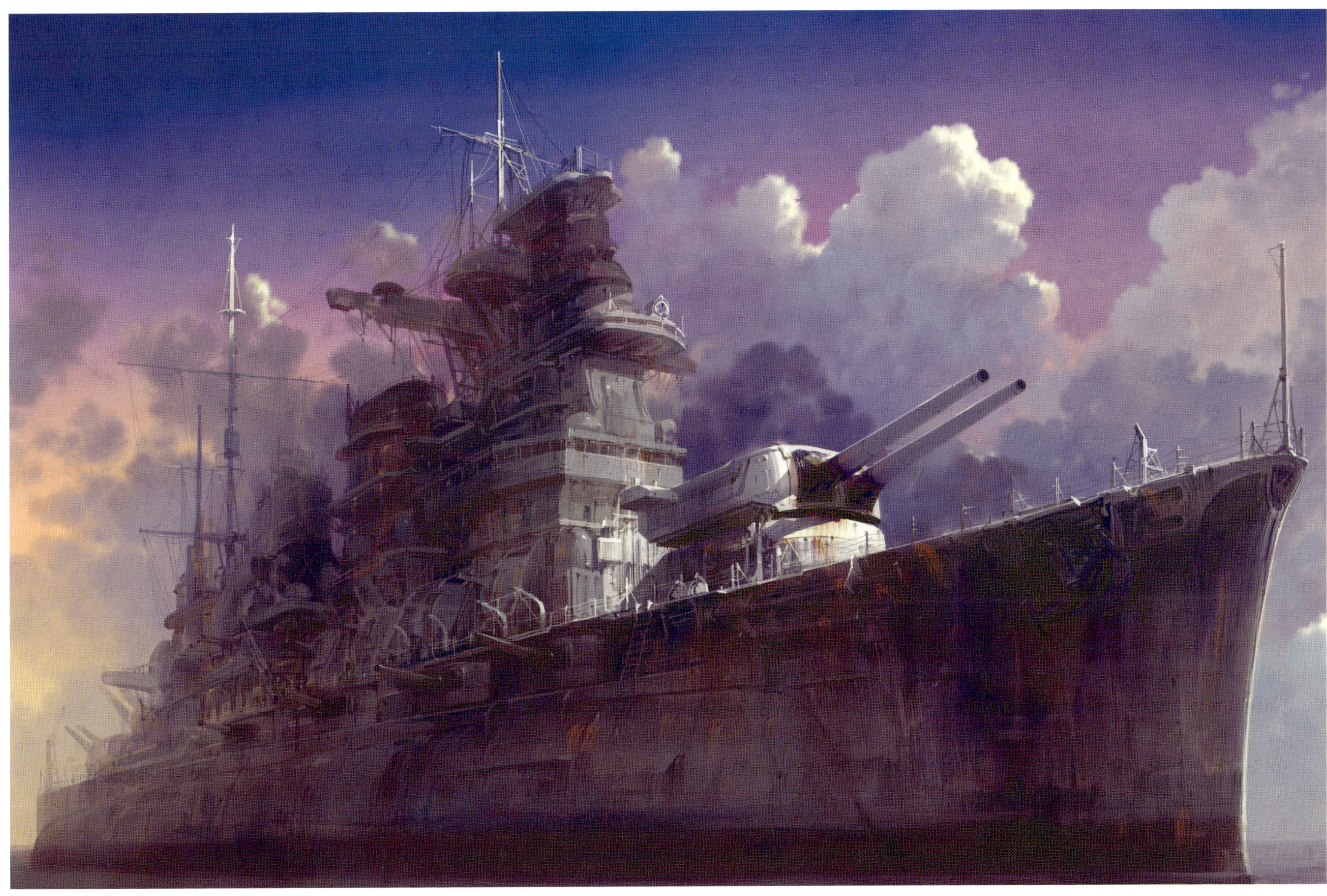

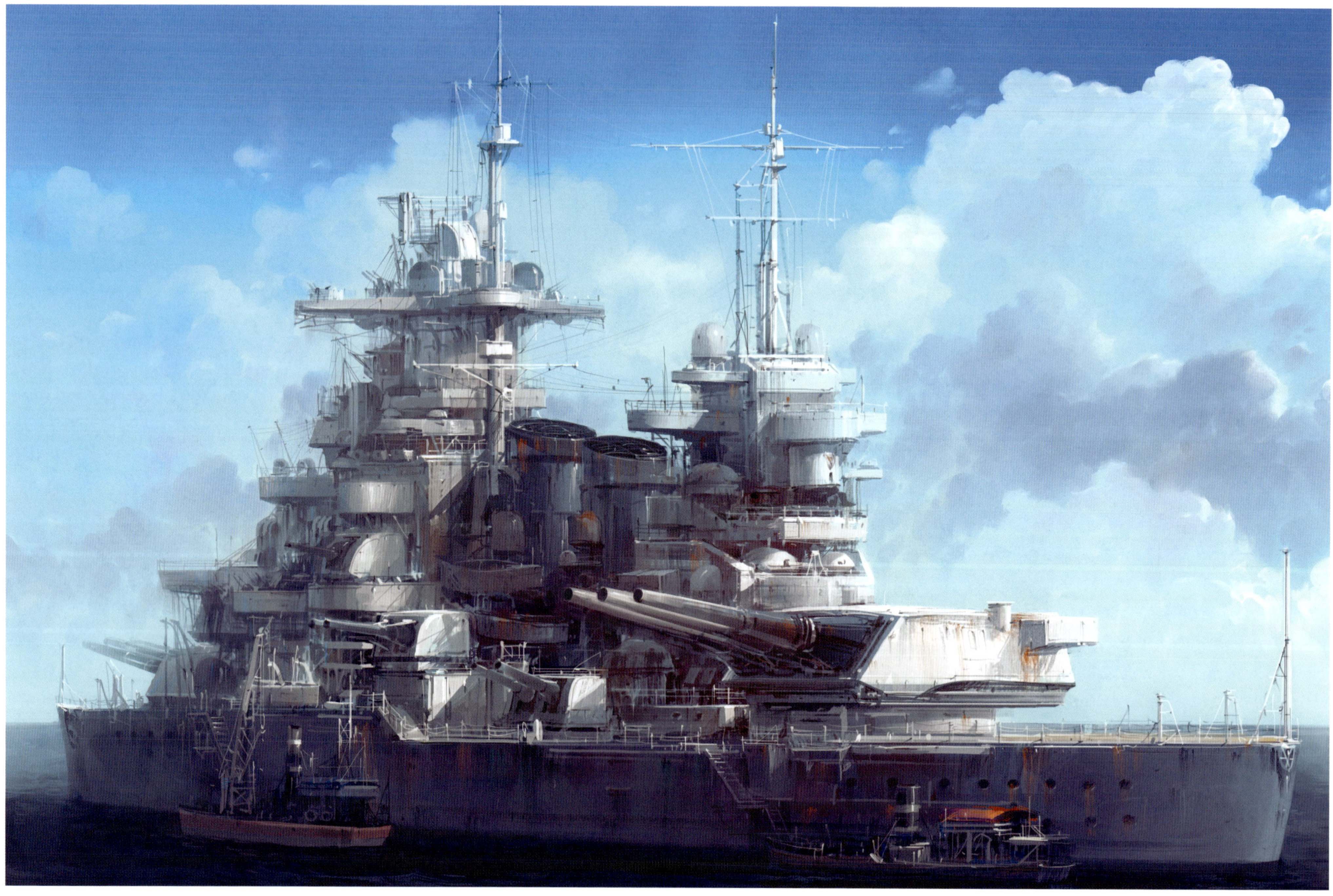

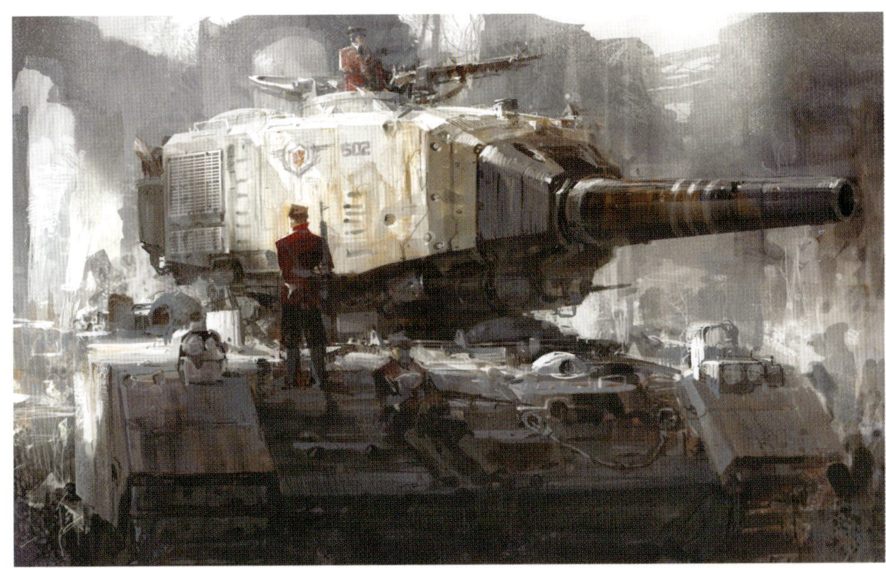 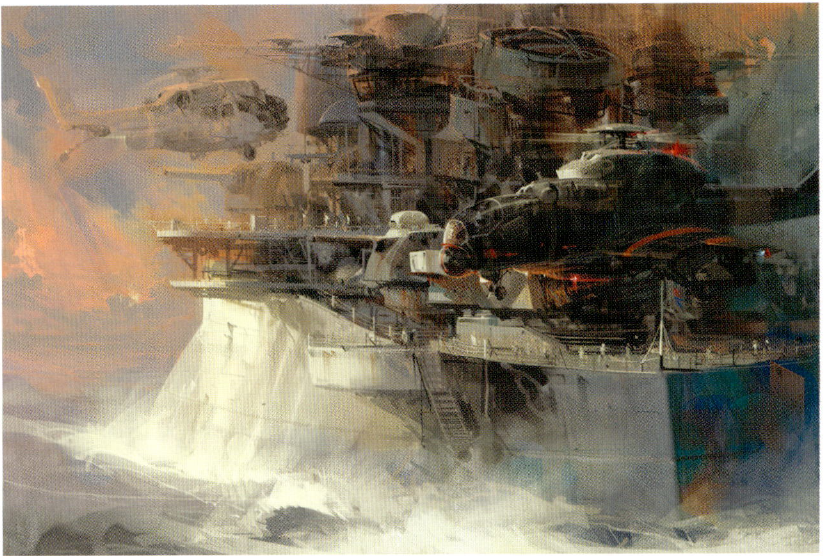

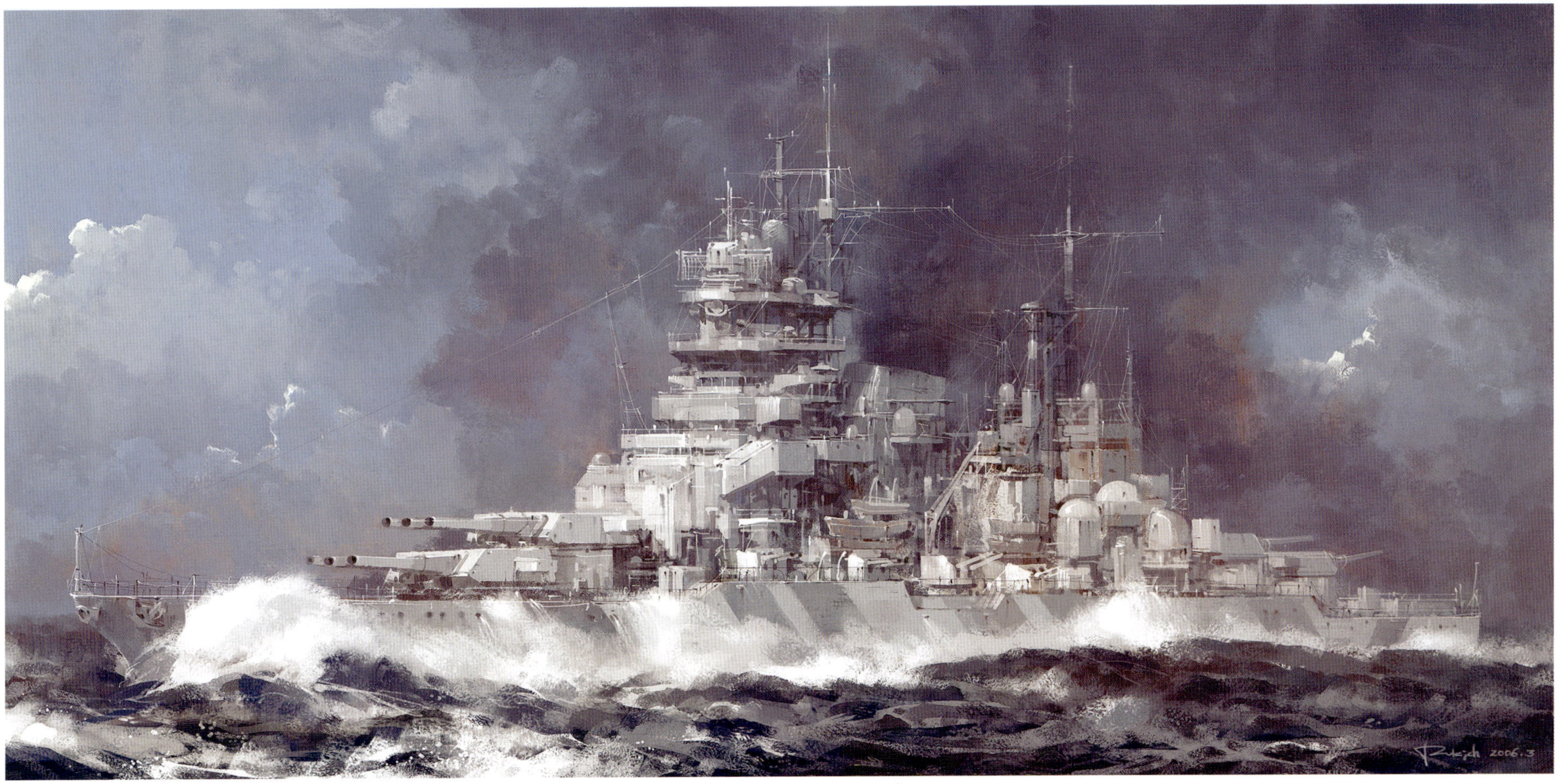

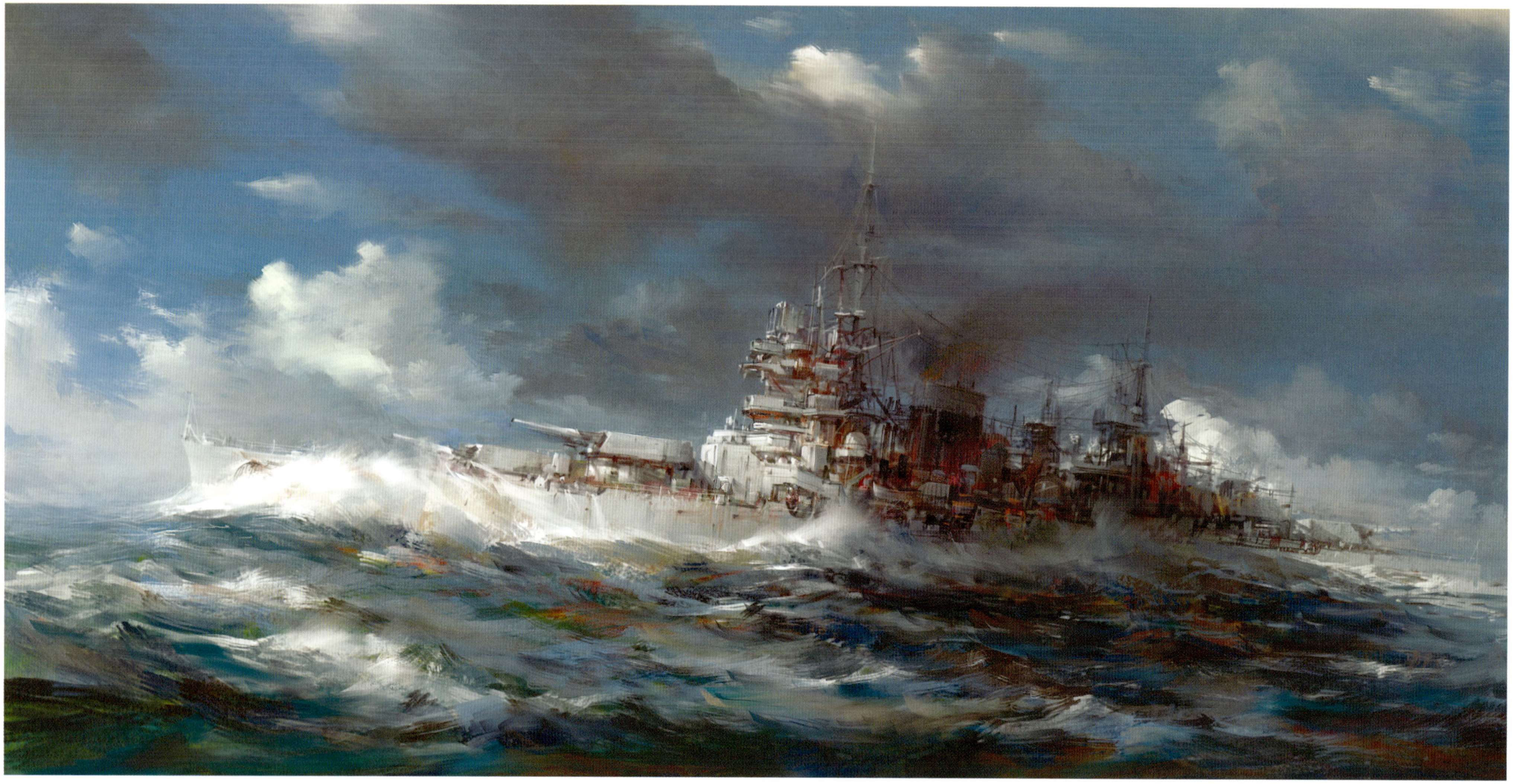

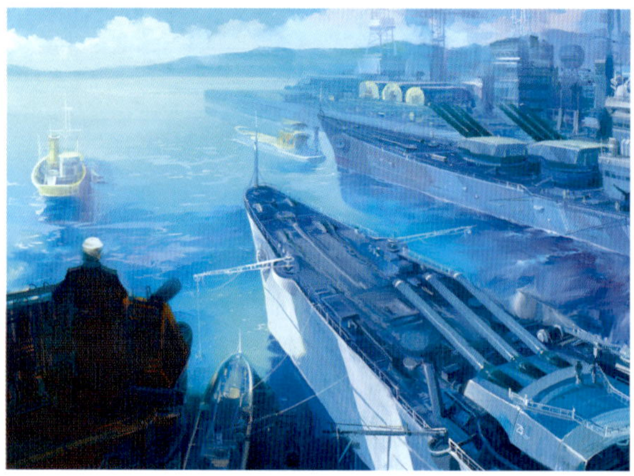

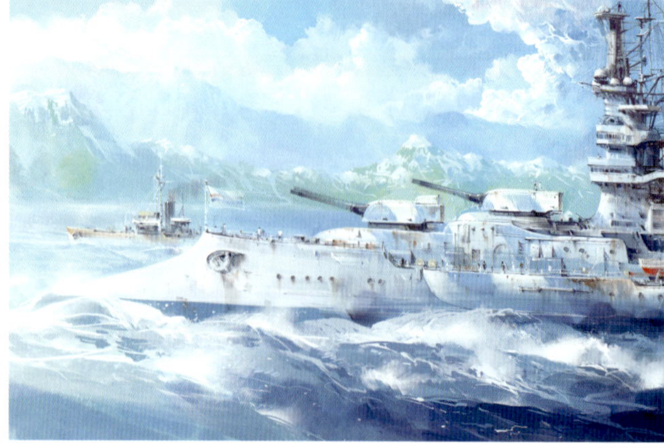

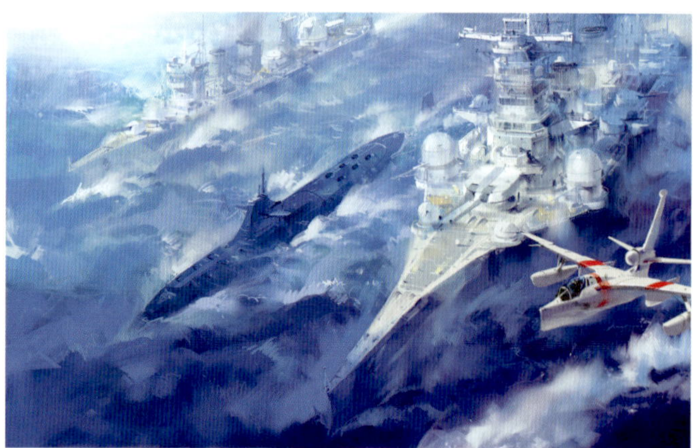

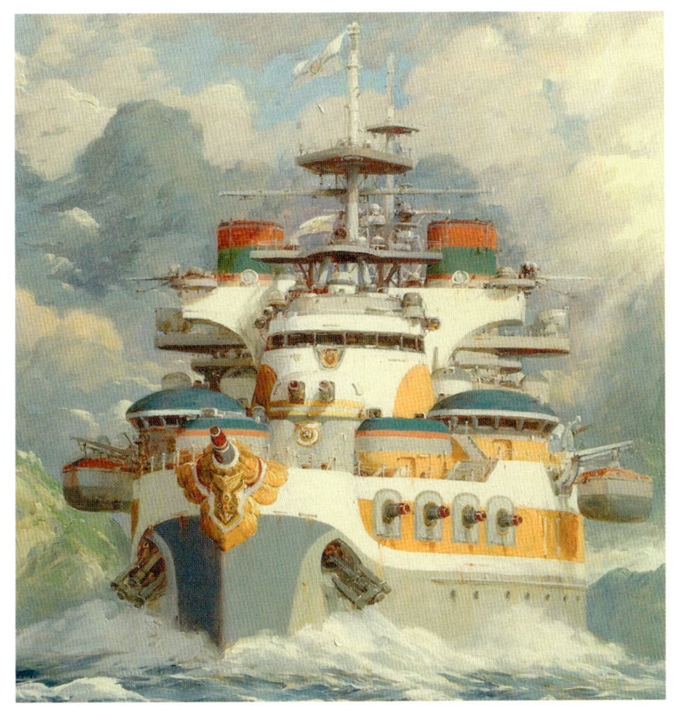

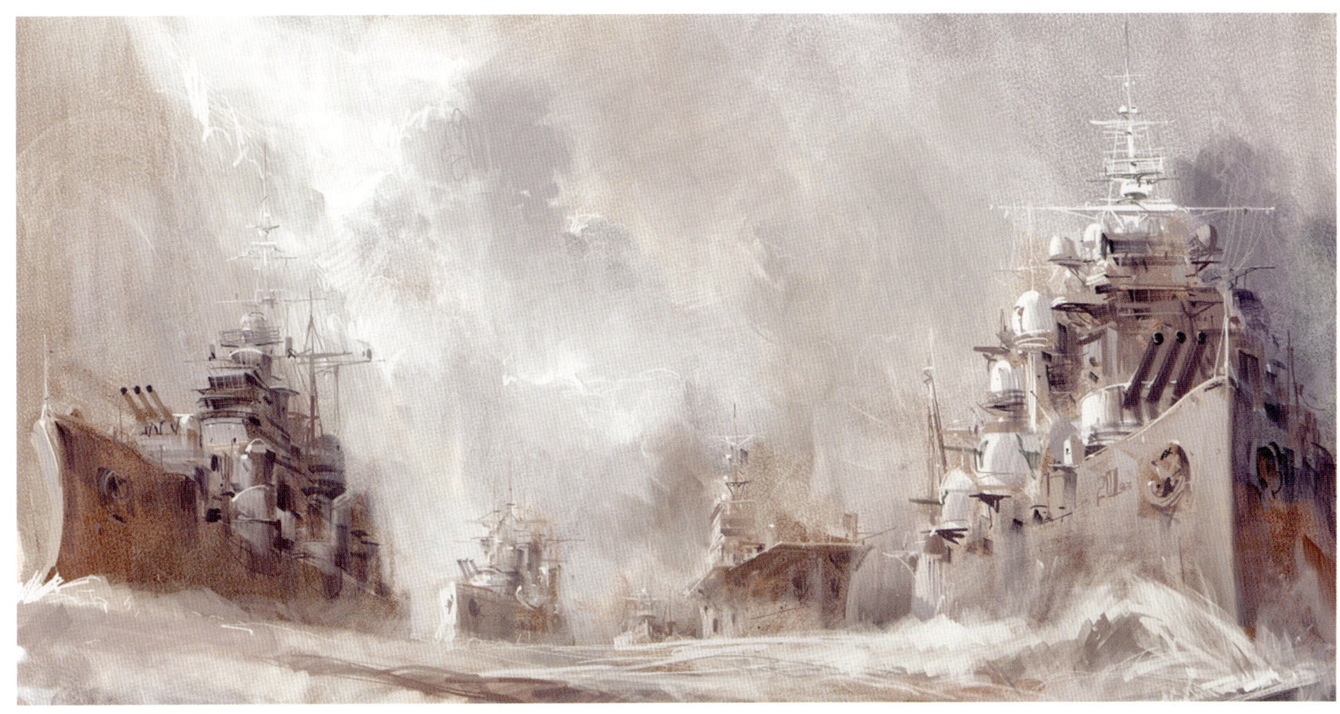

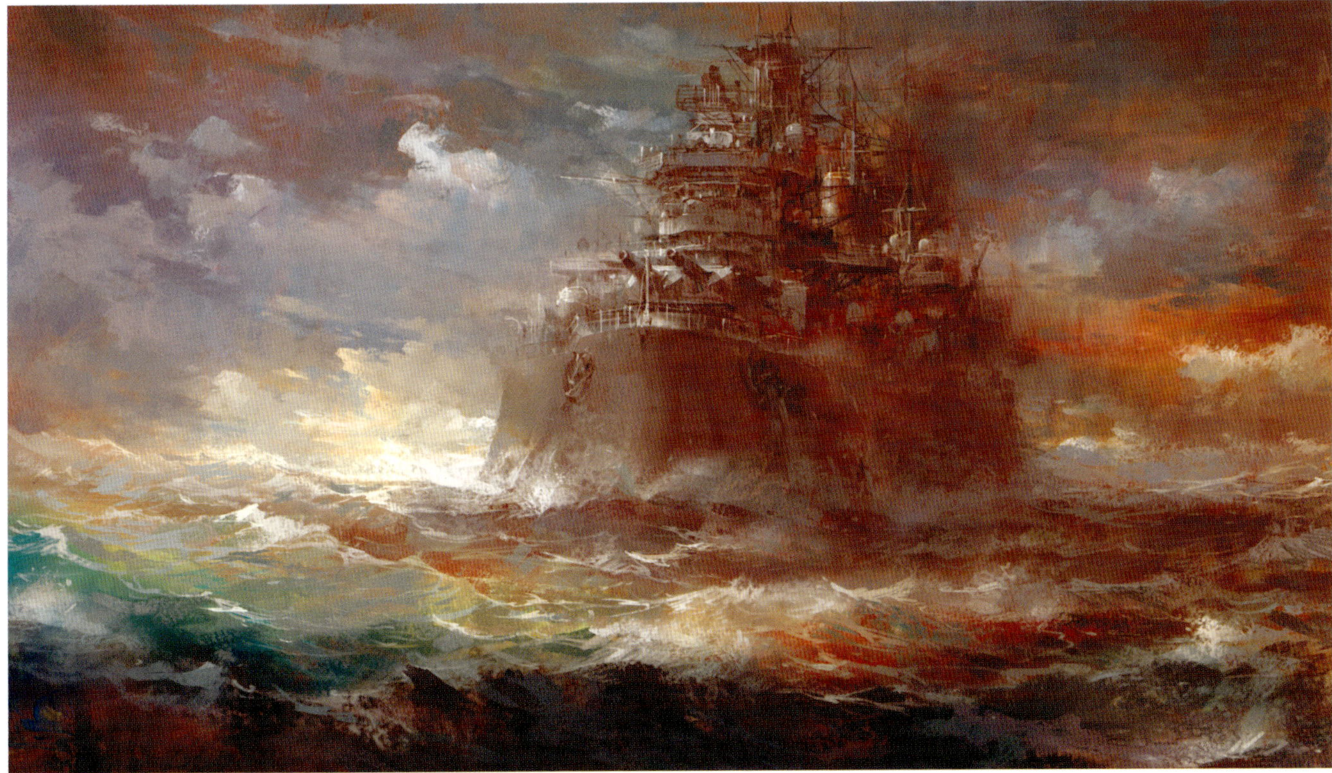

I use **CUSTOM BRUSHES** to **ADD** more interesting **TEXTURE** to a painting.

NEVERTHELESS, one should be careful not to overdo it.

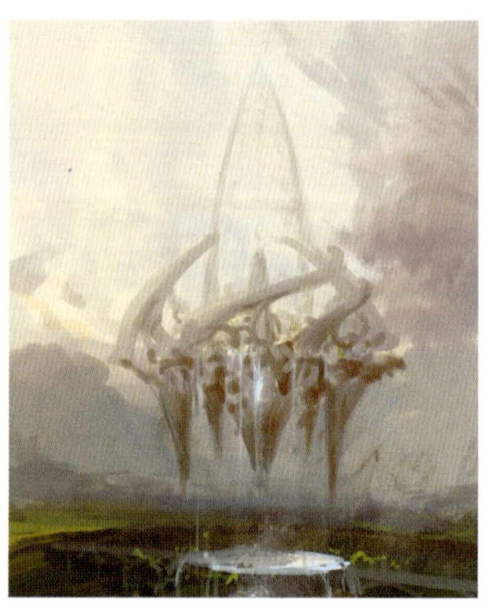

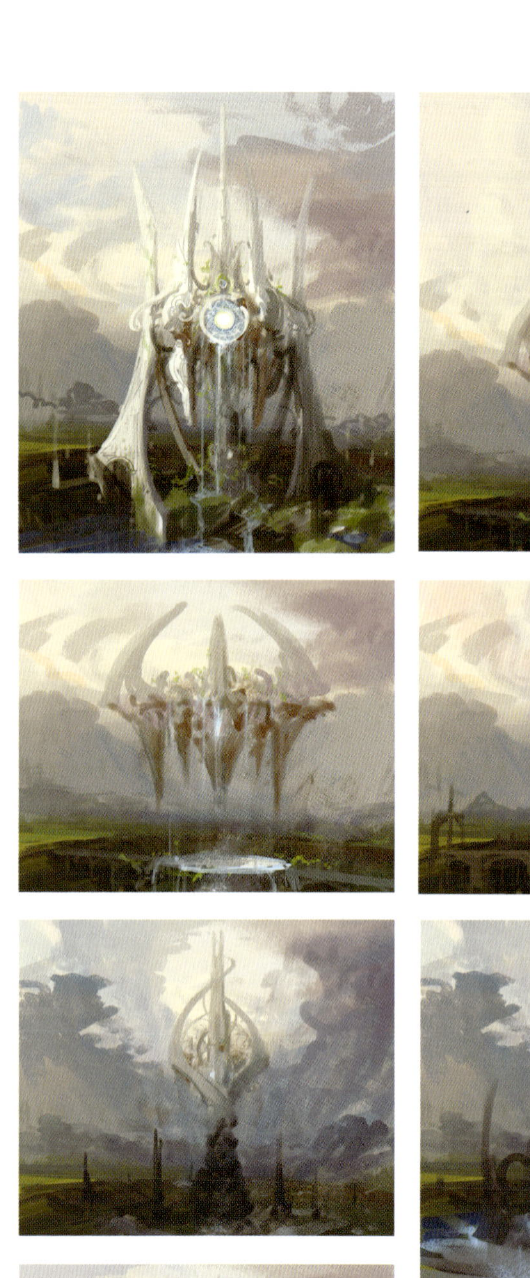

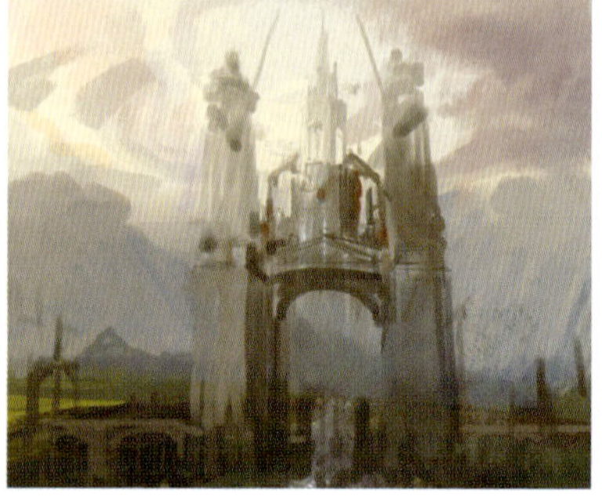

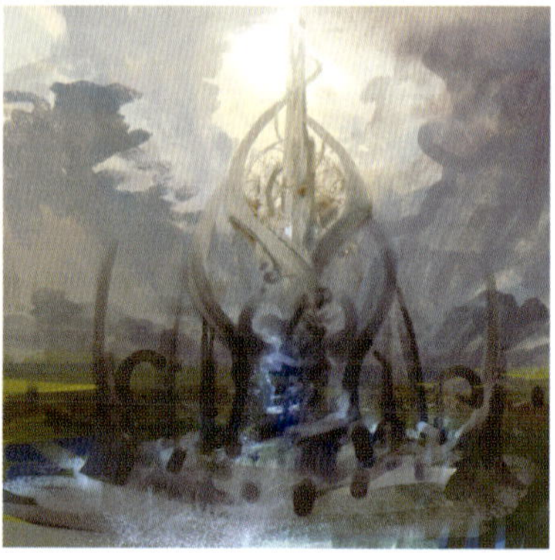

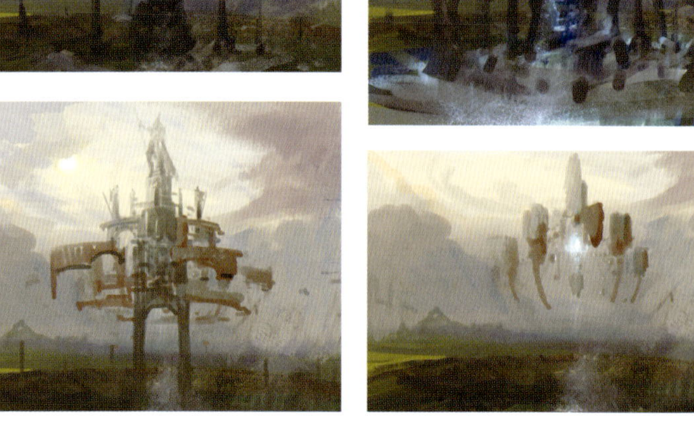

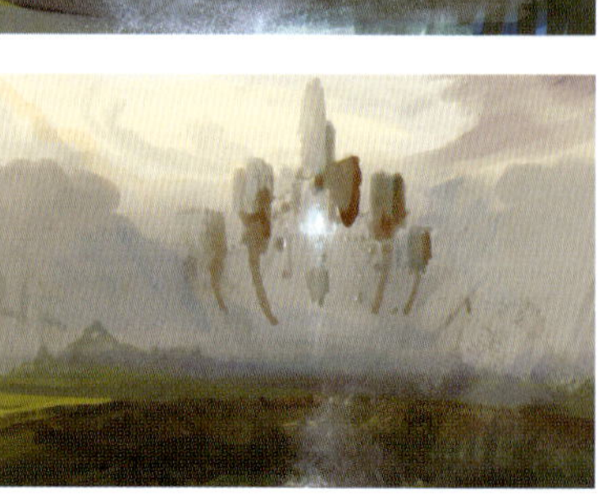

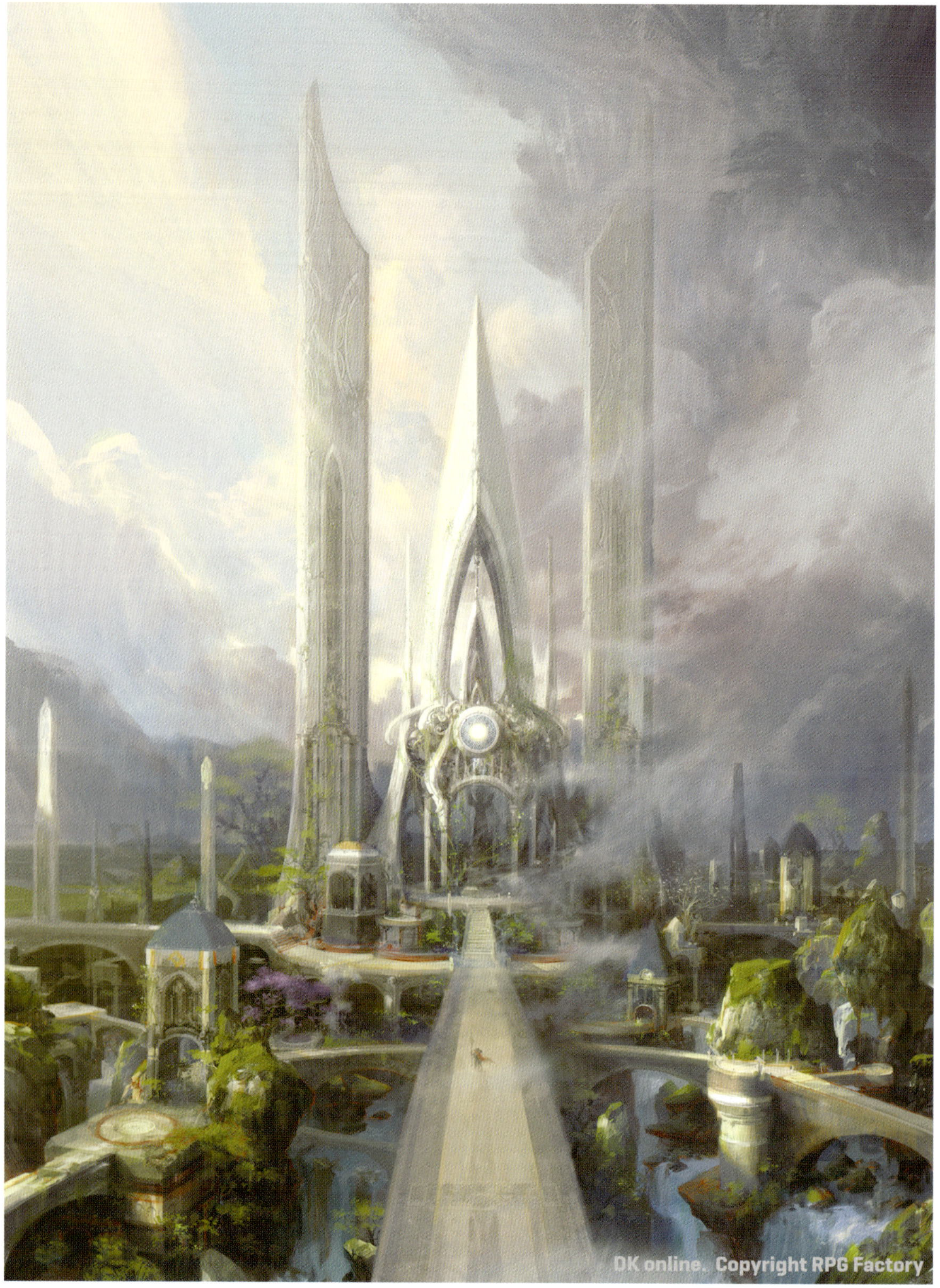

DK online. Copyright RPG Factory

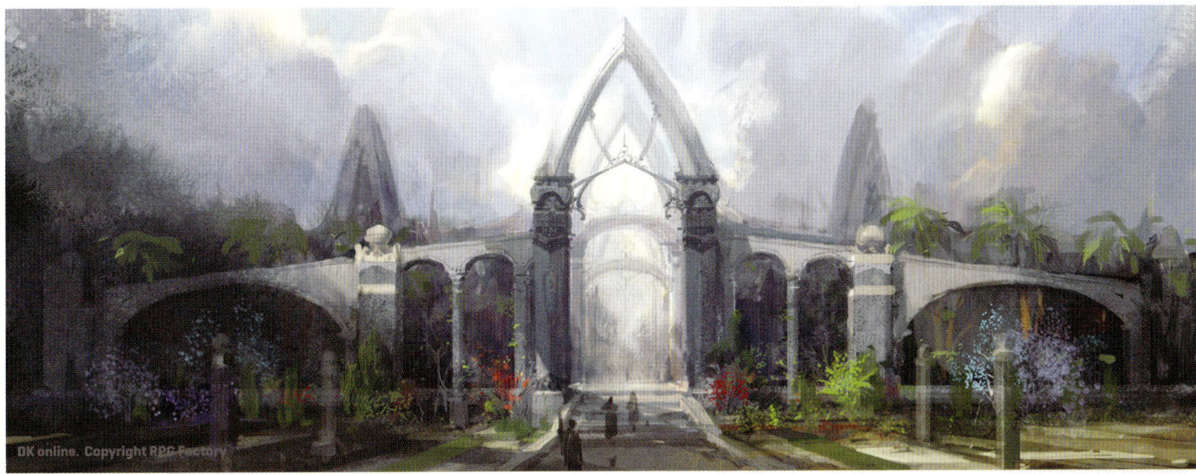

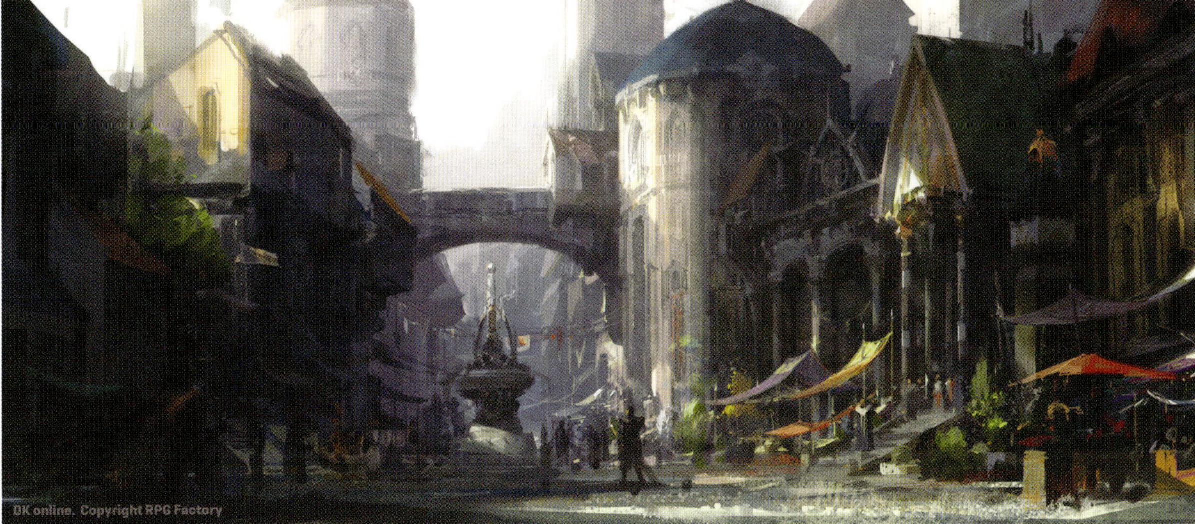

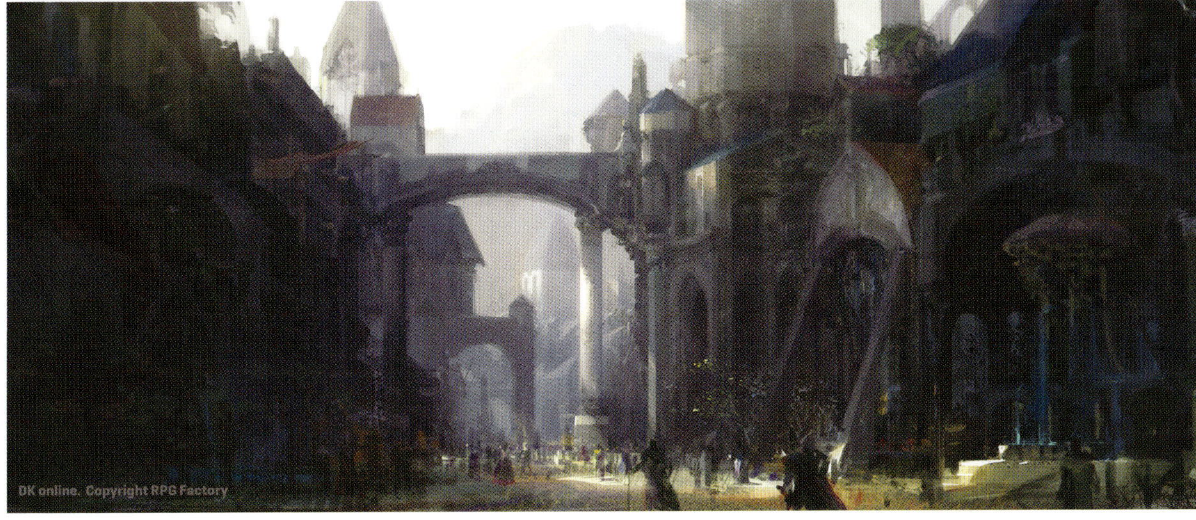

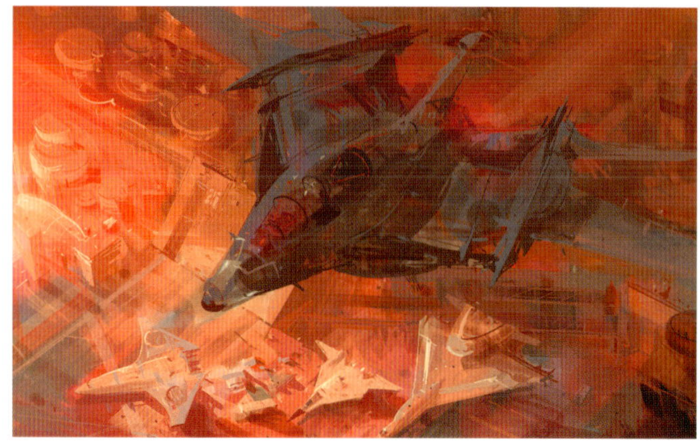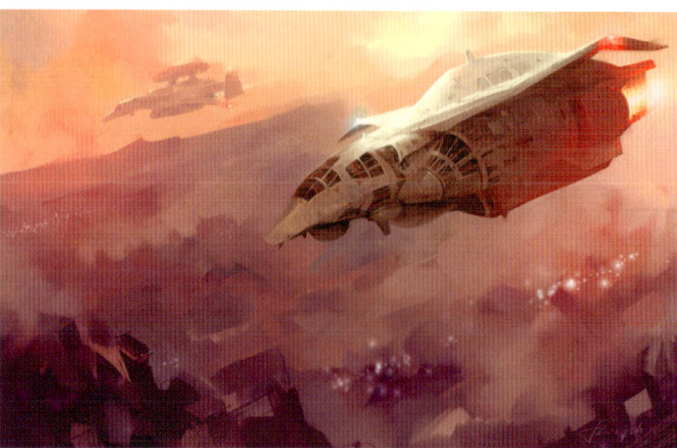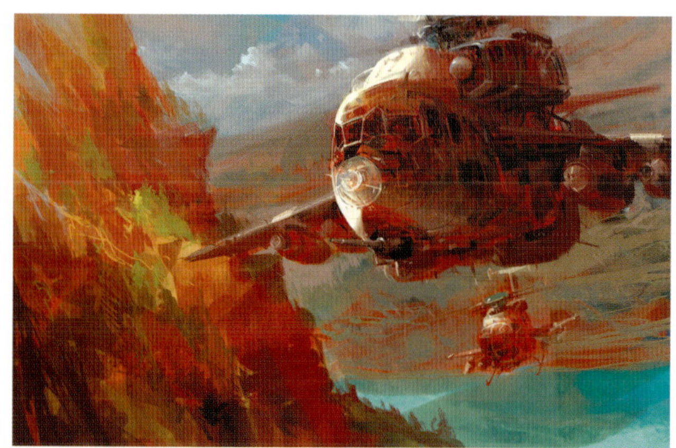

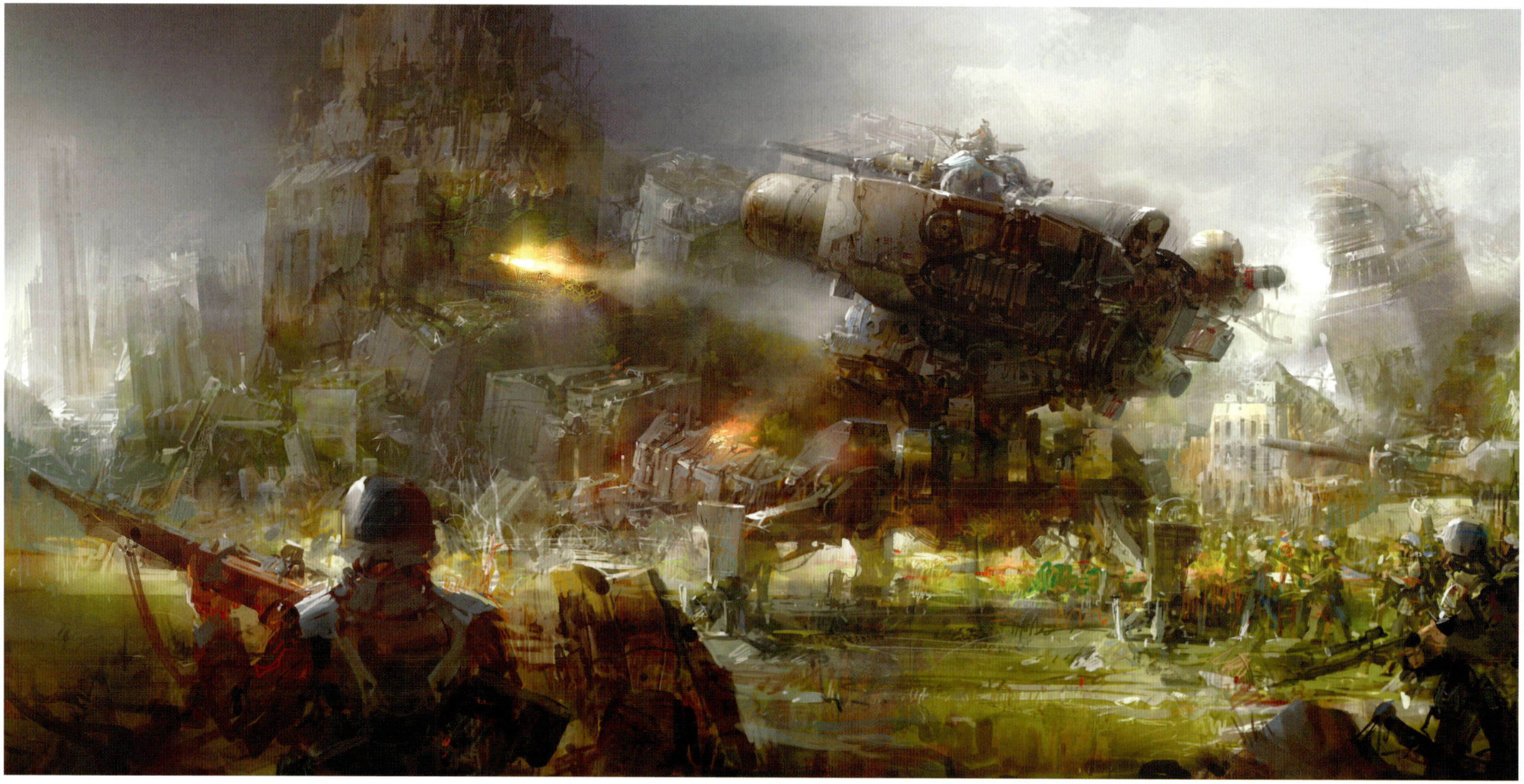

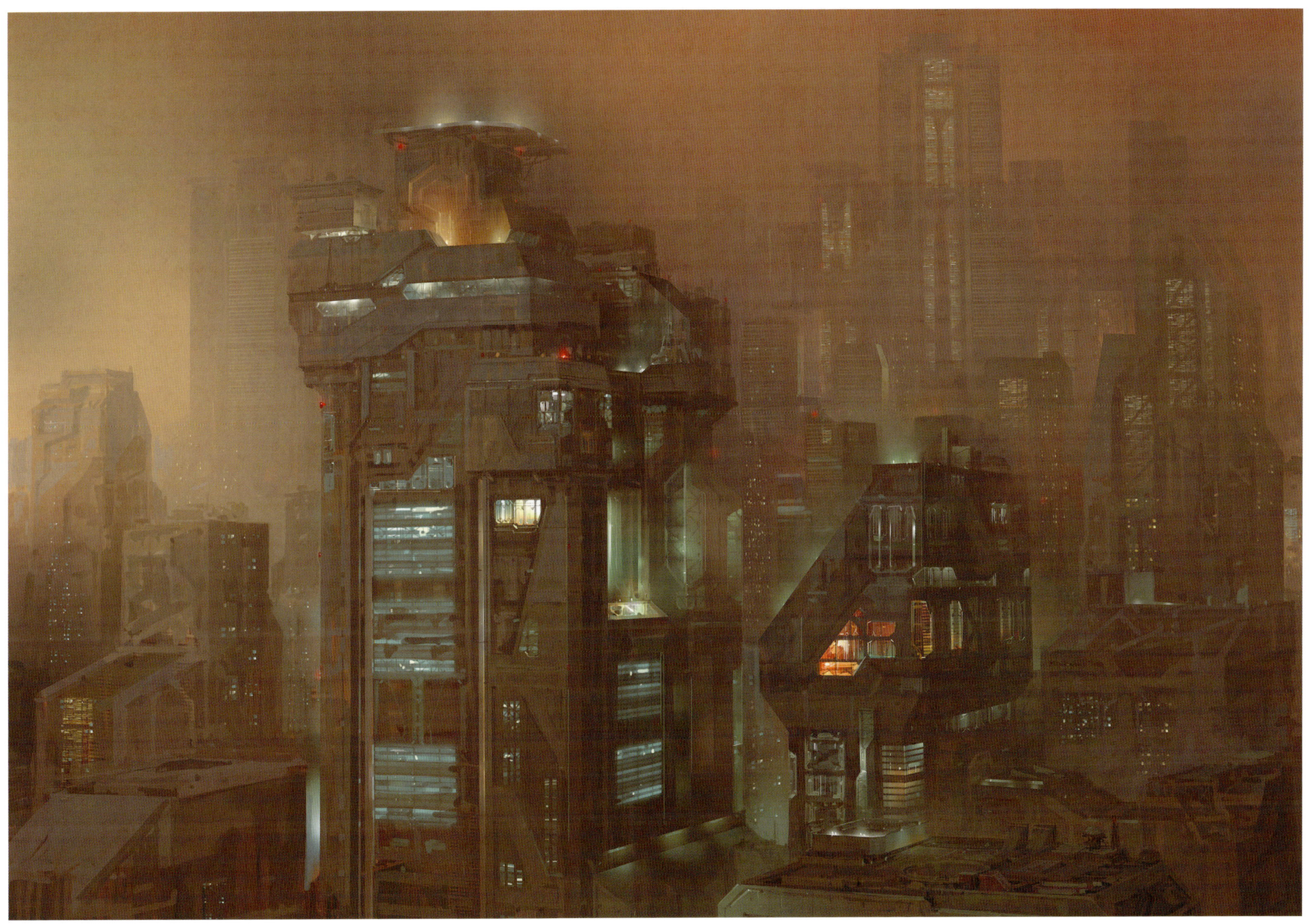

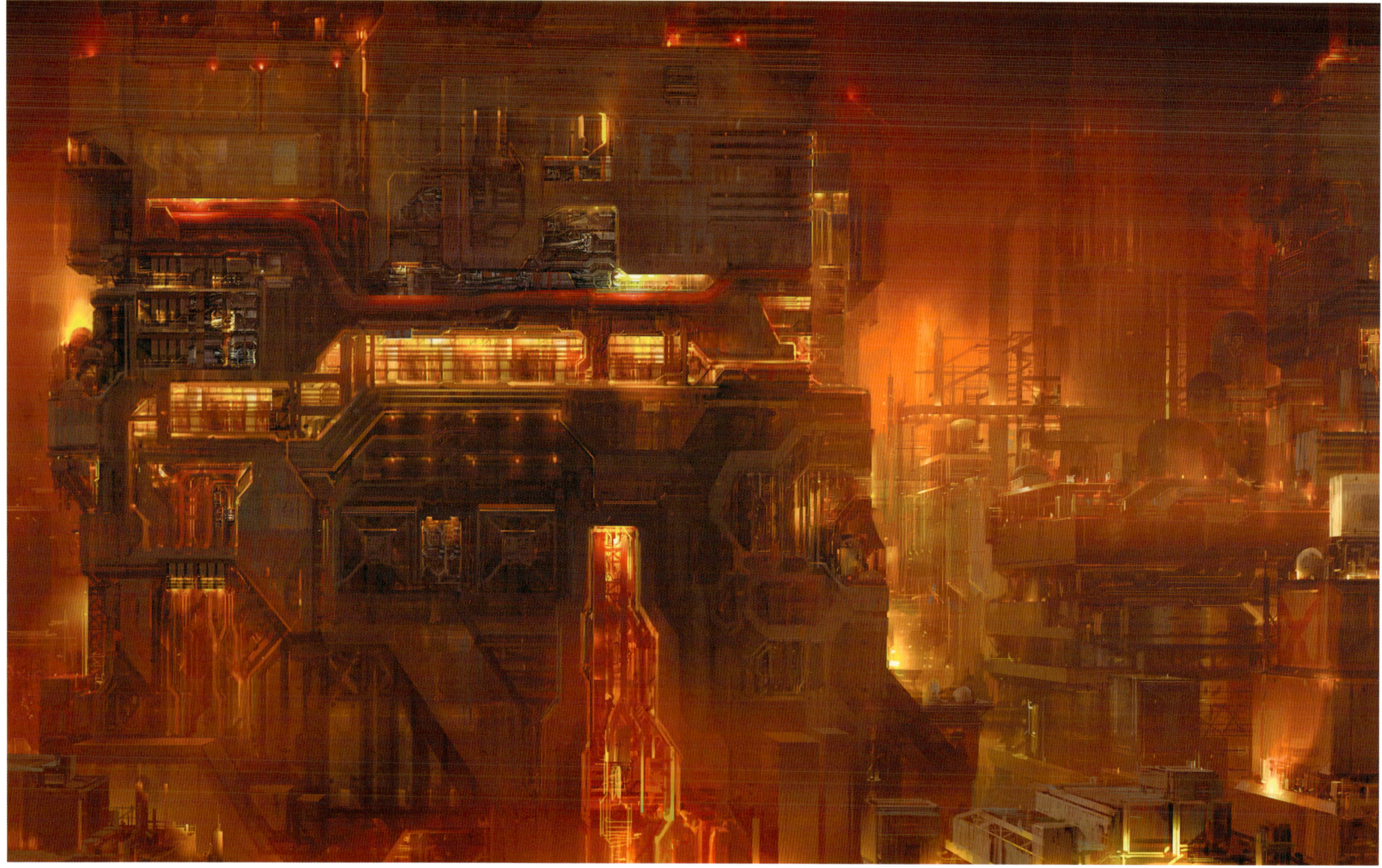

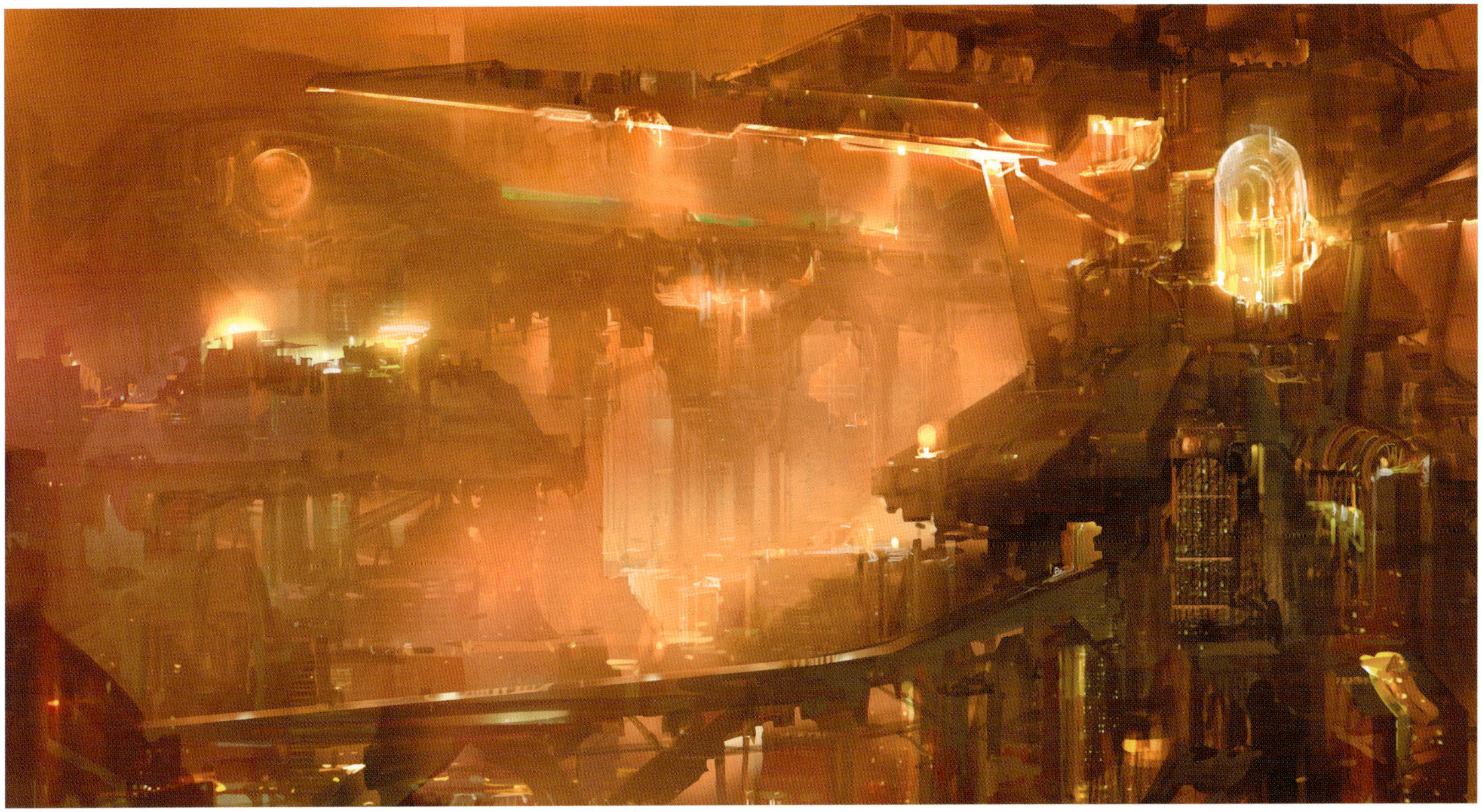

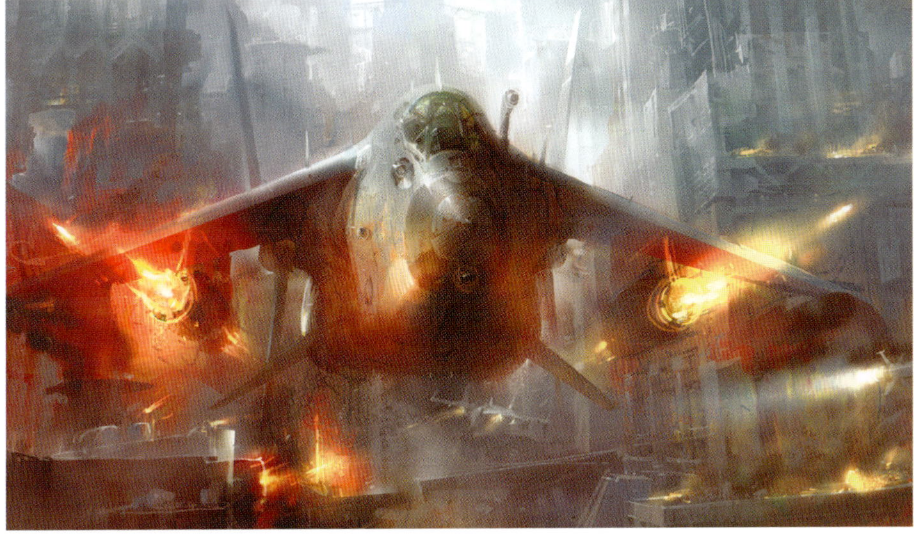

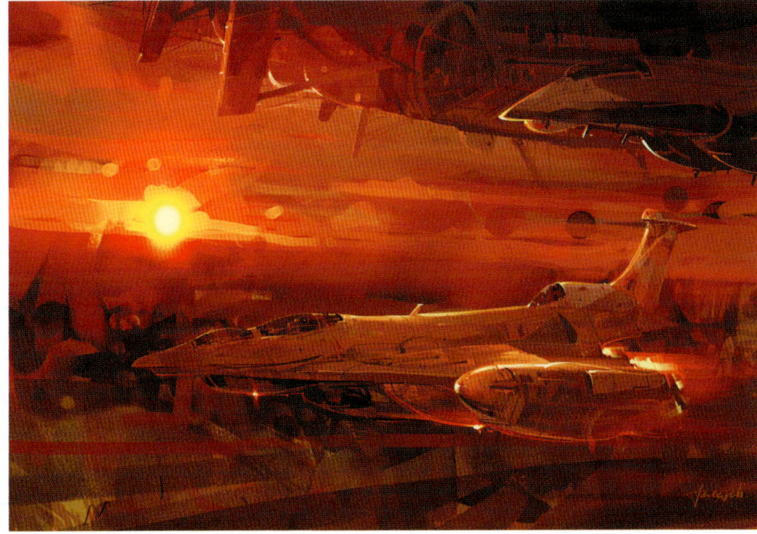

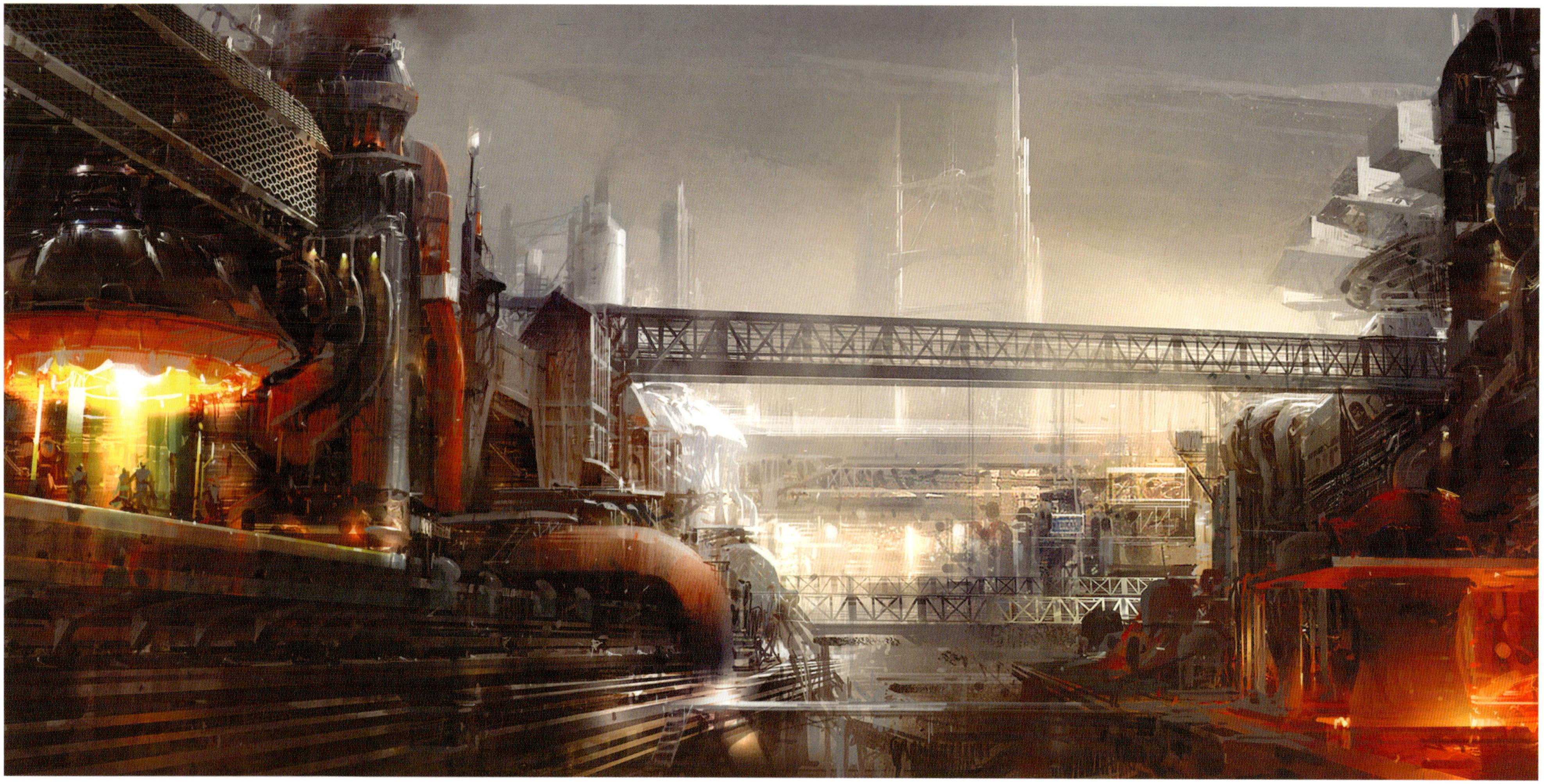

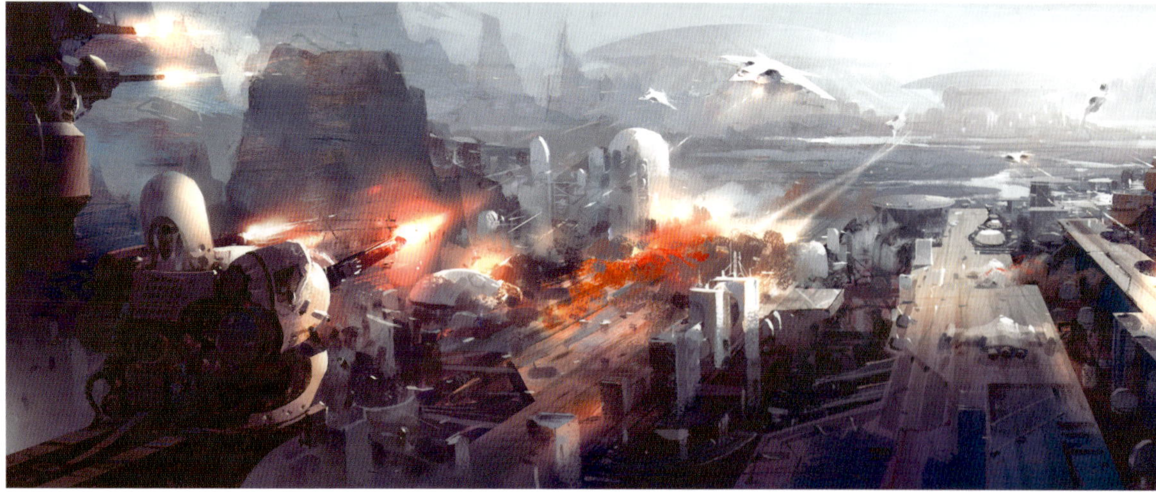

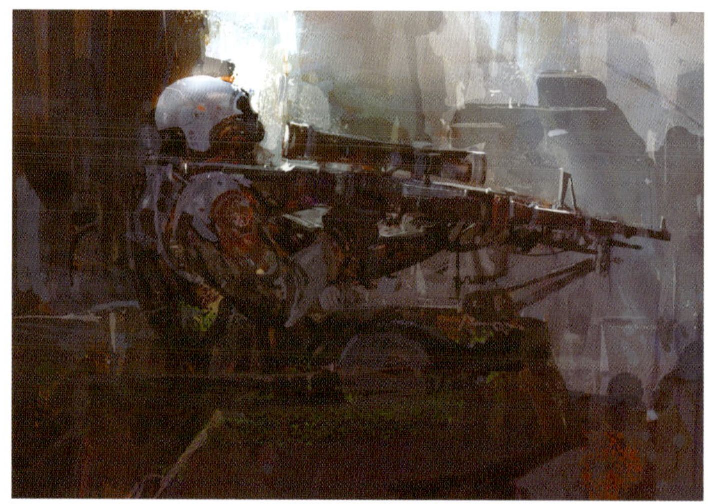

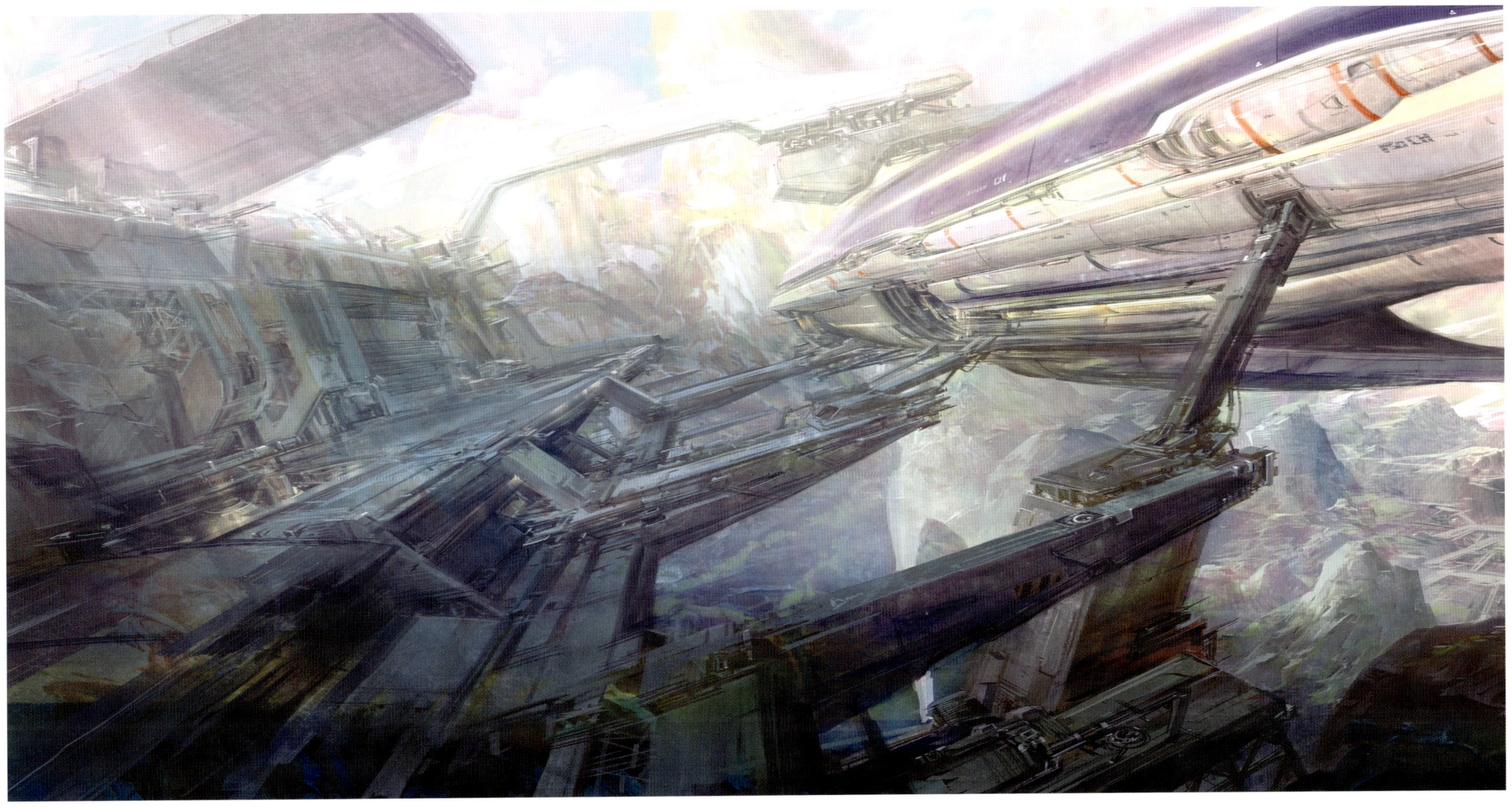

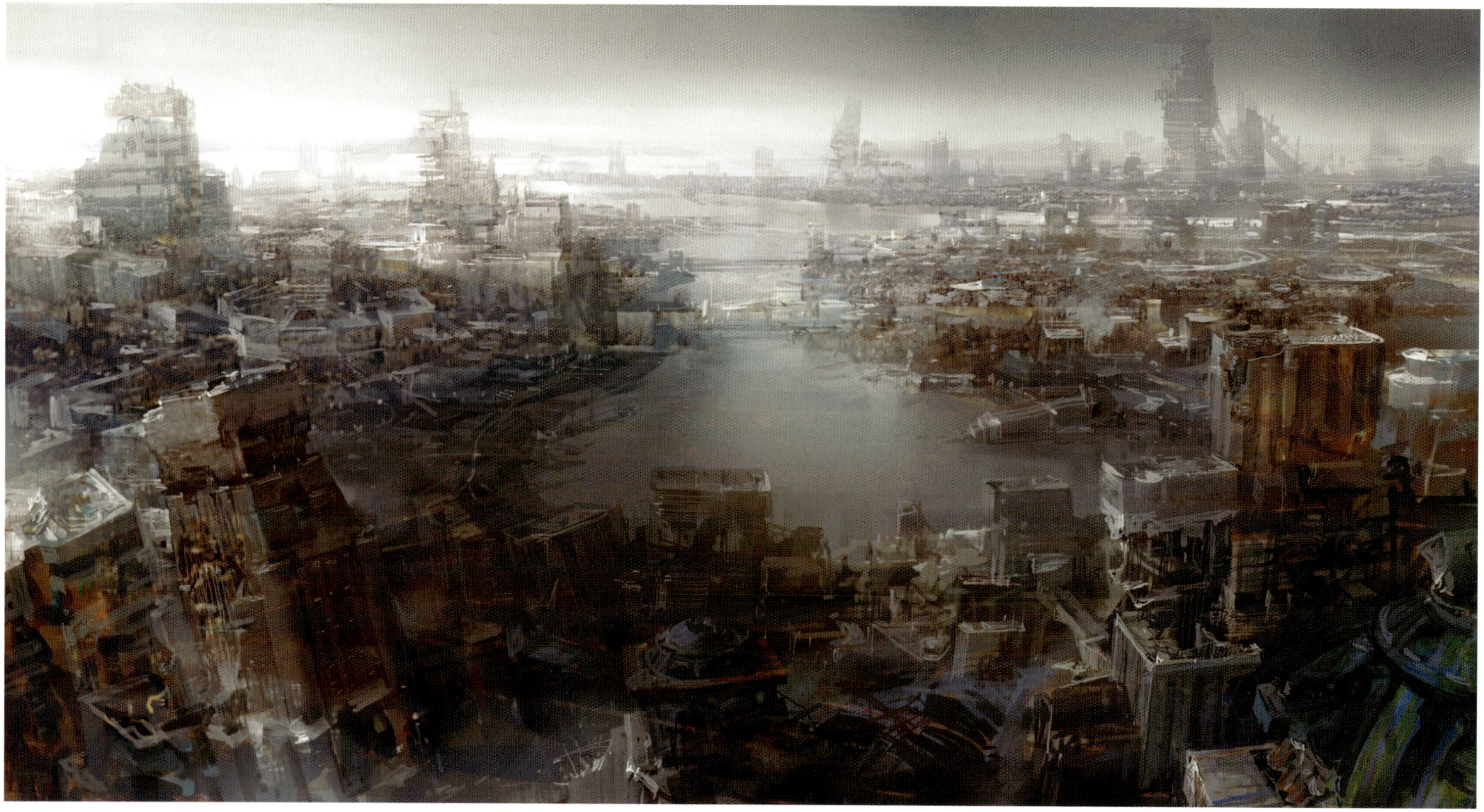

The **MORE VARIETY** that can be seen in a painting, the **MORE DYNAMIC** the painting.

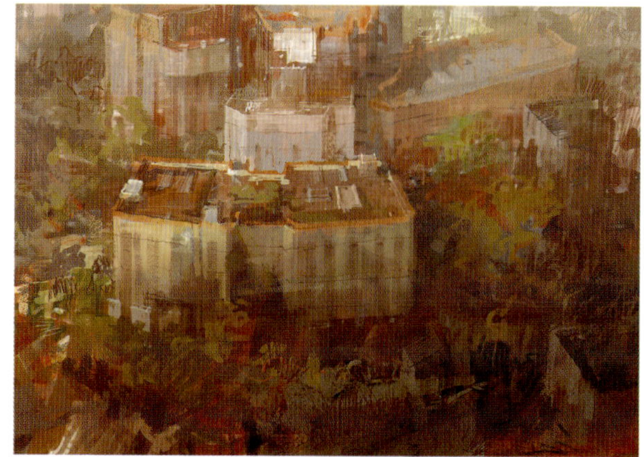

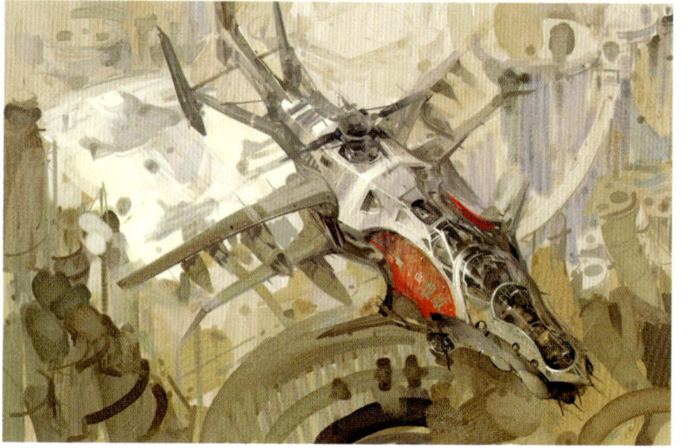

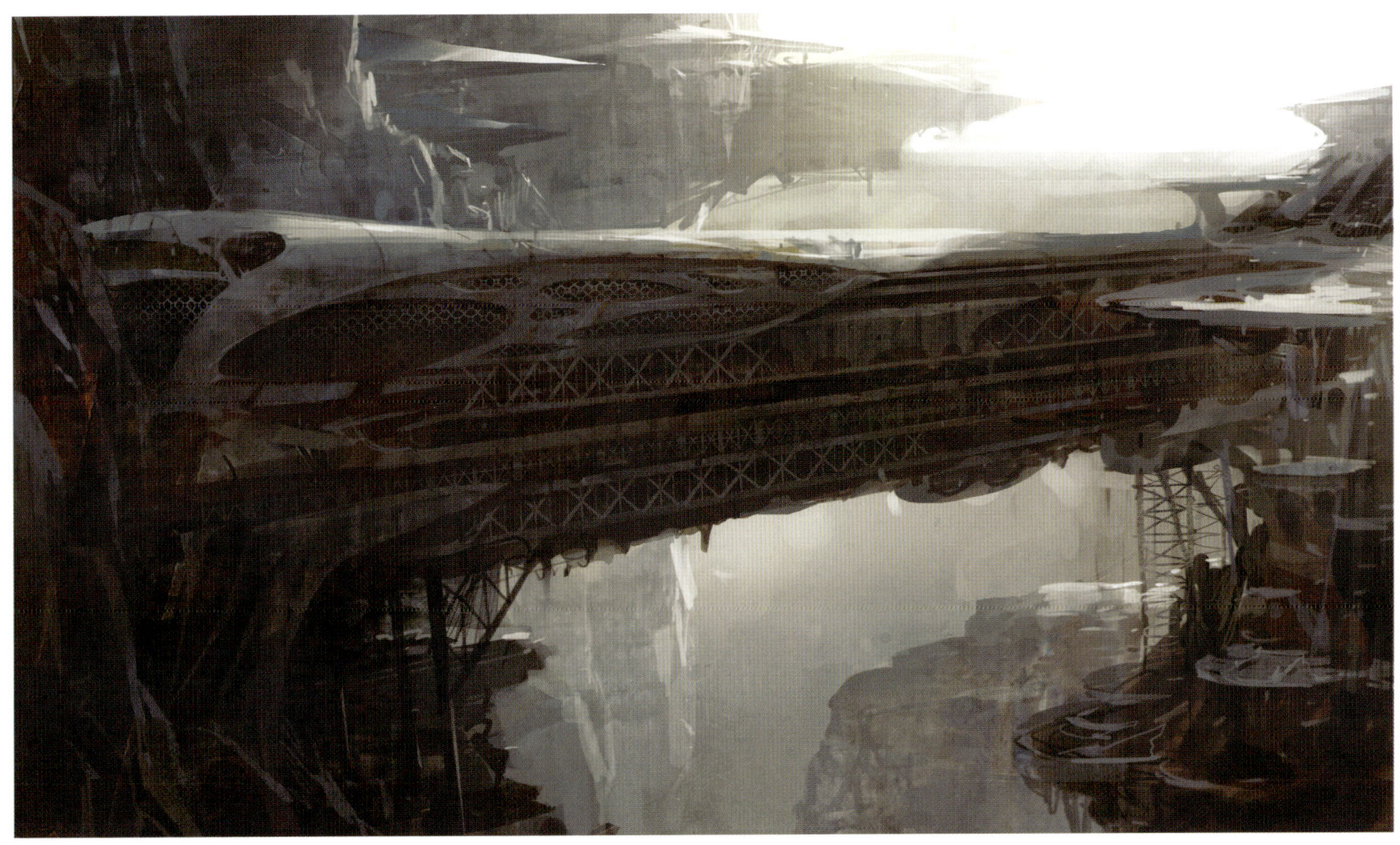

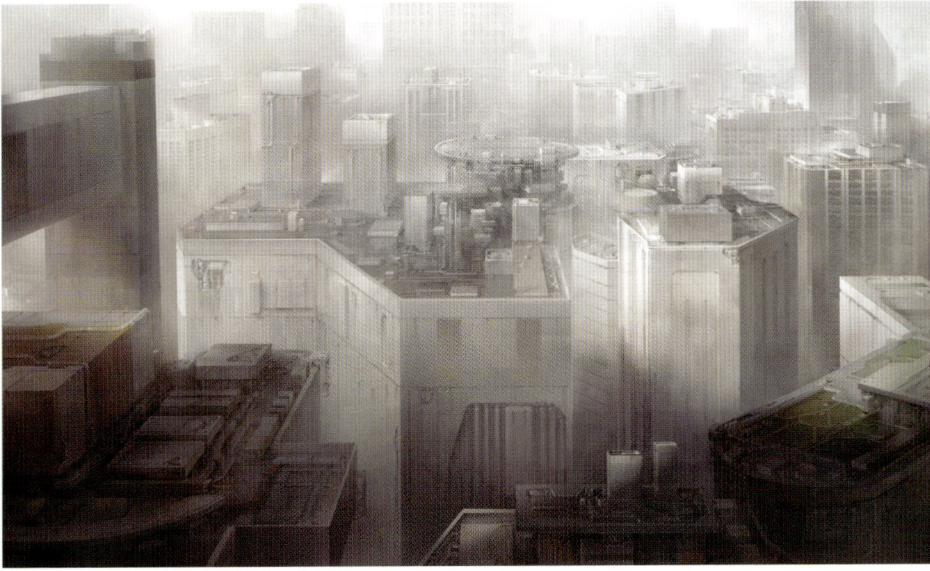

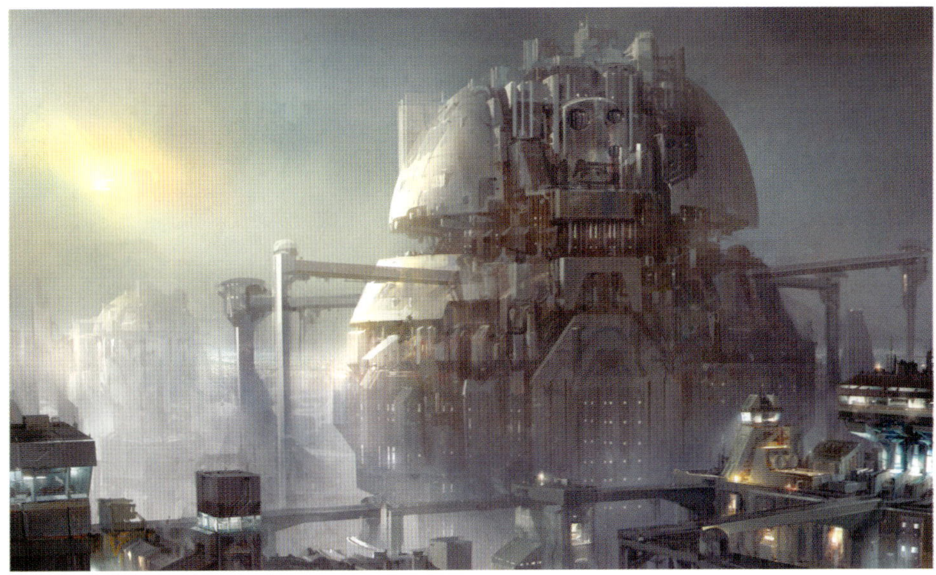

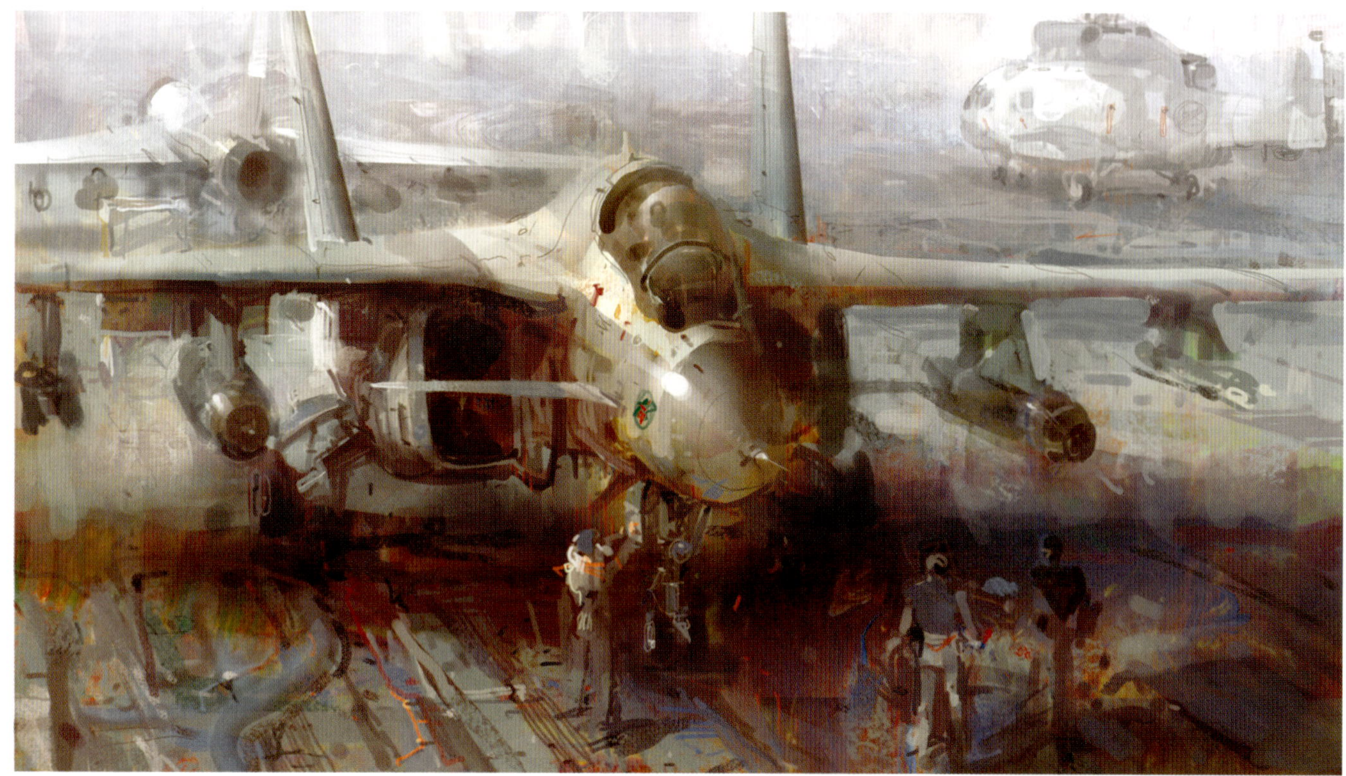

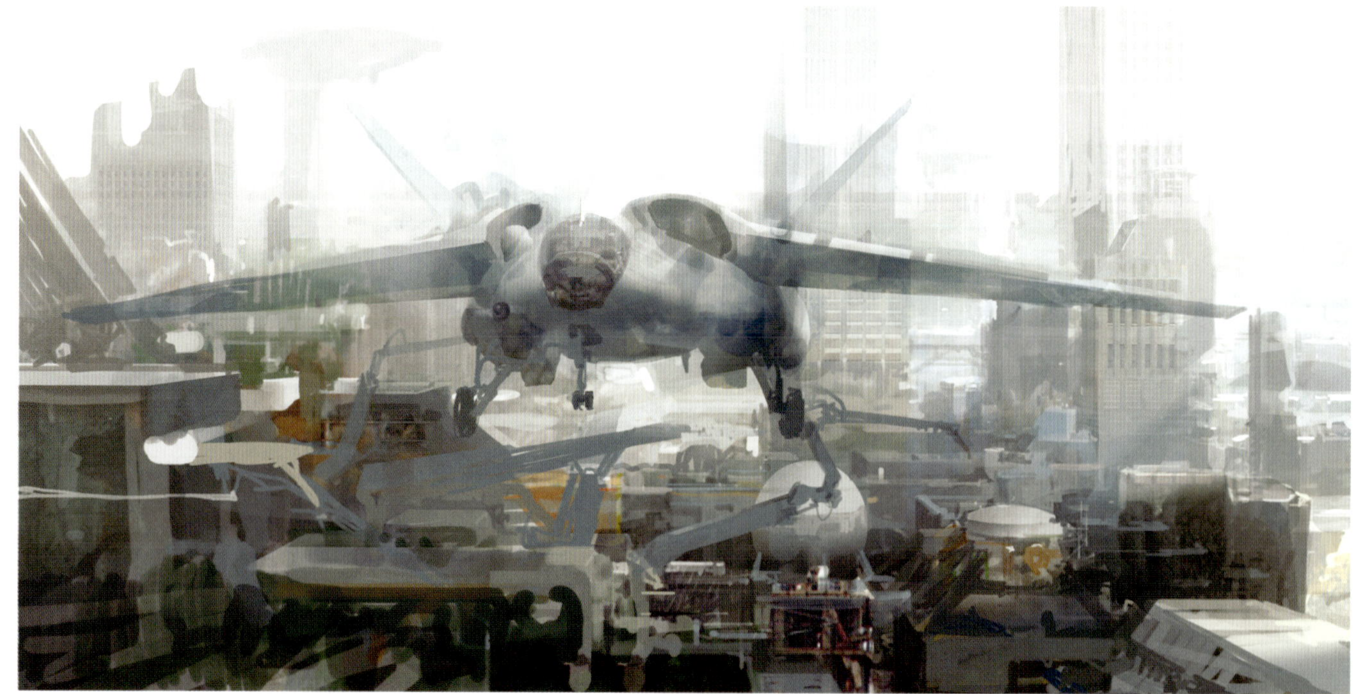

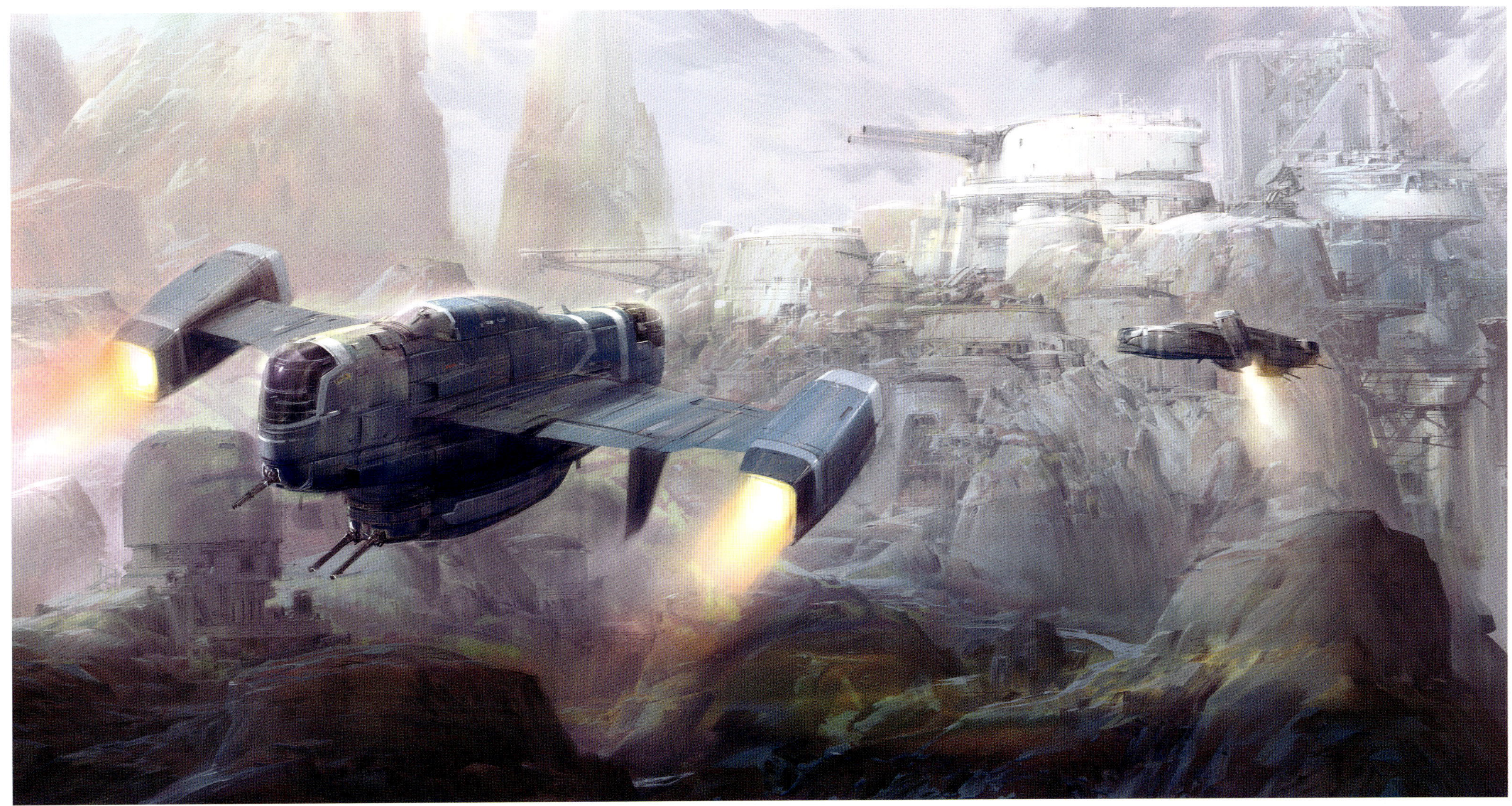

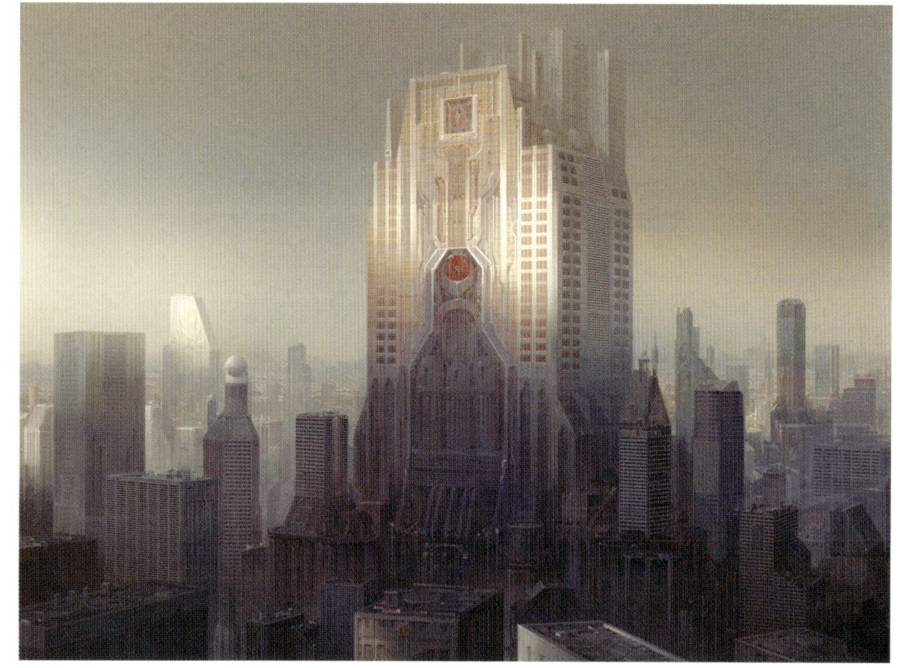

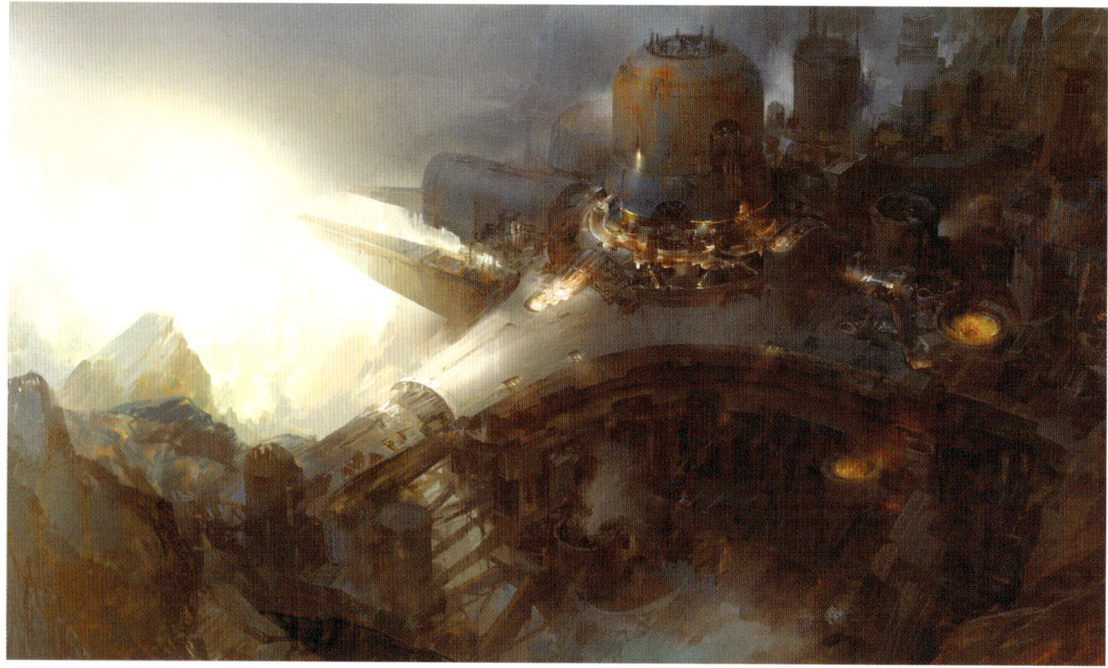

Select the section that gets the MOST light and make it SHARP and CLEAR.

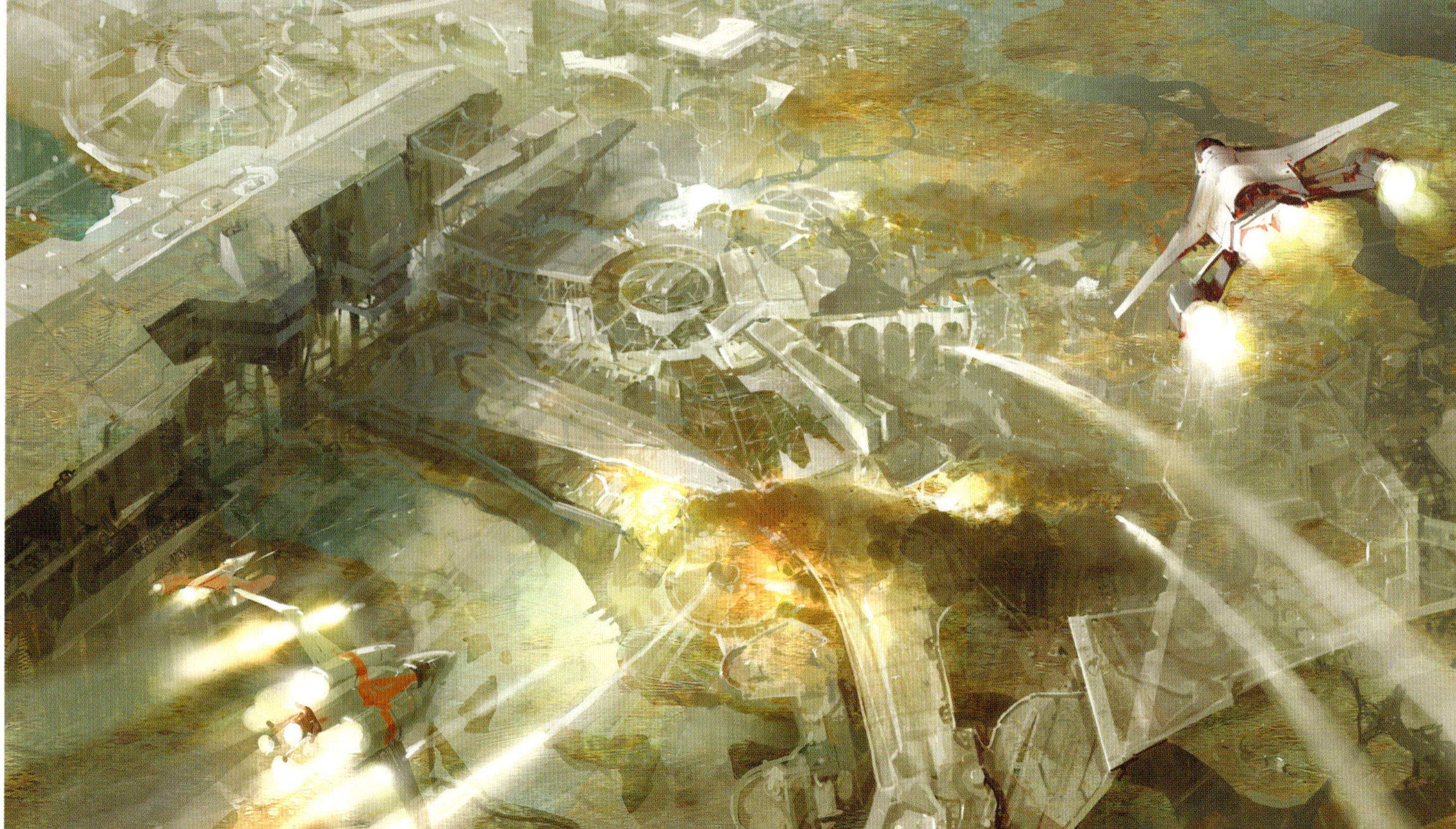

That will draw the viewer's attention and will make the painting look MORE DEFINED.

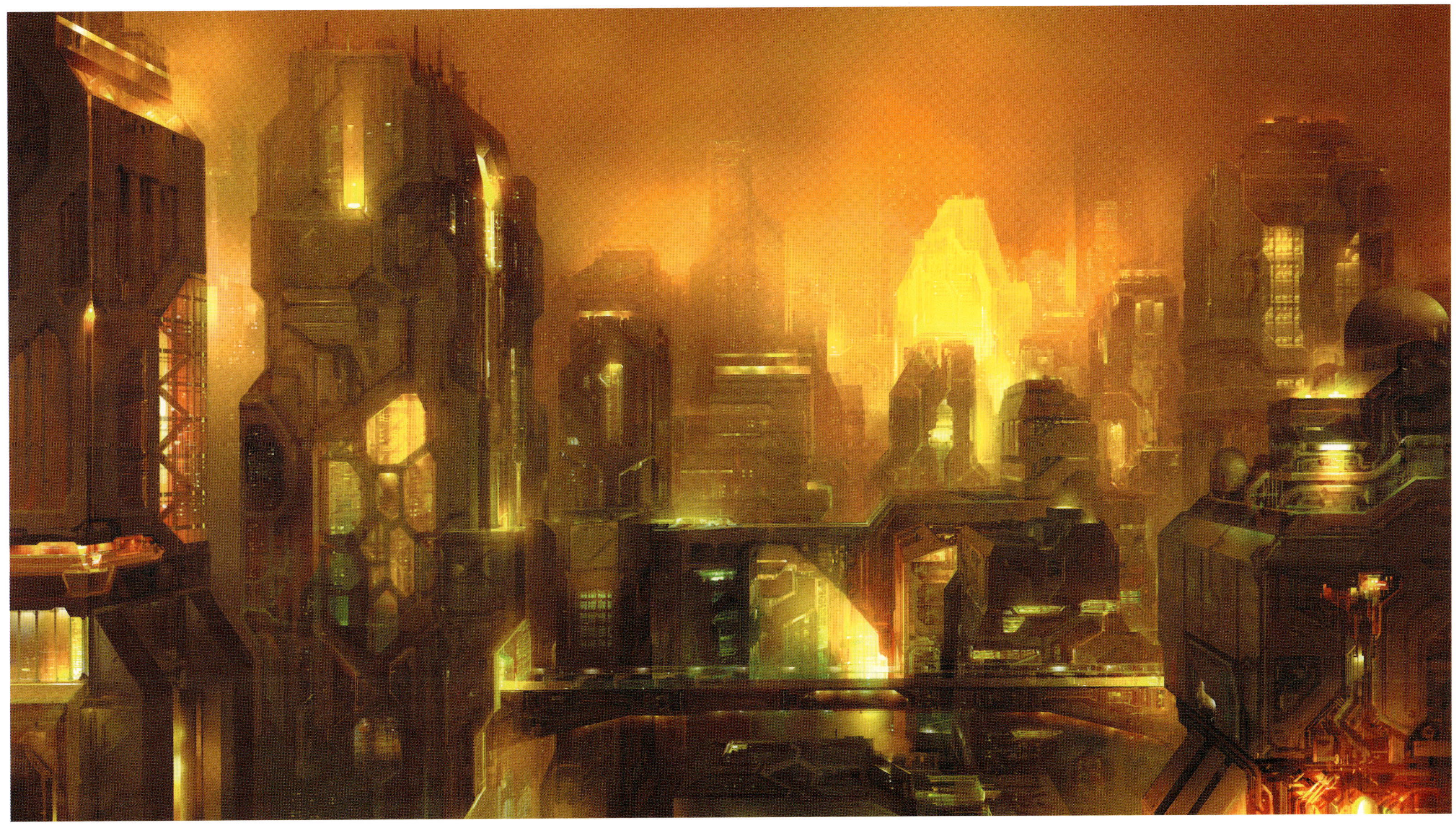

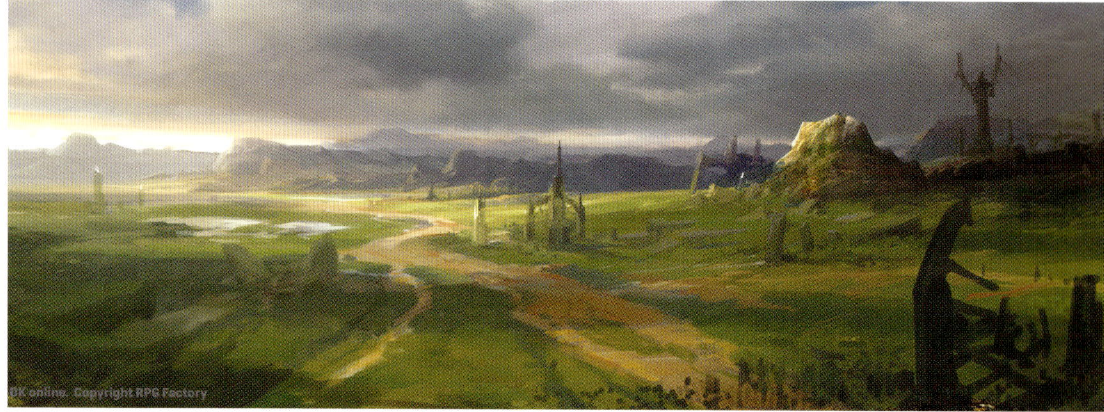

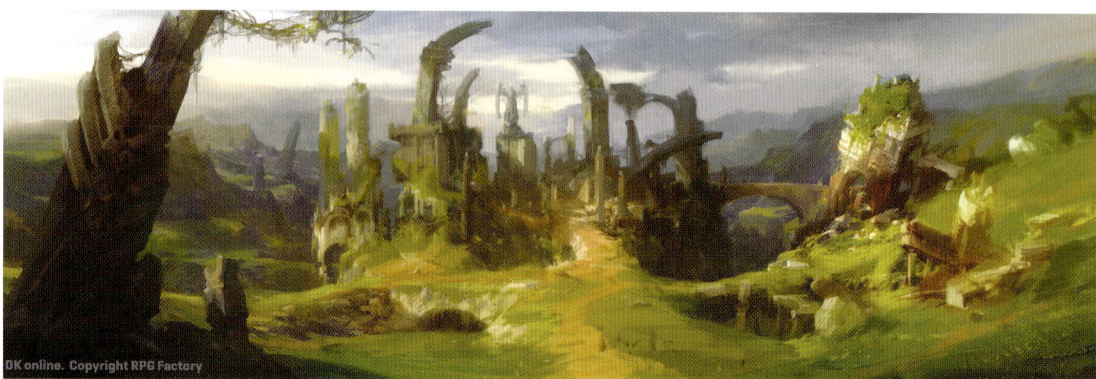

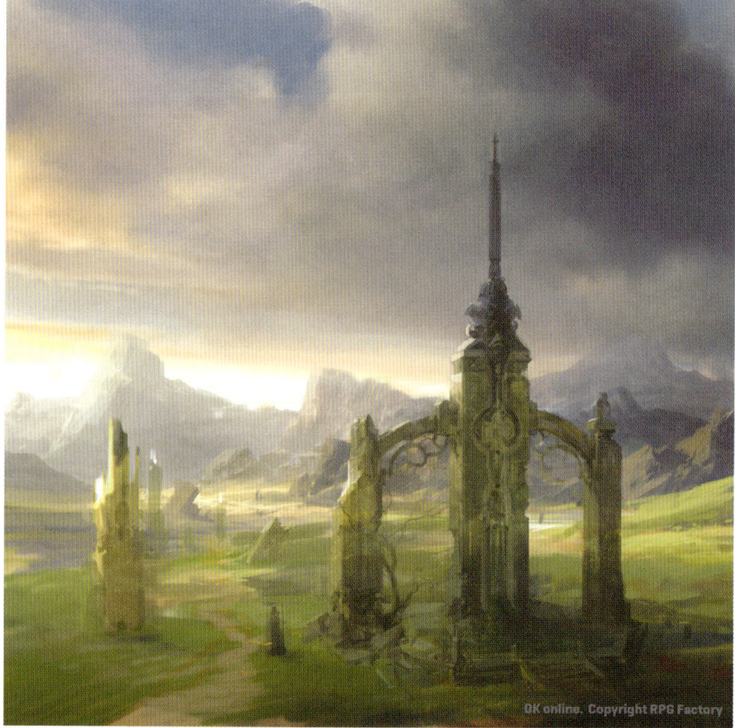

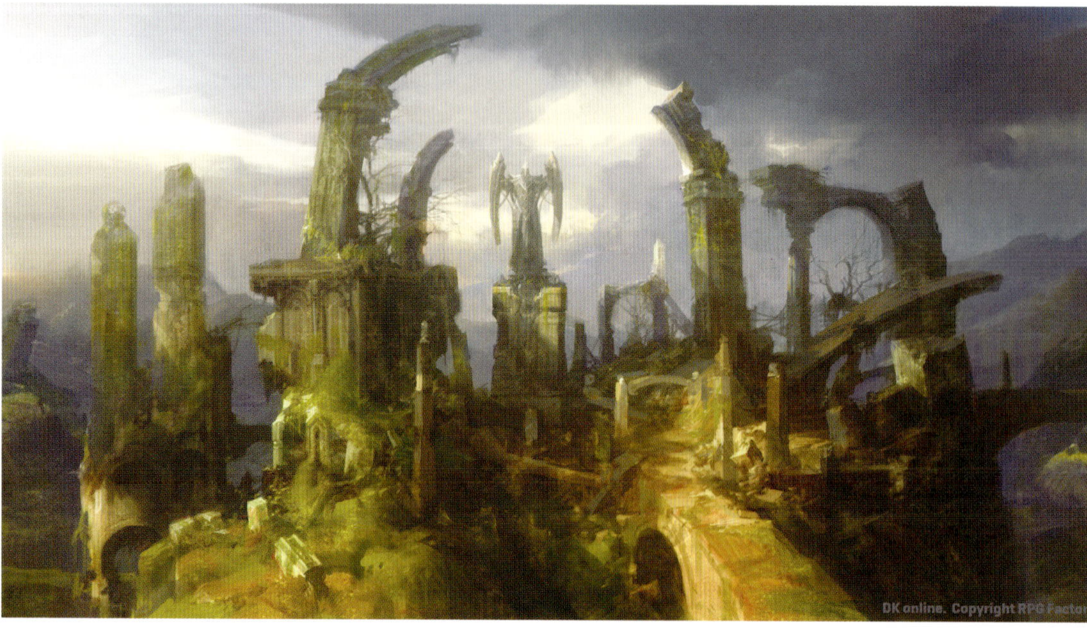

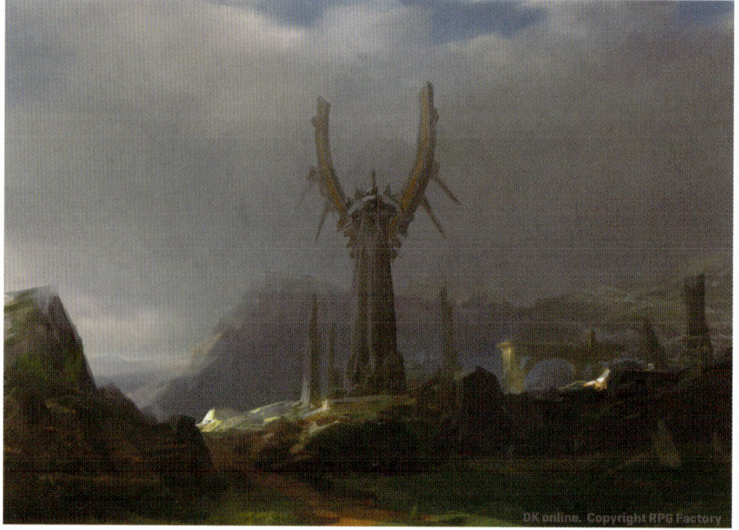

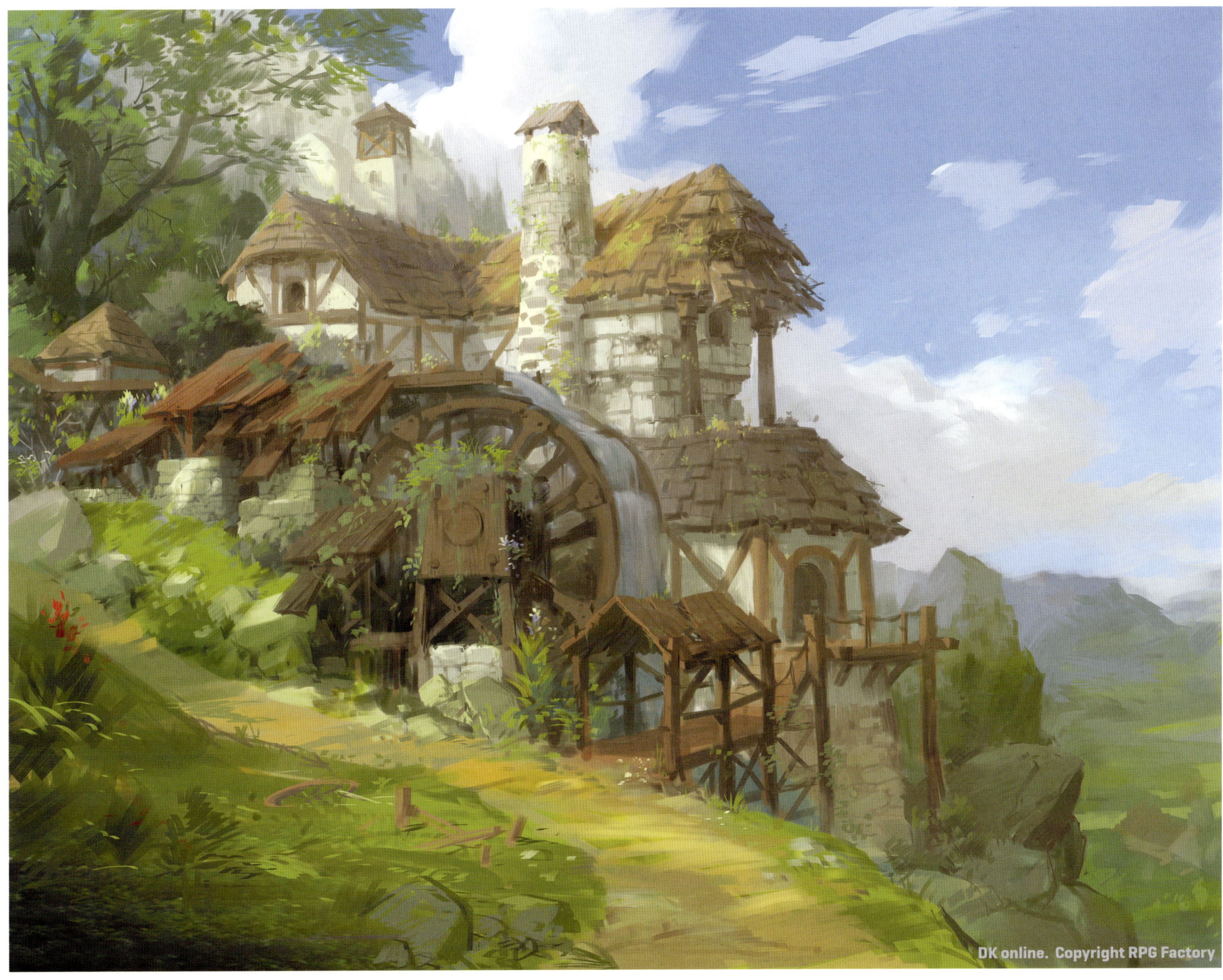
DK online. Copyright RPG Factory

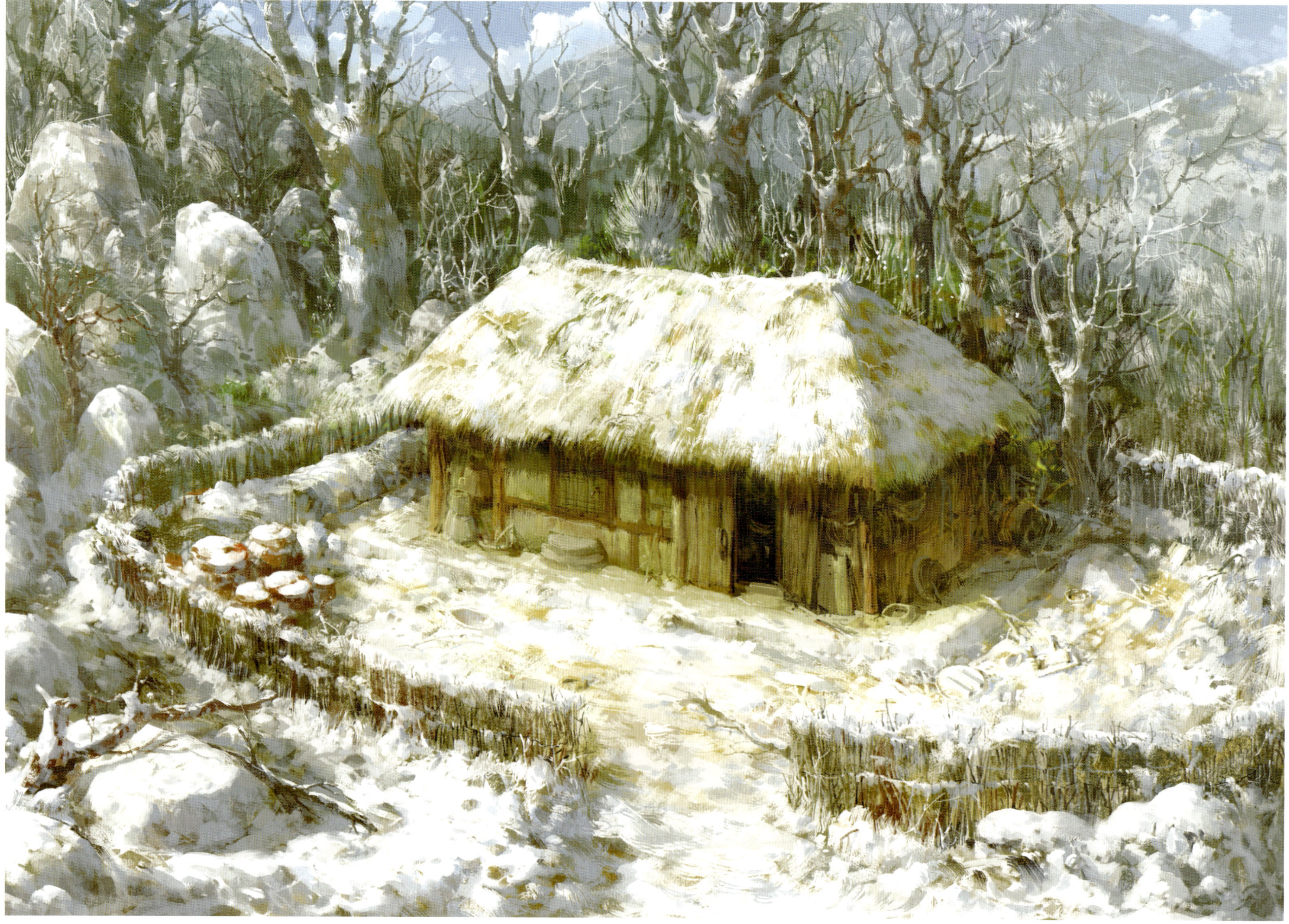

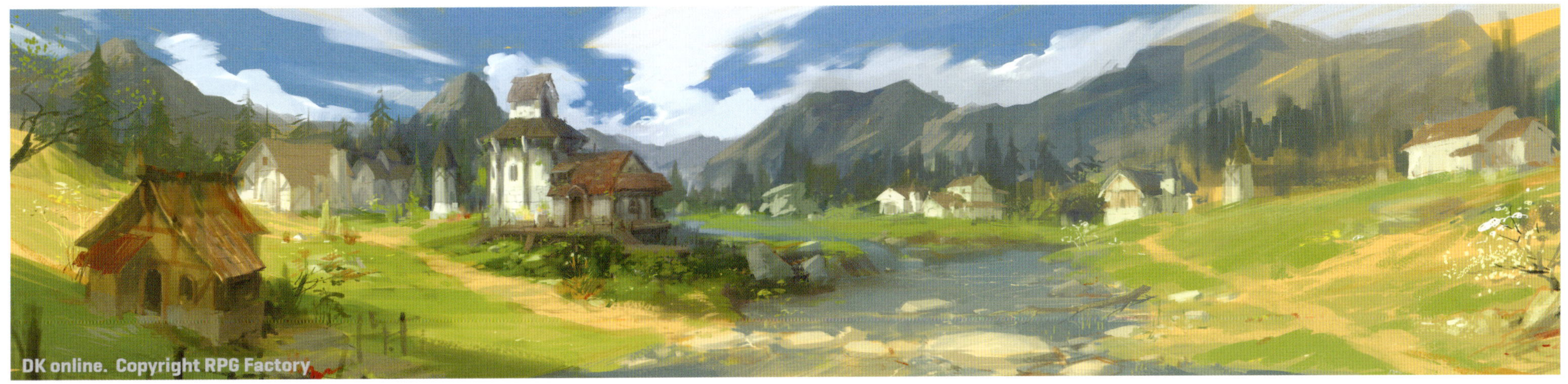
DK online. Copyright RPG Factory

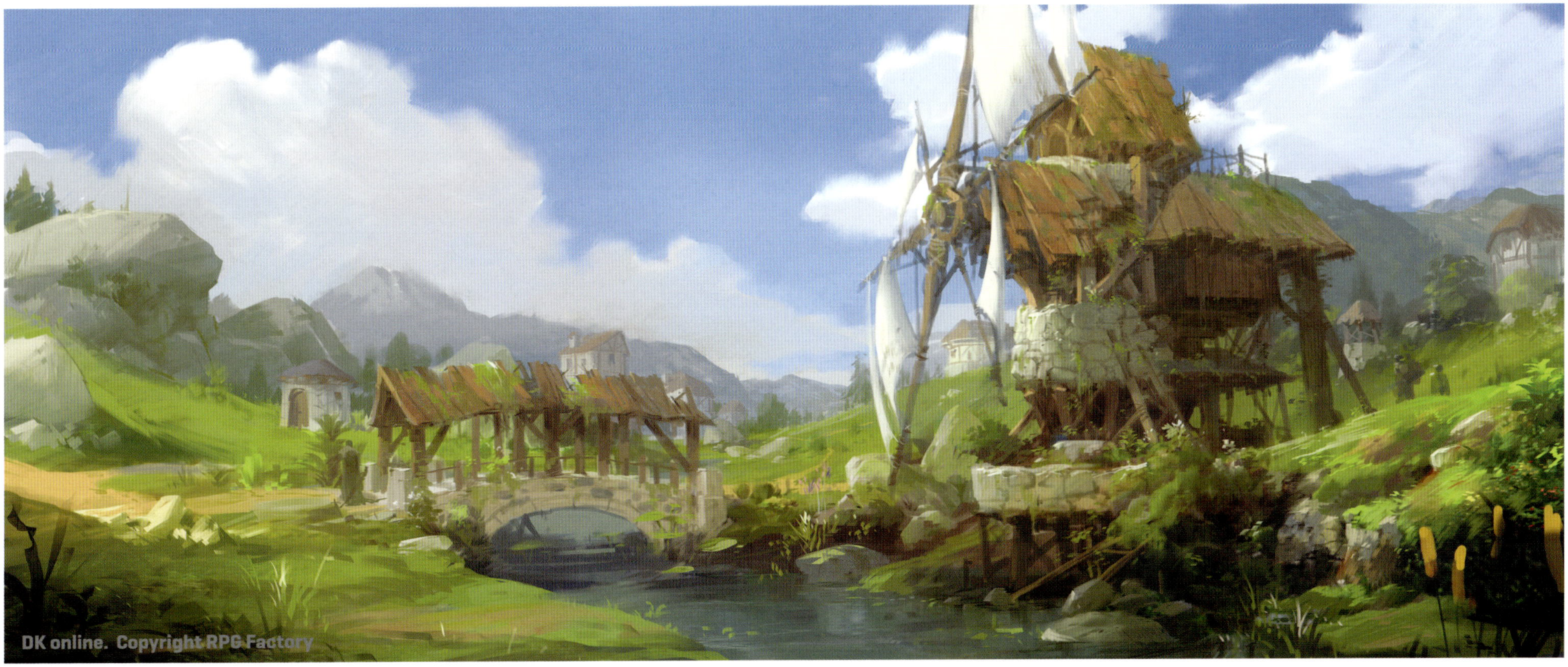

PAINTING a NATURAL SCENE is such a fun experience, and always gives me a very TRANQUIL feeling.

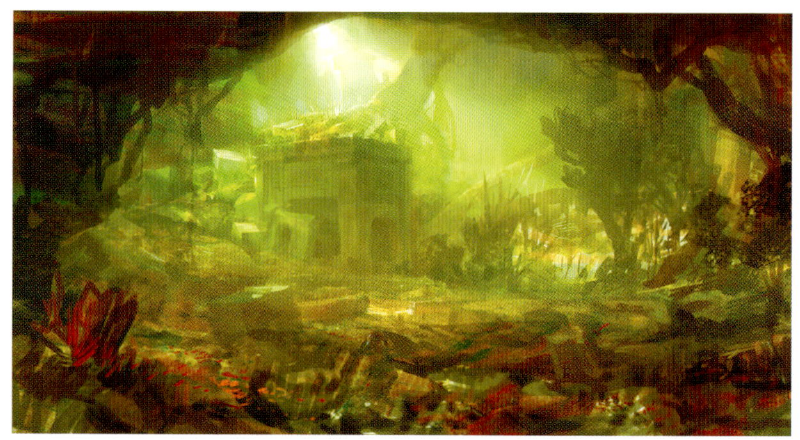

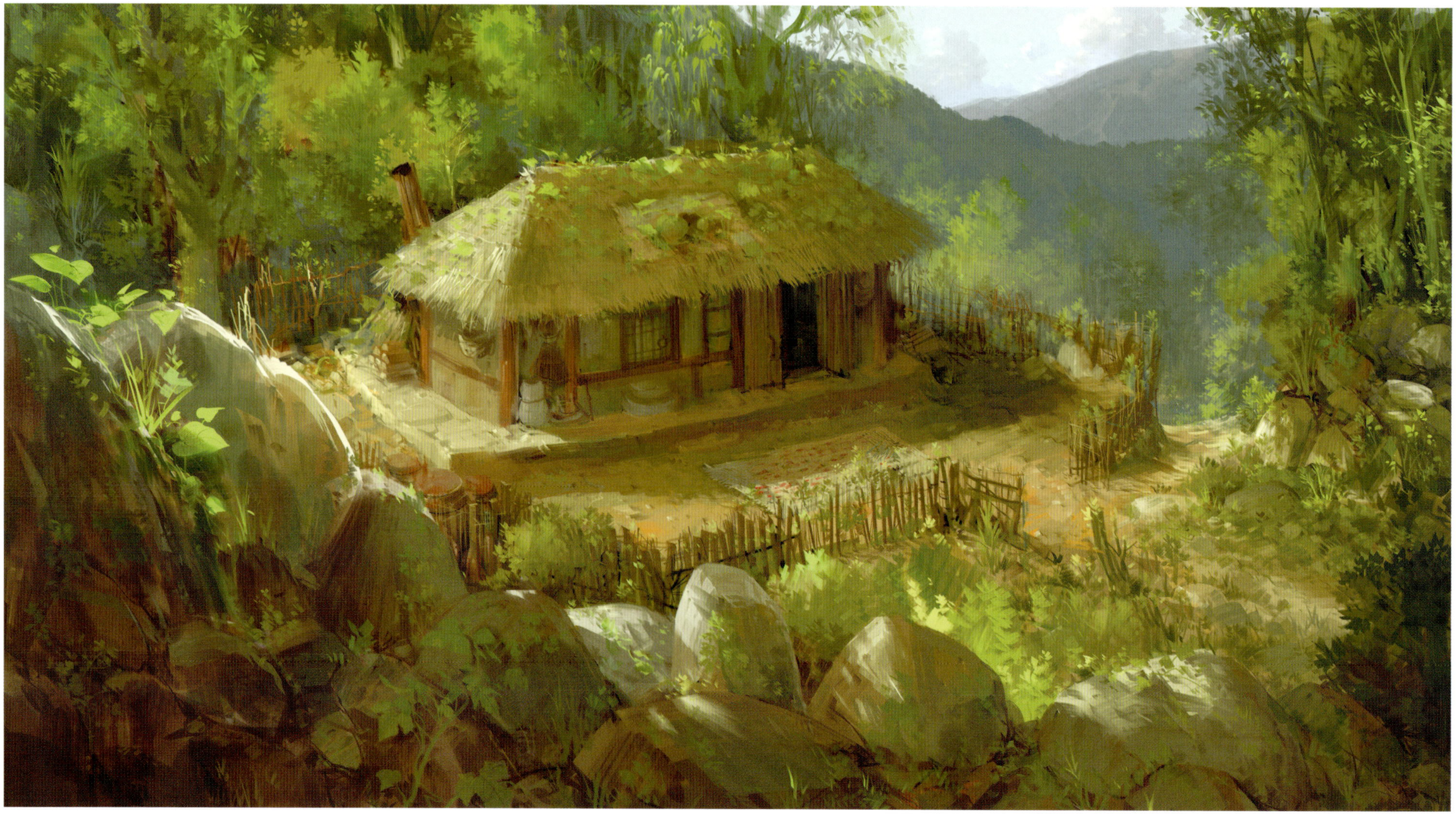

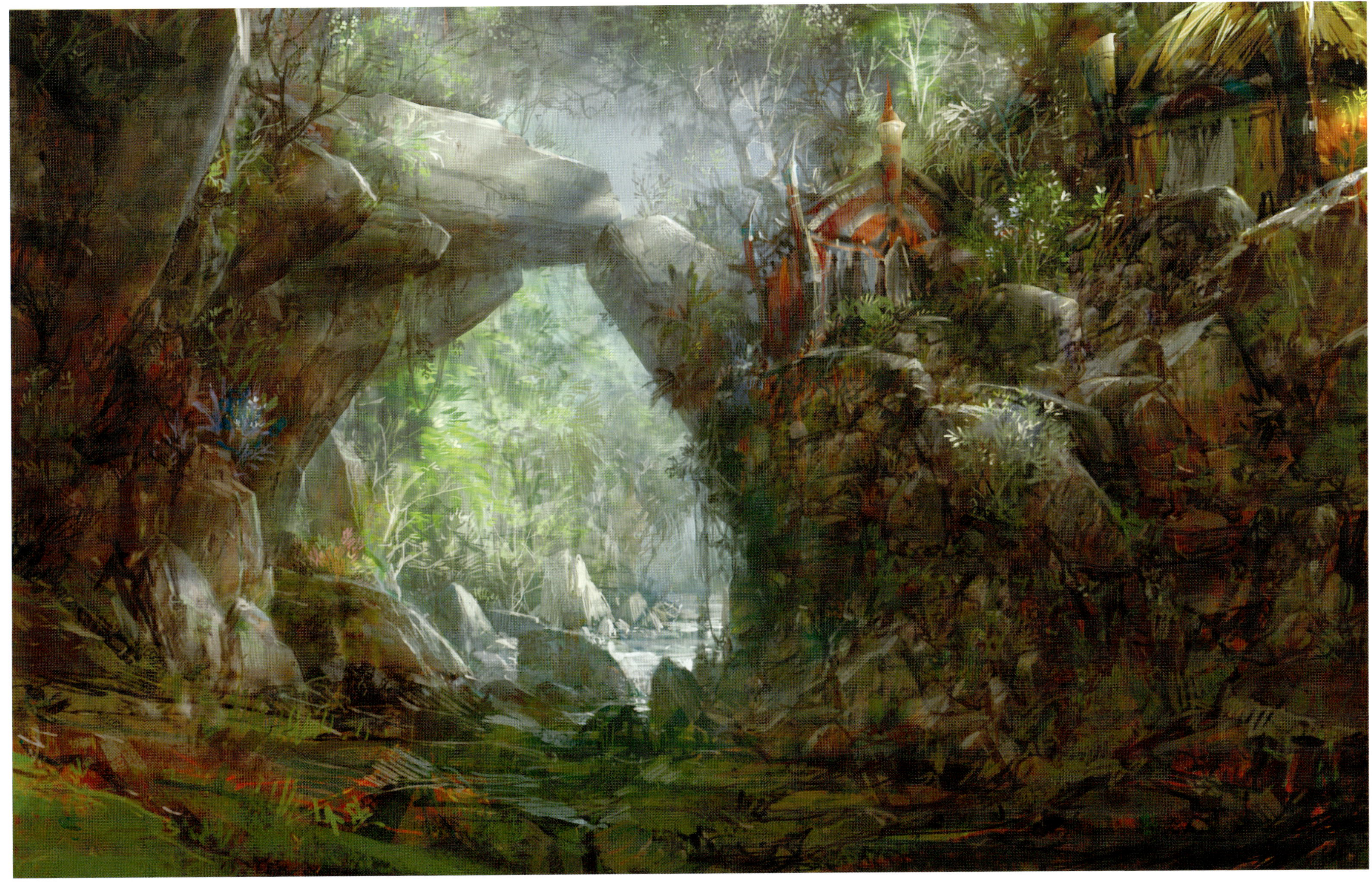

It is **AMAZING** how many different plants grow in **NATURE**.

Observe them **CAREFULLY**, and **MEMORIZE** their shapes, so that this information can be used **WHENEVER IT IS NEEDED.**

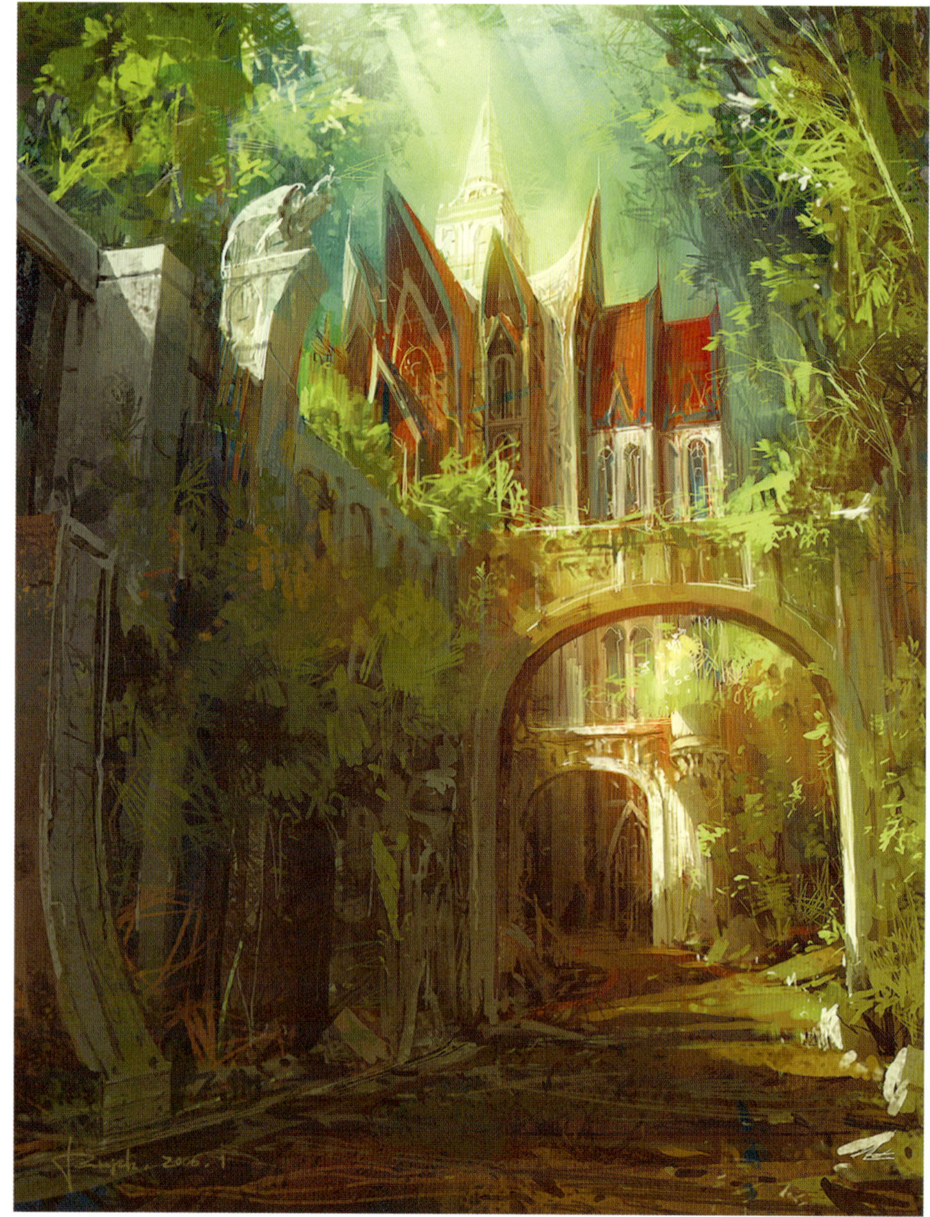

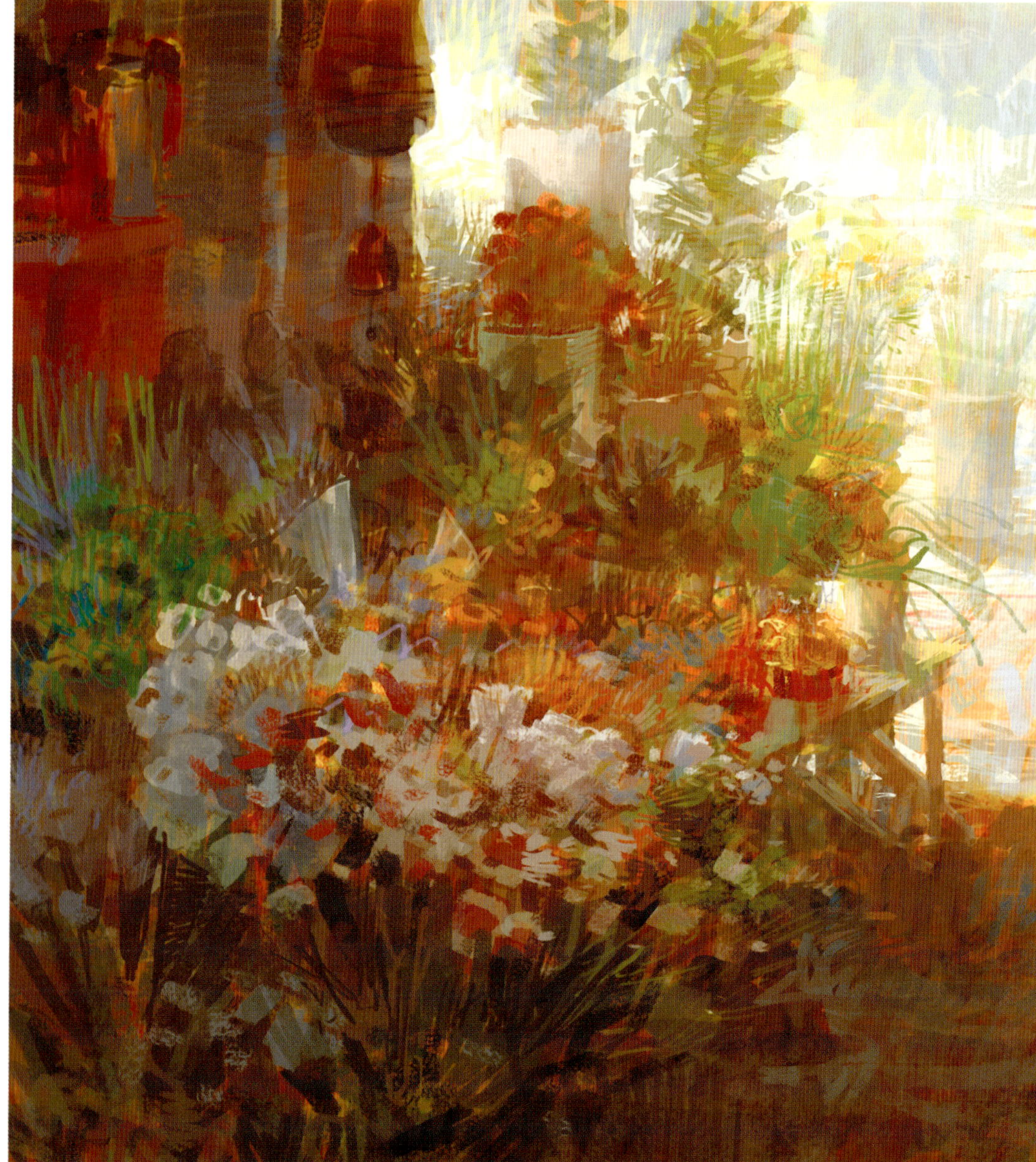

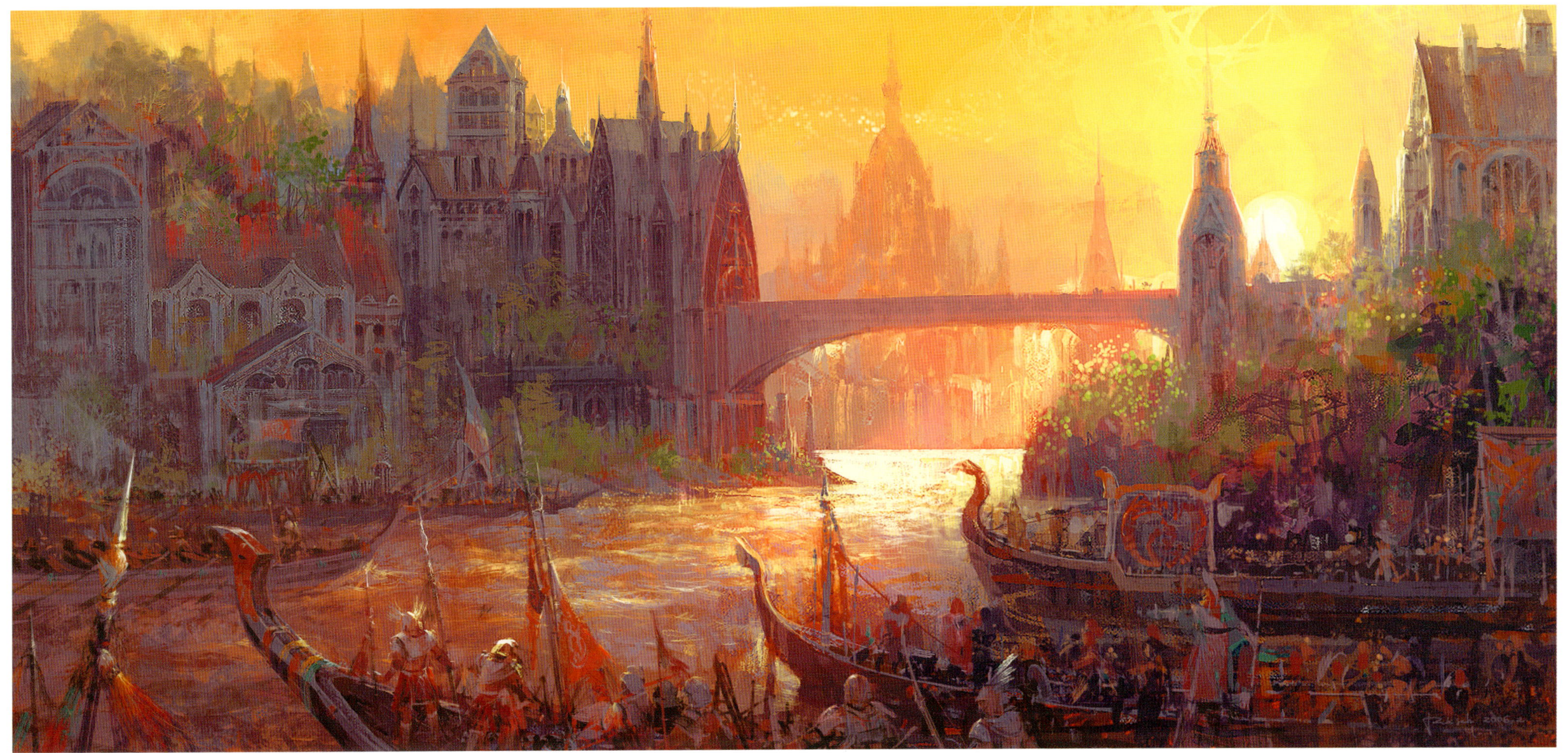

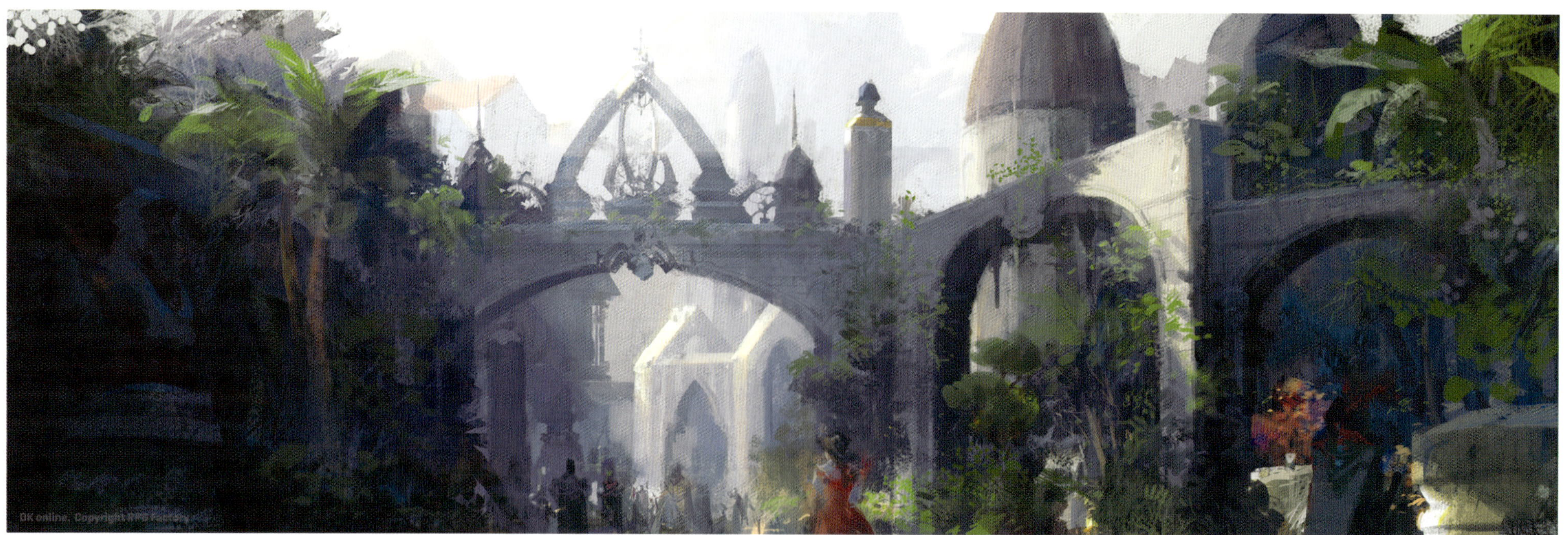

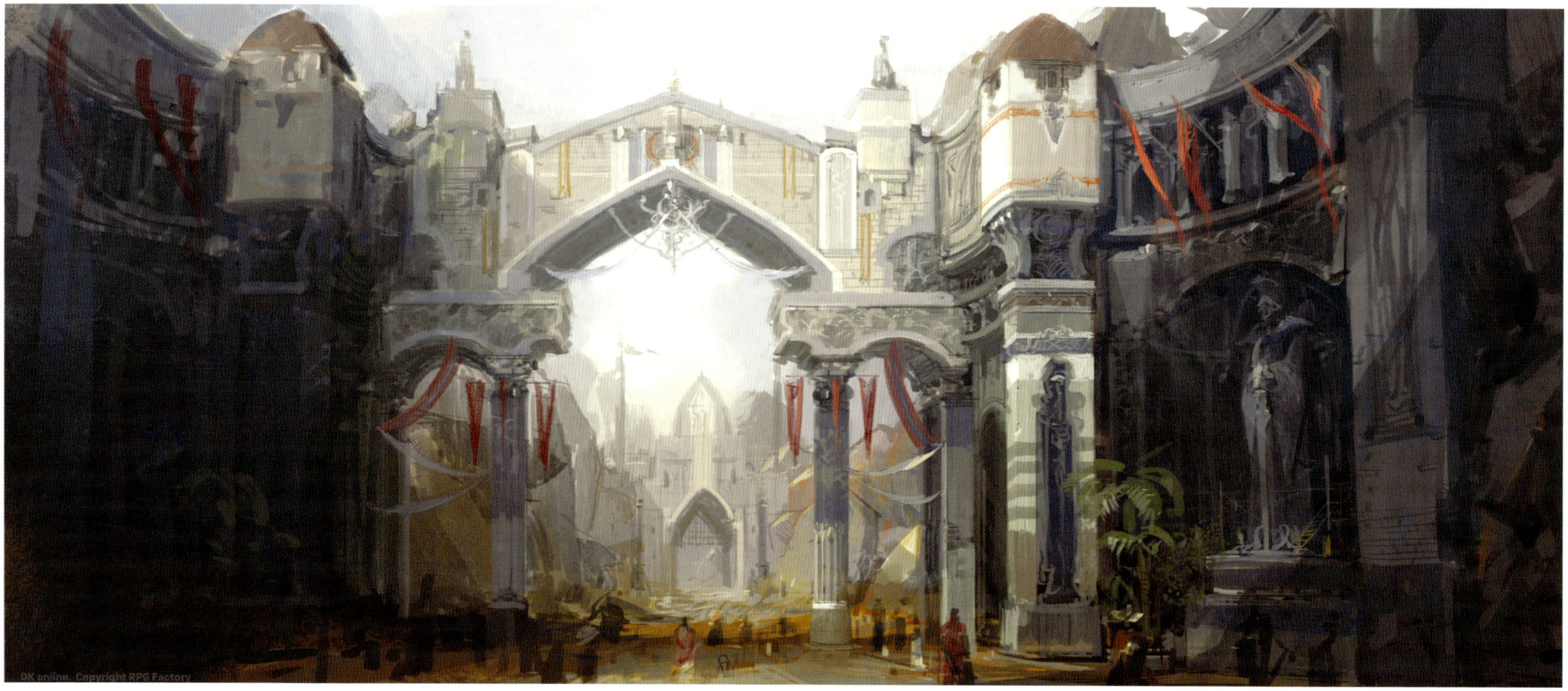

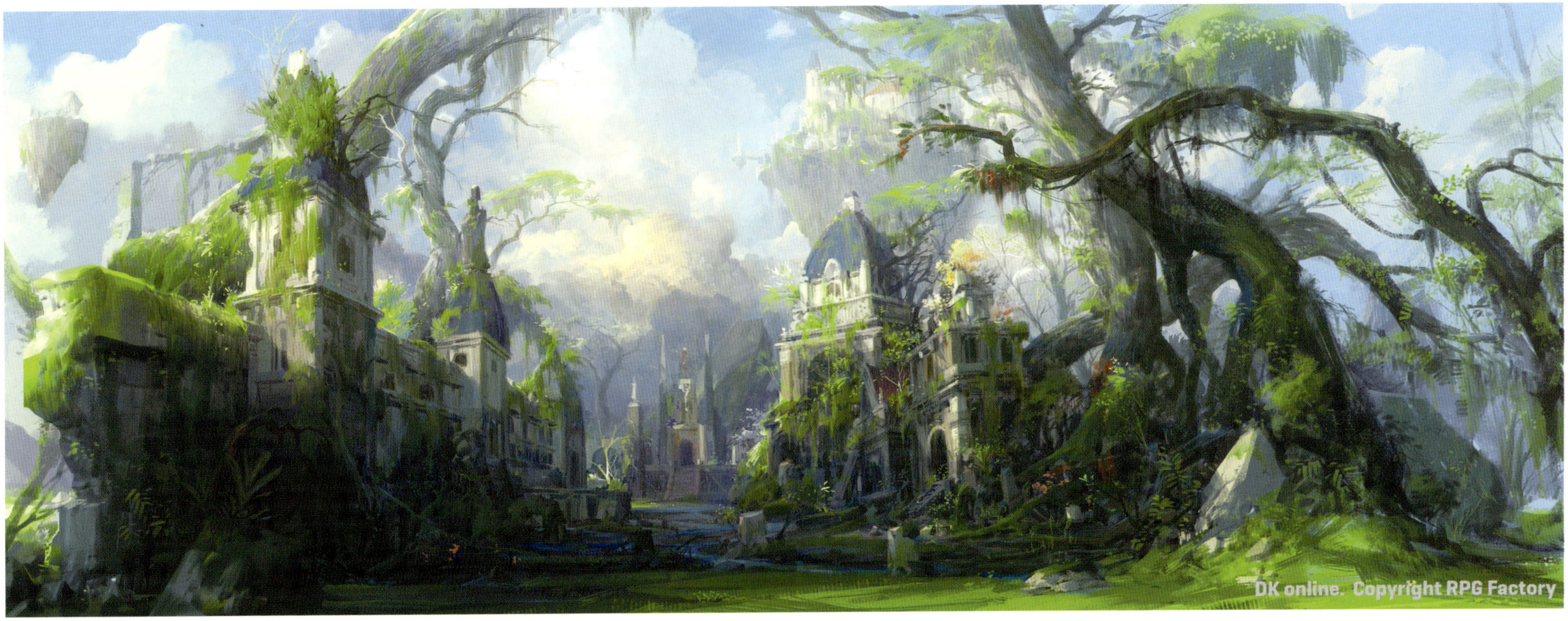

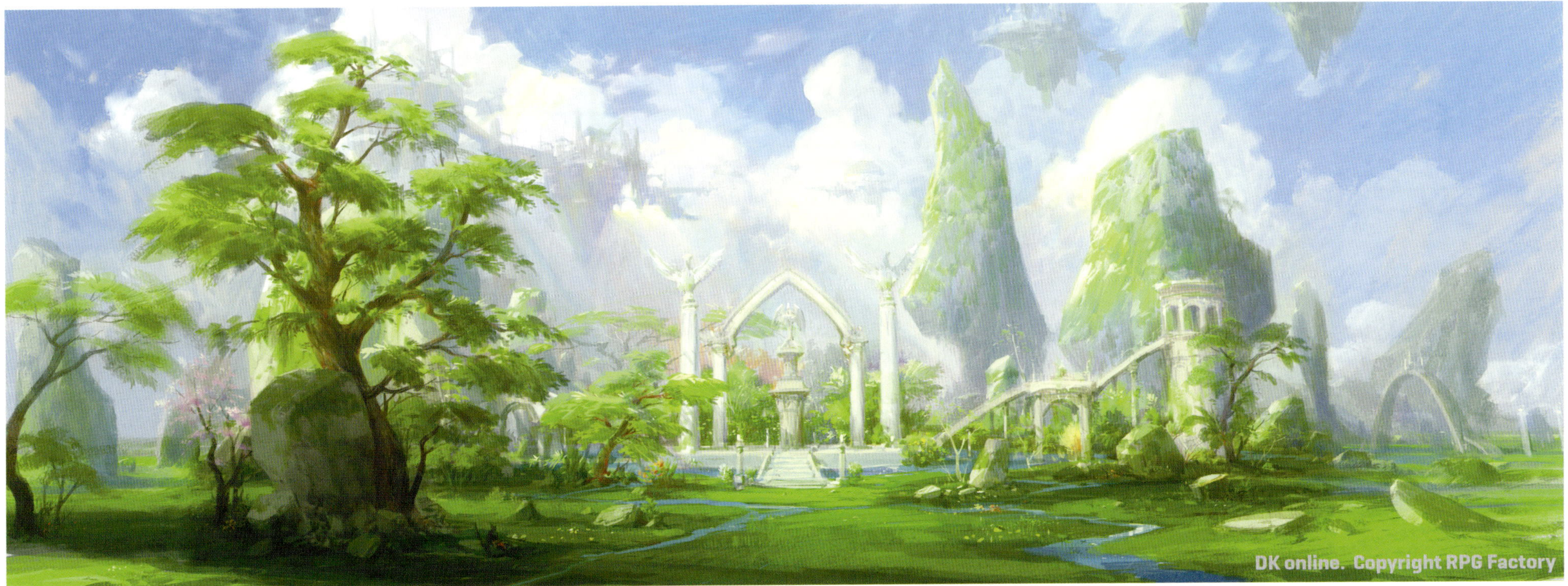

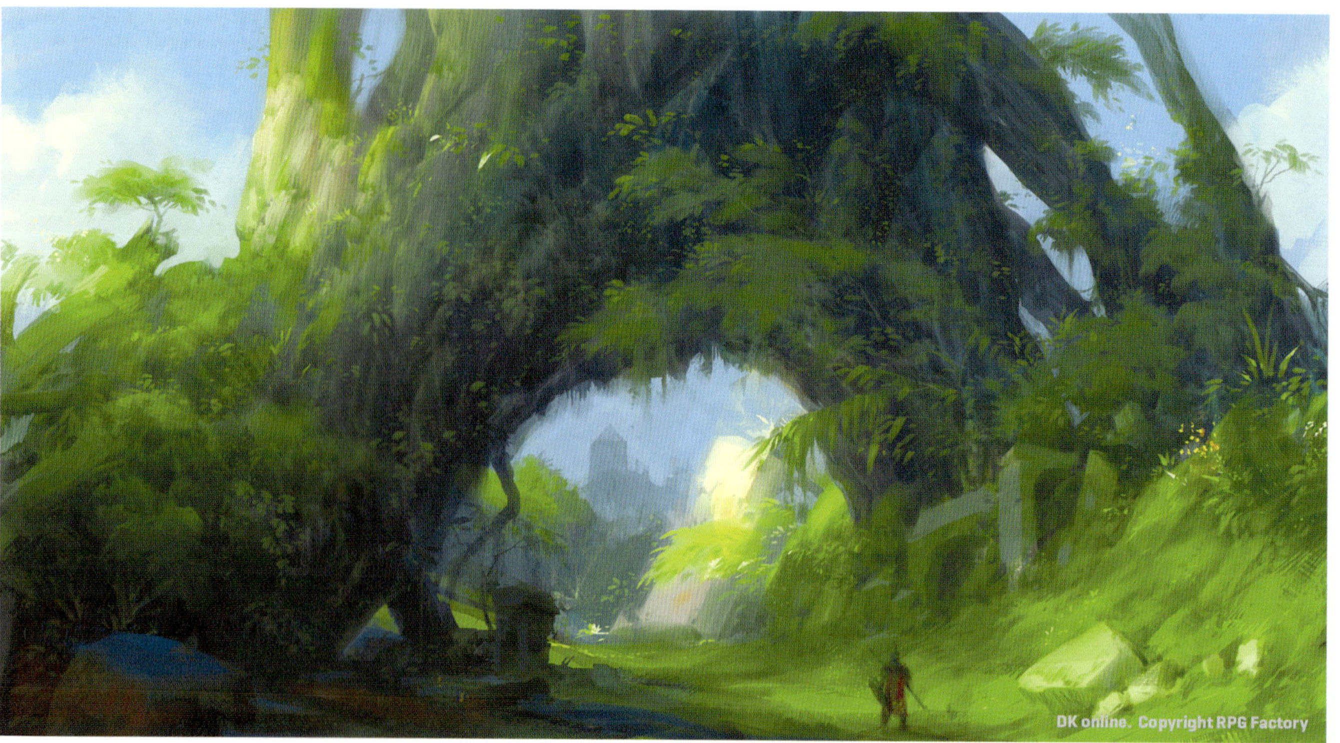

DK online. Copyright RPG Factory

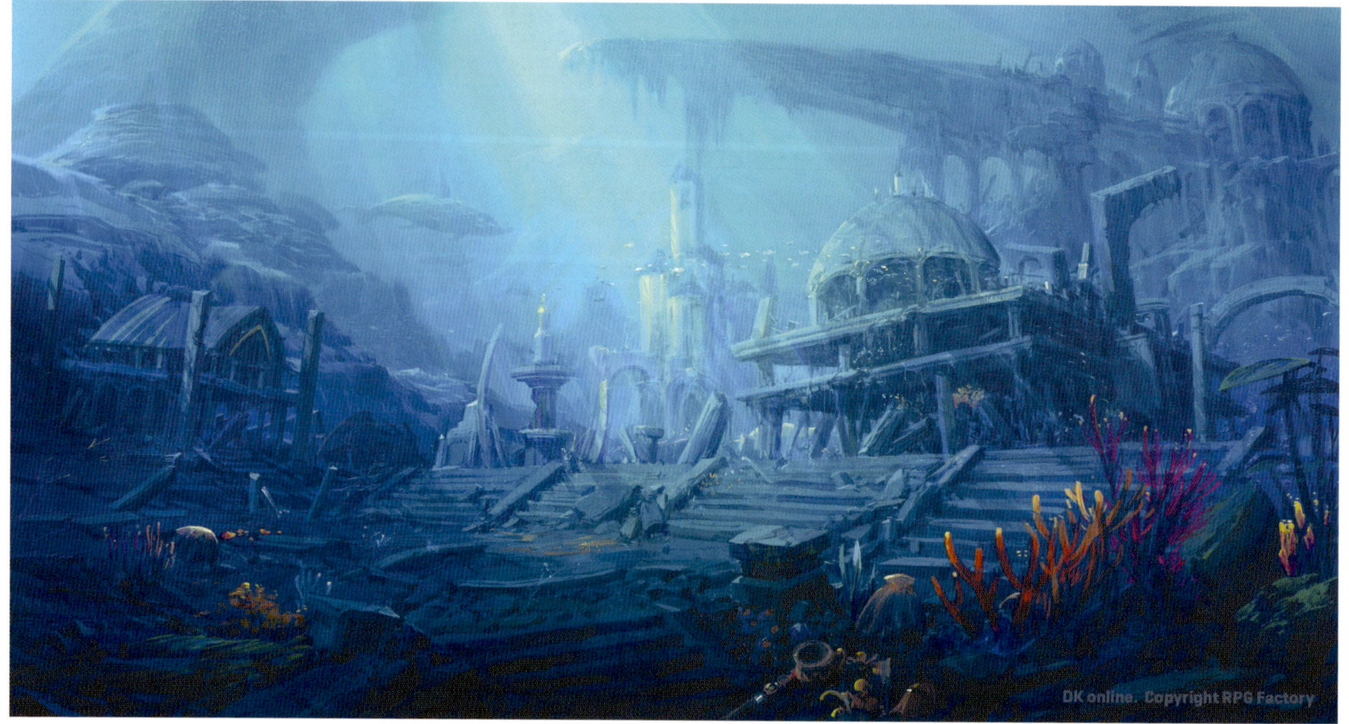

DK online. Copyright RPG Factory

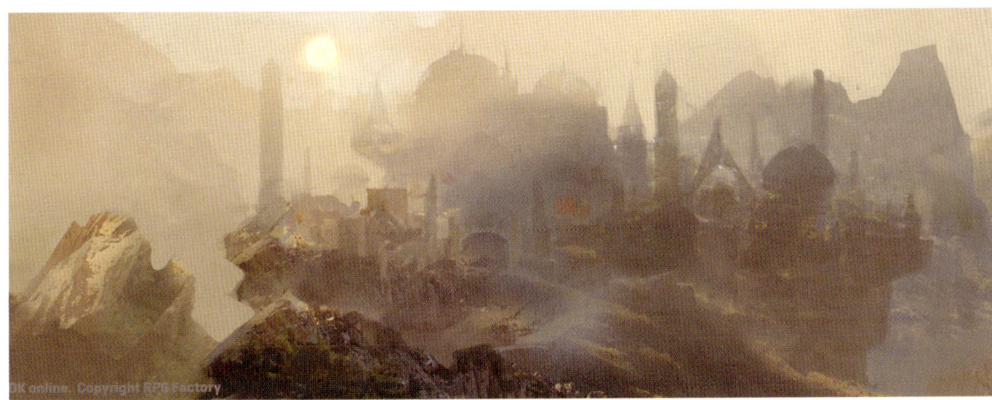

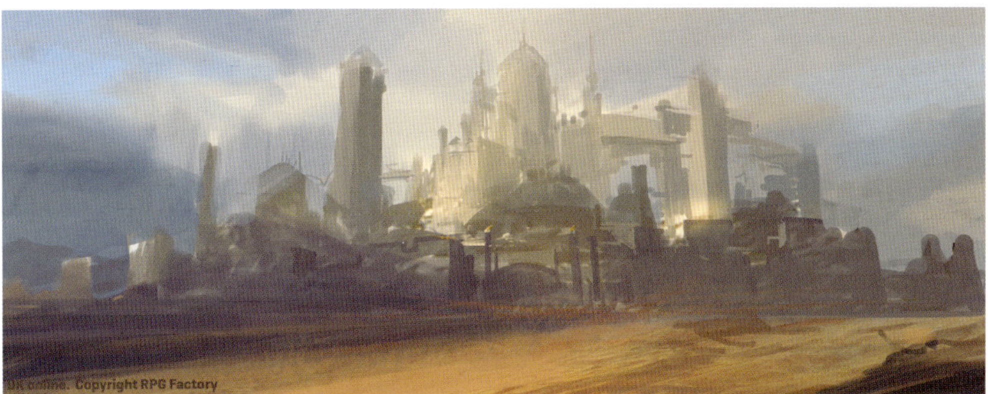

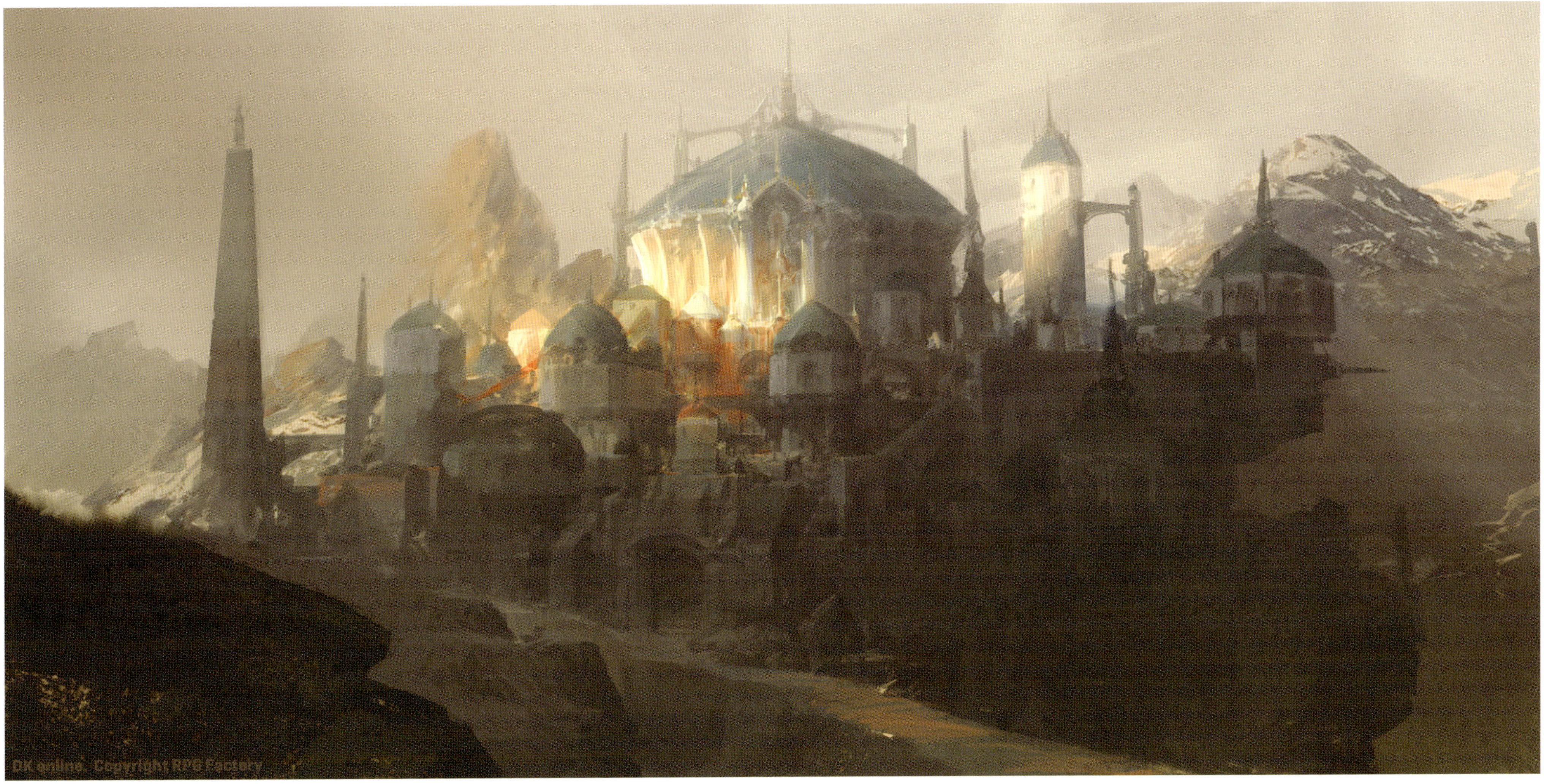

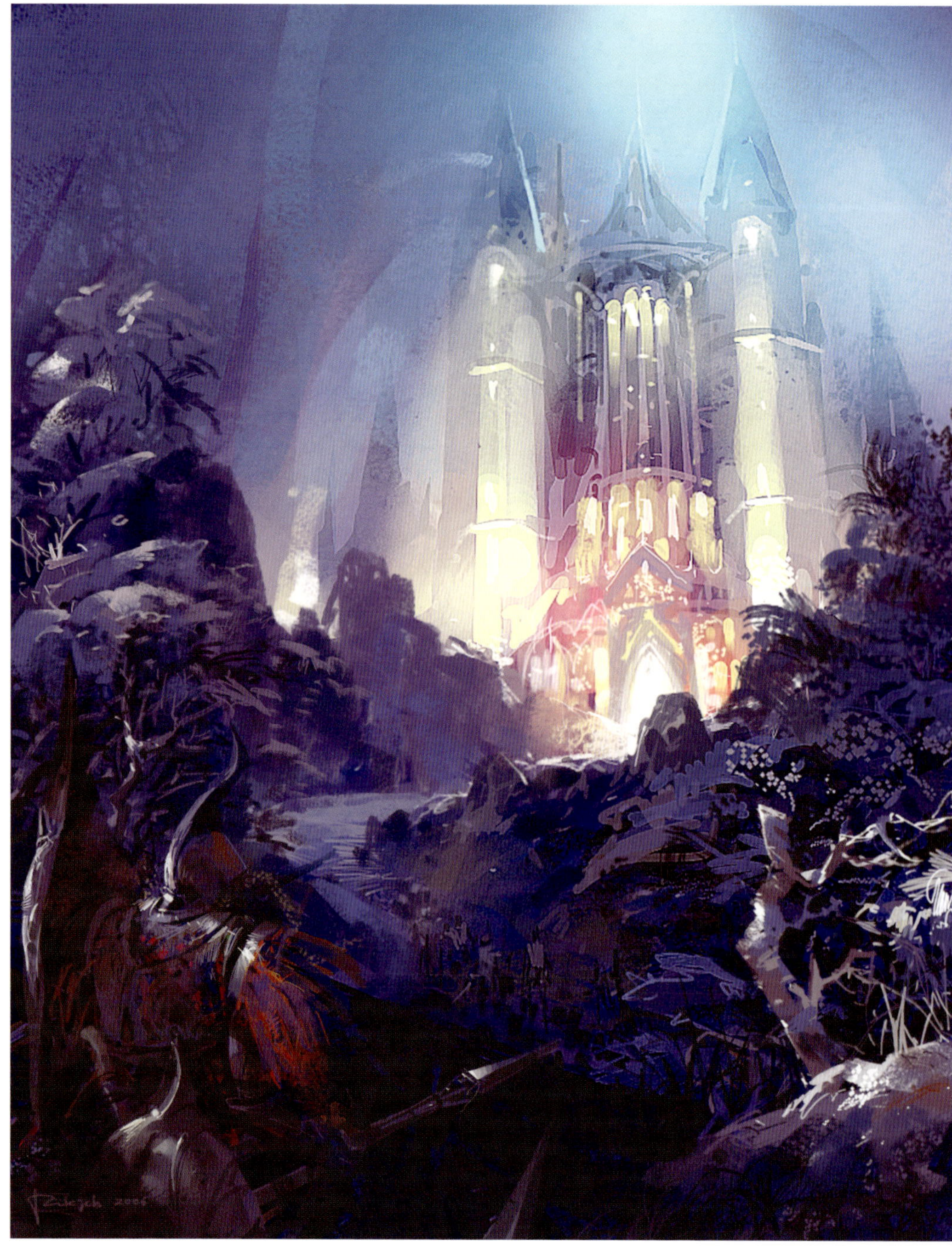

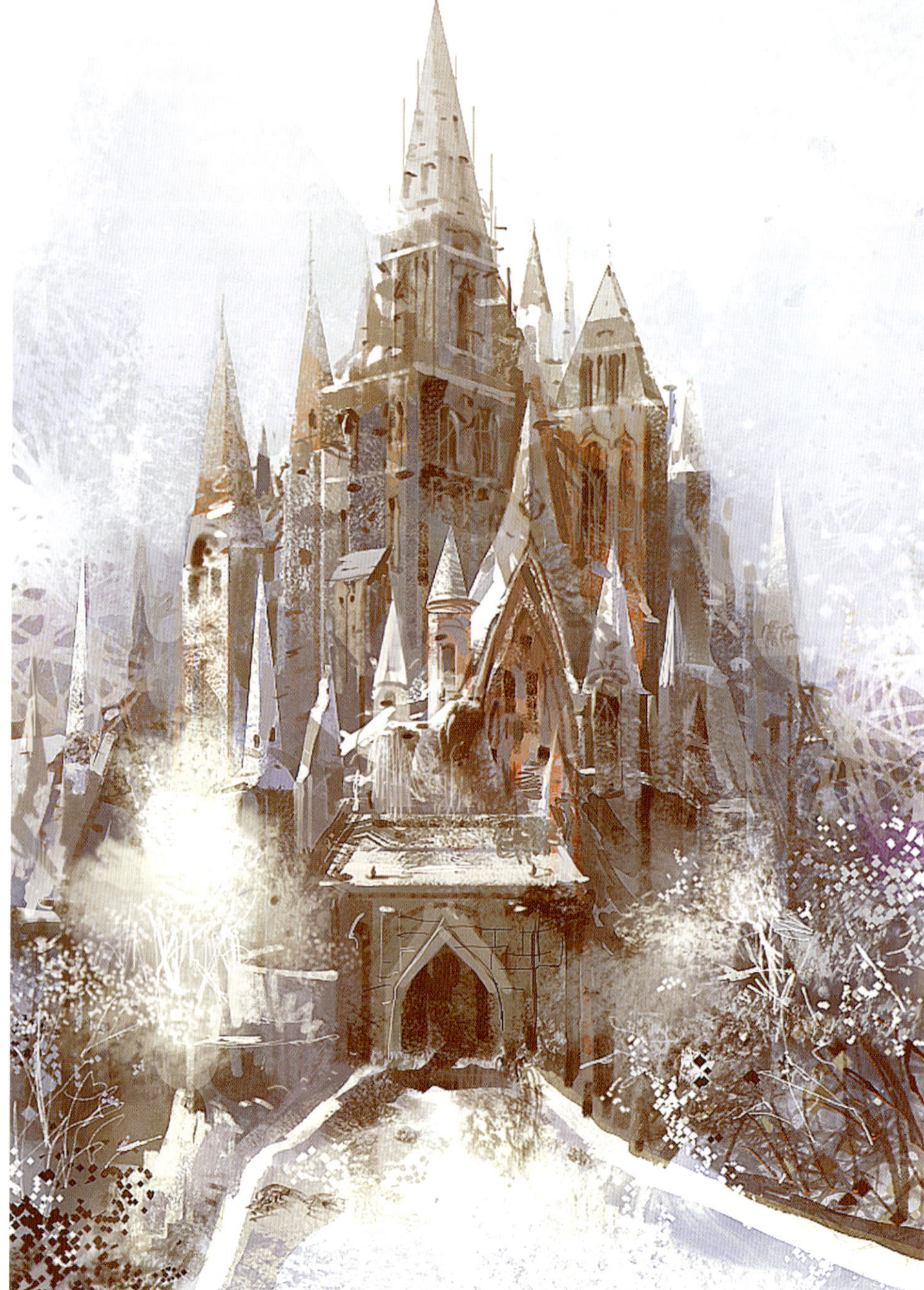

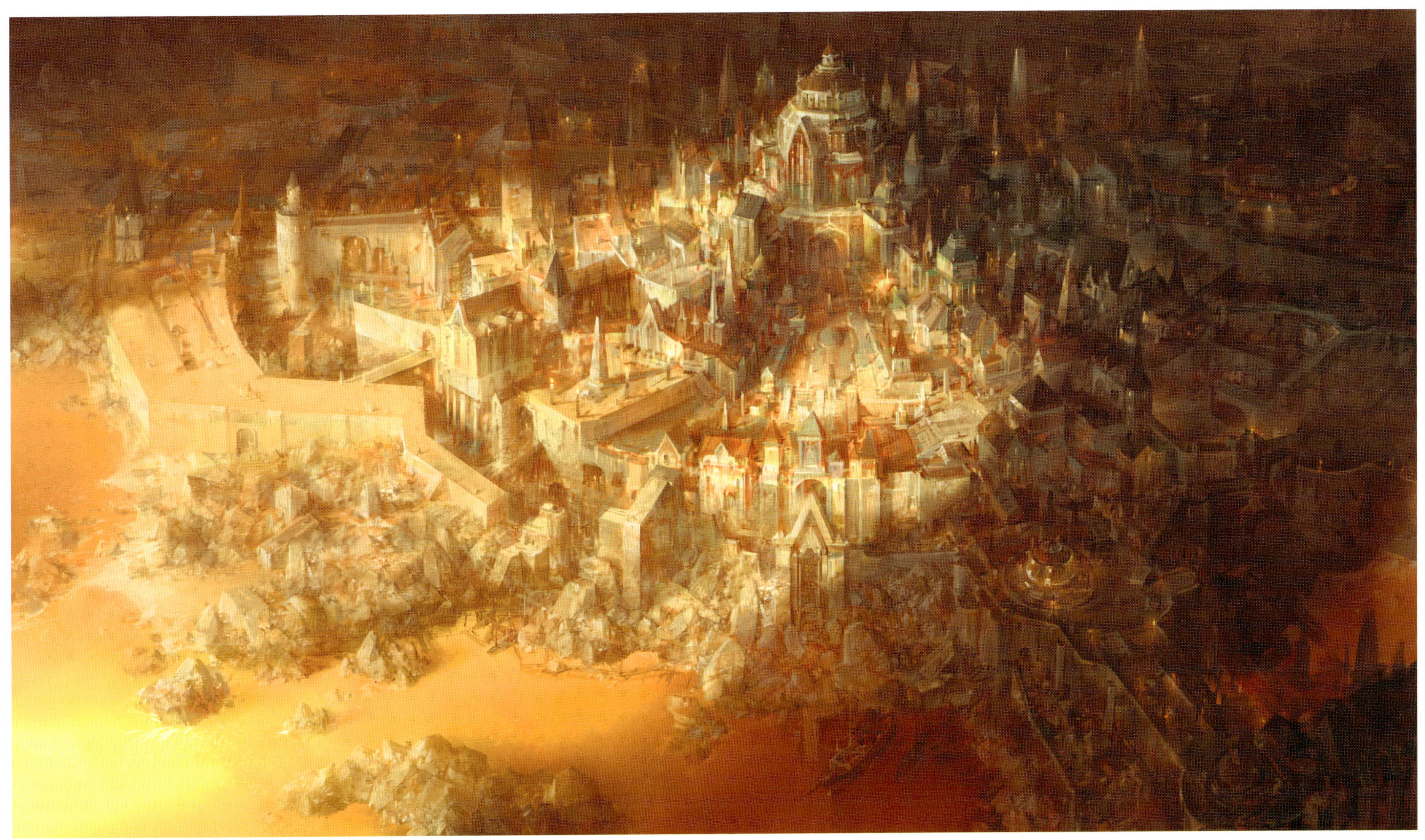

Sometimes, a
BRUSHSTROKE makes for
a **HAPPY ACCIDENT.**

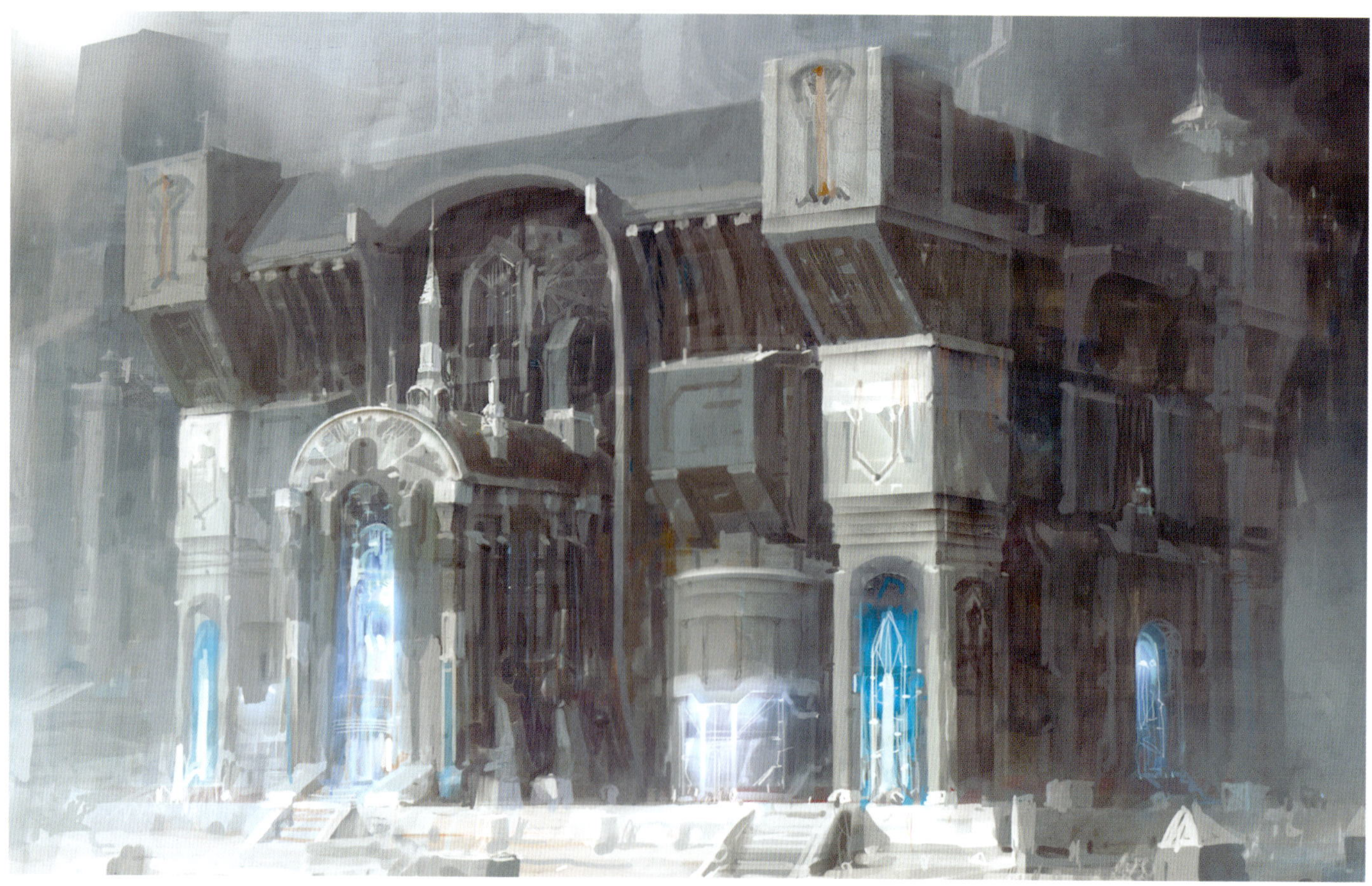

Remember this always: **Art is not about theory it is about feeling.**

Obviously having a good base knowledge is important, but what I want to say is, if you want to move someone's heart with your painting, you have to listen to your heart and follow the feeling of your heart.

Having good knowledge and/or a good technique is definitely needed in order to paint what you have in your mind, but the technique does not make your painting special—it is your heart that makes your painting special.

There are so many amazing things in this world that theory cannot explain. You have to observe carefully, feel it with your heart, and paint a lot. Practice, practice, and practice. Good luck!